Asset Price Bubbles:
The Implications for Monetary, Regulatory, and International Policies

Asset Price Bubbles:
The Implications for Monetary, Regulatory, and International Policies

edited by

William C. Hunter
Federal Reserve Bank of Chicago

George G. Kaufman
*Loyola University Chicago
and
Federal Reserve Bank of Chicago*

Michael Pomerleano
World Bank Group

The MIT Press
Cambridge, Massachusetts
London, England

© 2003 Massachusetts Institute of Technology

All rights reserved. No part of this book may be reproduced in any form by any electronic or mechanical means (including photocopying, recording, or information storage and retrieval) without permission in writing from the publisher.

Set in Times by Sztrecska Publishing for The MIT Press.
Printed and bound in the United States of America.

Library of Congress Cataloging-in-Publication Data

Asset price bubbles : implications for monetary, regulatory, and international policies / edited by William C. Hunter, George G. Kaufman, Michael Pomerleano.
    p. cm.
    Revised papers of a conference sponsored by the Federal Reserve Bank of Chicago and the World Bank.
    Includes bibliographical references and index.
    ISBN 0-262-08314-0 (hc. : alk. paper)
    1. Financial crises—Congresses. 2. Financial services industry—Congresses. 3. Monetary policy—Congresses. I. Hunter, W. Curt (William Curt). II. Kaufman, George G. III. Pomerleano, Michael.

HB3722 .A884 2003
338.5'42—dc21   2002032415

Table of Contents

Acknowledgements ix
Preface xi
Overview xiii

Part I: Keynote Addresses

1 Asset Price Bubbles, Information, and Public Policy
   Randall S. Kroszner 3
2 Asset Price Bubbles and Their Implications for Monetary Policy and Financial Stability
   Jean-Claude Trichet 15
3 Rational and Nonrational Bubbles
   Allan H. Meltzer 23
4 Diverse Views on Asset Bubbles
   Robert J. Shiller 35
5 Asset Prices and Monetary Policy
   Michael Mussa 41

Part II: Recent Experience with Asset Price Bubbles

6 U.S. Stock Market Crashes and Their Aftermath: Implications for Monetary Policy
   Frederic S. Mishkin and Eugene N. White 53
7 Japan's Experience with Asset Price Bubbles: Is It a Case for Inflation Targeting?
   Kunio Okina and Shigenori Shiratsuka 81
8 Lending Booms, Real Estate Bubbles, and the Asian Crisis
   Charles Collyns and Abdelhak Senhadji 101
9 Tropical Bubbles: Asset Prices in Latin America, 1980–2001
   Santiago Herrera and Guillermo E. Perry 127
10 Different Countries, Similar Experience
   Takeo Hoshi 163
11 Comments on Recent Experiences with Asset Price Bubbles
   Ignazio Visco 165

Part III: Theory and History of Asset Price Bubbles

12 Stocks as Money: Convenience Yield and the Tech-Stock Bubble
John H. Cochrane 175

13 Bubble Psychology
Werner De Bondt 205

14 Bubbles in Real Estate Markets
Richard Herring and Susan Wachter 217

15 Comments on: "Stocks as Money ..." and "Bubble Psychology"
Robert S. Chirinko 231

16 Comments on Theory and History of Asset Price Bubbles
Bertrand Renaud 239

Part IV: Empirical Dimensions of Asset Price Bubbles

17 Imbalances or "Bubbles?" Implications for Monetary and Financial Stability
Claudio Borio and Philip Lowe 247

18 Testing for Stock Market Overvaluation/Undervaluation
Ellen R. McGrattan and Edward C. Prescott 271

19 A Stochastic Index of the Cost of Life: An Application to Recent and Historical Asset Price Fluctuations
Michael F. Bryan, Stephen G. Cecchetti, and Róisín O'Sullivan 277

20 Comments on Empirical Dimensions of Asset Price Bubbles
Andrew J. Filardo 291

21 Bubbles, Inflation, and the Big One: Comments on "A Stochastic Index of the Cost of Life ..." and "Testing for Stock Market Overvaluation/Undervaluation"
Bruce Lehmann 299

Part V: International Transmission of Financial Shocks

22 Globalization and Changing Patterns in Crisis Transmission
Michael D. Bordo and Antu Panini Murshid 309

23 Asset Price Bubbles and Stock Market Interlinkages
Franklin Allen and Douglas Gale 323

24 Banking Policy and Macroeconomic Stability: An Exploration
Gerard Caprio, Jr., and Patrick Honohan 337

25 A Global Perspective on Extreme Currency Linkages
Philipp Hartmann, Stefan Straetmans, and Casper de Vries 361

26 Comments: Shifting the Risk after Shifting the Focus
Anna J. Schwartz 383

Part VI: Technology, the New Economy, and Asset Price Bubbles

27 Valuation and New Economy Firms
Steven N. Kaplan 391

28 Home Bias, Transactions Costs, and Prospects for the Euro
Catherine L. Mann and Ellen E. Meade 403

29 Comments on "Valuation and New Economy Firms"
Lawrence Slifman 419

Part VII: Implications of Bubbles for Monetary Policy

30 Asset Prices in a Flexible Inflation Targeting Framework
Stephen G. Cecchetti, Hans Genberg, and Sushil Wadhwani 427

31 Interest Rate Policy Should Not React Directly to Asset Prices
Marvin Goodfriend 445

32 Comments on Implications of Bubbles for Monetary Policy
Benjamin M. Friedman 459

Part VIII: Implications of Bubbles for Prudential Regulatory Policy

33 The Historical Pattern of Economic Cycles and Their Interaction with Asset Prices and Financial Regulation
Charles A. E. Goodhart 467

34 Asset Price Bubbles and Prudential Regulation
Jeffrey Carmichael and Neil Esho 481

35 The Morning After: Restructuring in the Aftermath of an Asset Bubble
Michael Pomerleano 503

36 Comments on "The Historical Pattern of Economic Cycles and Their Interaction with Asset Prices and Financial Regulation"
Joaquim Vieira Levy 517

37 Comments on "Asset Price Bubbles and Prudential Regulation"
Ramon Moreno 523

38 Comments on "The Morning after ... "
Eric Rosengren 529

Part IX: Looking Forward: Plans for Action to Protect against Bubbles

39 Banking Provisions and Asset Price Bubbles
   Jaime Caruana 537

40 Looking Forward on Monetary and Supervision Policies to Protect against Bubbles
   Takatoshi Ito 547

41 Planning to Protect against Asset Bubbles
   Vincent R. Reinhart 553

Conference Program 561

Index 569

Acknowledgements

Both the conference and this volume represent a joint effort of the Federal Reserve Bank of Chicago and the World Bank Group, and many persons at each institution aided in their preparation and successful execution. The three editors served as the principal organizers of the conference program. They would like to thank all the persons who contributed their efforts. At the risk of omitting some, in particular, we thank Ella Dukes, Shirley Harris, and Loretta Novak, who supervised the arrangements, and Julia Baker, Howard Deehan, Bob Dlotkowski, Lauren Fredericks, Jonathan Hao, Lana Henderson, Helen O'D. Koshy, Hala Leddy, Rita Molloy, Sally Sztrecska, Elizabeth Taylor, Barbara Van Brussell, and Karen Wagner, who helped in the preparation of the conference and the proceedings volume. Special mention must be accorded Kathryn Moran (Federal Reserve Bank of Chicago), who had primary responsibility for preparing the program information and shepherding the book from manuscript review to final copy, as well as to Jean Valerius and Loretta Ardaugh (Federal Reserve Bank of Chicago) and Colleen Mascenik (World Bank Group), who supervised the administrative procedures.

Preface

The Federal Reserve Bank of Chicago and the World Bank Group in Washington, DC, cosponsored a conference on "Asset Price Bubbles: Implications for Monetary, Regulatory, and International Policies," on April 22 through April 24, 2002, at the Federal Reserve Bank of Chicago. This was the fourth annual international conference sponsored by the Chicago Fed in partnership with a different major official international institution. Previous conferences were cosponsored with the Bank for International Settlements and the International Monetary Fund (IMF). The conference was originally planned to immediately follow the scheduled annual meeting of the IMF and the World Bank in Washington. When that meeting was cancelled, the conference was deferred to April, following the semi-annual meeting of the two organizations. Because of the timeliness of the topic and the high quality of the previous conferences, this year's gathering attracted participants from more than 30 countries. The papers published in this volume were presented at the conference by government officials, regulators, and academics representing a broad range of countries and institutions, from small emerging economies to large industrial economies.

A distinctive feature of the last two decades has been the prolonged buildups and sharp declines in asset prices in many markets (such as equity and housing) in both the industrialized and the developing world, with serious adverse consequences for the macroeconomies of these countries. This has sparked an intense debate in academic and policy circles regarding the appropriate monetary and regulatory response to these dramatic shifts. Identifying and analyzing lessons from this volatility that could be used to prevent, or, at least, mitigate the magnitude of future financial crises is of prime importance to the international community.

The conference sessions addressed the following areas.
- What has the experience of asset price bubbles looked like in different countries?
- What behaviors prolong asset price bubbles?
- Is there theory and history to explain asset price bubbles?
- How are financial shocks transmitted throughout the global marketplace?
- What is the interaction of the "new economy" and asset price bubbles?

- How will monetary policy respond to asset price bubbles?
- How will prudential regulatory policy respond to asset price bubbles?
- Are there actions that can be taken to protect against asset price bubbles?

The conference speakers were selected to represent a wide range of views on these subjects, so that all viewpoints would be heard and given a thorough airing. We were pleased to have the Honorable Jean-Claude Trichet, Governor of the Bank of France; Randall S. Kroszner, Council of Economic Advisers; Allan Meltzer, Carnegie Mellon University; Robert J. Shiller, Yale University; and Michael Mussa, Institute for International Economics, as keynote speakers. In addition to these distinguished speakers, we were fortunate to have gathered internationally recognized presenters, discussants, and audience members to participate in our conference. The conference provided a forum for an important free interchange of ideas that hopefully will serve to better macroeconomic and microeconomic policies in the future. It is in the pursuit of these objectives that the papers delivered at the conference are published in this volume to reach a larger audience.

William C. Hunter
George G. Kaufman
Michael Pomerleano
Editors

Overview: Asset Price Bubbles: The Implications for Monetary, Regulatory, and International Policies

The Context

The recent volatility in asset price markets has sparked an intense debate in academic and policy circles regarding the appropriate monetary and regulatory response to these dramatic shifts. Although the large gains and losses associated with asset bubbles have been well documented, surprisingly little consensus exists about the causes, characteristics, and behavior of asset bubbles. By unraveling the factors that lead to and amplify asset bubbles, the papers presented during the conference help to explain why some bubbles result in greater, more prolonged losses and what policymakers can do to safeguard economies from these costly, destabilizing episodes. This conference attempted to synthesize the various strands of analysis to offer policymakers a more complete picture of what asset price bubbles are, how we might identify them, and—most importantly—what we should do to avoid or limit the destructive havoc they may inflict on the financial system and economy. As Robert J. Shiller notes in his keynote address, researchers of various intellectual backgrounds have approached the bubbles question without agreement: "Microeconomists still rarely cite macroeconomists, economists rarely site psychologists, and academics rarely site news media stories." As a result, the conclusions of this research are fragmentary—each observer's analysis resembles the parable of blind men who are asked to describe an elephant by touching one part.

Currently, economies around the world are experiencing the financial distress brought about by excesses—the sharp run-up in debt and equity investments in high-tech, telecommunications, and other firms, including in the United States the failed energy trader Enron and telecom WorldCom—during the late 1990s. Shiller attributes the rapid rise of the U.S. stock market to optimism about the advent of the World Wide Web, to Western market economy "triumphalism" over other economic regimes, to capital gains tax cuts and the rise of pension plans such as 401(K) plans, to the lowering of transaction costs, and to the expanding volume of stock trades, among other factors. Similar exuberance prevailed in East Asia prior to 1997. The asset price bubble in these countries was amplified by the confidence expressed in the "East Asian miracle" as a paradigm for sustained economic growth. The bubbles were followed by increases in market risk premiums, tightening of credit standards and availability, and a fall in stock market and other asset prices.

Despite the similarities, the severity of the post-bubble losses and the potential for spillover into the real economy have varied. In "Asset Prices Bubbles, Information, and Public Policy," Randall S. Kroszner observes that asset bubbles are not a new phenomenon of the 1990s; witness the Dutch tulip mania in the 17th century and the South Sea bubble in the 18th century. However, the succession of asset price bubbles in the past two decades, coupled with faster and larger movements of capital and information across borders, fixed currency regimes, and weak banking systems in some countries, has created a serious policy challenge. Asset prices inflated and then collapsed, leading to crises first in Japan, subsequently in East Asia—particularly Thailand and Malaysia—and more recently in the United States. The macroeconomic losses were often substantial, resulting in fiscal costs, slower growth, and social costs, such as higher unemployment and poorer public health. In addition to these measurable losses, economies faced the opportunity costs in terms of development.

Allan H. Meltzer, in "Rational and Nonrational Bubbles," notes that theoretical general equilibrium models give no support to proposals urging policymakers to respond to asset price changes. The economics profession is not close to having a useful model of asset prices that separates the various sources of change. Furthermore, examinations of bubble episodes do not offer a consistent explanation of the behavior of buyers and sellers. He raises one policy lesson that has been reinforced by recent experience: Asset price declines, even large declines, need not be followed by output price deflation or by deep and lasting recessions. The U.S. stock market decline in 1987 and the NASDAQ decline in 2000 were not the prelude to major recessions or deflations, as in the United States in the 1930s or Japan in the 1990s. The difference is explained mainly by the decisions regarding policy actions. This experience suggests that expansive economic policies can compensate for any deflationary impact that asset prices have on output prices.

Jean-Claude Trichet raises the issue of the proper role of the central bank in his contribution, "Asset Price Bubbles and Their Implications for Monetary Policy and Financial Stability." He notes that asset price developments are a serious cause of concern for central banks since they may affect price and financial stability. However, he expresses the view that central banks should not introduce asset prices into their monetary policy reaction function. He advances two reasons: First, it is difficult to implement a sound monetary policy while focusing on highly volatile indicators; second, he doubts that asset prices can be determined scientifically. Trichet also emphasizes that measures aimed at improving market transparency and reducing herding behavior can improve the functioning of the financial system. The recommendations focused on regulatory, accounting measures, and tax rules and regulations, as well as of codes of good conduct and good practices.

In "Asset Prices and Monetary Policy," Michael Mussa echoes concerns about monetary policy. He observes that adjustments in monetary policy have broad effects on financial markets and the economy. Monetary policy is a blunt instrument for responding to a narrow class of asset markets. Therefore, the suppression of most asset price volatility through monetary policy is neither feasible nor desirable. He concludes that it is not practical to think of linking adjustments in monetary policy in some mechanical way to movements in asset prices. Further, he is skeptical about "rational bubbles." Nevertheless, his central thesis is that, beyond their general relevance as macroeconomic indicators, in exceptional times and circumstances, asset prices should exert a special influence on the conduct of monetary policy.

Recent Experience with Asset Price Bubbles

Various regional experiences provide historical perspectives on how asset price bubbles develop and the kinds of policy environments that tend to exaggerate or mitigate the impact of collapses.

In "U.S. Stock Market Crashes and Their Aftermath: Implications for Monetary Policy," Frederic S. Mishkin and Eugene N. White examine 15 episodes of stock market crashes in the United States throughout the 20th century and classify them by the extent of their impact on the rest of the financial system. Their findings corroborate the general consensus that bubbles are very difficult to identify *ex ante*. They argue that the U.S. Federal Reserve System does not have an informational advantage over investors and therefore is unlikely to recognize a developing bubble or to prick it in advance. Further, in their view, the link between monetary policy actions and stock prices is tenuous at best. Therefore, attempts to prevent bubbles through monetary policy might not be critical. Mishkin and White's data indicate that in the history of U.S. stock crashes many stock market bubbles have burst (for example, in 1946, 1962, and 2000) without causing financial instability. This has been especially true in cases where bank balance sheets and the financial system were sound before the onset of crashes. The authors conclude that the critical question facing monetary policymakers is not whether a stock market crash is coming or can be prevented, but whether financial instability is present. Central banks are therefore advised to focus their policy responses on financial regulatory measures that ensure the robustness of banking systems.

Although very different, Japan's experience with a bursting asset price bubble in the late 1980s illustrates some of the same conclusions. In "Japan's Experience with Asset Price Bubbles: Is It a Case for Inflation Targeting?," Kunio Okina and Shigenori Shiratsuka examine the Bank of Japan's policies in the late 1980s, when an asset price collapse initiated an economic downturn that has lasted more than a decade. They examine the common criticisms of Japanese monetary policy: excessive monetary easing in the late 1980s and a delayed policy reversal toward monetary tightening. Okina and Shiratsuka also recognize the challenge that policymakers face in identifying bubbles. In particular, various macroeconomic models for assessing Japan's inflation and output gap in the late 1980s suggest conflicting policy responses depending upon assumptions and modeling choices. Key among these choices are how to decompose the rising growth rate into cyclical and trend components, how to evaluate inflationary pressures and the fundamental value of asset prices, and how to identify the correct path for potential growth. The authors conclude that assets do not provide sufficient information for making real-time judgments about future growth, that the potential for "flexible interest rate targeting" is therefore limited, and that other guideposts are necessary for monetary policymaking.

Unlike the recent experience in the United States, the bursting of the Japanese asset bubble led to a long-term economic slowdown. Financial system vulnerabilities amplified the adverse impact of the bubble collapse. Banks continued to lend to unprofitable firms in an effort to prevent losses from materializing (evergreen lending). At the same time, the losses eroded the capital of the banks, reducing the capacity of financial institutions to take risks, leading to a credit crunch. As a result, the easing of monetary policy was not effective, and the effectiveness of monetary policy was hindered by the lack of new lending.

Waves of optimism, in the words of Charles Collyns and Abdelhak Senhadji in "Lending Booms, Real Estate Bubbles, and the Asian Crisis," led to large capital inflows in many East Asian countries, a fast-paced expansion of domestic credit by an underregulated banking system, and high rates of investment in the property sector. The subsequent outflows of capital were followed by extreme pessimism, investor flight, bank failures, and collapsing equity, housing, and debt markets. Often, the impact was not limited to the financial markets. East Asia's financial crisis quickly deteriorated into an economic and social crisis. Real wages plummeted, and the region's major cities filled with workers seeking jobs. In the countryside, rural credit evaporated and threatened the livelihood of many.

In East Asia prior to the 1997 crisis, Collyns and Senhadji find a strong link between the underestimation of risk, a "wave of optimism," and lending booms, especially in the real estate sector, on the one hand, and the asset price inflation that followed, on the other. The real estate sector provided a dramatic illustration of this cycle, because property values rose at an accelerating pace, while banks that lent out on the basis of collateral value showed increasing willingness and capacity to lend. Collyns and Senhadji describe an "asymmetric response" of property prices to credit, whereby "the response during periods of rising property prices is three times the response during periods of declining prices." They attribute this asymmetry in large part to opaque real estate markets. When the bubbles burst in East Asia, the outcomes were varied. Collyns and Senhadji emphasize that the extreme property price cycles were neither necessary nor sufficient to cause the subsequent crises that struck some of the countries' exchange markets and banks. For instance, Hong Kong SAR, Malaysia, and Singapore survived the real estate fallout and minimized damage to the rest of their economies. It is no coincidence that these economies had relatively strong banking regulatory frameworks before the bubbles formed and policymakers took immediate action to reduce and contain the disruptive impact when the bubbles burst. This experience again underscores the importance of sound banking regulation to buffer a financial system from severe losses after the collapse of a bubble.

In "Tropical Bubbles: Asset Prices in Latin America, 1980–2001," Santiago Herrera and Guillermo E. Perry document similar problems in Latin America. Bubbles in asset price markets deserve policymakers' attention, because they often precede sharp and costly crashes in financial markets, with potentially broader consequences. Herrera and Perry calculate that between 1980 and 2000, 14 of the 22 episodes of asset price bubbles in Latin America ended in crashes. Further, these crashes tended to produce currency crises in the region. Herrera and Perry document Latin America's experiences with the rise and collapse of asset price bubbles since 1980 and identify a set of common determinants. Domestic factors include rapid credit expansion and the volatility of credit growth and asset returns. External factors include changes in capital flows as a result of changes in short-term interest rates in the United States.

Asset price bubbles can, in part, be attributed to wealth effects in household consumption—rising perceptions about the future growth of incomes, increasing creditworthiness of households, and changes in corporate investment as a result of falling cost of new capital, rising expectations about future growth of earnings, and greater perceived creditworthiness of firms. Based on 21 years of evidence from Latin America, Herrera and Perry conclude that it would be extremely risky to predict or pre-emptively attempt to burst asset bubbles. Instead, they suggest that policymakers should focus on country-specific domestic factors to buffer against bubbles and mitigate their impact. Such measures include smoothing the cyclical behavior of credit for the private sector, restricting the use of stocks and real estate as loan collateral during booms, raising capital requirements for highly leveraged banks, imposing ceilings on credit growth, and, over the longer term, promoting the development of secondary markets, real estate investment trusts, and other market instruments for spreading risks.

The collective experiences of many countries suggest that policymakers face similar challenges around the world. First, bubbles are difficult to identify *ex ante*. There is always the possibility that asset appreciation reflects a favorable change in economic fundamentals. However, monetary policymakers possess incomplete and often ambiguous ex ante information in making that determination and are also subject to public and political pressures. Even countries with highly sophisticated supervisory institutions and central banks with extensive, highly transparent information resources have had difficulty identifying bubbles. Second, for the most part, bubbles have followed rapid expansion of credit. Third, the collapse of bubbles has produced various outcomes in different countries, with robust financial systems showing less systemic distress than weak systems. Fourth, advanced economic development does not make an economy immune to an asset price collapse. Finally, as these experiences warn, attempts to prick a bubble may backfire: Intervention may cause more harm than good.

What, then, should be the role of policy based on these experiences? In general, the collective works suggest that policymakers should strengthen regulatory and prudential policy to strengthen the financial system. Because credit booms often give way to asset bubbles, many of the authors suggest measures to contain rapid credit growth (such as higher collateral coverage), improve credit practices, and lessen reliance on stocks and real estate collateral as the basis for lending. Other authors suggest emphasizing the introduction of more contracyclical loan-loss provisioning.

Theory and History of Asset Price Bubbles

To provide a theoretical framework for understanding the causes and policy implications of asset price bubbles, various authors have proposed models to explain why these bubbles form. In "Stocks as Money: Convenience Yield and the Tech-Stock Bubble," John H. Cochrane analyzes price movements of U.S. technology stocks in the 1990s and advances a model of "Rational Behavior with Friction." He suggests that some stock prices vary based on a "convenience yield" that has to do with the availability of information and the velocity of trading. That is, the recent demand for tech stocks, despite their prices being well above the fundamentals, represented something similar to a demand for cash as opposed to irrational beliefs about future stock prices. Just as people hold paper money for short periods of time for its usefulness in making transactions, people would buy shares of a given stock, say Palm, in order to make future transactions with it. Because of the inability to sell short costlessly, betting one way or the other on the future of a company requires owning its stock. Palm's share outstanding were very limited, giving it the "convenience yield." Once the amount of shares outstanding increased significantly, the transaction value diminished, causing the share price to fall.

In "Bubble Psychology," Werner De Bondt approaches the same question from the perspective of behavioral and finance psychology to assess the motivations that drive the behavior of individual investors. Individuals derive knowledge, he argues, from experience, logic, and authority applied to mental frameworks that result in rather predictable patterns of behavior. For example, individual investors tend to place a premium on stocks that are glamorous or familiar; they also tend to manage risks poorly and lack adequate portfolio diversification, because their knowledge is narrow.

In his commentary, Bertrand Renaud notes that behavioral models are very difficult to test empirically. Further, he points out that De Bondt's model focuses on the individual investor, and he asks how valuable are behavioral analyses of individual investors in markets that are dominated by institutional investors, who have better information and possess professional skills and more sophisticated risk-management methods.

In their paper "Bubbles in Real Estate Markets," Richard Herring and Susan Wachter point out that real estate prices behave differently from equity or other asset prices. They develop a model for explaining the unusually dramatic cycles in this market. The model describes a cycle that takes place in bank-dominated financial systems: rapid expansion of bank credit into the real estate sector, which in turn leads to increased value of real estate prices. Higher real estate prices increase the perceived collateral value of these assets to banks and, in turn, decrease the banks' perception of risk in the real estate market. As such, banks are motivated to lend more to the real estate market, at greater risk and at lower cost to the borrowers. The authors offer several explanations as to why banks expose themselves to this increasing degree of risk: disaster myopia, perverse incentives (high leverage, implicit insurance, herd behavior, principal–agent conflicts), short-term players, poor data, and inadequate analysis.

The policy implications of these three models suggest several courses of action to address the problem of potentially destabilizing asset price cycles. The models of Cochrane and De Bondt suggest that a key role of policymakers is to improve the quality and quantity of information and transparency in order to minimize information gaps. Their models also suggest that boom and bust cycles are not easily identified *ex ante*. Herring and Wachter's model suggests that monetary policymakers should not expand credit too rapidly and that financial regulatory policies should take an active role in restricting the potentially hazardous, seemingly irrational, risk-taking in real estate markets.

Empirical Dimensions of Asset Price Bubbles

Applying theoretical models to asset price bubbles draws attention to the critical questions facing financial policymakers: What information is available regarding bubbles? What information is relevant? And what, if anything, should be done about it? Policymakers must make selective use of a large set of conflicting information and imprecise indicators. Moreover, they have to make decisions in real time regarding prospective economic growth and prices, without the benefit of hindsight.

In "Imbalances or 'Bubbles?' Implications for Monetary and Financial Stability," Claudio Borio and Philip Lowe examine the annual movements of asset prices in 34 countries beginning in 1962, looking at 38 crisis episodes. To replicate the perspective of a monetary policymaker, the authors select only data that were available *ex ante*; they examine the asset price gap, credit gap, and investment gap. Working from data that shows two completed asset price cycles since the 1970s, Borio and Lowe arrive at two key observations: 1) Credit and asset price cycles often proceed in tandem, and 2) cycles appear to be increasing in magnitude. Based on this analysis, they conclude that asset price information is useful and that central banks should use individual and aggregate asset prices as a tool for conducting monetary policy.

In "A Stochastic Index of the Cost of Life: An Application to Recent and Historical Asset Price Fluctuations," Michael F. Bryan, Stephen G. Cecchetti, and Róisín O'Sullivan argue that asset prices offer useful information for monetary policymakers and that they should eschew measures of inflation that focus only on the current cost of current consumption. This perspective, they contend, creates an "inter-temporal substitution bias" and should be revised to include the current cost of future consumption. To correct this bias, the authors create a "cost of life" index. Applying dynamic factor methodology, they use asset prices to measure the flow of future services and combine this with the cost of current consumption in a weighted average. Bryan, Cecchetti, and O'Sullivan's work has important messages: It underscores the importance of inter-temporal analysis, it warns against relying too heavily on current consumer price index prices, and it highlights the challenge of capturing the changing prices of nonfinancial assets. Unfortunately, there are no clearly marked road signs identifying asset bubbles. Hence, for every suggestion, there are qualifiers. Bryan, Cecchetti, and O'Sullivan warn that price information does not consistently tell the same story; during periods of real interest rate fluctuations, the information may be biased.

Ellen R. McGrattan and Edward C. Prescott, in "Testing for Stock Market Overvaluation/Undervaluation," develop a measure of capital stock and compare it to market capitalization to determine the presence of a bubble. By this measure, the authors conclude that the U.S. stock market was undervalued in 1929 and that there was no asset bubble. The subsequent crash was caused by severe tightening by the Fed, not the bursting of a bubble.

Implications of Bubbles for Monetary Policy

There is general consensus that asset prices offer at least some information that might be useful for monetary policymakers in the short term, but there are mixed views on whether asset prices have any significant relationship to output gaps and commodity inflation forecasts—the primary indicators for monetary policymakers. Therefore, the most important question is whether monetary policy should target asset prices.

In "Asset Prices in a Flexible Inflation Targeting Framework," Stephen G. Cecchetti, Hans Genberg, and Sushil Wadhwani argue that central bank action may be effective in certain circumstances in affecting asset prices. However, it is very difficult to apply. Cecchetti, Genberg, and Wadhwani argue that a buildup of asset price misalignments can lead to macroeconomic imbalances, misaligned exchange rates, and lost competitiveness. When there are shocks in asset markets, a policy of "leaning against the wind" of asset price changes may balance outputs. They qualify their support for central bank action. Central bank responses to asset price misalignment yield beneficial results only in very limited circumstances. Macroeconomic performance has improved after policy has reacted modestly to asset price misalignments when these misalignments are due to financial shocks. However, policy responses have not been useful when productivity shocks or a change in fundamentals are the underlying determinants. Therefore, responding mechanically to all asset price changes can produce worse outcomes than not responding to any at all. Cecchetti, Genberg, and Wadhwani also note that several factors may constrain the effectiveness of monetary policy actions—for example, the resiliency of the financial system, the openness of the economy, and the role of the banking sector.

In "Interest Rate Policy Should Not React Directly to Asset Prices," Marvin Goodfriend takes the view that asset price fluctuations provide useful information. But in his opinion there should be no presumption of a correlation between asset price movements and real short-term interest rate movements; a relationship between these variables may be positive or negative. He argues that attempts to target asset prices may be counterproductive and that the downside risks of inappropriate action outweigh the potential benefits of useful intervention. His discussion of asset bubbles and monetary policy highlights several practical problems that constrain central banks. First, the information is not perfect. Markets do not capture all available information, central bank information is drawn from imperfect measurements, and contradictory signals can come from different asset prices such as exchange rates, housing prices, and stock values. Monetary policymakers cannot hope to identify and address all inflation and output misalignments. Second, as Goodfriend points out, there is a credibility issue: Central banks rely heavily on reputation and credibility, both of which are jeopardized by inappropriate, unnecessary, or poorly executed policy actions. Shocks are often too hard to identify as misalignments, which increases the risk of selecting the wrong policy and losing credibility. With weakened credibility, central banks are even less capable of performing their core function—maintaining financial stability. In conclusion, he is skeptical about the usefulness of asset price information for influencing exchange rate or interest rate policy.

In "Comments on Implications of Bubbles for Monetary Policy," Benjamin M. Friedman is equally skeptical that univariate, mechanical extrapolations from asset prices are useful, given the risks of poor measurement and misinterpretation. Friedman captures the time constraint succinctly: "What did they know? When did they know it? What could they do about it?" Referring to the Central Bank of Japan in the late 1980s, Friedman notes that asset prices did not provide useful information in real time.

International Transmission of Financial Shocks

The challenge of responding to asset price bubbles is complicated by the fact that financial systems are increasingly interlinked across the world. By examining globalization in a historical context, Michael D. Bordo and Antu Panini Murshid, in "Globalization and Changing Patterns in Crisis Transmission," offer observations and predictions about the frequency and direction of financial shocks. Their analysis draws on a comparison of two periods of rapid financial globalization, 1880–1914 and 1990–2002, to arrive at the following conclusions. First, there is strong evidence of global co-movement of asset prices in the 1880–1914 period and less evidence of such today, with patterns being more regional than global. Second, there is less evidence of simultaneous shocks, but more evidence of shocks that are confined to groups of emerging or advanced countries. The probability of global crisis was lower in the most recent period than in the period from 1880 to 1914, but risks at the local and regional level were approximately the same in both periods. Unlike the earlier period of rapid globalization, when shocks generated in Western Europe extended to colonial territories, the shocks of recent periods tended to originate in emerging market countries and to spread within the immediate region.

Philipp Hartmann, Stefan Straetmans, and Casper de Vries, in "A Global Perspective on Extreme Currency Linkages," analyze currency markets over the past 20 years and find that the initial probability of a crisis occurring is higher in emerging markets than in developed economies. However, the analysis suggests that once a crisis has struck, the breadth of it is not more severe among emerging markets than among industrial countries. Today's economically advanced countries are more stable than before because they use better macroeconomic policies, are more transparent, have flexible exchange rate systems, and have reached a higher state of financial maturity and diversity of markets.

In "Asset Price Bubbles and Stock Market Interlinkages," Franklin Allen and Douglas Gale present a theoretical model based on an "agency problem" of the amount of credit provided for speculative investment. Their analysis recognizes that investors in real estate and stock markets borrow from banks. The authors' analysis of bubbles and crises in capital markets emphasizes the agency conflict that exists between borrowers and lenders when information is asymmetric. Risk is shifted if the ultimate providers of funds—banks—are unable to analyze their investments due to the lack of financial sector expertise and resulting opacity. The shifting of risk increases the return to investment in the assets and causes investors to bid up asset prices above their fundamental value.

In her discussion, Anna J. Schwartz takes issue with Allen and Gale, arguing that in today's economy borrowers may not be better informed than lenders when the investment is stock. Thus, in the United States, investors recently suffered larger losses than lenders when the stock market bubble burst. This casts doubt on the likelihood of agency problems being a major contributor of the U.S. stock market bubble.

In "Banking Policy and Macroeconomic Stability: An Exploration," Gerard Caprio, Jr., and Patrick Honohan examine the banking sector and arrive at very similar conclusions. They emphasize the important role of deep financial markets and well-developed regulatory and supervisory institutions, which buffer countries from shocks in the financial system. The policy conclusions are that emerging market policymakers need to focus on strengthening macroeconomic policy, increasing transparency of information, and building up regulatory and supervisory capacity in order to avoid and mitigate the effects of financial shocks. Caprio and Honohan suggest that allowing foreign participation in the financial system is essential to achieving these goals. Greater reliance on foreign participation, when combined with strong supervisory institutions and transparency, is seen as an important tool for insulating an economy from shocks. The authors qualify their recommendations with the warning that an effective regulatory environment with prompt corrective action may actually amplify short-term shocks.

Technology, the New Economy, and Asset Price Bubbles

The United States witnessed rapid growth of its high-tech sector in the 1990s, especially the infamous dot-com and telecom firms that soared in a frenzy of investment with unlimited access to capital and then crashed. In retrospect, many observers have called this phenomenon a bubble, where tech stocks were extremely overvalued. According to Steven N. Kaplan, in "Valuation and New Economy Firms," investors overestimated network effects and cost reductions and underestimated the effects of competition. The effects on the stock market are not clear, but some real effects are evident. Kaplan recognizes substantial improvements in productivity since 1990, as well as improvements in processes, many of which have come from outsourcing noncore labor functions, capital deepening, and a decline in transaction costs. Kaplan speculates that the U.S. economy will continue to reap these benefits over the next five to 10 years.

In "Home Bias, Transaction Costs, and Prospects for the Euro," Catherine L. Mann and Ellen E. Meade point to a transformation of the intermediation process in asset markets: buying and selling as well as clearing and settlement that have had an effect on the allocation of international portfolios since 1990. Although intermediation and settlement costs have fallen, Mann and Meade find that information costs are still significant and remain the greatest transaction cost in international asset markets. As a result, they find that U.S. investors maintain a strong "home bias." The implication is that foreign firms are well rewarded for listing in the U.S. securities markets and conforming to U.S. rules about information and disclosure.

Implications for Prudential, Regulatory, and International Policies

In light of the practical challenges in identifying and reacting appropriately to an asset price bubble with monetary policy, prudential policy offers possibly the best line of defense. Not only has historical analysis of bubbles and crashes linked frequency of crisis to weakness of regulatory policies, but economies have weathered the storm better when they have had strong supervisory and regulatory institutions.

Reviewing recent financial crises, both Charles A. E. Goodhart, in "The Historical Pattern of Economic Cycles and Their Interaction with Asset Prices and Financial Regulation," and Jeffrey Carmichael and Neil Esho, in "Asset Price Bubbles and Prudential Regulation," note that financial regulation tends to be inherently procyclical. Both papers find that capital adequacy and provisioning rules have not anticipated or responded adequately to boom–bust cycles. Capital adequacy has been inappropriately low or not sufficiently responsive to cyclical movements. Regulators do not "bite" during a boom, only during a low cycle. In banking, for example, the Value-at-Risk model for capital adequacy becomes a challenge when risks are perceived to be very high and credit contracts during a bust period. Likewise, since traditional loan-loss provisioning is based on backward-looking data, it eases during economic upswings and tightens during downswings, amplifying the scope of cycles.

To mitigate the problem so that regulation does not amplify bubbles, Goodhart suggests contracyclical provisioning for nonperforming loans. Similarly, Carmichael and Esho recommend dynamic loan-loss provisioning. For instance, following the Spanish approach, financial institutions would be compelled to build up loan-loss provisions in good times in order to mitigate the regulatory hit that they would suffer in bad times. Carmichael and Esho also emphasize the importance of stress testing; regulators would assess banks' vulnerability to a variety of shocks by subjecting bank balance sheets to various tests, both models-based and informal tests. They cite the methods used by the Australian Prudential Regulation Authority, which takes a consultative approach to prudential regulation, but notes that this approach is costly and requires sophisticated staff. By taking these prudential measures, the regulator can aim to strengthen bank balance sheets, monitor exposure to sectoral lending, and improve prudential rules to avoid exacerbating price cycles. (However, they equally observe that even the most sophisticated regulator cannot be expected to anticipate or counteract asset price cycles.)

Developing countries face significant practical hurdles to making these institutional and regulatory improvements work. In "The Morning After: Restructuring in the Aftermath of an Asset Bubble," Michael Pomerleano offers empirical evidence that the extent, severity, and duration of price bubbles hinge in part on the availability of financial sector skills and market-based instruments. Cross-country data point to a positive relationship between the development of financial sector skills and a reduction in the fiscal costs of crises. Where human capital is lacking in the financial sector, assets are inaccurately valued and restructuring proceeds slowly. Therefore, countries need to invest in developing the human capital and market-based instruments that help the developed economies avoid, mitigate, and recover from crises. The implication is that policymakers need to take an active role in investing in the development of the base of professionals—actuaries, financial analysts, appraisers, and insolvency experts—to perform these sophisticated functions. Illustrative initiatives that can facilitate the development of the professionals include the development of formal licensing and accreditation programs for professions, government outsourcing of contracts to the private sector, and increased foreign participation.

Looking Forward: Plans for Action to Protect against Bubbles

The final session, "Looking Forward: Plans for Action to Protect against Bubbles," represents a prospective effort to identify policy measures. Jaime Caruana, in "Banking Provisions and Asset Price Bubbles," concentrates on the procyclicality of loan-loss provisions due to inadequate recognition of latent credit risk. In order to reinforce the solvency of Spanish banks in the medium term, the Bank of Spain adopted statistical provisioning to supplement specific provisioning with the intent of capturing expected losses earlier in the cycle. The contracyclical provisioning offers several advantages. It provides banks with incentives for better risk management, and its anticyclical nature mitigates the tendency to reinforce cycles.

In "Planning to Protect against Asset Bubbles," Vincent R. Reinhart agrees that central banks must pay attention to asset prices but suggests that asset bubbles are difficult to identify in real time or even after the fact. Therefore, tightening monetary policy beyond desired macroeconomic goals in response to high and rising equity prices or other asset values would involve trade-offs. Reinhart observes that there are many ways to deal with systemic strains resulting from sharp declines in asset prices. Before the fact, Reinhart advocates working with supervisors to ensure that depositories maintain adequate standards, keeping mandatory capital ratios high enough, and requiring stress tests of critical systems. After the fact, he recommends injecting reserves to meet liquidity needs, lending freely at the discount window, and encouraging participants to continue taking on credit exposure. Finally, he notes that diversified financial systems tend to be more resilient. To an important extent, the U.S. economy is resilient to asset price shocks due to the existence of multiple channels of intermediation; therefore, policymakers should nurture the development of diversified financial systems.

In "Looking Forward on Monetary and Supervision Policies to Protect against Bubbles," Takatoshi Ito reiterates some of the key messages presented during the conference regarding the role of monetary policy and regulatory and supervisory initiatives. He notes that it is difficult to identify whether asset price increases reflect a permanent productivity increase or a bubble and that there is no theoretical framework to support the contention that interest rate increases would stop asset price increases. He explores several concrete proposals to strengthen regulatory and supervisory initiatives against bubbles. Foremost among these is ensuring market transparency and regulating the bank loan-to-value ratios. Ito observes that Japan was too late in establishing regulations designed to reduce the concentration of lending to real estate-related sectors. Moerover, the Japanese system created tax incentives to hold properties, and the inheritance tax, in particular, created incentives to increase demand when prices rose.

In addition to the participants' presentations summarized in this overview, a number of discussants provided excellent commentary for each session which is included in the text of this volume. These discussants include Takeo Hoshi, Ignazio Visco,

Robert S. Chirinko, Andrew J. Filardo, Bruce Lehmann, Lawrence Slifman, Joaquim Vieira Levy, Ramon Moreno, and Eric Rosengren.

Conclusions

The evidence, policy recommendations, and models presented in this volume differ about what monetary policy actions, if any, policymakers should take to protect against bubbles or mitigate their impact. However, several recurring themes and messages are emphasized:

- Asset price bubbles are very difficult to identify ex ante, because policymakers are constrained by imperfect information, limited effectiveness of policy instruments, the downside risks of misusing instruments, and time constraints.
- Although many bubble collapses are followed by crises, not all crashes lead to crises that destabilize the financial system; financial systems that have strong supervisory and regulatory institutions and macroeconomic stability before the onset of a bubble tend to weather a bubble's collapse better than systems that do not.
- Bubbles and crashes occur with greater frequency in emerging, rather than developed, economies because they are more likely to occur when financial markets are opaque, when regulation and supervision are poor, and when lending is based on collateral rather than expected cash flow due to poor accounting standards.
- Countries that suffer from longer, costlier, and more systemically destabilizing crashes tend also to suffer from poor transparency, weak macroeconomic policies, and microstructural weaknesses in advance of the asset price bubble. This suggests that even more important than the effort to identify bubbles is the effort to establish an effective prudential regulatory regime that will buffer the financial system against the impact of crisis.
- Transparency minimizes information asymmetries and potential agency problems. Development and enforcement of accounting and auditing standards, including the quality of disclosure and the frequency and means of dissemination, are desirable.
- Broader, more diversified financial systems spread risks and weather the storm of post-bubble collapses better than more narrow, less diversified systems. Promoting the development of risk-transfer instruments, such as securitized assets, index funds, stock borrowing, lending, and short-selling regimes, and regulated futures and derivatives markets—to allow for heterogeneity of opinions and allow investors to bet against bubbles—is warranted.
- Strong regulatory and supervisory institutions are always the best line of defense. In this context, maintaining the credibility and reputation of the central bank so that it will be able to carry out its core function—maintaining macroeconomic stability—is essential. In banking systems, a number of authors prescribe efforts to maintain mandatory bank capital ratios that are high enough to conduct obligatory "stress" tests of banking systems and individual banks, to regulate the

loan-value-ratio (as in the Hong Kong Monetary Authority), as well as to regulate banks to prevent concentration of lending to real estate-related sectors. Preventive measures are also recommended in the capital markets: Build the capacity of the technical skills of regulators and financial practitioners; promote investor education; conduct surveillance of concentrations and illicit activities and share information between regulators; institute prudential reporting and dynamic requirements geared to safe and sound clearing and settlements; redesign loan-loss provisioning rules to be less procyclical; assign investigatory and intervention powers and clear legal definitions for different species of property; and design effective disciplinary, civil, and criminal remedies against perpetuators of stock fraud.

William C. Hunter
George G. Kaufman
Michael Pomerleano
Editors

PART I
KEYNOTE ADDRESSES

Chapter 1
Asset Price Bubbles, Information, and Public Policy

Randall S. Kroszner*
Council of Economic Advisers

1. Introduction

The issue of asset price bubbles is by no means a new one. Studies of such well-known putative bubbles as the Dutch tulip mania in the 17th century and the South Sea bubble in the 18th century have long fascinated economists. Despite the persistent interest in such phenomena, asset price bubbles are still not well understood.

Asset price bubbles represent a challenge to researchers and policymakers because some fundamental questions have not been answered in a convincing manner: How does one define an asset price bubble in a practical way? How can we identify an asset price bubble? If a bubble could be identified and measured, how should a policymaker respond? I commend the conference organizers for putting together such an impressive list of academic researchers, policy researchers, and policymakers in order to address the important issue of asset price bubbles. I am confident that the conference will yield a better understanding of the policy implications of asset price bubbles.

I will discuss the issue of asset price bubbles, focusing on the role of information and implications for public policy. I will start with some observations about the difficulty of identifying asset price bubbles from a practical view as a policymaker. The ability to identify asset price bubbles would be critical if a policymaker were interested in pursuing a policy to deflate bubbles. Even though I will argue that identifying bubbles is fraught with peril, there is, nonetheless, an important role for policymakers in addressing the possibility of asset price bubbles. Asset price bubbles—if they exist in a meaningful way—represent a mispricing of asset values by the market. The well-established principles of market efficiency provide insights on how to design policies that could improve the flow and accuracy of information for pricing assets and, therefore, could help to reduce the likelihood that an asset price bubble could form. I will then close with a discussion of recent Bush administration policies that go a long way toward strengthening financial markets through a more effective exchange and provision of information in the marketplace.

2. Identifying Asset Price Bubbles

One way to understand the practical implications of asset price bubbles for public policy is to appreciate how much economists know, and do not know, about identifying asset price bubbles. To be sure, there are economists and many journalists who claim they "know" when an asset price bubble is forming. Such knowledge sells books and magazines. However, the research record on asset price measurement is far from being sufficient to build a policymaker's confidence.

Identifying asset price bubbles is quite difficult both *ex ante* and *ex post*. Kindleberger (1996), for example, maintained that asset price bubbles are often defined by their time series behavior. An asset price that soars and then subsequently crashes is the standard example of what many think of as bubble behavior. To motivate how such pattern recognition creates problems for policymakers, I prepared a few charts with which to play the game that I would like to call "Is it a Bubble?" We will look at a chart without its labels and try to guess whether it represents an asset price bubble. For example, figure 1 is a flat line. Is it a bubble? Most economists using the chartist view of bubbles might disagree that this is *prima facie* evidence of a bubble. Figure 2 helps to answer the question by revealing that the flat line represents the value of the Argentine peso from 1997 to 2002. During this period, the Argentine currency board established a fixed exchange rate between the peso and the U.S. dollar. This figure also shows that in January 2002, the Argentine peso depreciated sharply. I would agree that the depreciation moved the peso closer to the value that markets assessed the fundamentals to support. The Argentine situation illustrates how a flat asset price not only fails to indicate a lack of financial stress but also that a sharp change in an asset price can represent a restoration of an asset price toward a more appropriate market rate.

Further lessons can be learned by comparing the behavior of U.S. equity values over time. Figure 3 shows five periods in which the Standard & Poor's 500 rose rapidly. Which episodes represent bubble behavior? Once again, patterns can be deceiving. Figure 4 illustrates this point by showing that all the run-ups in stock prices are not followed by sharp and persistent collapses. From the vantage point of the peaks in 1956 and 1987, the rapid run-up in prices, which were of a similar size to those of 1929 and 1937, were not foreshadowing an imminent and precipitous decline.

The increase in equity prices in the 1990s presents a particularly apt example for this conference to consider. During the five-year period before the peak in 2000, the increase in equity prices was well within the historical movements of the other five earlier episodes. One question is whether there was some way to know that the asset price increase during the 1990s was a bubble or economic fundamentals. The increase in equity prices could have reflected fundamental changes in the U.S. economy as new technologies were altering the economic landscape. During this period, for example, labor productivity began growing at a much faster rate than in the past two decades (figure 5). The setback in 2000 may have reflected a change in fundamentals,

Asset Price Bubbles, Information, and Public Policy

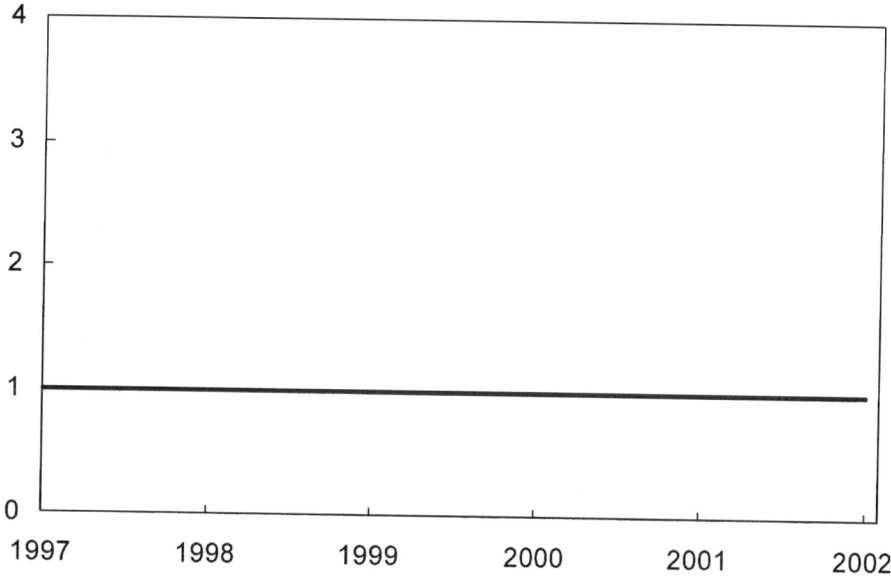

Figure 1: Is It a Bubble?

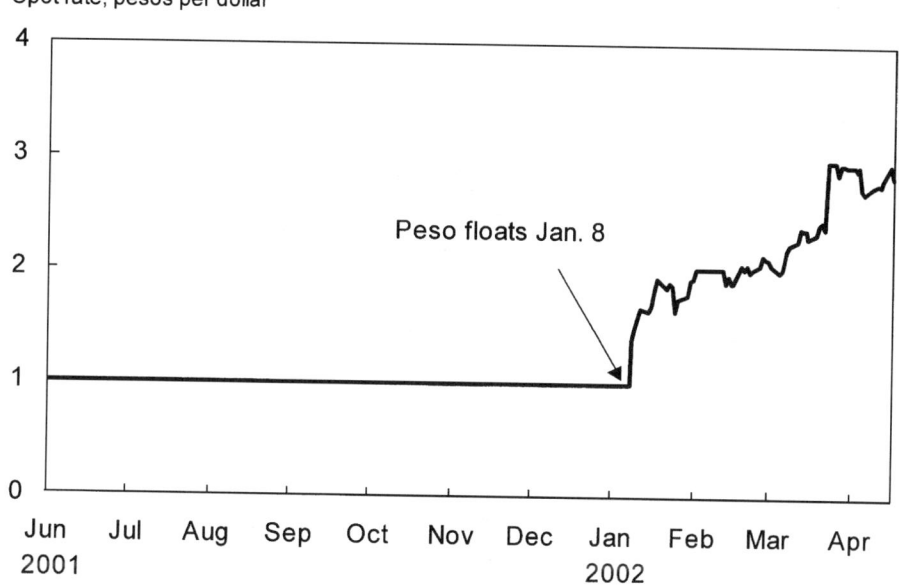

Figure 2: Argentine Peso

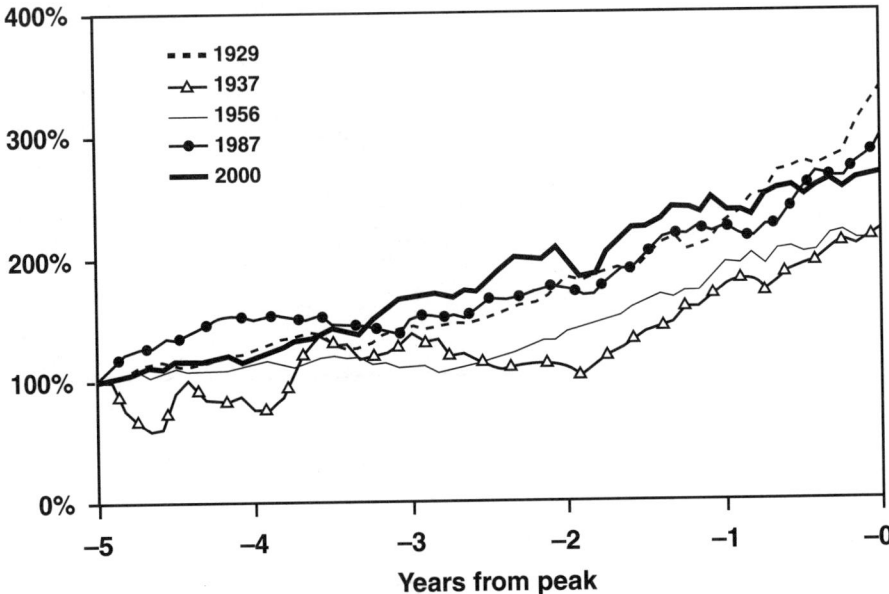

Figure 3: S&P 500: Five Years before Local Peak

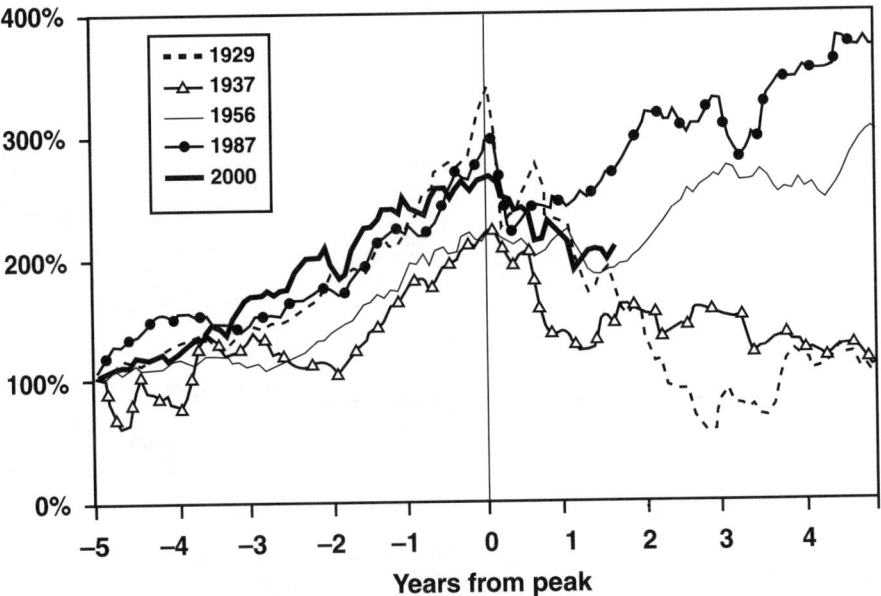

Figure 4: S&P 500: Five Years before and after Local Peak

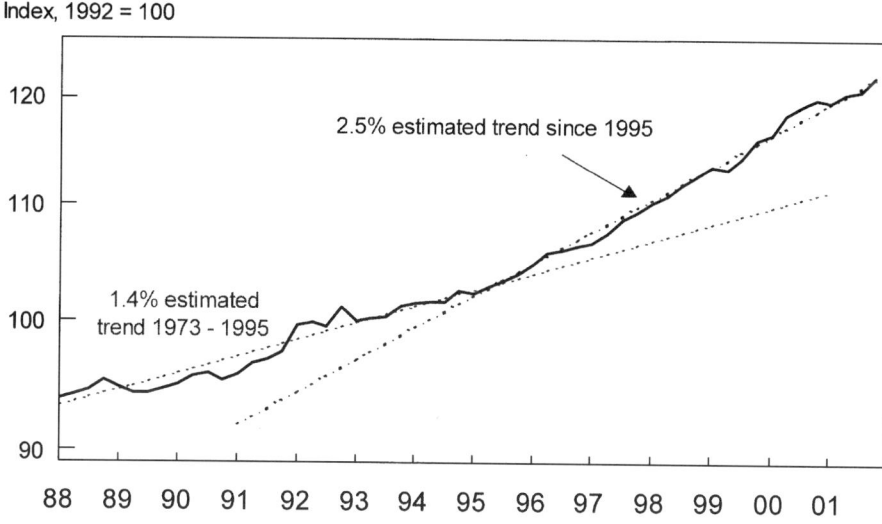

Figure 5: Nonfarm Labor Productivity

such as the information that the some overly optimistic possibilities of the "new economy" were less likely to occur. On the other hand, the dramatic rise in stock prices could have been the result of an asset price bubble. From a policy perspective, there is a big difference between the collapse of an asset price bubble and a change in economic fundamentals that leads rational investors to re-evaluate earnings potential. Without a doubt, policymakers in the 1990s were finding it difficult to determine if asset prices were exhibiting asset bubble behavior or simply reflecting economic fundamentals.

Another equally important question is whether with hindsight the run-up in asset prices in the late 1990s was a result of asset price bubble behavior. My reading of the academic literature leads me to conclude that this question is quite difficult to answer in a convincing way. In fact, McGrattan and Prescott's paper (2002) for this conference is a fascinating study because the authors raise doubts about whether the famous stock market crash of 1929 was a stock market bubble both from an *ex ante* and *ex post* perspective.

The inability to identify asset price bubbles *ex ante* should be sufficient reason for policymakers to be cautious about taking pre-emptive actions to deflate an asset price bubble. The inability to identify asset price bubbles *ex post* not only reinforces this cautious approach but also should cause policymakers to take pause about whether the rhetoric of asset price bubbles is a useful concept for policy discussions.

3. The Role of Public Policy

Given the difficulty of identifying asset price bubbles, the natural follow-up question is: What should be the role for policymakers? While knowing when to "deflate" an asset price bubble may be beyond the ability of economists, are there other policies that policymakers should pursue? To answer this question, we need to delve into the source of an asset price bubble—the mispricing of assets.

Having taught at the University of Chicago for more than a decade, I understand quite well that the issue of asset pricing—and their mispricing—is serious business. Standard finance theory offers several ways to think about how markets incorporate information into asset prices. The *weak-form market efficiency* criteria state that market asset prices reflect only information contained in the history of prices or returns themselves; the *semi-strong market efficiency* criteria state that market asset prices reflect all information known to all market participants (all public information); and strong-form market efficiency criteria state that market asset prices reflect all information known to any market participant (all public and private information). It is through this theoretical lens that policymakers can evaluate the appropriate responses to concerns about whether assets are being efficiently priced.

We can conceptualize these microfoundations of asset pricing by reflecting on the thought process that an investor undertakes when she sees that a firm's stock price has risen. The higher price has two possible explanations. The price could be the reflection of improved "fundamentals"—that is, new information about the firm's better prospects quickly embedded into its price. Alternatively, the higher price could be the reflection (at least in part) of "irrational exuberance" about the firm's prospects. This irrational exuberance creates a bubble, since the stock price does not reflect fundamentals alone. The investor's puzzle or inference problem is to determine which of these two possibilities is most likely correct and, therefore, whether to buy or sell that company's stock.

A public policy implication is that better information, easily accessible to *all* investors, makes bubbles more difficult to form and to be sustained. Reconsider our individual investor, attempting to infer (fundamental) information about a company's stock price. Improved public information has two reinforcing effects. First, the individual investor (or her financial advisor) can examine the firm's financial statements and Securities and Exchange Commission (SEC) filings and make a judgment about the firm's prospects compared to the current stock price. Second, the individual investor can be confident that she is not missing relevant information that is available to other market participants. When a price seems to outstrip fundamentals, an investor logically asks whether it is a bubble or whether she does not have access to important information about fundamentals. So it is important that information is available not only to select individuals, but to the general public.

Recent academic work suggests particular avenues through which public information can prevent bubbles from forming. For example, Allen and Gale's paper (2002) for this conference, building on their earlier work, identifies the agency relationship as a key transmission mechanism in the formation of bubbles. The authors' core agency example is that banks lend funds for projects without being able to observe the riskiness of the investments made by the project manager. Because of limited liability (in case of default), the agency problem initiates bubbles; the price of the risky asset can be driven above its fundamental value because the project manager does not fully bear the downside risk. Another application Allen and Gale offer is to the stock market. Here a major agency issue is that investment choices are largely made by institutional investors or other intermediaries. Indeed, the incentives for risk-taking by mutual fund managers due to the agency problem have been documented by Chevalier and Ellison (1997).

More broadly, the agency problem arises from an asymmetry of information. In Allen and Gale, for example, the project manager, acting as an agent of bank investors, has unobserved information and takes an unobserved action that affects investors' returns. In the current policy environment, the agency problem is exacerbated because of uncertainty about valuations due to well-publicized problems with accounting standards. If banks lack trust in the accuracy of the accounting standards, then the agency problem grows.

So, the clear policy lesson to be drawn from this literature is the importance of improving transparency. Better public information diminishes these agency problems, especially by reducing information asymmetry and uncertainty about the economic environment. With more accurate and complete information, heightened competition among intermediaries would enhance incentives to align the intermediaries' interests with those of their clients—the individual investor—and, therefore, lead to a more successful assessment of the risks taken with their clients' funds.

4. Two Administration Proposals to Strengthen Market Efficiency

Better disclosure of information and clearer rules have been a priority for the Bush administration. In a sense, the administration's recent efforts have been intended to improve market efficiency by moving financial markets closer to a strong form of market efficiency. Let me turn to two such proposals aimed at strengthening financial markets.

4.1 The President's Plan to Strengthen Retirement Security

At the 2002 National Summit on Retirement Saving, the president outlined the key components of his agenda to strengthen retirement security. One of the key components was a provision to expand workers' access to investment advice, a measure that encourages employers to make investment advice available to workers and allows qualified financial advisors to offer individualized investment advice only if they agree to act solely in the interests of the workers they advise. At present, the Employee Retirement Income Security Act (ERISA) generally impedes employers from obtaining investment advice for their employees from the financial institutions that often are in the best position to provide advice. In addition, federal liability standards on employer-sponsored investment advice are vague and confusing. As a result, millions of rank-and-file workers today are needlessly denied tools they could be using to make sound investment decisions and enhance their retirement security. Only 16 percent of 401(k) participants have an investment advice option available through their retirement plan. In other words, 84 percent do not. Breaking down these barriers in order to enable investors access to valuable information about their retirement funds is important.

The president's agenda for pension reform paves the way for employers to arrange for investment advice to be given to their employees—which will help to provide better information to investors, reduce uncertainty, and generally reduce the likelihood that deviations between market prices and fundamental valuations will arise. To this end, the administration supports H.R. 2269 (Retirement Security Advice Act) which would help American workers to better manage their retirement savings by expanding the availability of investment advice. This bill also would place advisers who have affiliations with investment products on a more equal footing with non-affiliated advisers, foster competition among firms, and promote lower costs to participants. H.R. 2269 would afford certain plan participants access to advice from fiduciary advisers, who are regulated by federal or state authorities. As fiduciaries under ERISA, these advisers would be held to the standard of conduct currently required by ERISA. H.R. 2269 also would add important protections to ERISA, by providing information to participants about fees, relationships that may raise potential conflicts of interest, and limitations on the scope of advice to be provided.

There are many important benefits to this bill. The bill updates an outdated federal law to allow employers to provide their workers with access to high-quality professional investment advice as a benefit to their employees. The measure clarifies employer liability, thereby removing the barrier to employers contracting with advice providers and their workers. No employee is under any obligation to accept or follow any advice. Workers, not their advisers, will have full control over their investment decisions. By modernizing an outdated section of ERISA, Congress can help workers plan for their retirement more wisely, maximize their retirement security, and minimize their risk. The more education investors receive, the better equipped they will be to deal with the risk of market volatility, make the choices that best serve their long-term needs, and protect and grow their hard-earned retirement dollars. The bill fosters a competitive, dynamic marketplace for investment advice that serves worker needs and establishes a strong, protective framework that safeguards their interests.

4.2 President Bush's 10-Point Plan on Financial Disclosure

In recent months the U.S. system of corporate financial disclosure has come under scrutiny. The U.S. capital markets remain the largest, most transparent, and most liquid in the world. Nonetheless, this system can and should be improved.

In his speech in March, President Bush outlined his 10-point plan (see appendix for details) to improve corporate financial disclosure and to enhance shareholder protection. This plan is guided by the following core principles: 1) providing better information to investors; 2) making corporate officers more accountable; and 3) developing a stronger, more independent audit system. Each of these elements will improve the access to information and make mispricing less likely in the future. The administration supports the enactment of H.R. 3763 (Corporate and Auditing Accountability, Responsibility, and Transparency Act of 2002) as an important step toward improving corporate responsibility and is consistent with the president's 10-point plan.

The president's plan provides better information to investors. First, the president has directed the SEC to require companies to disclose quarterly information in its control that a reasonable investor would find necessary to assess a company's value, without compromising competitive secrets (point No. 1). Disclosure practices have fallen behind advances in corporate finance. Moreover, too many firms have mistaken "check the box" compliance with GAAP (generally accepted accounting principles) for proper disclosure. The president's plan refocuses companies on what constitutes proper disclosure in today's business environment. Second, the president has directed the SEC to expand the list of significant events requiring disclosure between quarterly reporting periods (point No. 2). These steps will aid investors in understanding the underlying economics of public firms, and so help distinguish future business and investing opportunities from future speculative bubbles.

Enhancing the accountability of corporate leaders is also crucial to restoring trust in our system. Chief executive officers (CEOs) should personally vouch for the veracity, timeliness, and fairness of their companies' public disclosures, including their financial statements (point No. 3). In addition, CEOs should be forced to disgorge any bonuses or incentive based compensation in cases of accounting restatements involving misconduct (point No. 4) and should be barred from holding such positions in publicly traded companies in the future in cases of serious misconduct (point No. 5). The president is proposing that companies disclose stock transactions by officers and directors in company stock within two business days of execution (point No. 6). Currently corporate leaders can go as long as a year without disclosing personal transactions with the company and as long as 40 days for open market transactions.

Corporate governance remains largely an issue for state law and market discipline. But the federal government can play an important reinforcing role. For example, the growth of stock-based or incentive-based compensation for CEOs addresses a genuine interest of shareholders in aligning executives' interests with their own. But an imperfectly crafted compensation plan could lead some executives to engage in actions that manipulate the stock price to their own benefit. Forcing such gains to be returned to the shareholders in cases of misconduct ultimately serves shareholder interests by making incentive-based compensation plans more effective. Moreover, this mandatory disgorgement makes mispricing less likely, since CEOs will not reap rewards from misconduct that inflates the share price. Thus, market efficiency is strengthened.

Developing a stronger, more independent audit system is the final element of the president's plan. Investors also depend on the judgment, integrity, and competence of independent auditors. While auditors cannot prevent intentional deceit, they provide a critical external check on corporate management. Under the president's plan, audit company independence will be assured by SEC restrictions on providing services that compromise such independence. This addresses possible conflicts of interest. The president has directed the SEC to set forth prohibitions against the performance by an outside auditor of internal audit services for the same client. In addition, other non-audit services would not be prohibited under the president's plan, but clients would have to disclose in greater detail the fees paid to the auditing firm and its affiliates (point No. 7). Moreover, an independent regulatory board should ensure that the accounting profession is held to the highest ethical standards (point No. 8).

The authors of accounting standards must be responsive to the needs of investors (point No. 9). The president has called upon the SEC to exercise broader oversight of the Financial Accounting Standards Board, ensure its independence, and require promulgation of standards that reflect economic reality rather than compliance with GAAP. Finally, firms' accounting systems should be compared with best practices, not simply against minimum standards (point No. 10).

Although I have a great appreciation and respect for the role accountants play in the financial reporting system, as an economist I cannot help but smile at the notion that economic principles will play a larger role in accounting standards. The strengthening of accounting and auditing systems will provide greater information and transparency to investors. Indeed, my previous academic work (Kroszner and Rajan, 1994, 1997) suggests that the presence of conflicts of interest will result in the voluntary adoption of institutions that ameliorate such conflicts. And, in the present case we are already seeing market penalties that are acting to reward more transparent disclosure. The president's plan is helping to reinforce powerful market incentives.

5. Conclusion

The traditional questions associated with asset price bubbles continue to interest policymakers today. The economics literature on asset price bubbles, however, does not offer many convincing answers. Economists still have much research to do in order to improve our understanding of this phenomenon and its implications for public policy. The conference organizers should be commended for tackling an important, and vexing, policy issue.

A fundamental problem for policymakers in the past, the present, and probably the future is the ability to identify asset price bubbles *ex ante*, or even *ex post*. Without confidence that bubble conditions exist, policymakers must be wary about responding to an apparent asset price bubble because the response may result in more harm than good. This does not mean that there is no role for the public policymaker. As we have seen with the president's recent proposals, such as the 10-point plan for financial disclosure and reforms of rules governing 401(k) retirement accounts, public policies can help remove barriers to the effective exchange and provision of information, thereby strengthening markets and reducing the likelihood of asset mispricing.

*Randall S. Kroszner is a member of the President's Council of Economic Advisers. He is currently on leave from the University of Chicago's Graduate School of Business where he is a professor of economics and from his positions as editor of the *Journal of Law & Economics* and associate director of the George J. Stigler Center for the Study of the Economy and the State. He is also a faculty research fellow of the National Bureau of Economic Research.

References
Allen, F., and D. Gale, 2002, "Asset Price Bubbles and Stock Market Interlinkages," *Asset Price Bubbles: The Implications for Monetary, Regulatory, and International Policies*, William C. Hunter, George G. Kaufman, and Michael Pomerleano, eds., Boston: The MIT Press.

Chevalier, J., and G. Ellison, 1997, "Risk Taking by Mutual Funds as a Response to Incentives," *Journal of Political Economy*, December.

Garber, P., 2000, *Famous First Bubbles: The Fundamentals of Early Manias*, Cambridge, MA: The MIT Press.

Kindleberger, C., 1996, *Manias, Panics, and Crashes: A History of Financial Crises*, 3rd ed., New York: Wiley.

Kroszner, R., and R. Rajan, 1994, "Is the Glass-Steagall Act Justified? A Study of the U.S. Experience with Universal Banking Before 1933," *American Economic Review*, September.

Kroszner, R., and R. Rajan, 1997, "Organization Structure and Credibility: Evidence from Commercial Bank Securities Activities Before the Glass-Steagall Act," *Journal of Monetary Economics*, August.

McGrattan, E., and E. Prescott, 2002, "Testing for Stock Market Overvaluation/Undervaluation," *Asset Price Bubbles: The Implications for Monetary, Regulatory, and International Policies*, William C. Hunter, George G. Kaufman, and Michael Pomerleano, eds., Boston: The MIT Press.

Appendix

President Bush's 10-Point Plan on Financial Disclosure

1. Each investor should have quarterly access to the information needed to judge a firm's financial performance, condition, and risks.
2. Each investor should have prompt access to critical information.
3. CEOs should personally vouch for the veracity, timeliness, and fairness of their companies' public disclosures, including their financial statements.
4. CEOs or other officers should not be allowed to profit from erroneous financial statements.
5. CEOs or other officers who clearly abuse their power should lose their right to serve in any corporate leadership positions.
6. Corporate leaders should be required to tell the public promptly whenever they buy or sell company stock for personal gain.
7. Investors should have complete confidence in the independence and integrity of companies' auditors.
8. An independent regulatory board should ensure that the accounting profession is held to the highest ethical standards.
9. The authors of accounting standards must be responsive to the needs of investors.
10. Firms' accounting systems should be compared with best practices, not simply against minimum standards.

Chapter 2
Asset Price Bubbles and Their Implications for Monetary Policy and Financial Stability

Jean-Claude Trichet*
Bank of France

It is a great honor and pleasure to talk today in front of such a distinguished audience on the theme of asset price bubbles at the invitation of the World Bank and the Federal Reserve Bank of Chicago. As a central banker, my main focus will be on the implications of asset price developments and bubbles for both monetary policy and financial stability. The far-reaching changes observed over the last decade on financial markets, the growing role of these markets for the financing of the economy, and the evidence gathered over the recent period on the key role that financial factors may play in shaping and amplifying the business cycle have drawn attention to the relative importance of asset prices and wealth effects on the real economy.

There are at least two reasons why asset prices and wealth effects may have grown over the last decade:

1. First, changes in asset valuations, mainly driven by the rise in the new economy stock prices from the mid 1990s and their subsequent collapse in 2000, have been dramatic. This is well documented in the United States. But, even in Europe, where the influence of the so-called "new economy" is more modest, the rise in stock prices has also been significant.

2. Second, these changes have probably influenced private spending more than past asset prices movements did because of the more widespread share ownership observed in a number of industrialized countries. As far as France is concerned, market capitalization as a percentage of gross domestic product (GDP) increased approximately four-fold between 1990 and 2000 (28 percent to 110.5 percent), and we have some evidence that the share of households' equity holdings in financial assets has also risen.

All of these developments have recently raised the issue of whether monetary policy should react to financial asset prices and, more generally, to asset prices. The motivation is two-fold: *Not only could the large swings*, misalignments or even bubbles, *on asset prices endanger price stability,* which is the main objective of most central banks, *but also they could impinge upon financial stability,* which is an other important goal of central banks. Let me now develop these two points.

1. Implications for Monetary Policy

1.1 Transmission Channels of Monetary Policy

The role asset prices may play in the transmission mechanism of monetary policy is well known theoretically, although quite difficult to characterize empirically. Monetary policy mainly controls the interbank overnight rate, which is not directly relevant for any material economic decision. The way in which monetary policy affects the real economy is when it impacts on relevant financial prices, i.e., when it moves the whole yield curve or when it affects the exchange rate and other asset prices.

There might be several channels through which the policy rate can affect asset prices or asset valuations. First, changes in interest rate modify people's expectations about future economic growth, and, thus, their profit expectations. Second, monetary policy decisions may change the set of discount factors economic agents apply to their profit expectations or to the future stream of services or revenues from the asset they hold (housing, for instance). Finally, interest rate changes may induce portfolio shifts amongst assets that may, in turn, affect their relative prices.

Besides this, and for the sake of simplicity I will call it the "interest rate channel," changes in asset prices also generate wealth effects that may have a significant impact on several components of aggregate demand, namely consumption and investment. These wealth effects feed through to the economy via various channels, such as a direct increase in net wealth, which may lead to a rise in consumption because of households' intertemporal smoothing behavior; via Tobin's q, which activates firms' investment; or via an increase in the value of collaterals, which may reduce agents' external financing constraints and enhance final spending, in accordance with the "broad credit channel." Although the evidence is mixed about the effectiveness of the wealth channel, even in the United States (Lettau and Ludvigson, 2001), it is likely to have increased over recent years. Moreover, asset prices fluctuations or changes might also activate some confidence or expectations channels that may in turn influence the spending decisions of households or firms. For all of these reasons, asset prices have a particular role in the conduct of monetary policy.

1.2 How Should Central Banks React?

Does this mean that monetary policy should react directly to asset prices? Or, more precisely, should asset prices be directly taken into account by the central bank's reaction function? This issue is still debated amongst researchers and academics; my feeling is that *we should remain extremely cautious about it,* perhaps because it would be like opening Pandora's box if we started setting our key policy rates according to asset price changes. Another reason for being extremely cautious is that assessing asset price valuations is a very challenging exercise. And, *what matters is not only the asset price level per se,* or the pace of its change, *but also its deviation from a highly hypothetical fundamental value,* which basically is hard to measure or determine.

Although, from time to time, it may seem that asset price dynamics are not really correlated to overall economic development, it is generally hard to assess whether these dynamics are rooted in some deep fundamental changes or whether asset prices evolve according to some "pathological path." The recent "tech stock bubble" provides us with an illustration of such a difficulty: While one was witnessing the "irrational exuberance" in 1996, the surge in capital spending associated with the development of new technologies resulted in a faster productivity growth, which, in turn, boosted equity prices. At that time, uncertainties about fundamentals (was there an American miracle?) made a proper assessment of asset valuations difficult, although the large movements in asset prices were a concern for central banks.

However, *when expectations reverse,* for example, due to the reassessment of expected profitability in the economy, *and consequently asset prices decrease, the point is to determine whether the attitude of the central bank ought to be different in order to preserve monetary and financial stability.* That is, some could argue that the central bank's response should be asymmetric. In the booming phase, as long as price stability is not endangered, central banks do not react to the rise in asset prices. Conversely, in the recession phase or when a bubble bursts, central banks could consider reacting if they deem that monetary and financial stability is endangered. *What could then restrain them from doing it?* Such an asymmetric reaction, all the more if it seems to be systematic, *has actually a cost,* pointed out in the literature, since it may generate some *moral hazard problems:* As long as economic agents believe the central bank will ultimately make use of its "safety net," there is an incentive to invest on riskier projects in order to magnify expected returns, keeping in mind that potential losses are likely to be limited.

Would then, a systematically symmetric reaction by a central bank to asset price changes *solve this problem? I would not share that view*, because central banks cannot accurately assess the deviation of asset prices from their highly hypothetical fundamental value. To illustrate my point, let us consider a situation in which the central bank fails to diagnose the presence of a bubble and, therefore, does not react appropriately to the surge in asset prices; then, agents may become involved in riskier projects without having consciously taken the decision to accept greater risk, but on the ground of what they have interpreted as a sound financial and economic environment. As a result, we have shifted to another problem, which is close to the idea of "disaster myopia" (Guttentag and Herring, 1986).

1.3 The Issue of Measuring Price Stability

However, this raises another issue, especially in the current context of muted inflationary pressures but ample fluctuations in asset prices: Are we measuring inflation accurately? Is price stability being ensured, in the context of large movements in asset prices? Shouldn't asset prices be taken into account when defining price stability? Up to now, this debate has focused on the role asset prices may play as leading indicators of inflation. One rationale behind this thinking may be that asset valuation is computed in a forward-looking manner and, therefore, asset prices embed expectations about future economic growth and future inflationary pressures. Empirical evidence gathered on such an issue tends to support the idea that some asset prices, housing prices in particular, may actually play such a role. However, this theory has to be qualified by the fact that, as I mentioned earlier, wealth effects are difficult to establish in a definitive manner. This is probably less true for the United States, although this is debatable and could be discussed in this conference, but this is more likely to be true for the euro area. Moreover, there might be a danger that asset prices diverge from the Consumer Price Index (CPI), as this was observed over the last few years. There might be an internal conflict here if the objective of price stability is defined by aggregating the changes in the CPI and the changes in asset prices, and this is a crucial issue since the nature of both types of prices is fairly different.

So, do asset prices have a key role to play in the conduct of monetary policy? To answer this question, I will briefly describe the way we deal with asset prices in the conduct of the European single monetary policy. As you already know, the European Central Bank's (ECB) monetary policy strategy is based on a two-pillar approach. This concept of monetary policy was designed to promote the conduct of a sound monetary policy whilst coping with the complexity of the set of major determinants of inflation, fully recognized by the governing council of the ECB. That is why we rely upon a binocular vision of the factors of inflation, i.e., as a monetary phenomenon according to pillar one and as the result of short-term to medium-term developments of inflation according to pillar two. This framework is also well suited to addressing the asset price bubble issue.

In this context, the *first pillar is very* helpful for analyzing how ample liquidity is within the euro area, that is to say, how much the broad monetary aggregate (M3) deviates from its reference value and how economic agents make use of this liquidity: Credit and loan developments are carefully monitored, in line with economical and financial developments. Portfolio shifts are also an important part of the monetary analysis. Too rapid a credit expansion to the private sectors associated with large portfolios shifts towards equities and a strong rise in stock or asset prices would, under normal economic conditions, signal the risk of a bubble formation.

The *second pillar* consists of a wide range of economic and financial indicators: Stock and bond prices, housing prices, and exchange rates are also analyzed in-depth. Obviously, their assessment is made in the context of maintaining price stability over the medium term, and the ECB does not react to their signals unless price stability is endangered. To recap, if monetary policy does not react directly to asset price developments or to an asset price bubble, it has clearly to take under consideration all the consequences of these developments on aggregate demand and aggregate supply and on economic agents' confidence and expectations, since they may at some point affect price developments.

Let me now turn to my second point—the implications of asset prices bubbles for financial stability.

2. Implications for Financial Stability

Over the last decade, we have experienced several financial crises and contagion episodes—just to name a few episodes, the Mexican crisis in 1994–95, the Russian Long-Term Capital Management in 1998, the "tech bubble" that ended in 2000, or more recently the financial crises in Argentina and Turkey. However, recent research (Bordo et al., 2000) has shown that, if the frequency of financial crises is not significantly different from what was observed in previous periods over the long run (1883–1998), recent episodes were certainly shorter, but perhaps more severe.

Although financial globalization has brought about improved macroeconomic efficiency, via a more efficient allocation of resources and capital, liberalized capital flows, increased competition on financial markets, increased transparency (apart from the recent Enron episode!), and changes in asset prices have also become more pronounced and have experienced clear misalignments or deviations from their "equilibrium" levels. Moreover, credit seems to have played a greater role in asset prices fluctuations. Initially observed during the "speculative bubbles" of the 1980s and early 1990s, this trend has persisted, if not amplified.

Several factors may explain these recent and abnormal patterns in asset prices. I shall give a few examples.

1. First, "short-termism:" Some market participants may have become more inclined to be mostly preoccupied with their short-term results. This trend might result, in particular, from growing pressure to yield good results immediately. However, these results are not necessarily sustainable. Marking-to-market financial products may also have contributed to this widespread focus on immediate financial performances. This emphasis on short-term performance may result in increased volatility in the price formation process: The shorter the investment horizon of markets participants, the bigger the impact of any new information on prices.

2. Second, herding or mimetic behavior: Mimetic behavior is, of course, by no means a new phenomenon on financial markets. Technological developments on markets may, however, have gradually reinforced this type of behavior, as participants are under increasing pressure to follow their peers through matching the performance of a benchmark. There is no doubt that the spread of benchmarking allows fund managers and clients to better assess their performance against that of other funds. But, in a context of growing competition within the sector, it may well have increased mimetic behavior. Some market participant operators (whose own compensation is closely linked to the relative, rather than absolute, profit and losses they generate) may indeed have come to the conclusion that it would be better to be wrong along with everybody else, rather than running the risk of being right alone. A striking example of rational mimetic behavior is the influence that hedge funds enjoyed as "opinion leaders" and trendmakers. By its nature, trend-following amplifies the imbalance that may at some point affect a market, potentially leading to vicious circles of price adjustments and liquidation of positions. Moreover, more and more participants are able to access financial markets directly, while the expertise to deal with a larger set of technical information is not evenly distributed. This may also reinforce the role of "gurus."

3. Third, index management: As a fund management technique, it has proved to be very popular on equity markets and may have contributed to exacerbating movements in financial asset prices. Because their goal is to mimic the performance of indices, "passive managers" try constantly to match the composition of their benchmark. They, thus, help to amplify market trends, buying more as the market rises

and liquidating more as the market drops. It can be argued that index funds distort the price of the targeted indices and that, as a result, the indices end up creating rather than measuring performance.

4. Last but not least, the impact of risk management techniques on market dynamics is particularly enlightening with regard to the question of asset price overshooting. Value-at-risk (VaR) calculations have become a crucial element of the standard approach used by market participants to evaluate the risk inherent in their market activities and to set up exposure limits. Of course, central banks and financial institutions should continue to encourage the use of these instruments. But, in times of financial turmoil, the growing use of sophisticated risk management techniques by financial intermediaries might have had the paradoxical effect of amplifying the initial shock, exhausting liquidity, and contributing to contagion phenomena. Regardless of the intrinsic qualities of these risk management tools, we see that their growing use in the same fashion by all market participants may have produced pernicious effects. When market players rely on converging risk evaluations, they tend to take the same decisions at the same time, thus, amplifying the initial shock to prices and trading volumes.

All these factors have one consequence in common: They encourage homogenous behavior and reactions to the detriment of the diversity that is indispensable to the smooth functioning of financial markets.

So, what are the possible policy implications of these recent patterns or trends on financial markets? My opinion is that financial authorities might reflect on some ways to foster behavioral diversity in financial markets. As we have just seen before, some specific factors, such as short-termism, mimetic behavior, etc. ... have tended to make "contrarians" less proactive on financial markets. As a consequence, in order to safeguard the smooth functioning of the markets, the diversity of participants' behaviors must be protected or even reinforced. This necessary diversity should logically reflect natural differences in time horizons, strategies, and reaction functions of market players. On this point, I would like to explore amongst many others three possible avenues for future action for both monetary or financial authorities and the financial industry.

Avenue 1: Strengthen the Continuing Efforts Aimed at Market Transparency

Experience shows that uncertainty and incomplete information are determining factors in mimetic behavior. These shortfalls in market transparency make mimetic behavior seem rational to agents, who prefer to follow bigger participants who are thought to be better informed, rather than develop their own analysis. Therefore, strengthening transparency continues to be the priority. In the same vein, attention should be paid to expand the skills and competencies required for the analysis of more detailed and complex information. Transparency is useless if only a limited number of experts are able to deal with it.

One of the objectives of transparency is to enable better differentiation of borrower creditworthiness. A key feature of mimetic behavior is that all borrowers are "tarred with the same brush." So when one emerging economy encounters difficulties, all neighboring countries are treated in the same way—regardless of their actual economic and financial situation. The same applies to businesses operating in the same economic sector. Transparency may have improved since the Asian crisis, which may explain why contagion effects are nowadays rather subdued (see Argentina). Let us continue and reinforce these efforts.

Avenue 2: Take into Account the Medium- and Long-term Perspective of Some Market Participants

Some investors, such as pension funds and insurance companies, have to invest funds in order to enable their customers to build up wealth over the medium- and long-term, notably in preparation for retirement. Consequently, these types of investors are supposed to behave differently from traders and short-term investors, who are working on a very different time horizon. But at times it seems that they are all pushed to behave in much the same way—on the basis of a very short-term horizon.

To preserve, and even restore, their specific investment approach, these investors might be more shielded from excessive short-term pressures. This objective raises considerable difficulties, because it touches on the way in which the performances of medium- and long-term funds and life insurance companies are assessed. In other words, this objective concerns the accounting standards and practices they use. It might imply that some rules and standards would be adapted to the medium- and long-term horizons used by these entities.

Avenue 3: Diversify the Risk Management Tools of Financial Institutions

As I mentioned earlier, even the best techniques can have adverse effects when used on a standard basis and by all participants. To some degree, this is perhaps what has happened to VaR-based techniques, which have been, for very good reasons, massively adopted by the financial industry. Because they use more or less similar parameters and suffer from the same weaknesses—for example, they did not take market liquidity into account adequately at the time of the 1998 crisis—such tools might tend to give converging signals to those that use them. They, thus, encourage the mimetic behavior that I discussed previously.

Of course, the fact that some market participants are more sophisticated than the average is a guarantee that standardization will remain limited, since these participants will develop techniques that are little used by others.

However, supervisors might help and obviously are already helping to spread the idea that financial institutions should round out their current range of risk management tools to include extensive use of stress testing. This technique offers a better reflection of the varying situations of institutions and of the diverse perceptions that institutions have of exceptional events. The application of stress testing techniques and their results are, thus, inherently more diversified than those resulting from methods based on the VaR approach.

3. Conclusion

Asset price developments are a serious cause of concern for central banks since they may impinge upon both price and financial stability. And, I would like to stress what I feel is the highly complementary nature of price stability and financial stability objectives: Price stability is the bedrock on which financial stability is built.

However, in my opinion, it is clearly not opportune to introduce asset prices into a monetary policy rule the central bank should commit to or into a reaction function of the bank. Aside from the reasons I already mentioned, another issue is: Which asset price should we take into account? Should we limit the rule to stock prices, or extend the rule to housing prices, exchange rates, the cost of capital, and so on? I would also not support the idea of introducing asset prices into the measurement of inflation or the definition of price stability. My first reason is that the nature of goods and services on the one hand, and assets on the other hand, are quite different and so is the information contained in their prices. Another reason is that asset prices are highly volatile, much more volatile than other prices, especially in the current context of low inflation. Consequently, it might be difficult to implement a sound monetary policy by focusing on highly volatile indicators. Finally, it is highly questionable that one could determine scientifically what an asset price equilibrium value is. Some participants will probably address some of these issues, which are of great interest for central bankers, during the conference.

I also provided you with some examples of possible options monetary and financial authorities may take to help improve the functioning of the financial cycles. There is a lot of merit in embarking upon an overall review of regulatory, accounting, and tax rules and regulations, as well as of codes of good conduct and good practices, and, finally, upon structural developments of markets themselves. I am convinced that this review, triggered not only by macrofinancial considerations but also by dramatic micro observations, like Enron, is likely to help identify possible amendments and improvements that could protect and enhance not only the integrity but also the behavioral and conceptual diversity that should make up the essential characteristics of modern financial markets.

*Jean-Claude Trichet is governor of the Bank of France.

References

Bordo, M., B. Eichengreen, D. Klingebiel, and M. S. Martinez-Peria, 2000, "Is the Crisis Problem Growing More Severe?" Center for Economic Policy Research, September.

Guttentag, J. M., and R. J. Herring, 1986, "Disaster Myopia in International Banking," in *Essays in International Finance*, Vol. 164, Princeton University.

Lettau, Sydney, and Sydney Ludvigson, 2001, "Understanding Trend and Cycle in Asset Values: Bulls, Bears and the Wealth Effect on Consumption," Center for Economic Policy Research, discussion paper, No. 3104, December.

Chapter 3
Rational and Nonrational Bubbles

Allan H. Meltzer*
Carnegie Mellon University
and American Enterprise Institute

The subject of this conference is an esoteric issue in rational expectations, general equilibrium modeling. The issue arises because it is not possible to show that models of this kind converge to a unique, stationary equilibrium or dynamic equilibrium path. There are potentially multiple equilibria, and among them are some in which prices of assets or output do not converge to finite values. Prices can explode. A technical reason why a model may have bubble solutions is that there may not be an infinitely lived rational decisionmaker who breaks the bubble.

We have all heard of the German, Hungarian, and other hyperinflations studied by Cagan (1956) and subsequently by many others. The price level explodes upward in his model, as it did in practice. As long as the Reichsbank, or other central banks, allowed the money stock to accelerate, the price level accelerated. Indeed, this is the point of Cagan's model, and its success in explaining hyperinflations is evidence that there was *not* a bubble in these cases.

The first lesson about bubbles is that all explosive movements are not bubbles. It was entirely rational for people to observe the Reichsbank's monetary acceleration and conclude that the price level would also accelerate as a systematic response to monetary acceleration.

Economists use different definitions of "bubble" in their analytic work. The common element is that asset or output prices increase at a rate that is greater than can be explained by market fundamentals (Kindleberger, 1992). Or, a price is above its fundamental value today *only* because investors believe it will be higher tomorrow. The equilibrium of these models is a rational expectations equilibrium.

Popular use of "bubble" shares with economic usage the emphasis on anticipations. However, the Japanese stock market in the late 1980s and the U.S. stock markets in 1929 and 1999–2000 are usually described as driven by irrational, or nonrational, anticipations. Alan Greenspan used the term "irrational exuberance" to describe what he thought had driven stock prices. A recent *Wall Street Journal* article about the dollar quotes a market participant: "Another rate cut by the Fed ... will help a slight recovery of the dollar, but will not reverse the view that the dollar bubble has been pricked," (McCarthy, 2001). Robert Shiller's (2000) much-discussed book develops this line of reasoning, as did Charles Kindleberger (1978) and many others earlier. I discuss these two meanings separately because each raises some different issues.

One problem with almost any bubble explanation of asset prices is the difference in the behavior of buyers and sellers. If buyers are rationally or irrationally exuberant, how can we characterize sellers? More on that later.

1. Rational Bubbles

The standard model of asset prices values the asset as the present value of the stream of dividends that the owner expects to receive. Strictly speaking, the horizon must be infinite, but much of the literature discusses bubbles that collapse within a finite period. In the standard asset price model, the only systematic force driving asset prices is the expected dividend stream.[1] If prices conform to this expectation, the rational expectations equilibria are said to be driven by fundamentals.

Many other rational expectations equilibria are possible in principle. These equilibria depend on expectations that are unrelated to the dividend stream, or other fundamentals. They are called "bubble solutions," or bubbles. To preserve a rational expectations solution, the value of the bubble expected today must equal the discounted value of next period's anticipated value and be independent of fundamentals. By iterated substitution, today's value depends on all future bubble values discounted to the present. Thus, the price today has two parts—the contributions of the systematic and bubble components.

At this stage in the development of economic theory, we must regard the rational bubble hypothesis as devoid of empirical content, or empty. The main reasons are that we do not observe expectations and we cannot exclude other, entirely rational, non-bubble alternative explanations of prices. I believe it is for these reasons that attempts to test the rational bubble hypothesis have not produced compelling evidence. Peter Garber (1990) casts doubt on some major past bubbles, including the famous tulip mania in the 17th century and the Mississippi and South Sea bubbles. After reviewing the evidence from empirical tests, Flood and Hodrick (1990, p. 99) conclude that, "Current empirical tests for bubbles do not successfully establish the case that bubbles exist in asset prices." And, the strict version of the bubble hypothesis does not pass the eyeball test: We do not observe asset prices that become infinite. Long before an infinite value is reached, the asset value would exceed expected gross domestic product (GDP), hardly a rational outcome. Further, Paul Weller (1992, p. 272) points to another problem: The theory "provides no clue" about the conditions initiating or terminating bubbles.

One reason that a bubble hypothesis is difficult, if not impossible, to test is that expectations are measured relative to some maintained hypothesis and, with rational expectations, exploit all of the information that is relevant according to the maintained hypothesis. Bubble phenomena are what remain unexplained by the hypothesis. In this sense, bubbles are a name assigned to phenomena that may be explained by an alternative hypothesis.

This brings me to the second reason that we should be skeptical about rational bubbles. Suppose the euro-dollar exchange rate depreciates steadily. After a time, your hypothesis, based on fundamentals, predicts that the dollar is overvalued, so you sell the dollar short and buy the euro. The dollar appreciates. This happens repeatedly, suggesting to some that a bubble is present. Since there is both evidence and theory that nominal exchange rates overshoot their equilibrium values, others continue to bet that the fundamentals will drive down the price. Additional appreciation strengthens the expectation of a large profit when the euro-dollar exchange rate corrects.

Suppose the euro-dollar rate eventually rises. There is no way to distinguish the entirely rational expectation that the dollar was overvalued from the rational bubble explanation. The two differ only in that one predicts the devaluation from a structural hypothesis, while the bubble describes the same events as a result of a collapse of self-fulfilling expectations operating independently of the structural hypothesis. It is difficult, and perhaps impossible, to distinguish between nonlinear dynamics of fundamental values and a bubble.

The fact that, ex post, forecast errors appear to be serially correlated does not discriminate between the two explanations. Exchange rate theories are not sufficiently precise to predict when devaluations will occur. Random movements in relative GDP values, anticipated inflation, stock prices, or interest rates may delay depreciation without changing the structural model's forecast.

Several years ago Alex Cukierman and I (1982) explored a closely related model. Suppose there is a permanent change in the level or growth rate of one of the variables in the exchange rate model or in the asset-pricing model. Those who think that a permanent change occurred, and that future earnings or profits will increase, bid for assets and dollars to invest in the industries or firms that are expected to profit in the future. Those who doubt that a permanent change has occurred will regard assets as overvalued, so they sell. An econometrician using available data may find that errors are serially correlated and independent of the variables in the model. To the econometric researcher the rise in asset prices may look like a bubble; the serially correlated errors may suggest that the price rise is independent of the fundamental hypothesis. The speculator who believes that new technology has made possible a permanent increase in the profit rate will regard the rise in the stock price as the rational response to a fundamental change in expected future profits. Since profit or earnings anticipations are subjective, and not observable, it is possible to reject the true hypothesis and accept the bubble.

To use a current example, suppose there has been a positive change in U.S. productivity. In the light of recent experience, it should not require much effort to convince yourself that it takes considerable time—years—to establish that a productivity change is permanent, longer still to be confident whether the change is a one-time change in level, distributed over time, or a permanent change in the productivity growth rate.

If we date the start of the current U.S. productivity increase as 1995, the earliest that we could date recognition by policy officials that a change in productivity had occurred is 1997 or 1998, when Federal Reserve Chairman Alan Greenspan began to support that interpretation. Recall, however, that many forecasters predicted rising inflation at the time, based on models in which the non-accelerating inflation rate of unemployment (NAIRU) was above 5 percent. They did not believe that productivity or productivity growth had lowered NAIRU and the expected inflation rate. As to when we will know whether the productivity change is a change in level or growth rate, after six years, that date continues to be in the future.

It took more than three years to recognize that a change in productivity had occurred. I say more than three years because at first, econometric research found little evidence of a permanent change in productivity. Research by Gordon (1998) showed very little response of economy-wide productivity to the higher productivity in the computer industry. Productivity typically rises in economic expansions without raising trend productivity or productivity growth. Oliner and Sichel (2000) were among the first to find a productivity change affecting large parts of the economy (as opposed to a single sector). Their paper first circulated about 1999. I will generalize this set of issues after discussing a different type of bubble.

2. Nonrational Bubbles

Popular discussion refers to the behavior of the Japanese economy in the late 1980s as a "bubble economy." The reference is not to the type of bubble just discussed but to a nonrational bubble, called a mania in the writings of authors like Kindleberger (1978) or Minsky (1982). The rise in U.S. stock prices in 1929 and 1999 is often described in a similar way. A loose definition is a rise in the price of an asset or asset class that generates additional increases, a rapid upward price movement based on exaggerated beliefs about the potentials of a new technology or organizational structure to generate earnings. The rise is followed by a collapse. Examples from the pricing of many technology stocks in 2000 are familiar. Everyone can provide an example of rising share prices for companies without earnings, and in some cases without prospect of earnings for three to five years or longer.

There is always an alternative hypothesis. For Japan in the 1980s, a rational explanation is that Japan had large annual current account surpluses early in the decade. The intergovernmental decision to fix exchange rates, made at the Louvre early in 1986, meant that, instead of appreciating the yen, the Japanese external balance would increase growth of Japan's monetary base. The proper inference was that initially nominal interest rates would fall and asset prices would rise. Speculators were not disappointed, at least not right away. With rapid base money growth, a real interest rate of about 1 percent and soaring earnings, land and equity prices rose rapidly. The 1990–91 recession and a more restrictive monetary policy ended the asset price boom.

Governor Hayami of the Bank of Japan agrees with part of this explanation. He has written: "Monetary easing was a necessary condition for the emergence of a bubble," (Hayami, 2001, p. 10). He continued:

> "As a matter of fact, it is extremely difficult to identify whether it is a bubble or not when we are actually experiencing bubble expansion. One of the reasons for this difficulty is that we can not exclude from the observed reality the impact of changes in economic structure," (ibid. p. 10).

In my words, "bubble" is a name we assign to events that we cannot explain with standard hypotheses. After the event, we may rule out some explanations that appeared plausible earlier, but we are unlikely to exclude all alternatives except the bubble explanation.[2]

The rational story for the United States in 1929 starts by noting that capitalization rates for corporate earnings increased in 1926, with rising profit anticipations. The capitalization rate remained between 40 and 50 until the fall of 1929, after the recession began. The stock price increase in the first eight months of 1929 accompanied rapidly rising economic activity that suggested continued profit growth. The index of industrial production rose at a 19 percent annual rate in the first half of 1929. This followed nine months of double-digit annual growth. By April 1929, automobile production was 67 percent above the 1928 average. There are few comparable periods in U.S. history from 1919 to the present, and most of the others follow deep recessions, while 1928–29 did not.

Then, as now, there was much talk about a new economy and a new era, and there is some basis for both. In the 1920s, the new economy included automobiles, radios, adding machines, and the spread of telephones. Between 1922 and 1929, the number of registered automobiles more than doubled, from 12.2 million to 26.7 million. The number of radios increased from 60 thousand to more than 12 million, and the number of telephones in service, an older technology, rose from 14 to 20 million, (*Historical Statistics*, 1960). Changes in industrial practice also contributed to belief in the new economy. This was the era of scientific management, assembly line production, and expansion of consumer credit to purchase durable goods.

The new era supplemented and strengthened the idea of a new economy. The success of the Federal Reserve in preventing both inflation and banking panics encouraged the belief that risk had been reduced., Although there were recessions in 1923–24 and 1926–27 and many failures of country banks, the financial system avoided the major disruptions or banking panics of the pre-Federal Reserve period. Restoration of the gold standard added to the sense of stability and orderly adjustment at the end of the decade. At the time, economists, bankers, and much of the public put great faith in the stabilizing properties of the gold standard. Many of them shared the belief that Federal Reserve policy had reduced the risk of financial panic, a frequent event from 1890 to 1910. In 1927, Congress gave the Federal Reserve a permanent charter, a sign that the long struggle between the populists and bankers or commercial interests had been resolved.

One can also tell a story about the 1990s relating new technology to expected future earnings of technology stocks. As long as investors and speculators expected the new technologies to generate ever-larger future profits, share prices rose. Once investors or speculators started to doubt that the new technologies would create large rents or future profits, stock prices fell. With hindsight, it is now easier to believe that new technology has changed productivity growth much more than it changed profit rates, especially for firms, many of them called dot-coms, that apply the new technology.

That said, there is reason to be skeptical about the extent to which such stories are more qualitative than quantitative. Economists do not claim that their models explain or predict the exact price at which the market clears. The pricing of some of the dot-com stocks required extreme beliefs about future earnings and profitability. Even for Amazon, one of the more successful companies, it is difficult to reconcile the anticipated future growth of earnings from the online sale of books and records, necessary to explain the stock price, with the historical record of earnings and profits by large book or record chains that operate in the more conventional way. And, if the new technology would make the historical record obsolete, what would prevent other large chains from building warehouses and competing away the rents from the new technology?

There are many similar examples of investor behavior in recent years that can only be reconciled with the valuation models that economists use by invoking wildly optimistic expectations of sustained profit growth rates. Since we do not know the model or models that investors used and we cannot retrieve their expectations, it is unlikely that economists will find evidence that persuades neither believers in nonrational bubbles, nor nonbelievers, to change their opinions.

Explaining asset market outcomes as the result of euphoric anticipations creates a problem. Who are the sellers, and what do they think and do? In rising markets, there are always Cassandras predicting collapse, but they must have sold out earlier. Perhaps they now sell short. Short sales are too small to explain the volume of purchases in asset markets like the foreign exchange market for dollars and the NASDAQ or the Tokyo stock exchanges during their meteoric rise.

I do not doubt that a clever economist can invent a consistent story about buyers and sellers. I am less optimistic about the story's truth content and its ability to explain the data. Perhaps there are degrees of euphoria, so that the less euphoric increasingly sell to the more euphoric. But this would suggest that holdings become more concentrated as the bubble expands. Evidence does not support this implication.

3. An Alternative Model

There are other ways of modeling expectations that remain consistent with rational expectations and full use of available information but do not involve bubbles.[3] Suppose that the process governing asset prices or other variables is

1) $x_t = A_t e^{\alpha(t) t} u_t,$

where t is time, and A, α, and u are random walks with zero mean and constant variance.

Instead of a single random shock with zero mean and constant variance, let's assume that asset prices (or other variables) are subject to three types of shocks, each with zero mean. First, there are transitory, random deviations around a fixed trend or stationary value (u_t). This is the familiar random walk. Second are permanent changes in level, ΔA_t, and third are permanent changes in growth rates, $\Delta \alpha_t$. Investors cannot observe the errors directly and cannot separate them initially, and for some time after. They can only infer from a series of observations whether the level has changed permanently, thereby temporarily altering the measured growth path. A single observation does not permit the investor to know whether a current change is a temporary deviation that will revert to the prior mean, a persistent change that permanently changes the mean level but not the growth rate, or a permanent change in the growth rate. Frank Knight (1921) used a model similar to this to explain economic profits as a reward for bearing uncertainty. For Knight, uncertainty differed from risk. Risk referred to drawings from a known distribution. Uncertainty did not.

If the variance of the transitory component is relatively large, several observations are required to be modestly confident that a change in the mean is permanent. And, additional observations may be needed to decide whether the mean will continue to change, i.e., that the observed change is a change in growth rate not a permanent change in level. Series like profits, stock prices, and productivity are examples of relatively noisy series. After five years of productivity growth above the average or trend of the previous 20 years, we can only guess whether there has been a permanent change in trend productivity growth and profits, in one but not the other, or in neither. The length of time needed to gain confidence about the permanence of the change depends on relative variances of transitory and permanent shocks.

As a model of asset prices, this model differs from the bubble model. It views the investor as using incomplete and noisy information to infer the future path of profits and asset prices. Investors or speculators do not trade mainly on noise. They try to infer future patterns or trends, and they pay for the services of professional letter writers and advisers, or the services of professional investors, who use different types of models and procedures to reduce not just risk but uncertainty. They hire economists to forecast the future because, despite the mediocre record of such forecasts, they are the best forecasts available.

Knight (1921) distinguished between uncertainty and risk on the basis of the probability distribution governing outcomes. Risk refers to uncertain events, where the distribution of outcomes is known. We know the distribution of outcomes when we throw the dice or flip a coin. Uncertainty refers to events for which the distribution of outcomes is unknown and the basis for classification is tenuous. What is the probability that some of the technologies in which we invest today will be obsolete tomorrow? How can we know whether someone, somewhere, is working on a better solution or product? When making decisions, we act as if the probability distributions are well behaved, when they are not.[4]

Forecasting changes in productivity growth is not risky in Knight's sense. It is uncertain. We do not know, and cannot know, how many new innovations will be built on existing knowledge. How many will be successfully introduced? How many will be initiated, with economic rents competed away, raising productivity growth but not economic profits?

Unlike the rational bubble model, in this model expectations are based on imperfect knowledge of future fundamentals such as profits. Unlike the irrational exuberance model, systematic changes in fundamentals are critical. Investors and speculators may grossly overestimate (or underestimate) future profits and dividends, but they rely on their imprecise knowledge of the future and correct, perhaps over-correct, when new information becomes available.

4. Policy Implications

I have sketched the alternative model because its policy implications are very different from the implications of the bubble explanation of asset prices. I will compare the two.

If the bubble model is correct, much of the rise in stock market valuations in the past few years was unrelated to economic fundamentals. Since asset prices affect decisions to merge, invest, and consume, these decisions, basic to any rational allocation, were distorted. It makes sense, indeed it would be desirable, for the government or the Federal Reserve to prevent the rise in asset prices caused by the bubble, or, failing that, to break the bubble.

This line of reasoning presupposes that our models, or the government's, can identify the bubble component with enough accuracy to improve on the market's decisions. Or, failing that, policymakers can tell the public that they regard the rise in asset prices as independent of fundamentals.

In 1996, at an American Enterprise Institute dinner, the Federal Reserve, in the person of Alan Greenspan, did exactly that. He suggested to the public that the rise in the prices of shares traded on U.S. exchanges was due, in considerable part, to irrational exuberance. His statement circulated widely but had no lasting impact.

I had spent part of the previous summer and fall in the library of the Board of Governors' building. Several staff members questioned me about whether I thought there was a bubble in stock prices. I suspect that their models suggested an affirmative answer to that question. I cannot be certain, but I can attest that several of the staff worried about a repeat of the 1929 stock market break.

Some market participants explain that the Federal Reserve's failure to raise interest rates after the chairman's speech is the reason that the market's response to Chairman Greenspan's 1996 statement was short-lived. This explanation suggests that the initial decline occurred because investors and speculators anticipated an increase in interest rates. When the increase did not come, market prices resumed their increase. Notice that this explanation suggests that the change in interest rates, a systematic force or its absence, not just expectations, was one of the driving forces for stock prices. The other was the expectation of a continued high rate of earnings growth. When estimates of earnings growth collapsed for firms using the new technology, such as dot-coms, so did their share prices.

The alternative explanation emphasizes uncertainty about the future and the incomplete information that characterizes estimates of future earnings and asset prices. Policymakers do not typically have superior information, so they have no basis for intervening in asset markets. I believe the emphasis this model places on uncertainty, in the Keynes-Knight sense, corresponds well to behavior on asset markets. The model emphasizes the difficulty of separating purely random changes from the systematic forces governing earnings and asset prices. It recognizes that investors may misread signals and, as a result, misallocate capital. But it recognizes also that these errors are found only ex post and cannot be prevented. It is only after the fact that we clearly see the upper and lower turning points and can be reasonably certain that a given change was a transitory, random movement around a fixed mean rather than a permanent change in the mean or its growth rate.

A very different line of reasoning suggests that asset prices contain information about future inflation. This is certainly an implication of the models I worked on for many years with Karl Brunner (Brunner and Meltzer, 1989). In those models, asset prices respond to monetary and fiscal policy actions and also to changes in the expected return to real capital and the size of the capital stock. These general equilibrium models of money, bonds, and capital give no support to recent proposals urging policymakers to respond to asset price changes. These models can be consistent with the "fat tails" found in most asset price distributions.

It is true in these models, as I believe it is in fact, that asset prices reflect anticipations of inflation and that the response of asset prices with low transaction costs typically occurs before there is an increase in the prices of many goods and most services. But asset prices also rise for reasons unrelated to inflation. There is no reason to presume that policymakers are more capable of extracting the response of asset prices to monetary expansion or identifying inflationary and noninflationary components as they arise. One can imagine, and perhaps hope, that, in the future, economists will develop techniques that reliably separate the determinants of asset prices. When a reliable rule of this kind can be written, the information in asset prices can be used to increase the accuracy of inflation forecasts.

We are not there. We are not even close to having a useful model of asset prices that separates the various sources of change. Bubble explanations do not offer a consistent explanation of buyers and sellers. The absence of serious discussion of alternatives to rational bubbles, or irrational bubbles, may suggest how far we have to go. I have sketched such an alternative. Doubtless there are others. Testing those alternative hypotheses could do more to advance our discipline than continued work on empty propositions about rational bubbles or irrational behavior.

One policy lesson has been reinforced by recent experience. Asset price declines, even large declines, need not be followed by output or consumption price deflation or by deep, and lasting, recessions. The stock market decline in 1987 and the NASDAQ decline in 2000 were not the prelude to major recessions or deflations, as happened in the 1930s and, in Japan, in the 1990s. The difference is explained mainly by the difference in policy action. Expansive policies, especially monetary policy, prevented a recession in 1987 or 1988 and possibly in 2001.

The decline in the NASDAQ index after March 2000 is of similar order to the decline in the Nikkei beginning in 1990. The policy response was very different. This comparison, and the 1987 experience, suggest that expansive economic policies can compensate for any deflationary impulse on output prices coming from asset prices.

*Allan H. Meltzer is the Allan H. Meltzer University Professor of Political Economy and Public Policy at Carnegie Mellon University and a visiting scholar at the American Enterprise Institute. He is indebted to Bennett McCallum and Kevin Hassett for several helpful discussions.

Notes

1. Tomorrow's price depends on expected one-period dividends plus the expected capital gain. The latter depends on expected future dividends and gains. Repeated substitution yields a formula in which today's price depends on the entire future dividend stream.

2. Before leaving postwar Japanese experience, I note that Japan experienced two other periods in which asset prices rose rapidly, then collapsed—the IWATO boom of 1958–61 and the Tanaka boom of 1972–73. Prolonged recessions did not follow the earlier booms in land and stock prices. See Okina and Shiratsuka (2001).

3. A more complete exposition of the model in this section is Meltzer (1982).

4. John Maynard Keynes held a similar interpretation of risk and uncertainty to Knight's.

References

Brunner, Karl, and Allan H. Meltzer, 1989, *Monetary Economics*, Oxford: Basil Blackwell.

Cagan, Phillip, 1956, "The Monetary Dynamics of Hyperinflation" in *Studies in the Quantity Theory of Money*, M. Friedman, ed., Chicago, pp. 25–117.

Cukierman, Alex, and Allan H. Meltzer, 1982, "What Do Tests of Market Efficiency Show?," Carnegie Mellon University, unpublished paper.

Flood, Robert P., and Robert J. Hodrick, 1990, "On Testing for Speculative Bubbles," *Journal of Economic Perspectives*, Vol. 4, Spring, pp. 85–101.

Garber, Peter M., 1990, "Famous First Bubbles," *Journal of Economic Perspectives*, Vol. 4, Spring, pp. 85–101.

Gordon, Robert J., 1998, "Foundations of the Goldilocks Economy: Supply Shocks and the Time-Varying NAIRU," *Brookings Papers on Economic Activity*, Vol. 2, pp. 297–346.

Hayami, Masaru, 2001, "Opening Speech," *Monetary and Economic Studies*, Bank of Japan, 19, S-1, February, pp. 9–11.

Historical Statistics of the United States, 1960, Washington: Government Printing Office.

Kindleberger, Charles P., 1992, "Bubbles" in *The New Palgrave Dictionary of Money and Finance*, P. Newman et al., eds., London: Macmillan.

_____, 1978, *Manias, Panics and Crashes: A History of Financial Crises*, New York: Basic Books.

Knight, Frank H., 1921, *Risk, Uncertainty and Profit*, Boston: No. 16 in Series of Reprints of Scarce Traits in Economics, London School of Economics.

McCarthy, Grainne, 2001, "Dollar May Get Short-Term Lift from Rate Cut," *The Wall Street Journal*, August 20, p. C14.

Meltzer, Allan H., 1982, "Rational Expectations, Risk, Uncertainty, and Market Responses" in *Crises in the Economic and Financial Structure*, P. Wachtel, ed., Lexington, MA: Heath, chapter 1.

Minsky, Hyman P., 1982, *Can 'It' Happen Again?: Essays on Instability and Finance*, Armonk, NY: Sharpe.

Okina, Kunio, and Shigenori Shiratsuka, 2001, "Asset Price Bubbles, Price Stability, and Monetary Policy: Japan's Experience," Bank of Japan, Institute for Monetary and Economic Studies, discussion paper, No. 2001-E-16.

Oliner, Stephen D., and Daniel E. Sichel, 2000, "The Resurgence of Growth in the late 1990s: Is Information Technology the Story?" *Journal of Economic Perspectives*, Vol. 14, Fall, pp. 3–32.

Shiller, Robert J., 2000, *Irrational Exuberance*, Princeton, NJ: Princeton University.

Weller, Paul A., 1992, "Rational Bubbles," in *The New Palgrave Dictionary of Money and Finance*, P. Newman et al., eds., London: Macmillan, pp. 271–273.

Chapter 4
Diverse Views on Asset Bubbles

Robert J. Shiller*
Yale University

We had an exceptional conference today. There is a great diversity of information in these papers. I was particularly interested in some of these papers that relate to the fundamental concept that underlies the title of this conference: asset price bubbles. These are the papers that tackle the question of whether stock prices have become "overpriced" during bubble periods and then "crash" when the bubble bursts. These papers attracted my attention particularly since there appears to be a fundamental disconnect in our thinking about these bubbles. Highly educated people seem to differ at fundamental levels.

Let me first be clear on what I think a speculative bubble is. By a bubble, some seem to mean any period when asset prices rise and then fall. In their paper for this conference, Mishkin and White define a crash in just such terms, and this is fine for their purposes, I suppose. But I think that the troublesome concept of a bubble requires more than this. The traditional notion of a speculative bubble is, I think, a period when investors are attracted to an investment irrationally because rising prices encourage them to expect, at some level of consciousness at least, more price increases. A feedback develops—as people become more and more attracted, there are more and more price increases. The bubble comes to an end when people no longer expect the price to increase, and so the demand falls and the market crashes.

This traditional story of a bubble seems obviously at work in actual markets, according to many observers. And yet, it seems very unsatisfactory to many other observers. I try to put myself in the frame of mind of these other observers. Obviously, they will admit, there are some foolish people who might be vulnerable to exaggerated expectations in response to past price increases. But, there are also some very smart people who seem to be going along with the bubbles, not betting heavily against them. Thus, it does not seem right to attribute foolish behavior to the market. Moreover, these other observers will think that the idea that people are just foolish is too vague a concept, too nonspecific to allow us to gain any real understanding.

I sometimes find myself squarely in this very same frame of mind, and I write papers that rely on perfect rationality. But, personally, I find that I just cannot stay exclusively with such theories since they seem to abstract too much from the obvious and ignore so much evidence about what is going on in the "real world" in bubble periods. And, these theories ignore the well-established cognitive limitations of even the very smart people.

Stock market bubbles are an especially difficult topic. They are a difficult thing to explain in part just as history is difficult to explain. There are so many different forces that shape large historic events.

Bubbles are also difficult to explain, relative to other historic events, since the stock market phenomenon that we focus on involves a complicated game in which people try very hard to outsmart each other. Explaining the stock market is not like explaining aggregate consumption behavior. Deciding whether to buy a new sofa is not so strategic as deciding whether to invest in the stock market.

There are so many different ways of looking at the stock market and the real estate market that have been presented today at this conference. For example, McGrattan and Prescott have emphasized rational reactions in the markets to tax law changes. Allen and Gale have emphasized rational reactions to agency problems. Cochrane has stressed the convenience yield of speculative assets. In a different direction, De Bondt has emphasized an array of psychological factors. This diversity is a reflection of the complexity of the speculative markets. I believe, though, that the diversity is also a reflection of the diversity of intellectual traditions that may be applied to understanding speculative markets.

There are, in fact, very many intellectual traditions that I find relevant to understanding asset price bubbles. Of course, there is the tradition represented by the fundamental paradigm of economics and finance, which is the expected utility maximization model. There are other traditions represented in economics departments, such as the macroeconomics tradition, which has often not relied at all on the expected utility paradigm. Beyond this, however, I would mention intellectual traditions in other academic departments—psychology, sociology, and history. The ways these people have of gaining an understanding of human behavior are very different. Moreover, there are yet different traditions in our law schools. Lawyers, through their handling of disputes, acquire a very different understanding of these markets, which gives them particular strength in appreciating the fine points of investor strategies that exploit the complexity of our laws and institutions, along with a particular strength in appreciating the role of malicious and deliberate misrepresentation. I would also add the people in our news media, such as newspapers and magazines. Their methods often involve talking on a daily basis with people who are heavily involved in the action and trying to understand each day what is happening that day. This gives these media people, if not a broad long-run perspective, a rich source of understanding of day-to-day events.

I believe that all of these intellectual traditions have tool kits that can help us to understand economic phenomena like speculative bubbles. There is something of a movement in academic economics and finance these days to try to access some of these other intellectual traditions. We have today a growing interest in behavioral finance and an emerging interest in behavioral macroeconomics.

But, despite these efforts at integrating diverse approaches to understanding economic phenomena, there is still today a great divide across people from different intellectual backgrounds. Microeconomists still rarely cite macroeconomists, economists rarely cite psychologists, and academics rarely site news media stories.

Thinking about all this diversity of approach served to remind me of the parable of the blind men and the elephant. Since it is such a good story, and relevant to the issue I am describing, forgive me for a little diversion. This story was popularized by American poet John Godfrey Saxe (1816–87). However, the story actually originates in the ancient Buddhist religious text called the *Udana*. Saxe was merely a popularizer of this old story; he adapted it to American audiences by excising Buddha from the story, so that there was no cognitive dissonance imposed by religious background. He did this, in fact, by substituting himself for Buddha. The last verse in Saxe's poem is a moral, essentially Buddha's moral as seen in the *Udana*, which Saxe presents in the first person in the last verse of his poem.

If we read the original text of the *Udana*, we see that the story goes like this: "I have heard that on one occasion the Blessed One was staying near Savatthi, in Jeta's Grove, Anathapindika's monastery. Now at that time there were many priests, contemplatives, and wanderers of various sects living around Savatthi with differing views, differing opinions, differing beliefs, dependent for support on their differing views ... And they lived arguing, quarreling, and disputing, wounding one another with weapons of the mouth, saying, 'The Dhamma is like this, it's not like that. The Dhamma's not like that, it's like this.'"

Buddha then told them the following story:

"Once, in this same Savatthi, there was a certain king who said to a certain man, 'Gather together all the people in Savatthi who have been blind from birth ... show the blind people an elephant.'

'As you say, your majesty,' the man replied and he showed the blind people an elephant. To some of the blind people he showed the head of the elephant, saying, 'This, blind people, is what an elephant is like.' To some of them he showed an ear of the elephant, saying, 'This, blind people, is what an elephant is like.' To some of them he showed a tusk ... the trunk ... the body ... a foot ... the hindquarters ... the tail ... the tuft at the end of the tail, saying, 'This, blind people, is what an elephant is like.'"

The king then asked: 'Now tell me, blind people, what the elephant is like.'

The blind people who had been shown the head of the elephant replied, 'The elephant, your majesty, is just like a water jar.'

Those who had been shown the ear of the elephant replied, 'The elephant, your majesty, is just like a winnowing basket.'

Those who had been shown the tusk of the elephant replied, 'The elephant, your majesty, is just like an iron rod.'"

And Buddha, with the evidence from this story, concluded: "In the same way, monks, the wanderers of other sects are blind and eyeless."[1]

Well, I think the same conclusion applies in intellectual disputes today. We all are blind to certain aspects of complex phenomena like the asset price bubbles that are the subject of this conference.

In my 2000 book *Irrational Exuberance,* I presented a view of speculative markets that was in many ways an attempt to synthesize a lot of diverse information, but, in reflecting on today's papers, I must admit that there is a lot that I missed. Still, I think that the basic framework that I gave in that book is a good perspective from which to view bubbles.

In my model of speculative bubbles, I distinguish between precipitating factors for the bubble and amplification mechanisms that enhance the effect of these factors. Moreover, I consider the cultural factors that mediate the bubble and the psychological factors that provide the human substrate on which the bubble can grow.

The amplification mechanisms that make a bubble grow strong are just that price increases beget more price increases, through human psychology. As I said before, initial price increases attract investor interest and demand, and the new demand begets more price increases. We can find ourselves in a vicious circle, whereby prices accelerate upward. The price increase cannot go on forever, and eventually the halting of price increases disrupts the investor motivation for holding the highly priced stocks. At that point, the price increase may be sharply reversed, the bubble is burst, and there can be downward feedback, leading to lower and lower prices. This simple amplification mechanism is well known and has been talked about for centuries, but, curiously, is rarely mentioned by economists in their scholarly papers. From this lack of discussion, one might easily assume that such amplification is discredited by some scholarly work, while, in fact, no such scholarly work exists.

In *Irrational Exuberance,* I gave what I thought was a long list of precipitating factors for the stock market bubble that began in 1982, accelerated in the late 1990s, and peaked in early 2000. I gave 12 factors:

- the advent of the World Wide Web and its psychological impact,
- triumphalism in the West as Western free market solutions are adopted around the world,
- an emerging culture of business success,
- a Republican U.S. Congress and capital gains tax cuts,
- the baby boom from 1946 to 1966 and its delayed effect on the demand for stocks,
- expanded news media coverage of business news,
- a trend towards increasingly optimistic stock-market analysts' reports,
- the rise of pension plans such as 401(K) plans,
- the rise of mutual funds,
- the worldwide decline in inflation,
- the lowering of transactions costs and the expanding volume of stock market trade, and
- the increasing public interest in gambling and the association of self-esteem with winning.

Some of the papers presented today reminded me that the list of precipitating factors is even longer than the list I gave in my book. It is, in fact, the bewildering variety of changes that affect stock markets that makes it so hard for us to understand asset price bubbles. I believe, however, that there are certain things that we understand about speculative markets that incline them towards a large response to large price changes, notably the amplification mechanisms I discussed above. Beyond this, we learn from the diverse arguments about the direction of the stock market a little humility in trying to predict its future movements.

*Robert J. Shiller is the Stanley B. Resor Professor of Economics in the Cowles Foundation at Yale University and a fellow at the International Center for Finance at the Yale School of Management.

Note
1. Udana VI. Jaccandhavagga, translation by Thanissaro Bhikkhu.

Chapter 5
Asset Prices and Monetary Policy

Michael Mussa*
Institute for International Economics

It is a pleasure to return once again to Chicago and to this annual conference cosponsored by the Federal Reserve Bank of Chicago.

The topic of this year's conference, asset price bubbles, is certainly provocative, and several of our presenters and discussants have already been suitably provoked. It might have been timelier, however, to have convened this conference two years ago when, arguably, there was somewhat more of a bubble in U.S. asset markets than—hopefully—there remains today. Indeed, I would humbly suggest that the International Monetary Fund (IMF) was perhaps somewhat more timely in focusing on the topic of "Asset Prices and the Business Cycle" in the May 2000 edition of the *World Economic Outlook*—an analysis that is still worthwhile reading today.

However, our organizers, Curt Hunter and George Kaufman, have already suffered the rightful wrath of Anna Schwartz, and there is no need to add to their woes. Indeed, mindful of Anna's complaint about the relevance of several papers to the theme of this conference, I have selected a topic for these remarks that is clearly relevant to the conference theme (and to its location): asset prices and monetary policy. I hope that the topic makes Anna happy, for I fear that what I shall say about it may not entirely do so. My central thesis is that asset prices can, should, and actually do play a significant role in the responsible conduct of monetary policy.

Two qualifications should immediately be noted. First, prices of key assets including equities, bonds, real estate, and foreign exchange are important macroeconomic variables, and their behavior generally has implications for the things that monetary policy is fundamentally concerned with—namely, the maintenance of reasonable price stability and, more generally, the stability and growth of the economy. In particular, asset prices are among the leading indicators that help predict the likely future behavior of the price level and the level of economic activity. Accordingly, the behavior of asset prices should normally have some effect on monetary policy, along with that of a host of other useful economic indicators. My point is that beyond their general relevance as macroeconomic indicators, asset prices should—in some times and circumstances—exert a special influence on the conduct of monetary policy. (If these remarks were directed to an audience from a relatively small and open economy where the exchange rate is a far more important economic variable than it is for the United States, I would put particular emphasis on the exchange rate as an asset price that should sometimes exert a special influence on monetary policy. Here, however, the exchange rate is unlikely, except in rare circumstances, to have special importance for monetary policy. Rather, the focus is on those occasional situations where the behavior of equity or real estate prices may become unusually important for monetary policy.)

Second, my point is not that the behavior of asset prices should be targeted as one of the key objectives of monetary policy or that monetary policy should seek to stabilize asset prices. Asset prices, especially equity prices, jump around a lot. The reasons for all of the asset price volatility that we observe are not entirely understood—although an important part of it relates to market responses to the receipt of new information. Suppression of most asset price volatility is neither feasible nor desirable. Nor is it relevant to think of linking adjustments in monetary policy in some mechanical way to movements in asset prices (i.e., to include asset prices as a determinant of monetary policy, as might be suggested by some extensions of the Taylor rule). Rather, the issue is whether there are identifiable circumstances—not necessarily frequently occurring or always easy to describe precisely in advance—when monetary policy should adjust in the light of developments in asset prices. I shall argue that there are such circumstances and that their occurrence is not so implausible as to be practically irrelevant, although their idiosyncratic nature is such that it is difficult to describe a rule to govern the appropriate monetary policy response.

1. The Relevance of Asset Price Bubbles

How does this relate to the central topic of our conference—asset price bubbles? Like Alan Meltzer in his luncheon speech yesterday, I have long been skeptical about so-called "rational bubbles." Did the Good Lord teach people how to solve, intuitively, difference and differential equations but forget to imbue them with the insight to impose the relevant boundary conditions? That's not rationality—its lunacy.

On the other hand, after a decade working on the practical, operational side of economic policy, I find that academic economists are irrationally attached to the theoretical assumption that economic agents are perfectly rational. Undoubtedly, this is a particularly powerful and analytically fruitful assumption, and one should be reluctant to give it up in favor of some vaguely specified alternative. However, in my observation, everyone is at least a little bit crazy about something, and it would be an amazing triumph of hope over experience to believe that averaging out the craziness of many people leads inevitably to collective rationality. Indeed, common sense suggests that circumstances where there is credible reason to believe that the result of the collective behavior of private economic agents is not entirely rational may be important candidates for public sector intervention—recognizing, of course, the danger that irrationality may afflict the public as well as the private sector.

Is it possible to identify asset price bubbles and similar anomalies with some reasonable degree of reliability? After the fact—after the collapse—a bubble often seems obvious. And, ex post evidence is surely relevant and legitimate in assessing whether asset price bubbles and similar anomalies do occur. But, what about before the collapse? If policy is to try to do something about asset price bubbles, other than respond after the collapse, then it would seem important to be able to diagnose bubbles as they are developing.

Let me tell you two anecdotes. You may not think that anecdotes are evidence. But for two years I worked for Ronald Reagan who firmly believed in the probative and persuasive power of anecdotes, and he was the only man since George Washington to see his two-term vice president elected to succeed him as president.

On Tuesday, March 14, 2000, Working Party 3 of the Organization for Economic Cooperation and Development held its regular meeting in Paris. The main subject at the secretary general's luncheon that day was equity prices and whether we should worry about them—the NASDAQ had, in fact, reached its historic peak of over 5,000 the preceding Friday. The debate was intense, if not heated. Leaving the meeting, I told the Federal Reserve's representative, Governor Ferguson, that if there was not a bubble in the NASDAQ, I had never seen one.

The other anecdote is a favorite story of my father. It concerns an old actor, down on his luck and searching for work. (Not a story that I used to tell while serving in the Reagan administration.) He reads in *Variety* that a former friend is directing a revival of one of Shakespeare's plays, and he goes to see him about a role. With some trepidation, the director agrees to cast the old actor, but explains that the part is a small one with only a single speaking line, "Hark, I hear the cannons roar!"

Thankful for his new opportunity and anxious to make the most of it, the old actor spends several hours practicing the single line with which he hopes to revive has career. He tries different words to emphasize: "*Hark*, I hear the cannons roar." Or, "Hark, I hear the *cannons* roar." Or perhaps, "Hark, I hear the cannons *roar.*"

Absorbed in his practice, the actor loses track of time, and is barely able to run down the street and rush up the alley to the stage door before his scene. Bundled into his costume and pushed onto center stage, he seems somewhat startled by the boom, boom, boom of the kettledrums behind the curtains. Glaring out dramatically at the audience, he declaims—"What the [heck] was that?"

Now, the point is that there are times when the cannons actually do roar, when asset prices do diverge substantially from values reasonably associated with economic fundamentals. Central bankers and other policymakers should not be ideologues on this issue; they should keep their ears open and be prepared to act appropriately.

2. How Should Monetary Policy Respond?

If there are asset price bubbles or other similar anomalies, what should monetary policy attempt to do about them? There is no single, pat answer. Sometimes, the right answer is to do nothing. Take the case of the dot-com equity price bubble. As detailed in Steve Kaplan's paper for this conference, from 1999 through early 2000 there was a mania to invest in a large number of firms with involvement in the Internet. In a number of cases, firms with few employees, little actual capital, very limited revenues, and negative earnings reached equity market valuations in the billions of dollars.

Could and should monetary policy have attempted to do something to rein in the dot-com bubble before its collapse. I shall argue that the Federal Reserve should have tightened policy somewhat earlier and more aggressively in 1999 and early 2000 than it actually did—for broad reasons of macroeconomic stabilization reinforced by concerns about a general bubble in U.S. equity markets. But, the more specific and more obvious problem of the dot-com bubble was not, by itself, a plausible concern of monetary policy. Adjustments in monetary policy have broad effects on financial markets and the economy; they are too blunt of an instrument to attack even obviously aberrant behavior in a relatively narrow class of asset markets. Moreover, there was relatively little reason to fear that either the dot-com bubble or its probable collapse would have grave macroeconomic consequences. Investors who saw spectacular gains might well have come to recognize equally spectacular losses on their dot-com holdings. Consumption spending might have been somewhat affected, but not to an appreciable extent relative to the size of the U.S. economy on the normal disturbances with which standard monetary policy should be expected to contend. Real investment spending by dot-com firms was not very large, and its probable decline in a collapse of the dot-com equity price bubble was not a serious concern for monetary policy. Nor were there large extensions of credit to dot-com firms that might create serious problems for the financial system in the event of a collapse of the dot-com equity price bubble.

In contrast, the broader "bubble" in U.S. equity prices in 1999 through early 2000 was, arguably, a concern for monetary policy. Clearly, equity prices were escalated relative to most normal measures of equity valuation such as price earnings ratios. This was especially the case with the telecommunication, media, and technology (TMT) sector, which dominated the NASDAQ, and less so with rest of the equity market. And, although the run-up in equity values was primarily concentrated in some sectors of the market, the effect on the total market valuation of all equities was substantial. Strong growth of consumption spending, despite an already low personal savings rate, suggests that high equity values were having an important impact on aggregate demand. Real investment spending also appeared to be pumped up by high equity values, particularly in the TMT sector. And, substantial debt issuance was being used to finance both real investment and corporate mergers and takeovers. Moreover, the general macroeconomic situation was one where additional impetus to aggregate demand from highly valued equities was not particularly welcome. Although still subdued, inflationary pressures were beginning to show some resurgence, as indicated by rising labor compensation and increases in the core consumer price index. Also, with unemployment falling to barely 4 percent and many firms reporting shortages of skilled labor as a key problem, labor markets were the tightest they had been since the acceleration of inflation in the late 1960s. Indeed, the Federal Reserve responded to these developments with a modest tightening of monetary policy during 1999.

My position then and my position now is that the Federal Reserve should have moved somewhat more aggressively to tighten monetary policy during 1999 and early 2000. The standard concerns of an appropriately forward-looking monetary policy—specifically, evidence of modest increases of inflationary pressures—might alone have justified somewhat more aggressive tightening, without any particular emphasis on asset prices. (As discussed later, were there not such traditional concerns, it is questionable whether the behavior of equity prices alone should have motivated monetary tightening.) But the escalation of equity prices beyond the normal bounds of reasonable valuation and the macroeconomic effects of this behavior clearly strengthened the case for monetary tightening beyond the relatively timid steps actually undertaken by the Federal Reserve through the end of 1999.

If the Federal Reserve made a mistake in 1999 by not tightening monetary policy somewhat more aggressively—partly in response to unreasonable escalation in equity prices—how serious was this error? Clearly, it was not very serious. If monetary policy had been tightened somewhat more aggressively during 1999 (and perhaps somewhat less by late 2000), the surge in the U.S. economy in the second half of 1999 and the first half of 2000 would probably have been more subdued; and, the subsequent slowdown in economic growth after the middle of 2000 would also probably have been more moderate. But, even the best monetary policy cannot reasonably be expected to eliminate all of the bumps and wiggles from the growth rate of the economy, and, by historical standards, the present cycle of speed-up and slow-down appears quite mild. A monetary policy that paid more attention to the unreasonable escalation of asset prices would probably have made it even milder—a worthwhile but not enormous gain. (It should also be noted that in late 1999, the Federal Reserve was concerned with the potentially disruptive effects of the Y2K problem and provided ample liquidity at year-end to forestall such problems. In fact, no significant problems emerged, but this could not have been known in advance.)

There are two other relatively recent instances where U.S. monetary policy should and did give special importance to developments in asset markets: after the stock market crash of October 1987 and in the autumn of 1998 in the face of the disruption in financial markets following Russia's sovereign default and the near-collapse of the hedge fund Long-Term Capital Management (LTCM). In both of these cases, the issue was not an unreasonable escalation of asset prices, but rather sharp declines in asset values that appeared unjustified by changes in economic fundamentals.

Few would dispute that the Federal Reserve acted properly and successfully in response to the stock market crash of October 1987, both in the initial emergency supply of liquidity to keep markets open and functioning and in easing monetary policy after the crash to counteract its likely undesirable effects on economic activity. There is somewhat greater controversy (wrongly, I believe) about the Federal Reserve's role in arranging for LTCM to meet with its principal creditors and counterparties so that a restructuring could be arranged without formal bankruptcy, but there is relatively little dispute that the Federal Reserve's easing of monetary policy in the autumn of 1998 was important in quelling unwarranted financial market turbulence and in reducing the risks to U.S. and global economic growth.

From these cases (and others), it appears to be broadly accepted that, at least in some circumstances, the Federal Reserve should respond to apparently unreasonable and potentially disruptive downward movements in asset prices. Why, then, is there more controversy about some role for monetary policy in resisting, in selected circumstances, upward movements in asset prices that appear unwarranted by economic fundamentals and also potentially threaten financial and economic disruption (including through the possibility of their rapid and disorderly reversal)?

Part of the answer is suggested by Federal Reserve Chairman Alan Greenspan's response to a similar question at a recent conference in Jackson Hole, WY. Sharp downward movements in asset prices often threaten severe disruption of the financial system (as they did in October of 1987 and the autumn of 1998), and it is important for the central bank to act to countervail such potential disruption. In contrast, (positive) asset price bubbles tend to build up relatively gradually and typically do not immediately threaten disruption of the financial system. This surely supports the view that, when needed, the monetary policy response to sharp asset price declines—increases in liquidity to keep markets functioning and urgent monetary easing—should be different from the response to large and apparently unwarranted escalations in asset prices that occur more gradually.

Such asymmetry, however, does not imply that monetary policy should respond only to anomalous asset price declines and never to price increases. Indeed, such extreme asymmetry in monetary policy would raise the concern that this policy itself might contribute to undesirable asset price volatility. Markets would come to expect that the central bank would step in with increased liquidity when asset price declines seem to threaten financial stability, but markets would not be discouraged from inflating asset prices by any concern that monetary policy would seek to limit the (generally less immediate) dangers to financial and economic stability from unwarranted upsurges in asset prices and the dangers of their rapid reversal. In contrast, appropriate but not extreme asymmetry would allow for urgent monetary easing to counteract market declines that threaten immediate financial market instability, but would leave open the option of more gradual monetary tightening in the face of asset price upsurges that appear increasingly out of line with underlying economic realities.

As already emphasized, the case for modest monetary tightening to countervail the apparent U.S. equity price bubble of 1999 and early 2000 was marginal, and the mistake from failing to undertake such tightening was not serious. If we go back to the late 1920s and early 1930s, however, there is clearly a case where the errors of monetary policy were much more substantial. Here, I disagree with the paper of Ed Prescott and Ellen McGrattan at this conference—there was a bubble in the U.S. stock market before the 1929 crash. The fact that stock prices collapsed after the supposed bubble is, admittedly, ex post evidence of the prior existence of the bubble. But this ex post evidence is, nevertheless, highly relevant and very powerful. Moreover, widespread commentary at the time certainly indicated that many people perceived that the stock market was being driven, to some important extent, by speculative mania.

Despite the fact that consumer prices were declining in the late 1920s, it is at least arguable that somewhat earlier monetary tightening might have helped to forestall the stock market bubble and lessen the subsequent danger of a catastrophic financial and economic downturn. The principal error of monetary policy in this episode, however, was the failure of the Federal Reserve to ease sufficiently aggressively as the economy spiraled downward into depression and deflation. One does not need to accept entirely analysis of Milton Friedman and Anna Schwartz in their *Monetary History of the United States* to recognize that the Federal Reserve made an enormous blunder in not easing monetary policy more aggressively during the great contraction of 1929 to 1933.

Indeed, I would characterize the mistakes of U.S. monetary policy in the late 1920s and early 1930s as the Mount Everest of monetary policy mismanagement. In comparison the mistakes made in responding to the equity price bubble of 1999–2000 have more the proportions of Capitol Hill—a promontory whose political significance vastly exceeds its geographic importance.

3. Experience beyond the United States

Outside of the United States, there are a number of more recent episodes where it may credibly be argued that monetary policy would have been improved by paying somewhat more attention to the apparently anomalous behavior of asset prices. The May 2000 edition of the IMF's *World Economic Outlook* (referred to earlier) discusses some of these episodes. Notably, several of these episodes involved unusual escalations in real estate prices—more so than equity prices—and were also associated with substantial expansions of credit particularly to the real estate sector, but were not accompanied by significant increases in general inflation of goods and services prices. When the collapses came, the liquidity and solvency of financial institutions was impaired, and this tended to deepen and spread the damage from the correction in asset prices. In these episodes, it can reasonably be argued that earlier attention of monetary policy to the dangers of escalations in asset prices, fueled to an important degree by credit expansion, would have helped to contain the bubble on the upside and subsequently limit the damage on the downside.

The outstanding case is clearly Japan in the late 1980s. With good reason this period is often referred to as "the bubble economy." Equity prices shot up, with the Nikkei peaking at 39,000 in late 1989. Real estate prices, especially in Tokyo, surged to a similar extent; the square kilometer occupied by the Imperial Palace and gardens in central Tokyo was at one time estimated to be worth more than all of California. Real investment spending also surged, not only in construction, but also across the broad front of Japanese industry. In fact, real business investment in Japan grew 9.6 percent in 1987, 11.9 percent in 1988, and 9.3 percent in 1989, and posted an 8.8 percent rise on a year-over-year basis in 1990 despite the beginning of the economic slowdown during the course of that year. Goods and services price inflation, however, remained generally subdued, with consumer prices increasing at an average annual rate of barely one-half of 1 percent in 1986 through 1988 and picking up to a still modest 2.3 percent for 1989.

During most of the period of the expanding bubble, Japanese monetary policy maintained a relaxed stance. The discount rate was held at 2.5 percent until May of 1989 and was raised to 4 percent late that year. Subsequently, after equity prices were already headed downward, the discount rate was raised further to 6 percent by the summer of 1990 and held at that level until mid 1991—when equity prices were well down from their peaks. (Real estate prices had also clearly peaked by this stage, but rather than showing sharp subsequent declines, the market essentially dried up. The downward correction in real estate prices has, in fact, dragged on for a decade while private construction activity has remained depressed.) The Bank of Japan (BOJ), however, did not reduce the discount rate to 4 percent until the spring of 1992, and the rate was will above 3 percent at the end of that year—by which time the Japanese economy was clearly in recession.

After the peak in asset prices, general price inflation continued to pick up in Japan, with consumer prices rising 3.1 percent in 1990 and 3.3 percent in 1991, before falling back to 1.7 percent in 1992. Thus, it might have appeared that the significant tightening of monetary policy after the peak in the Nikkei and the gradual shift toward an easier policy only after mid 1991 could be justified by the traditional focus of monetary policy on general price inflation, rather than on the behavior of asset prices.

However, monetary policy should be forward looking. As a huge asset price bubble was developing in Japan in the late 1980s and as this asset price bubble was clearly pumping up the broad macroeconomy on an unsustainable basis, despite subdued consumer price inflation, Japanese monetary policy could have and should have moved earlier to a more restrictive stance. If meaningful monetary tightening had begun even as late as the second half of 1988, an important part of the buildup of the bubble economy might have been forestalled, and the subsequent economic and financial correction from the collapse of the bubble might well have been significantly less severe.

The mistake of delaying the monetary policy response to the buildup of the bubble was compounded by the delay in the monetary policy response to the bubble's collapse. Despite the somewhat uncomfortable rate of consumer price inflation, it was becoming increasingly clear during the second half of 1990 that the falloff in equity prices and the slowdown in the real estate market was likely to take a fair bit of steam out of the Japanese economy, thereby lessening the need for a tight monetary policy. By the middle of 1991, forward-looking monetary policy should have begun to anticipate that a sharp slowdown in the Japanese economy was a prospect (although not yet a fact), and a move to a less tight monetary policy stance could have been justified. Clearly, in light of the very weak growth of the Japanese economy during 1992 and the prospect of further weakening in 1992, monetary policy remained too tight for too long.

Perhaps the arrangements for the governance of Japanese monetary policy contributed to these mistakes. In this period, the final authority over monetary policy rested with the Ministry of Finance (MOF), although senior officials (especially the governor) at the BOJ had significant influence, particularly in resisting policy changes. In the late 1980s, officials at the MOF wanted to keep the Japanese economy growing robustly, while maintaining a restrained fiscal policy. (The MOF was also under pressure from the U.S. Treasury to maintain strong domestic-demand led growth in Japan.) An easy monetary policy was useful to achieve the MOF's objectives. Senior officials at the BOJ might have preferred an earlier move toward monetary tightening in 1988 or 1989, but with little evidence of accelerating consumer price inflation, they were in a weak position to press the MOF for a change in monetary policy. This situation was reversed in 1990–92. After monetary policy had been tightened in the face of evidence of rising inflation, the BOJ was then in a position to resist pressures to ease monetary policy in advance of clear evidence that inflation was abating (whatever might have been happening to asset prices). And, the BOJ may have tended to offer such resistance partly out of the concern that once policy was eased, it might prove difficult to tighten again if inflation did not continue to recede as expected.

Whatever the explanation is for the decisions that determined Japanese monetary policy during 1988 through 1992, it is abundantly clear in hindsight—and should have been apparent at the time—that policy tightening was too late and too slow in

1988–89 and that once policy was tightened, the subsequent easing was insufficiently aggressive in 1991–92. These were not minor policy errors. An important part (although surely not all) of the difficulties of the Japanese economy during the past decade derive from how monetary policy dealt with the bubble economy of the late 1980s and its collapse in the early 1990s. Indeed, if the errors of the Federal Reserve in the late 1920s and (especially) the early 1930s are the Mount Everest of monetary policy mismanagement, then the errors of Japanese monetary policy in the late 1980s and early 1990s probably qualify as the Mount Fuji of mismanagement.

The point of this criticism from the perspective of this conference is that paying greater attention to the behavior of asset prices (beyond that normally accorded in the conduct of monetary policy) would have helped to avoid these serious errors. If Japanese monetary policy had paid greater attention to the buildup of the asset price bubble in equities and real estate (and to its effects on the macroeconomy), there would have been good reason to start tightening more aggressively before clear signs of overheating finally showed up in consumer price inflation. Symmetrically, if greater attention had been paid to the drop in equity values and the falloff in the real estate market, there would have been good reason to ease monetary policy more aggressively in anticipation of the usually lagged decline in consumer price inflation.

4. Public Explanation of the Role of Asset Prices

If, as the preceding discussion suggests, asset prices can play a useful role in helping to guide monetary policy, how should this be explained to the public? Or, to put the question somewhat more provocatively, why is it that central bankers generally appear so reluctant to admit that the behavior of asset prices might influence their decisions about monetary policy when many (but not all) outside analysts of monetary policy suggest that there should be such an influence?

In dealing with these questions, it is first relevant to note that at least some prominent central bankers are prepared to confess that monetary policy may have some role in responding to sharp drops in asset prices, particularly when they threaten to create disorderly conditions in financial markets. Indeed, as previously discussed, the Federal Reserve's policy easings after the stock market crash of 1987 and in the autumn of 1998 were undertaken and explained at least partly for this reason. And, no one complained. Easing of monetary policy is almost always more popular than tightening and probably especially so when easing is seen as counteracting sharp drops in peoples' wealth. In contrast, monetary tightening is often not so popular. The long-time former Federal Reserve Chairman Bill Martin used to observe that the key task of a central bank is to take away the punch bowl just as the party is starting to get interesting. But, as I liked to remind the IMF Executive Board, "Party poopers are not popular."

This is particularly likely to be the case if monetary tightening is explained as an effort to prick what the central bank perceives to be an asset price bubble—especially if the effort is successful. While consumer price inflation is generally unpopular, asset price inflation is much appreciated by those who own the assets. A central bank that proclaims an effort to depress asset prices makes few friends and many enemies. Thus, aside from the legitimate substantive reasons to treat seemingly anomalous asset price declines and asset price increases somewhat asymmetrically (as discussed earlier), there are important public relations reasons why a central bank might want to explain these actions is somewhat different terms. Indeed, even an independent central bank needs to be politically responsible through some mechanism, and it needs to maintain public support of its general policy behavior, if not necessarily for every individual policy action.

The way to deal with this issue is not, in my view, to focus on explaining the role of asset prices in the conduct of monetary policy, but rather to emphasize the responsibility of monetary policy to contribute to general macroeconomic stability. As former President Clinton's political guru, James Carville, put it, "It's the economy—stupid."

If asset prices appear to be behaving in an anomalous manner, but this behavior has no meaningful effect on the macroeconomy, then monetary policy should not be concerned. For example, as discussed earlier, the bubble in the dot-com equities in 1999–2000 was not, by itself, a reason to tighten U.S. monetary policy. In contrast, the broader escalation of U.S. equity prices, which was giving meaningful stimulus to investment and aggregate demand in a situation of very tight labor markets and incipient upward pressures on inflation, strengthened the rationale for more aggressive monetary tightening during 1999. Even more clearly, the bubble in Japanese equity and real estate prices was associated with broad indications of macroeconomic overheating by 1988, even though that overheating was not yet apparent in rising consumer prices. Monetary tightening by no later than the second half of 1988 could have been justified on broad grounds of preserving macroeconomic stability—with the bubble in asset prices contributing to the evidence that overheating was likely to continue and eventually bring an acceleration of consumer price inflation.

Of course, tying monetary policy to the broad objective of preserving macroeconomic stability will not necessarily make monetary tightening popular. People tend to like an economic boom, at least up to the point that it begins to translate into higher consumer price inflation. When memories of relatively high inflation were fresh and inflation itself tended to begin to accelerate at a somewhat earlier stage of an economic expansion, it was possible for central banks to point credibly to the threat of reviving the demon of inflation as justification for timely tightening of monetary policy. However, if monetary policy remains generally successful in keeping consumer price inflation subdued and the tendency for inflation to give early signs of acceleration further ameliorates, people may come to doubt that there really is a demon. Then, it may well become more difficult for central banks to persuade a skeptical public of the need to restrain a popular economic boom. In this situation, escalations of asset prices may become a more valuable signal and symptom of growing macroeconomic imbalances that warrant a monetary policy response. If so, central banks will simply have to face up to the fact that their fundamental task is not to maximize their popularity. Rather, their inspiration must come from Missouri's great pre-Civil War senator, Thomas Hart Benton, who said, "I despise the bubble of popularity."

---

*Michael Mussa is a senior fellow at the Institute for International Economics.

PART II

RECENT EXPERIENCE WITH ASSET PRICE BUBBLES

Chapter 6
U.S. Stock Market Crashes and Their Aftermath: Implications for Monetary Policy

Frederic S. Mishkin*
Columbia University and National Bureau of Economic Research

and

Eugene N. White
Rutgers University and National Bureau of Economic Research

1. Introduction

In recent years, there has been increased concern about asset price bubbles and what monetary policymakers should do about them. For example, the stock market collapse in Japan in the early 1990s, which is seen as the bursting of a bubble, has been followed by a decade of stagnation. Federal Reserve Chairman Alan Greenspan expressed concerns about a stock market bubble in the United States in his December 5, 1996, speech when he raised the possibility that the stock market was displaying "irrational exuberance."

To understand what the implications of stock market bubbles might be for monetary policy we pursue a historical approach. Because it is far from obvious when the stock market is undergoing a bubble, we look at historical episodes in the United States over the last 100 years of major stock market crashes. Although we cannot be sure that all these crashes were bubbles, a bursting of a bubble surely results in a stock market crash, and so analyzing the aftermath of stock market crashes can provide some clues as to the impact of a bursting bubble and what policymakers should do about it.

The paper is organized as follows. First we describe the data and the procedures we used to identify the stock market crashes in the United States over the last 100 years. Then we pursue a narrative approach to discuss what happened in the aftermath of these crashes. We end by drawing out the implications for monetary policy.

2. The Data and Choosing Episodes of Stock Market Crashes

Whether stock market crashes may be attributed to expectations of an economic decline or a loss of "irrational exuberance," they are believed to have an independent effect on economic activity. The shock is transmitted via the effect that a large loss in wealth has on consumer spending and through effects on the cost of capital on investment, both of which are standard channels in the monetary transmission mechanism.[1] Because stock price movements have an important impact on economic activity through these standard transmission mechanisms, central banks that are trying to conduct monetary policy in an optimal manner will necessarily react to them. However, the question arises as to whether the monetary authorities should react to stock market fluctuations over and above that indicated by their effect on the economy through the standard transmission mechanisms. For example, Cecchetti, Genburg, Lipsky, and Wadhwani (2000) argue that central banks should at times react to stock prices in order to stop bubbles from getting out of hand.[2] Alternatively, the monetary authorities might want to try to prop up the stock market after a crash by pursuing expansionary policy greater than that which would be indicated by simply looking at the standard transmission mechanisms of monetary policy. Such strategies might be appropriate if stock market crashes produce additional stress on the economy by creating financial instability.

As pointed out in Mishkin (1997), financial instability may arise when shocks to the financial system increase information asymmetries so that it can no longer do its job of channeling funds to those with productive investment opportunities. Whether this happens depends on the initial condition of financial and nonfinancial firms' balance sheets. If balance sheets are initially strong, then a stock market crash might not increase asymmetric information substantially because the shock from the crash will still leave them in a healthy condition. On the other hand, if balance sheets start out in a weakened condition, a stock market crash will leave them in a precarious state, which can lead to financial instability and a sharp decline in economic activity.

Stock market crashes may heighten informational problems arising from adverse selection and moral hazard. A stock market crash when balance sheets are initially weak increases adverse selection in credit markets because net worth of firms falls to very low levels (or may even be negative) and no longer functions as good collateral for loans. As pointed out in Calomiris and Hubbard (1990) and Greenwald and Stiglitz (1988), this worsens the adverse selection problem because the potential loss from loan defaults is higher, leaving the lender uncertain about whether a borrower is a poor credit risk. Uncertainty, which often accompanies a stock market crash in the form of increased volatility of asset prices, will also make it more difficult for lenders to screen out good from bad borrowers. The result of the increase in adverse selection will be that lenders pull out of the credit market, which, in turn, will result in a sharp contraction in lending and economic activity.

A stock market crash, which leaves firms' balance sheets in a weakened state, also increases the moral hazard problem. As demonstrated by Bernanke and Gertler (1989), when a stock market crash leaves firms with low net worth, they then have little at stake and so are likely to take risks at the lender's expense. The resulting increase in moral hazard, thus, also produces a contraction in lending and economic activity. Furthermore, if there is no deposit insurance, stock market crashes might also reduce financial intermediation by promoting a bank panic in which depositors, fearing for the safety of their deposits, withdraw them from the banking system, causing a contraction of bank loans. Given that banks perform a special role in the financial system (Battacharya and Thakor, 1993) because of their capacity to more closely monitor borrowers and reduce problems generated by information asymmetries, shocks that force them to curtail lending will also promote financial instability and a contraction.

The stress on the financial system from a stock market crash should become visible in interest rate risk premiums. The mechanisms above suggest that an important manifestation of financial instability would be a large rise in interest rates for borrowers for whom there is substantial difficulty in obtaining reliable information about their characteristics. There would be a much smaller effect on interest rates to borrowers for whom information about their characteristics is easily obtainable. Low quality borrowers are more likely to be those firms for which information about their characteristics is difficult to obtain, while high quality borrowers are more likely to be ones for which the asymmetric information problem is least severe. Consequently, a stock market crash that produces financial instability should lead to a rise in interest rate spreads for low versus high quality bonds.

To examine whether stock market crashes are associated with financial instability, we look at all stock market crashes in the 20th century, examining what happens to interest rate spreads and real economic activity. On the face of it, defining a stock market crash or collapse is simple. When you see it, you know it. However, attempting a more precise definition and measurement over the course of a century is more difficult. The choice of stock market index, the size of the collapse, and the time frame of the decline are key factors. To select the biggest stock market declines in this paper we have examined the behavior of three well-known stock indices: the Dow Jones Industrials, the Standard and Poor's (S&P) 500 and its predecessor, the Cowles Index, and the NASDAQ.[3] Crashes are discussed in nominal terms, except when there were significant differences in real and nominal movements.[4]

As October 1929 and October 1987 are universally agreed to be stock market crashes, the procedure to identify stock market crashes uses them as benchmarks. On October 28 and 29, 1929, the Dow Jones declined 12.8 percent and 11.7 percent, respectively, and on October 19, 1987, the Dow Jones fell 22.6 percent. As both fell slightly over 20 percent, a 20 percent drop in the market is used to define a stock market crash. The fall in the market—the depth—is, however, only one characteristic of a crash. Speed is another feature. Therefore, we look at declines over windows of one day, five days, one month, three months, and one year. For the effects that a crash can have on the market, the duration of the crash is also important. To cast a fine net to capture the features of speed and depth, we sorted the percentage changes for each window and looked at the 50 largest declines.

According to our procedure, we find 15 major stock market crashes in the 20th century, which are presented in figures 1 to 13. These show monthly stock market indices centering on the crash with windows of three years before and after the crash. The stock market index is set at 100 in the month prior to the month conventionally identified as the crash, even though the downturn may have begun well before this date. The Dow Jones index is used for 1903 to 1940. In 1946, we shift to the S&P 500 when it is first reported.

To examine the effects of stock market crashes on credit markets, we needed a measure of real activity for the economy. For this purpose, we selected the quarterly series for real gross domestic product (GDP) produced by Nathan Balke and Robert Gordon (1986) and measured in 1972 dollars. No interest rate series covered the whole of the century that could have produced an interest rate premium. The interest rate spread for the 1920s onward is the difference between Moody's AAA corporate bond rate and Moody's BAA corporate bond rate.[5] However before 1919, an alternative measure is required. The spread used here was constructed by Mishkin (1991) using Macaulay's (1938) data by subtracting the average yield on the best one-fourth of the bonds from the average yield on the worst one-fourth of the bonds.

3. Stock Market Crashes and Their Aftermath

The effects of a stock market crash on the pricing and availability of credit is not easily modeled econometrically. Over the course of a century, there are few series available over long spans of time. Even when series are available, their interpretation may change dramatically. Furthermore, some key factors, like the strength of the financial system, are difficult to measure. Thus, in this paper we follow a narrative approach to pull together the complex stories of the consequences of stock market crashes on the credit markets.

Whether a stock market crash will have a distinct and severe effect on the terms of credit that are offered to higher risk borrowers, thereby transmitting an independent shock to the economy, depends critically on two factors. First, the initial condition of the financial system is important. If the financial system is weak, being highly leveraged or having experienced cumulative shocks, it is more likely that a crash will induce lenders to raise rates to higher risk borrowers relative to low risk ones and produce financial instability. Second, given that a shock transmitted from the stock market crash promotes financial instability, how the monetary authorities react is critical. They can ignore the shock, in which case interest rate spreads will rise sharply, or they can inject liquidity into the system and dampen its effects. Lastly, it should be added that the more rapid and violent the crash, the more likely it will be a surprise, and intermediaries will have less time to make adjustments other than altering the terms of credit.

1903

The first crash of the 20th century occurred in 1903, an event often referred to as the "rich man's panic" and identified as occurring in October 1903. However, as can be seen in figure 1, the decline in the market began much earlier. The Dow Jones fell by 7.5 percent in July 1903 and by almost the same amount, 8.2 percent, in October. By the end of October, the index was down 16 percent over the year. By the Cowles Index, the biggest monthly decline, 12.9 percent, was in August 1903, and the yearly decline to September 1903 was a cumulative 26.8 percent. Whether the stock market

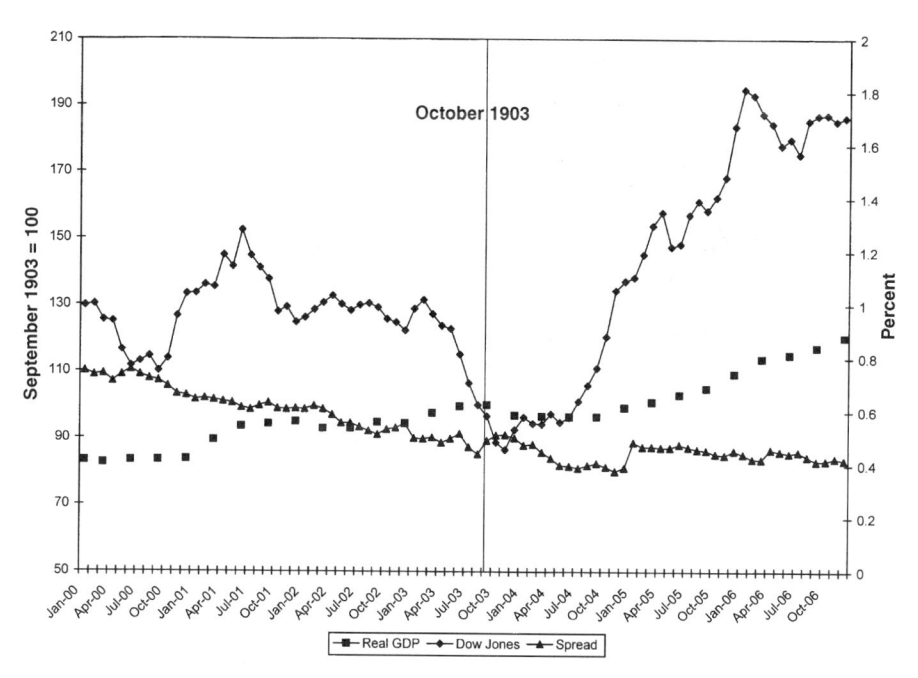

Figure 1: Crash of 1903

anticipated or followed the business cycle is unclear. The National Bureau of Economic Research (NBER) dates the peak of the cycle in the last quarter of 1902, while the real gross domestic product (GDP) data, shown in figure 1, indicates that the decline began a year later. This difference is the result of the fragile nature of economic data in the early 20th century. In any event the economic contraction was relatively mild, and the banking system had experienced no prior stress.

The stock market collapse began when banks called in the loans of underwriting syndicates, which had sponsored new issues in the previous two years. The syndicates responded by selling the unsold underwritten securities plus older higher-grade stocks and bonds. This liquidation in the last quarter of 1903 helped to drive down the market. According to Friedman and Schwartz (1963) railroads found it difficult to borrow, and other companies and financial houses failed. The effect of the collapse on spreads was relatively mild. Using Mishkin's (1991) spread, as seen in figure 1, there is no significant movement in the spread, even as interest rates rose. However, looking at the difference between high-grade industrial bonds and high-grade railroad bonds, where the former would have been considered riskier in this period, there is a rise in the spread of 25 basis points.[6] Part of this mild effect of the stock market may be attributed to the actions of then Secretary of the Treasury Leslie M. Shaw. In the absence of a central bank, he anticipated the November payment of interest on outstanding bonds, bought bonds for the sinking fund at high premiums, and increased government deposits at national banks, adding significantly to funds available to the money market (Friedman and Schwartz, 1963). Although the stock market crash of 1903 represented a large fall in stock prices, the initial soundness of the financial system and the monetary response of the Treasury led to a result in which there was little evidence of financial instability.

1907

The crash of 1907 is the first stock market collapse of the 20th century that had a discernable effect on the credit markets. After a sustained boom in the stock market from 1904 through 1906, the market began to collapse in early 1907, as seen in figure 2. As measured by the Dow Jones, the market sustained losses of 9.7 percent in March 1907, 8.2 percent in August 1907, and then 11.3 and 10.9 percent in October and November, respectively, of that year.[7] Real GDP continued to grow through the end of the second quarter of 1907, before falling 1 percent by the third quarter and then a shocking 5.5 percent in the last quarter. The NBER dates the peak of the business cycle as May 1907, with a long slide to the trough in June 1908.

The rapidly declining stock market, well in advance of the economy, may have been an important factor stressing the financial system, and spreads began moving upwards. The financial system appears to have been much more susceptible than in 1903, with banks becoming involved in more risky ventures and a serious rivalry emerging between banks and their newest competitors, trust companies. One speculative venture, the manipulation of shares of copper companies in the midst of a boom in the price of copper, failed. On October 14, eight banks associated with this activity were forced to seek assistance from the New York Clearing House, which in the years before the establishment of the Federal Reserve provided some limited lender-of-last-resort support. When the Knickerbocker Trust Company was discovered to have been involved in this venture, the New York Clearing House, composed of commercial banks, refused to come to its assistance. Knickerbocker was then forced to suspend payment

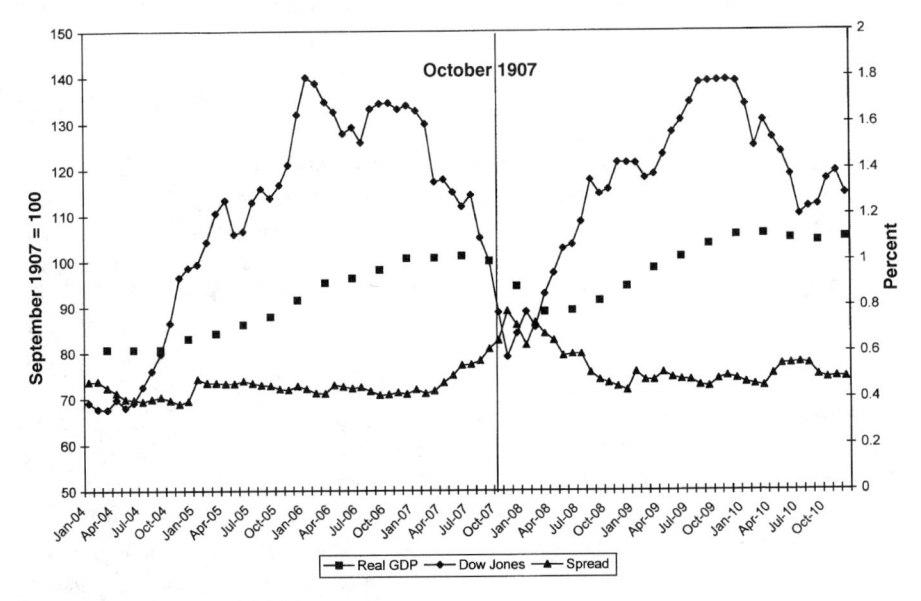

Figure 2: Crash of 1907

on October 22, creating a banking panic first in New York and then throughout the country. A nationwide suspension of specie payments to depositors quelled the panic, and payments were not resumed until January 1908 (Sprague, 1910; Friedman and Schwartz, 1963; Mishkin, 1991; Wicker, 2000).

The clearinghouses in New York and other cities began to issue clearinghouse loan certificates, a partial substitute for high power money, in late October 1907. However these institutions were not full-fledged lenders of last resort; their inability to halt the crisis eventually led to the creation of the Federal Reserve. The delay in the action of the clearinghouse was not compensated by the actions of then Secretary of the Treasury George Cortelyou. As in 1903, the Treasury tried to increase funds to the money market, depositing government funds in banks and exempting them from the legal reserves against these deposits while stimulating the importation of gold. But these actions were limited and late (Wicker, 2000).

Friedman and Schwartz (1963) identify a 2.5 percent drop in the money stock from May to September 1907 as putting downward pressure on the economy. They point to the fall in the money stock following the panic as a key factor turning a mild recession into a severe one that lasted until June 1908. However, while the banking panic clearly contributed to the economic decline, the spreads had been widening well before October 1907. The first phase of the stock market decline and rise in the risk premium was not accompanied by a falling money stock. It appears that the declining value of firms on the stock markets independently increased the adverse selection and agency problems for borrowers, effectively lowering their net worth. Numerous examples from the financial press indicate that these became severe problems early in the crisis. In March 1907, the price of Union Pacific shares, which were widely used to collateralize finance bills, fell by 50 points in less than two weeks. Then in June, New York City's new bond offering of $29 million failed with only $2 million being purchased (Sprague, 1910). In general, as seen in figure 2, most of the increase in the spread occurred in advance of the banking panic, although there was a sharp increase in October and November. Once the stock market began to rebound, the risk premium started to decline, in advance of the economic recovery.

Given the exposure of the banking system, and the late and limited response of the Treasury, the crash of 1907 thus might have been an important factor that increased risk premiums in the credit markets, thereby contributing to a severe recession.

1917

World War I and its aftermath produced huge fluctuations in the stock market. At the outset of the war, the market began a rapid descent. This drop was terminated when all markets were closed from the beginning of August to December 12, 1914, in fear of a banking and financial crisis. Figure 3 shows the crash in the second half of 1917. In nominal and real terms (taking into account the high wartime inflation), these were huge declines. In the 12 months ending November 1917, the Dow Jones fell 33.8 percent in nominal terms and 44.4 percent in real terms.

The crash of the market in late 1917 is stunning. It is notable, especially as the economy was booming. Real GDP in figure 3 is clearly on the rise, and the peak of the NBER business cycle was only reached in August 1918. The rising spread as the

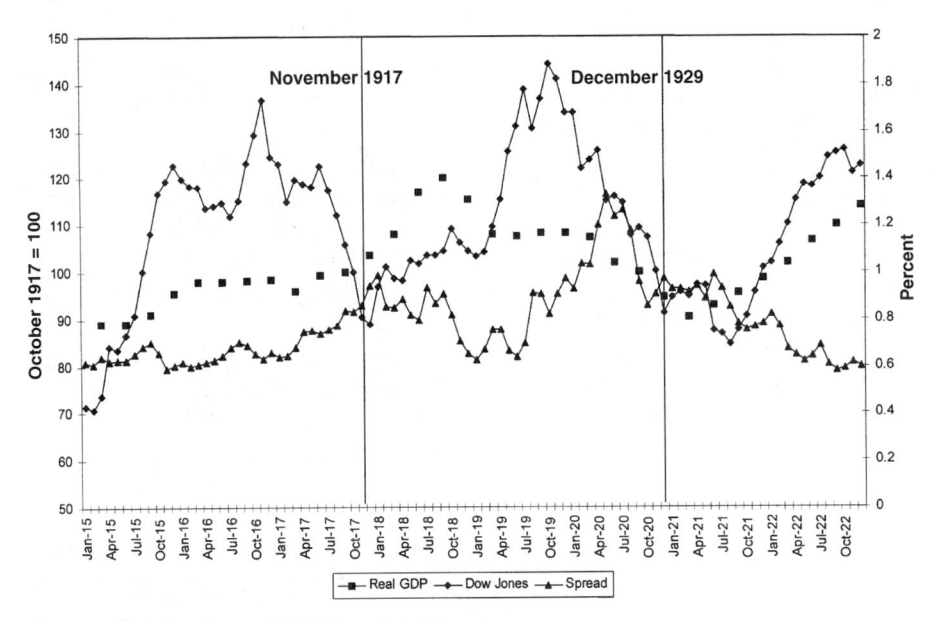

Figure 3: Crashes of 1917 and 1920

collapse of the market proceeded is, thus, noteworthy. Other spreads also increased in this downturn including the Junk-AAA spread, which increased more than 1 percent (Basile, 1989). The market decline, although large in magnitude, has been virtually ignored by historians. However, it would appear that the fall in share prices might be attributed in part to generally rising interest rates and controls on new capital issues. Furthermore, there were strong efforts to divert financial resources to the purchase of government bonds to finance the war (Friedman and Schwartz, 1963).

1920

The post-World War I fall in the market, although spread over a long period, was quite large, as viewed in figure 3. For the 12 months ending December 1920, the Dow Jones index fell 31.8 percent and 31.5 percent in nominal and real terms, respectively. The Cowles Index mirrors the Dow Jones for 1917, but for the 1920 collapse the Cowles Index is not in the top 50 crashes in nominal or real terms. In the quickly declining market of late 1920, the economy was entering a very steep recession. The peak of the business cycle, according to NBER dating, was reached in January 1920, with the economy spiraling downwards until July 1921. As the world economy moved into a recession, the decline in the United States was driven onwards by the Federal Reserve's efforts to halt inflation, raising discount rates sharply from January to June 1920 (Romer and Romer, 1989). Although gold inflows offset some of its efforts, the Fed managed an 11 percent decline in total high-powered money from September 1920 to the trough of the business cycle in July 1921. This contraction did not produce a banking panic, but it did induce a rise in bank failures from 63 in 1919 to 506 in 1921. Declining asset values rather than liquidity problems were at the root of most of these failures. The spread (figure 3) rose very quickly as the market dropped but then stabilized, while the Junk-AAA (Basile, 1989) spread remained at the high level it had reached following the 1917 crash. The BAA-AAA spread (which is available from 1919 on) also rose by 95 basis points from a low of 1.57 in October 1919 to a high of 2.52 in August 1921. With the recovery of the market and the economy, the spreads again fell to lower levels. The weakened condition of the banking system and the tight monetary policy of the Fed contributed to the substantial rise in the interest rate spread.

1929 and 1930–33

Although we will treat them separately, the two "great" crashes of 1929 and 1987 are an important pairing. The pattern of the crashes—with spectacularly rapid declines in stock prices—were similar, as was the Federal Reserve's successful lender-of-last-resort intervention to prevent effects of a crash from spilling over to the rest of the financial system (Mishkin, 1991). The monetary authorities response subsequently, however, offers an important contrast. After the crash of 1929, the Federal Reserve Board maintained its tight monetary policy, helping to push the economy into deeper recession. The stock market continued to collapse and distress to the financial system led to the highest ever risk premiums. Well aware of the aftermath of 1929, the Fed did not allow its concern for the market to distort its policy after October 1987. The economy continued to grow, and the market recovered.

The stock market crash of October 1929 was one of the sharpest and most abrupt collapses. On two days, October 28–29, the Dow Jones fell a total of 24 percent, down 19.6 percent for the month and down a further 22 percent in November. The Cowles Index was down 10 percent in October and 25 percent in November 1929. Although figure 4 shows that there was a brief recovery in the market in early 1930, it continued

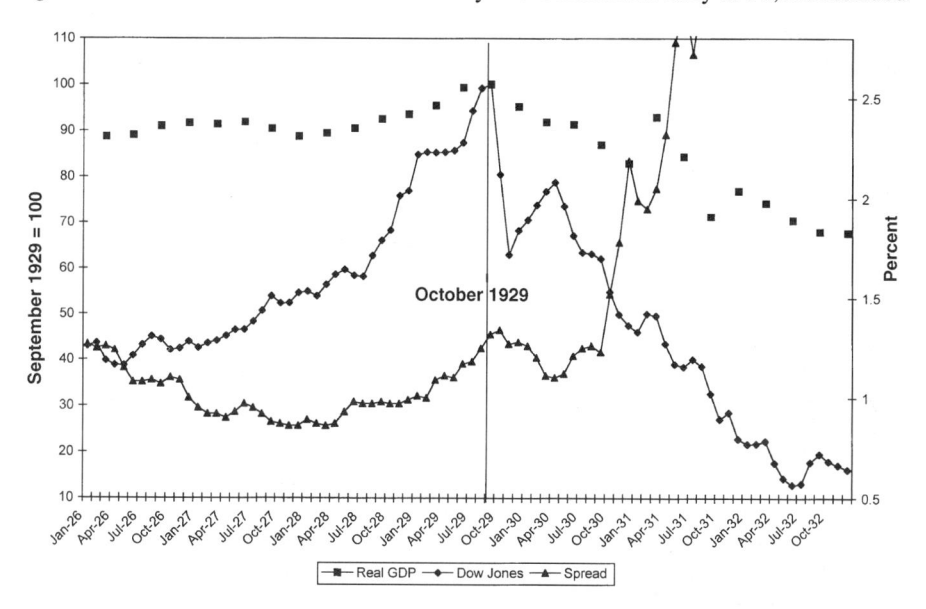

Figure 4: Crash of 1929

to bounce downwards almost continuously for the next two years, producing the greatest long-term market declines by any measure.

Given the magnitude of the shock, the behavior of the spread at first glance is puzzling; it rises as the market moved upwards in late 1928 and 1929 and then falls when the market plunges. Only when there is a slow sustained drop in share prices from mid 1930 onwards do spreads begin to soar off the chart. However, the behavior of the spreads in the crux of the crisis can be largely explained by the actions of the Federal Reserve. Operating under a gold standard where gold flowed to France and there was a perceived need to aid the weak British pound, the Fed began a tight monetary policy in early 1928, with the discount rate rising from 3.5 to 5 percent (Friedman and Schwartz, 1963; Hamilton, 1987). This policy was reinforced by the Federal Reserve's fears that excessive credit was fueling the boom in the stock market.

In February 1929, the Fed stepped up its policy of "direct pressure," instructing its member banks to limit "speculative loans," that is, loans to brokers. Finally, the Fed raised the discount rate in August 1929. However, higher rates and direct pressure did not suppress the demand for credit to buy stock, which was supplied by other intermediaries. Nevertheless, the market did extract a premium for brokers' loans, reflecting lenders' concerns that the rise in the market was not sustainable. Rates on brokers' loans had traditionally been similar to those on bankers' acceptances and commercial paper, relatively safe assets. But, in the boom, a premium of 2 to 3 percent arose for brokers' loans and the margin demanded climbed from 25 to 50 percent (White, 1990; Rappoport and White, 1993 and 1994). Some markets, like commercial paper, which declined by half in volume, and new foreign bonds, which almost disappeared, were squeezed by the flow of funds to brokers' loans. All risk premiums also moved upwards, including the BAA-AAA depicted in figure 4.

When the market collapsed in October 1929, banks and lenders of New York rushed to liquidate their call loans to brokers. In order to keep the call loan market from freezing up, the Federal Reserve Bank of New York engaged in a classic lender-of-last-resort operation, very similar to one conducted in 1987. The New York Fed let it be known that member banks could borrow freely from the New York Fed in order to take over the brokers' loans called by others (Friedman and Schwartz, 1963). In addition, the New York Fed made open market purchases of $160 million during this period, even though this amount was far in excess of what was authorized by the Federal Reserve System's Open Market Investment Committee. As a result, New York City banks stepped into the breach and increased their loans. The crisis was contained, and there were no panic increases in money market rates or threats to banks from defaults on brokers' loans. The premium on brokers' loans collapsed, as the market believed that there was no further danger. This decline in perceived risk was mirrored in fall in other risk premiums, including the BAA-AAA spread.

Unfortunately, the Federal Reserve Board did not approve of the New York Fed's intervention. It censured the New York bank and in spite of the recession that had begun during the summer and was in full swing by the end of the year, the Federal Reserve Board maintained its tight monetary policy. The tentative recovery in 1930, seen in GDP movements in figure 4, was aborted by this policy. The continued decline in the stock market from 1930 through early 1933 reflected the economy's policy-aggravated slide into depression. The collapsing economy placed enormous stress on the banking system. The banking crises of 1930, 1931, and 1933 undermined intermediation (Friedman and Schwartz, 1963; Bernanke, 1983; Mishkin, 1991), contributing further to the decline of the economy. In these circumstances, risk premiums soared, as seen in figure 4, as lenders fled from risky borrowers.[8]

The stock market collapse beginning in 1929 shows in high relief the importance of the two factors we have identified. In 1929, the banking system was relatively weak and the drop in the market was large and sudden. However, the effects were quickly contained by the response of the New York Fed. Yet, the further though less sudden decline in stocks and other asset values in the 1930s appears to have contributed to the rising risk premiums as the Fed stuck to its tight money policy.

1937

The stress imposed on financial markets is perhaps most evident in 1937. As shown in figure 5, the stock market plunged during this time as the economy moved into recession, while the interest rate spread increased much more sharply than in any other crash in the 20th century. The decline in the market was steep but not greater than in other episodes. In three consecutive months, the market bounced downward, losing a total of 22.4 percent by December 1937 as measured by the Dow Jones and 22.8 percent by the Cowles Index. By April 1938, both indices had fallen by another 10 percent. The peak in the business cycle was reached in May 1937 and hit bottom in June 1938; over its course real GDP declined 10 percent. The leap in the risk premium, shown in the spread variable in figure 5, was in plain evidence elsewhere. The Junk-AAA premium increased from 4.1 percent to 10.4 percent from April 1937 to April 1938.

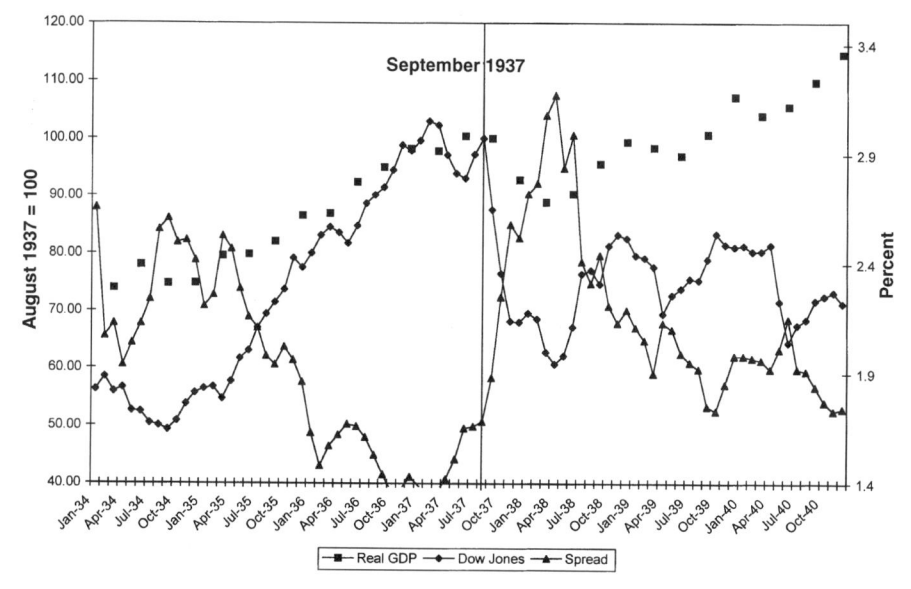

Figure 5: Crash of 1937

In early 1937, the Federal Reserve believed that it was time to tighten monetary policy. There had been steady economic expansion for two years, wholesale prices were up 50 percent, and stock prices had doubled. Focusing erroneously on the nominal level of interest rates, which seemed extremely low, the Fed concluded that policy was easy. This conclusion was buttressed by the fact that commercial banks held very large excess reserves. Instead of using open market purchases or increases in the discount rate, the Fed decided that it should increase reserve requirements beginning in July 1936 (Friedman and Schwartz, 1963). In a series of actions in August 1936 and March and May 1937, the Fed doubled reserve requirements, jacked up margin requirements for stock purchases, and cut slightly the discount rate. Banks responded by cutting lending to restore their excess reserves, which contributed to the sharp contraction.

The decline in the stock market reflects the seriousness of the economic downturn. However, the decline in asset values may have been a key part in the increase in the interest rate spread. The banking system had taken a pounding during the banking crises of 1930, 1931, and 1933. In June 1929, there had been 24,504 commercial banks with $49 billion of deposits. After the banking panics, and the March 1933 bank holiday, the number of banks had been winnowed to 14,440 with $33 billion of deposits by December 1933. The rush for liquidity by the banking public had been accompanied by an effort by the banks to increase their liquidity, as well. They slashed their lending and vastly increased their holdings of cash and bonds. Savings banks, savings and loan associations, and insurance companies had suffered similar collapses and had moved to augment their liquidity (White, 2000).

In this dramatic rush to cut lending, banks and other intermediaries would have sought even more strenuously to avoid risky borrowers. Increased adverse selection and moral hazard problems would have then propelled risk premiums to higher levels, as is evident in figure 5. The dramatic fall in asset values would have exacerbated this development. The lower value of firms would have made it increasingly difficult for anyone perceived to be risky to borrow either from an intermediary or on a financial market. The existing weakness of the banking system, tight monetary policy, and the decline in the stock market and other asset values were probably all factors in the rise of risk spreads, contributing further to the severity of the 1937–38 recession.

1940

In May and June 1940, with the defeat of France by the Germans and the Dunkirk evacuation, the Dow Jones and the Cowles Index lost 20 percent of their value, as seen in figure 6. While real GDP declined in the first quarter of 1940, there was no recession, and expansion continued until February 1945. Although small by comparison to jumps in the interest rate spread in 1937, there was a small but obvious increase during the collapse of the market. However, the spread still did not rise above levels reached in 1938 and 1939, and immediately fell to the pre-crash levels and then continued to decline. The economy and the financial system were in no immediate threat from the crash of the market. In September 1939 when war broke out in Europe, the Federal Reserve purchased $400 million of government securities to offset the big fall in the price of U.S. government bonds. This action was regarded by the Federal

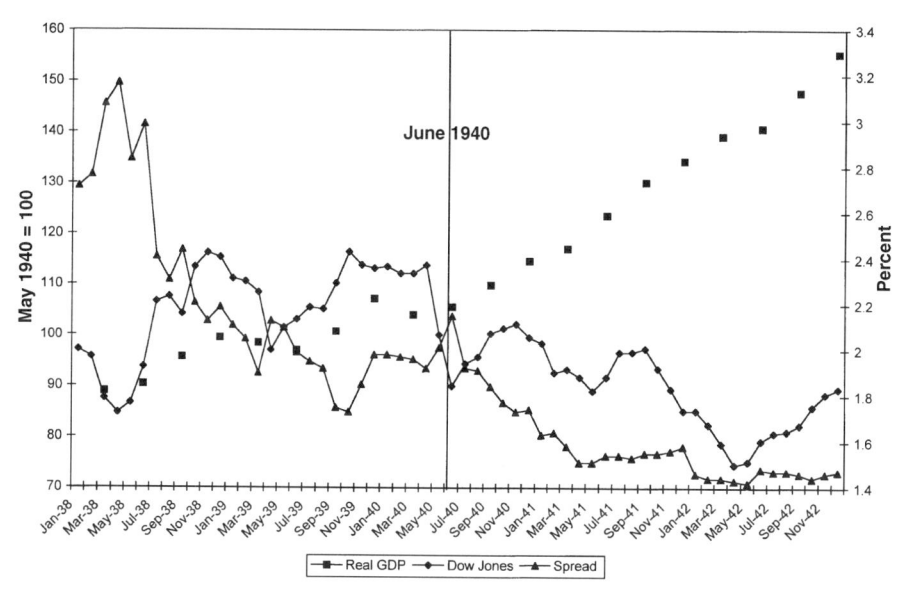

Figure 6: Crash of 1940

Reserve Board, and probably the markets as well, as a break from past practice. The professed aim was to protect member bank portfolios and to ensure an "orderly" capital market for economic recovery (Friedman and Schwartz, 1963). This action and the steady growth of the money stock from rising gold flows may have limited the reaction of the credit markets to the stock market crash.

By 1940, the weaker financial institutions had been eliminated and the balance sheets of most banks and firms had been substantially strengthened. These actions improved initial conditions, and the Fed's early policy intervention meant that the credit markets reacted very little to the stock market crash.

1946

After several months of slow decline, in September 1946 there was an abrupt drop in the stock market of 12 percent measured by the Dow Jones and 14.7 percent by the S&P 500. This collapse is quite surprising as it came after the severe post-World War II recession. According to NBER dating, the peak of the previous boom was in February 1945 and the bottom was hit in October 1945. The crash, thus, appears to be unrelated to the recovery of the economy. What is also striking is that there is almost no effect of the crash on the interest rate spread, as shown in figure 7. The lack of response of the debt markets to the collapse in equity prices may be attributed to the continuance of the government's wartime policy of supporting the price of government bonds. The posted rate on Treasury bills was three-eighths of 1 percent and 2.5 percent on long-term securities (Friedman and Schwartz, 1963). Any upward pull on these rates by higher rates elsewhere in the market was offset by open market operations by the Fed, which only decided to fight inflation in October 1947 (Romer and Romer, 1989).

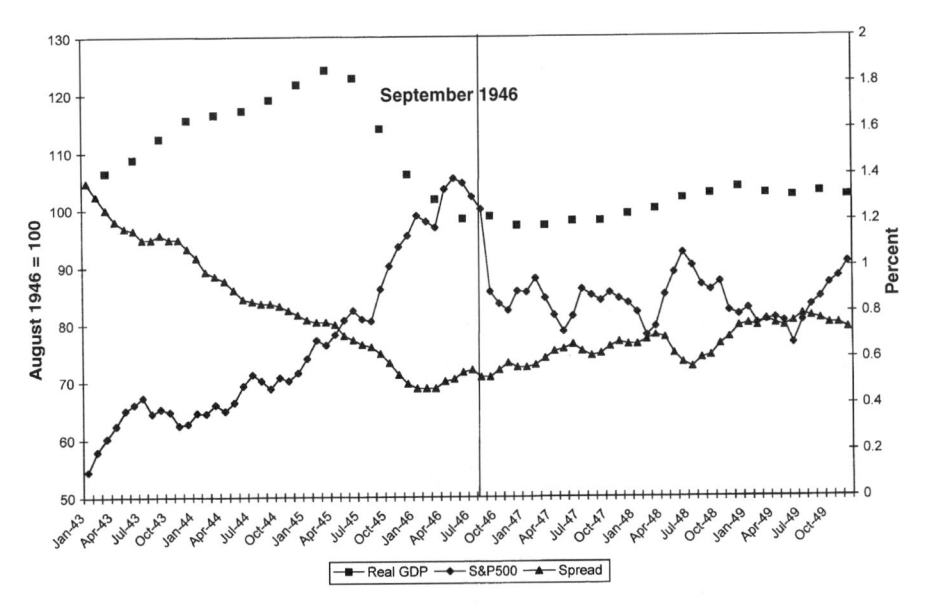

Figure 7: Crash of 1946

The continued growth of the money stock and the bond price supports helped insulate the credit markets from the stock market crash. In addition, by the end of World War II, the financial system had been purged of almost any risk, except that derived from holding government bonds. Thus, not surprisingly, the collapse in stock prices in 1946 was not followed by significant rises in interest rate spreads.

1962

The stock market crash in 1962 occurred at a time when the economy was expanding. Real GDP, as seen in figure 8, was rising, and the expansion begun in February 1961 continued until December 1969. Beginning in April 1962, the market had lost 20.6 percent of its value as measured by the Dow Jones by June and 20.9 percent by the S&P 500. Yet, this shock did little to drive the interest rate spread upward. In fact, it appears to have been remarkably steady. The banking system was very stable; there had been no significant loan losses or bank failures in decades. The Federal Reserve was concerned about maintaining orderly markets for treasury securities and kept interest rate movements modest. There was no monetary surprise from the Fed; contractionary actions were only undertaken in 1955 and 1966 (Romer and Romer, 1989). Thus, this shock from a stock market crash appears to have had little effect on interest rate risk premiums in credit markets.

1969–70

The sharp decline in the stock market in mid 1970 occurred at the time of a very mild recession. Although the economy had peaked in December 1969, the slowdown has been referred to as a "hiatus" rather than a recession (Gordon, 1980). However, the expansion was also quite sluggish. The market peaked in advance in November 1968, then began to drift downwards, declining abruptly in May 1970, as seen in figure 9.

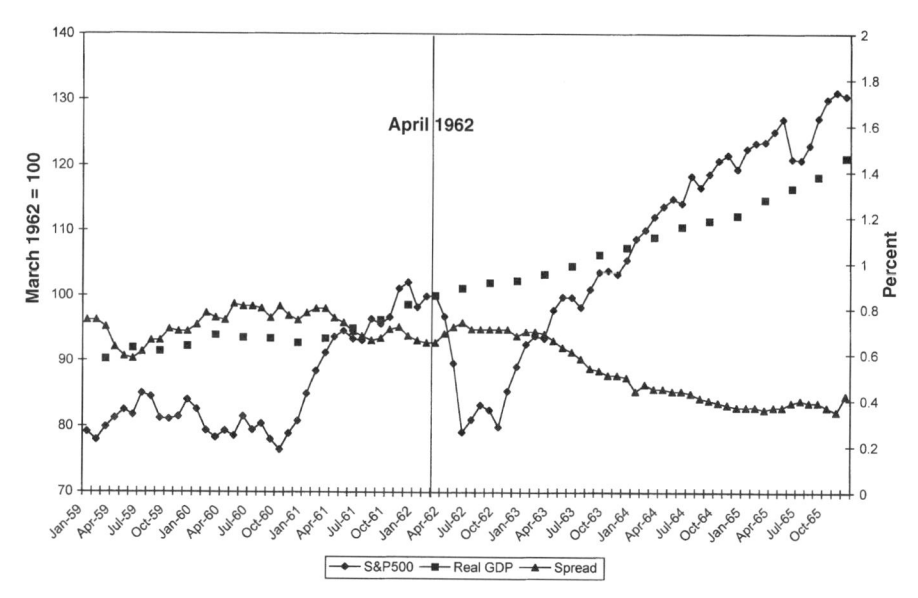

Figure 8: Crash of 1962

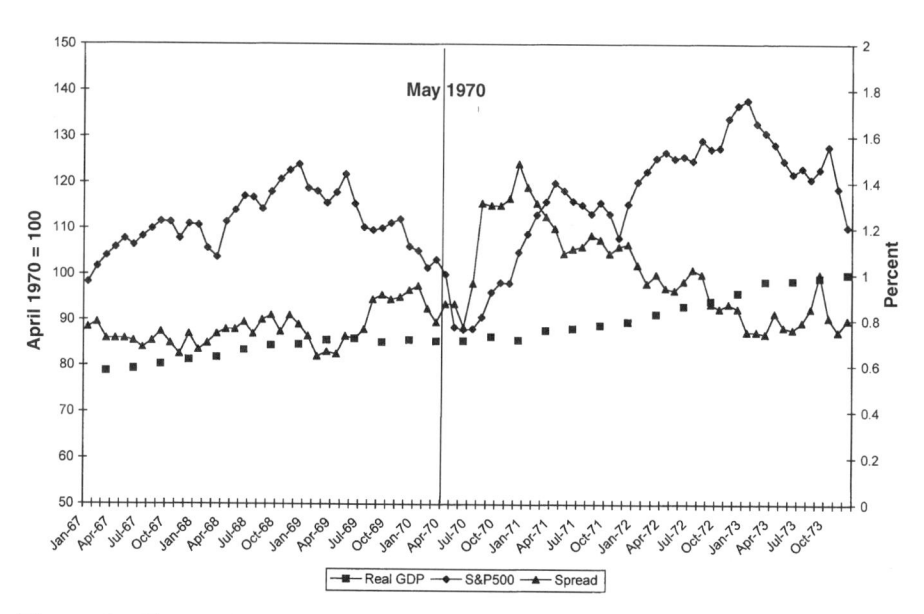

Figure 9: Crash of 1970

Eventually, the market hit bottom in June 1970, for a 30.6 percent drop. In this uncertain atmosphere when there was a decrease in the valuation of firms from a fall in net worth, adverse selection problems began to appear in credit markets and the spread began to widen.

By May 1970, Penn Central Railroad was on the verge of bankruptcy. The railroad asked for assistance first from the Nixon Administration and then the Federal Reserve. Both these requests were rebuffed, and on June 21, 1970, Penn Central was forced to declare bankruptcy. As a major issuer of commercial paper, the Federal Reserve was concerned that this default would make it impossible for other corporations to roll over their commercial paper, producing further bankruptcies and perhaps a panic. To prevent this from happening, the Fed encouraged money center banks to continue lending, promising that the discount window would be available to them (Mishkin, 1991).

In spite of the Fed's actions in response to a potential problem in the commercial paper market, interest rate spreads widened. Not only did the commercial paper–Treasury bill spread rise (Mishkin, 1991), but so also did the BAA-AAA spread (figure 9). The general rise in risk premiums indicates that problems of the commercial paper market had the potential for spreading to parts of the capital market. However, the increase in the spread variables from the Penn Central bankruptcy were not large by standards of other crises and were likely to have been dampened by the prompt action of the Fed.

1973–74

One of the largest and longest stock market collapses, viewed in figure 10, occurred in the early 1970s. Beginning with a monthly fall in the Dow Jones of 14 percent and the

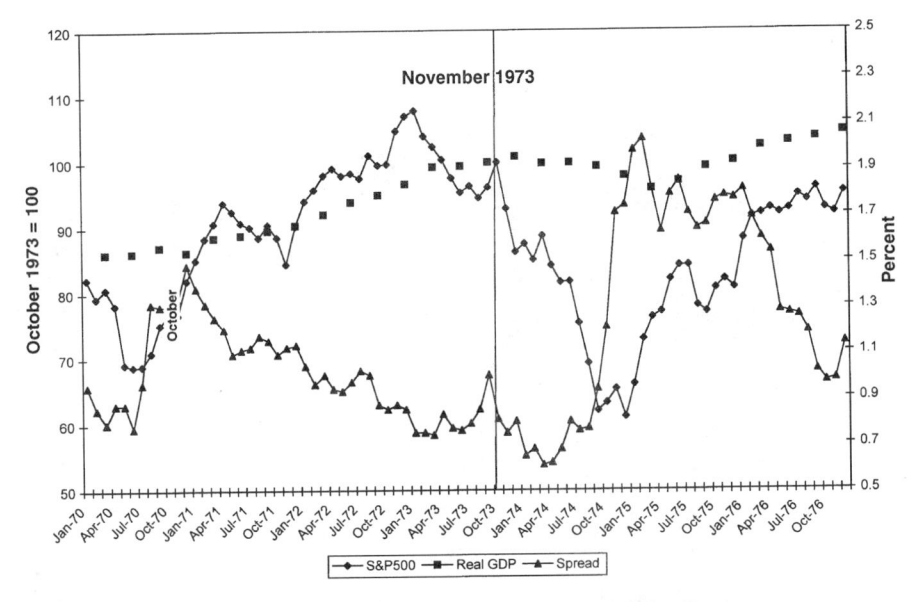

Figure 10: Crash of 1973

S&P 500 of 7 percent in November 1973, the 12-month declines ending in October 1974 were 30.4 percent and 36.8 percent for the two indices, respectively. At the same time as the market dropped, the economy moved into a recession that lasted until March 1975. The market crash was accompanied by a large increase in the interest rate spread (figure 10). However, the increase occurred mostly after the stock market had hit its bottom. Unlike the earlier post-World War II decades, the financial markets and institutions were forced to cope with rising inflation and inflation uncertainty following the OPEC (Organization of Petroleum Exporting Countries) oil price shock. The large decline in asset values also contributed to making low quality borrowers seem to be even worse risks. The existing condition of the banking system was not as favorable to the absorption of any shock. With a recession and inflation, bank earnings fell as borrowers failed to make payments and loan losses rose. Banks found increased difficulty in funding, as market rates moved well above the Regulation Q ceilings that set rates for bank deposits. Banks found themselves troubled by real estate loans and loans made to non-oil-producing countries. In the previous two decades bank failures had been very rare and involved only small institutions. In October 1973, the first large bank failure since the depression occurred in San Diego, followed by failure of the nation's 20th largest bank, Franklin National, in October 1974. These failures highlighted the generally weakened state of the banking system (Sinkey, 1979; Spero, 1980; White, 1992).

The stock market crash in this environment aggravated the problems of agency costs, thereby reducing the willingness of lenders to provide low quality borrowers with credit and driving up the interest rate risk premiums. However, the fact that a majority of the increase in the spread occurred well after the market had turned upward suggests that the other factors were important in producing financial instability.

1987

The October 1987 crash had the largest one-day decline in stock market values in U.S. history. On October 19, the Dow Jones fell 22.6 percent, and for the month the index was down 23.2 percent. As measured by the S&P 500, the market fell 12.1 percent in October and 12.5 percent in November. Thus, the pattern of the rise and fall of the market for 1926–29 in figure 4 and 1984–87 in figure 11 look remarkably similar.

Unlike the 1920s, the Fed in the 1980s was no longer preoccupied by speculation, but after the 1970s it was concerned about inflation and tightened policy to prevent any acceleration. At the outset of the stock market boom, monetary aggregates had increased at a fairly rapid pace. But, in the first six months of 1987, their growth slowed considerably. Worried about rising foreign interest rates, a poor trade balance, and a weak dollar, interest rates in the United States rose in anticipation of action by the Fed, which increased the discount rate from 5.5 percent to 6 percent on September 4 (Mussa, 1994). These actions did not slow down the economy, and it continued to grow steadily, as seen in the real GDP movement in figure 11. The risk premium was steady, and the spread appears to have declined even when the market moved into the last phase of the boom in mid 1987.

The sharp decline on October 19 put the financial system under great stress because in order to keep the stock market and the related stock index futures market

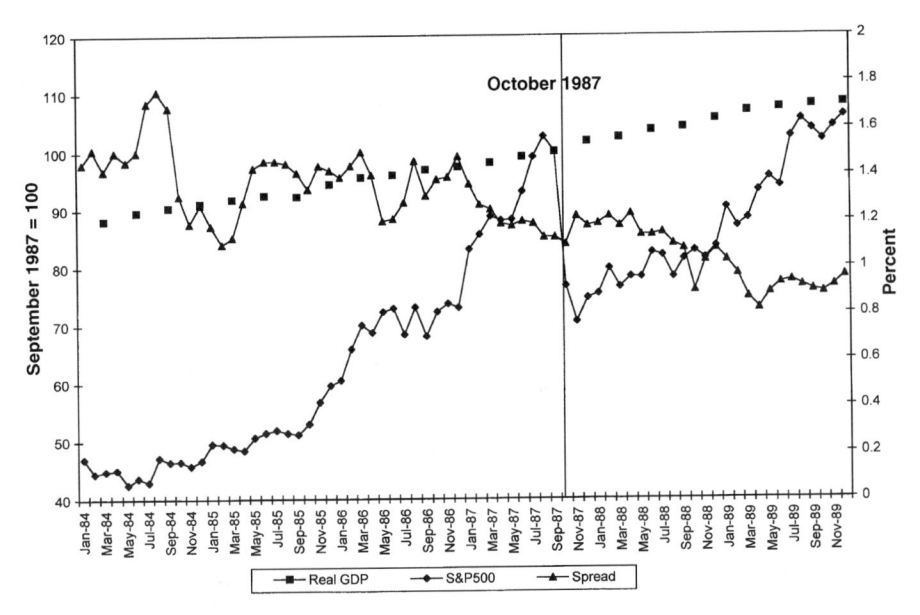

Figure 11: Crash of 1987

operating in an orderly fashion, brokers needed to extend huge amounts of credit on behalf of their customers for margin calls. The magnitude of the problem is illustrated by two brokerage firms, Kidder, Peabody and Goldman, Sachs, who by themselves had advanced $1.5 billion in response to margin calls on their customers by noon on October 20. Clearly, brokerage firms as well as specialists were severely in need of additional funds to finance their activities. Despite the financial strength of these firms, there was so much uncertainty that banks were reluctant to lend to the securities industry at a time when it was most needed. The Federal Reserve, thus, began to fear that there would be a collapse of securities firms and a breakdown in the clearing and settlement systems. To prevent this from happening, before the market opened on October 20, Chairman Greenspan announced the Federal Reserve System's "readiness to serve as a source of liquidity to support the economic and financial system." The Open Market Desk then supplied $17 billion to the banking system, or more than 25 percent of bank reserves and 7 percent of the monetary base. In addition, commercial banks were told that they were expected to continue supplying other participants of the financial system with credit, including loans to broker-dealers to ensure that they could carry their inventories of securities.[9] Spreads widened at the outset of the crisis, but then quickly decreased in response to the actions of the Fed. Although stock prices continued to oscillate violently for the remainder of 1987, financial markets gradually calmed down. The Fed carefully withdrew most of the high-powered money that it had provided, ensuring that the federal funds rate was stable at 6.75 percent, or about 1 percent below the level before the crash.

Thus, cushioned by the Federal Reserve's action, which was reminiscent of the New York Fed's behavior in the October 1929 episode, the crash was not seen as a threat to the stability of the financial system or borrowers despite the large loss in equity values. Bank failures and loan losses were rising rapidly in the late 1980s, and yet the crash was prevented from damaging the susceptible financial system. There was almost no movement in the spread, shown in figure 10, from mid 1987 to mid 1988.[10] The Fed's lender-of-last-resort operation was again successful, but this time there was no overreaction to the boom in the market and monetary policy was focused on economic activity, not the stock market.

1990

In August 1990, a major stock market decline began with the Dow Jones falling 10 percent and the S&P 500 declining 8.1 percent. By October 1990, the market had fallen 15.9 percent and 14.7 percent by these measures, respectively. The decline in the market closely followed the movement of the economy into a recession, the peak of the expansion having been reached in July 1990. Yet, although the 1990–91 recession was a relatively mild one and the stock market decline was moderate, the interest-rate spread did rise substantially, as seen in figure 12. A likely source of this widening of the spread was the very weak initial condition of depository institutions. The savings and loans already required a bailout from the government on the order of $150 billion, while loan losses were increasing and commercial bank failures had risen to more than 200 per year by the late 1980s (White, 1992).

2000

Lastly, figure 13 shows the most recent gyrations in the market. The sharp short slump beginning in July 1998, although it was not large enough to pass the simple test of a 20 percent drop, fell 12.7 percent in two months. The GDP kept rising, but the spread widened considerably. The current decline in the S&P 500 began in August 2000, falling 23 percent by December 2001. The collapse mirrored the slowing economy that

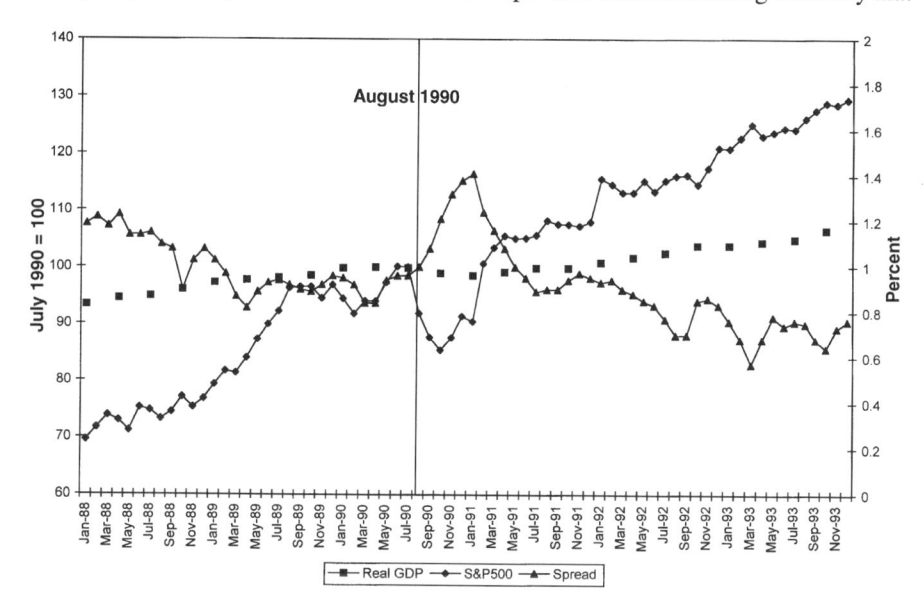

Figure 12: Crash of 1990

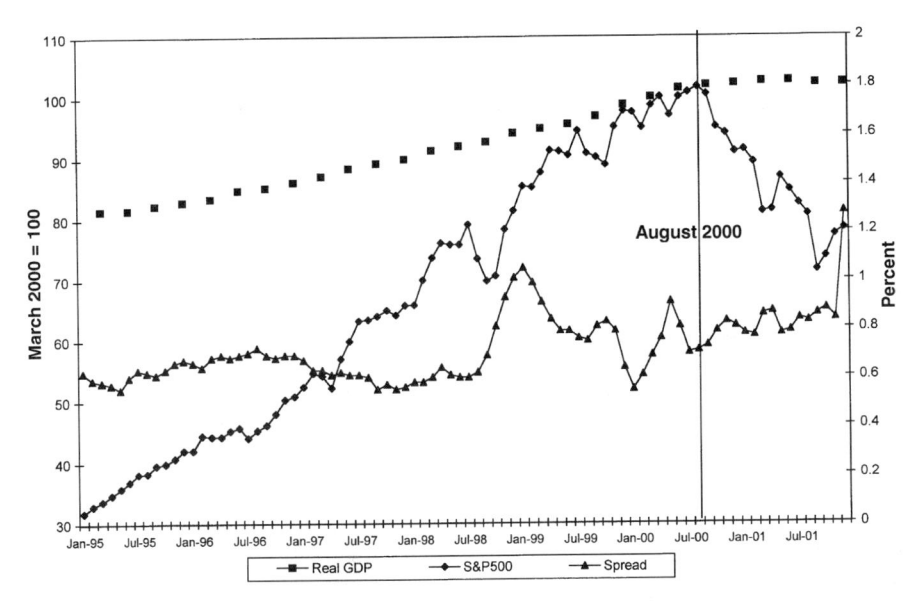

Figure 13: Crash of 2000

moved into a recession in March 2001. However, it important to note that the collapse in stock prices has not been evenly felt across the market. Between August 2000 and December 2001, the Dow Jones dropped approximately 11 percent, the S&P 500 fell 23 percent, and the NASDAQ, nearly 49 percent. The higher tech, higher risk stocks took a beating. Yet, this did not immediately translate into a higher risk premium for these borrowers even in the aftermath of the September 11 terrorist attacks and the recession, which had started six months earlier. One explanation for this stability is that the financial system has been stronger than at any time since the 1960s. The weak banks have been culled out by failure and merger, and new regulations and a long period of growth made intermediaries stronger and less susceptible to a sudden decline in asset values. Thus, there was no reason for a squeeze on the less creditworthy customers, despite the decline in the stock market. However, there was a sharp increase in the spread in December 2001 continuing into 2002. This development did not reflect any change in the stock market but rather the effects of the Enron scandal. The revelations of fraud and misleading accounting indicated that the quality of information about corporations was weaker than the markets had supposed. Given the revelation of greater information asymmetries, it is not surprising that risk premiums rose.

4. Implications for Monetary Policy

The description of the 15 episodes of 20th century stock market crashes suggests that we can place them into four categories.

1. Episodes in which the crashes did not appear to put stress on the financial system because interest rate spreads did not widen appreciably. These include the crashes of 1903, 1940, 1946, 1962, and 2000.

2. Episodes in which the crashes were extremely sharp and which put stress on the financial system, but where there was little widening of spreads subsequently because of intervention by the Federal Reserve to keep the financial system functioning in the wake of these crashes. These include the crashes of 1929 and 1987.
3. Episodes in which the crashes were associated with large increases in spreads suggesting severe financial distress. These include the crashes of 1907, 1930–33, 1937, and 1973–74.
4. Episodes in which the crashes were associated with increases in spreads that were not as large as in the third category, suggesting some financial distress. These include the crashes of 1917, 1920, 1969–70, and 1990.

Obviously, deciding which crashes go into categories 3 and 4 is somewhat arbitrary. For example, the 1920 crash episode does have a substantially greater increase in the spread than 1917, using the Mishkin measure, but the increase for the BAA-AAA spread (which was available from 1919 on) is similar to that in 1990 and is less than in the other category 3 episodes.

Looking at these four categories of crash episodes, what conclusions can we draw? First is the fact that many stock market crashes (category 1) are not accompanied by increases in spreads, which suggests that stock market crashes by themselves do not necessarily produce financial instability. These episodes also are ones in which the balance sheets and the financial system are in good shape before the onset of the stock market crash. Furthermore, in these cases where financial instability does not appear, economic downturns tend to be fairly mild. Second, very sharp stock market crashes like those in 1929 and 1987 (category 2) do have the potential to disrupt financial markets. But actions by the central bank to prevent the crashes from seizing up markets—not to prop up stock prices—are able to prevent financial instability from spinning out of control. Third, situations in which financial instability becomes severe, when spreads widen substantially (category 3), are associated with the worst economic downturns.

Because stock market crashes are often not followed by signs of financial instability, we must always be cautious about assigning causality from timing evidence. Certainly, one cannot make the case that stock market crashes are the main cause of financial instability. Indeed, in many episodes, a case can be made that the source of financial instability might have been caused by other factors, such as the collapse of the banking system or the severity of the economic contraction. Only in the cases of the extremely sharp market crashes in 1929 and 1987 do we have more direct evidence that some financial markets were unable to function as a result of the stock market crash. The theory of how stock market crashes can interfere with the efficient functioning of financial markets suggests that the impact of a stock market crash will be very different depending on the initial conditions of balance sheets in the economy.

What then are the monetary policy implications of the analysis of the stock market crashes examined here?[11] The first is that financial instability is the key problem facing the policymaker and not stock market crashes, even if they reflect the bursting of an asset price bubble. If the balance sheets of financial and nonfinancial institutions are initially strong, then a stock market crash (bursting of the bubble) is unlikely to lead to financial instability. In this case, the effect of a stock market crash on the economy will operate through the usual wealth and cost of capital channels, only requiring the monetary policymakers to respond to the standard effects of the stock market decline on aggregate demand. In this situation, optimal monetary policy, which focuses solely on minimizing a standard loss function, will not respond to the stock market decline over and above its effects on inflation and output. Indeed, a regime of flexible inflation targeting, which is what all so-called inflation targeters actually pursue (see Bernanke, Laubach, Mishkin, and Posen, 1999), is consistent with this type of optimal monetary policy (Svensson, 1999). Also Bernanke and Gertler (1999) have shown that a regime of flexible inflation targeting is likely to make financial instability less likely and to be stabilizing in the presence of asset price bubbles.

However, central banks may see the need to directly respond to a stock market crash when the crash puts stress on the financial system in order to prevent financial instability. We have seen exactly this response of the Fed in the crashes of 1929 and 1987, when the Fed had direct evidence that financial markets were unable to function in the immediate aftermath of the crashes. What is important about both these two episodes is the nature of the stress on financial markets. The source of stress had more to do with the speed of the stock market decline than the overall decline of the market over time, which has often been far larger with little impact on the financial system. Furthermore, in both episodes, the focus of the Federal Reserve was not to try to prop up stock prices but, rather, to make sure that the financial markets, which were starting to seize up, would begin functioning normally again.

A focus on financial instability also implies that central banks will respond to disruptions in financial markets even if the stock market is not a major concern. For example, as described in Maisel (1973), Brimmer (1989), and Mishkin (1991), the Fed responded aggressively to prevent a financial crisis after the Penn-Central bankruptcy in June 1970 without much concern for developments in the stock market even though the market had an appreciable decline from its peak in late 1968. In the aftermath of the Penn-Central bankruptcy, the commercial paper market stopped functioning and the Fed stepped in with a lender-of-last-resort operation. The New York Fed got in touch with money center banks, encouraged them to lend to their customers who were unable to roll over their commercial paper, and indicated that the discount window would be made available to the banks so that they could make these loans. These banks then followed the Fed's suggestion and received $575 million through the discount window for this purpose. In addition, the Fed, along with the Federal Deposit Insurance Corporation and the Federal Home Loan Banks decided to suspend Regulation Q ceilings and the Fed supplied liquidity to the banks through open market operations.

Similarly, in the fall of 1998, the Fed supplied liquidity to the system and lowered the federal funds rate sharply by 75 basis points even when the market was at levels that were considered to be very high by Federal Reserve officials. The Fed's intervention stemmed from its concerns about the stress put on the financial system by the Russian crisis and the failure of Long-Term Capital Management. A spectacular lender-of-last-resort operation was also carried out in the aftermath of the destruction of the

World Trade Center on September 11, 2001. Because of the disruption to the payments system, the liquidity needs of the financial system skyrocketed. To satisfy these needs and keep the financial system from seizing up, within a few hours of the incident, the Fed made a similar announcement to that made after the crash of 1987, stating, "The Federal Reserve System is open and operating. The discount window is available to meet liquidity needs."[12] The Fed then proceeded to provide $45 billion to banks through the discount window, a 200-fold increase over the previous week. When the stock market reopened on Monday, September 17, trading was orderly, although the Dow Jones average did decline by more than 7 percent.

These examples suggest the importance of having a central bank focus on the potential of financial instability per se. Too much of a focus on the stock market rather than on the potential for financial instability might lead central banks to fail to take appropriate actions as in 1970, 1998, and 2001, when the level of the stock market was not a primary concern.

Too great a focus on the stock market also presents other dangers for central banks. Too much attention on asset prices, in this case common stocks, can lead to the wrong policy responses. The optimal response to a change in asset prices very much depends on the source of the shock to these prices and the duration of the shock. An excellent example of this pitfall of too much focus on an asset price is the tightening of monetary policy in Chile and New Zealand in response to the downward pressure on the exchange rate of their currencies in the aftermath of the East Asian and Russian crises in 1997 and 1998 (see Mishkin and Schmidt-Hebbel, 2002). Given that the shock to the exchange rate was a negative terms of trade shock, it would have better been met by an easing of policy rather than a tightening. Indeed, the Reserve Bank of Australia responded in the opposite direction to the central banks of New Zealand and Chile, and eased monetary policy after the collapse of the Thai baht in July 1997 because it was focused on inflation control and not the exchange rate. The excellent performance of the Australian economy relative to New Zealand and Chile's during this period illustrates the benefit of focusing on the main objective of the central bank rather than on the asset price.

A second problem with the central bank focusing too much on stock prices is that it raises the possibility that the central bank will be made to look foolish. The linkage between monetary policy and stock prices, although an important part of the transmission mechanism, is still, nevertheless, a weak one. Most fluctuations in stock prices occur for reasons unrelated to monetary policy, either reflecting real fundamentals or animal spirits. The loose link between monetary policy and stock prices, therefore, means that the ability of the central bank to control stock prices is very limited. Thus, if the central bank indicates that it wants stock prices to change in a particular direction, it is likely to find that stock prices may move in the opposite direction, thus making the central bank look inept. Recall that when Alan Greenspan made his speech in 1996 suggesting that the stock market might be exhibiting "irrational exuberance," the Dow Jones average was around 6,500. This did not stop the market from rising, with the Dow subsequently climbing to above 11,000.

A third problem with focusing on stock prices is that it may weaken support for a central bank because it looks like it is trying to control too many elements of the economy. Part of the recent success of central banks throughout the world has been that they have narrowed their focus and have more actively communicated what they can and cannot do. Specifically, central banks have argued that they are less capable of managing short-run business cycle fluctuation and should, therefore, focus more on price stability as their primary goal. A key element of the success of the Bundesbank's monetary targeting regime was that it did not focus on short-run output fluctuations in setting its monetary policy instruments.[13] By narrowing their focus, central banks in recent years have been able to increase public support for their independence. Extending their focus to asset prices has the potential to weaken public support for central banks and may even cause the public to worry that the central bank is too powerful, having undue influence over all aspects of the economy.

A fourth problem with too much focus on the stock market is that it may create a form of moral hazard. Knowing that the central bank is likely to prop up the stock market if it crashes, the markets are then more likely to bid up stock prices. This might help facilitate excessive valuation of stocks and help encourage a stock market bubble that might crash later, something that the central bank would rather avoid. This begs the question of whether monetary authorities should try to prick asset price bubbles, because subsequent collapses of these asset prices might be highly damaging to the economy, as they were in Japan in the 1990s. Cecchetti, Genburg, Lipsky, and Wadhwani (2000), for example, argue that central banks should at times react to asset prices in order to stop bubbles from getting too far out of hand. However, there are serious flaws in this argument. First, is that it is very hard for monetary authorities to determine if a bubble has actually developed. To assume that they can is to assume that monetary authorities have better information and predictive ability than the private sector. If the central bank has no informational advantage, if it knows that a bubble has developed that will eventually crash, then the market knows this too and then the bubble would unravel and, thus, would be unlikely to develop. Without an informational advantage, the central bank is as likely to mis-predict the presence of a bubble as the private market and, thus, will frequently be mistaken, thus, frequently pursuing the wrong monetary policy.

5. Conclusions

This paper has examined 15 episodes of stock market crashes in the United States in the 20th century. The basic conclusion from studying these episodes is that the key problem facing monetary policymakers is not stock market crashes and the possible bursting of a bubble, but rather whether serious financial instability is present. Indeed, the situation depicted in figure 13, which shows that the recent stock market crash has had little impact on interest-rate spreads, appears to be an episode in which the stock market crash is not associated with financial instability. Thus, the current environment does not appear to be one that requires an unusual response to the stock market decline. With a focus on financial stability rather than the stock market, the response of central banks to stock market fluctuations is more likely to be optimal and, therefore, support for the independence of the central bank can be maintained.

*Frederic S. Mishkin is the Alfred Lerner Professor of Banking and Financial Institutions at the Graduate School of Business at Columbia University and a research associate at the NBER. Eugene N. White is a professor in the Department of Economics at Rutgers University and a research associate at the NBER.

Notes

1. See Mishkin (1995) and the other papers in this symposium for discussion of how changes in stock prices affect aggregate economic activity.

2. For an opposing view, see Bernanke and Gertler (1999).

3. For details on how crashes were defined and the use of the stock indices, see Mishkin and White (2002).

4. Although most observers consider only the nominal value of stocks when they describe a crash, over long periods of time, the real value of securities is a concern. To obtain the real value of the indices, the consumer price index (1982–84 = 100) was employed.

5. These series were obtained from the FRED database maintained by the Federal Reserve Bank of St. Louis. See www.frstls.gov.

6. Both series are from Standard & Poor's. The high-grade railroad bonds and the high-grade industrial bonds are available on the Macro History data set on the NBER's web site (www.nber.org) as series 13024 and 13026.

7. The Cowles Index showed similar movements with declines of 15.2, 18.6, and 17.0 percent in March, October, and November 1907, respectively.

8. Bank loans also began to carry large premiums relative to bankers' acceptances, Treasury securities, or any other safe assets, rising from just over 0.5 percent in 1929 to 2 percent to 4 percent in the worst years of the depression (*Banking and Monetary Statistics*).

9. See Brimmer (1989) and Mishkin (1991) for a description of the Fed's lender-of-last-resort role in this episode.

10. However, as shown in Mishkin (1991), there was a sharp but brief increase in the junk bond Treasury spread when the crash occurred. This suggests that there was the potential for the crash to lead to substantial financial instability, but this did not occur because of the quick action by the Federal Reserve.

11. There are other implications for other types of policy besides monetary policy that are beyond the scope of this paper. For example, concerns about preventing financial instability lead to the need to focus on financial regulation and supervision, as is discussed in Mishkin (2000).

12. "Economic Front: How Policy Makers Regrouped to Defend the Financial System," *The Wall Street Journal*, Tuesday, September 18, 2001, p. A1.

13. See Bernanke, Laubach, Mishkin, and Posen (1999).

References

Balke, Nathan, and Robert J. Gordon, 1986, "Historical Data, Appendix B," in Robert J. Gordon, *The American Business Cycle: Continuity and Change,* Chicago: University of Chicago, pp. 781–850.

Basile, Peter, 1989, "The Cyclical Variation of Junk Bond Risk Premiums in a Historical Perspective: 1910–1955," master's thesis, Rutgers University.

Battacharya, Sudipto, and Anjan Thakor, 1993, "Contemporary Banking Theory," *Journal of Financial Intermediation,* October, pp. 2–50.

Bernanke, Ben S., 1983, "Non-Monetary Effects of the Financial Crisis in the Propagation of the Great Depression," *American Economic Review,* Vol. 73, June, pp. 257–276.

Bernanke, Ben S., Thomas Laubach, Frederic S. Mishkin, and Adam S. Posen, 1999, *Inflation Targeting: Lessons from the International Experience,* Princeton: Princeton University Press.

Bernanke, Ben S., and Mark Gertler, 1989, "Agency Costs, Collateral, and Business Fluctuations," *American Economic Review,* Vol. 79, pp. 14–31.

Brimmer, Andrew F., 1989, "Distinguished Lecture on Economics in Government: Central Banking and Systemic Risks in Capital Markets," *Journal of Economic Perspectives,* Vol. 3, Spring, pp. 3–16.

Board of Governors of the Federal Reserve System, 1943, *Banking and Monetary Statistics, 1914–1941.*

Calomiris, C. W., and R. G. Hubbard, 1990, "Firm Heterogeneity, Internal Finance, and 'Credit Rationing,'" *Economic Journal,* Vol. 100, pp. 90–104.

Cecchetti, Stephen G., Hans Genburg, John Lipsky, and Sushil Wadhwani, 2000, *Asset Prices and Central Bank Policy,* Geneva Reports on the World Economy, London: International Center for Monetary and Banking Studies and Center for Economic Policy Research.

Dow Jones, Inc., 2001, "Economic Front: How Policy Makers Regrouped to Defend the Financial System," *The Wall Street Journal,* Tuesday, September 18, p. A1.

Economagic, stock indices, www.economagic.com.

Federal Reserve Bank of St. Louis, FRED, www.frstls.gov.

Freelunch, stock indices, www.economy.com.

Friedman, Milton, and Anna Jacobson Schwartz, 1963, *A Monetary History of the United States, 1867–1960,* Princeton: Princeton University Press.

Greenwald, B., and J. E. Stiglitz, 1988, "Information, Finance Constraints, and Business Fluctuations," in *Financial Constraints, Expectations and Macroeconomics,* M. Kohn and S.C. Tsiang, S.C., eds., Oxford: Oxford University Press.

Macaulay, Frederick R., 1938, *The Movements of Interest Rates, Bond Yields and Stock Prices in the United States Since 1856,* New York: National Bureau of Economic Research.

Maisel, Sherman, 1973, *Managing the Dollar,* New York: Norton.

Mishkin, Frederic S., 2001, "Financial Policies and the Prevention of Financial Crises in Emerging Market Countries," National Bureau of Economic Research, working paper, No. 8397, forthcoming in Martin Feldstein, ed., *Economic and Financial Crises in Emerging Market Countries,* Chicago: University of Chicago Press.

_____, 1997, "The Causes and Propagation of Financial Instability: Lessons for Policymakers," *Maintaining Financial Stability in a Global Economy,* Kansas City, MO: Federal Reserve Bank of Kansas City, pp. 55–96.

_____, 1995, "Symposium on the Monetary Transmission Mechanism," *Journal of Economic Perspectives*, 9, No. 4, Fall, pp. 3–10.

_____, 1991, "Asymmetric Information and Financial Crises: A Historical Perspective," in R. Glenn Hubbard, *Financial Markets and Financial Crises,* Chicago: Chicago University Press, pp. 69–108.

Mishkin, Frederic S., and Klaus Schmidt-Hebbel, 2002, "One Decade of Inflation Targeting in the World: What Do We Know and What Do We Need to Know?" in *Inflation Targeting: Design, Performance, Challenges,* Norman Loayza and Raimundo Soto, eds., Santiago: Central Bank of Chile, pp. 117–219.

Mishkin, Frederic S., and Eugene N. White, 2002, "U.S. Stock Market Crashes and Their Aftermath: Implications for Monetary Policy," National Bureau of Economic Research, working paper.

Mussa, Michael, 1994, "Monetary Policy," in Martin Feldstein, ed., *American Economic Policy in the 1980s,* Chicago: Chicago University Press.

National Bureau of Economic Research, Macro History Database.

Pierce, Phyllis, 1991, *The Dow Jones Averages, 1885–1990,* Homewood, IL: Business One Irwin.

Rappoport, Peter, and Eugene N. White, 1993, "Was There a Bubble in the 1929 Stock Market?" *Journal of Economic History* 53, (3) September, pp. 549–574.

_____, 1994, "Was the Crash of 1929 Expected?" *American Economic Review* 84, (1), March, pp. 271–281.

Romer, David H., and Christina D. Romer, 1989, "Does Monetary Policy Matter?" A Test in the Spirit of Friedman and Schwartz," *National Bureau of Economic Research Macroeconomics Annual,* Olivier Blanchard and Stanley Fisher, eds., Cambridge: MIT Press, pp. 121–170.

Romer, Christina, 1990, "The Great Crash and the Onset of the Great Depression," *Quarterly Journal of Economics,* Vol. 105:3, August, pp. 597–624.

Sprague, O. M. W., 1910, *History of Crises Under the National Banking System,* Washington, DC: U.S. Government Printing Office.

Svensson, L., 1997, "Inflation Forecast Targeting: Implementing and Monitoring Inflation Targets," *European Economic Review*, Vol. 41, pp. 1111–1146.

White, Eugene N., 2000, "Banking and Finance in the Twentieth Century," in S. Engerman and R. Gallman, eds., *The Cambridge Economic History of the United States,* Vol. III, Cambridge: Cambridge University Press, pp. 743–802.

_____, 1992, *The Comptroller and the Transformation of American Banking, 1960–1990* Washington, DC: Office of the Comptroller of the Currency.

_____, 1990, "The Stock Market Boom and Crash of 1929 Revisited," *Journal of Economic Perspectives,* Vol. 4 (2), Spring, pp. 67–83.

Wicker, Elmus, 2000, *Banking Panics of the Gilded Age,* Cambridge: Cambridge University Press.

Chapter 7
Japan's Experience with Asset Price Bubbles: Is It a Case for Inflation Targeting?

Kunio Okina*
Bank of Japan

and

Shigenori Shiratsuka
Bank of Japan

1. Introduction

Since the latter half of the 1980s, Japan's economy has experienced extremely large swings against the backdrop of the emergence, expansion, and bursting of asset price bubbles. When looking back at this episode from the viewpoint of monetary policy management, should the Bank of Japan (BOJ) have given more consideration to asset price fluctuations in formulating its monetary policy? Or, should the BOJ not have been focused on asset price fluctuations and conducted policies focusing only on the general price level?

A rise and fall in asset prices affects real economic activity mainly through the following routes: 1) via consumption through the wealth effect, and 2) via investment through a change in external finance premium due to changes in collateral and net asset values.[1] Therefore, when asset prices are rising, they affect the economy in a favorable way even though such rising is occasioned by a bubble and the adverse effects are not thoroughly recognized.

However, once the economy enters a downturn, the above favorable cycle reverses and the economy will face a severe reaction. That is, the harmful effects of a bubble will emerge, exerting stress on the real side of the economy and financial system. In such a case, if intensified bullish expectations that previously supported the bubble are left unchecked, expansion and subsequent bursting of the bubble will become bigger, affecting the real economy directly or, by damaging the financial system, indirectly. In light of Japan's experience, it seems to be characteristic that effects of a bubble are asymmetrically larger in the bursting period than in the expansion period.

During the asset price bubble in the late 1980s the measured inflation was relatively moderate, but expectations that low interest rates would continue over time had been generated in the meantime, making economic agents' expectations extremely bullish.[2] What should be noted about the asset price bubble in Japan is that it was not a rational bubble as modeled in Blanchard and Watson (1982), which is expressed as a divergence from economic fundamentals and the probability of its bursting is recognized among economic agents and, thus, incorporated into asset price formation. Rather the bubble was characterized by euphoria, that is, excessively optimistic expectations with respect to future economic fundamentals, which last for several years and then burst. Hence, in light of Japan's experience, it seems to be extremely important to accurately analyze what asset price fluctuations imply and to accurately evaluate how "expectations" illustrated in such fluctuations are sustainable.[3]

This paper is composed as follows. Section 2 summarizes the characteristics of asset price bubbles in the late 1980s based on Japan's experience of asset price booms in the postwar period. Section 3 verifies the relationship between monetary policy management and asset prices in the process of the emergence of the bubble based on a standard view of policy rules. In section 4, after summarizing the effects of the bursting of the bubble on financial system stability, the impact on monetary policy is considered. Section 5 rounds up the discussion and presents a conclusion.

2. Japan's Asset Price Booms in the Postwar Period

Let us review the major characteristics of asset price booms in the postwar period. Figure 1 plots major financial and economic indicators: stock prices and land prices as indicators for asset prices (upper panel) and the Consumer Price Index (CPI) and growth rate of real gross domestic product (GDP) (lower panel). This figure shows the three major boom-bust cycles in asset prices: 1) the Iwato boom in the second half of the 1950s; 2) the boom beginning with Prime Minister Tanaka's "remodeling the Japanese archipelago"[4] project to the first oil crisis; and 3) the Heisei boom in the late 1980s to early 1990s.

First, at the time of the Iwato boom, while investment demand due to technological innovation replaced post-World War II reconstruction demand as the main driver and ushered in the high economic growth period, asset prices increased rapidly and, on the price front, consumer prices rose while wholesale prices remained generally stable, thus, leading to so-called "productivity difference inflation." However, the real economic growth rate exceeded 10 percent per annum, and the increase in asset prices mainly reflected technological progress.

Second, during the period from the "remodeling the Japanese archipelago" boom to the first oil crisis, asset prices first increased and then the general price level sharply increased due to the excessively high growth of money stock and oil price hikes stemming from the first oil crisis, while real economic growth rapidly declined marking an end to the high economic growth period.

Finally, in the Heisei boom, asset prices increased dramatically under long-lasting economic growth and stable inflation; this period is frequently referred to

Japan's Experience with Asset Price Bubbles 83

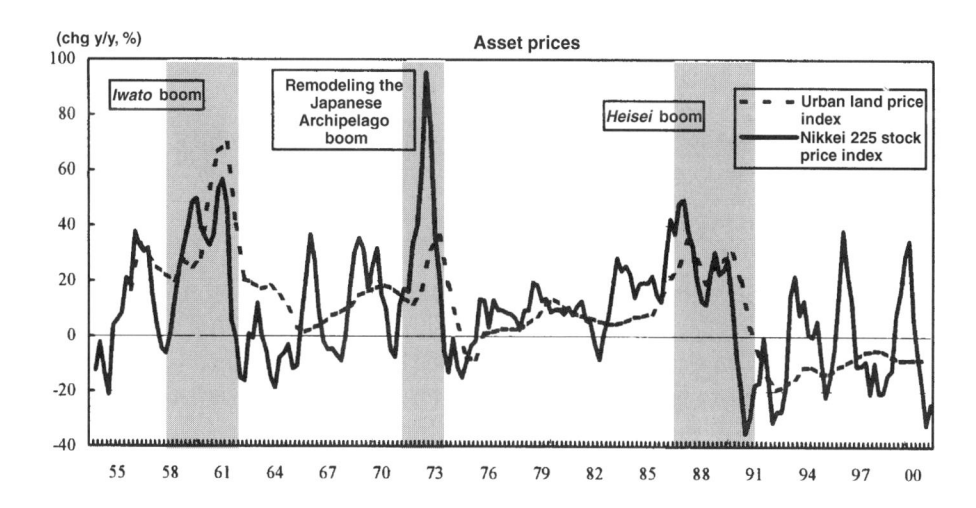

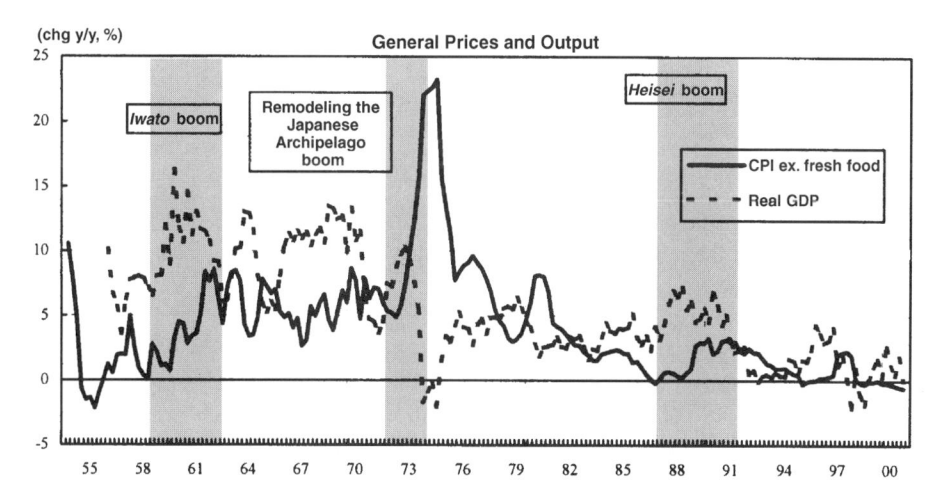

Sources: Bank of Japan, *Financial and Economic Statistics Monthly*

Notes:
1. Urban land price index is figure for commercial land in six major cities.
2. Regarding CPI before 1970 and domestic WPI before 1960, the prewar base series are connected with the current series.
3. Unemployment rate is seasonally adjusted.

Figure 1: Asset Prices, General Prices, and Economic Environment

as the "bubble era." The phenomena particular to this period are stable CPI inflation parallel with the expansion of asset prices and long adjustment periods after the peaking of asset prices. Asset prices skyrocketed during the bubble era but then declined rapidly from their peaks at the period from the end of 1989 to 1990, and land prices continued declining while stock prices remained stagnant with unstable fluctuation.

3. Monetary Policy and Asset Prices Bubbles

Japan's stagnant economy in the 1990s was conspicuous, and, against such a backdrop, the BOJ's monetary policy during the period has often been criticized. However, some sort of objective benchmark becomes necessary to evaluate such criticisms. In this regard, what is most interesting is a verification of Japan's monetary policy based on the Taylor rule and its variant. We selected the Taylor rule as a benchmark because it is currently the most popular policy reaction function and there is abundant literature, such as Bernanke and Gertler (1999, 2001) dealing with it in relation to the role of asset prices in monetary policy formulation.

3.1. Criticism on Japan's Monetary Policy

A typical criticism based on the Taylor rule can be found in McCallum (2001) shown in figure 2. The main point of his criticism is that monetary policy had been consistently too tight since 1993. However, when looking at the period of expansion of the bubble, the policy rule used by McCallum suggests interest rates would have declined in 1987, and after the bursting of the bubble the policy reversal toward monetary easing would have lagged compared with actual policy.[5]

However, such results do not accord with the general criticism of the BOJ's policy during the bubble period: the protracted period of excessive monetary easing and delay in lifting monetary tightening after the bursting of the bubble. What does this signify? One perspective holds that the BOJ should have focused more on asset prices.[6]

Against such a view, Bernanke and Gertler (1999, 2001) hold a negative view on assigning monetary policy to control asset price fluctuations. The authors argue that a central bank aiming to stabilize asset prices is problematic for various reasons, one of which is that it is difficult to distinguish whether asset price fluctuations are induced by fundamentals or other factors, or both. Upon such reasoning, Bernanke and Gertler present simulation results showing that the BOJ should have been able to achieve better performance if it had pursued a Taylor-type rule (figure 3). What is especially striking and interesting about these results is that, despite focusing only on the inflation and output gap, Bernanke and Gertler's policy rule implied the need for rapid tightening in 1988. In response, BOJ Deputy Governor Yamaguchi commented: "I don't see how a central bank can increase interest to 8 percent or 10 percent when we don't have inflation," (Yamaguchi, 1999).

3.2. Assessment of Policy Rule Simulation

Why, then, do the estimation results of Bernanke and Gertler (1999) shown in figure 3, despite focusing only on the inflation and output gap, seem to imply early and rapid

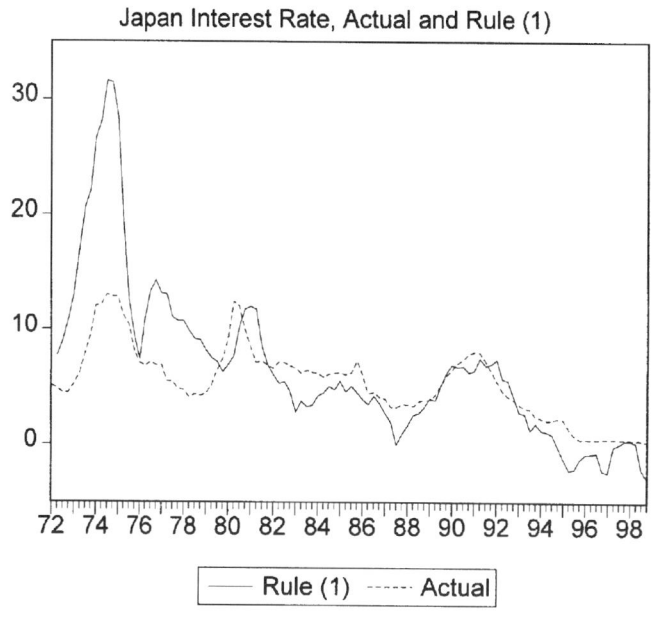

Source: McCallum (2001)

Figure 2: Policy Rule (1): McCallum's Estimation

Source: Bernanke and Gertler (1999)

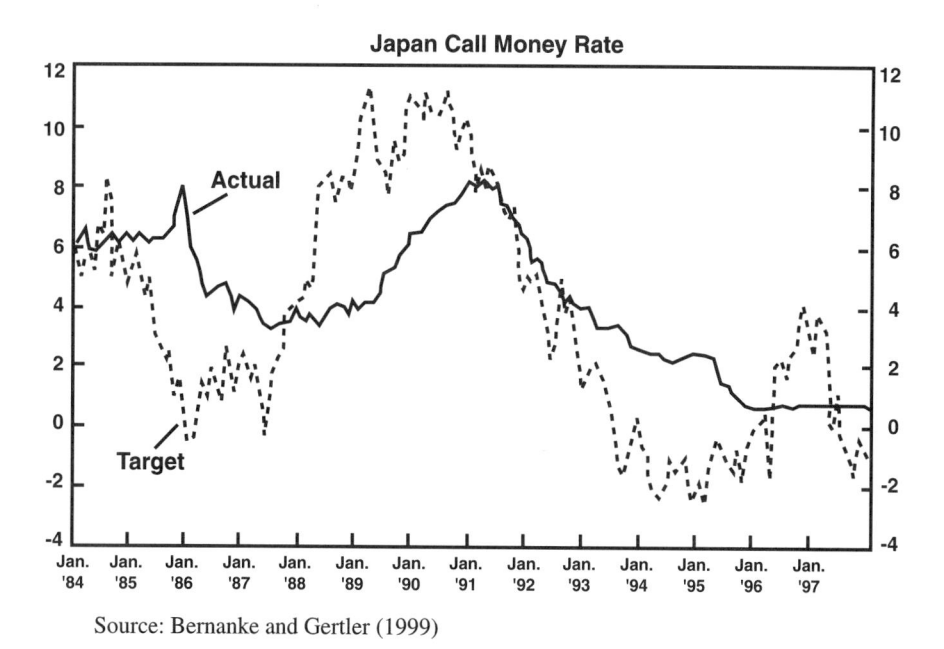

Figure 3: Policy Rule (3): Bernanke-Gertler's Estimation

monetary tightening, which is in contrast to the estimation results derived from the standard Taylor rule, as in figure 2?

First, let us look at developments in Japan's CPI and output gap, both of which form the basis for a Taylor-type policy rule (figure 4). As a whole, the CPI shows smooth swings, but it rapidly rose in 1989 and 1997, reflecting the introduction of a 3 percent consumption tax and then an increase to 5 percent, respectively. With respect to the output gap, we use the difference between real GDP and its trend obtained by applying the Hodrick-Prescott filter (HP filter). We will later describe problems with respect to estimating the output gap.[7]

Next, when we compare the McCallum formula and Bernanke-Gertler formula, the largest difference is that the former uses a backward-looking Taylor rule based on realized inflation, while the latter uses a forward-looking Taylor rule, which assumes perfect foresight with respect to the inflation for one year ahead. In addition, the Bernanke-Gertler formula puts greater weight on inflation and less on the output gap. As a result, in a simulation using the Bernanke-Gertler formula, "future" fluctuations of inflation strongly affect the current target value of the policy interest rate.

By following the Taylor rule formulas, which McCallum (2001) and Bernanke and Gertler (1999) assumed in their estimations, we have used the above mentioned CPI and output gap and tried to reproduce the target rate, as shown in figure 5. The top panel of figure 5 shows our estimated results of a backward-looking Taylor rule, which corresponds to what McCallum estimated (figure 2), and the bottom panel shows our estimated results of a forward-looking Taylor rule, which corresponds to the estimate by Bernanke and Gertler (figure 3).[8] You can see that our estimates have reproduced qualitatively similar results compared with those of McCallum and Bernanke and Gertler.

In our backward-looking Taylor rule, target policy rate is as a whole higher than that of McCallum, which results in a substantially shorter zero interest rate period and implies rather tighter monetary policy overall, but, as in the case in Japan, can avoid the impractical consequence of embarking on zero interest rates for as early as 1987. On the other hand, our forward-looking Taylor rule, despite quarterly and monthly differences, well follows the estimation results of Bernanke and Gertler as a whole.

During the period of expansion of the bubble, there were two humps in the estimate of McCallum, from 1989 to 1990, and in those of Bernanke and Gertler, from 1988 to 1989. When we look at the basic data, the first hump seems to have resulted from the introduction of the consumption tax (3 percent) in April 1989. If we adjust for it, the first hump disappears for both backward- and forward-looking Taylor rules. Since a one-time price rise induced by an introduction of the consumption tax should not be offset by monetary tightening, one cannot say the BOJ delayed tightening. One can only say the bank delayed tightening if perfect foresight of core inflation rates for one year ahead is practically feasible, while it might have been difficult to insist on the pursuit of rapid monetary tightening such as raising the interest rate from 4 to 8 percent in 1988.[9]

3.3 Measuring the Output Gap and Asset Price Bubbles

The above discussion reveals that in accurately assessing monetary policy management, it is crucial to gauge inflationary pressure by carefully examining its basic data

Japan's Experience with Asset Price Bubbles 87

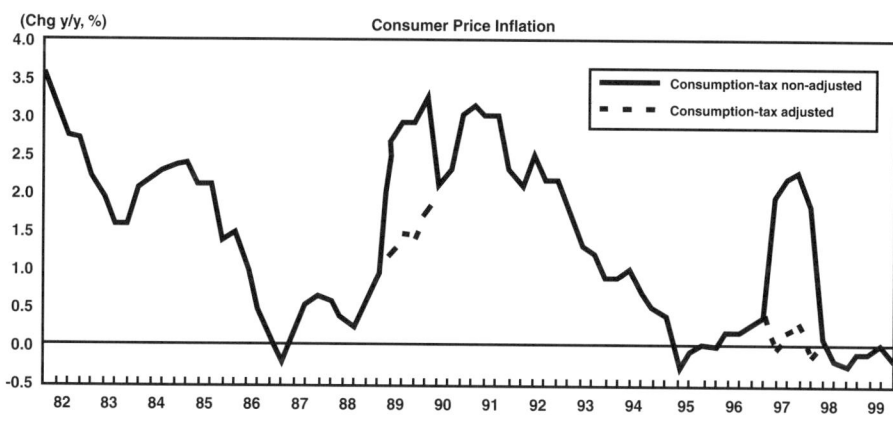

[1] Consumer Prices

[2] Output Gap

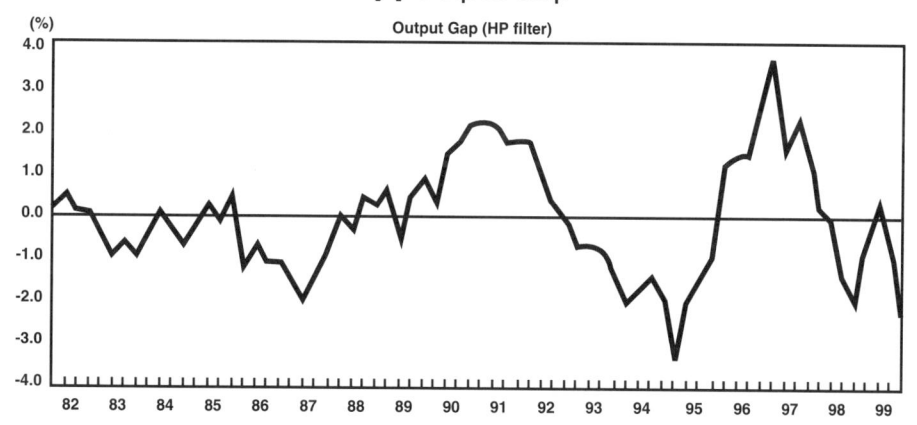

Sources: Ministry of Public Management, Home Affairs, Posts and Telecommunications, *Consumer Price Index;* Cabinet Office, *Annual Report on National Accounts*

Notes:
1. Figures for the CPI are adjusted for the impacts of consumption tax.

2. Output gaps are computed as a difference between actual and HP-filtered series for the Real GDP. HP-filtered series computed for the sample period from 1955Q2 to 2000Q4 with the smoothing parameter $\lambda = 1,600$.

Figure 4: Data for Estimating Taylor Rule

[1] Backward-Looking Taylor Rule

(%) Actual and Target Call Rate (Backward-Looking Taylor Rule)

— Target (cons. tax adjusted)
— Target (cons. tax non-adjusted)
■ ■ ■ Actual

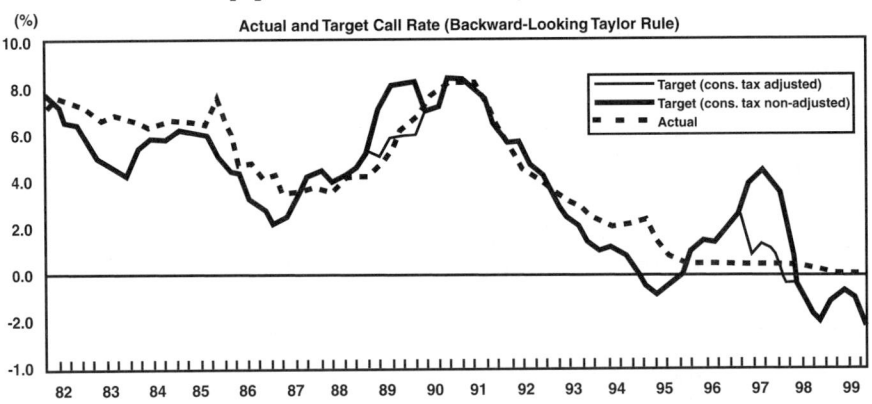

[2] Forward-Looking Taylor Rule

(%) Actual and Target Call Rate (Forward-Looking Taylor Rule)

— Target (cons. tax adjusted)
— Target (cons. tax non-adjusted)
■ ■ ■ Actual

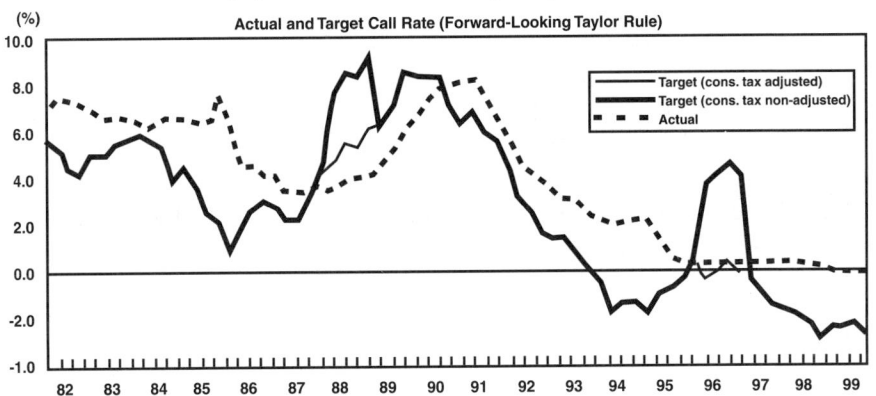

Sources: Bank of Japan, *Financial and Economic Statistics Monthly*; Ministry of Public Management, Home Affairs, Posts and Telecommunications, *Consumer Price Index*; Cabinet Office, *Annual Report on National Accounts*

Notes:
1. Taylor rule is defined as follows:
   Basic equation: $R_t = r^*_t + \pi^* + \alpha \times (\pi_{t+T} - \pi^*) + \beta \times (Y_t - Y^*)$
   r^*_t: equiribrium real short-term interest rate at period t
   π^*: targeted rate of inflation
   R_t: uncollateralized overnight call rate at period t
   π_{t+T}: rate of CPI inflation at period t
   $Y_t - Y^*$: output gap at period t.
2. The rate of inflation in the second term of the right-hand side are that for the current period ($T=0$) and one year ahead ($T=4$), respectively.

Figure 5: Examination of the Taylor Rule

of prices and real GDP. In so doing, a serious problem is that, since the level of the output gap will vary depending on the estimates of potential GDP, the derived optimal target rate might differ, even from the same observed inflation and real GDP. The path of optimal interest rates will differ whether one adopts the optimistic expectations at the time to revise the potential growth path upward or accepts the potential growth rate based on the hindsight that such expectations were nothing more than euphoria.

What typically shows this point is the evaluation of the real GDP growth path on a real-time basis (the upper panel of figure 6). Quarter one of 1987 is the bottom prior to the bubble period, and a linear trend line from 1977Q4 to 1987Q1 almost corresponds to the 3.5 percent growth path. However, from 1987Q1 to mid 1991, real GDP expanded following the 5 percent growth trend. With the benefit of hindsight, most of the trend shift was temporary and should not have been accommodated. It should be noted that continued economic expansion makes it difficult to decompose a rising growth rate into cyclical and trend components.

In this regard, Bernanke and Gertler (2001) state that "[A]dmittedly, the output gap is difficult to measure, but we are more confident in economists' ability to measure the output gap than to measure the fundamental component of stock prices," and "[I]n addition, the behavior of inflation provides a real-time indicator of the magnitude of the output gap, whereas there is no analogous indicator to provide confirmation of estimates of stock fundamentals." However, Japan's experience shows that central banks are unlikely to evaluate potential inflationary pressure stemming from asset price fluctuations "without getting into the business of deciding what is a fundamental and what is not," (Bernanke and Gertler, 1999); their argument, thus, seems to be too optimistic. First, the inflation rate itself should not necessarily be a predominant real-time indicator of the magnitude of the output gap. Second, one could not have estimated, therefore, a correct potential growth path without identifying whether then prevailing expectations were euphoria or not.

Similar argument seems to be applicable to the recent U.S. experience (the lower panel of figure 6). Meyer (2000) states that a major challenge for U.S. monetary policy as of March 2000 was to determine how "to allow the economy to realize the full benefits of the new possibilities while avoiding an overheated economy." He also emphasizes the importance of assessing the level of potential GDP in evaluating inflationary pressure against the background of enormous changes in economic structure (namely the "new economy") behind rising U.S. stock prices.

4. Monetary Policy during the Bursting of the Bubble

4.1. The Bubble and Japan's Financial System

Looking back at Japan's experience of the period when the bubble burst, it can be characterized by the fact that financial system instability was intensified, thereby seemingly amplifying the adverse impacts of the bursting of the bubble.

There was a temporary economic recovery until around 1997 despite the economy having shouldered the adverse effects in the financial system due to asset price

[1] Japan

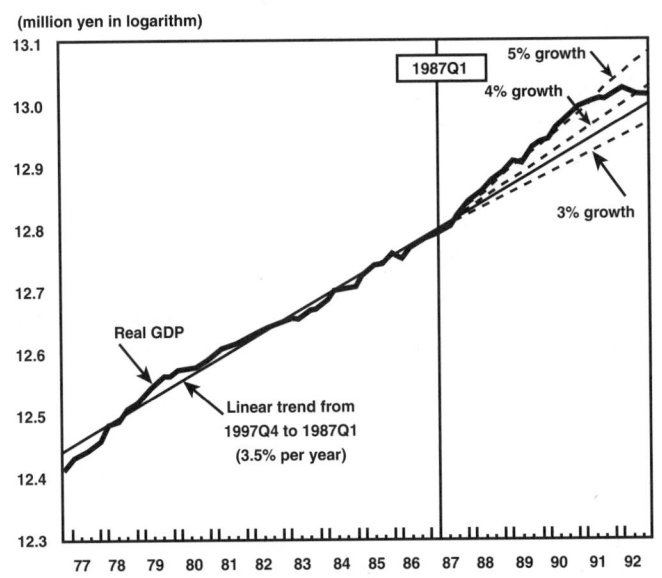

(million yen in logarithm)

- 1987Q1
- 5% growth
- 4% growth
- 3% growth
- Real GDP
- Linear trend from 1997Q4 to 1987Q1 (3.5% per year)

[2] USA

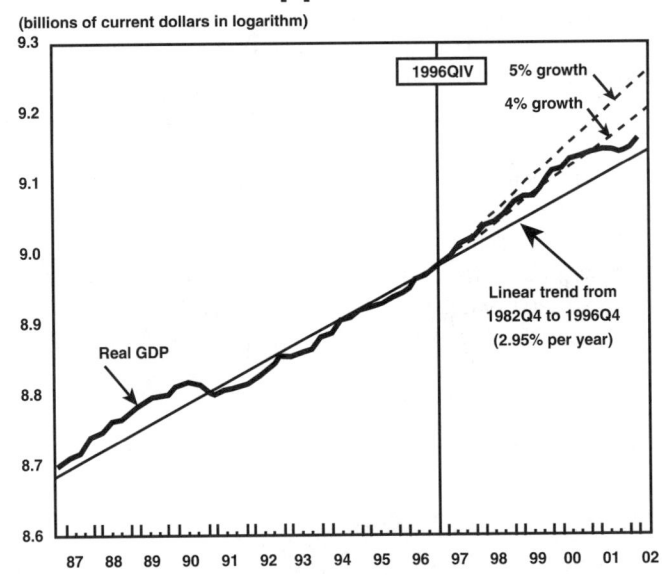

(billions of current dollars in logarithm)

- 1996QIV
- 5% growth
- 4% growth
- Real GDP
- Linear trend from 1982Q4 to 1996Q4 (2.95% per year)

Sources: Japan: Cabinet Office, *Annual Report on National Accounts*
USA: Bureau of Economic Analysis, U.S. Department of Commerce (http://www.bea.gov)

Figure 6: Impact of Trend Shift in Real GDP

declines. Economic recovery from late 1995 was relatively robust, and the growth of business investment in particular turned positive in fiscal 1995 after an interval of three years, led mainly by electronic and telecommunications-related investment. Stock prices also rapidly rallied from mid July and recovered the 20,000 level in the Nikkei 225 at year-end. In fiscal 1996, in addition to public investment, favorable private sector performance strongly propelled the economy, resulting in a high growth rate of 5 percent.

Reflecting such developments in the real economy, the target interest rate according to the backward-looking type Taylor rule (figure 5) that had once reached the zero bound by early 1995, rose rapidly up to 1997. On the other hand, the actual BOJ's policy rate had promptly declined since 1995 and crossed the target rate. The background to such divergence seems to be the concerns over the serious balance sheet adjustment, which constrains the economic recovery. In fact, even though Japan's economy had been recovering at a rather rapid pace, the nonperforming loans of financial institutions had been increasing (figure 7), thus indicating that balance sheet adjustment had not necessarily progressed during the period of this recovery.

Why were there conflicting moves between real economic activity and the financial system? One possible answer is that Japan's financial system had historically heavily relied on bank-based financing (figure 8). Under a bank-based financial system, banks accumulate internal reserves when the economy is sound and absorb losses stemming from firms' poor business performance or bankruptcy during recession, and, hence, financial intermediation plays a buffer role against short-term shocks.[10] However, such a risk smoothing function of the financial system will be suddenly lost if the system encounters a shock that erodes banks' net capital to the extent that it threatens their soundness. Therefore, the effects of the bursting of the bubble on the financial system seem to be invisible headwind up to a certain "critical point" after which they suddenly materialize.[11]

As such, a characteristic of bank-based financial systems where financial effects stemming from the bursting of the bubble rapidly materialize beyond a certain critical point, together with lack of disclosure and underdeveloped safety net measures, make it all the more difficult to promptly deal with the nonperforming loan problem. However, in Japan's case, until effects of the financial instability materialized, the financial supervisory authorities had concern over the possibility of financial crisis triggered by the disclosure of actual financial conditions of the banking sector. With such lack of disclosure, the public was apathetic to the injection of public funds and, consequently, the financial system problem was forborne. It was from 1997 to 1998 when the financial system was driven to the brink of malfunctioning that public recognition changed; but, by then, the magnitude of the problem had become so extensive that drastic steps were increasingly difficult to take.

4.2 Financial System Instability and Monetary Policy

Next, let us examine to what extent monetary easing effects were offset during the period when the bubble burst because of financial system problems.

It is difficult, however, to give a direct answer to this question. But, Japan's high growth of monetary base and contrasting continuous decline in private lending

(ratio to nominal GDP, %)

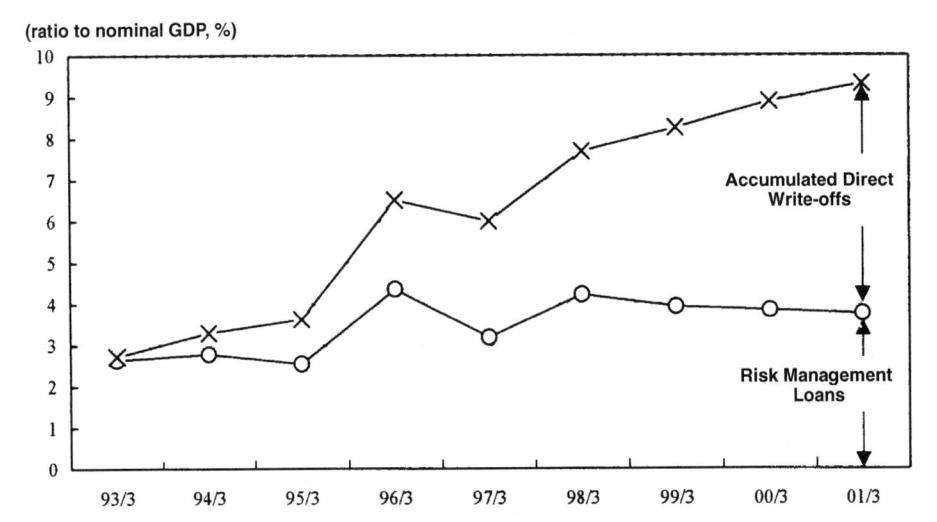

[Chart showing two lines from 93/3 to 01/3. "Accumulated Direct Write-offs" line (X markers) rising from about 2.5 to about 9.5. "Risk Management Loans" line (O markers) ranging from about 2.5 to about 4.5.]

Sources: Financial Service Agency (http://www.fsa.go.jp); Cabinet Office, *Annual Report on National Accounts*

Notes:
1. Figures are summations of city banks, long-term credit banks, and trust banks (figures for all banks and all deposit-taking institutions are impossible to retroact before the fiscal year of 1995).

2. Risk management loans are summations of loans to borrowers in legal bankruptcy, past due loans in arrears by six months or more, and loans in arrears by three months or more and less than six months.

Figure 7: Nonperforming Loans

(figure 9), plus the rigidity in lending to low profit industries, such as real estate and construction (figure 10), strongly imply that problems that hamper the effectiveness of monetary policy lie, rather, in malfunctioning of the financial system stemming from balance sheet problems of firms and financial institutions. This suggests the possibility of two mechanisms: 1) An increase in nonperforming loans erodes the net capital of financial institutions, resulting in a decline in risk-taking ability (credit crunch), and 2) Even though firms become unprofitable, financial institutions continue lending to them to prevent losses from materializing (forbearance lending). Under such circumstances, loans to unprofitable firms become fixed and funds are not channeled to growing firms, holding down economic activity.

As such, when the financial system carries problems stemming from the bursting of a bubble, effectiveness of the central bank's monetary easing will be substantially counteracted. Once a financial system tumbles into a critical situation, the boundary between monetary and prudential policies be comes extremely ambiguous.

During financial crises, financially stressed banks tend to have serious difficulties not only with lending, but also with arbitraging and dealing. This hampers the

[1] Financial liabilities held by nonfinancial corporations (ratio to total financial liabilities)

Unit: %

	Japan	U. S.	Germany
Borrowing	38.8	12.1	33.3
Bonds	9.3	8.2	1.3
Shares & equities	33.8	66.6	54.3
Others	18.1	13.0	11.0

[2] Financial assets held by households (ratio to total financial assets)

Unit: %

	Japan	U. S.	Germany
Currency & deposits	54.0	9.6	35.2
Bonds	5.3	9.5	10.1
Investment trusts	2.3	10.9	10.5
Shares & equities	8.1	37.3	16.8
Insurance & pension	26.4	30.5	26.4
Others	3.9	2.2	1.1

Source: Bank of Japan, Research and Statistics Department (2001)

Notes: 1. Figures are those for the end of 1999.
2. Regarding financial debt for enterprises, stocks are evaluated at the market value, and, thus, do not necessarily correspond to the accumulated funding by enterprises. In addition, U.S. figures include those for sole proprietorships, and regard their net worth as proprietors' equities in household sector. Thus, it should be noted that the ratio of equities to total assets are likely to be higher, compared to those for other countries. For the details, see Bank of Japan, Research and Statistics Department (2001).

Figure 8: Financial Structure

transmission mechanism from the policy-targeted rate to longer-term rates, resulting in segmentation among various financial markets. Thus, it could be extremely important for a central bank to intervene in various financial markets to fix segmented markets, thereby restoring market liquidity and the proper transmission mechanism.[12] This monetary operation may be rather different from that of a normal situation. Such an operation would require not only adjusting the aggregate amount of liquidity in financial markets by changing short-term interest rates, but also fixing the allocation of liquidity among financial markets. It should be noted, however, that in Japan's case such easing effects only mitigated the liquidity constraint of financial institutions and failed to be transmitted outside the financial system since the transmission channel between financial and nonfinancial sectors was not functioning sufficiently.

4.3 Early Response to Financial Crises

The pace of the BOJ's reduction of interest rates from late 1993 to autumn 1995 was slowed when the BOJ was about to face a record low official discount rate of 2.5 percent during the period of expansion of the bubble, suggesting the possibility that the BOJ was rather reluctant to pursue additional easing.[13] There are conflicting views

94   Chapter 7

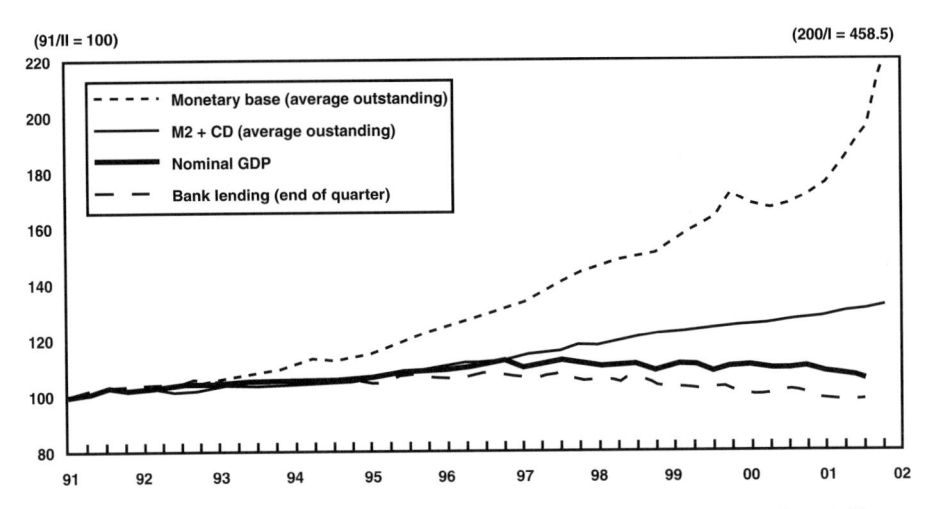

(91/II = 100)   (200/I = 458.5)

- - - - Monetary base (average outstanding)
—— M2 + CD (average outstanding)
—— Nominal GDP
— — Bank lending (end of quarter)

Sources: Bank of Japan, *Financial and Economic Statistics Monthly*; Cabinet Office, *Annual Report on National Accounts*

Notes: Figures for monetary base, M2+CD, and nominal GDP are seasonally adjusted. Figures for bank lending are seasonally non-adjusted

Figure 9: Monetary Aggregates

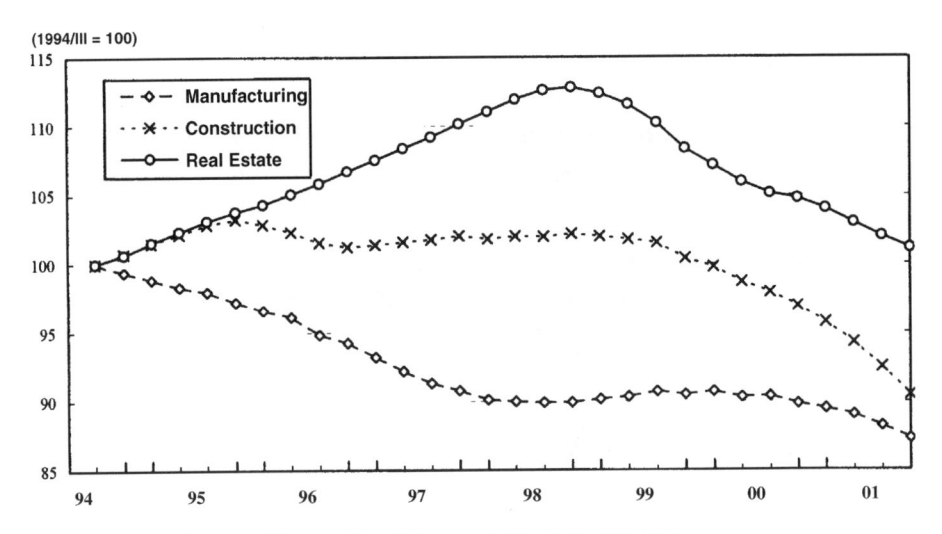

(1994/III = 100)

— ◇ — Manufacturing
· · ✶ · · Construction
—○— Real Estate

Source: Bank of Japan, *Financial and Economic Statistics Monthly*

Figure 10: Loans Outstanding by Industries

with respect to the delay in the pace of interest rate reduction since 1993: One argument holds that interest rates should have been reduced at a quicker pace, while another advocates that even if interest rates had been reduced more quickly the effects would have been limited since the financial system was already substantially wounded. In light of the subsequent development of Japan's economy, a view that prompt interest rate reduction more faithful to the Taylor rule was desirable seems to be convincing, as McCallum (2001) suggested.

However, based on an observation that the financial system was substantially wounded in the period after 1993 and the effectiveness of monetary easing was limited, what might have been worth trying was a more drastic than normal interest rate reduction before 1993, even though it was adequate in light of the Taylor rule. In the previous section, in line with Okina et al. (2001), we pointed out that expectations become extremely bullish during a period of euphoria and, thus, a substantial increase in interest rates would have been necessary to induce a change in such expectations. Put differently, even if interest rates had been high, the effect of monetary tightening would not have materialized to any great degree until such expectations had been adjusted downward. If such expectations had been adjusted downward, the adverse effects on the economy would inevitably have been quite large due to the combined effect of the rise in interest rates themselves and the revision of euphoric expectations.

The above presumption might lead us to the conclusion that an early interest rate reduction was indeed necessary. However, here again an important point is predictability of the effects of a bubble bursting, and, therefore, it seems that the BOJ, during the expansion of the bubble, should have made a judgment as to what extent the potential output path would perpetually shift downward because of effects arising from the bursting of the bubble on the financial system (i.e., to what extent a decline in asset prices would be permanent).[14]

5. Conclusions

In this paper, we have reviewed the process of the emergence, expansion, and bursting of Japan's asset price bubbles since the late 1980s to date, from the viewpoint of monetary policy management.

First of all, Japan's experience does not necessarily suggest that asset prices need to be included in the targets of monetary policy. In this regard, the conclusion of Bernanke and Gertler (1999) is correct. However, their assertion that a central bank can accomplish effectively and comprehensively both macroeconomic stability and financial system stability by adopting a strategy of "flexible inflation targeting" is not automatically guaranteed.

A critical point is that, as it had been in Japan during the bubble period, a bubble is based on excessively optimistic expectations with respect to the future, which might be described as euphoria with the benefit of hindsight, rather than a rational bubble, as modeled by Blanchard and Watson (1982). Under continued price stability, the perceived potential output path has shifted upward as economic expansion prolonged, resulting in the emergence of euphoria and underestimation of inflationary pressure in view of the output gap. However, increases in asset prices during this period also failed to deliver a sufficient clue to assess whether such increases were the consequence of an advent of a new economy or just euphoria. After all, a central bank cannot take an appropriate policy response without evaluating whether or not expectations for a new stage of development induced by asset price hikes are euphoric and forecast a correct path for the potential growth rate. In this sense, it cannot reasonably be assumed that direct inclusion of asset prices into policy targets could have lead to more appropriate policy judgment.

In addition, Japan's experience seems to suggest that trying to carry out early and drastic monetary easing when a bubble bursts would be worth trying. However, in the case of Japan, a characteristic of a bank-based financial system where effects of the bursting of the bubble on the financial front suddenly materialize at a stage beyond a certain critical value made it difficult for the central bank to recognize that the shock of the bubble bursting would have a prolonged impact beyond the normal business cycle at an early stage of the bursting. To this end, as is similar with the case during the period of emergence and expansion of the bubble, the central bank cannot make a policy judgment without evaluating to what extent the potential output path will perpetually shift downward by taking account of effects of the bubble bursting on the financial front.

*Kunio Okina is the director of the Institute for Monetary and Economic Studies of the Bank of Japan. Shigenori Shiratsuka is a senior economist at the Institute for Monetary and Economic Studies of the Bank of Japan. The authors thank the participants in this conference, especially two discussants, Takeo Hoshi and Ignazio Visco, for their helpful discussions and Michio Kitahara, Ryoji Koike, and Tomiyuki Kitamura for their assistance. The views expressed in the paper are those of the authors and do not necessarily reflect those of the Bank of Japan or the Institute for Monetary and Economic Studies.

Notes

1. Bernanke and Gertler (1995) explain that frictions in financial markets, such as imperfect information and costly enforcement of contracts, generate a difference in costs between external funds, such as bond financing, and internal funds, such as retaining earnings. They call this wedge the external finance premium and emphasize that it fluctuates coincidentally with business cycles, thereby propagating the conventional effect of interest rates on aggregate demand.

2. Okina et al. (2001) examine this point in detail.

3. If an increase in asset prices is caused by a rational bubble, evaluation on economic fundamentals will remain unchanged, and thus existence of the bubble will not affect assessment on an output gap. On the contrary, since euphoria cannot be generated independent of recognition that economic fundamentals have shifted upward, assessments on economic fundamentals and an output gap are inevitably two sides of one coin. Such difference between a rational bubble and euphoria is crucially important in considering the implications of the asset price hikes on the monetary policy management. See Okina et al. (2001) and Shiratsuka (2001a, 2001b).

4. Kakuei Tanaka, who became Prime Minister in 1972, effected extremely aggressive public investment based on his belief (remodeling the Japanese archipelago) it was necessary to resolve overpopulation and depopulation problems by constructing a nationwide *shinkansen* railroad network, which led to an overheated economy.

5. Such a lagged tendency is commonly observed in Taylor's (2001) own estimate.

6. However, information content of asset prices is not necessarily high in terms of forecasting the rates of inflation and real GDP growth. For detail, see Okina and Shiratsuka (2001). Another standpoint is to insist that there are problems with the Taylor rule itself. McCallum (2001) also presents results obtained by the McCallum rule, which utilizes base money, but comparison between other policy rules and the Taylor rule goes beyond the main topic of this paper.

7. There is no explanation in McCallum (2001) of how he measured potential GDP or the output gap. However, since he assumes the equilibrium real interest rate as constant (3 percent), it is highly likely that he used the difference between a log-linear trend and real GDP as the output gap. Bernanke and Gertler (1999) measured the output gap using monthly data, namely the difference between the Industrial Production Index (output) and its quadratic trend.

8. Backward- and forward-looking Taylor rules were derived following formulations of McCallum (2001) and Bernanke and Gertler (1999). They used weights for the inflation rate and output gap of 1.5 and 0.5, and 2.00 and 0.33, respectively. While McCallum (2001) and Bernanke and Gertler (1999) made their estimation assuming the equilibrium real interest rate as constant, this paper estimates the output gap by using an HP filter, and thus, considering the effects of a declining potential growth rate since entering the 1990s, we regarded the growth rate of the HP-filtered trend for the past one year as the real interest rate to derive the Taylor rule.

9. Another concern regarding the substantial rise in interest rates might be the potential adverse effects on financial system. For example, as a reason for interest rate smoothing, Goodfriend (1991) points out the possibility that financial institutions' portfolios would incur huge capital losses when the interest rate has been unexpectedly and substantially raised. For further discussion on this point, see Okina and Shiratsuka (2001).

10. Baba and Hisada (2002) discuss the characteristics of Japan's financial system in detail.

11. In fact, in autumn 1997 when the economy experienced a slowdown parallel with the government's moves toward fiscal consolidation and coincided with East Asian economic crises, financial instability materialized triggered by collapse of major financial institutions such as Sanyo Securities, Hokkaido-Takushoku Bank, and Yamaichi Securities. Such financial system instability, together with other factors, seems to have exerted extremely strong deflationary pressure on the economy. As a consequence, Japan experienced a serious recession where real GDP (68SNA basis) declined for five consecutive quarters from the fourth quarter of 1997.

12. In this regard, the money market operations conducted by the BOJ since 1997 can be interpreted as being motivated by both the sufficient provision of liquidity and the proper allocation of liquidity among segmented markets. First, during the financial crisis from 1997 to 1998, as Saito and Shiratsuka (2001) point out, the BOJ implemented a so-called dual operation in order to facilitate year-end and fiscal year-end funding, that is, injected longer term funds while absorbing excess funds in the overnight transactions. Second, with respect to the zero interest rate policy conducted from February 1999 to August 2000, Fujiki and Shiratsuka (2002) empirically show that it had a powerful easing effect, mitigating the liquidity constraints of financial institutions, as witnessed by a significant reduction in term spreads.

13. Mori et al. (2001) examine this question based on four criteria, i.e., monetary aggregates, equity yield spread, the Taylor rule, and real short-term interest rates and point out that "the reaction of monetary policy was rather swift to the extent it was taken against the background of a normal business contraction with stock adjustments."

14. In making such a difficult judgment, the usefulness of asset price information is unlikely to be significantly high, compared with other information variables. See Okina and Shiratsuka (2001) for further discussion.

References

Baba, Naohiko, and Takamasa Hisada, 2002, "Japan's Financial System: Its Perspective and the Authorities' Roles in Redesigning and Administering the System," *Monetary and Economic Studies* Vol., 20 (2), Institute for Monetary and Economic Studies, Bank of Japan, pp. 43–93.

Bank of Japan, Research and Statistics Department, 2001, "Japan's Financial Structure: In View of the Flow of Funds Accounts," *Quarterly Bulletin*, Vol. 9 (1), Bank of Japan, pp.105–142.

Bernanke, Ben S., and Mark Gertler, 1995, "Inside the Black Box: The Credit Channel of Monetary Policy Transmission," *Journal of Economic Perspectives*, Vol. 9 (4), pp. 27–48.

_____, 1999, "Monetary Policy and Asset Price Volatility," in *New Challenges for Monetary Policy*, Federal Reserve Bank of Kansas City, pp.77–128.

_____, 2001, "Should Central Banks Respond to Movements in Asset Prices?," *American Economic Review*, Vol. 91 (2), pp. 253–257.

Blanchard, Oliver J., and Mark Watson, 1982, "Bubbles, Rational Expectations and Financial Markets," in *Crises in the Economic and Financial Structure*, P. Wachtel, ed., Lexington: Lexington Books, pp. 295–315.

Fujiki, Hiroshi, and Shigenori Shiratsuka, 2002, "Policy Duration Effect under the Zero Interest Rate Policy in 1999–2000: Evidence from Japan's Money Market Data," *Monetary and Economic Studies,* Vol. 20 (1), Institute for Monetary and Economic Studies, Bank of Japan, pp. 1–31.

Goodfriend, Marvin, 1991, "Interest Rates and the Conduct of Monetary Policy," *Carnegie-Rochester Conference Series on Public Policy*, Vol. 34, pp. 7–30.

McCallum, Bennett T., 2001, "Japanese Monetary Policy," mimeo.

Meyer, Laurence, 2000, "Structural Change and Monetary Policy," available on the Internet at http://www.bog.frb.fed.us/boarddocs/speeches/2000/20000303.htm.

Mori, Naruki, Shigenori Shiratsuka, and Hiroo Taguchi, 2001, "Policy Responses to the Post-Bubble Adjustments in Japan: A Tentative Review," *Monetary and Economic Studies*, Vol. 19 (S-1), Institute for Monetary and Economic Studies, Bank of Japan, pp. 53–102.

Okina, Kunio, and Shigenori Shiratsuka, 2001, "Asset Price Bubbles, Price Stability, and Monetary Policy: Japan's Experience," Institute for Monetary and Economic Studies, discussion paper series 2001-E-16, Bank of Japan.

Okina, Kunio, Masaaki Shirakawa, and Shigenori Shiratsuka, 2001, "Asset Price Bubble and Monetary Policy: Experience of Japan's Economy in the Late 1980s and its Lessons," *Monetary and Economic Studies*, Vol. 19 (S-1), Institute for Monetary and Economic Studies, Bank of Japan, pp. 395–450.

Saito, Makoto, and Shigenori Shiratsuka, 2001, "Financial Crises as the Failure of Arbitrage: Implications for Monetary Policy," *Monetary and Economic Studies*, Institute for Monetary and Economic Studies, Bank of Japan, Vol. 19 (S-1), pp. 239–270.

Shiratsuka, Shigenori, 2001a, "Is There a Desirable Rate of Inflation? A Theoretical and Empirical Survey," Monetary and Economic Studies, Institute for Monetary and Economic Studies, Bank of Japan, Vol. 19 (2), pp. 49–83.

_____, 2001b, "Asset Prices, Financial Stability and Monetary Policy: Based on Japan's Experience of the Asset Price Bubble," in *Marrying the Macro- and Microprudential Dimensions of Financial Stability*, Bank for International Settlements, working paper, No. 1, pp. 261–284.

Taylor, John B., 1993, "Discretion versus Policy Rules in Practice," *Carnegie-Rochester Conference Series on Public Policy*, Vol. 39, pp. 195–214.

Taylor, John B., 2001, "Low Inflation, Deflation, and Policies for Future Price Stability," *Monetary and Economic Studies*, Institute for Monetary and Economic Studies, Bank of Japan, Vol. 19 (S-1), pp. 35–51.

Yamaguchi, Yutaka, 1999, "Asset Price and Monetary Policy: Japan's Experience," in *New Challenges for Monetary Policy*, Federal Reserve Bank of Kansas City, pp. 171–176.

Chapter 8
Lending Booms, Real Estate Bubbles, and the Asian Crisis

Charles Collyns*
International Monetary Fund

and

Abdelhak Senhadji
International Monetary Fund

The liberalization of financial systems and the globalization of capital markets have improved the provision of financial services and the allocation of resources; they also have increased the scope for pronounced financial cycles. These cycles have often involved dramatic fluctuations in asset prices, amplifying the business cycle and occasionally culminating in banking and exchange market crises. Although both industrial and emerging market economies have been affected, emerging markets have incurred the heaviest costs.

Typically, these financial cycles are generated by a wave of optimism underpinned by favorable developments in the real side of the economy. This optimism contributes to the underestimation of risk, overextension of credit, excessive asset price inflation, overinvestment in physical capital, and buoyant consumer expenditures. When expectations realign with fundamentals, the imbalances are corrected abruptly, as excessive optimism gives way to excessive pessimism, disrupting both the financial system and the real economy.

Recent research has shown how the procyclical character of bank credit can amplify the magnitude of the business cycle (see Bernanke, 1983, on the Great Depression; Bernanke and Gertler, 1995; Kiyotaki and Moore, 1997). The property market plays a central role in such cycles because increases in real estate prices tend to boost banks' willingness and capacity to lend, while a number of factors allow persistent deviations from efficient pricing. In a globally integrated financial world, large capital inflows can exacerbate these credit cycles. Where a surge in capital flows combines with lax regulation of the financial sector, the credit cycle can particularly end in severe financial crisis.

The Asian crisis of the late 1990s followed this pattern. Key features of the buildup included heady belief in an "East Asian miracle" capable of delivering rapid economic growth over an extended period; capital account and financial market liberalization that contributed to heavy capital inflows intermediated in considerable part through the banking system; and high rates of investment and rapid increases in asset prices, especially in the property sector as underregulated banking systems expanded domestic credit at a tremendous pace. Subsequently, economic growth suffered setbacks, asset markets reversed, and both financial and corporate balance sheets deteriorated. Eventually, investor sentiment turned negative, exacerbating this process and generating a series of banking and exchange crises across the region.

Within this familiar story, there were considerable differences in experiences across countries. Thailand, and to a lesser extent Malaysia, experienced an extreme property price cycle, while Korea experienced a much more subdued one (table 1). Singapore and Hong Kong experienced dramatic property price booms and slumps, yet did not suffer long-lasting damage. Property price cycles were, in practice, neither *necessary* nor *sufficient* to produce an exchange and banking crisis.

This paper examines the link between lending booms, property price cycles, and financial crisis across the range of East Asian countries. Two closely related papers look at these issues. Herring and Wachter (1999) explain real estate cycles and banking crises by focusing on the interaction of credit cycles and banking behavior. Hilbers, Lei, and Zacho (2001) examine the relationship between developments in real estate markets and the financial sector to determine under what circumstances, and to what extent, booms and busts in the real estate sector affect the health and stability of the financial system.

Country	Capital inflow surge	Real credit growth	Property price bubble	Stock market bubble	Banking crisis	Exchange crisis
Indonesia	√√	√	√	√√	√√	√√
Korea	√	√	√	√√	√√	√√
Malaysia	√	√√	√√	√√	√	√√
Philippines	√√	√	√	√	√	√
Thailand	√√	√√	√√	√√	√√	√√
Hong Kong SAR (China)	√√	X	√	√	X	√
Singapore	√	√	√	√	X	X
Taiwan (China)	X	√	√√	√	√	X

Note: √ indicates a moderate capital inflow or a bubble/crisis, √√ indicates important capital flows or a severe bubble/crisis, and X indicates minimal bubble/crisis. The specific calibration is explained in Collyns and Senhadji (2002).

Table 1: Incidence of Asset Price Bubbles and Banking and Exchange Rate Crises in East Asia

This paper builds on the work of the two other papers to examine the extent to which fast-growing bank lending contributed to property price inflation in Asia and ultimately to the crisis that followed a severe correction in asset prices. The paper differs from the other two by focusing on the Asian experience and by offering different empirical evidence. Section 1 reviews the theoretical literature on the determinants of real estate cycles. Section 2 examines the extent of asset price bubbles, the role of the banking sector in the formation of bubbles, and the link between bubbles and financial crisis. Section 3 examines empirically the determinants of real estate prices and presents the results of regressions testing the importance of the credit channel in asset price inflation in Asian economies. Section 4 draws some policy lessons.

1. Determinants of Real Estate Cycles

Imperfect information, supply rigidities, and imperfect financial markets make the market vulnerable to prolonged periods in which actual prices may deviate from their fundamental value (see Herring and Wachter, 1999). Since the price of a real estate asset depends on the future value of fundamentals, investors may either underestimate or overestimate the fundamental price in an environment with imperfect information. In particular, investors becoming overoptimistic about expected growth could drive the price above its replacement cost. In efficient financial markets, these deviations from the fundamental price are countered by sophisticated investors selling real estate short until the price reverts back to its fundamental value. However, there is no futures or options market for land. Optimistic investors remain in the market as long as prices are rising and financing is available. Long construction lags prevent a quick supply response, so prices keep rising for a protracted period and a price bubble develops. Finally, as prices move further and further away from their fundamental value, more and more investors move to the sell side, dampening price inflation. As this process gathers momentum, prices drop abruptly.

Moral hazard and adverse selection in the banking system exacerbate such price fluctuations in the real estate sector. Moral hazard arises from explicit or implicit deposit guarantees and weak financial regulation, which encourage banks to take on riskier loans without adjusting their cost of funds (see Bernanke and Gertler, 1995; Mishkin, 1996; Krugman, 1998; Allen and Gale, 2000). Moral hazard induces excessive risk-taking by banks, overinvestment, and excessive asset prices. The problem is particularly acute for large banks, which often are seen as "too big to fail." Adverse selection is an asymmetric information problem arising when the riskiest investors are the ones most actively seeking loans. Thus, investors who are the most likely to produce an *adverse* outcome are most likely to be *selected*. In periods of real estate price booms, adverse selection can exacerbate price bubbles.

Increases in the price of real estate may increase both the value of bank capital, to the extent that banks own real estate, and increase the value of real estate collateral, leading to a downward revision of the perceived risk of real estate lending (see Herring and Wachter, 1999; Bank for International Settlements, 2001, Chapter 7). Consequently, an increase in real estate prices may increase the supply of credit to the real estate industry, which further increases the price of real estate. These feedback effects go into reverse when real estate prices start to decline. A decline in the price of real estate decreases bank capital directly by reducing the value of banks' own real estate assets and indirectly by reducing the value of loans collateralized by real estate (the precise effect depends on country-specific accounting standards). Furthermore, a decline in real estate prices is likely to reduce the costs of default and increase the perceived risk of real estate lending. Real estate lending declines, putting even more downward pressure on real estate prices, which in turn feeds back to bank lending. As the banking sector weakens, banking supervision and regulation may increase capital requirements and impose stricter rules for classifying and provisioning against real estate loans, squeezing lending to real estate investors even further.

2. Property Prices, Credit Cycles, and the Asian Crisis

This section presents evidence of the extent of asset price cycles in East Asia in the 1990s, focusing on developments in the property market. It considers the role of the financial system in the buildup of asset prices during the first six years of the decade and examines how falling property prices contributed to the banking and exchange crises in the final years of the decade. The discussion covers the five crisis countries (Indonesia, Korea, Malaysia, the Philippines, and Thailand) as well as Hong Kong, Singapore, and Taiwan, which also experienced major price cycles but weathered the storm with less severe dislocation.

2.1 Asset Price Cycles in East Asia

Given the scarcity of reliable data on property, we begin by sketching developments in equity markets, which provide a clearer picture of investor expectations and have more accessible data (data on property prices and stock market indexes are from the CEIC database; details are given in Collyns and Senhadji, 2002). East Asian stock markets trended upward through the first part of the decade, peaking around 1997 at an average 165 percent higher than their value at the start of the decade (figure 1). Thailand's stock peaked much earlier than the others—on January 4, 1994—after a particularly dramatic run-up in prices. This buildup in stock prices was reflected in profit to earnings (P/E) ratios well above historical norms.

Regional stock prices generally fell sharply from mid 1997 through the end of 1998, the crisis period. Korea, Malaysia, and Thailand suffered declines of more than 70 percent, while the other five countries suffered declines of more than 50 percent from the peak (table 2). Equity markets recovered in 1999 as the economies turned around, but then subsided again as the global economy (especially the electronics cycle) turned down. Equity prices in most East Asian countries in mid 2001 were not far from their level 10 years earlier.

Evidence on property prices is much less readily available. Some countries collect property price indexes, but coverage is not uniform, the length of series is often limited, and the series can be highly volatile. Moreover, the data are not defined uniformly across countries—for example, the property price index covers official land

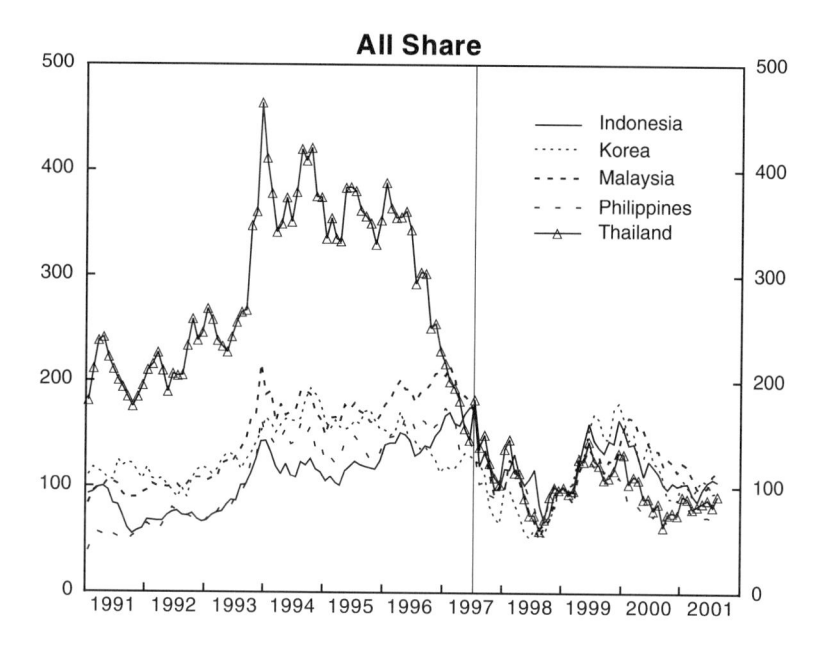

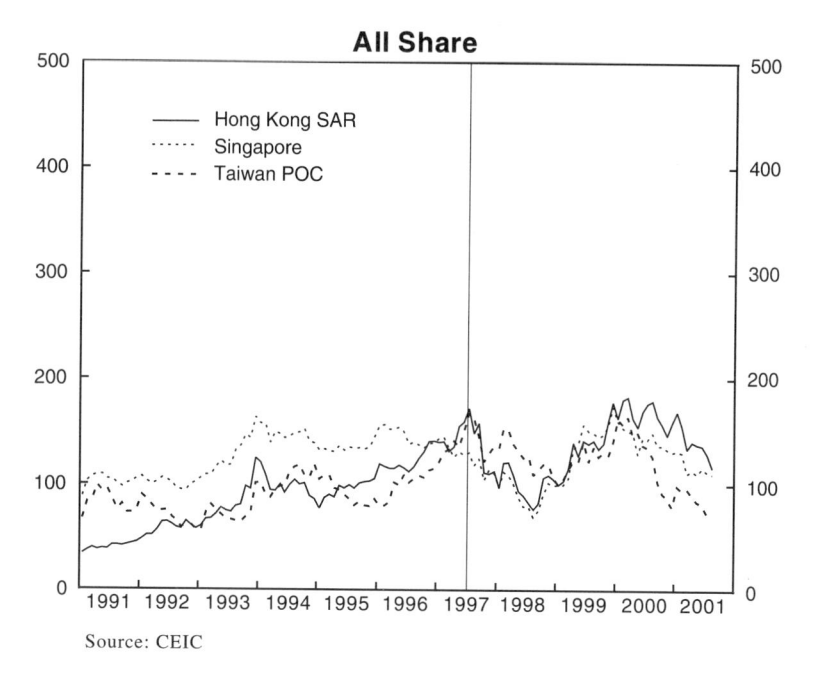

Lending Booms, Real Estate Bubbles, and the Asian Crisis

Source: CEIC

Figure 1: Selected Asian Countries: Stock Market Indices—Panel One (January 1999 = 100)

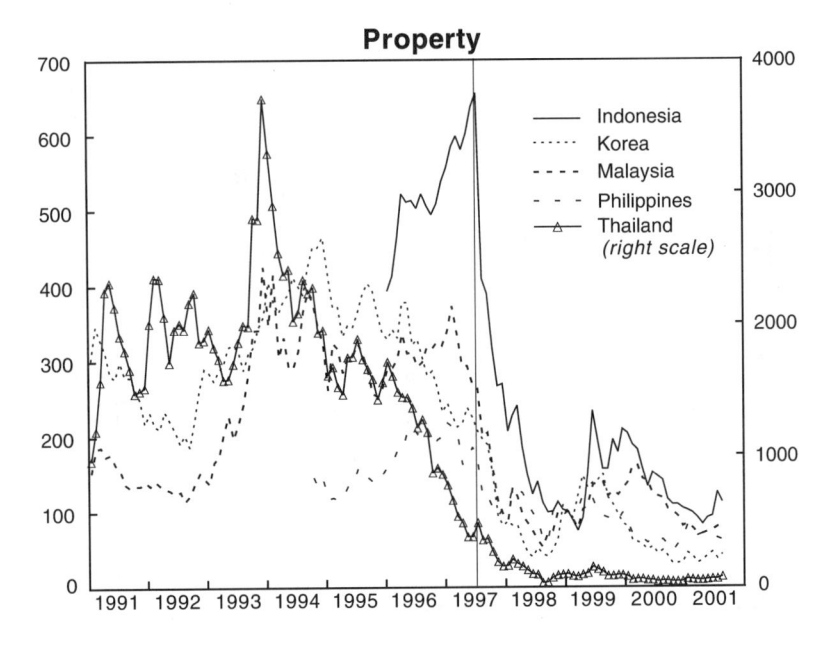

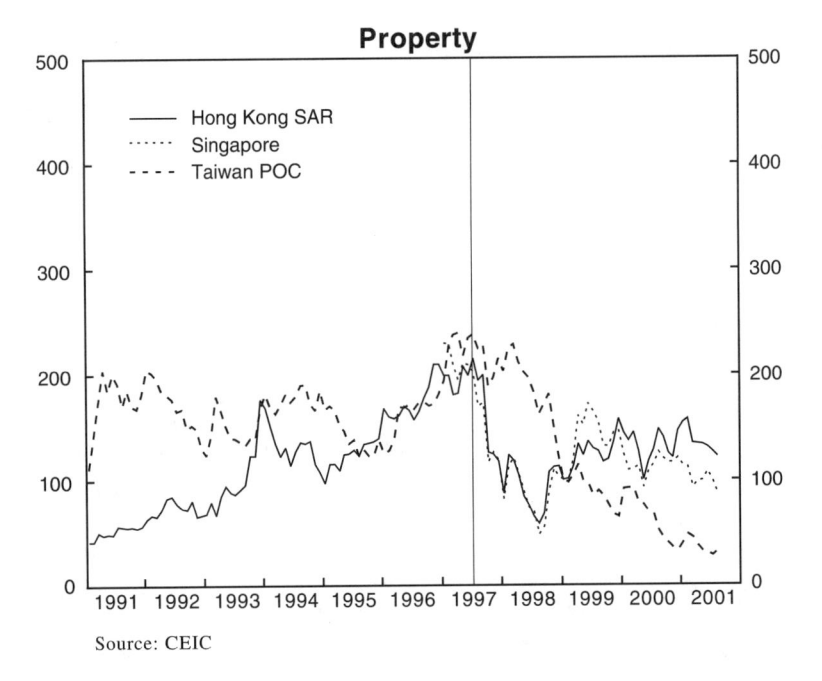

Figure 1 *(continued)*: Selected Asian Countries: Stock Market Indices—Panel Two (January 1999 = 100)

Source: CEIC

Ratio of property to all share

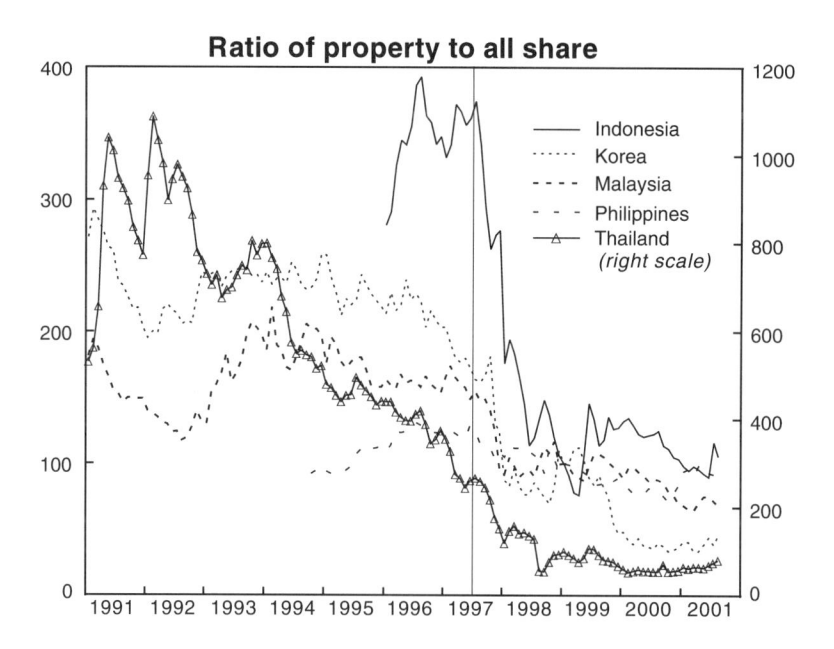

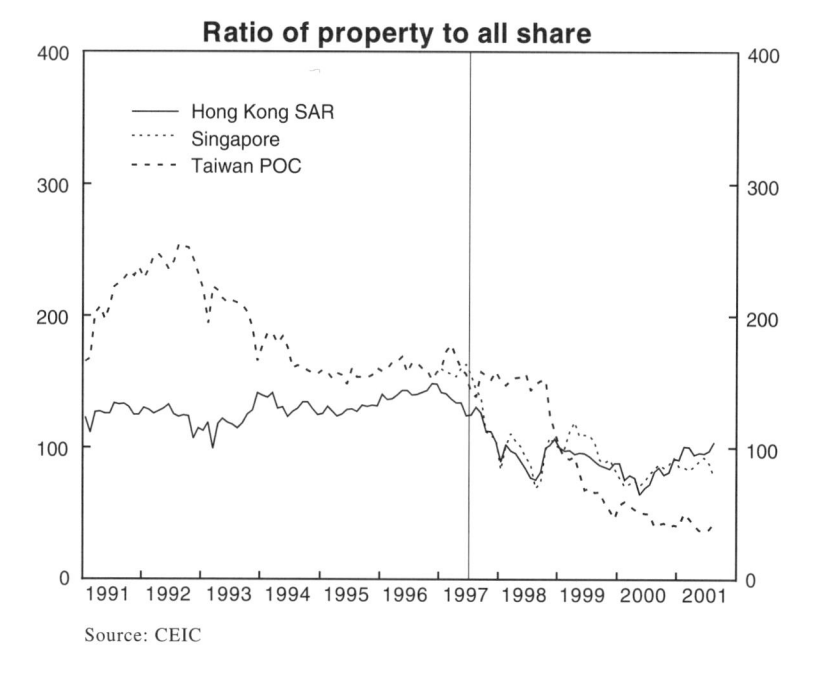

Source: CEIC

Figure 1 *(continued)*: **Selected Asian Countries: Stock Market Indices—Panel Three (January 1999 = 100)**

Table 2: Property Stock Index in Equity Markets in East Asia in the 1990s

Country	Peak Date of peak	Peak P/E ratio at peak	Peak Increase from January 1991 to peak[a]	Trough Date of trough	Trough P/E ratio at trough	Trough Decline from peak to trough[b]
Indonesia	July 1997	20.0	66.5 (January 1996)	March 1999	–6.0	–88.7
Korea	October 1994	n.a.	49.7	June 1998	n.a.	–91.2
Malaysia	February 1997	28.6	145.1	August 1998	16.5	–86.0
Philippines	January 1997	38.7	49.6 (October 1994)	September 1998	7.2	–72.5
Thailand	January 1994	54.9	285.3	August 1998	5.8	–99.1
Hong Kong SAR	July 1997	16.2	413.7	August 1998	4.0	–73.0
Singapore	January 1997	n.a.	n.a. (January 1997)	August 1998	5.4	–79.0
Taiwan POC	April 1997	59.5	115.7	July 2001	n.a.	–88.5

Note: a = percentage change in the stock price index between January 1991 (or if data cover a shorter span, from the first observation available, given in parentheses) and the last peak before the crisis; b = first trough after the crisis; and n.a.= not available.
Source: CEIC and authors' calculations

prices for Korea, residential property prices for Indonesia, and housing prices for Thailand and Malaysia. Given these deficiencies, it is useful to supplement these data with a) the Consumer Price Index (CPI) for housing, which reflects rents, and b) information from stock market indexes for the property subsector (second panel of figure 1). Such data must be interpreted with care and can only be a rough proxy for real estate prices.

Movements in property prices in East Asian countries in the 1990s were more diverse than movements in stock prices. Hong Kong and Singapore, which have the most complete and reliable data on property prices, experienced a buildup in both commercial and residential markets through 1996 for Singapore and 1997 for Hong Kong, followed by a sharp decline through 1999 (figure 2). This pattern, which is also evident in the CPI for housing, is consistent with real estate price bubbles, a hypothesis supported by empirical work in Kalra, Mihaljek, and Duenwald (2000).

Malaysia and Thailand also experienced large commercial real estate cycles. Stock price data suggest that, like equities, the property market peaked in Thailand in late 1993, although property price series are volatile and suggest a further price surge in 1997. In Malaysia, property prices rose steadily through 1997, before subsiding. The CPI for housing also shows significant rent inflation in Malaysia prior to the crisis. However, the CPI for housing in Thailand did not exhibit significant inflation during the early 1990s, highlighting the limitations of the CPI in capturing property price inflation.

For Korea, Indonesia, and the Philippines, property price data either are not available or do not show strong cyclical behavior. Nevertheless, share price data for the property sector suggest pronounced boom-bust swings in these countries, most notably in Indonesia. In Korea, a pronounced property price bubble was associated with the construction boom leading up to the Seoul Olympic Games in 1988, but a further price run-up occurred in the early 1990s. Furthermore, the CPI for housing shows an important increase in rents up to the crisis. Only in the Philippines were stock prices in the property sector considerably less volatile than stock prices of all shares (third panel of figure 1).

2.2 Asset Price Booms and Credit Cycles

Optimistic expectations of growth, heavy capital inflows, inadequate corporate governance, and dependence on intermediation by underregulated banks and finance companies led almost inevitably to rapid growth in credit, particularly for the property sector.

First, a period of rapid economic growth without the apparent emergence of fundamental macroeconomic imbalances generated optimistic expectations that such annual growth rates could be sustained for an extended period. Four of the five crisis countries (Indonesia, Korea, Malaysia, and Thailand) achieved annual growth rates greater than 7 percent during 1991–96. Current account deficits rose but were easily financed by surging private capital inflows. Significant real exchange rate appreciation was avoided through tight fiscal and monetary policies aimed at sterilizing excess liquidity. Only the Philippines experienced a moderate fiscal deficit (around 1.5 percent of gross domestic product (GDP) on average over 1991–96).

Property prices (Q1 1999=100)

- - - - Korea - Land price - whole nation
------- Malaysia - whole nation
———— Thailand - grade A office

Property prices - commercial (Q1 1999=100)

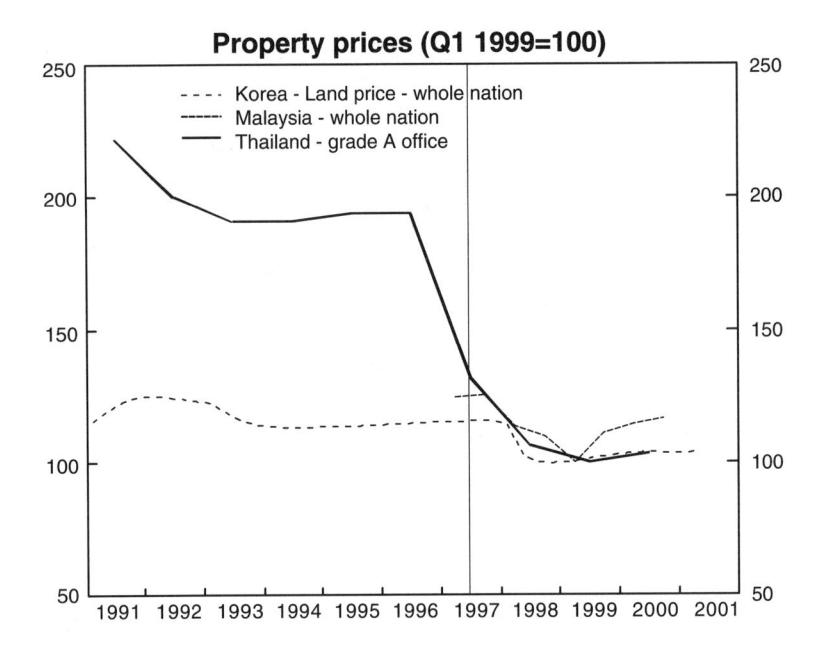

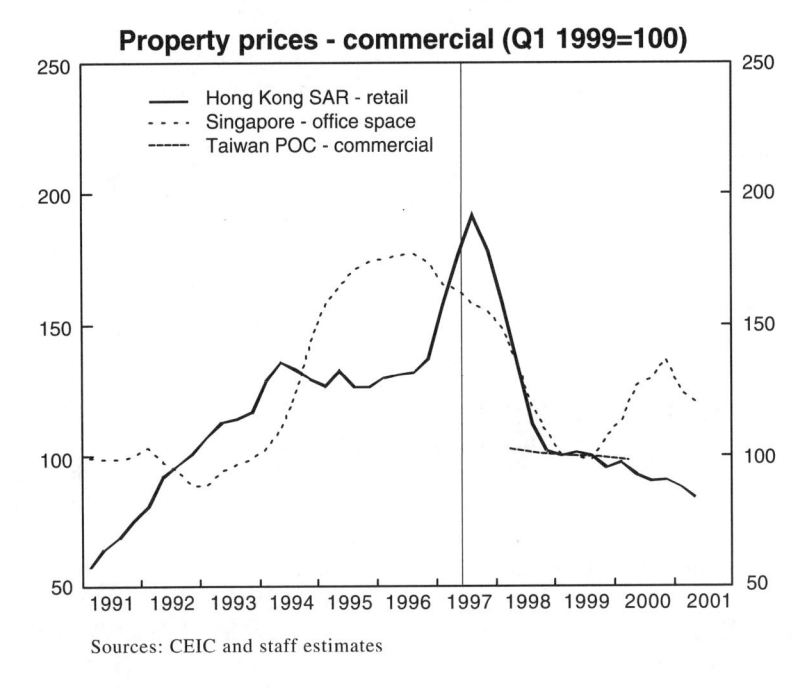

———— Hong Kong SAR - retail
- - - - Singapore - office space
------- Taiwan POC - commercial

Sources: CEIC and staff estimates

Figure 2: Selected Asian Countries: Property Price Indices—Panel One

Property prices - residential (Q1 1999=100)

— Indonesia - residential
······ Thailand - high residential condominium

Property prices - residential (Q1 1999=100)

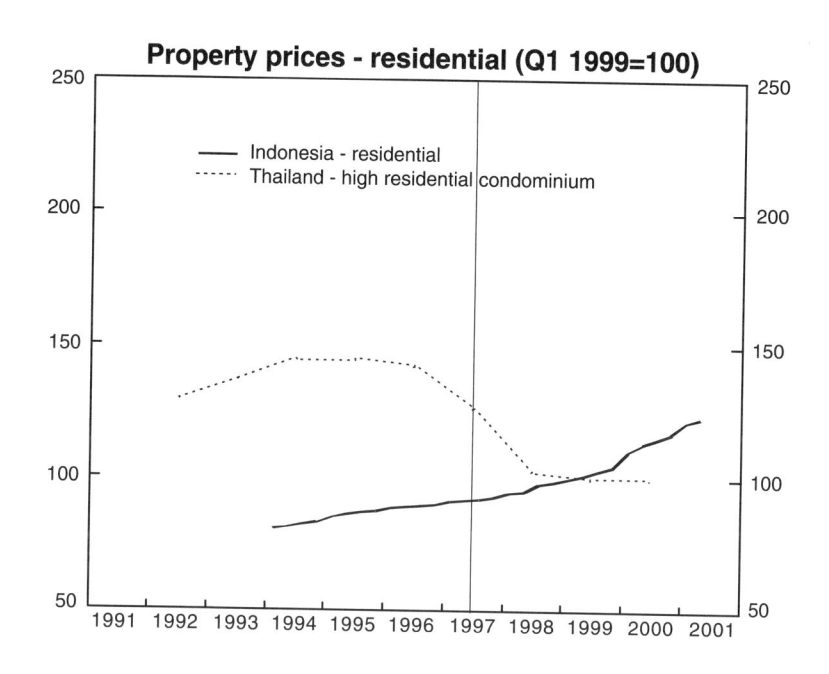

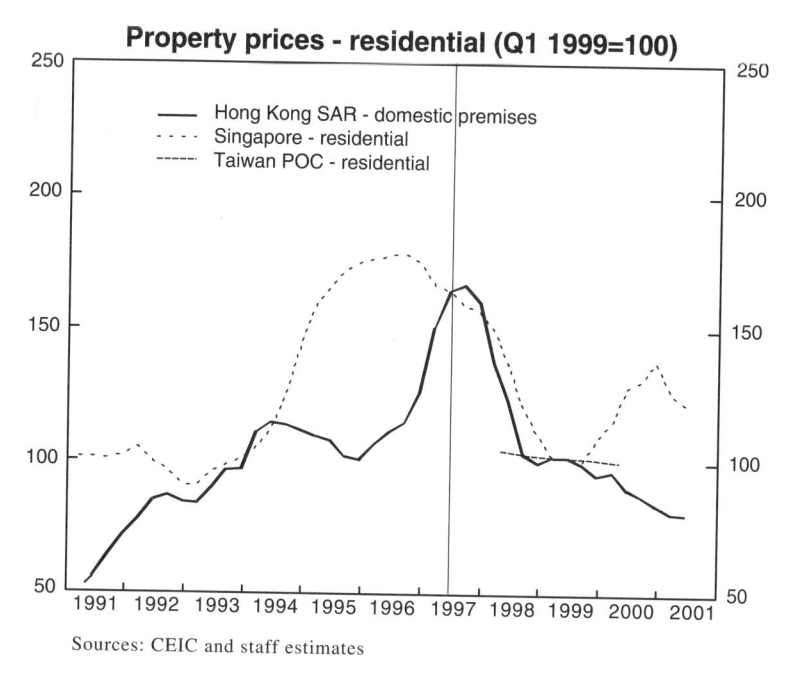

— Hong Kong SAR - domestic premises
- - - Singapore - residential
----- Taiwan POC - residential

Sources: CEIC and staff estimates

Figure 2 (*continued*): **Selected Asian Countries: Property Price Indices— Panel Two**

Second, a structure of public policies and corporate governance encouraged the rapid accumulation of capital. In most of the East Asian economies, public policies emphasized state support—including subsidies and directed credit—to favored firms or industries, particularly in export sectors. De facto fixed exchange rate pegs against the U.S. dollar, capital account liberalization, and financial market deregulation allowed firms easy access to low-cost external funding. However, mechanisms were not in place to ensure adequate rates of return. Cross-holding share structures allowed wealthy families owning a small percentage of shares to exert corporation control. Although, theoretically, borrowing from abroad can be optimal for an undercapitalized economy, the end result was low profitability of investment projects over much of East Asia. For instance, the 20 to 30 largest conglomerates in Korea achieved a rate of return on invested capital well below the cost of capital.

Third, the dominant role of the banking system exacerbated the scope for moral hazard. In most East Asian countries, equity and bond markets were relatively underdeveloped, and capital inflows were largely intermediated by domestic banks channeling funds to local firms (figure 3). In some cases—for example, the Bangkok International Banking Facilities (BIBF) in Thailand—offshore banking markets were set up to facilitate such flows. Typically, techniques for credit assessment by banks were weakly developed, and banks tended to rely heavily on property collateral (and, to some extent, equity collateral) in making loan decisions.

Fourth, regulatory structures lagged behind the rapid growth of bank intermediation. Most countries adopted Basel Committee recommendations on capital adequacy requirements, but without stringent credit assessment such requirements provided little discipline, and, where performance fell short, corrective measures were typically inadequate. Out of 240 Indonesian banks in April 1996, 15 did not meet the required 8 percent capital adequacy ratio, and 41 did not comply with the legal lending limit; 12 of the 77 licensed foreign exchange banks did not meet the rules on overnight positions (see Corsetti, Pesenti, and Roubini, 1998). Moreover, while most countries avoided explicit deposit guarantee schemes, in practice depositors were not required to take losses when banks ran into difficulties, implying at least implicit deposit insurance and eroding barriers to moral hazard (see Herring and Wachter, 1999). In some countries (for example, Thailand), the rapid growth of nonbank financial intermediaries, partly funded by the banks themselves, allowed regulations on bank lending to be circumvented. The government usually intervened with failing banks, which were forced to restructure or were merged with other banks; typically, they were not closed (see Dekle and Kletzer, 2001).

As shown in table 3, by 1997 property exposure was particularly high—more than 30 percent of total bank loans—in Hong Kong, Malaysia, Singapore, and Thailand. In Singapore, an important factor in the high levels of property exposure was the government's decision to relax the rules allowing foreigners to purchase subsidized government housing from the resale market. Elsewhere, the concentration was less striking, notably Korea, where capital inflows tended to be channeled directly to the large industrial conglomerates (chaebols), and the Philippines, where growth was less dramatic. Rapid growth of bank lending went hand-in-hand with escalating real estate prices.

Lending Booms, Real Estate Bubbles, and the Asian Crisis   113

Capital flows (in percent of GDP)

- Indonesia
- Korea
- Malaysia
- Philippines
- Thailand

Capital flows (in percent of GDP)

- Hong Kong SAR
- Singapore
- Taiwan POC

Sources: IFS, APDCORE, World Economic Outlook, and staff estimates

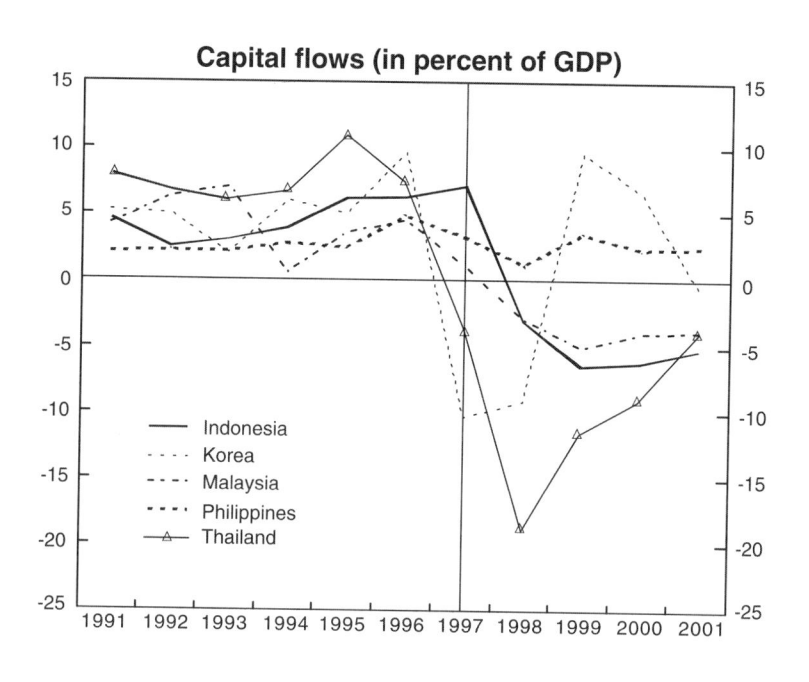

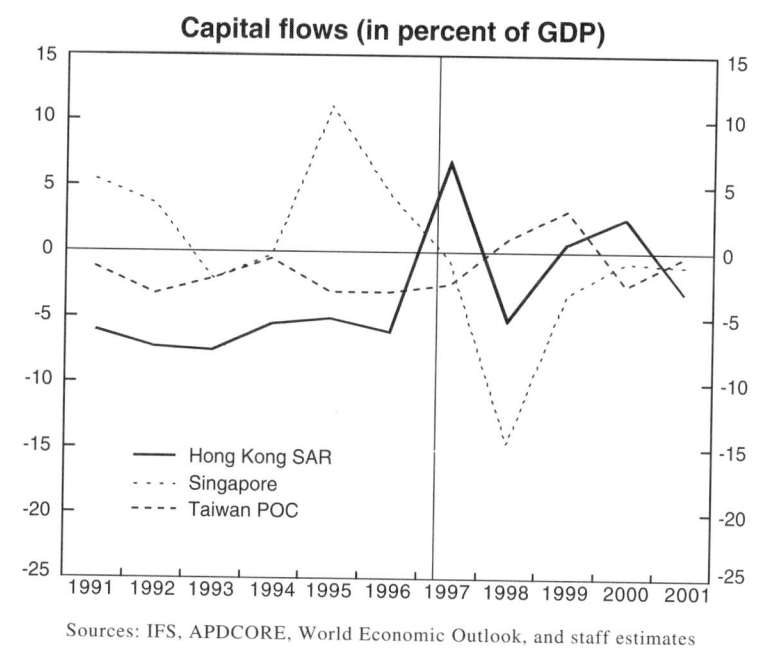

Figure 3: Selected Asian Countries: Capital Flows and Credit Growth—Panel One

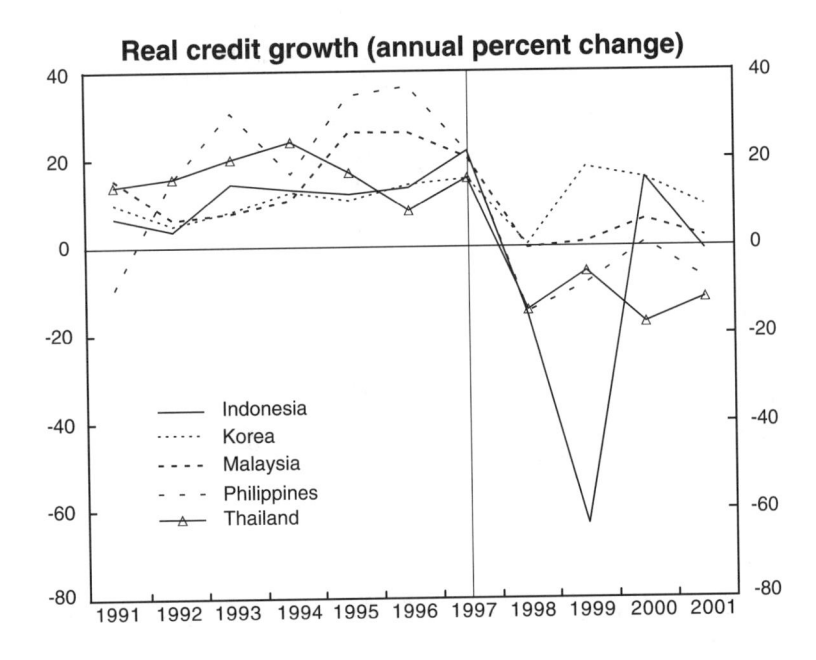

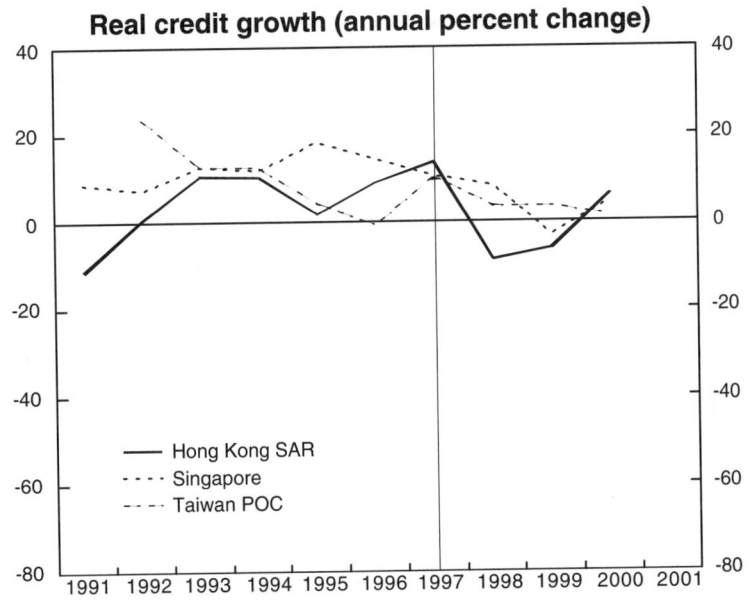

Sources: IFS, APDCORE, World Economic Outlook, and staff estimates

Figure 3 (*continued*): **Selected Asian Countries: Capital Flows and Credit Growth—Panel Two**

Country	Property exposure, 1997	Collateral valuation, 1997	Nonperforming loans, 1997	Nonperforming loans, 1998	Capital-asset ratio, 1998
Korea	15–25	80–100	16.0	22.5	6–10
Indonesia	25–30	80–100	11.0	20.0	8–10
Malaysia	30–40	80–100	7.5	15.0	8–14
Philippines	15–20	70–80	5.5	7.0	15–18
Thailand	30–40	80–100	15.0	25.0	6–10
Hong Kong SAR	40–55	50–70	1.5	3.0	15–20
Singapore	30–40	70–80	2.0	3.5	18–22

Source: Corsetti, Pesenti, and Roubini (1998)

Table 3: Exposure of Banking Systems to the Real Estate Sector in Asian Countries (Percentage of Assets at the End of 1997)

2.3 Property Price Declines and Financial Distress

The dramatic turnaround in the 1990s reflected a deterioration of performance in the real sector of these economies. Starting in 1996, the growth of export volume began to slow, particularly in Indonesia, Korea, Malaysia, and, especially, Thailand, as these countries faced greater competition from elsewhere (for example, China, Vietnam, and México). Terms of trade losses occurred in response to a decline in world semiconductor prices and a hike in oil prices.

With some slowing of growth and incipient investor concerns about the sustainability of the growth record, asset prices came under pressure in both equity and property markets. Nonperforming loans began to rise, especially in Thailand where the property market downturn had started earlier in response to both increased supply following a construction boom and tighter monetary policy initiated in 1994. Markets began to be concerned with the health of bank balance sheets, as demonstrated by falling market value of the banking sector in Korea, Malaysia, and Thailand (figure 4).

By early 1997, reserves came under pressure in the context of increasingly negative investor sentiment and concern about overvaluation of regional currencies (figure 5). These pressures culminated in a successful speculative attack on the Thai baht on June 2, 1997. Speculative attacks then spread to other economies perceived as suffering from similar fragilities. Some countries adopted an interest rate defense, but the policy lacked credibility given perceptions that high interest rates would be difficult to sustain given highly leveraged balance sheets (Kaminsky and Reinhart, 1999).

Corporate and financial balance sheets—already weak—were undermined further by the impact of sharp declines in exchange rates on the local currency value of debt, a sharp regional recession, as well as losses on their exposure to the property sector. Banks also suffered heavy losses on loans to an overleveraged corporate sector, against which real estate collateral provided security of declining value. The results were widespread corporate bankruptcies, collapse of confidence in domestic banking systems, and further declines in asset prices.

Stock market index - finance/bank (January 1999=100)

Indonesia
Korea
Malaysia
Philippines
Thailand

Stock market index - finance/bank (January 1999=100)

Hong Kong SAR
Singapore
Taiwan POC

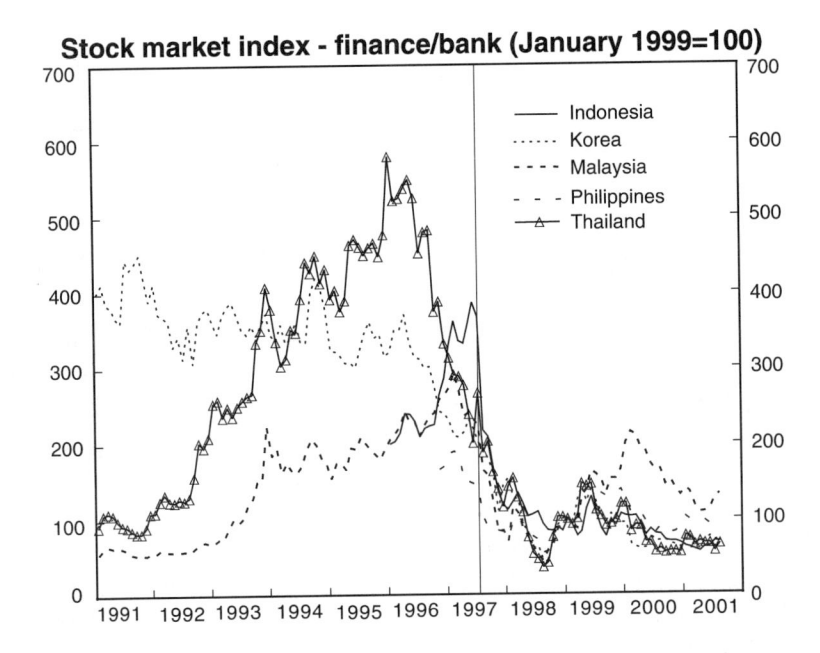

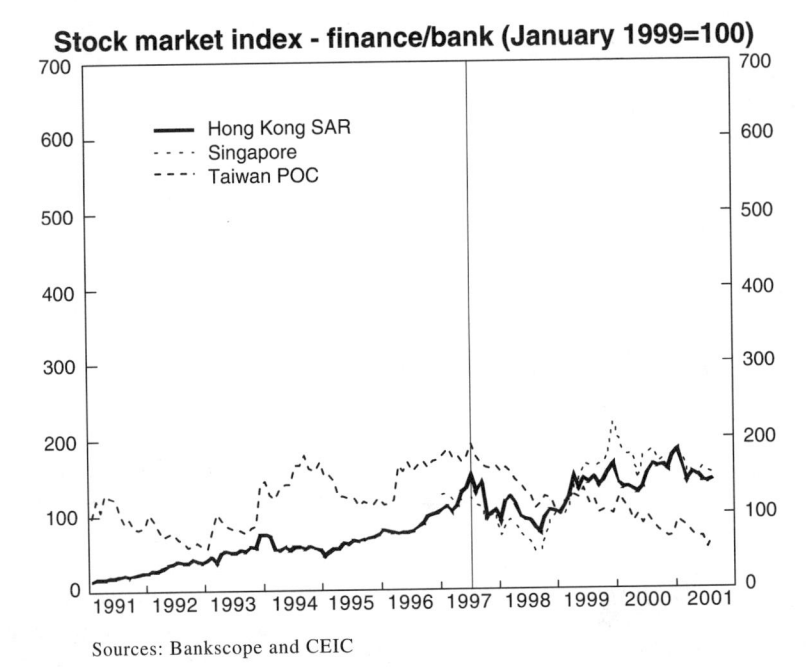

Sources: Bankscope and CEIC

Figure 4: Selected Asian Countries: Stock Market Indices and Nonperforming Loans—Panel One

Nonperforming loans (in percent of gross loans)

— Indonesia
······ Malaysia
- - - - Philippines
- - - Thailand

Nonperforming loans (in percent of gross loans)

— Hong Kong SAR
- - - Singapore
- - - Taiwan POC

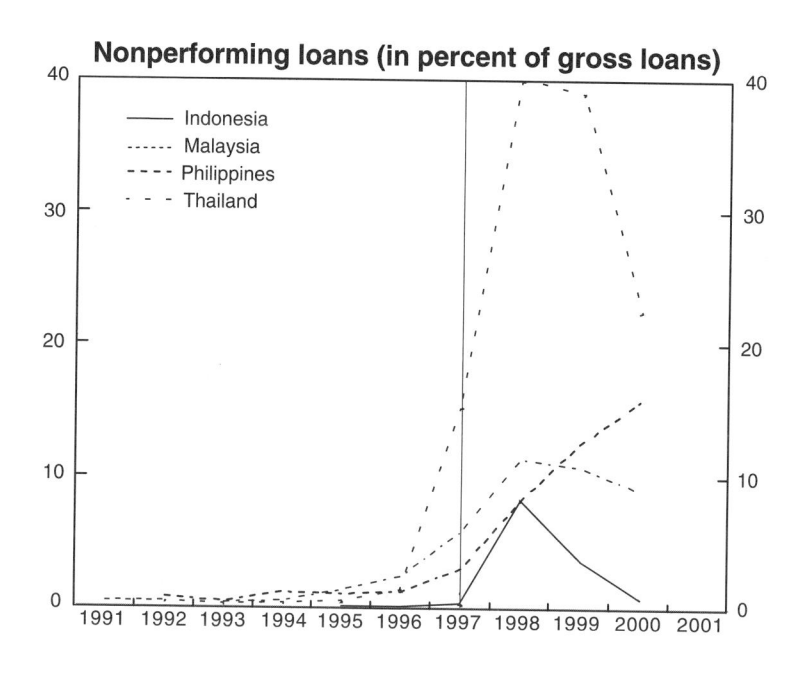

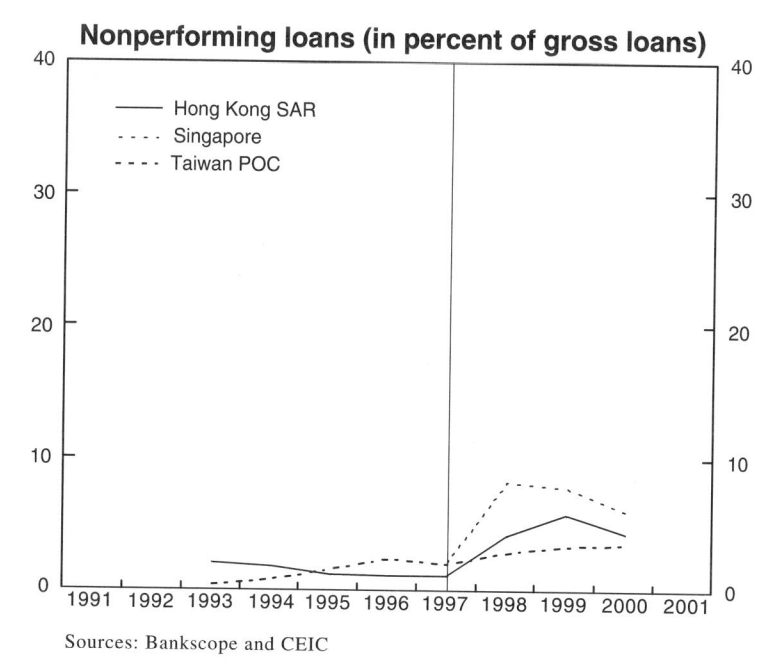

Sources: Bankscope and CEIC

Figure 4 (*continued*): Selected Asian Countries: Stock Market Indices and Nonperforming Loans—Panel Two

Sources: APDCORE, CEIC, WEFA INTLINE

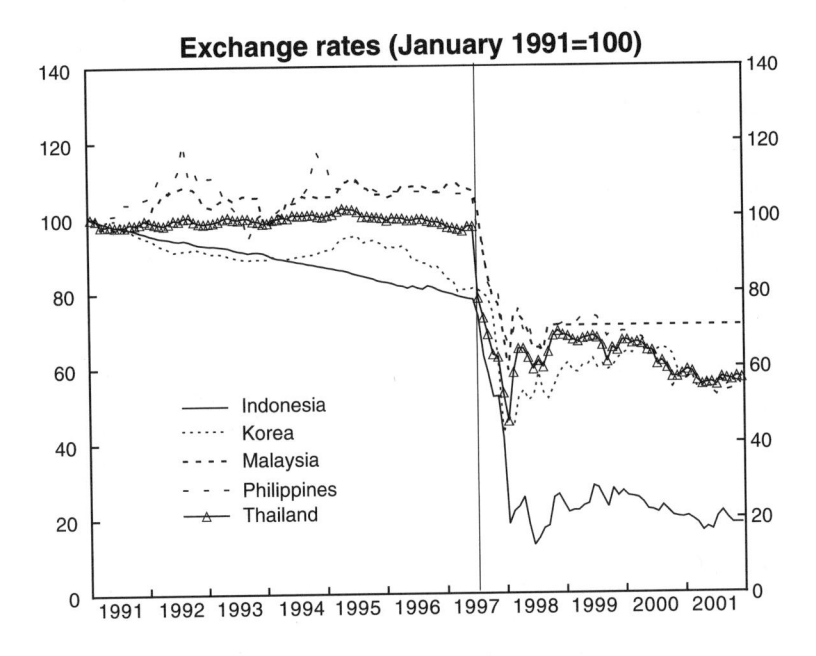

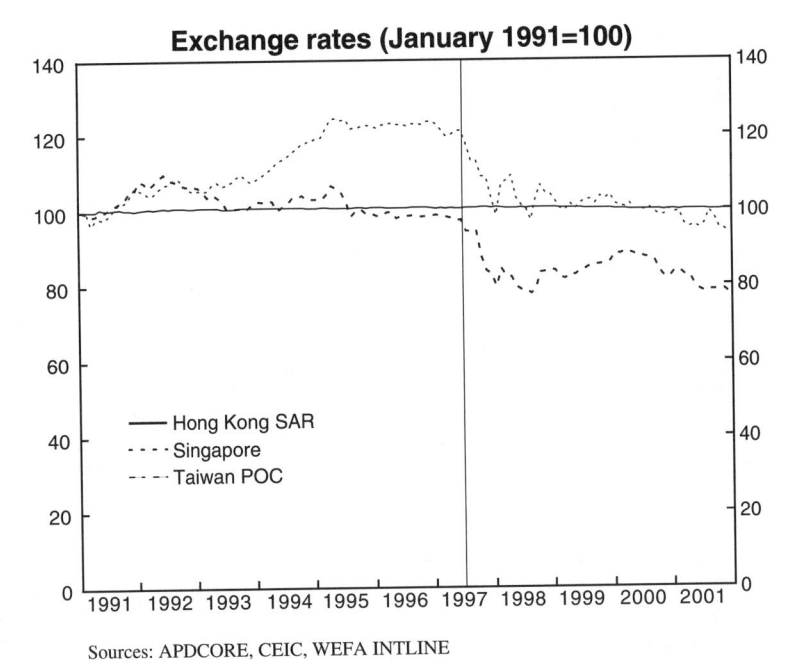

Figure 5: Selected Asian Countries: External Indicators—Panel One

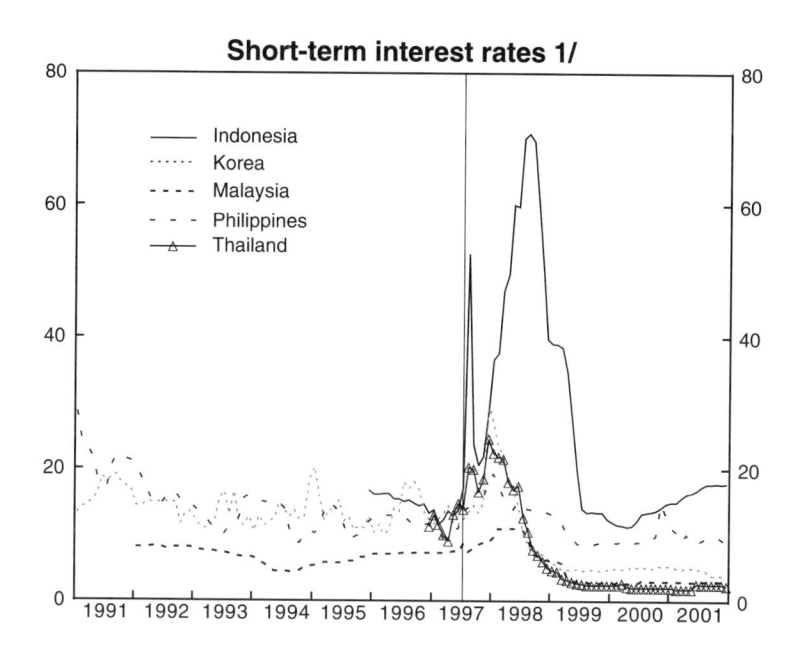

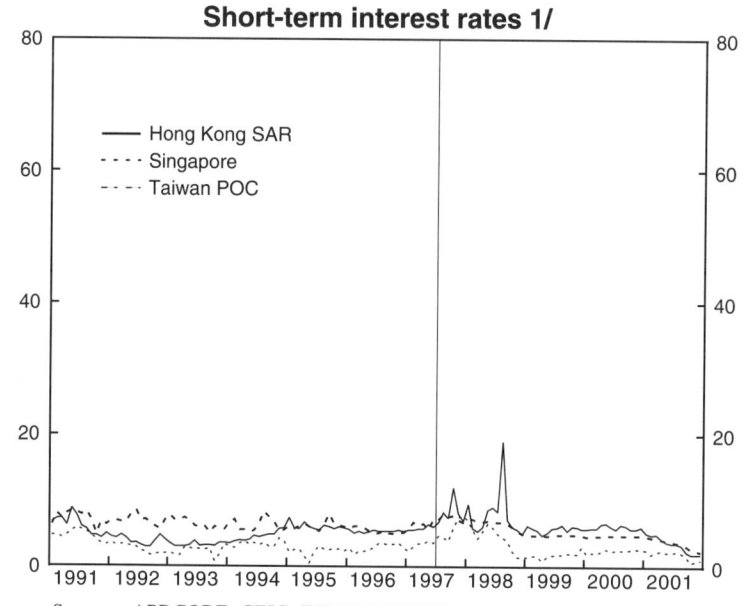

Short-term interest rates 1/

- Indonesia
- Korea
- Malaysia
- Philippines
- Thailand

Short-term interest rates 1/

- Hong Kong SAR
- Singapore
- Taiwan POC

Sources: APDCORE, CEIC, WEFA INTLINE
1/ Hong Kong SAR, 1-month HIBOR; Indonesia, 1-month JBOR; Korea, overnight call market rate; Malaysia, 1-month KLIBOR; Philippines, 91-day Treasury bill rate; Singapore, 1-month SIBOR; Taiwan POC, overnight interbank; Thailand-1month repo

Figure 5 (*continued*): Selected Asian Countries: External Indicators—Panel Two

Beyond this broad regional story, there were significant cross-country differences in how the crisis period played out. These differences reflected differences in the extent of asset price overvaluation and the underlying strength of domestic banking systems.

Thailand was heavily hit because the property price bubble was large and the financial system was weak. Losses were particularly heavy in the largely unregulated finance company sector, which had sharply accelerated lending to the real estate and property sectors, financed mainly by domestic banks from funds channeled through the BIBF. While the peak in property prices occurred in December 1993, strong investment in the real estate sector continued until the crisis, reflecting time-to-build lags or a perception by investors that declining prices would be short-lived.

Malaysia also experienced a sharp decline in real estate prices and a heavy buildup in nonperforming loans. However, Malaysian financial institutions were better regulated and better capitalized, so the stress on the exchange rate, while marked, was not as dramatic as in Thailand. Moreover, a blanket guarantee of deposits announced at the end of 1997 was credible, helping to avoid a general bank run (Meesook et al., 2001).

Indonesia and Korea both underwent severe foreign exchange and banking crises, but the banking crisis in both countries was generated largely by defaults on dollar-denominated loans extended to highly leveraged connected firms. The property sector played a smaller role, reflecting less obvious property price bubbles and smaller bank exposure to the property sector. In Korea, the bubble in both equities and property prices burst before the crisis.

The Philippines experienced a moderate economic upswing in the first half of the 1990s and a less severe downturn during the crisis period. As in Indonesia and Korea, in the Philippines, developments in the property sector played a smaller role in the economy.

Hong Kong and Singapore experienced pronounced upswings in the property market in the first half of the 1990s, with very heavy bank exposure to the sector (see Hilbers, Lei, and Zacho, 2001). In Singapore, property prices surged 30 percent in 1994–95, and in 1996 the authorities took steps to discourage speculation, imposing capital gains taxes and stamp duties, limiting bank loans to 80 percent of the purchase price, and increasing the supply of government land for residential development. Similarly, in Hong Kong in mid 1997, the authorities made more public land available for private development. Both economies experienced pressure in the exchange market during the crisis period, but responded effectively to contain the pressures—in Singapore through increased exchange rate flexibility and in Hong Kong through an aggressive interest rate defense of the currency board regime combined with equity market intervention to counter speculative attacks by hedge funds. Property prices dropped sharply in both economies, contributing to some increase in nonperforming loans. Nevertheless, the rise in problem loans was relatively modest compared to that in other East Asian countries, while the robust capitalization of major banks, together with the avoidance of deep recession and healthier balance sheets, allowed these banking systems to weather the storm without experiencing bank runs or other forms of major distress.

3. The Credit Channel to Asset Price Inflation in Asia: Some Empirical Results

The thrust of the discussion so far is that bank lending in the Asian economies has contributed to excessive asset price inflation, in particular in the real estate market, and the bursting of the bubble in these markets contributed significantly to the financial crisis in Asia. This section presents the major results of an effort to assess quantitatively the relationship between credit growth and real estate prices using both panel regressions and individual country Value-at-Risk (VaR) meaures (see Collyns and Senhadji, 2002, for details of the regressions and estimations).

The specification was kept parsimonious and follows the empirical literature, which finds that GDP per capita is the main determinant of property prices. It captures both the procyclical behavior of property prices and the economy's income, which is a determining factor for the demand for business and residential property. The dependent variable is a composite property price index reflecting both residential and commercial property prices, deflated by the CPI (ppi). Independent variables include credit to the private sector deflated by the CPI (c_p), real GDP per capita ($gdppc$), and a dummy variable in some equations. The dummy variable d_1 takes one for the period 1979:1 to 1996:4, and zero thereafter. The dummy variable d_2 takes one when the quarterly growth rate of ppi is positive and zero otherwise. The $dlog$ operator indicates first difference in logs. The notation with FE and w/o FE indicates whether the equation has been estimated with or without fixed effects, respectively.

Interest rates (both domestic and foreign) were included in the regression but were found to be statistically insignificant and, therefore, were dropped from the final specification. In other words, interest rates do not significantly increase the explanatory power of the model once the credit variable is included in the regression.

The panel regression results are presented in table 4. Equation 1 is estimated without fixed effects. Both coefficients are statistically significant at 1 percent and the magnitude of the coefficient estimate on real credit seems to suggest a powerful effect of credit on property price inflation: An increase in real credit by 10 percent implies an increase in property prices by 8 percent. Considering that real credit has been growing annually in the 9 percent to 36 percent range during the period 1990–97 in the five crisis countries (Indonesia, Korea, Malaysia, the Philippines, and Thailand), the cumulative effect of this credit boom on property prices has been substantial. As expected, property prices are strongly procyclical.

To test the robustness to potential omitted variables, the same equation was estimated using fixed effects (equation 2). Including fixed effects does not significantly alter the results. Equation 3 tests whether the response of property prices was different before and after the crisis. The response of property prices to real credit during the period 1979Q1–96Q4 was 2½ times larger than the response during the period 1997Q1–2001Q1 (the coefficient on real credit declined from 0.961 during the first period to 0.393 during the second period). Finally, equation (4) tests wether the relationship between property prices and real credit is asymmetric. Interestingly, the response of property prices to real credit is much stronger during periods of rising property prices than during periods of decline. A 10 percent increase in real credit will boost property prices by 12.4 percent during periods of rising property prices but by only 4.4 percent

	Dependent variable: $dlog(ppi/ppi(-4))$			
Independent variables	(1) w/o FE	(2) with FE	(3) w/o FE	(4) w/o FE
d_2				0.10 (3.70)*
$dlog(c_p/c_p(-4))$	0.805 (4.55)*	0.748 (4.56)*	0.393 (1.89)***	0.442 (2.50)*
$d_1*dlog(c_p/c_p(-4))$			0.568 (2.15)**	
$d_2*dlog(c_p/c_p(-4))$				0.800 (2.65)*
$dlog(gdppc/gdppc(-4))$	1.789 (7.66)*	1.782 (7.07)*	1.749 (7.13)*	1.210 (5.11)*
N	213	213	213	213
R^2	0.32	0.35	0.33	0.45

Note: t-statistics using White's heteroskedasticity-consistent standard errors are given between parentheses. Statistical significance at 1, 5, and 10 percent is indicated by *, **, and ***, respectively.

Table 4: Determinants of Real Estate Prices

during periods of decline. This may reflect the fact that banks tend to reduce the share of credit to the property sector and, therefore, decrease their exposure to the real estate market once the real estate price bubble bursts. It may also reflect data problems as the decline in credit during bust periods may be exaggerated because of write-offs during crises. Finally, it can also reflect downward rigidity of property prices, at least in the short term as investors may be reluctant to sell property at a price lower than the purchase price.

While the above results are suggestive, the specifications adopted in table 4 neglect two important issues. First, they assume that causality runs only from real credit to property prices, but not vice versa (a formal Granger-Causality test for each country generally fails to reject causality in both directions). Second, there is no dynamics in the chosen specifications. To address these issues, these results were complemented by running individual-country VaRs using the same specification. The results from this VaR exercise tend to confirm the results from the panel estimation in table 4 (for details, see Collyns and Senhadji, 2002).

To sum up, the empirical results suggest that a) property prices are strongly procyclical, b) bank lending has indeed significantly contributed to property price inflation in Asia during the period prior to the crisis, c) the response of property prices was significantly stronger before the crisis, and d) the response of property prices to credit was asymmetric in the sense that the response during periods of rising property prices was three time the response during periods of declining prices.

4. Policy Lessons

This paper does not provide scope for a full assessment of the policy lessons from the Asian crisis. Nevertheless, this section underlines a number of important policy lessons drawn from the paper and elsewhere (see, for example, Herring and Wachter, 1999; Lane et al., 1999; for a more comprehensive analysis, see International Monetary Fund (IMF), 1997; Kochhar, Lougani, and Stone, 1998; Berg 1999; Meesook et al., 2001).

Most important, the Asian experience with property price booms and busts and the consequences for financial stability reinforce the *critical importance of strong bank regulation*, both to reduce risks that a bubble will develop and to contain the disruptive costs when a bubble bursts.

In particular, restraining the growth of bank credit to the property and related sectors discourages the development of real estate bubbles. Steps in this direction include the following:

- strengthening credit assessment and reducing reliance on collateral as the basis for credit decisions by encouraging banks to look more broadly at the soundness of a borrower's business prospects and capacity for loan repayment in credit risk assessment, while tightening underwriting standards for real estate lending (for example, maximum loan to value ratios), especially when property prices are rising rapidly and may be deviating significantly from fundamental values;

- reducing moral hazard in the banking system by a) establishing a transparent and credible framework for deposit insurance and bank resolution to ensure that large creditors and depositors can suffer losses (to improve market discipline), b) imposing stringent capital adequacy requirements to ensure that bank owner's capital is truly at risk, and c) adopting more demanding accounting standards (particularly to provide more realistic information on asset valuation to strengthen market discipline by investors and creditors);

- applying a comprehensive approach to bank regulation: the Thai experience clearly demonstrates the systemic dangers of allowing a lightly regulated banking sector with wide lending power to play an important part in financial intermediation; moreover, sophisticated risk management systems (including rigorous stress testing) discourage banks from taking on large exposure to market risk (for example, in the property market); and

- encouraging alternative sources of financing for the real estate sector, including development of the real estate investment trust, similar to that in the United States, in order to broaden the investor base and increase the availability of equity financing for this sector.

Of course, even with generally well-managed banks and strong regulations, asset price bubbles may emerge. Lending decisions inevitably are influenced by a human tendency to follow what others are doing, and moral hazard can never be entirely excluded from bank intermediation. However, the experience of Hong Kong SAR and Singapore during the late 1990s demonstrates that highly capitalized banks can better absorb the costs of the subsequent asset price deflation than undercapitalized ones.

The Asian experience also supports the view that well-balanced macroeconomic and related policies help to avoid asset price bubbles and contain the disruptive impact of subsequent collapses. The difficulty, of course, is to recognize bubbles in real time. Nevertheless, as seen in Thailand, Korea, and Indonesia, the potentially enormous costs arising from mistakes suggest a conservative policy erring on the side of caution. In particular:

- Capital account liberalization should be carefully phased in, in line with domestic financial regulation and requires a sound macroeconomic environment. Recently, some observers have recommended taking a much more restrictive approach to debt flows, particularly in Asia, where internal saving generation is already strong (for example, Krueger, 2000; Horiguchi, 2001).
- There is also clearly benefit to a conservative approach to monetary policy that takes account of asset price developments in reaching judgments on short-term policy settings.
- Finally, there is room to manipulate policy settings that directly affect the property sector as a means to moderate property price movements before they become extreme. Singapore followed this route in 1996, increasing public land sales and taxes on capital gains from real estate and limiting bank loans to 80 percent of the purchase price, thus, helping to deflate the buildup in land prices and reducing the country's vulnerability during the Asia crisis in 1997–98.

*Charles Collyns is a senior advisor and Abdelhak Senhadji is a senior economist in the Asia and Pacific Department of the International Monetary Fund. The authors are grateful to Kalpana Kochhar for making critical suggestions on various preliminary drafts, Youkyong Kwon for superb research assistance, and Anita Jupp for efficient editing. They also thank Jahangir Aziz, Raymond Brooks, Ralph Chami, Ajai Chopra, Vikram Haksar, Paul Hilbers, Roberto Rosales, and participants in an Asia and Pacific Department seminar for very helpful comments. In addition, the authors thank the Monetary Authority of Singapore, Bank of Indonesia, Bank Negara Malaysia, and Bank of Thailand for providing useful comments. The authors are solely responsible for any remaining errors. The views expressed in this paper are those of the authors and do not necessarily represent those of the IMF.

References

Allen, Franklin, and Douglas Gale, 2000, "Bubbles and Crises," *Economic Journal*, Vol. 110, No. 1, pp. 236–255.

Berg, Andrew, 1999, "The Asia Crisis: Causes, Policy Response, and Outcomes," Washington, DC: International Monetary Fund, working paper, No. 99/132.

Bernanke, Ben, 1983, "Nonmonetary Effects of the Financial Crisis in the Propagation of the Great Depression," *American Economic Review*, Vol. 73, pp. 257–276.

Bernanke, Ben, and Mark Gertler, 1995, "Inside of a Black Box: The Credit Channel of Monetary Policy Transmission," *Journal of Economic Perspectives*, Vol. 9, No. 4, pp. 27–48.

Bank for International Settlements (BIS), 2001, *Annual Report, June 2001,* Chap. 7., Basel: BIS.

Collyns, Charles, and Abdelhak Senhadji, 2002, "Lending Booms, Real Estate Bubbles, and the Asian Crisis," Washington, DC: International Monetary Fund, working paper, No. WP/02/20.

Corsetti, Giancarlo, Paolo Pesenti, and Nouriel Roubini, 1998, "What Caused the Asian Currency and Financial Crisis? Part I: A Macroeconomic Overview," pp. 1–39, mimeo.

Dekle, Robert, and Kenneth Kletzer, 2001, "Domestic Bank Regulation and Financial Crises: Theory and Empirical Evidence from East Asia," Washington, DC: International Monetary Fund, working paper, No. 01/63.

Herring, Richard, and Susan Wachter, 1999, "Real Estate Booms and Banking Busts: An International Perspective," Washington, DC: Group of Thirty, occasional paper, No. 58.

Hilbers, Paul, Qin Lei, and Lisbeth Zacho, 2001, "Real Estate Market Developments and Financial Sector Soundness," Washington, DC: International Monetary Fund, working paper, No. 01/129.

Horiguchi, Yusuke, 2001, "Should External Borrowing be Restrained?" Washington, DC: International Monetary Fund, unpublished paper.

International Monetary Fund (IMF), 1997, *World Economic Outlook,* Chap. 3, Washington, DC: IMF, December.

Kalra, Sanjay, Dubravko Mihaljek, and Christoph Duenwald, 2000, "Property Prices and Speculative Bubbles: Evidence from Hong Kong SAR," Washington, DC: International Monetary Fund, working paper, No. 00/2.

Kaminski, Graciela, and Carmen Reinhart, 1999, "The Twin Crises: The Causes of Banking and Balance-of-Payments Problems," *American Economic Review,* Vol. 89, No. 3, pp. 473–500.

Kiyotaki, Nobuhiro, and John Moore, 1997, "Credit Cycles," *Journal of Political Economy,* Vol. 105, No. 2, pp. 211–248.

Kochhar, Kalpana, Prakash Lougani, and Mark Stone, 1998, "The East Asian Crisis: Macroeconomic Developments and Policy Lessons," Washington, DC: International Monetary Fund, working paper, No. 98/128.

Krueger, Anne, 2000, "Conflicting Demands on the International Monetary Fund," *American Economic Review,* Vol. 90, No. 2, pp. 38–42.

Krugman, Paul, 1998, "What Happened to Asia?" unpublished paper.

Lane, Thimothy, Atish Ghosh, Javier Hamann, Steven Phillips, Marianne Schultze-Ghattas, and Tsisi Tsikata, 1999, *IMF-Supported Programs in Indonesia, Korea, and Thailand,* Washington, DC: International Monetary Fund, occasional paper, No. 178.

Meesook, Kanita, Il Houng Lee, Olin Liu, Yougesh Khatri, Natalia Tamirisa, Michael Moore, and Mark Krysl, 2001, *Malaysia: From Crisis to Recovery,* Washington, DC: International Monetary Fund, occasional paper, No. 178.

Mishkin, Frederic, 1996, "Understanding Financial Crisis: A Developing Country Perspective," Cambridge, MA: National Bureau of Economic Research, working paper, No. 5600.

Chapter 9
Tropical Bubbles: Asset Prices in Latin America, 1980–2001

Santiago Herrera*
World Bank Group

and

Guillermo E. Perry
World Bank Group

1. Introduction

The past decade began in a festive mood in Latin America, with policymakers welcoming the future that had finally arrived with its rewards: growth, rising asset prices, rising investment to gross domestic product (GDP) ratios, strong capital inflows, and booming domestic credit.[1] The decade ended, however, on a gloomy note: stagnant growth, falling investment ratios, stagnant or falling asset prices, sluggish domestic credit, and several crippled banking systems. How do we account for this disappointing reversal? Can it be traced to the relationship between the credit boom (external and domestic) and the behavior of asset prices? Is the bust related to the boom? Is the behavior of asset prices governed by fundamentals, or do asset prices in Latin America reflect the presence of bubbles, as in other emerging market economies? We address these issues and their policy implications in the following four sections of this paper.

Section 2 describes the evolution of asset prices in Latin America and identifies periods of significant asset overvaluation, as well as crash episodes. Stock market prices and, to a lesser extent, real estate prices provide the basis for the analysis. Using Froot and Obstfeld's (1991) intrinsic bubbles model as a benchmark, periods of asset overvaluation are identified for the region and the no-bubbles hypothesis is rejected. We find that stock market crashes follow most bubbles, with the resulting prices being lower than those before the bubble formed. Crash episodes often led to or coincided with currency crises (Kaminsky, Lizondo, and Reinhart, 1997).

Section 3 identifies the regularity of bubble episodes in Latin America and examines several factors that affect the probability of bubble occurrence, focusing on the contrast between the country-specific variables and the common external factors. The country-specific variables include both the level and the volatility of domestic credit growth, the volatility of asset returns, capital flows to each country, and the terms of trade. The common external variables include the degree of asset overvaluation in the U.S. stock and real estate markets and the term spread of U.S. Treasury securities. We estimate a logit model for a panel of five Latin American countries from 1985 to 2001 to assess the relative importance of each factor. Generally, we find that the marginal probabilities of both common and country-specific variables are roughly of the same order of magnitude. This finding contrasts with those of previous studies that real asset returns in Latin America are dominated by local factors (Harvey, 1995; Hargis and Maloney, 1997). We also find that the U.S. term spread is the single most important determinant of bubbles.

Section 4 explores the main empirical channels through which asset prices affect real economic activity, with the most important being the balance-sheet effect and its impact on bank lending. We show how the allocation of bank lending across different sectors responded sensitively to real estate prices during the boom years in countries that experienced banking crises. Thus, asset price bubbles have long-lasting effects in the financial sector, and, through this channel, on growth. Another channel through which asset prices—particularly stock market prices—affect long-run growth is investment. We find a strong positive association between stock prices and investment and a negative effect of stock price volatility on investment. To the extent that stock prices incorporate information about future aggregate demand, the central bank may monitor them as a means of anticipating the future course of inflation. An additional motive for the central bank to monitor asset prices is the general coincidence of the crash episodes identified in this paper with currency crises in the region in the past two decades.

Finally, in section 5, we present our conclusions and discuss the key policy implications of bubbles for the region.

2. Do Tropical Bubbles Exist? What Do They Look Like?

2.1 Evolution of Asset Prices in Latin America

Since the 1980s, stock prices in Latin America (LAC) have fallen into two subperiods.[2] First, during the 1980s, prices showed no clear trend, though there were some spikes in Argentina, Brazil, and, to a lesser extent, México. The price spike episodes of the 1980s were preceded by high and rising inflation. A second period, during the 1990s, initially witnessed a substantial price increase that was stabilized and then reversed by the latter part of the decade. Only in Brazil did the rising trend continue throughout the entire decade. Stock prices in LAC—particularly in Argentina, Brazil, and México—experienced recurrent crashes. In Chile and Colombia, these sudden falls were less frequent.

Returns in stock markets across the region were positively and highly correlated. The highest correlation coefficients are between Chile and México (0.92), Colombia and México (0.87), Chile and Colombia (0.86), Argentina and Chile (0.82), México and Argentina (0.81). Across time, however, there are changes in these correlations. Computing the correlation coefficients with a 24-month rolling window, we observe that, for the biggest three countries, these coefficients are stationary; however, there is a structural change in the generating processes in the early 1990s (figure 1).[3]

There also is a positive association between stock prices and dividends (normalized) in most countries (figure 2). Both variables tend to move together, although there are periods when they diverge. Colombia seems to be the only case in which the series are clearly divergent.

Comparing these results with those for East Asian countries—Indonesia, Korea, Malaysia, and Thailand—we find that, for most countries, correlations of stock returns are around 0.50 or lower. The only exception is the correlation between Malaysia and Thailand of 0.86 (table A1 in appendix A). Thus, stock return correlations are lower in Asia than in LAC. As for change in these East Asian correlations over time, there is no clear evidence of structural breaks in the correlations as was the case in the LAC countries (figure A1 in appendix A.)

We built proxies for Argentina, Colombia, and México using the rent component of the Consumer Price Index, deflated by the overall index. In the case of México, there is a strong correlation between this proxy and the index of the value of urban land in México City constructed by Banco de México (Guerra, 1997). A boom in real estate prices occurred in México in 1988–91, in Argentina in 1990–93, and in Colombia in 1993–96. We also present real estate prices in two affluent neighborhoods of Santiago de Chile in 1975–82,[4] as reported by Conley and Maloney (1995). Figures 3a and 3b show the evolution of returns on real estate investment in México and the United States, as captured by our proxies.[5] For the entire sample period, there is no correlation (figure 3a); however, there is a correlation of 0.70 after 1995 (figure 3b).

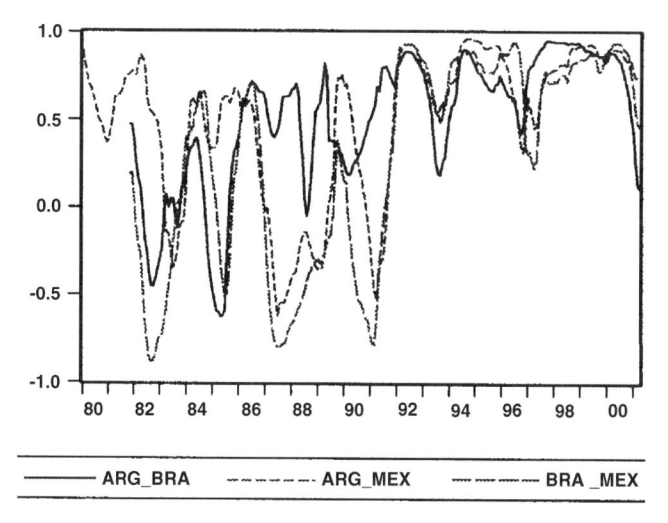

Figure 1: Correlations of Stock Market Returns 24-Month Rolling Window, 1978–2001

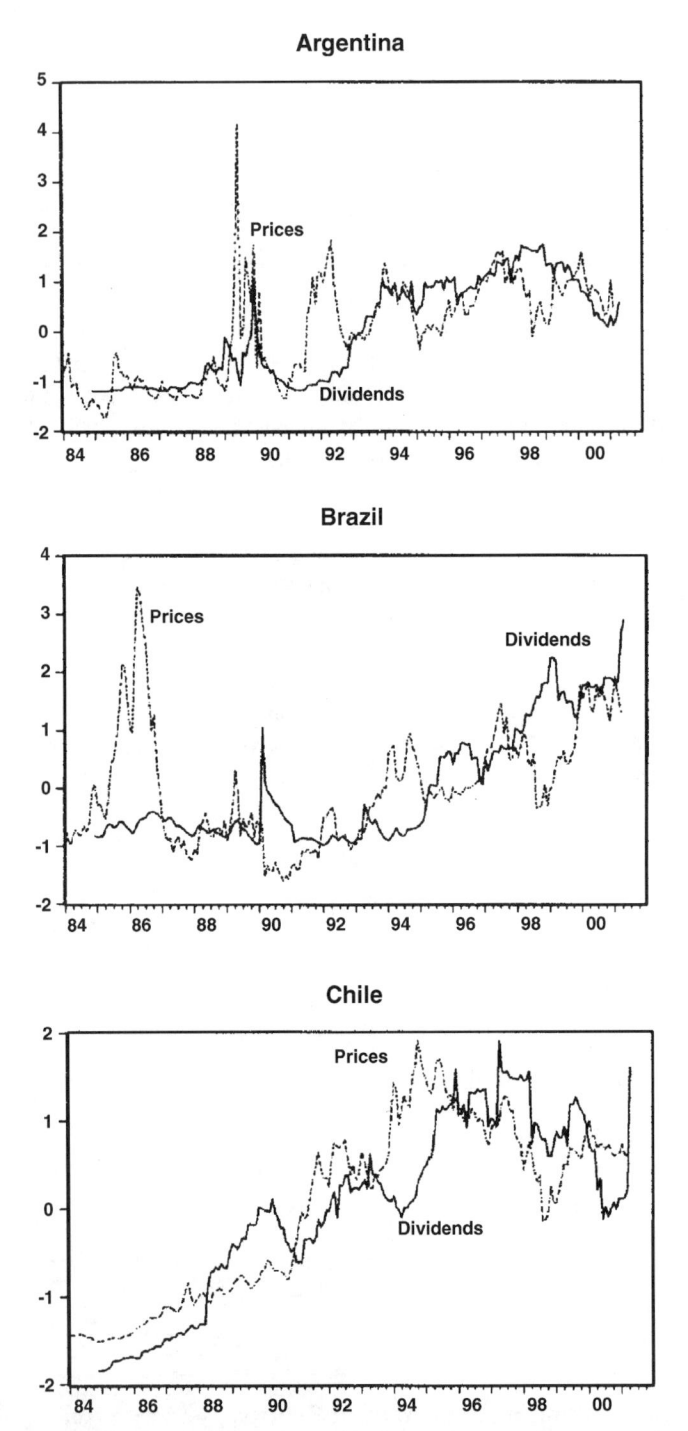

Figure 2: Stock Market Prices and Dividends (1984–2001, Normalized Data)

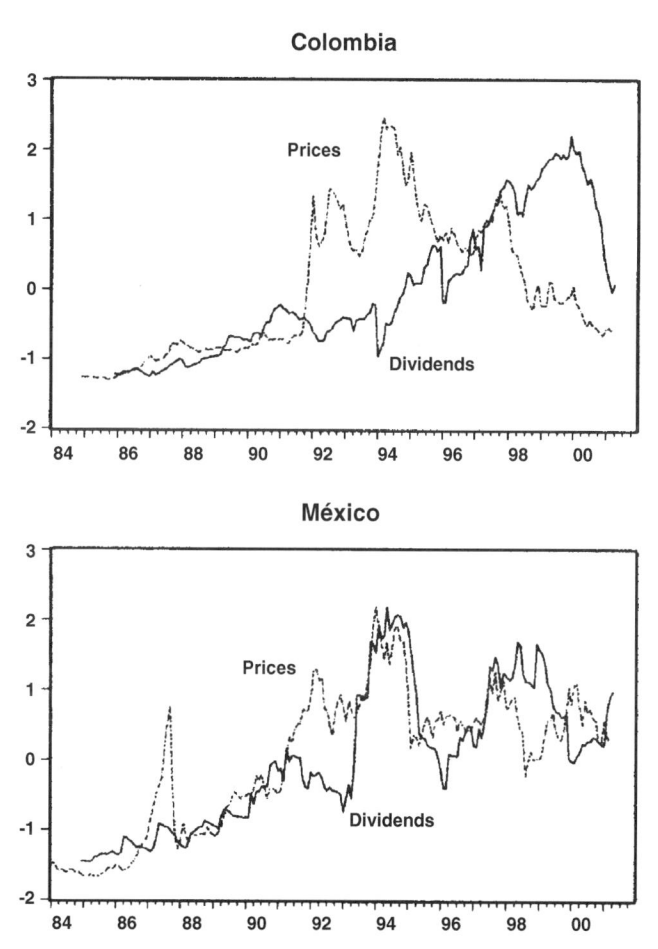

Tropical Bubbles: Asset Prices in Latin America, 1980–2001   131

Colombia

México

Figure 2 (*continued*): **Stock Market Prices and Dividends (1984–2001, Normalized Data)**

2.2 Testing for Bubbles: The Latin American Case

Theoretical and empirical work on bubbles is extensive, including some well-known surveys (Camerer, 1989; Flood and Hodrick, 1990; and Campbell, 2000). In general, a bubble (B_t) is defined as the difference between the fundamentals-determined price (P^{PV}_t) and the observed price (P_t). In the case of stocks, the fundamentals price can be expressed as the sum of discounted expected future cash flows—or dividends—to the holder of the asset.[6]

1) $P_t = P^{PV}_t + B_t$

The bubble term, B, if it exists, can be expected to grow at the real rate of interest.[7]

In the case of Latin America, testing for bubbles has been scarce. For our purposes, therefore, we chose the tests with the simplest structure (Campbell, Lo, and

Graph 3a, 1976–2001

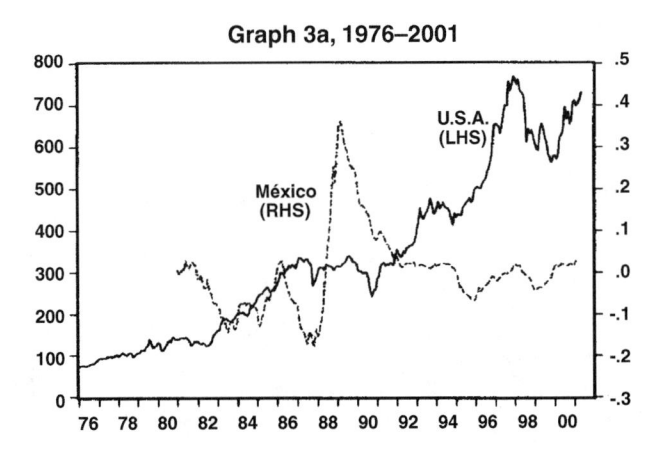

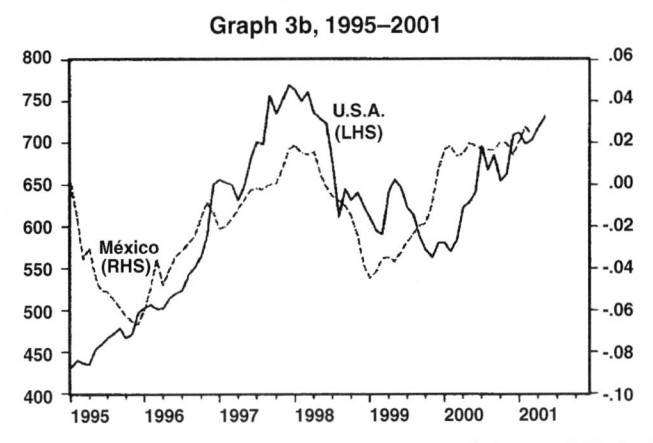

Graph 3b, 1995–2001

Figure 3: Return to Real Estate Investments in México and United States

McKinlay, 1997), and those used to test for bubbles in other emerging market economies (Sarno and Taylor, 1999). The general idea is to verify or reject the existence of a stable (nonexplosive) relationship among stock prices, dividends, and returns.

The equation that establishes the basis for the tests (see appendix B for a derivation) is:

2) $$d_t - P_t = -\frac{k}{1-\rho} + E_t \sum_{j=0}^{\infty} \rho^j (-\Delta d_{t+1+j} + r_{t+1+j}),$$

where d_t = log dividends, p_t = log prices, and r_t = return.

Given the accounting identity nature of the above equation,[8] if prices go up, either dividends go up, or expected future returns go down to maintain the dividend-to-price ratio stationary. Hence, the tests are oriented toward examining the stationary (or explosive) behavior of the log dividend-price ratio and the existence of a stable relationship among dividends, prices, and returns.

Accordingly, we perform two types of tests. First, we check for unit roots in the log dividend-price ratio and in the real return series. If dividends follow an I(1) (shown in table 1) process, their difference is stationary, and the return series must be of the same order of integration as the dividend-price ratio. If the series have unit roots, the "no-bubble" hypothesis is rejected. Second, we check for a cointegrating relationship between the log dividend-price ratio and returns. If a stable (equilibrium) relationship is rejected, then the "no-bubble" hypothesis also is rejected.

Beginning with the unit root tests, we note that the Standard Augmented Dickey-Fuller tests (ADF) for series with bubbles may result in accepting stationarity, even though the series are, in fact, explosive, because the recurrent collapse of the bubble may resemble a mean reversing process (Evans, 1991). Results for the ADF (unit root) tests are in table B1 of appendix B. For most countries, total return and (log) dividend yields have a unit root. The standard ADF tests reject the unit root hypothesis in Argentina (both series) and México (dividend yield), although the results are not robust to the inclusion of a deterministic time trend. Hence, for most countries, the bias toward accepting stationarity due to periodically collapsing bubbles is not a problem, except for the possible exceptions of Argentina and México.[9]

To correct the potential bias in the standard unit root and cointegration tests, Taylor and Peel (1998) propose a residuals-augmented least squares (RALS), briefly described in appendix B. The main idea is to introduce into the standard ADF tests an auxiliary term that mitigates the skew and kurtosis originating from the collapsing prices.

Results for the RALS unit root test are shown in table B.3 (appendix B) and summarized in table 1. These results are similar to those obtained with the ADF test. Total returns and log dividend yield are nonstationary series in most countries (Brazil, Chile, Colombia, and Peru). However, the unit root hypothesis is rejected for stock returns in Argentina and for the dividend yield in México.[10] In most countries, therefore, we are unable to reject the unit root hypothesis, implying bubble behavior in stock prices during the sample period. We proceed to verify these conclusions with the cointegration tests.

To verify (or reject) the hypothesis of the existence of a long-run relationship between the log dividend-price ratio and real returns, we use three alternative conintegration tests: the standard Johansen cointegration test, the RALS cointegration test, and the autoregressive distributed lag (ARDL) method. Given that the tests are valid regardless of the order of integration of the variables, the ARDL has the advantage of circumventing the issue of pre-testing for unit roots (Pesaran et al., 1999).

Table 1 summarizes the results.[11] Both the standard Johansen and the RALS cointegration tests reject the hypothesis of a long-run relationship between total returns and the log of dividend yield in all the countries.[12] Finally, the ARDL method rejects the existence of a long-run relationship, except for the case of Argentina, in the specific case in which the regression includes time trend.

Thus, the main results and conclusions of this section are:

- Returns are nonstationary when performing ordinary ADF tests. This result is confirmed by the Taylor-Peel RALS test, with the possible exception of Argentina, when a deterministic time trend is included.

	RALS: Unit Root Test		RALS: Cointegration Test	Johansen Cointegrating Vectors*		ARDL: Test on Long-Run Relationship
	Total Returns	Log of Dividend Yield		No Data Trend	Linear Data Trend	
ARGENTINA	I(0)[a]	I(1)	Not cointegrated	0	2	Long-run relationship[b]
BRAZIL	I(1)	I(1)	Not cointegrated	0	0	No long-run relationship
CHILE	I(1)	I(1)	Not cointegrated	0	0	No long-run relationship
COLOMBIA	I(1)	I(1)	Not cointegrated	0	0	No long-run relationship
MÉXICO	I(1)	I(0)	Not cointegrated	0	2	No long-run relationship
PERU	I(1)	I(1)	Not cointegrated	0	0	No long-run relationship

[a]Results are sensitive to the inclusion (or not) of constant and trend. The series are I(1) when constant and trend are not included in the regressions.
[b]Results are sensitive to the inclusion (or not) of constant and trend. There is no long-run relationship when trend is not included in the regressions.

Table 1: Unit Root, Cointegration and Tests for Long-Run Relationship between Returns and (Log) Dividend Yields

- Log dividend yield is nonstationary with ADF and the RALS tests, with the possible exception of México, when a deterministic time trend is included in the regression.
- Log dividend-yield and returns are not cointegrated according to the standard Johansen tests, and, using the ARDL method, we reject the hypothesis of a long-run relationship between these variables. Argentina is an exception when the null includes a time trend.

All of the tests lead to a rejection of the hypothesis of no-bubbles in stock prices for our sample between 1980 and 2001, though there is some ambiguity regarding the case of Argentina.

2.3 When Have Bubbles Occurred, and How Persistent Are They?

Given the rejection of the "no-bubble" hypothesis for stock prices in Latin America, we now identify periods when observed prices differed significantly from the fundamentals-determined price based on Froot and Obstfeld's (1991) intrinsic bubbles model. Froot and Obstfeld set up the basic model of the stock price-dividend relationship[13] and arrive at the following expression for stock prices described in equation 1:

$$P_t = P_t^{PV} + B_t$$

where P_t, the stock price, is equated to P_t^{PV}, the present discounted value of expected future dividend payments,[14] and B_t, the bubble term (if it exists), is expected to grow at the real interest rate.[15]

To find a simple, closed-form solution for P^{PV}, an assumption has to be made about future dividend growth or the dividend-generating process. Froot and Obstfeld show that if the log dividend process is generated by

3) $\quad d_{t+1} = \mu + d_t + \xi_{t+1}$

where μ is the trend growth in dividends and ξ_t is a $(0, \sigma^2)$ normal random variable, then the present value price is proportional to dividends:

4) $\quad P_t^{PV} = \kappa D_t$

where, $\kappa = (e^r - e^{\mu + \sigma/2})^{-1}$,

r = return on stocks over the whole sample period, and μ, σ are, respectively, the trend growth rate of log (dividends) and the standard deviation of the residuals of an AR(1) process describing the dividends (equation 3).[16]

Since, for each country, we have r and can obtain estimates of μ, σ from a regression of equation (3), we calibrate the value of κ.[17] Hence, the bubble component can be approximated by the difference between the observed price and the P^{PV}.[18] Figure 4 shows the (normalized) observed prices and the present-value prices for Argentina, Brazil, Chile, and México. This indicates that during the 1990s there were persistent deviations of the observed price from the estimated present-value price. Argentina is the only exception, but, even in this case, there were significant, although very transitory, deviations in the 1980s.

Froot and Obstfeld estimate a more complicated version of their model, where bubbles depend not only on dividends, but also on time,[19] of the following type:[20]

5) $\quad P_t/D_t = c_0 + c_1 D_t^{\lambda-1} + c_2 D_t^{\lambda^1-1} + gX_t$

where P = prices, D = dividends, and X = a linear term on dividends or a time trend. We also included a quadratic time trend; and λ, λ^1 are the positive and negative roots, respectively of the dynamic system $\lambda^2\sigma^2/2 + \lambda\mu - r = 0$ described above. The estimation of the nonlinear equation was done restricting the values of these roots.

Besides allowing the quantification of the divergence of observed values from the predicted values, this model is useful to verify the existence of bubbles. The null hypothesis of no bubbles implies that $c_1 = 0$, while the alternative implies $c_1 > 0$. The estimations (appendix C) lead to rejection of the "no-bubble" hypothesis in all the cases except Argentina. Moreover, in all cases (figure 5), deviations of the observed price from the predicted one are persistent, frequent, and significant in size. Argentina is the only country that does not have a bubble after 1992. These results are similar to

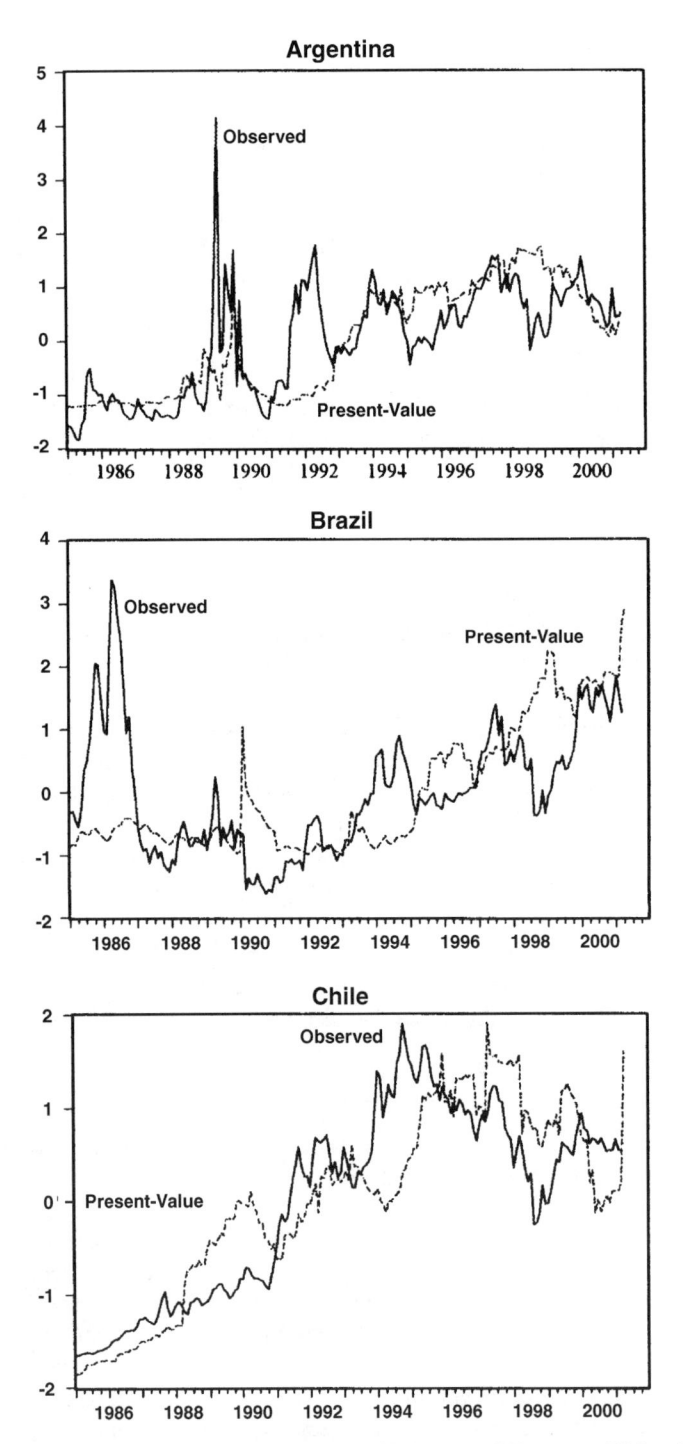

Figure 4: Divergence between Observed Prices and Present-Value Prices

Figure 4 (*continued*): **Divergence between Observed Prices and Present-Value Prices**

those of the simpler model. The timing of the bubbles tends to coincide in both approximations.[21] In Argentina, there is evidence of bubbles during the periods of hyperinflation from 1985 to 1989. Hall, Psaradakis, and Sola (1999) identify bubbles for money supply, exchange rate, and prices in 1985 and 1989, years for which we also find bubbles in the stock market.

Following the same procedure, we estimate the intrinsic bubble model for the United States and obtain interesting results (figure 6). First, like Froot and Obstfeld (1991) and Bonds and Cummins (2000), we cannot reject the hypothesis of bubble behavior. Second, the deviations of the observed price from the predicted one show two periods of significant stock price overvaluation. One begins in 1986 and ends in 1987 (the crash of 1987). The second one occurs in the second half of the 1990s. The significant deviation of late 1997 was (temporarily) corrected in 1998, while the overvaluation in 2000 had not been corrected by the end of the year.[22] These results are very similar to Reinhart's (1998) quantification of overvalued U.S. stock prices.[23]

Having quantified the over/undervaluation of assets for the Latin American countries and the United States,[24] we examine the correlation of these measures across time. For the period 1980–2001, we note very low correlation coefficients, recalling that stock returns were highly correlated. We also note the negative sign between deviations from the model in the United States and in the Latin American countries, except in Mexico, where it is negligible. These correlations are significantly lower than those found among industrialized nations for a similar time period (IMF, 1998).[25] For example, the correlation coefficients were of the following order: U.S.–Canada, 0.58; U.S.–UK 0.65; U.S.–Germany, 0.44; Germany–France, 0.49.

Restricting the sample period to 1995–2001, we observe that correlation coefficients increase, with the most notable changes being the rise in the México–U.S. coefficient to 0.40 and the negative coefficient of Brazil–U.S., –0.27. Similarly, others (Harvey, 1995) have found a negative correlation between Brazil and other Latin American countries, although for a different sample period.

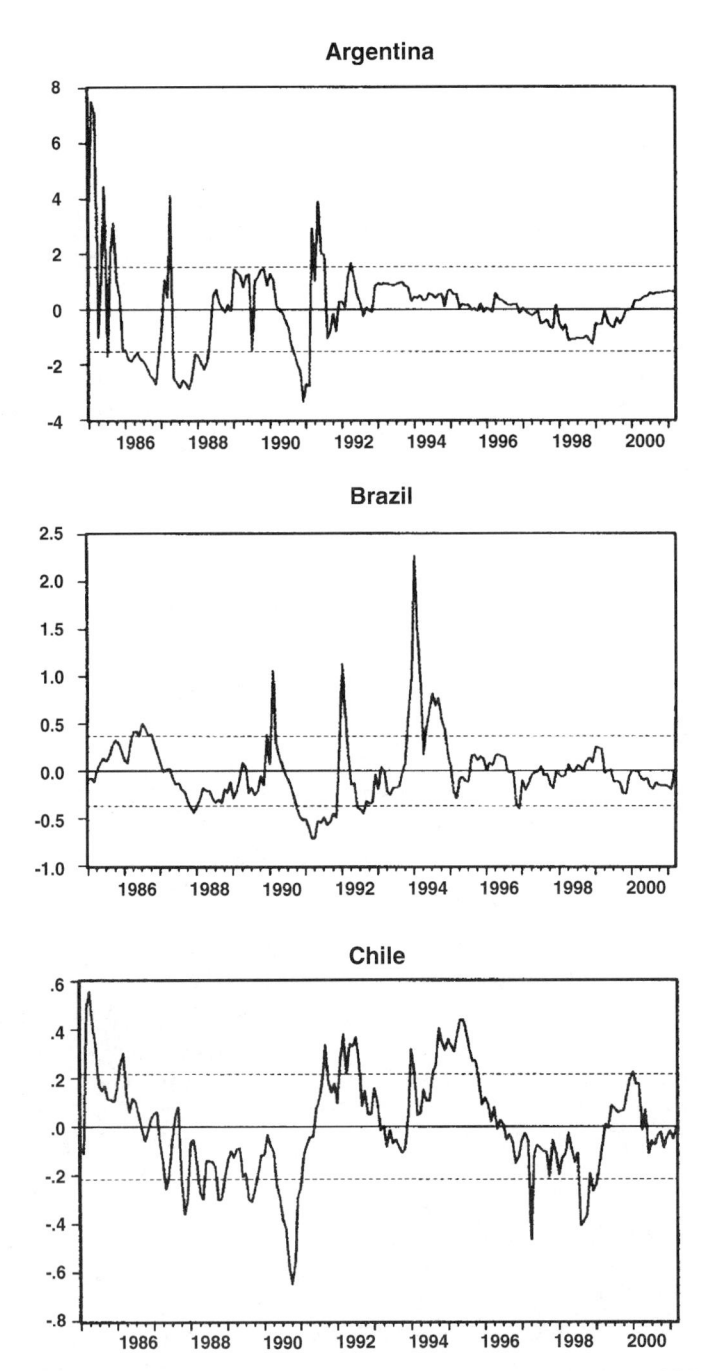

Figure 5: Deviation of the Observed Price from the Intrinsic Bubble Model Predicted Price in Several LAC Countries

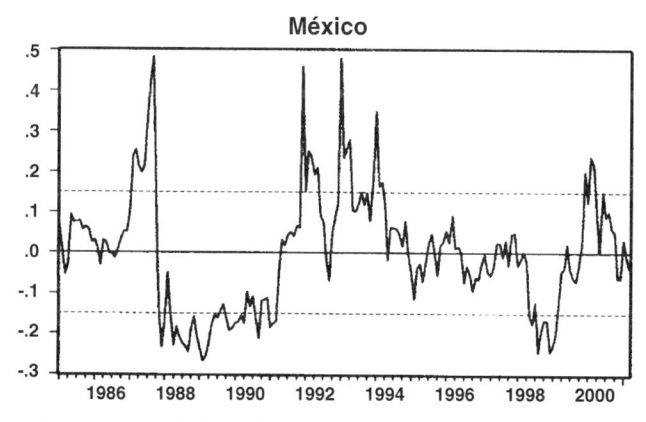

Tropical Bubbles: Asset Prices in Latin America, 1980–2001   139

México

Figure 5 (*continued*): **Deviation of the Observed Price from the Intrinsic Bubble Model Predicted Price in Several LAC Countries**

Based on this section's results, we built a dummy variable for bubble periods. The dummy takes the unit value whenever there is a significant departure of stock prices from their present-value price or from the price predicted by the intrinsic bubble model.[26] Leaving the negative deviations aside,[27] we label these as bubble episodes (table 2).

Regarding real estate prices, apart from noting periods of rapid growth, we are unable to identify departures of observed prices from the fundamentals, because we are using one of the most important fundamentals, rent, to build our price proxy.[28]

2.4 Most (but Not All) Bubbles End in Crashes, and There Are Crashes without Bubbles

Following Patel and Sarkar (1998), we construct an auxiliary variable, defined as the ratio of the stock market price to the maximum value of the series up to that time

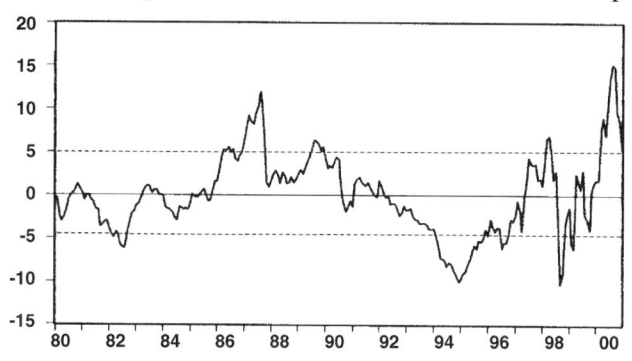

Figure 6. Deviation of the Observed Price from the Intrinsic Bubble Model Predicted Price in Several LAC Countries

LAC	BUBBLE	CRASH 1-*CMAX*	CRASH 2-*DLPRICE*
Total	22	24	41
Total bubbles ending with a crash	14	11	24
Independent bubbles and crashes	6	9	13
Crashes during bubbles or vice versa	2	4	4

Table 2: Number of Bubbles and Crashes

period, to trace the evolution of stock prices and determine crash periods. This variable, referred to as *CMAX*, is bound to take values between zero and one. Patel and Sarkar define a crash period for Latin America when the price index falls more than 35 percent relative to the historical maximum. This provides a benchmark to compare our results.

We endogenously determined the country-specific thresholds such that, if the *CMAX* fell below this level, the episode was catalogued as a crash. The endogenous threshold selection was done by means of the Self-Exciting Threshold Autoregression (SETAR) mechanism (Potter, 1995).[29] In this fashion, events were classified as crashes if the *CMAX* fell below the following threshold levels: Argentina, 31 percent; Brazil, 63 percent; Chile, 79 percent; Colombia, 87 percent; and México, 70 percent.[30]

As an alternative to working with the *CMAX* variable, we used the monthly percentage changes of the stock price indices in real terms and determined endogenously the country-specific threshold using the SETAR method. The monthly percentage falls exceeding the following threshold levels were considered crash episodes: Argentina, 34 percent; Brazil, 22 percent; Chile, 11 percent; Colombia, 11 percent; and México, 11 percent.

We combine the information on crash and bubble periods for Argentina, Brazil, Chile, Colombia, and México. Table 2 shows results for bubbles and crashes identified by each of the methodologies. Crash type 1 identifies crash periods with the *CMAX*, while crash type 2 identifies crashes with the monthly percentage changes of the stock prices.

We observe that there are more crashes than bubbles. While there are 22 bubbles in the 1980–2001 period, there are between 24 and 41 crashes depending on the method of identification. Bubbles and crashes have similar average durations: Bubbles persist for 8 months, while crashes last 10 months.[31] The average price increase during bubbles is 173 percent,[32] while the average price fall in crashes is 181 percent.

Most bubbles end in crashes: 14 out of 22 bubbles (64 percent) end up bursting. For this type of bubble episode, the stock market price resulting after the crash is lower than that prevailing before the bubble; in 12 out of the 14 episodes, prices were lower after the crash than before the bubble.

We also note that there are crashes not preceded by bubbles. Most of these episodes are related to foreign crises. Brazil, Chile, Colombia, and México show crashes not proceeded by bubbles during the Asian crisis (1997:10) and the Russian crisis (1998:08). The U.S. stock market crash in 1987 also is reflected in crashes in Brazil, Chile, and México.

Similarly, most countries register a crash in the first or second quarter of 1994, when there was a shift in U.S. monetary policy: Between February and June, the Federal Reserve Funds Rate was increased four times, signaling a clear change in policy direction. Based on these findings, the Tequila crisis can be understood as beginning with the bursting of a bubble in the Méxican stock market by the second quarter of 1994 and the intervention of two banks in September 1994. Later, in the first months of 1995, after the devaluation of the peso, there is evidence of a second crash in México. In Brazil, Chile, and Colombia, there are also price crashes in the first quarter of 1994, clearly associated with the same external event.

Most crash periods led to or coincided with currency crises documented elsewhere (Kaminsky, Lizondo, and Reinhart, 1996) (appendix C), and this explains why including the stock market price improves the performance of early warning systems of currency crisis (Herrera and Garcia, 1999).

3. Determinants of Bubbles

3.1 Stock Prices, Capital Flows, Domestic Credit Growth, and Terms of Trade: Stylized Facts and Motivating Evidence

For the largest LAC countries, stock prices show a nonstationary behavior, with a significant change in level in the early 1990s. To clarify the timing of these changes, we use Andrews and Zivot (1992) and Vogelsang and Perron (1998) tests for structural breaks. Additionally, we use SETAR methods to determine approximate break-points in the series. Different methods yield different results (table 3), but in Argentina, Chile, Colombia, and México, we identify a structural break in the stock price series in mid 1991.

Capital flows are mean-reverting processes with a change in mean. This change took place in 1991 in Argentina, Chile, and México. Domestic credit growth also is stationary with structural breaks taking place in the early 1990s, except in México, where it happened in 1988.

There are two other interesting empirical regularities. First, the relationship between terms-of-trade positive shocks and the occurrence of bubbles (figure 7) seems to have been important in Argentina, Chile, Brazil, and Colombia. Second, the realization of the relationship between domestic credit growth and the bubble episodes (figure 8) seems to take place with a long lag. Almost all of the bubble episodes were preceded by a cycle of credit boom, but in México the bubble surges once the acceleration has ceased.

3.2 Determinants of Bubbles in Latin America

To gauge the relative importance of the different factors affecting the divergence of asset prices from their fundamentals-determined prices, we follow the international business cycle theory that analyzes the relationship between stock returns in one country and foreign indicators of economic activity and foreign financial variables (Canova and De Nicolo, 1995). Based on information sets that contain both local and global variables, this approach has been used to explain asset returns in emerging markets (Harvey, 1995; Hargis and Maloney, 1997).

	Log of stock market prices in real terms (*LGPRLCR*)	6-month moving average of capital flows proxy (*KFLO6*)	Domestic credit in real terms (*DCR*)	Domestic credit growth in real terms (*DCRG*)
Argentina	89:02, 91:06	91:09	82:08, 84:05 89:06, 90:04	91:05
Brazil	86:11, 90:10, 93:04	92:01	89:11, 91:09	92:02
Chile	91:07	91:09, 96:07, 97:09, 97:12	83:07, 89:05 91:02	82:06
Colombia	91:11, 94:05, 98:02	97:02	97:01	91:10
México	86:05, 91:11, 94:10, 97:10	91:10, 94:03	92:07	88:08
Peru	97:10	94:03, 96:09	88:02, 89:12	90:08

Table 3: Tests of Unit Roots for Series with Structural Breaks

Among the country-specific factors, we include domestic credit expansion, volatility of credit growth, and volatility of asset returns. Other country-specific variables are capital flows and terms-of-trade shocks,[33] though they are "external." The common external factors are the degree of overvaluation in U.S. asset prices[34] and the spread between 10-year bonds and three-month Treasury bills.[35] This last variable is included to incorporate agents' expectations of future real interest rates in the United States, or of the future course of economic activity (Estrella and Mishkin, 1997; Fama, 1990). If future output is expected to be high, consumption-smoothing agents will borrow against it and bid up interest rates (Chen, 1991). Alternatively, if the term spread is a good predictor of inflation, a rise in the spread anticipates future falls in real interest rates (Fama, 1990). Both effects lead to a positive expected sign in the coefficient of the term spread.

Pooling monthly data for five countries since 1985, we estimate a logit model[36] (table 4) with satisfactory results.[37] All of the domestic variables are significant and have the expected sign. Volatility of domestic credit and volatility of asset returns affect positively the probability of bubble occurrence, as predicted by the Allen–Gale model. Likewise, terms-of-trade (positive) shocks and capital flows have the same effect. Domestic credit growth has a negative sign 12 months prior to the bubble, but the sign is positive 18 months prior to the bubble. This reflects the nonlinear effect of this variable.

Particularly noteworthy is the opposite sign of the overvaluation proxies for stock markets and real estate. When U.S. stock markets are overvalued, the

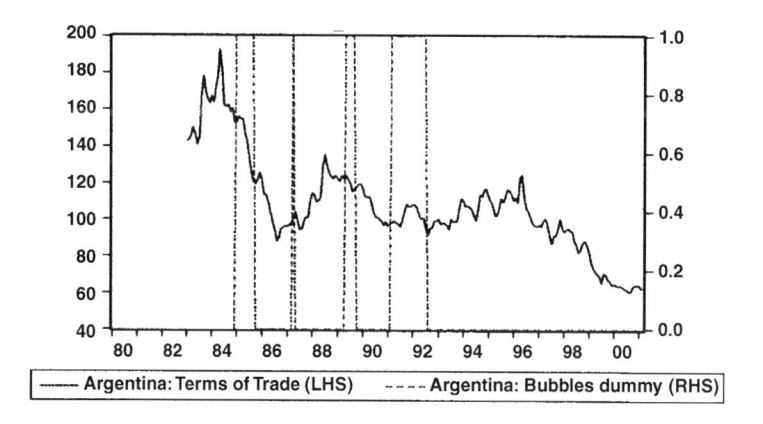

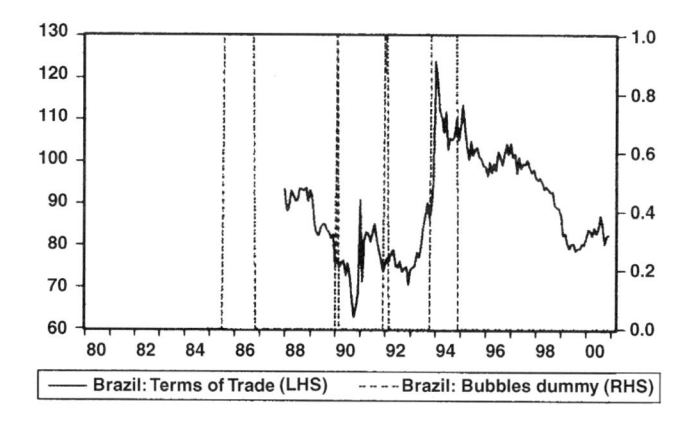

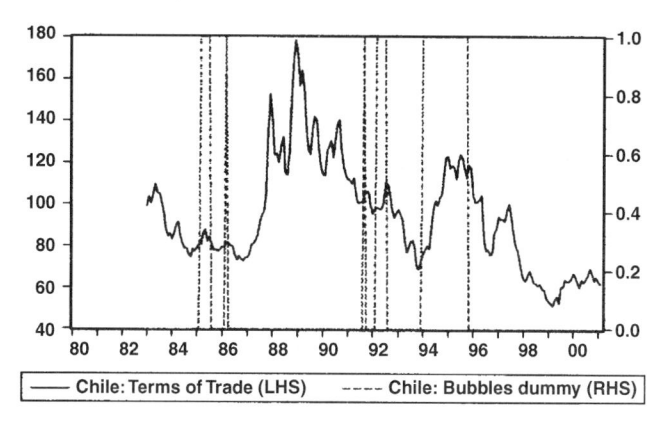

Figure 7: Positive Terms of Trade Shocks and Bubbles

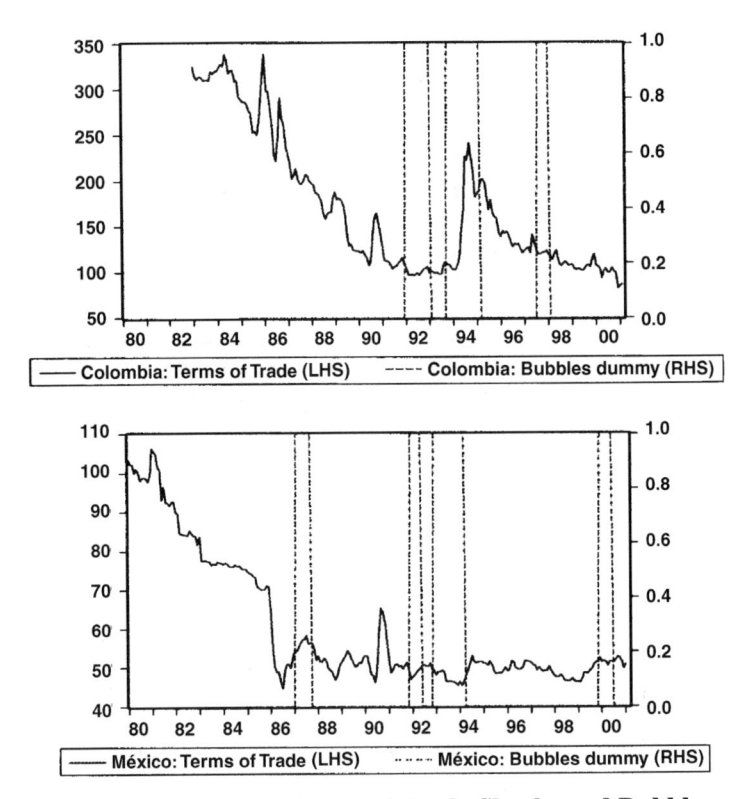

Figure 7 (*continued*): Positive Terms of Trade Shocks and Bubbles

probability of a bubble occurrence in Latin American stock markets declines. However, the probability increases with overvaluation in real estate markets. The only way to reconcile this result is through the negative or low positive correlation between these asset classes in the United States. The term structure spread is significant and has the expected sign. Thus, higher-term structure spreads are leading indicators of expanding economic activity or lower future real interest rates (Estrella and Mishkin, 1997; Fama, 1990).

Marginal probabilities tell us how the probability of a bubble changes with a unit change in each individual variable. We calculated these probabilities by estimating the marginal effect at each observation and then taking the sample average. The differences across countries arise because of the fixed-effects coefficient, and because the values of the explanatory variables are different for each country. The term spread in the United States has the largest marginal impact on bubble probability. This statistical result is confirmed by observing the correlation between the term spread and the residuals of the intrinsic bubble model (figure 9), which is surprisingly close in the Méxican case. The second most influential variable is domestic credit growth; the volatility of real asset returns and terms-of-trade shocks are of similar importance.

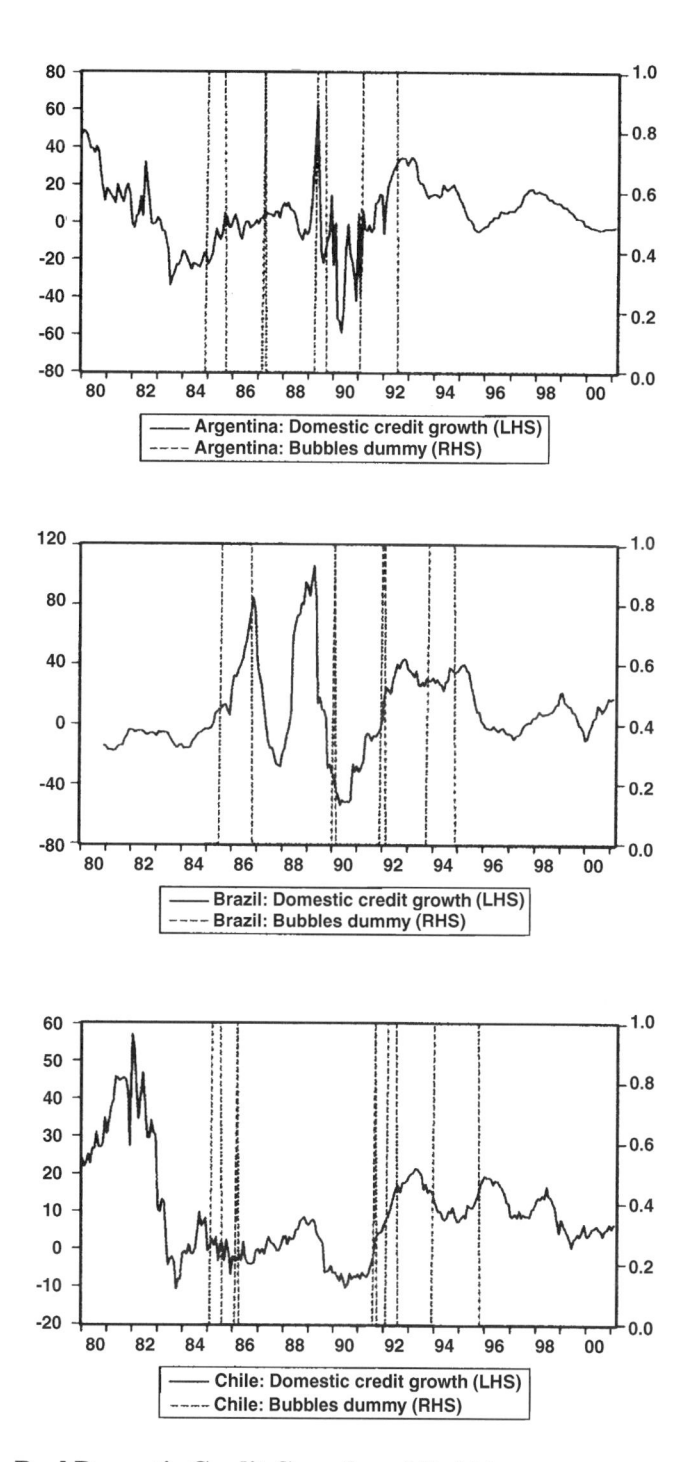

Figure 8: Real Domestic Credit Growth and Bubbles

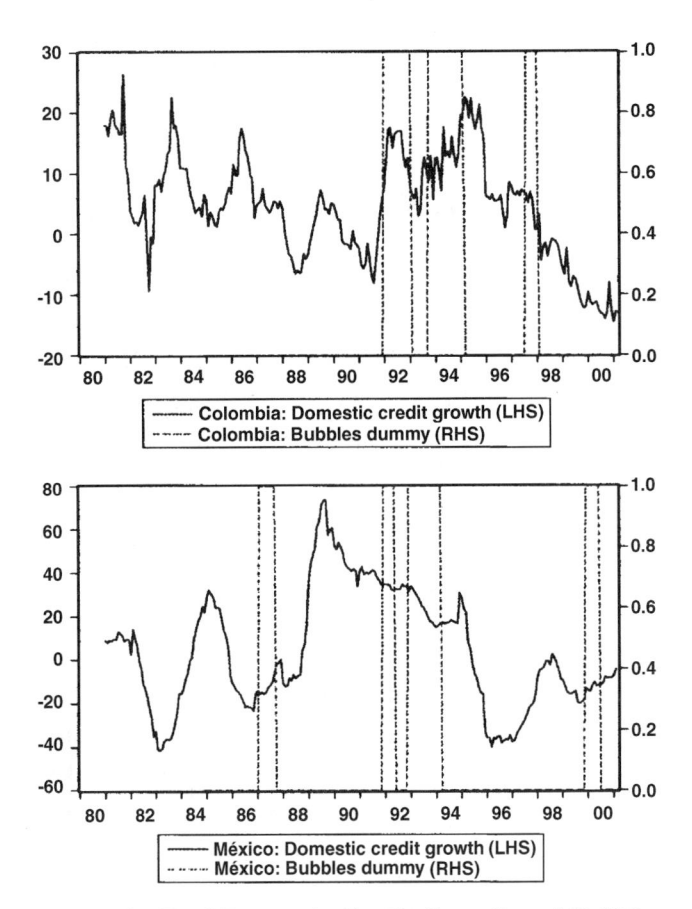

Figure 8 (*continued*): **Real Domestic Credit Growth and Bubbles**

4. Asset Prices, Economic Activity, and Growth

4.1 Stock Prices and Economic Activity: Consumption and Investment

In LAC countries, we find a clear direction of causality running from stock market returns to consumption and investment. There are several explanations for the causality between stock market returns and consumption. First, there exists the wealth effect, according to which agents' consumption decisions depend on wealth, which in turn is affected by stock price movements. However, given that stocks are not a widespread form of saving in LAC, this effect is unlikely to explain the observed statistical result. Second, stock prices might be signaling the future growth of the economy and, hence, the future growth of labor income (Ward, 1999), which will affect consumption. Third, as the perceived wealth of individuals changes positively, so does their creditworthiness, allowing agents to increase their indebtedness and/or to receive credit at a lower cost.

The observed causal relationship between investment and stock prices can be explained by Tobin's q theory. According to this theory, as stock prices change the

Variable	Coefficient	Std. Error	z-Statistic	Prob.
10-year and 3-month U.S. T-bill spread	1.481	0.176	8.407	0.000
Residual of U.S. intrinsic bubble	-0.282	0.135	-2.098	0.036
Deviations of equity real estate variable	0.637	0.151	4.217	0.000
Real domestic credit growth (-12)	-0.426	0.195	-2.184	0.029
Real domestic credit growth (-18)	0.530	0.143	3.696	0.000
Capital flows proxy	0.408	0.210	1.938	0.053
Terms of trade deviation	0.659	0.107	6.150	0.000
Domestic credit volatility*	0.367	0.227	1.614	0.107
Asset returns volatility**	0.600	0.301	1.996	0.046
Argentina dummy	-3.281	0.328	-10.006	0.000
Brazil dummy	-3.465	0.429	-8.085	0.000
Chile dummy	-1.395	0.275	-5.070	0.000
Colombia dummy	-1.079	0.226	-4.775	0.000
México dummy	-2.117	0.270	-7.843	0.000
Mean dependent var	0.189	S.D. dependent var		0.392
S.E. of regression	0.324	Akaike info criterion		0.706
Sum squared resid	84.322	Schwarz criterion		0.787
Log likelihood	-273.880	Hannan-Quinn criter.		0.737
Avg. log likelihood	-0.336			

Notes: All series were normalized.
*24-month moving window of a standard deviation of the differenced log of domestic credit in real terms.
** 24-month moving window of a standard deviation of the first difference of the log of the real global total return series.

Dependent Variable: Bubbles dummy
Method: Binary Logit

Table 4: Panel Data: Logit Results (Argentina, Brazil, Chile, Colombia, and México)

ratio between the market valuation of existing capital and the cost of new capital (Tobin's q) changes. As stock prices rise, the cost of new capital falls relative to that of existing capital, and firms acquire new capital (invest). Stock prices also convey information regarding the future growth of the economy and, therefore, affect investment. The balance sheet effect may also operate here. As asset prices change, firms' perceived creditworthiness changes, and hence their access to credit.

Quarterly stock price and investment data for the 1990s (figure 10) reveal a clear positive relationship. For a longer run view, we estimate a panel for five Latin American countries from 1980 to 1999 with SUR methods (table 5). The dependent variable is the ratio of gross domestic investment to GDP, while the explanatory variables are foreign direct investment (Borensztein, De Gregorio, and Lee, 1998), situations of state failure (from the Polity International database) as expressed in a dummy variable, government consumption expenditure, government capital

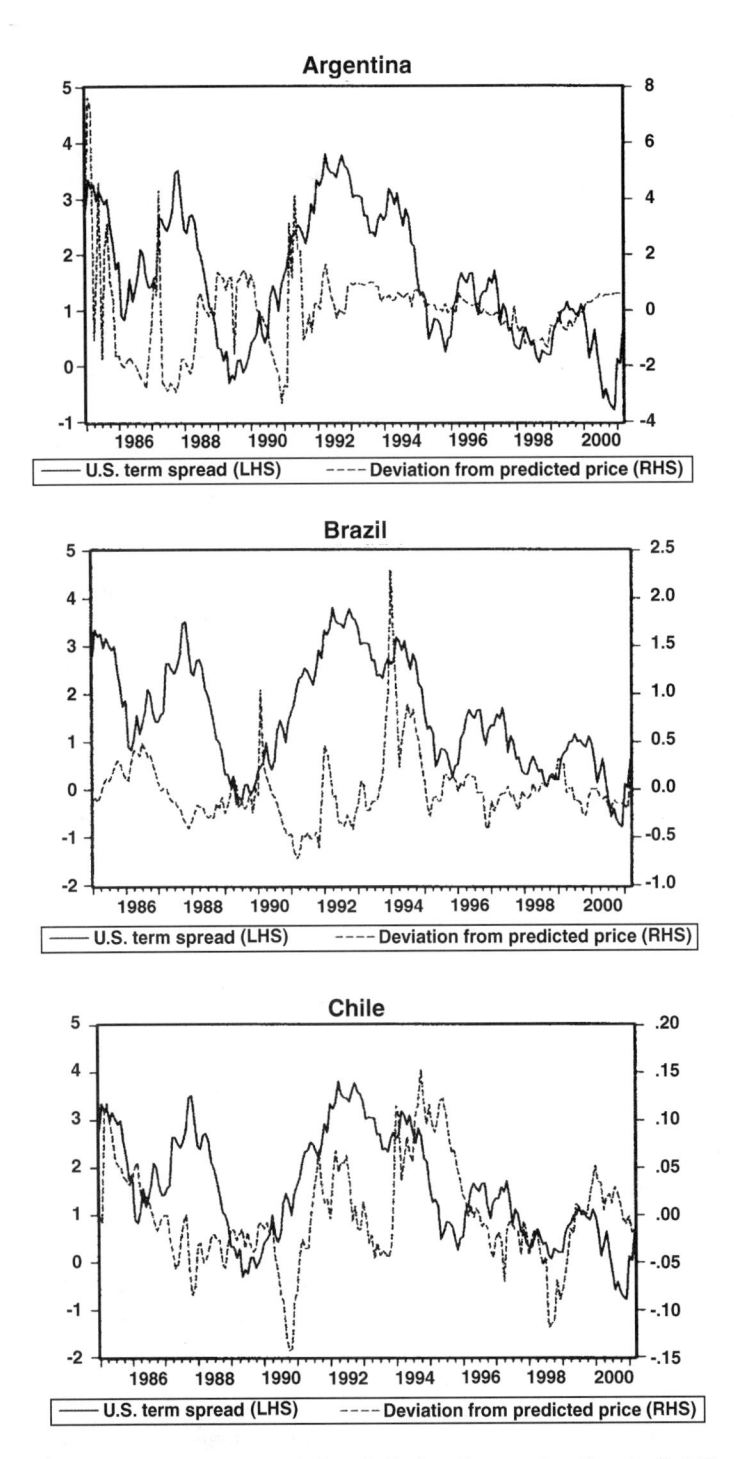

Figure 9: U.S. Term Spread and Stock Price Overvaluation in LAC

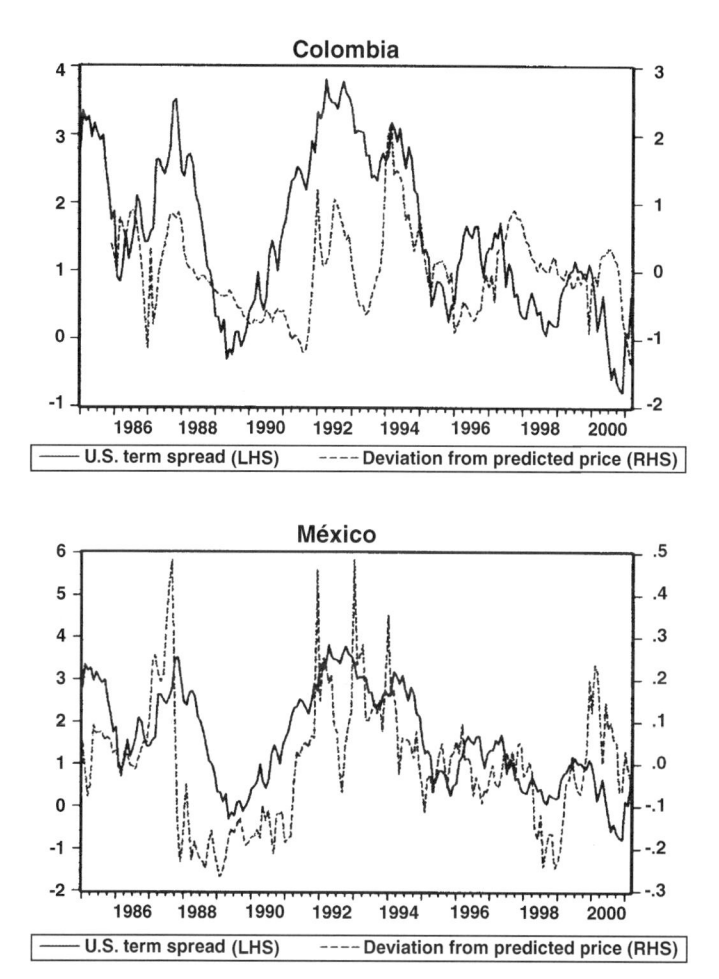

Tropical Bubbles: Asset Prices in Latin America, 1980–2001 149

Figure 9 (*continued*): **U.S. Term Spread and Stock Price Overvaluation in LAC**

expenditure, the log of stock prices, the volatility of stock returns, and lagged growth (Seven and Solimano, 1993; Cardoso, 1993).[38] All of the variables have the expected sign, with stock prices having a positive sign and the volatility variable having a negative one. Hence, while bubbles may have a positive effect through increases in stock markets, prices generally end up lower than before the bubble started. Other negative effects on investment are transmitted by the increased volatility effect. Additionally, the adverse effect of bubbles on the financial sector lasts for many years, negatively affecting growth, given the relationship between financial intermediation and growth (Beck, Levine, and Loayza, 2000).

In addition to these effects, a bubble episode may lead to overinvestment, which, combined with the effect on consumption, can lead to poor domestic saving. Together these two factors should produce larger current account deficits as asset prices tend to be overvalued. Some of our figures (appendix E) show this is likely to be true in the

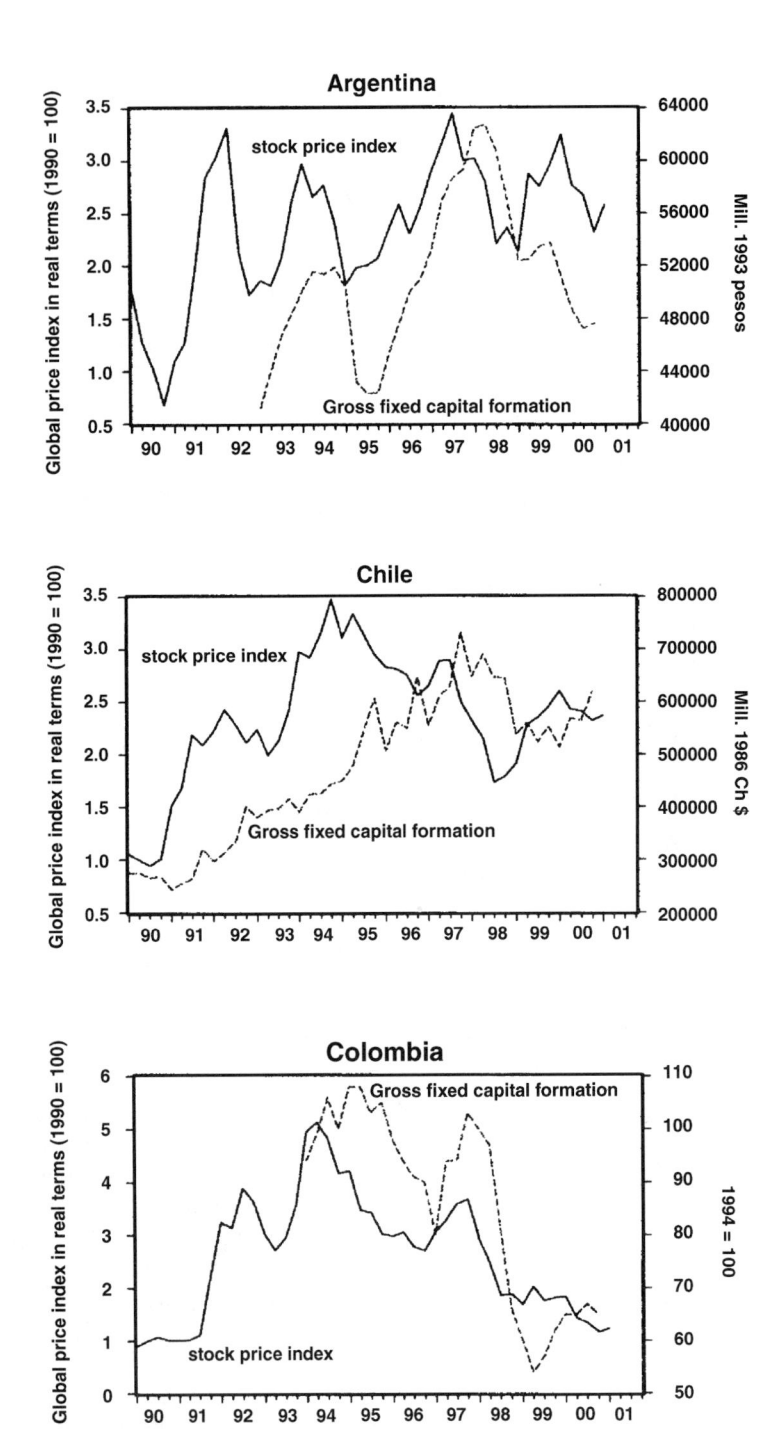

Figure 10: Stock Market Prices and Investment

México

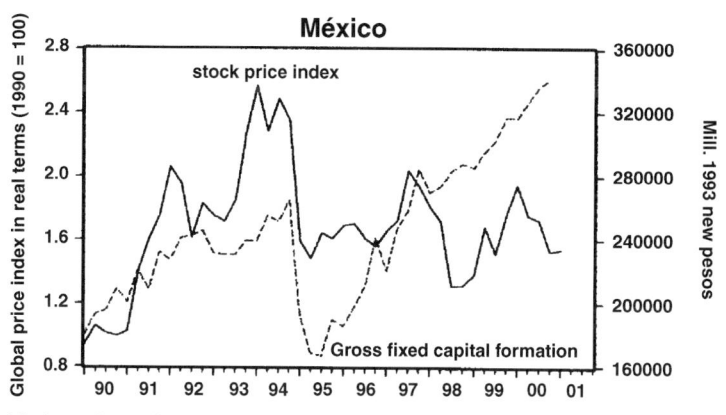

Figure 10 (continued): Stock Market Prices and Investment

United States and México. However, other Latin American countries do not show any discernible relationship, therefore, further work is required.

4.2 Housing Prices and Domestic Credit

Asset price changes affect economic activity through the balance sheets of agents that change their creditworthiness as asset prices change. More specifically, there exists a close relationship between housing prices and domestic credit growth in the three countries where we could get more complete series, namely Argentina, Colombia, and México (figure 11), and Chile in the late 1970s and early 1980s before the banking crisis.[39]

Variable	Coefficient	Std. Error	t-Statistic	Prob.
C	20.735	1.758	11.795	0.000
Foreign Direct Investment (% to GDP)	0.50	0.275	1.817	0.073
Government Consumption (% to GDP)	–0.099	0.034	–2.908	0.005
Public Capital Expenditures (% to GDP)	0.454	0.110	4.124	0.000
Log of Stock Market Price in real terms	0.923	0.361	2.559	0.012
Real Total Returns Volatility	–10.133	4.585	–2.210	0.030
GDP growth (–1)	0.364	0.155	2.348	0.021
STATEFAILAVG	–12.071	1.861	–6.487	0.000
R-squared	0.393			
Adjusted R-squared	0.341			

Notes: STATEFAILAVG = Average of "Episodes of State Failure" as defined by the State Polity 98 from the University of Maryland. It includes ethnic wars, revolutionary wars, abrupt or disruptive regime changes, and genocides/politicides.

Dependent Variable: Gross Domestic Investment (% to GDP)
Method: Seemingly Unrelated Regression, 1980–99
Number of cross sections used: Argentina, Brazil, Chile, Colombia, and México

Table 5: Panel Results: SUR Estimation

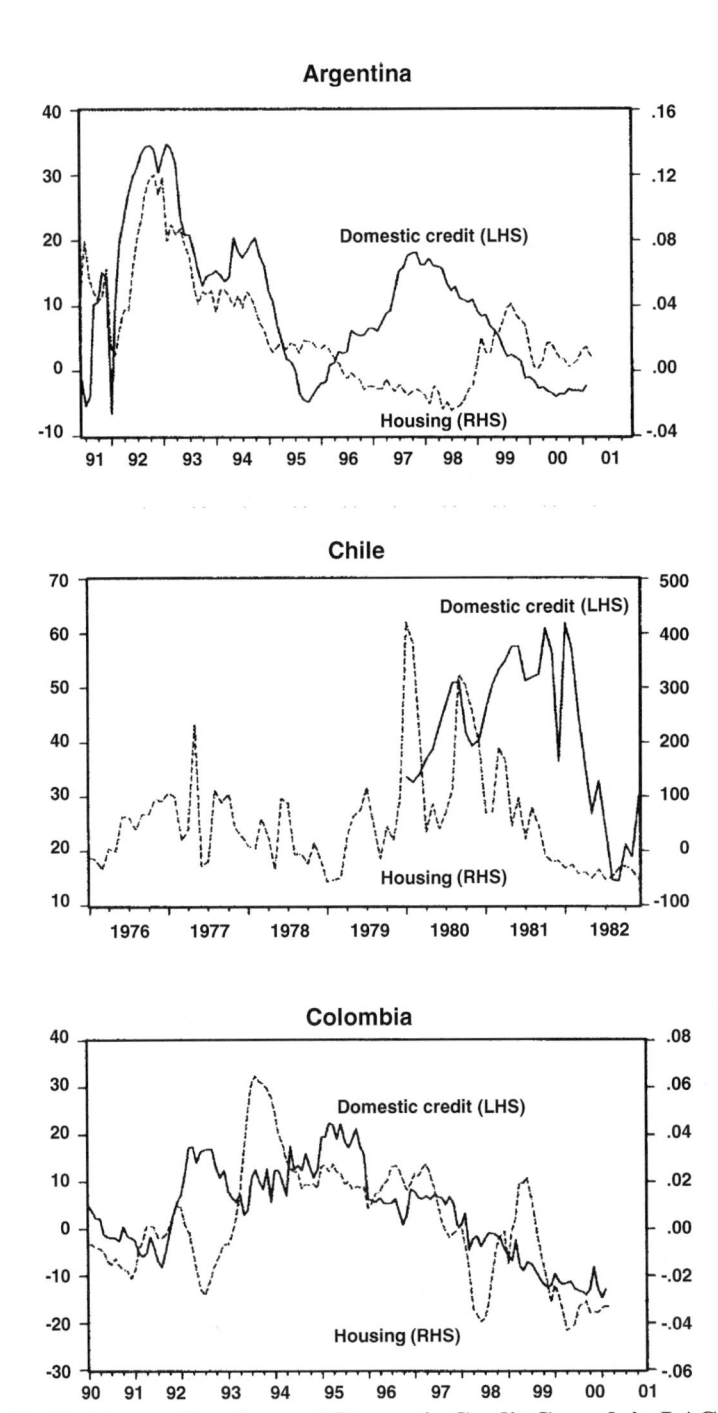

Figure 11: Return on Housing and Domestic Credit Growth in LAC

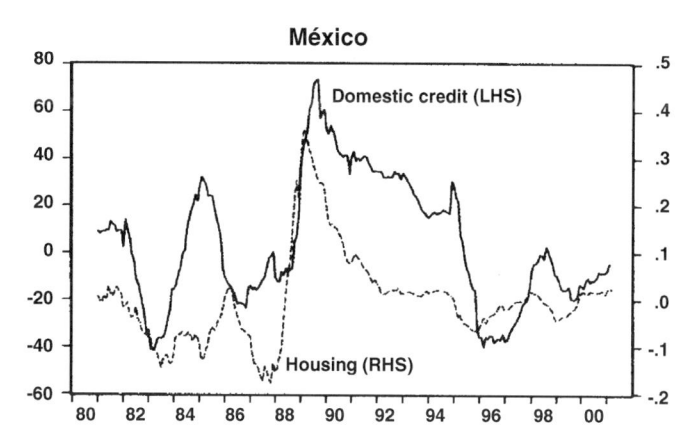

Figure 11 (*continued*): Return on Housing and Domestic Credit Growth in LAC

Granger causality between asset prices and domestic credit goes in both directions; however, when restricting the sample to the 1990s only, the causality is stronger (larger f-statistics) from housing prices to domestic credit (table F1 of appendix F). Regarding the relationship between stock prices and domestic credit, we found evidence of Granger casuality from the stock returns to domestic credit growth (table F2 of appendix F).[40]

Balance-sheet effects appear to operate as described by Bernanke, Gertler, and Gilchrist (1998). In their model, an agent's external finance is more expensive than internal financing, and the premium for external finance varies inversely with the net worth of potential borrowers. So, as asset prices fall—in this case, real estate prices—the net worth of borrowers falls, and banks are less willing to lend.

When asset prices rise, banks tend to lend more to the sectors affected by the bubble. The case of México is revealing. In this case, as real estate prices fell in the early 1980s, lending to the construction and housing sectors fell as a percentage of total bank lending. When real estate prices rose, the proportion of bank lending to these sectors doubled, reaching a peak in 1995, when real estate prices stopped growing and reversed the trend. In Colombia, a similar relationship between real estate prices and credit to housing and construction is observed.

When a crash occurs, nonperforming loans rise as borrowers become insolvent, and the ratio of nonperforming loans is greater in the housing sector. In Colombia, nonperforming loans jumped from 6 percent at the end of 1997 to 10 percent in 1999 and to 13 percent at the end of 2000.

Argentina did not have a banking crisis of the magnitude experienced by México or Colombia.[41] In this country, credit to the construction sector did not increase with the rise of real estate prices. On the contrary, it fell and a similar trend occurred in housing mortgage credit. In the first quarter of 1991, credit to the construction sector was 6.7 percent of total credit; by the second quarter of 1994 it had fallen to 4.0 percent. Once the Tequila crisis hit in late 1994, the nonperforming loans of this sector increased from 20 percent of total loans to the sector to 24 percent, which is much smaller than the Méxican case and slightly larger than in the Colombian case.

Another difference in banking practices between Argentina, on the one hand, and, Colombia and México on the other concerns the nonperforming loans coverage ratio.[42] While Argentina's banking sector coverage was 55 percent in December 1994, it quickly rose to 68 percent in 1996. In México, the coverage ratio was 49 percent in 1994, and it had risen to 55 percent by 1997. When the crisis began in 1998, Colombia had an extremely low 38 percent coverage ratio, which then increased to 46 percent by the end of 2000.

Finally, the Chilean case, as derived from the Conley-Maloney data on housing prices, shows that its bubble was accompanied by rising domestic credit. In this case, the credit explosion took place in 1976–79, prior to the rise in property prices.[43] However, a credit contraction followed the fall in real estate prices and a banking crisis in late 1981 followed the collapse in real estate prices. This is another example of the balance sheet effect. The bubble and the credit expansion occurred immediately before the banking crisis of the early 1980s.

4.3 Bubbles Have Long-Lasting Consequences on Poverty Issues

Evidence from México and Colombia (appendix G) shows that, after the bubble bursts and domestic credit contracts, the proportion of people who own the house in which they live falls. This phenomenon tends to be more acute in the poorest quintiles. In 1995 in Colombia, 68 percent of households fully owned the houses in which they lived; by 1999, following the crisis, this figure fell to 58 percent. In México, the same statistic fell from 72 percent to 66 percent between 1995 and 2000. If middle-class and poor people lose their main asset during crises, they become less creditworthy, since they lose their only source of collateral. The fact that this phenomenon more often affects middle- and lower-income families suggests increasing income distribution inequality and, through this channel, potential declines in long-run growth (Barro, 2000).

5. Policy Implications and Conclusions

Given the existence of bubbles in Latin America and their negative effect on the financial sector, on investment, on income distribution, and, hence, indirectly, through all these channels on long-run growth, the case for intervention to avoid bubbles is warranted. There are several problems, however, beginning with the identification of bubbles, or asset price misalignments. The main difficulty arises from equating a bubble with the expected future changes in fundamentals. Setting aside this discussion, however, is there anything authorities can do, based on our findings concerning bubble determinants?

First, there is little that policymakers in Latin America can do to influence the course of common external factors. Similarly, there is little that can be done about country-specific external factors such as capital flows and terms-of-trade shocks. While there is ample literature about insulating the economy from capital flows volatility, the evidence is mixed regarding its effectiveness and costs (Dooley, 1996; Montiel, 1999). Our results, though, show that there is room for improvement of stabilization funds and savings mechanisms that buffer recurrent terms-of-trade shocks.

Country-specific domestic factors are a different story. Given the difficulty of identifying the imminence of bubbles, authorities should permanently aim at smoothing the cyclical behavior of credit for the private sector. To achieve this end, several tools are available. First, policymakers can adopt the countercyclical provisioning of credit such that, during expansion phases, financial intermediaries create capital cushions, beyond the specific credit loss risks, to absorb potential losses during the crash. This generic provision would apply to all loans. Other types of restrictive policies to restrain the use of stocks and real estate as collateral during booms are available. Alternatively, by placing higher capital requirements for highly-leveraged customers, authorities can limit the potential for bubble generation and posterior damage. Credit growth ceilings, widely used in the past, may also prove to be helpful. Unfortunately, the problem with nearly all of these restrictive policies, with the exception of the generic countercyclical provision, lies in the difficulty of monitoring. Hence, they are subject to regulation arbitrage.

Another policy proposal concerns the fact that most developing countries have inefficient secondary markets for family housing units. The functioning of this imperfect market is impaired even more during crises, when negative shocks hit the economy, and banks are stuck with repossessed collateral, which they pretend to dump in the market to obtain liquidity. In response, analysts (Holmstrom and Tirole, 1998) have proposed restraints on the disposition of real estate by commercial banks to prevent prices from falling further during crisis situations. In this setting, both borrowers and banks are insured against price collapse and consumers pay higher prices for real estate, although insurance raises an ex-ante social surplus.

Rather than adopting these types of policies that "throw sand into the wheels," others propose the expansion of the number and variety of markets required to stabilize prices. For example, Shiller (1993) argues for the creation of "macro markets." These are international markets for long-term claims on the incomes of countries or different occupational groups or markets for highly fixed assets such as single-family homes. Recently developed, these complex securities are of very limited use. An example of one of the few cases where this has been applied is Bulgaria, which recently issued GDP warrants as part of the Brady renegotiation.

Along this line, real estate investment trusts (REITs), which are passive portfolio managers of real estate properties (Herring and Wachter, 1999), are an option to develop real estate markets and diversify risk. These agents, whose shares are publicly traded, act as mutual funds that hold property and generate income and tax-free capital gains for individual investors.[44]

A final option, puncturing a bubble, is very risky. Even "talking down" a bubble is a difficult task, however, as time goes by, authorities may be forced to intervene directly in this way. Recent experience in the United States shows that this policy intervention has costs. Another good example of the costs of bubble puncturing is the Brazilian episode of the *real* depreciation undertaken until July of 2001. The depreciating trend of the *real* (figure 12) took the currency to around 2.50 per dollar by the third week of June 2001. Because this movement was interpreted as being driven by a speculative bubble, the central bank abandoned its nonintervention (in the foreign exchange market) policy, in effect since 1999, and sold dollars to "irrigate" the

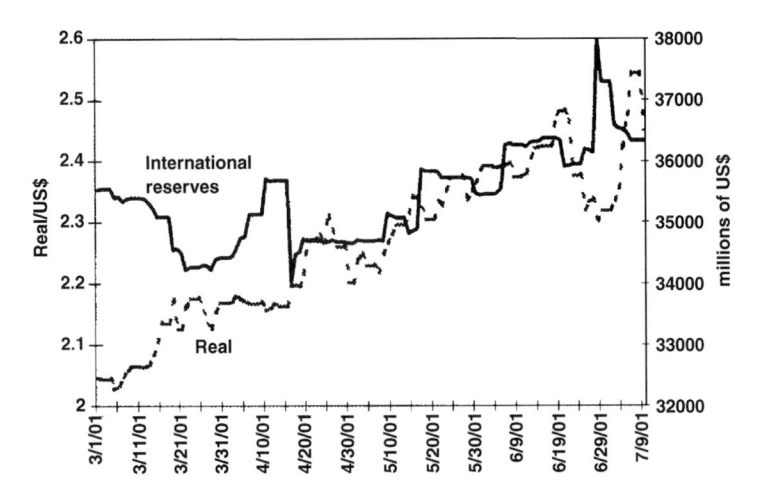

Figure 12: Brazil: Real, April–July 2001

market. Selic interest rates were simultaneously raised by 150 basis points. The market welcomed the "Fraga moves" and the *real* appreciated to 2.30 per dollar. Two weeks later, in the first week of July, the *real* had fallen back to 2.55 per dollar, and the central bank lost approximately US$2 billion of reserves that the IMF had disbursed in the last week of June (figure 12). Additionally, on June 27, the central bank sold a total of $4 billion *reales* (approximately US$1.7 billion) in one-year, dollar-indexed bonds to stabilize the currency. Summing up the entire episode, the central bank's net debt in foreign currency increased by US$4 billion, and the exchange rate was at about the same level as before the attempt to puncture the bubble. However, by year's end the *real* was about 2.32, implying that, after all, the central bank may have been right.

*Santiago Herrera is a staff member of the World Bank Group. Guillermo E. Perry is chief economist for the Latin America and the Caribbean region of the World Bank Group. The authors thank Conrado Garcia and Ana Maria Menendez for research assistance. Comments by Luis Serven, Bill Maloney, and Daniel Lederman are gratefully acknowledged.

Notes

1. A longer version of this paper is available in the World Bank Policy Research Working Papers Web site, Policy Research, working paper, No. 2724, November 2001, and the appendices cited in this paper are available from the authors upon request.

2. A full description of the variables used in this paper and their sources is presented in appendix A, which is available from the authors.

3. The tests for stationarity and structural change are those of Perron (1994). For the correlation between Brazil and México, the structural change is in 1991:11, while that for Argentina

and México is in 1991:06. The Argentina-Brazil break occurs at an earlier date—1985:06. The figure for the correlations in changes in stock market returns is similar to that reported here.

4. The data were extracted weekly from *El Mercurio*. The authors thank Bill Maloney for making the data available.

5. For the United States, we consider the return index of REITS as computed by the NAREIT. For Mexico, it is the year on year growth rate of the housing price index constructed by us.

6. $P_t^{PV} = \Sigma_{s=t} e_t^{-r(s-t+1)} E_t[D_s]$ is one solution to the equation $P_t = e^{-r} E_t[D_t + P_{t+1}]$. It is the particular solution attained after imposing a transversality condition.

7. The bubble term is generally described as $B_{t+1} = B_t(1 + r) + b_t$, where b_{t+1} is the innovation in the bubble at time $t + 1$ (Flood and Hodrick, 1990).

8. Campbell (2000) notes that this equation is derived from an identity, solved forward imposing the restriction of a transversality condition and taking expected values.

9. The rejection of the unit root hypothesis in both Argentina and México depends on whether the trend or the constant is included. In Argentina when a constant, but no trend, is included, the unit root cannot be rejected. This is simply noted to show the ambiguity of the results concerning the "no-bubble" hypothesis in these two countries.

10. Argentina's result is sensitive to the inclusion of a constant and a time trend in the regression of the null hypothesis.

11. See tables B2 to B5 in appendix B for detailed results.

12. The Johansen test (table 1) shows two cointegrating vectors for Argentina and Mexico. Given that the test is for cointegration between two variables, this problem is not present in the RALS test.

13. $P_t = e^{-r} E_t[D_t + P_{t+1}]$.

14. $P_t^{PV} = \Sigma_{s=t} e_t^{-r(s-t+1)} E_t[D_s]$.

15. $B_t = e^{-r} E_t[B_{t+1}]$.

16. Sellin (1998) also uses this assumption on the dividend process to obtain a simple solution for the present-value price.

17. Appendix C, table C1, shows coefficients for Latin American countries and the United States.

18. An important assumption is that dividends at time t are known before setting the price. Any "news" effect is captured immediately by the present-value price. However, because of timing issues, (distributed) dividends do not necessarily reflect all the news, and as a result we may identify as a bubble something that is simply the price responding to news that the dividend series did not incorporate. To examine the extent of this problem, we ran Granger causality tests between the (differenced) log prices and log dividends up to 12 lags, and only in Argentina did we find robust significant evidence of prices Granger-causing dividends. In the other four countries, we reject the hypothesis that prices contain useful information beyond that in current dividends. Froot and Obstfeld reject causality from prices to dividends in the case of the United States.

19. Their simplest model, where bubbles depend on fundamentals (dividends) only, is of this type: $B(D_t) = cD_t^\lambda$ where λ is the positive root of the dynamic system $\lambda^2\sigma^2/2 + \lambda\mu - r = 0$ and c is a constant. By adding the present value price and the bubble term we get $P(D_t) = P_t^{PV} + B(D_t) = kD_t + cD_t^\lambda$ which is a price with the bubble driven by fundamentals.

20. This is the model reported in Froot and Obtfeld's table 4, augmented with the negative root part as indicated in their footnote 28.

21. The residuals are the difference between the observed price and the predicted price. Since the predicted price already has a bubble component, this approximation underestimates the size of the bubble and might lead us to overlook a bubble episode when it actually existed. This residual can be considered as the innovation in the bubble.

22. The data come from Robert Shiller's book, *Irrational Exuberance*, and can be found on his Web page. He has dividend data until December 2000, and hence the model was estimated until that date.

23. Reinhart uses a cointegration approach to verify the equilibrium relationship between the price-to-earnings ratio and fundamentals for the period 1980–96. Departures from the predicted model are summarized in figure 1.

24. We quantified for the East Asian countries the degree of departure from the benchmark cases, and we did not obtain any significant departures after 1995. This is a strange result, given that we reject, as Sarno and Taylor do, the no-bubbles hypothesis. The only explanation seems to be that all the bubbles happened before 1995. Future versions of this paper will present this, together with the crashes in East Asian countries.

25. In the 1998 *World Economic Outlook*, the IMF computed deviations of actual prices from predicted stock prices and calculated the correlations between 1985 and 1999.

26. Appendix C presents the details.

27. The literature has generally ruled out the existence of negative bubbles, because they would imply negative stock prices (Diba and Grossman, 1988, Froot and Obstfeld, 1991). However, Allen and Gale (2000b) consider the case where stock prices fall below their fundamental values.

28. In the case of the United States, we consider deviations of the proxy from a Hodrick Prescott trend later in this paper.

29. Patel and Sankar worked in nominal figures, while we use real stock prices. The variable is regressed against its own lags, each time with a different dummy "threshold" variable. The threshold selected corresponds to the regression with a lower likelihood ratio or Akaike information criterion. See Appendix C for a detailed explanation and tables of the *CMAX* variables for each country.

30. In the United States, the threshold *CMAX* was 94 percent.

31. The crash duration refers to the time elapsing between the point when the threshold is surpassed and the moment the *CMAX* reaches a minimum.

32. This percentage increase is computed by comparing the prices at the beginning and end of the bubble. However, the price increase is larger if you consider the percentage change between the maximum price during the bubble and the beginning price. This happens because the maximum price is reached before the bubble ends.

33. Terms of trade were introduced in deviations from a Hodrick-Prescott trend.

34. As a proxy of stock overvaluation in the United States, we took the residuals from the intrinsic bubble model. As a proxy of real estate overvaluation, we considered deviations from a Hodrick-Prescott trend of the returns of equity REITs.

35. The spread between 10-year bonds and three-month bills contains information about future changes in interest rates (Campbell and Shiller, 1987; Mishkin, 1988) or future changes in economic activity (Estrella and Hardouvelis, 1991; Chen, 1991). On the use of stock market prices and a proxy for real estate simultaneously, several studies have found a negative correlation between stock returns and real estate returns in the United States (Ibbotson and Siegel, 1984; Hartzell, 1986; and Worzala and Vandell, 1993). For this reason, some analysts recommend real estate investment as a hedging instrument for stock investments (NAREIT, 2000). We did not include real interest rates as an explanatory variable, since they are used in the construction of the bubble indicator to estimate the present-value price (to calibrate the value of K).

36. We estimate both logit and probit models, and the results are almost identical (see appendix D). However, we present the logit exercise in the main text of this section, given the possibility that in some cases probit models do not produce consistent estimators with fixed-effects panel methods (Hsiao, 1997 and Green, 1999).

37. The model was estimated with instrumental variables to control for potential endogeneity of the domestic variables. Additionally, to avoid difficulties in the interpretation of the marginal probabilities, as well as to facilitate comparison across variables, we employed standardized variables (subtracting the mean and dividing by the standard deviation of the series) to circumvent the units problem. This does not alter the signs or significance of the results obtained with the raw data.

38. Seemingly unrelated regressions (SUR) estimate the panel. Appendix D shows that estimation with the original data does not alter the sign or significance of any of the results, and changes in the parameter values are relatively minor.

39. Conley and Maloney (1995) figure date series for housing prices and consumer loans, but do not link their behavior relative to each other; they also do not link these data to the banking crisis that followed. They see the behavior of these series as separate elements of the euphoria prevailing in Chile during the period.

40. The causality direction changes when other transformations are used (i.e., month-to-month growth rates instead of year-to-year).

41. World Bank staff estimates that the fiscal cost of the banking sector crisis in México amounted to about 19 percent of GDP, and IMF staff estimates Colombia's banking sector rescue costs to be around 8 percent of GDP, while there were no fiscal costs in Argentina.

42. The ratio of provisions for loan losses to nonperforming loans.

43. We were unable to find a uniform data series of credit for the nonfinancial private sector, and, therefore, we present only nonmanipulated series. However, all the available series show the credit explosion in 1975–79.

44. The National Association of REITS (NAREIT) Web site presents detailed descriptions of the types of trusts that exist.

References

Allen, Franklin, and Douglas Gale, 2000, "Bubbles and Crises," *The Economic Journal*, Vol. 110, January, pp. 236–255.

Andrews, D. W. K., and E. Zivot, 1992, "Further Evidence on the Great Crash, the Oil-Price Shock, and the Unit-Root Hypothesis," *Journal of Business & Economic Statistics*, Vol. 10, pp. 251–270.

Barro, R., 2000, "Inequality and Growth in a Panel of Countries," *Journal of Economic Growth*, Vol. 5, pp. 5–32.

Beck, T., R. Levine, and N. Loayza, 1999, "Finance and the Sources of Growth," World Bank, Policy Research, working paper, No. 2057.

Bernake, B., M. Gertler, and S. Gilchrist, 1998, "The Financial Accelerator in a Quantitative Business Cycle Framework," in *Handbook of Macroeconomics*, J. Taylor and M. Woodford, eds., Amsterdam: North Holland.

Bonds, S., and J. Cummins, 2000, "The Stock Market and Investment in the New Economy: Some Tangible and Intangible Fictions," Brookings Papers on Economic Activity, No.1, pp. 61–108.

Campbell, J. Y., 2000, "Asset Pricing at the Millennium," *The Journal of Finance*, Vol. 55, pp. 1515–1567.

Campbell, J. Y., A. W. Lo, and A. C. McKinlay, 1997, *The Econometrics of Financial Markets*. Princeton: Princeton University Press.

Campbell, J. Y., and R. J. Shiller, 1987, "Cointegration and Tests of Present Value Models," *The Journal of Political Economy*, Vol. 95, pp. 1062–1088.

Canova, F., and G. De Nicolo, 1995, "Stock Returns and Real Activity: A Structural Approach," *European Economic Review*, Vol. 39, pp. 981–1015.

Cardoso, E., 1993, "Macroeconomic Environment and Capital Formation," in *Striving for Growth after Adjustment: The Role of Capital Formation*, L. Serven and A. Solimano, eds., World Bank Regional and Sectoral Studies, Washington DC.

Chen, N., 1991, "Financial Investment Opportunities and the Macroeconomy," *The Journal of Finance*, Vol. 46, pp. 529–554.

Conley, J., and W. Maloney, 1995, "Optimal Sequencing of Credible Reforms with Uncertain Outcomes," *Journal of Development Economics*, Vol. 48, pp. 151–166.

Diba, B. T., and H. I. Grossman, 1988, "Explosive Rational Bubbles in Stock Prices?," *American Economic Review*, Vol. 98, pp. 746–754.

Dooley, M., 1995, "A Survey of Academic Literature on Controls over International Capital Transactions," National Bureau of Economic Research, working paper, No. 5352.

Estrella, A., and G. Hardouvelis, 1991, "The Term Structure as Predictor of Real Economic Activity," *The Journal of Finance*, Vol. 46, pp. 555–576.

Estrella, A., and F. Mishkin, 1997, "The Predictive Power of the Term Structure of Interest Rates in Europe and the United States: Implications for the European Central Bank," *European Economic Review*, Vol. 41, pp. 1375–1401.

Evans, G. W., 1991, "Pitfalls in Testing for Explosive Bubbles in Asset Prices," *American Economic Review*, Vol. 81, pp. 746–754.

Fama, E. F., 1990, "Term Structure Forecasts of Interest Rates, Inflation and Real Returns," *Journal of Monetary Economics*, Vol. 25, pp. 59–76.

Flood, R., and R. Hodrick, 1990, "On Testing for Speculative Bubbles," *Journal of Economic Perspectives*, Vol. 4, pp. 85–101.

Froot, K. A., and M. Obstfeld, 1991, "Intrinsic Bubbles: The Case of Stock Prices," *American Economic Review*, Vol. 81, pp. 1189–1214.

Green, W., 1994, *Econometric Analysis*, New York: Prentice Hall.

Guerra, A., 1997, "La Relevancia Macroeconomica de los Bienes Raices en Mexico," Banco de México, Research Department, working paper, No. 9707.

Hall, S. G., Z. Psaradakis, and M. Sola, 1999, "Detecting Periodically Collapsing Bubbles: A Markov-Switching Unit Root Test," *Journal of Applied Econometrics*, Vol. 14, pp. 143–154.

Hargis, K., and W. Maloney, 1997, "Emerging Equity Markets: Are They for Real?" *Journal of Financial Research*, Vol. 20, pp. 243–262.

Harvey, C., 1995, "Predictable Risk and Returns in Emerging Markets," *Review of Financial Studies*, Vol. 8, pp. 773–816.

Herrera, S., and C. Garcia, 1999, "User's Guide to an Early Warning System for Macroeconomic Vulnerability in Latin American Countries," Policy Research, working paper, No. 2233, World Bank.

Herring, R., and S. Wachter, 1999, "Real Estate Booms and Banking Busts: An International Perspective," processed, The Wharton School, University of Pennsylvania.

Holmstrom, B., and J. Tirole, 1998, "LAPM: A Liquidity-Based Asset Pricing Model," National Bureau of Economic Research, working paper, No. 6673.

Hsiao, C., 1996, "Logit and Probit Models," in *The Econometrics of Panel Data—A Handbook of the Theory with Applications*, L. Matyas and P. Sevestre, eds., Boston: Kluwer Academic Publishers.

Ibbotson, R., and L. Siegel, 1984, "Real Estate Returns: A Comparison with other Investments," *AREUEA Journal*, Vol. 12, pp. 219–241.

Kaminsky, G., S. Lizondo and C. Reinhart, 1997, "Leading Indicators of Currency Crises," The World Bank, Policy Research, working paper, No. 1856.

Mishkin, F., 1998, "The Information in the Term Structure: Some further Results." *Journal of Applied Econometrics*, Vol. 3, pp. 307–314.

Montiel, P., 1999, "Policy Responses to Volatile Capital Flows," paper presented at the World Bank-International Monetary Fund-World Trade Organization conference on Capital Flows, Financial Crises, and Policies.

National Association of Real Estate Investment Trusts, 2000, *Real Estate Performance*, special issue, available on the Internet at www.nareit.com/.

Patel, S., and A. Sarkar, 1998, "Stock Crises in Developed and Emerging Markets," Federal Reserve Bank of New York, research paper, No. 9809.

Pedroni, 1999, "Critical Values for Cointegration Tests in Heterogeneous Panels with Multiple Regressors," *Oxford Bulletin of Economics and Statistics*, No. 61.

Pesaran, M. H., Y. Shin, and R. J. Smith, 1999, "Bounds Testing Approaches to the Analysis of Long Run Relationships," processed, available on the Internet at www.econ.cam.ac.uk/faculty/pesaran/.

Reinhart, V. R., 1998, "Equity Prices and Monetary Policy in the United States," in *The Role of Asset Prices in the Formulation of Monetary Policy*, Bank of International Settlements, conference papers, Vol. 5.

Sarno, L., and M. P. Taylor, 1999, "Moral Hazard, Asset Price Bubbles, Capital Flows, and the East Asian Crisis: The First Tests," *Journal of International Money and Finance*, Vol. 18, pp. 637–657.

Sellin, Peter, 1998, "Asset Prices and Monetary Policy in Sweden," in *The Role of Asset Prices in the Formulation of Monetary Policy*, Bank of International Settlements, conference papers, Vol. 5.

Serven, S., and A. Solimano, 1993, "Economic Adjustment and Investment Performance in Developing Countries: The Experience of the 1980's," in *Striving for Growth after Adjustment: The Role of Capital Formation*, L. Serven and A. Solimano, eds., Washington, DC: World Bank Regional and Sectoral Studies.

Shiller, R., 2001, "Bubbles, Human Judgment and Expert Opinion," Yale University, Cowles Foundation, discussion papers, No. 1303.

_____, 2000, *Irrational Exuberance*, New York: Broadway Books.

_____, 1993, *Macro Markets: Creating Institutions for Managing Society's Largest Economic Risks*, Oxford: Oxford University Press.

Taylor, M. P., and D. A. Peel, 1998, "Periodically Collapsing Stock Price Bubbles: A Robust Test," *Economic Letters*, Vol. 61, pp. 221–228.

Vogelsang, T. J., 1998, "Additional Tests for a Unit Root Allowing for a Break in the Trend Function at an Unknown Time," *International Economic Review*, Vol. 39, pp. 1073–1100.

Vogelsang, T. J., and P. Perron, 1992, "Nonstationarity and Level Shifts with an Application to Purchasing Power Parity," *Journal of Business & Economic Statistics*, Vol. 10, pp. 301–321.

Worzala E., and K. Vandel, 1993, "International Direct Real Estate Investments as Alternative Portfolio Assets for Institutional Investors: An Evaluation," paper presented at the AREUEA meeting.

Chapter 10
Different Countries, Similar Experience

Takeo Hoshi*
University of California, San Diego

I have enjoyed reading the four papers that examine the experiences with asset price bubbles in the United States, Japan and other Asian economies, and Latin American countries. Each paper deals with an experience from a different part of the world, but when we read all four papers at the same time, we find that all of them make similar findings. In this sense, each paper reinforces the results of the other papers. The four papers collectively reach a very convincing conclusion on the impact of bubbles on the economy and the implications for monetary and regulatory policies. In these comments, I summarize the major findings of these papers and discuss their policy implications.

First, bubbles are everywhere. The papers find bubbles in the United States at several points in the 20th century, in Japan in the late 1980s, in other Asian economies in the early 1990s, and in many Latin American countries in the 1990s. No country seems immune from asset price bubbles.

Second, the papers find a strong correlation between rapid credit growth, especially bank credit, and the emergence of bubbles. The relation was especially clear in many Asian economies, including Japan, and the Latin American countries.

Third, when a bubble crashes, the economy often suffers tremendously. The Herrera–Perry paper finds that in Latin American countries, stock market crashes were associated with low investment. Also, in the other economies a crash often led to financial instability and recession. The Great Depression in the United States, the Asian financial crisis in the late 1990s, and the Japanese economy in the last decade are all clear examples of such devastating effects of crashes.

In some cases, however, crashes did not cause financial or real crises. The Mishkin–White paper finds several episodes in the United States where a crash did not lead to financial instability. The Collyns–Senhadji paper points out that Singapore and Hong Kong successfully avoided the Asian financial crisis even though they experienced asset price bubbles in the 1990s.

An obvious question is, "Why the difference?" Why can one economy sometimes escape from seriously negative impacts of crashes, while another does not? Mishkin and

White provide a clear answer. They argue that the key differences are the policy response of the central bank after the crash and the health of the financial system before the crash.

For example, Mishkin and White find the liquidity provision by the Federal Reserve was crucial in maintaining the financial stability after the crash of 1987 in the United States. Okina and Shiratsuka make a similar argument. The Bank of Japan provided ample liquidity following the crisis of November 1997. During the financial disruption after a crash, the "boundary between monetary and prudential policies becomes ambiguous," Okina and Shiratsuka argue.

Finally, the four papers identify a robust financial system as a key difference between a costly crash and a less costly crash. The crash of bubbles in technology stocks in the United States did not lead to financial instability because the U.S. financial system was healthy. An interesting case is Malaysia, which was influenced by the Asian financial crisis, but didn't feel the effects as much as Thailand, Indonesia, or Korea did because Malaysian financial institutions were relatively better capitalized, according to Collyns and Senhadji.

What do these findings imply for monetary and regulatory policies? If a crash is often costly, as the four papers found, policymakers may want to prevent asset price bubbles from starting at all, or stop bubbles if they have started, or do something when bubbles burst. The papers' findings are useful in examining what policymakers can do and should do about bubbles.

Can policymakers do something to prevent a bubble from starting? The papers find a strong correlation between rapid credit growth and a bubble. Hence, policymakers may want to contain a rapid credit growth. Collyns and Senhadji report some success of such policies in Singapore and Hong Kong. As Herrera and Perry argue, however, such restrictive policies are difficult to monitor. The fact that we observe bubbles everywhere seems to suggest it is extremely difficult to eliminate bubbles entirely.

If it is difficult to prevent bubbles, how about stopping a bubble when it is under way? The problem here is in identification. How can policymakers tell it is a bubble and not an adjustment to a new fundamental? As Okina and Shiratsuka stress, it is very difficult to identify a bubble when we are in the middle of one. Even worse, policymakers' attempts to stop a bubble may backfire, as Herrera and Perry argue using the Brazilian episode.

Finally, can policymakers do something after a crash? Here, the central bank can definitely help by supplying ample liquidity to stabilize the financial system. The experience of the Bank of Japan in 1997–98 suggests, however, that providing emergency liquidity may not be sufficient to restore the financial system.

In the end, it comes down to the health of the financial system. Bubbles may not be preventable or stoppable once they have started, but a robust financial system can reduce the cost of a crash. All four papers point to the importance of regulatory policy in creating and sustaining a robust financial system. This seems to be the most important policy implication noted in all of the papers.

---

*Takeo Hoshi is a professor of economics at the Graduate School of International Relations and Pacific Studies at the University of California, San Diego.

Chapter 11
Comments on Recent Experiences with Asset Price Bubbles

Ignazio Visco*
Organization for Economic Cooperation and Development

The papers before us examine a number of asset price bubbles, or in some cases booms, following Kindleberger's well-known distinction. Particularly interesting is the breadth of the experiences described here, involving various assets (equities, real estate, land, currencies) in rather different countries (from advanced Organization for Economic Cooperation and Development [OECD] countries to emerging economies to less developed countries [LDCs]). As a result, I shall concentrate my discussion on some possible common themes between these varied experiences. More specifically, I shall concentrate on the identification of bubbles and the role of policy in bubble episodes.

1. On the Identification of a Bubble

In order to identify a bubble, we first need to define what constitutes one. A well known definition is the one proposed by Kindleberger (1987): A bubble is "a sharp rise in price of an asset or a range of assets in a continuous process, with the initial rise generating expectations of further rises and attracting new buyers—generally speculators—interested in profits from trading in the asset rather than its use or earning capacity." This definition implies that, in a bubble, the price of the asset deviates from its "fundamental value," and that a reversal of expectations and a sharp decline in prices (a crash) would usually occur.

Most authors have here concentrated on this misalignment from fundamentals (the "euphoria" of Okina and Shiratsuka). However, bubbles may be rational to the extent that changes in asset prices may be self-fulfilling, or, to put it differently, that "sunspots" may be continuously incorporated in market expectations. In such cases one might argue, perhaps, not only that a bubble is indeed very difficult to identify but also that there is little that traditional policy can do to prevent a bubble. The issue then becomes a different one: how to organize institutions and market conditions (the rules of the game) so that possible sharp movements in asset prices would cause as little damage as possible to the economy.

If a bubble reflects growing misalignments from fundamental values, the difficulty in identifying it coincides with that of ascertaining "permanent" changes (or lack thereof) in the fundamental determinants. Even if there might at times be some definite views on the possibility of such changes, it generally takes time before these views find empirical confirmation. On the other hand, as Mishkin and White observe, identifying a stock market crash is easy: "When you see it, you know it." This explains perhaps why there is more consensus on a role for policy in the aftermath of a crash. Indeed, it is more difficult to "see" and "recognize" a bubble than a crash, even *ex post*.

With that in mind, I find it interesting that most papers "assume" that particular episodes were bubbles. The only exception is the paper by Herrera and Perry, who actually look at the evolution of fundamentals and test (*ex post*) for the existence of a stable relationship between this evolution and changes in asset prices. I believe this is a promising route, even if not always a conclusive one. It is definitely worth looking at the fundamentals. Unfortunately, however, bubbles are identified from the fact that a crash has occurred, even if not all crashes are the result of the burst of a bubble. In that context, it is clear that simple data observation is insufficient to spot a bubble. It is, however a necessary starting point. I thus invite you to a visual exercise, a look at three types of assets (figure 1).

If not bubbles, the prices of some of these assets certainly look like they have sharply deviated at times from some sort of historical averages. An important question to ask is whether these deviations are justified by observed changes in fundamentals. Going one step further, one could then consider the evolution of more complex entities, such as price–earnings (P/E) ratios (figure 2). We may then observe, for instance, that many, but not all, the crashes identified by Mishkin and White are also visible here, and perhaps some other episodes (such as the sharp pick-up most recently observed) should be also considered.

Indeed, P/E ratios are often used to assess deviations from fundamentals. Changes in (expected) earnings can justify price movements, as P/Es are affected by changes in discount factors, opportunity costs, and risk premiums. Practitioners and policymakers, including those at the OECD, devote much time to the discussion of these issues. Indeed, at the OECD we have had long discussions, using calculations based on the discounted dividend model or Gordon formulae; this is similar to the more sophisticated econometric analysis and tests conducted by Shiller, Campbell, and others, including Herrera and Perry in their paper.[1] On the basis of these calculations, already in early 1998, the OECD had warned of the risk of substantial deviation of U.S. equity prices from some historical norms, and the implicit anticipated return to those norms (see, for a published analysis, OECD, 1998). This analysis was repeated in 1999 and 2000, in the context of discussions within the OECD Economic Policy Committee and Working Party 3, where we reflected on the reasons for possible permanent deviations from historical norms (see, for example, OECD, 2000, p. 29).

Even acknowledging that something new might have occurred in the United States and in some other economy, the high-tech stocks synthesized in the NASDAQ index undoubtedly looked substantially overvalued. This was also evident in a visual inspection (figure 3). The conclusion was that, unless we were prepared to accept that

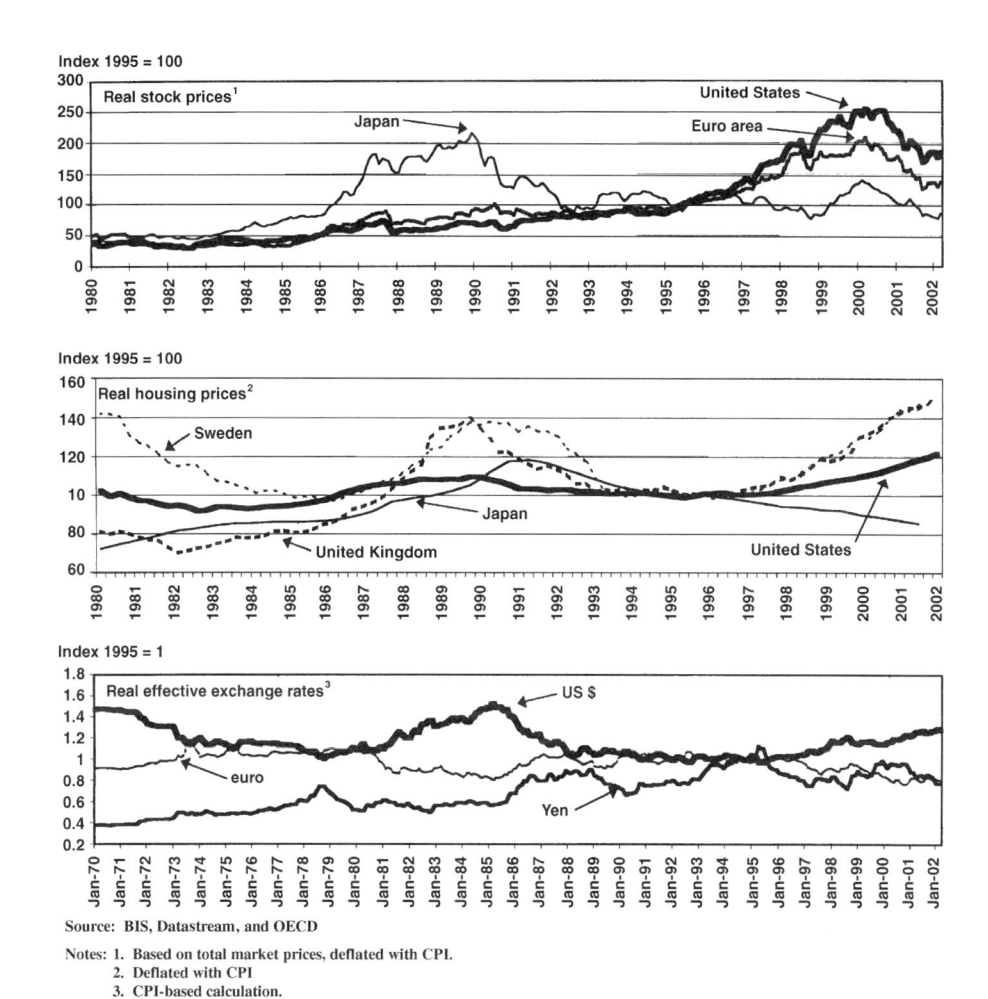

Comments on Recent Experiences with Asset Price Bubbles 167

Figure 1: Real Asset Price

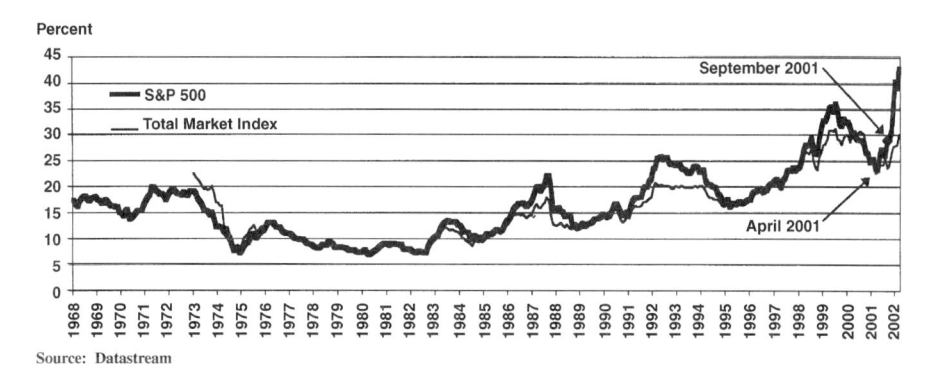

Figure 2: Price Earnings Ratios in the United States

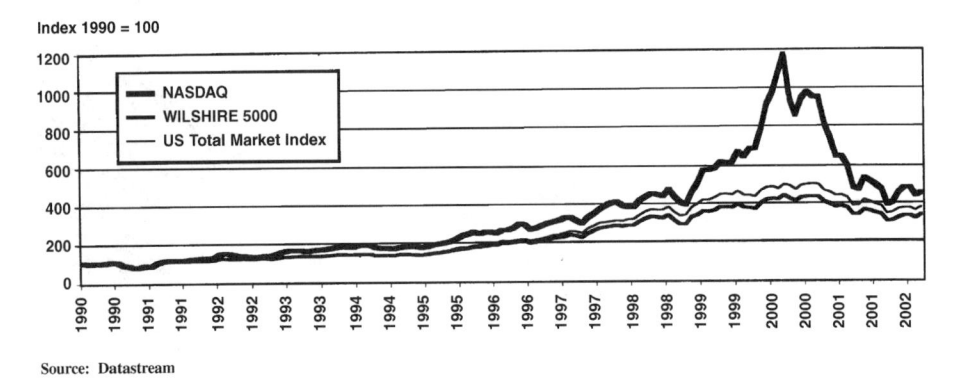

Figure 3: Stock Prices in the United States

the risk premium had fallen permanently and drastically below the historical average or that the growth in earnings would turn out to be much higher than the (already substantially upwardly revised) potential rate of growth of the U.S. economy, stocks were indeed at a risk of a substantial correction. Neither of those assumptions was widely shared, and the main question was then when, not if, the correction would take place. This leads to a further question: Are stocks still overvalued? The adjustment in overall stock prices has been substantial since mid 2000, but doubts still remain as to whether it has been completed, especially relative to actual and prospective earnings.[2] In sum, a bubble might be difficult to identify, but an informed discussion (one that relates to fundamental values) can and should certainly take place *ex ante*. And perhaps some consensus might emerge (even *ex ante*). I would venture to suggest, for instance, this being the case for Japan stock and land prices in the 1980s, the NASDAQ in the late 1990s, and real estate prices in London at present.

2. On the Role of Policy

This brings us to the discussion on the role of policy. One can derive from the papers before us a number of ideas worth sharing:

It may be justified to intervene to counter systemic problems linked to financial instability induced by sharp corrections of asset price bubbles. This is the role (often as "lender of last resort") performed by the Federal Reserve Bank of New York in 1929, but not followed by the Fed in subsequent years. As observed by Mishkin and White, however, this role is not confined to risks related to bubble-bursting, as attested by the examples of Penn Central in 1970 and Long-Term Credit Management (LTCM) in 1998.

To reduce the consequences and the number of crashes, effective regulatory frameworks, and good financial structures, including healthy balance sheets, are fundamental. This was not the case, as exemplified in the papers by Collyns and Sehadji and by Herrera and Perry, in East Asia or in most of Latin America in past crises. It was not the case either in Nordic countries in the 1980s. The problem with this uncontroversial prescription is that it is not obvious to implement. In order for efficient prudential oversight to exist, one needs internal/external surveillance, effective transparency and disclosure rules, and good corporate governance, among other things. In sum, one needs resilient institutions.

A bubble is dangerous to prick, since there is a risk of creating further financial instability. Indeed, being in Chicago, how can we deny that markets know better than governments? Still, one should not ignore that different perspectives may exist, as market participants may have more limited life spans and as horizons and discount factors may differ. So there may be a role for governments, after all, in coordinating expectations when these are heterogeneous or when market failures occur (after all, not only governments fail). In that context, I agree with the consideration that there are circumstances when some action to prevent the worst consequences of a bubble should not be *a priori* excluded. This may be justified in order to avoid relatively rare, but possibly very damaging, consequences. Financial instability can negatively impact on overall objectives, such as price stability and the proper allocation of economic resources. If we act in the aftermath of a crash, we may make this aftermath less sharp. The question concerning government intervention is then: when, how, and with which policy instruments? But this, fortunately, will be discussed in other sessions.

At this stage, I would just observe that a verdict on proposals such as those advanced by Blanchard (2000) and Cecchetti et al. (2000) and more generally on Taylor "augmented" policy rules (for example allowing for extreme deviations of P/Es from historical or other norms) is still open. The role of asset price movements in monetary policymaking is not obvious, as their deviations from possible "equilibrium" levels are certainly not as cyclical as, say, those of output gaps. But at times bubbles and their bursting may end up in substantial fluctuations with obvious effects on prices and output, the variables that should be targeted. Careful consideration of asset price developments is therefore relevant, even if we still need to understand more on the way they impact on the economy. So, perhaps, Mishkin and White conclude a bit unfairly on the Cecchetti et al. Center for Economic Policy Research–International Center for Monetary and Banking Studies (CEPR–ICMB) report, which is probably more cautious and less naïve than they suggest. In that regard, a comparison between Japan in the 1980s and the United States in the 1990s is interesting (figure 4).

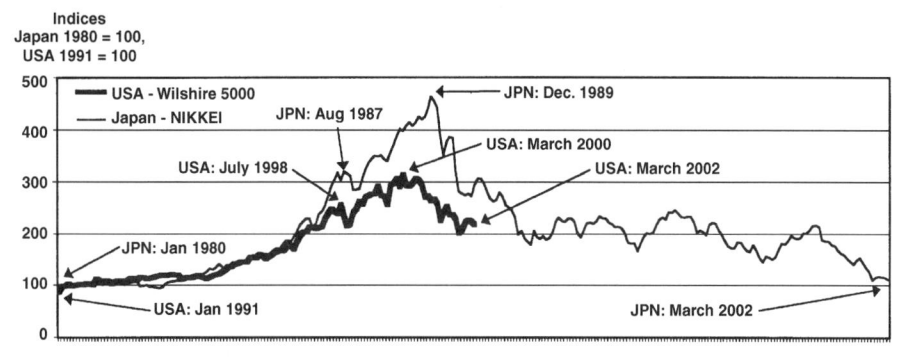

Figure 4: Real Stock Prices—Superimposed

Graphically the cases seem similar, but underlying conditions are different. On fundamentals, although there was a long discussion at the time of a possible permanent change in Japan's productivity growth, in reality it did not happen. In the United States, the rise in tech stocks may have been exaggerated, but some "new economy" is still quite visible in productivity results. Indeed, the productivity gains have passed the recession test, or so it seems. But even more interesting are differences in monetary policy. Japan's monetary policy was perhaps behind the curve and the crash was followed by stagnation—the causes are well described by Okina and Shiratsuka. Perhaps something could have been done, even if made difficult by exchange rate constraints and lack of effective central bank independence. Instead, rates were kept too low for too long during much of the bubble, and then were raised and kept high exactly when the bubble burst.

In the United States, after the LTCM episode in 1998, the Fed lowered rates from 5.50 percent to 4.75 percent, while claiming that it was not looking at the stock market. One could not say, however, that monetary policy was "easy" even in 1998. Furthermore, rates were raised subsequently, while the bubble continued to inflate. One may ask why. Forward-looking anti-inflation behavior? Many would have preferred, looking at the stock market and possible consequences of a sharp adjustment, for this tightening to have taken place even earlier. In any case, the federal funds rate reached 6.50 percent in spring 2000. While not targeting the stock market, the demand effects and possible inflationary consequences of what many considered to be at the time excessive equity price levels, even in the presence of a "new economy" rise in productivity growth, might have played a role. And the bursting of the tech stocks bubble has been accompanied by a substantial easing of monetary conditions.

What can we conclude from this? On one side, with the correction in the stock market, the real economy has also slowed down considerably. But the downturn has been very limited and shallow, and the acceleration in productivity seems to be real. The mildness of the adjustment might then be related to the good health of balance sheets, as Mishkin and White seem to claim. Perhaps the verdict is still open, however. Indeed, as shown in figure 2, the stock market correction might not yet have run its full course. Corporate and especially household indebtedness are also far from negligible. In any case, the issue at hand is whether and how the Fed reacted to the NASDAQ bubble. Of course, asset prices were not directly targeted. But central banks look at everything and, when all said and done, the notion that central banking is as much art as science is ever more true.

*Ignazio Visco is head of the Economics Department and chief economist for the Organization for Economic Cooperation and Development.

Notes

1. See, for the discounted dividend model and derivations, Gordon (1962). On econometric tests of stock market bubbles, I refer to the discussion in the paper by Herrera and Perry.

2. Indeed at 1.5 percent the implicit risk premium in the first quarter of 2002 (given a return to equity holders of 2.4 percent, inclusive of the yield from net repurchases, a potential growth rate of 3.1 percent and a real rate of interest of 4 percent) is half the 1986–93 average and two-thirds the 1994–2001 average.

References

Blanchard, O. J., 2000, "Bubbles, Liquidity Traps, and Monetary Policy: Comments on Jinushi et al. and on Bernanke," *Japan's Financial Crisis and its Parallels to the U.S. Experience*, Washington DC: Institute for International Economics.

Cecchetti, S., H. Genberg, J. Lipsky, and S. Whadwani, 2000, *Asset Prices and Central Bank Policy*, report on the World Economy 2, Geneva: CEPR and ICMB.

Gordon M., 1962, *Investment, Financing and Valuation of the Corporation*, Homewood, IL: Irwin.

Kindleberger, C. P., 1987, "Bubbles," in *The New Palgrave: A Dictionary of Economics*, J. Eatwell, M. Milgate, and P. Newman, eds., London: MacMillan.

Organization for Economic Cooperation and Development, 2000, *OECD Economic Outlook*, Paris, No. 68, December.

_____, 1998, "Recent Equity Market Developments and Implications," *OECD Economic Outlook*, Paris, No. 64, December, Chapter 5.

PART III

THEORY AND HISTORY OF ASSET PRICE BUBBLES

Chapter 12
Stocks as Money: Convenience Yield and the Tech-Stock Bubble

John H. Cochrane
University of Chicago

1. Introduction

What caused the rise and fall of tech stocks in the late 1990s? I suggest that a mechanism much like the transactions demand for money drove many stock prices above the "fundamental value" they would have had in a frictionless market.

During the boom, there was an intense demand for short-term trading in tech stocks. As a result of market frictions, such trading requires shares of the stock—if no shares are outstanding, there's no way to bet one way or the other on the future of a company. Few shares were available for trading, so the available shares gave a convenience yield: People were willing to hold them for a little while for short-term trading, even though they knew that the shares were overvalued as a long-term investment, just as people will briefly hold money even though it depreciates rapidly in a hyperinflation.

As Ofek and Richardson (2001) document, tech stocks fell when many more shares became available due to a combination of initial public offerings (IPOs), expiration of lock-up periods, and increasing ability to sell short, while at the same time the speculative demand for shares mirrored in share volume declined dramatically. As increasing money supply and declining transactions demand led to lower interest rates—money less overpriced relative to bonds—these events sharply reduced the convenience yield of shares.

This paper simply documents the analogy between tech stocks and conventional money demand. I start with a microcosm, the 3Com/Palm event, and then I extend the lessons of that microcosm to the NASDAQ/tech-stock experience as a whole. I verify that the elements of a trading-related convenience yield are there in each case, in particular that high prices are associated with high volume and low share supply. I conclude with a review of various theories. The key point is that in the tech-stock boom and bust, as in the famous historical "bubbles," high prices come along with a trading frenzy. None of the alternative theories says anything about this linkage—they can predict high prices just as easily with no volume. The convenience yield inextricably links the rise and decline of prices with the rise and decline of trading.

This paper is an interpretive review. Most of the empirical work is either taken directly from or closely inspired by the work of Lamont and Thaler (2001) and Ofek and Richardson (2001, 2002). My interpretation of the evidence is quite different.

2. 3Com, Palm, and Convenience Yield

3Com and Palm

On March 2, 2000, 3Com sold 5 percent of its shares of Palm in an initial public offering. It retained 95 percent of the shares, and announced that it would give those shares to 3Com shareholders by the end of the year. Each 3Com share would get approximately one and a half shares of Palm. (Most of the data and facts about this event come from Lamont and Thaler, 2001.)

There were two ways to end up with a share of Palm at the end of 2000: You could buy one share of Palm directly, or you could buy 1/1.5 shares of 3Com. At the end of trading on March 2, a share of Palm bought directly cost $95.06. 3Com closed at $81.81, so a share of Palm bought by buying 3Com cost $81.81/1.5 = $54.54—a much lower price for an apparently identical security, and you get the rest of 3Com for free.

Figure 1 plots daily data on the price of Palm stock and 1/1.5 times the price of 3Com stock. As figure 1 shows, through mid May it was cheaper to buy Palm "implicitly" by buying 3Com than it was to buy it directly. The prices in figure 1 imply that the *rest* of 3Com (the "stub") was valued by the market at a *negative* amount—minus $22 billion at the end of the day on March 2. (The sharp drop in 3Com in late July, shown in figure 1, comes on the day that it spun off its remaining Palm shares. The market apparently had no problems adding and subtracting on that day!)

This event seems a clear violation of the law of one price. 3Com should always be worth *at least as much* as its holdings of Palm.

This event is an interesting microcosm in which to start thinking about the stock market events of the end of the decade. The value of Palm embedded in 3Com is an easily-measured lower bound on the "fundamental value," so this event allows us pretty cleanly to look at a case of a security (Palm) whose price was above such a "fundamental value." Then, we can see to what extent the same lessons might apply to other stocks, and the tech or the NASDAQ index, for which "fundamental value" measures are much harder to estimate.

Similar Events, Obvious Objections

The 3Com/Palm event was not isolated. Lamont and Thaler document six additional carve-outs with negative stub values in the 1996–2000 period. Mitchell, Pulvino, and Stafford (2002) find 82 cases in a longer sample in which the implied value of a parent company is less than the value of its holdings of a publicly traded subsidiary. More generally, there have been many puzzling circumstances in which a rapid rise in the

Palm and 3Com/1.5

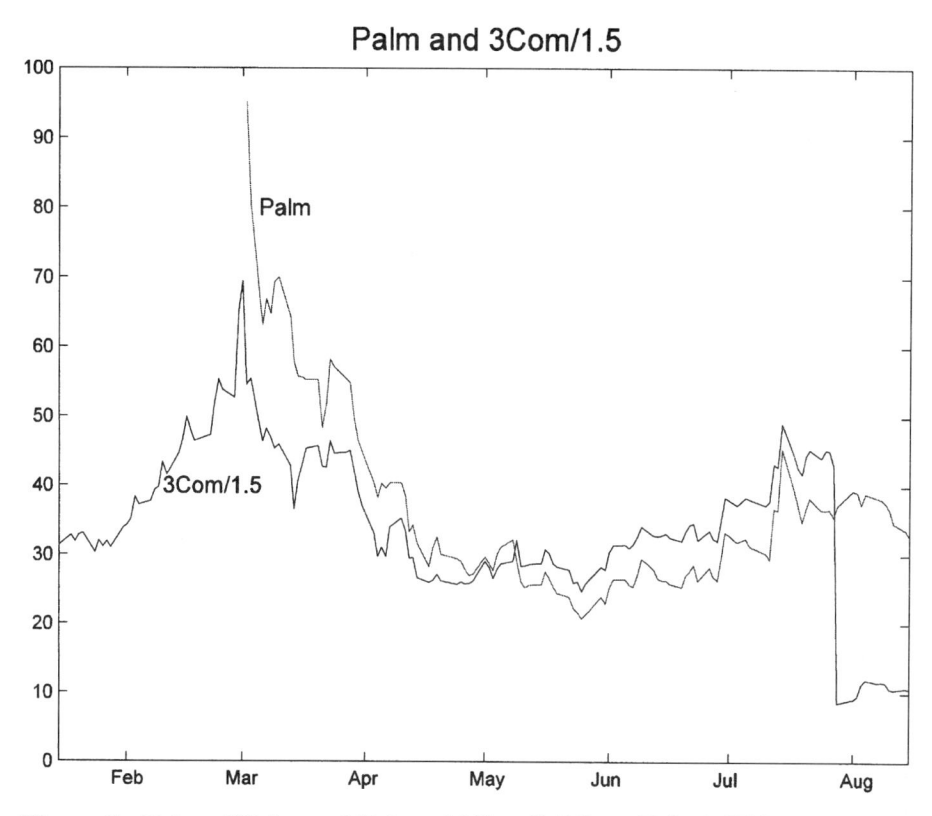

Figure 1: Price of Palm and Price of 3Com/1.5 from Palm's IPO to the Eventual Spinoff

stock price of a partially owned subsidiary does not affect the parent's stock price. For example, in 1999, General Motors (GM) had issued tracking stock for its Hughes Electronics unit and also had a 20 percent stake in publicly traded Commerce One (Lamont, 2000). Between September 1999 and January 2000, Hughes stock rose 97 percent and Commerce One stock rose 413 percent. General Motor's stock was barely affected. Lamont cites analyst calculations that this move left GM's auto business a price/earnings ratio of only 1.5, at the same time Ford's price/earnings ratio was 7 and DaimlerChrysler's was 12. The value of the rest of GM did not fall below zero, but the frictionless model is on thin ice if we have to assume that shocks to GM's fundamentals are strongly *negatively* correlated with shocks to Hughes and Commerce One fundamentals and uncorrelated with those of Ford and DaimlerChrysler.

These and related observations suggest to many observers that a downward sloping "demand for shares" is at work. The prices of the *available* shares are being set as if the unavailable shares—Palm Shares held by 3Com, Hughes shares held by GM, tech stock shares held by insiders, etc. ...—did not exist.

Why aren't such price differences arbitraged away? The Lamont and Thaler, Mitchell, Pulvino, and Stafford, and other investigations of these events carefully document the institutional details that prevent arbitrage. In the real world, you cannot "costlessly" short Palm and buy 3Com shares, in anticipation of your arbitrage profits after spinoff. Short sales require you to borrow stock before you sell it. In the 3Com/Palm case, 3Com stock was often simply not available for borrowing. If your broker could find some, you may have had to pay dearly for the privilege, unlike the textbook case that you receive interest on the proceeds of the short sale. Furthermore, if the spread widens, you may be wiped out before the price finally rights itself. The short loan may be called, and you may be unable to re-establish the short position—short loans must be re-established *daily*.

In the end, though, the fact that it could not be arbitraged away does not resolve the puzzle. The puzzle is: *Why are Palm and 3Com prices different in the first place? Who is buying overpriced Palm shares and why? What is the source of the "demand for shares?"*

All results in finance are controversial, and this one is, as well. One can quarrel whether it really was an arbitrage. True, fundamental stub values can be negative. Though stock is a limited liability security, stubs are not. $P \geq 0$ and $P + C \geq 0$ do not imply $C \geq 0$. For example, 3Com may borrow, using Palm shares as collateral, and then go bankrupt. In addition, the spinoff is not 100 percent sure to happen. 3Com can postpone the spinoff or cancel it (as they can and did advance it from December to July). 3Com may be acquired, and the new parent may cancel the spinoff. Note in figure 1 the sudden end of the negative stub value on the day that the Internal Revenue Service approved the tax-free status of the spinoff. This fact alone suggests that there is at least some real risk that the spinoff will not happen. Mitchell, Pulvino, and Stafford discuss all the ways in which apparent negative stub arbitrages can fail to work out and find that a surprising 30 percent of their negative stub "arbitrage opportunities" terminate without removing the mispricing. This story is strained for 3Com/Palm. It's hard to imagine that the correct valuation of 3Com less Palm was negative $22 billion in March and then recovered steeply to the spinoff in July.

Treasury Bills and Dollar Bills

On March 2, 2000, the one-year Treasury bill (T-bill) sold for $94.17.[1] A Treasury bill is, of course, a sure promise to receive $100 in a year's time. One could also get a claim to $100 in a year's time by buying $100 directly and holding it for a year. *Two ways of getting exactly the same payoff have a different price.* Why does anybody hold an overpriced dollar (Palm) when they could hold a cheaper Treasury bill (3Com) instead?

We have lots of good stories for this clear-cut violation of the law of one price makes sense. We don't need an irrational, psychological, or behavioral attachment to "dollars" rather than "Treasury bills" to explain it. People hold money because it provides "liquidity services" that make up for its poor rate of return. A poor rate of return is the same thing as a "too high" price. Much of the point of monetary economics is devoted to explaining "rate of return dominance."

This analogy is not just creative residual-naming. Monetary economics makes some quite sharp predictions about when this "mispricing" can occur. If Palm/3Com is "like" dollars/Treasury bills, we must see the standard predictions of money demand hold true.

2.1 Money-Like Facts About 3Com and Palm

Huge Turnover and Small Short-term Losses

Nobody holds dollars today as a way of getting dollars a year from now (except drug dealers, and so on, who value the anonymity of dollars, but the traditional theory of money demand is the right analogy for stocks). We each hold dollars for a short time between trips to the bank and transactions. We're happy to hold dollars for these short times, despite the fact that they depreciate relative to Treasury bills, because we need to hold dollars briefly. Dollars turn over quickly, and as interest rates rise—as dollars rise in price relative to Treasury bills—dollars turn over more quickly.

Palm turned over quickly. Lamont and Thaler (table 8) report that on average 19 percent of the available Palm shares changed hands *every day* in the 20 days after the IPO. The even more dramatic case of Creative/Ubid had a 106 percent average daily turnover, and Lamont and Thaler's six cases average 38 percent *daily* turnover (table 8). Figure 2 plots Palm daily turnover. As you can see, there are many days with huge turnover. Volume on the first day was one and a half times the total issue, as prices fell quickly

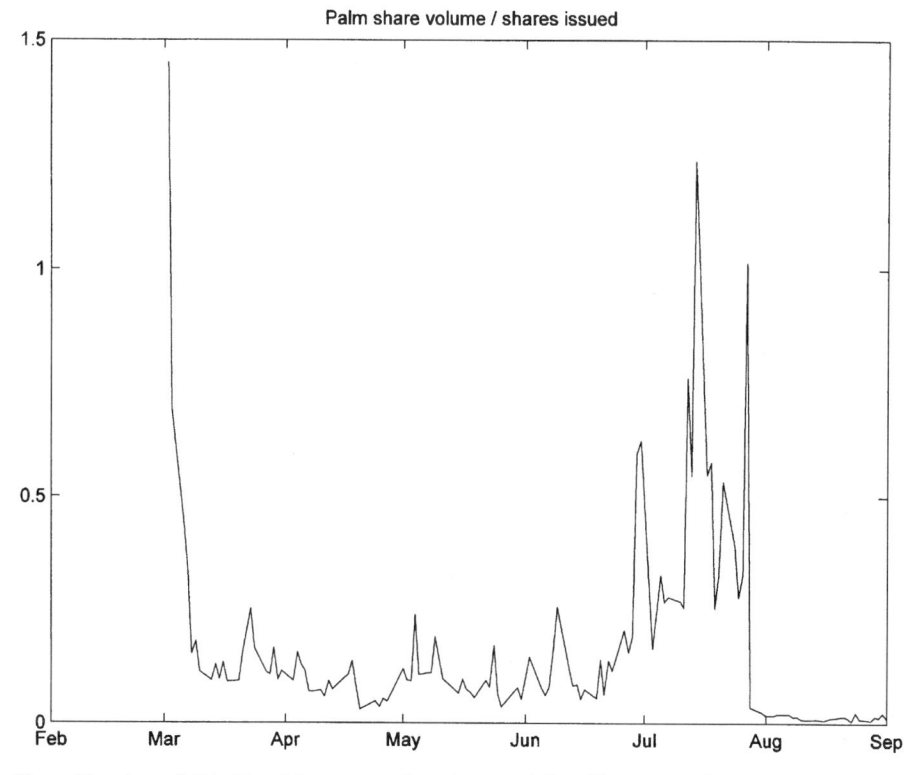

Note: The sharp fall in late July comes when the remaining 95 percent of shares are spun off by 3Com.

Figure 2: Palm Daily Turnover (Volume/Shares Issued)

from as much as $160 to the $92 close. By comparison, only 4.5 percent of 3Com shares were traded every day in the same period, and daily share volumes for typical stocks are 2 percent or less. This means that on average, Palm shareholders held the stock for less than five days, and during peak periods average holdings were much shorter than that![2]

Lamont and Thaler conclude that people who bought Palm rather than 3Com were "irrational" and "just making a mistake." They could have gotten Palm a lot cheaper by buying 3Com and waiting for the spinoff, a massive version of buying the name brand rather than the generic. But these turnover rates suggest that few Palm buyers did, in fact, make that mistake, and the vast majority of Palm shares were held for very short times.

At a five-day horizon, holding Palm rather than 3Com is not so obviously stupid. Take at face value that the Palm share at $95.06 will decline to the implicit $54.54 value from buying 3Com in nine months. This means a negative 42.6 percent relative return over nine months—pretty bad. But it is only a negative .2 percent *daily* return, or a negative 1 percent *five-day* return. Now, losing on average .2 percent as a day trader, or 1 percent as a five-day trader isn't *bright*, but it's much further from idiotic than the huge loss of buying Palm rather than 3Com and holding it for a year.

Palm stock was also tremendously volatile during this period, with a 7.15 percent standard deviation of daily returns and a 15.4 percent standard deviation of five-day day returns. The latter is about the same as the volatility of the Standard & Poor's (S&P) 500 index over an entire year. Figure 3 plots the distribution of one- and five-day Palm returns. Imagine that you are betting on the movements of Palm over a few days. Clearly the fact that Palm will on average drift down .2 percent per day is completely drowned out by the typical movements. Only a small bit of information about the short-term movements will swamp the information of a negative .2 percent daily drift down, and make Palm a smart investment. The drift is a small loss, of the same order of magnitude as the bid/ask spread, commissions, or the loss from taking a short-term rather than long-term capital gain. The *Good Housekeeping* guide to careful investing warns you to minimize these losses, but we usually don't jump to "irrationality" to explain why people are a bit sloppy about managing small losses, especially when quick decisions can bring such large gains.

Price and Volume

A crucial prediction of monetary economics is that velocity increases at higher interest rates, or as the spread between the value of a dollar and a T-bill increase. As interest rates rise, people pay more attention to economizing cash holdings, and so turnover increases. If some sort of transactions demand is behind "overvalued" Palm shares, then the "overvaluation" should be associated with huge volume.

We already know that Palm's volume was, in fact, huge on average. Figure 4 shows that time variation in Palm volume also lines up with time-variation in Palm's prices. (The plot presents a five-day centered moving average of share volume. Volume varies enormously from day to day. Prices incorporate expected returns for a long time in the future, so prices will be associated with longer-run movements in volume. Dollar volume is the economically more meaningful measure, but I plot share volume to emphasize that the positive correlation between volume and price does not just come from a constant share volume multiplied by varying prices.)

Distribution of Palm returns

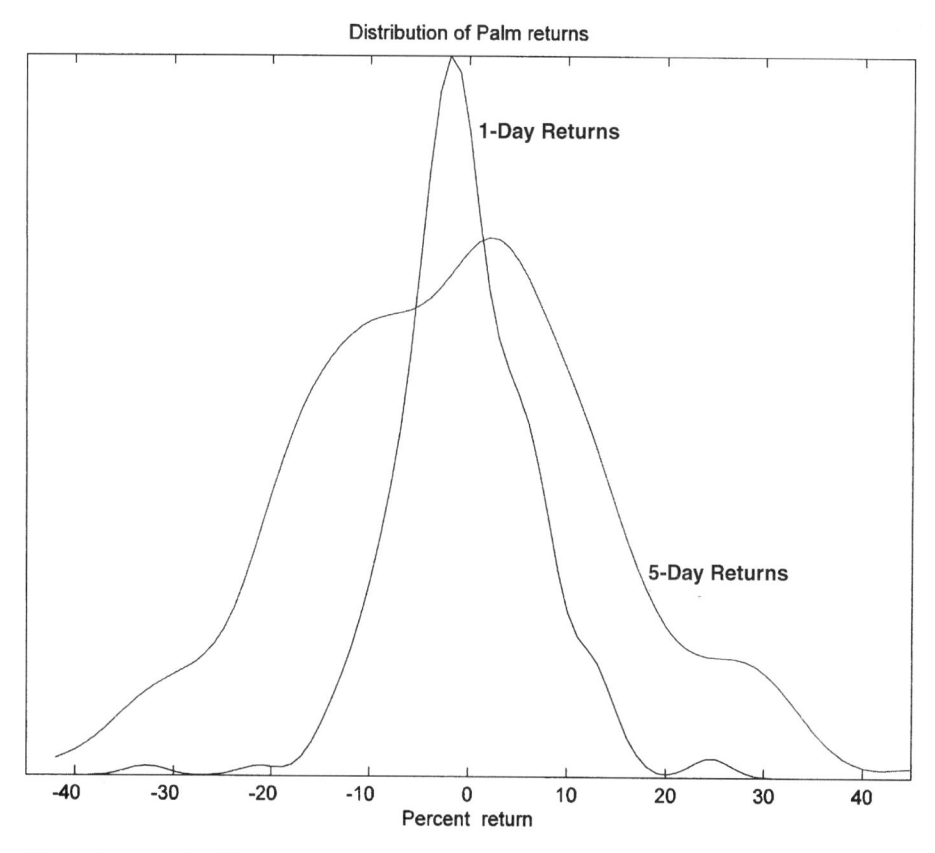

Note: The smoothed histogram uses a normal distribution window with a 2 percent standard deviation window width. The returns are actual, with an arbitrary placement.

Figure 3: Distribution of Palm Daily Returns, 2002

A positive correlation between price and volume is not a common stylized fact of the market microstructure literature. For example, Gallant, Rossi, and Tauchen's (1992) comprehensive study lists four stylized facts, starting with the correlation of volume with volatility, but do not mention a broad-based correlation of volume with price.

The correlation isn't unknown—for example, Brennan and Subrahmanyam (1996) and Jones (2001, table 2) find that high share turnover (and other liquidity measures) forecast low subsequent returns, which is the same thing as a high price—but it isn't one of the most commonly studied effects. The spike in volume surrounding the sharp price decline in late December is a more typical volume event. The spike in volume around mid July comes contemporaneous to the 3Com spinoff and is, therefore, also unlikely to be primarily driven by a transactions demand. It is significant that a positive correlation between price and volume does show up. It suggests an unusual case in which the transactions-based relation between price and volume can stick out above all the other more usual effects.

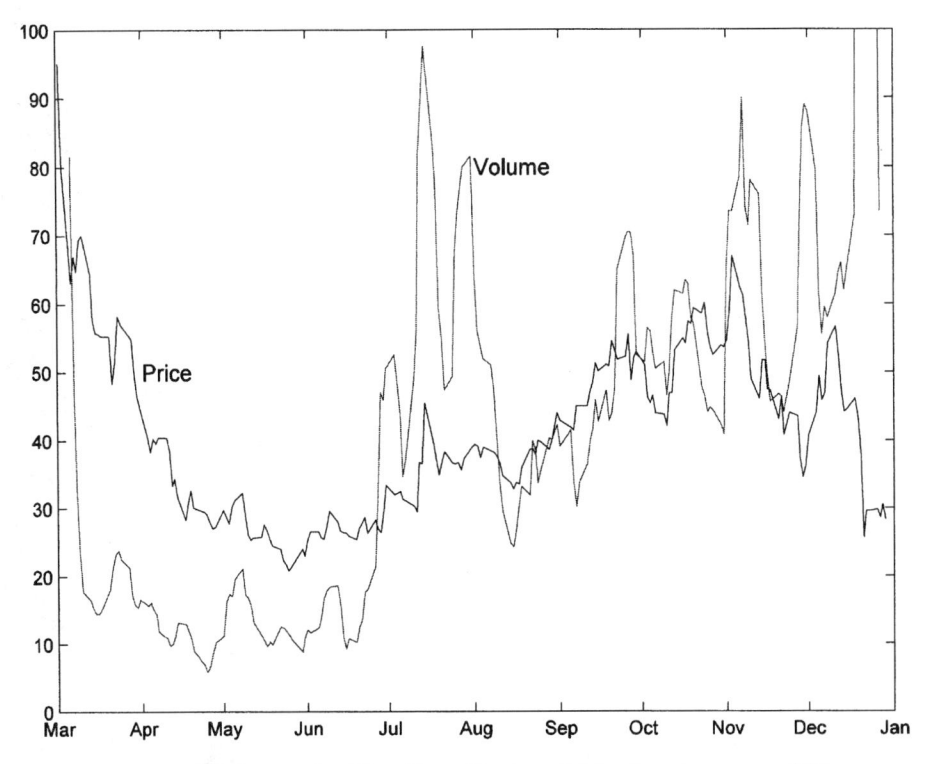

Figure 4: Palm Price and a Five-Day Centered Moving Average of Share Volume

Arbitrage and Short Sales Constraints

As we have seen, a crucial feature of Palm/3Com was that short selling was at first impossible, then very expensive.

A restriction on short selling is vital to maintaining the dollar/Treasury bills spread, as well. Why doesn't arbitrage remove the price difference between dollars and Treasury bills? The arbitrage is to short dollar bills and buy Treasury bills. Alas, you can't short dollar bills—printing them is illegal. Printing close substitutes—banknotes, or small denomination bearer bonds—is also illegal.

Share Supply and Short Sales

Money is more overpriced—interest rates are higher—when money supply is lower. In this context it is interesting that the Palm "overvaluation" happened while only 5 percent of Palm stock was outstanding and 95 percent was retained by 3Com. If you wanted to bet on Palm computers, up or down, you had to compete for one of the very small number of shares outstanding. (Actually, what matters is the "float," the number of shares easily available for trading. Many shares are not actively traded or available to be lent for short even though in private hands. Low float can come from a small amount issued or from a small amount of a large issue available for trading. Unfortunately, we don't have a clean definition and even less data on float.)

Short selling can act like inside money (bank account) creation as a way to increase the supply of shares. If A lends shares to B and B sells to C, then both A and C have long positions even though there is only one share outstanding.

Despite the costs of short positions, Palm short sales were massive, increasing steadily to 147 percent of available shares in July. That means that on average each share was bought, lent to short, sold, and then half were bought, lent, and shorted again. (After the spinoff, the total number of Palm shares sold short did not change, but the supply of available shares jumped so that the fractions returned to normal. Interestingly, Lamont and Thaler show that *parents* averaged 3.7 percent short interest. While much lower than the subsidiaries, it is a testament to the divergence of opinion on tech stocks and the emphasis on high-frequency trading that anyone was short the long end of an arbitrage opportunity!)

Figure 5 plots Palm's "overpricing" relative to 3Com, i.e., Palm/(3Com/1.5) − 1, against the share supply induced by shorting, 1 + short interest/shares issued. You can see the nice pattern—as share supply increased, the "overpricing" decreased steadily.

It is a little surprising that Palm prices did not fall when the spinoff occurred and a huge new volume of shares was available for trading. However, this event was widely anticipated, so the price decline would have to be slow and hard to measure. The

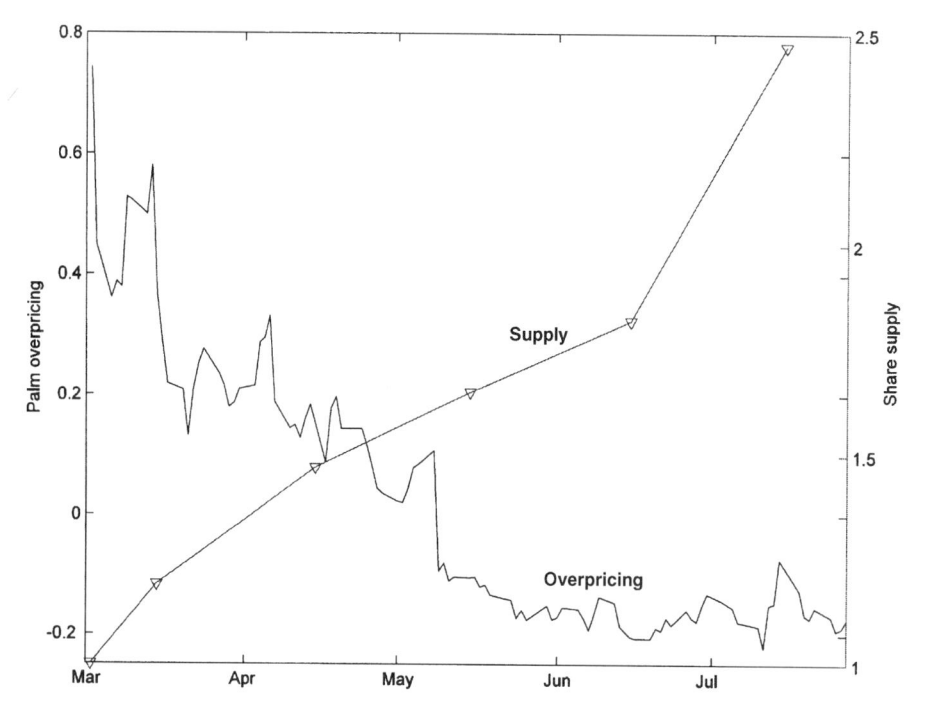

Note: "Palm overpricing" is Palm price/(3Com price/1.5) − 1. "Share supply" is 1 + short interest/shares issued.

Figure 5: Palm Overpricing and Share Supply

explosion in shorting in July indicates many people expected such a price decline, and the massive short interest may have gone a long way to providing the required extra share supply before the spinoff.

Poor Substitutes—If You Want to Trade, You Have to Trade Palm

There can only be a money premium if money is a "special asset," if there are no good substitutes such as private banknotes. There can only be a convenience yield for Palm stock if there are no good substitutes for the purposes of high frequency trading. Are there?

3Com and Palm Are Poorly Linked

The obvious substitute for Palm is 3Com, since 3Com holds 95 percent of Palm stock. If you want to bet on Palm for a few days, why not buy 3Com instead and save the 1 percent negative drift? Surely, any news that impacts Palm's prospects will affect 3Com, as well.

Table 1 evaluates this option. The first row runs Palm returns on 3Com returns. This is simple, but the two returns may have a spuriously high correlation, as they will both rise when the market rises. The right strategy for betting on Palm is to hedge the Palm investment with an investment in the market index, for a beta zero strategy that bets only on Palm's fortunes. Thus, in the second row I estimate a beta on the NASDAQ index for each of Palm and 3Com and then run a regression of the Palm market model residual on the 3Com market model residual. The bottom set of rows evaluates the Palm/3Com return correlation at a five-day horizon. We know Palm and 3Com will converge at a six-month horizon, perhaps the delinking at a one-day horizon disappears by the typical five-day horizon.

Table 1 shows that buying or selling 3Com is a very poor way of betting on Palm at short horizons. While the regression coefficients b are gratifyingly close to one, the R^2 are surprisingly low, given that all of 3Com's value (and then some!) is attributable to its Palm shares. Of the 7 percent daily Palm volatility and 13 percent to 15 percent five-day Palm volatility, 4.5 percent daily Palm volatility and 8 percent to 10 percent five-day Palm volatility are missed by the strategy of buying 3Com in place of Palm.

One-day returns:	b	R^2	$\sigma(y)$	$\sigma(\varepsilon)$
$Palm_t = a + b3Com_t + \varepsilon_t$	0.96	0.60	7.2	4.5
$(Palm_t - \beta Nasdaq_t) = a + b(3Com_t - \beta Nasdaq_t) + \varepsilon_t$	0.93	0.53	6.9	4.6
Five-day returns:				
$Palm_t = a + b3Com_t + \varepsilon_t$	1.03	0.69	15.0	8.3
$(Palm_t - \beta Nasdaq_t) = a + b(3Com_t - \beta Nasdaq_t) + \varepsilon_t$	0.95	0.54	13.4	10.0

Note: σ units are daily percent returns.
Sample: March 3 to July 27, 2000

Table 1: Regressions of Palm Returns on 3Com Returns

Volatility and Delinking

Table 1 demonstrates that something really weird (or really monetary) is going on in the Palm and 3Com valuation. All of 3Com's value is due to its Palm shares. The only way that 3Com and Palm returns can diverge is if there is news about the rest of 3Com. But when the stub is small, it would take astounding volatility of news about the rest of 3Com to account for the poor correlation between 3Com and Palm shares.

Here is the argument quantitatively. The value of 3Com should be (if the law of one price holds) the value of its components:

1) *3Com value = value Palm shares held by 3Com + 3Com stub value*

Equation 1 implies that the 3Com stub return can be inferred 3Com and Palm returns by:

$$3Com\ Stub\ Return_t = \frac{(Total\ 3Com\ value)_{t-1}}{(3\ Com\ stub\ value)_{t-1}} 3Com\ Return_t$$

$$- \frac{(value\ of\ Palm\ shares\ held\ by\ 3Com)_{t-1}}{(3Com\ stub\ value)_{t-1}} Palm\ Return_t.$$

As the stub value declines to zero, any deviation between Palm returns and 3Com returns implies infinite variation in the 3Com stub return.

Figure 6 shows the imputed 3Com stub return before the spinoff and the actual 3Com return after the spinoff, together with 15-day moving average standard deviations. It's clear that the "3Com stub risk" before the spinoff is much greater than the actual 3Com stub risk revealed after the spinoff. The overall standard deviation of the 3Com stub return is 32.2 percent (daily return!) before the spinoff and only 6.72 percent afterwards.

At short horizons, Palm prices and 3Com prices are delinked. If you buy 3Com in order to bet on Palm shares, you are taking on much more than the true risks to the stub value of 3Com. You are taking on the risk that when the exact moment comes to sell, the price move in the 3Com market will be delinked from the price move in the Palm market. *If you want to bet on Palm, you have to buy Palm.*

High Frequency Delinking

High frequency traders can't trade at the closing prices graphed in daily data, and they spend a lot of time looking at intraday prices, figuring out exactly when the right time is to buy and sell. Figure 7 shows a very close-up shot of one afternoon, March 14. (I chose the date at random among days other than the opening day, rather than select for a pretty plot. The opening day is completely chaotic.) The figure presents the NYSE TAQ (trade and quote) data of every single trade. There is a wide trading band at any point in time—good execution is important for day traders! The figure also shows substantial lack of correlation between 3Com and Palm. In this case 3Com is moving around in ways not followed by Palm. From the perspective of a high frequency trader,

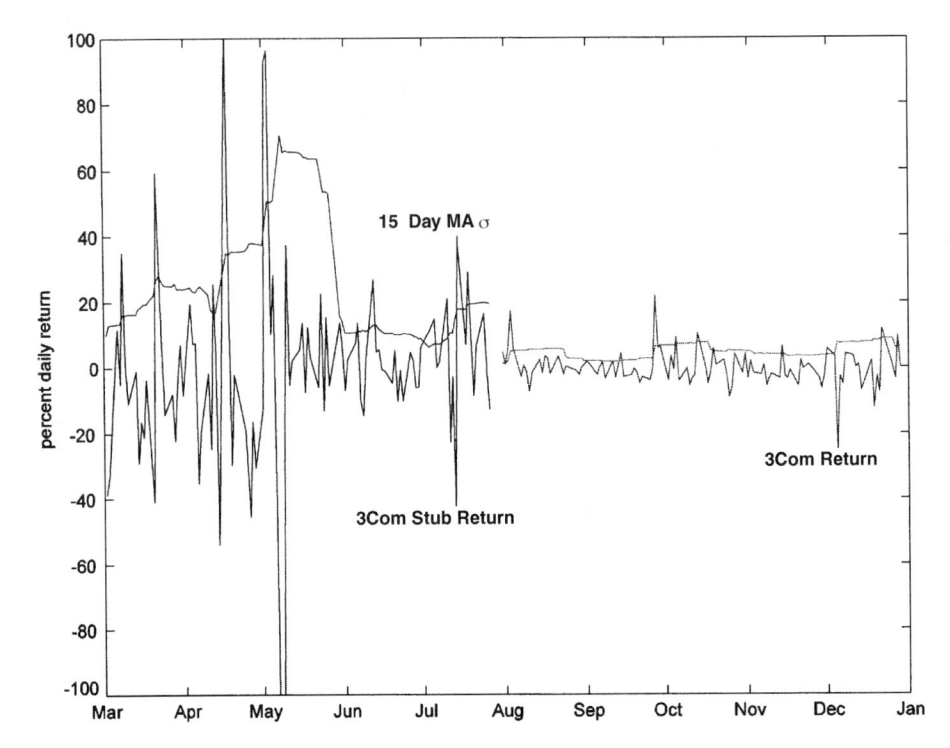

Note: 3Com Stub is 3Com less the value of Palm shares held by 3Com.

Figure 6: Return of the 3Com Stub before the Spinoff and Returns of 3Com Itself after the Spinoff

3Com is a very poor substitute for Palm—even though all of 3Com's value and more is due to its holding of Palm shares.

Options Are Delinked

What about options? Rather than buy Palm directly or buy 3Com, why not synthesize Palm with a long call and short put—or just buy the naked option corresponding to the direction in which you think Palm will go?

Lamont and Thaler (2001) look at options and find massive violations of put-call parity. The synthetic 3Com stub is almost never negative. The synthetic Palm price is typically far below the actual Palm price and does not allow an arbitrage. For example, they report in their table 6 that on March 17, the synthetic Palm was between 8 percent and 30 percent (depending on maturity) less than the actual Palm. They do not report a time series (and I have not yet constructed one), but if the level of synthetic Palm can be so far away from actual Palm, it seems likely that changes are also poorly correlated, in the same way that 3Com and Palm are poorly correlated. If you bet on Palm by buying much cheaper synthetic Palm, when the news you anticipate hits actual Palm it may not hit the synthetic Palm equally.

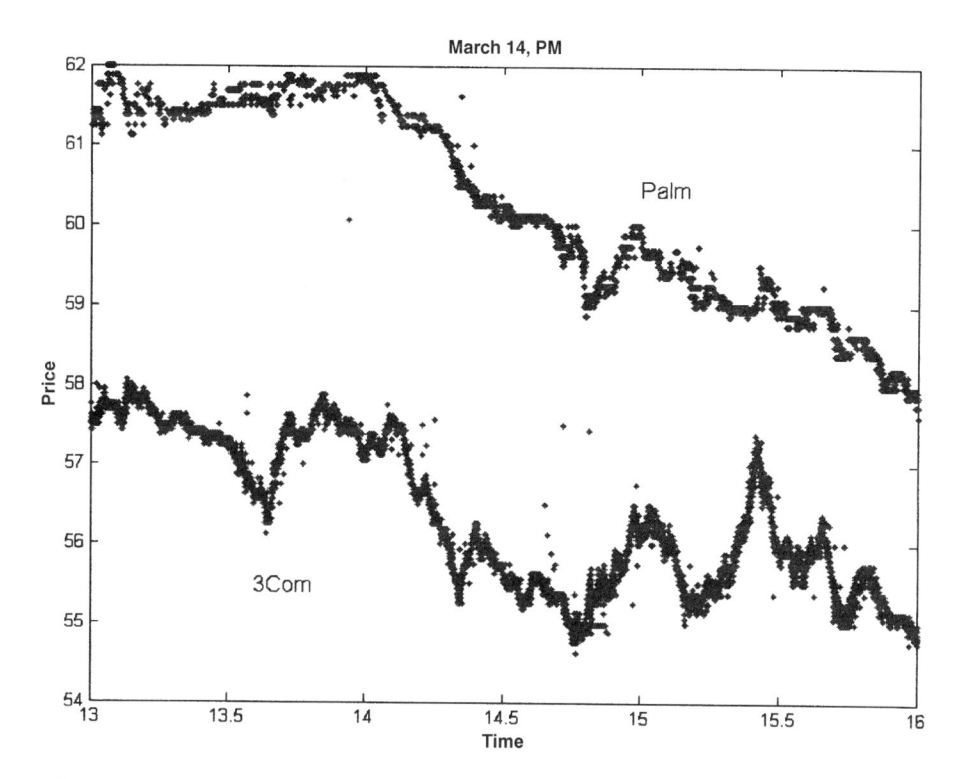

Stocks as Money: Convenience Yield and the Tech-Stock Bubble 187

Figure 7: Trade by Trade Prices for 3Com and Palm on the Afternoon of March 14, 2000

Why Did 3Com Fall?

It's interesting that on the day of the Palm IPO, 3Com fell 21 percent. One would think that the surprising good news about the value of Palm would lift 3Com, since 3Com holds 95 percent of Palm's shares. Where is the bad news for 3Com (including 95 percent of Palm)?

A convenience yield view gives a reason for 3Com to fall. Until Palm is issued, the only way to bet on the prospects of Palm is to buy 3Com. The minute Palm starts trading, however, you can start to bet on Palm by buying and selling Palm directly. If the day-traders abandon 3Com and head off to trade Palm stock, 3Com loses much of its potential convenience yield, its required return rises, and its price falls. Of course, there must be some surprise in this shift in trading. Any perfectly predictable event should already be reflected in the price, leading to a slow relative decline in 3Com rather than a one-day 21 percent drop, as the perfectly predictable event of the actual spinoff did not seem to give a huge decline in Palm. Still, it's possible that it was unclear whether the massive pre-IPO trading in 3Com would all move to Palm, given how few shares would be issued, and that there was some surprise in this event.

Summary

Table 2 summarizes many of the empirical similarities between the 3Com/Palm "mispricing" and the dollar/T-bill "mispricing," to show the many common features of the two phenomena.

2.2 Making Sense of a Convenience Yield for Stocks

Does a trading-related convenience yield for stocks make any economic sense? If so, can it possibly be large enough to explain events such as 3Com/Palm or the NASDAQ?

Similar Effects and the Size of Convenience Prices

The Size of Monetary Spreads

While we usually think of interest rates and convenience yields as small, the money/bond price spread has, historically, far exceeded the Palm/3Com spread. All it takes is a hyperinflation. For example, with a 100 percent inflation rate, the price of a one-year bond is one-half (I assume a zero real rate to keep computations simple), so money is overpriced relative to one-year bonds by 100 percent! And, hyperinflations of many hundreds and thousands of percent have been common even in the 20th century. The Palm/3Com spread—arguably one of the largest convenience yields in a century of asset price data—is, at about a 50 percent per year relative return, mild by these standards.

It may seem strange to think of money as overvalued in a hyperinflation, but that is, in fact, the case—money suffers a high rate of depreciation, so its price today is "too high" relative to its price tomorrow. People hold a small amount of money, for a *short* time, because it is in fact extraordinarily *valuable* in a hyperinflation. I highlight the adjectives, as all three elements show up for Palm.

Convenience Yields in Finance

Transactions-related price spreads and convenience yields in rates of return are not a novelty to finance. Of course, the commodity convenience yield is the heart of commodity futures pricing. Something about having grain in a warehouse, rather than relying on your ability to buy it if needed, must be valuable.

	3Com/Palm	Dollar/T-bill
Law of one price violated	x	x
Restrictions on long-term short	x	x (no banknotes)
High turnover, short horizon in "expensive" end	x	x
Turnover higher as price spread higher	x	x (velocity)
High price security is "special" for trading	x	x
Price spread higher as quantity lower	x	x
Price spread lower as substitutes arise	x	x
Much shorting substitutes despite cost	x	x (checking accounts)
Size can be large	x	x (hyperinflations)

Table 2: Summary of the Similarities Between 3Com/Palm and Dollar/T-bill Mispricing

Krishnamurthy (2001) documents the spread between 30-year bonds, which are actively traded, and 29-year bonds, which are not. The 30-year bonds are "overpriced," which is explainable by a similar transactions demand or convenience yield for holding them. As with Palm/3Com, Krishnamurthy documents short constraints in the form of a "special repo rate."

Krishnamurthy finds the overpricing is typically about 10 basis points. This is not as small as it seems. Ten basis points for a 30-year coupon bond is about $1.50 per $100 face value. In addition, the 29/30 year yield spread vanishes in a year, so the expected return spread is about one and a half percentage points.

Mason (1987) and Boudoukh and Whitelaw (1991, 1993) document the benchmark" effect in Japanese bonds. Bond traders usually focus on a single issue called the "benchmark," which can trade as much as one percentage point above bonds with nearly identical terms. When the benchmark changes, the old benchmark declines in value and the new benchmark gains, in a manner reminiscent of 3Com's fall and Palm's rise when Palm opened. One percentage point on a 10-year (par, coupon, 5 percent yield) bond is an $8 price difference.

These numbers are smaller than Palm/3Com, but so is bond volatility. Furthermore, we expect that the differences in opinion or information about the value of government bonds are much smaller than that for a tech-stock IPO in March 2000. Therefore, we expect smaller convenience yields.

Fernald and Rogers (2001) examine the relative prices of the two classes of shares of Chinese companies that can be held by domestic residents and foreigners, respectively. Though identical in other respects, the shares available to foreigners have traded for as little as *one-fourth* of the price of domestic shares. They also document that the domestic shares have as much as twice the price volatility as the foreign shares, and domestic shares average 2.4 percent daily turnover, compared to 0.3 percent for foreign shares. A natural interpretation is that the domestic share market is where the high frequency trading takes place, so domestic shares inherit a convenience yield not given to the foreign shares. One-fourth seems like a lot, but Fernald and Rogers calculate that the price difference only translates to about a four percentage point per year difference in expected return, since stocks are long-lived securities.

The Gordon growth formula $\dfrac{p}{d} = \dfrac{1}{r-g},$

reminds us that stocks whose prices are already high, due to high growth g or low required return r, are especially sensitive to changes in required return. For example, a stock with $r - g = 2$ percent has $p/d = 50$ while a stock with $r - g = 5$ percent has $p/d = 20$. A one percentage point reduction in required return raises the high priced stock to $p/d = 100$ while it only raises the low priced stock to $p/d = 25$. Based on this simple argument, it at least is not a surprise that convenience yield effects seem most dramatic among "growth stocks" whose prices are already high relative to book value, earnings, or dividends.

3. Theories of a Convenience Yield

One's first objection to the T-bill/ dollar bill analogy might be that money is special because it is the medium of exchange. You don't use Palm stock to buy your morning coffee. However, the medium of exchange need not have a convenience yield, and a convenience yield is not limited to the medium of exchange. If every point of sale had a debt card reader, we could arrange our transactions without holding any money. Money would lose its convenience yield, even though it remained medium of exchange. Conversely, bond liquidity spreads, commodity convenience yields, and depreciating inventories of all kinds remain, though they are not media of exchange.

Money's convenience yield comes because you have to hold some money as an inventory, or buffer stock. That feature is generated by the medium of exchange function when markets are not constantly available, but lots of other trading frictions can generate an inventory demand.

Trading requires some shares of stock. Obviously, you can't buy stock if there is none. You can't short it either. To short stock, you have to find someone to borrow it from, and then you have to find someone to sell it to. You have to hold stock for a short time in order to short it. Duffie, Gârleanu, and Pedersen (2001) model these short selling mechanics. In the model, everyone wants to short. An equilibrium short rebate keeps each agent happy to hold depreciating stock for the time it takes to find a borrower or a purchaser. The stock price falls slowly as short sales build up.

Scheinkman and Xiong (2002), following Harrison and Kreps (1978), present a model close to the verbal analysis I have presented. They show how a limited number of shares plus a large volume of trading based on differences of opinion can drive prices up above the frictionless "fundamental value."

So far, fully rational models have not derived the extraordinary volume of trading. Traders say they act on differences of information, or differences of opinion (different processing of the same information). Yet every trader can't have better than average information. Scheinkman and Xiong rely on "overconfidence"—each trader thinks his signal is more accurate than it really is. Baker and Stein (2002) present a model based on irrational investors who under react to news contained in order flow. Their model predicts that high turnover will be associated with low returns, i.e. high prices. Other models rely on "noise traders" or other less than fully rational behaviors.

Yet "irrationality" seems a superficial response to the deep problem posed by volume. Even hyper-rational finance professors and Nobel Prize winners run to high frequency trading when they go off to Wall Street. Without high frequency trading, the NYSE and NASDAQ would disappear, as retail life-cycle investing could not support them. Do we really believe that the NYSE and NASDAQ are temples to irrationality—that they would disappear if traders would only take to heart the fact that we can't all be better informed than average? Furthermore, when we write models that make arbitrary behaviors structural, we risk repeating the ill fate of Keynes' consumption function and Phillips' static curve.

I don't propose to solve the volume mystery here. It seems a productive first step to note that there is a lot of high frequency trading. Let us see if trading can induce a convenience yield and inventory demand for shares sufficient to explain puzzling price patterns and worry about micro foundations later. If irrational *trading*, but not irrational *valuation*, is behind puzzling price anomalies, that is already news.

It may give some comfort to remember that the microfoundations of money demand are also an enduring theoretical puzzle. Obviously, a dollar is helpful in arranging transactions, but vaguely realistic models of optimal transactions demand do not come close to the $500 per capita of actual U.S. cash holdings. The puzzles are the same: "Why don't people use foreign currencies, or credit cards?" sounds a lot like "Why didn't Palm traders use options, or 3Com?"

A basic theorem of frictionless finance (essentially, the Modigliani-Miller theorem) is that the value of the company should not depend on the number of shares issued to the public. Even if 99 percent of the shares are locked up, or held passively by some other company, the total market value should not be affected by the number of shares publicly issued. The convenience yield violates this theorem; it gives rise to a downward sloping "demand for shares," especially in times of huge volume and much high frequency trading.

4. The Rise and Fall

The Palm/3Com event is a microcosm of a larger puzzle—the NASDAQ rise and subsequent fall. Price volatility was large, share turnover enormous, short interest large, and many stocks, and especially many of the unusually highly priced stocks, also had the curious feature that only a small fraction of total shares were issued to the public. Did a convenience yield explain or at least contribute to the events? I review the same suggestive litany of facts in the larger experience.

The "Bubble" Was Concentrated

Figure 8 compares three indices, the NYSE, the NASDAQ, and an index of NASDAQ tech stocks. (The tech index is composed of NASDAQ stocks with SIC code 737. I did not want an index composed of surviving stocks. The 737 code is the most common SIC code for stocks on various tech or Internet stock indices. This is a narrow index—for example, it leaves out eBay—but for this purpose it is better to be too narrow than too wide.)

The figure makes clear that if there was a "bubble," or some behavioral overenthusiasm for stocks, it was concentrated on NASDAQ stocks, and NASDAQ tech and Internet stocks in particular.

Prices and Volume Are Correlated in Time Series and Cross Section

Figure 9 presents dollar volume for the three indices of figure 8. The pattern is clear—both in the time series and in the cross section, prices are high where dollar volume is high. (Ofek and Richardson, 2001, figures 1 and 2 present a narrower and even more dramatic Internet index. Their index rises 10 times more than the S&P 500 and shows the same strong correlation with volume as between the figures here.)

Dollar volume is the economically right measure. A high dollar volume will naturally result from a constant share volume and higher prices. That is still economically important higher volume, but it is interesting to verify whether this is the case. Figure 10 verifies that, in fact, share volume, as well as dollar prices of a given share volume, rose and fell.

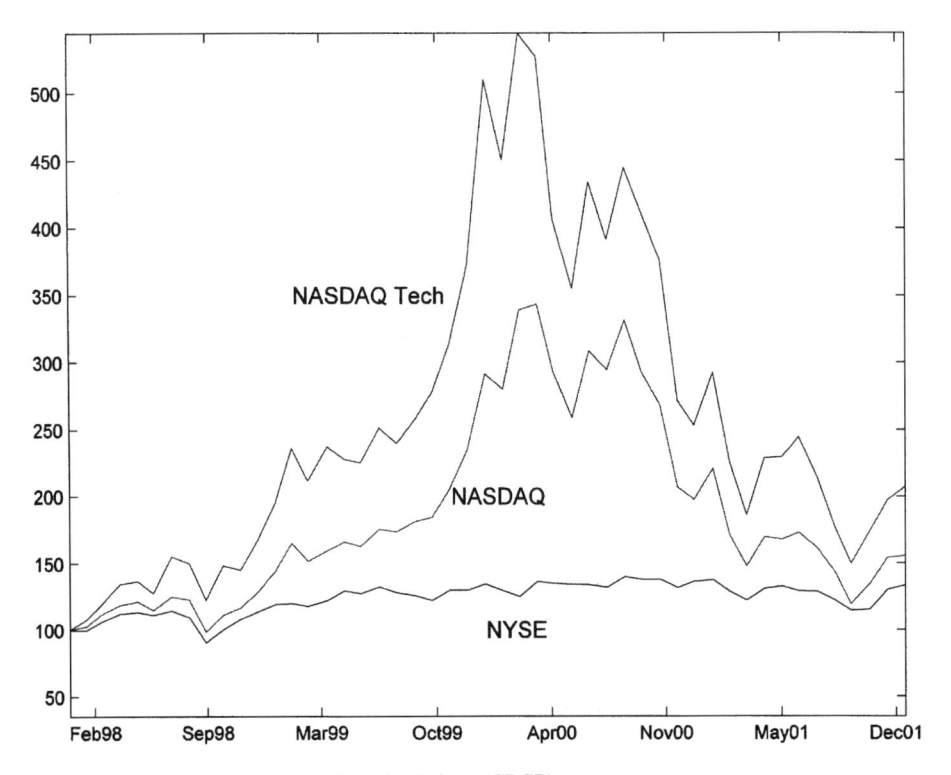

Source: Center for Research in Security Prices (CRSP)
Note: SIC code 737 = computer processing and data processing. Each index is based at 100 in January 1998.

Figure 8: Total Market Value (Price × Shares) of the NYSE, the NASDAQ, and NASDAQ Stocks with SIC Code 737

The association of price and volume is a generic feature of the historical "bubbles," though not of most theories applied to them. For example, figure 11 shows a surprising time-series correlation between the NYSE index and NYSE volume through the 1929 boom and crash. The graph presents share volume; dollar volume rose and declined even more calamitously. (Jones, 2001, also notes the sharp decline in volume with the great crash. Jones shows that other measures of liquidity including bid/ask spreads also declined sharply.) Any value that shares had in high frequency trading in 1929 had evaporated by 1933. The South Sea bubble and tulip bubble similarly came and went with trading frenzies (Garber, 2001).

Cross-sectional Relation Between Price and Volume

There is also a cross-sectional relation between price and volume. To quantify this relationship, I run cross-sectional regressions of market equity/book equity on share turnover. Book equity is an easily available, though imperfect, proxy for the frictionless fundamental value. Table 3 presents the cross-sectional regressions, and figure 12

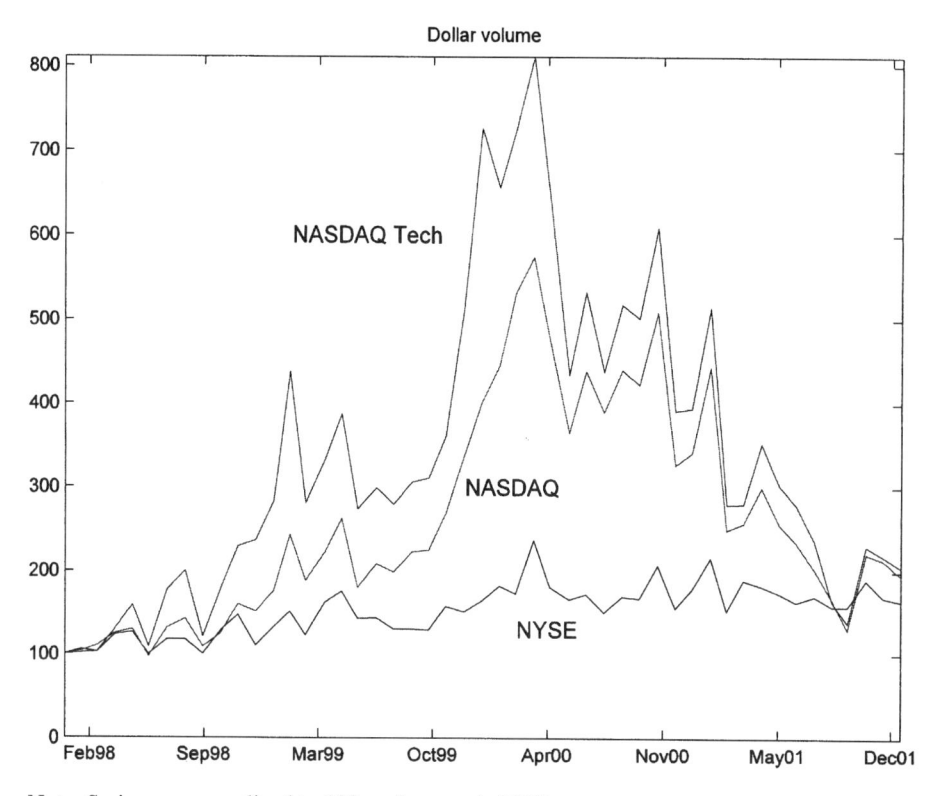

Stocks as Money: Convenience Yield and the Tech-Stock Bubble 193

Note: Series are normalized to 100 on January 1, 1998.

Figure 9: Dollar Volume on the NYSE, NASDAQ, and NASDAQ with SIC Code 737

plots the cross-sectional correlation between log market/book and log turnover at each month. (For a single regression, the coefficient, R^2, and correlation all carry the same information.)

Both the figure and the table show an important cross-sectional correlation between value and turnover, as a convenience yield predicts. Figure 12 shows interesting variation over time in the cross-sectional correlation. The correlation is highest during the boom year 1999. That is consistent with a positive correlation induced by a convenience yield sticking out more over the noise, in the year that convenience yield was most important to prices. (The plot also shows year effects, due to the once per year changes in book value. I don't have a story why changes in book value should change the cross-sectional correlation so much.)

The regressions also suggest that the correlation is statistically significant. The ordinary least squares (OLS) t statistics in the cross-sectional regressions are large, though the errors are undoubtedly cross-correlated. The Fama-MacBeth t statistics are also large, even given the short time dimension of the sample. (Since there is such a strong year effect visible in the plot, and as a rough correction for the time-series

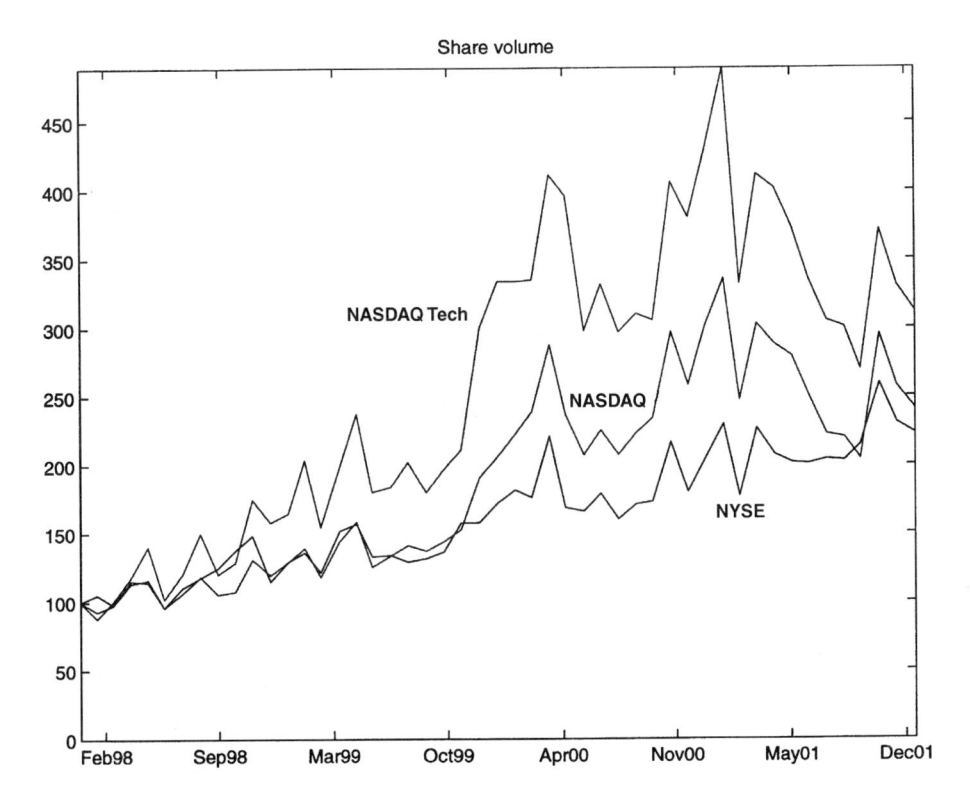

Note: Series are normalized to 100 in January 1998.

Figure 10: Share Volume on the NYSE, NASDAQ, and NASDAQ with SIC Code 737.

correlation of the cross-sectional regression coefficients, I formed Fama-MacBeth standard errors by dividing the time series variance of the cross-sectional coefficients by five, the number of years, rather than 60, the number of months.)

Other Predictions for the Internet Bubble
Ofek and Richardson (2001) survey Internet stocks in the late 1990s. In addition to the strong correlation between price and volume, they document all the other pieces of the convenience yield picture.

Short Sales Constraints
In addition to the usual problem that it is difficult and costly to maintain a long-term short position for years, and that you may get wiped out in the mean time by arbitrage opportunities (Liu and Longstaff, 2000), Ofek and Richardson document the exceptional difficulty of shorting Internet stocks during the boom. Rebate rates were low, violations of put/call parity common, as was the case with Palm/3Com.

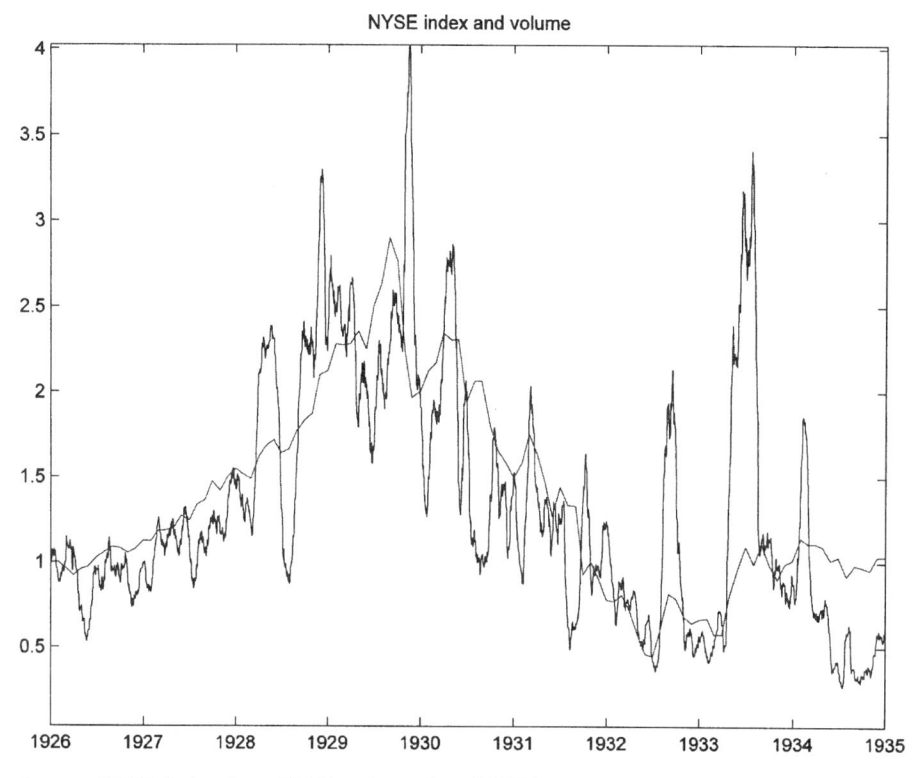

Source: NYSE index from CRSP; volume from NYSE
Note: Volume is the more volatile series. Both series normalized to 1 in 1926.

Figure 11: Share Volume (20-Day Moving Average) and NYSE Index in the Great Crash

Small Number of Shares Available

Most of the Ofek and Richardson Internet index consists of new companies, and, as with Palm, small fractions of the total shares are initially available for trading. Insiders are typically "locked out" of selling for a fixed period, usually 180 days, after the IPO.

Price Declines When Shares Become Available

One source of "share supply" is insider sales after lock-up expiration. Many observers commented on the puzzle that prices fell when the lock-up period ended, as if the market had been assigning value to traded shares ignoring the presence of shares held by insiders. Ofek and Richardson (figure 5) show that Internet firms lost 12 percent of value (cumulative abnormal return) from 20 days prior to the end of lock-up to 20 days after the end of lock-up. They document a large fraction of shares removed from lock-up between December 1999 and March 2000, coincident with the dot-com peak (figure 4). In addition, to the extent that traders want to bet on the Internet as a whole

Sample	a	b	t	FM*t*	R²	ρ
All CRSP Dec 1999	0.85	0.33	27		0.12	0.34
NASDAQ Dec 1999	0.89	0.38	23		0.13	0.37
All CRSP 1996–2000 (averages)	0.83	0.21	18	7.5	0.06	0.24
NASDAQ 1996–2000 (averages)	0.85	0.23	16	7.2	0.07	0.27

$$\ln\left(\frac{ME}{BE_i}\right) = a + b \ln\left(\frac{\text{share volume}}{\text{shares outstanding}}\right) + \varepsilon_i$$

Note: The first two rows present a single cross-sectional regression for December 1999. The second two rows present averages over cross-sectional regressions run in every month from January 1996 to December 2000. *t* gives the OLS cross-sectional regression *t* statistic, and the average of the monthly *t* statistic in the second two rows. FM*t* presents the Fama-MacBeth *t* statistic, calculated from the time-series standard deviation of the cross-sectional regression coefficients b_t dividend by $\sqrt{5}$. ρ is the correlation between log market/book and log turnover. Book values follow Fama and French (2002).

Table 3: Cross-sectional Regressions of Market Value/Book Value on Share Turnover

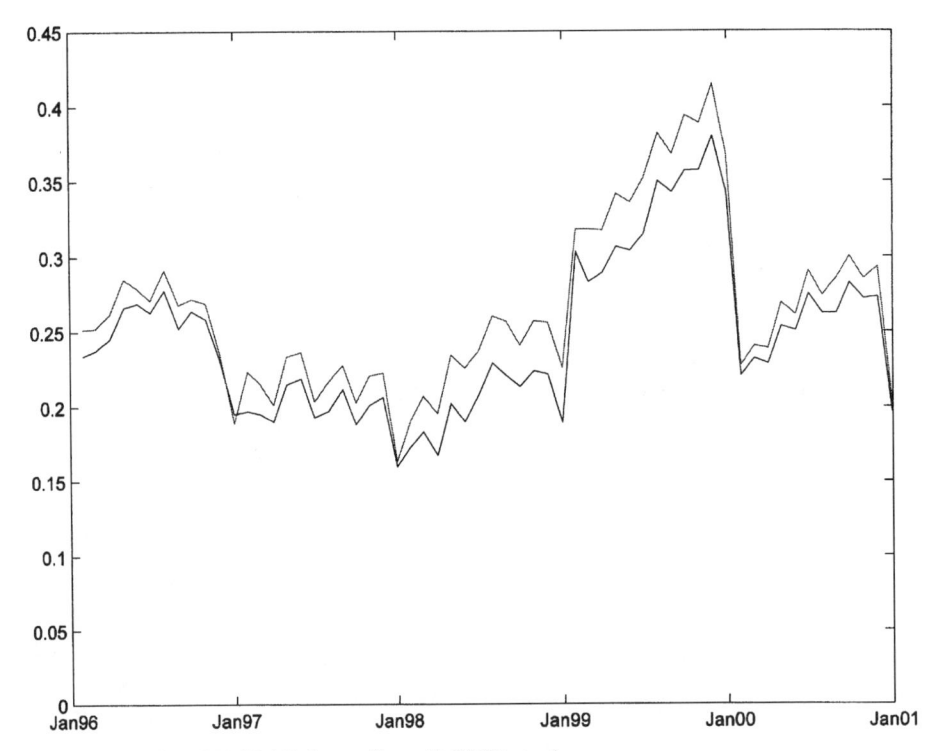

Note: Upper line: NASDAQ; lower line: all CRSP stocks.

Figure 12: Cross-sectional Correlations of Log (Market/Book) with Log Turnover

rather than company specific events, the huge supply of new shares via IPO counts to satisfy the transaction demand. The total supply of Internet shares via IPO, seasoned equity offerings, and insider sales grew rapidly to a peak in March 2002, just as the price peaked, as well (figure 5).

5. A Comparison of Theories

What theories account for the curious behavior of tech stock prices? How many of the facts do they capture? Table 4 summarizes.

Frictionless Rational Pricing—High Earnings

The standard model of frictionless pricing, for example the simple Gordon growth model with constant growth g and expected return r,

$$\frac{p_t}{d_t} = \frac{1}{r-g},$$

can generate huge price rises if people expect huge earnings growth g. The Internet was surely a once-in-a-generation technological novelty, a discovery on par with the automobile or the computer itself. Couldn't prices have risen on rational expectations of earnings growth?

Many observers noted that the earnings growth required to support Internet valuations was astronomically high. While fine on a story-telling, qualitative basis, this theory is difficult to match quantitatively. We now know that these observers were right. However, being *wrong* once is not the same thing as being *irrational*. Was it irrational to believe that the Internet was a much bigger phenomenon than it turned out to be?

Fact	Theory					
	1	2	3	4	5	6
Prices rise, decline	x	x	x	x	x	x
Prices do not forecast earnings		x	x	x	x	x
Long-term short difficult			x	x	x	x
Large dispersion of opinion					x	x
Price high with number shares low (ts & cs)					x	x
Price high with high volume (ts & cs)						x
Price high with volatility high (ts & cs)						x
Biggest in growth stocks						x

Note: "ts&cs" stands for "time-series and cross section."

Table 4: Summary of Theories and Which Facts They Account for
1: Frictionless model driven by earnings expectations
2: Frictionless model driven by risk premia
3: Rational bubble
4: Irrational valuation
5: Optimists' opinions only with short restrictions
6: Convenience yield, shares are needed for high frequency trading

Rational expectations can't be wrong all the time. If this time high prices were disappointed (so far) by *ex post* earnings growth, at some other time, high prices must have been *under*estimates of even better earnings growth. In fact, the lessons of the volatility test literature starting with Shiller (1982) and the return forecasting literature such as Fama and French (1988) are that, by and large, high prices correspond to lower future returns, not to higher earnings growth.

In addition, the association of price movements with volume, scarce shares, short restrictions, and so forth are just coincidences to this theory. That volume was high is as irrelevant as that the sky was blue.

Frictionless Rational Pricing—Low Returns
If not high g, perhaps low r is the explanation. If earnings grow at 5 percent, all it takes is a 5 percent required return to generate an *infinite* price. Absent an arbitrage opportunity, a time-varying risk premium can be invoked to explain any price pattern.

Fluctuations in the market as a whole might be sensibly understood as a time-varying risk premium. The top of the largest economic boom in postwar U.S. history is exactly when you'd expect a risk premium to be low and stock prices to be high. This view is also completely consistent with the volatility test and return regression evidence—high prices *are* followed by low returns, and low returns can be perfectly rational. (Campbell and Cochrane, 1999, is one model of this effect.)

Alas, while this story can easily explain procyclical variation in the market as a whole, it is much more strained to explain a boom in one particular segment of the market. Why should *Internet* stocks suddenly have a much lower risk premium? This would have to come from a dramatic change not in overall risk aversion and the market premium, but from a dramatic change in the perceived covariance (beta) of Internet earnings with respect to fundamental risk factors such as consumption, the market portfolio, and so on. And, then after March 2000, that beta changes back again. This is a hard story to swallow.

This model is also silent on a number of empirical regularities. Like all frictionless models, the huge volume of trading and the association with scarce shares are again irrelevant.

Rational Bubbles
A "rational bubble" occurs if everyone rationally holds stocks for any finite number of periods, but the "transversality condition" at infinity does not hold. For example, a stock with no dividend could satisfy

$$p_t + 1 = (1 + r)p_t + \varepsilon_{t+1}.$$

The expected return is $(1 + r)$, yet the price is not zero even though there are no dividends—the present value formula is violated. The price is expected to grow *forever*. Since we know the world will end in a few billion years, this model requires a small bit of irrationality—you're counting on someone, someday, buying an overvalued stock. However, that irrationality is pushed arbitrarily far in the future.

Rational bubbles can produce fascinating price paths with booms and crashes. They also produce price volatility that does not forecast earnings or returns. Rational bubbles require a short constraint, otherwise you would short the bubble, pay any dividends and turn an arbitrage profit at infinity into an arbitrage profit now.

However, though "bubble" has been invoked to explain everything from tulip prices, the South Sea company, the 1929 Dow, and 2000 tech stocks, this model is also silent on many common features of the events. Volume, again, is the most notable. In a "rational bubble" it is always rational to *hold* the stock for a period. There is no reason ever to buy or sell. It is also silent on all the other characteristics listed in table 3. There is no reason the bubble should happen in tech stocks and not coal stocks and no reason that "share supply" should seem to matter to prices.

Irrational Valuation

Many observers including Lamont and Thaler conclude that this event is prima facie evidence for "irrational" investors, who simply put too high a value on Palm. The trouble with this explanation is that it can explain too much. If prices were too low, they would be labeled "irrational depression" rather than "irrational exuberance." (And, they have—most of the time the finance profession struggles with the equity premium puzzle that prices seem too low leading to too high average returns.) The strength of any theory is the number of things it *can't* explain. I look forward to the day that behavioral finance can document structural patterns of behavior toward risk, well-understood evolutionary responses to our two million years of avoiding lions on the plains of Africa, that serve poorly in financial markets and can explain specific puzzles and not others. That day is not with us yet.

As with the other theories, irrational valuation is silent on many crucial attributes of the experience—above all, volume: If investors were irrationally attracted to Palm and bought too high, why did they get irrationally disgusted a day later and sell? Why did investors become irrationally attached to tech stocks and not coal stocks? Why did irrational attraction come and then go? Why did they lose their irrational attraction when insider's lock-up periods expired?

One of the key definitions of "irrational" behavior is that people recognize it when it's pointed out and change; education can overcome irrationality. This is one of the few ways to separate "irrationality" from just plain mistakes, or limited processing ability, and to give it some non-tautological content. The dog is not irrational for failing to short Palm; when the mistake is pointed out she just wags and pants as before. Yet the 3Com/Palm event was widely noted in the business press (and at the University of Chicago Graduate School of Business faculty lunchroom) on March 2, 2000; the overpricing was no secret. Similarly, story after story about how Internet stocks were "overpriced" from the point of view of long-term investors appeared in the business press. People bought anyway, *but not for the long term* as the volume numbers show. Many finance academics were actively trading Internet stocks—apparently, the best education in the world is not sufficient to overcome the desire to trade. Lamont and Thaler and Ofek and Richardson both document that institutional ownership was a little lower than usual in Internet stocks, but "educated" institutions still held large amounts. Thus, we cannot explain Palm/3Com or the NASDAQ by educable irrationality.

Short Constraints Mean We Can't See the Pessimists
Ofek and Richardson (2001) interpret their findings as evidence for models in which short sales constraints keep the pessimists' views from being expressed, as in Miller (1977). Chen, Hong, and Stein (2001) also advocate this view. This view also generates a "demand for shares." In particular, as stressed by Ofek and Richardson, it explains the concentration of high prices in stocks with few shares outstanding. However, this view is again silent on volume.

Of course there is some blurring of categories here, especially given the number of models currently being explored. Models such as Harrison and Kreps (1978) have some trading; their speculative demand comes from the possibility that an even more optimistic investor will come along, and then today's optimist will sell to him. Rather than categorize papers, it's more productive to categorize the underlying stories. One story focuses on the fact that with short constraints we don't see the pessimists. This story does not fundamentally involve any volume; we can all wake up the next morning and see the same thing with no trades happening. If one adds changes in opinions or changes in traders, some volume emerges and, potentially, some even higher prices.

Summary
Table 4 summarizes the facts and theories. All of the theories explain prices that rise and then decline. Only the convenience yield theory says anything about volume. The convenience yield theory can *only* explain high prices if there is a restriction on the number of shares or substitutes and a large trading volume. All of the other theories are silent on this observation; high volume is a coincidence.

6. Concluding Remarks

A substantial convenience yield or liquidity premium for stocks that are undergoing a trading frenzy, based on wide dispersion in opinion about a fundamentally new technology, is an attractive explanation for the high prices of NASDAQ tech stocks around 2000. This view not *only* explains the rise and fall of prices, which many stories do, but it also explains—indeed it *requires*—a wide variety of features common to this and similar experiences, including the association of high prices with high volume, high volatility, short sales frictions, and small numbers of available shares.

The possibility that some component of stock prices represents a trading-related convenience yield can help to explain a number of puzzles related to observations that demand curves seem to slope down at times. Among the most obvious, it suggests the long-run underperformance of IPOs (e.g., Loughran and Ritter, 1995), following the Palm pattern on a more subdued scale. It suggests trading-related price anomalies such as the S&P 500 inclusion effect on prices (Harris and Gurel, 1986; Shleifer, 1986) and betas (Barberis, Shleifer, and Wurgler 2002): Given the large number of index-linked contracts, stocks in the index will be traded a lot more than stocks out of the index.

The possibility of stock convenience yields is also interesting for policy and investment management. Obviously, buy-and-hold investors and institutions should avoid stocks with high convenience yields, or lend them when short rebates make it profitable to do so. If convenience yield induced price distortions are substantial, fewer restrictions on trading and short-selling and better substitutes, such as individual stock futures markets, can be important in limiting stock price volatility and helping stocks to send the proper signals about physical investment rather than share issue.

*John H. Cochrane is the Theodore O. Yntema Professor of Finance in the Graduate School of Business at the University of Chicago. The author thanks Thomas Chevrier for research assistance; Owen Lamont for data, extensive comments, and many helpful discussions; and Matthew Richardson for data. Revised versions of this paper (and this version with color graphs) can be found at http://gsbwww.uchicago.edu/fac/john.cochrane/research/Papers/.

Notes

1. Data from the Federal Reserve H.15 release, http://www.federalreserve.gov/releases/h15/data/b/tbsm1y.txt.

2. NASDAQ volume includes dealer trades, so one might argue that the correct number is 10 days rather than five. On the other hand dealers are people, too. More generally, there was surely great heterogeneity in holding times.

References

Barberis, Nicholas, Andrei Shleifer, and Jeffrey Wurgler, 2002, "Comovement," manuscript.

Baker, Malcom, and Jeremy C. Stein, 2002, "Market Liquidity as a Sentiment Indicator," Harvard University, manuscript.

Boudoukh, Jacob, and Robert Whitelaw, 1993, "Liquidity as a Choice Variable: A Lesson from the Japanese Bond Market," *Review of Financial Studies*, Vol. 6, pp. 266–292.

_____, 1991, "The Benchmark Effect in the Japanese Government Bond Market," *Journal of Fixed Income*, Vol. 1, pp. 52–59.

Brennan, Michael, and Avanidhar Subrahmanyam, 1996, "Market Microstructure and Asset Pricing: On the Compensation for Illiquidity in Stock Returns," *Journal of Financial Economics*, Vol. 41, pp. 441–464.

Campbell, John Y., and John H. Cochrane, 1999, "By Force of Habit: A Consumption-Based Explanation of Aggregate Stock Market Behavior," *Journal of Political Economy*, Vol. 107, pp. 205–251.

Chen, Joseph, Harrison Hong, and Jeremy C. Stein, 2001, "Breadth of Ownership and Stock Returns," National Bureau of Economic Research, working paper, No. 8151, and *Journal of Financial Economic,* forthcoming.

Duffie, Darrell, Nicolae Gârleanu, and Lasse Heje Pedersen, 2001, "Valuation in Dynamic Bargaining Markets," Stanford University, manuscript.

Fama, Eugene F., and Kenneth R. French, 2002, "Testing Tradeoff and Pecking Order Predictions about Dividends and Debt," *Review of Financial Studies,* Vol. 15, pp. 1–33.

_____, 1988, "Dividend Yields and Expected Stock Returns," *Journal of Financial Economics,* Vol. 22, pp. 3–27.

Fernald, John, and John H. Rogers, 2001, "Puzzles in the Chinese Stock Market," *Review of Economics and Statistics.*

Gallant, Ronald A., Peter E. Rossi, and George Tauchen, 1992, "Stock Prices and Volume," *The Review of Financial Studies,* Vol. 5, pp. 199–242.

Harris, Lawrence, and Eitan Gurel, 1986, "Price and Volume Effects Associated with Changes in the S&P 500: New Evidence for the Existence of Price Pressure," *Journal of Finance,* Vol. 41, pp. 851–860.

Harrison, Michael, and David Kreps, 1978, "Speculative Investor Behavior in a Stock Market with Heterogeneous Expectations," *Quarterly Journal of Economics,* Vol. 92, pp. 323–336.

Jones, Charles, 2001, "A Century of Stock Market Liquidity and Trading Costs," Columbia University, manuscript.

Jones, Charles, and Owen Lamont, 2002, "Short Sale Constraints and Stock Returns," *Journal of Financial Economics.*

Krishnamurthy, Arvind, 2001, "The Bond/Old-Bond Spread," Northwestern University, manuscript.

Lamont, Owen, 2000, "Guilty as Charged: Violations of the Law of one Price in Financial Markets," University of Chicago, manuscript.

Lamont, Owen, and Richard H. Thaler, 2001, "Can the Market Add and Subtract? Mispricing in Tech Stock Carve-outs," University of Chicago, manuscript.

Liu, Jun, and Francis Longsta, 2000, "Losing Money on Arbitrages: Optimal Dynamic Portfolio Choice in Markets with Arbitrage Opportunities," University of California, Los Angeles, manuscript.

Loughran, Tim, and Jay Ritter, 1995, "The New Issues Puzzle," *Journal of Finance,* Vol. 50, pp. 23–51.

Ofek, Eli, and Matthew Richardson, 2002, "The IPO Lock-Up Period: Implications for Market Efficiency and Downward Sloping Demand Curves," New York University, manuscript.

_____, 2001, "Dot Com Mania: The Rise and Fall of Internet Stock Prices," New York University, manuscript.

Miller, Edward, 1977, "Risk, Uncertainty and Divergence of Opinion," *Journal of Finance,* Vol. 32, pp. 1151–1168.

Mitchell, Mark, Todd Pulvino, and Erik Stafford, 2002, "Limited Arbitrage in Equity Markets," *Journal of Finance,* Vol. LVII, pp. 551–584.

Scheinkman, José, and Wei Xiong, 2002, "Overconfidence, Short-Sales Constraints and Bubbles," Princeton University, manuscript.

Shiller, Robert J., 1981, "Do Stock Prices Move too Much to be Justified by Subsequent Changes in Dividends?" *American Economic Review,* Vol. 71, pp. 421–436.

Shleifer, Andrei, 1986, "Do Demand Curves for Stocks Slope Down?" *Journal of Finance,* Vol. 41, pp. 579, 590.

Chapter 13
Bubble Psychology

Werner De Bondt*
University of Wisconsin, Madison

During the last 20 years, it has become apparent to everyone—individual and institutional investors, money managers, academicians, and policymakers—that we know far less about the behavior of financial markets and asset valuation than it was thought earlier.

In retrospect, perhaps the most striking development was strong and unanticipated price volatility in stock, bond, currency, and real estate markets. The performance of equity markets in particular left many intelligent people in disbelief. The powerful rise and subsequent decline of these markets in the United States, Europe, and Japan was a humbling experience, both in terms of discredited theory and practical challenge. Asset price bubbles are worrisome because they misallocate scarce resources and because they may lead to economic stagnation. Even if a bubble at first remains confined to one sector, contagion and spillover effects can cause further damage. Bubbles also redistribute wealth. Sometimes, good people get hurt. Financial earthquakes undermine the public's trust in the integrity of the market system.

Although movements in interest rates played a role in stock market instability, changing forecasts of economic prospects were the main source. Much of what happened during the 1980s and the 1990s was not forecasted, and much of what was forecasted did not happen. As always, the quality of judgment was the most critical factor in asset valuation. After all, "what is news" depends on the expectations embedded in prices.

Of course, it is difficult to identify a stock market boom, *ex ante*, as "a bubble that is about to burst." One of the lessons from history is that even very impressive changes in stock prices elude easy interpretation. Yet, during the 1980s and the 1990s, the collective judgment of the investing public went wrong in many ways. We certainly know so, *ex post*, with the benefit of hindsight. Consider, for instance, the multitude of financial myths surrounding the technology boom in the United States. Until a year ago, it was said confidently that high-tech companies would generate breathtaking, accelerating gains in economic productivity. It was said that, in the valuation of high-tech firms, the outlook for growth mattered more than did immediate earnings. It was said that some of these firms were already monopolies, with unbeatable advantages, and that they were not subject to the business cycle. High-tech companies, for all these reasons, were touted as superior investments. Across the nation, many financial advisers convinced their clients that there was "no price too high" to pay for a good high-tech company.

In academic finance, the most striking development of the last two decades was how dearly held notions of market efficiency, the positive relationship between return and nondiversifiable risk, and dividend discount models were put into question. For instance, it appeared that the volatility in equity returns could not readily be rationalized by subsequent movements in dividends and interest rates (Shiller, 1989). The long-term return premium of equity over bonds was a second much investigated puzzle. Among others, investor myopic loss aversion seemed a plausible explanation. It also became clear that, in the cross section of stocks, returns were somewhat predictable—but not by beta as the capital asset pricing model suggests. In the time-series dimension, many studies documented short-term reversals, intermediate-term momentum, and long-term reversals in stock prices, all in contradiction to the random walk hypothesis (De Bondt, 2000).

Where do these developments leave us today? Surely, with more respect for the traditional view that price and value are not always one-and-the-same thing. "The stock market is not a weighing machine, on which the value of each issue is recorded by an exact and impersonal mechanism. Rather [it] is a voting machine, whereon countless individuals register choices which are the product partly of reason and partly of emotion," said Benjamin Graham and David Dodd in *Security Analysis* (1934). Indeed, as long as there have been organized stock markets professional traders have emphasized the psychology of investors, market imperfections, and the limits of rational arbitrage (Mackay, 1841; Harrison, 1998; Chancellor, 1999). Investment decisions, John Maynard Keynes (1936) declared, are motivated by "animal spirits." He went on to portray the stock market as a beauty contest. Maybe, through careful fundamental analysis, some investors can pin down the intrinsic values to which prices gravitate in the long run. In the near term, however, such calculations may well be fruitless. Crowd sentiment has its own dynamics, and the "state of the market" drives a wedge between price and value. Money managers can choose to ignore these realities but they do so at the peril of their own jobs. According to Keynes, "There is nothing so dangerous as the pursuit of a rational investment policy in an irrational world."

1. Modern Finance

Contrary to the understanding of Keynes, Graham, and Dodd, and most practitioners, modern finance was built on the twin assumptions of "perfect markets and perfect people." Markets are efficient.[1] In its most stringent form, this paradigm takes a purely functional approach and dismisses institutional arrangements as neutral mutations—ultimately irrelevant to economic outcomes. Modern finance also snubs the human factor. It was conceived as a logical, normative model of an idealized decisionmaker. All behavior is reduced to the axioms of rationality that define *economic man*, that is, expected utility maximization, risk-aversion, rational expectations, and Bayesian updating. Under complete rationality an individual is able to view the full consequences of each possible action at once and choose objectively what is best for him or for her. In other words, the theory does not treat cognition as a scarce resource. Herbert Simon (1983) calls this approach "the Olympic model."

The rational paradigm fails in at least two major ways. First, as mentioned, its predictions of market behavior prove unsatisfactory. In an interview with *The Economist* (April 23, 1994), Merton Miller admitted this lack of success with unusual candor. He stated, "The blending of psychology and economics ... is becoming popular ... because conventional economics has failed to explain how asset prices are set." (Indeed, a series of well-documented anomalies first brought to light by behavioral hypotheses now dominates asset pricing research.) A second failure of the rational paradigm is that the underlying assumptions are descriptively false. Few people, it turns out, are Olympians. This is easily seen in laboratory experiments. For instance, risk-taking depends at least as much on situational as on personality factors. Or, contrary to the principle of "decision frame invariance," alternative descriptions of an identical problem give rise to different choices (Tversky and Kahneman, 1986). Subjects in many cases willingly violate the axioms of rationality. The normative logic of choice, therefore, may not be a suitable starting point for a descriptive theory of decisionmaking. The deviations from that model are widespread, systematic, and fundamental. What we need, it seems, are new descriptive theories of financial behavior and asset pricing.

2. Behavioral Finance

The new field of behavioral finance takes up this challenge. It is the study of financial decisionmaking with the help of concepts borrowed from psychology. Behavioral finance follows an empirical, inductive approach. It is built on the notion of "bounded rationality" and it focuses on observed behavior. Of course, what an individual does may be very different from what, in principle, he should do. Richard Thaler and myself (1995) and Karl-Erik Warneryd (2001) offer surveys of the literature. The central insight of behavioral finance is that "decision processes shape decision outcomes." If we want to understand and influence what people do, we better first investigate how people think. Under bounded rationality, the decisionmaker does not contemplate in every instant the whole range of possible actions that lie ahead. People are human. Their "true nature" is such that attention, memory, habit, social influences, emotion, visceral responses, and task complexity all contribute to decision processes. For instance, when people move to a new city, most stop searching for an apartment when they find one that satisfies their needs. They do not optimize in a literal sense. Suboptimality in decisionmaking is usually traced to one of three sources: problems of cognition, emotions (for example, wishful thinking), and conformism. My discussion below centers on cognitive issues—mostly relating to the psychology of judgment.[2]

A simple way to think about investment decisionmaking is as a series of present value calculations. Everything depends on the expected future cash flows, the opportunity cost of capital, and the required investment. Of course, it may be very difficult to get an accurate estimate of, say, the earnings of a telecommunications company five years from now. Actions depend on beliefs, however. The questions "how intuitive forecasts are made" and "how sophisticated man, as an intuitive statistician, really is" are fundamental.

The psychological research has produced some disheartening results. (For a literature review, see Gilovich, 1991.) For instance, simple regression models that capture an individual's weighting policy for major predictor variables and that apply it consistently often lead to better forecasts than the subject himself. This phenomenon occurs because any misconception that the subject has is less detrimental than his inconsistencies in applying a given decision rule (Dawes, 1979). Outcome feedback often induces response inconsistency and it may not help accuracy. Neither does prediction accuracy improve with experience, incentives, and the amount of available information. Many experts falsely believe that they can beat decision rules, which yield the correct choice in a large proportion of cases. Highly motivated subjects grow impatient. They do not easily tolerate errors without resorting to a strategy shift. Finally, the prime effect of extra information is to make the subjects feel more confident, without improving the quality of their judgment (Oskamp, 1965). More generally, people are prone to experience confidence in highly fallible judgments.

Two significant concepts relating to "how people think" are mental frames and heuristics. In the first instance, most reasoning occurs with the help of *mental frames*. A frame refers to the decisionmaker's simplified perspective on a complex real world problem, that is, his conceptual model. The frame defines how the problem is formulated and how actions and outcomes are experienced relative to certain aspiration levels. In many cases there is no unitary model of truth, even though there are degrees of knowledge. (For instance, by and large, company hiring practices reflect the belief that good university students become productive employees. This intuitive theory may well be correct although I cannot offer evidence.) As a rule, the tacit models that people use are fluid; they can be misleading, and they need not be internally consistent. Much of what people know they accept on faith. (Is milk rich in calcium? Is Chile a country in South America? Are stocks the best investment for the long run?) Every newborn child cannot possibly recreate from scratch all of our collective knowledge about the universe. Mental frames are socially shared. To a significant degree, they are fabricated by educators, opinion leaders, and men in advertising. ("At Ford, quality is job one.")

Precisely because our intuitive knowledge structures are influenced by what others say and do, we are social animals. Mental frames have great influence. When people interpret their lives or look for guidance, impressions of this kind may well trump experience and logic. Sometimes, there is no alternative. Major personal decisions, say, relating to career choices, are not repeated so often that people can learn much from their own experience. What is troubling, however, is that many frames are both mistaken and resistant to change. Ideally, we would like to understand the sources of illusions and the mind processes that sustain them. In fact, all the pseudo-science, myth, and superstition that envelop us (say, on the benefits of herbal medicines) seem to disprove the descriptive relevance of the economic concept of rational expectations. The issue is not easily reduced to a debate about learning. Self interest matters, too. For instance, pressure groups in society spend large sums of money to shape the content of news reports. To create a world dominated by particular problems is to create support for particular solutions. Marcia Angell (1996) analyzes the clash between law and junk science in the breast implant case and the economic interests that motivate it. Elaine Showalter (1997) studies chronic fatigue, Gulf War, and other syndromes as imaginary epidemic illnesses of the 1990s.

Heuristics are shortcuts for coping with new information. Generally, heuristics produce the desired outcome but, on occasion, they lead to foreseeable errors in judgment. Few people are aware of these biases. In a series of classic papers (reprinted in Kahneman et al., 1982), Amos Tversky, Daniel Kahneman, and others analyzed three major rules of thumb: representativeness, availability, and anchoring-and-adjustment. Judgment by *representativeness* occurs when people assess the likelihood of an event by its superficial similarity to a well-known stereotype. The unjustified neglect of base rates that follows implies that man can hardly be viewed as a Bayesian decisionmaker. Representativeness also supports the mental structuring of random sequences, and it explains the failure to appreciate the statistical phenomenon of "regression-to-the-mean." These experimental findings motivated the original studies of stock market overreaction. Judgment by *availability* takes place whenever a probability is judged by vividness and by the ease with which an event is brought to mind. The *anchoring-and-adjustment* heuristic explains the power of first impressions. People start from an initial value and adjust if to yield an inference, but the adjustment is typically insufficient so that different anchors produce different conclusions. People, we find, are active interpreters of new information; that is, they constantly go beyond the data that are given. Hence, human cognition is conservative. Beliefs tend to sustain themselves despite evidence to the contrary.[3]

3. Financial Behavior

I have described some of the nonreflective strategies that people use in intuitive judgment. It is of decisive importance to establish that these strategies, and the biases associated with them, influence day-to-day decisionmaking. For this reason, behavioral finance has collected many new facts about how financial forecasts are made, how portfolios are managed, and how stocks are traded.[4] Below, I briefly illustrate some of the new findings as they relate to the behavior of amateur investors (also called noise traders) and experts (security analysts).

In prior work (1998), I have sketched "a portrait of the individual investor." The portrait is unimpressive. I list four classes of anomalies relating to irregular perceptions of the dynamics of equity prices, perceptions of value, risk management, and trading practices. Perhaps the best-established stylized fact is that many investors see price patterns where there are none. In various ways, traders take pains to justify their decisions.[5] There is a strong extrapolation bias, that is, the expected continuation of past price changes, as well as a strong optimism bias.[6] Subjective perceptions of price variability are typically too narrow. This reflects overconfidence. Perceptions of value depend in large measure on popular models, that is, what is in fashion. Many people do not distinguish between good stocks and good companies. They are also willing to pay more for assets that are familiar to them and, therefore, make them comfortable. What is surprising is the failure to infer basic investment principles from years of experience, for example, the benefits of diversification. It is widely believed that risk can be managed by knowledge and trading skill after funds have been committed. This encourages investors to put their wealth in relatively few assets.[7] Finally, while some investors procrastinate and others trade too much, nearly all have a psychological aversion to realize losses. Some investors tend to take gains on past winner stocks early.

Many studies have examined the quality of security analysts' stock recommendations and earnings forecasts (see, for example, De Bondt and Thaler, 1990; De Bondt and Forbes, 1999). On the whole, these studies find that the analysts are decidedly human. The data suggest 1) excessive optimism (for example, "low" earnings forecasts are often more accurate than the consensus), 2) excessive use of popular models (that is, forecasts of earnings changes that are too extreme, up or down, especially for long-term predictions), 3) excessive confidence, 4) excessive rationalization (that is, the tendency to give too little weight to earnings news and to miss turning points), and 5) excessive agreement among analysts (that is, herding behavior). The range of forecasts, in the cross section of analysts, is surprisingly narrow. Most actual earnings per share numbers fall outside the range of the "high" and "low" forecasts. Yet, agreement among analysts is always so strong that it barely increases further as we get closer to the time of the earnings announcement.

4. Market Behavior and Asset Price Bubbles

Besides decision anomalies (seen in experimental data) and anomalies in financial behavior (seen in survey and trading data), behaviorally inspired research has also discovered a list of market anomalies, for example, the long-run underperformance of initial public offerings, excess volatility in stock prices, the predictive power of the book-to-market value ratio in the cross section of asset returns, intermediate-term price momentum, and long-run price reversals (the winner-loser effect) (for a survey, see De Bondt and Thaler, 1995). All these findings support the view that investor psychology influences stock returns and that sophisticated agents may benefit in a methodical way from other people's cognitive and emotional shortcomings.[8] I (De Bondt, 2000) show that many of the results first established with U.S. data also hold in international markets.

What causes predictable momentum and reversals in stock prices? The most likely explanation is that analysts and traders naïvely extrapolate past earnings trends.[9] Investor under- and overreaction may be accounted for by the unwarranted use of stereotypes. For instance, investors freely talk about "growth firms" and "declining industries" even though annual earnings changes provide little evidence of reliable time-series patterns (except for reversals in the tails of the distribution). All too often, the life-cycle metaphor proves persuasive. No wonder, then, that when an earnings surprise hits, many traders refuse to believe it. Underreaction occurs when new evidence runs counter to a firmly held view. People persevere in their beliefs. They filter the data to confirm what they think they already know. Consistent with this interpretation of the data, three- to five-year stock market losers are more likely than not to experience subsequent positive earnings surprises, and past market winners are more likely than not to report subsequent negative surprises.

Modern finance has responded to the new facts in different ways. It either reinterprets them as nonanomalous (for example, the abnormal profits compensate for time-varying risk), it questions their pervasiveness and robustness (Fama, 1998), or it argues that markets may yet be minimally rational, in the sense that markets fail to supply opportunities for abnormal profits. The most common counterargument is rational arbitrage. "Even if we accept the notion that many investors misinterpret the news," it is said, "a relatively few individuals sensitive to arbitrage may make markets work as the standard theory predicts." My reading of the literature is that there are no compelling reasons to give that argument decisive weight (for a lengthy discussion, see Brunnermeier, 2001).

One way to think about the matter is to ask for the minimal set of restrictions on heterogeneous beliefs and information sets that even in frictionless markets are necessary for the existence of rational, arbitrage-free equilibrium prices. Russell and Thaler (1985) and others show that investors are not allowed to form different opinions based on the same substantive information. They must agree on the value implications of any conceivable state. When there is such divergence of opinion, rational prices may yet prevail if, at some future time, the true mapping of events into value is revealed to all and if, in the meantime, only rational investors sell short. Neither of these assumptions applies to the stock market.

Institutional factors, such as short sales constraints or capital gains taxes, are likely to change the situation for the worse rather than for the better. In a world with nontrivial trading costs and heterogeneous beliefs, every individual not only chooses the size of his holdings in each asset but also in which assets to invest. Equilibrium involves the simultaneous determination of asset prices and the identity of investors trading in each asset. Some economic agents never reveal their information via trade, except by abstaining. As a result, market prices cannot reflect it (Mayshar, 1983).

A pure arbitrage opportunity does not exist unless it is certain that share prices will eventually revert to their fundamental underlying values. However, to affect prices, investors with superior forecasting ability or with inside information must assume increasing amounts of diversifiable risk. In practice, arbitrageurs face financial constraints (Shleifer and Vishny, 1997). Second, it may be rational for these traders to ride the trend rather than to go against it. Third, the resilience of a bubble may stem from the inability of rational arbitrageurs to coordinate their selling strategies. Fourth, a market may rationally launch itself onto a speculative bubble with prices being driven by an arbitrary self-confirming element in expectations (Tirole, 1982). There is no choice-theoretic rationale for singling out equilibrium price paths that do not suffer this extrinsic uncertainty.

What are the common behavioral elements in the various interpretations of asset price bubbles? To answer that question, I go back to Charles Kindleberger's (1978) scenario of the canonical financial crisis. In the prelude to crisis, Kindleberger distinguishes three stages: 1) an economic shock that reflects structural change outside the experience of most people and that objectively justifies higher prices (a "new era");

2) rising investor confidence, leading to the increased use of leverage and speculative instruments; and 3) a herding effect, where demand increases because prices are going up. Similarly, when the bubble bursts, an outside shock first reduces demand. Next, prices drop more as demand slows because even lower prices are expected in the future. The central puzzle is the excessive optimism and overconfidence that start the cycle, as well as the positive feedback trading that keeps it going. After the success stories have become widely known and accepted by the public, unrealistic hopes for rapid wealth accumulation draw many newcomers into the market. These players tend to naïvely duplicate strategies that produced high profits in the past. An interesting aspect of herding behavior is the illusion of universal liquidity, that is, the belief of any individual trader that in a downturn he will be able to get out while others take losses.[10] Surveying bubbles from the 17th century to the 1987 crash, White (1990) concludes: "The principal factor that leads to [their] emergence ... is that the ... fundamentals of the assets ... cease to be well identified. Another feature ... is the appearance of ... inexperienced investors." Shiller (2000) also defends the feedback theory. He ascribes a prominent role to the mass media in the Internet bubble. Evidently, many other self-interested parties (top managers, auditors, investment bankers, analysts, brokers, lawyers, and politicians) stoked the fire.

5. Conclusion

Much is learned about the behavior of investors and markets by studying how people solve financial problems. Substantively, behavioral finance shows that:

1. *Intuitive judgment is fragile*. Basic investment principles, such as portfolio diversification, are not learned from everyday experience. In fact, as the Enron debacle and recent accounting scandals show, many investors are financially illiterate. The timely, full, and transparent disclosure of information helps to maintain trust in the capital markets, but, by itself, may not be enough. Because the state at present plays a lesser role in protecting people from the hazards of life (for example, sickness and old age) than it did before, financial education and easy access to reliable, independent financial advice are important agenda items for policymakers.[11]

2. The *speculative dynamics of stock prices* are broadly consistent with the position taken by Graham and Dodd (1934) that, in the long run, prices gravitate to economic fundamentals but that, in the short run, investor psychology may drive a wedge between price and value. The valuation errors of noise traders create risk but they may be a profit opportunity for sophisticated, patient investors.

Behavioral finance has already proved itself to be a productive, pragmatic, and intuitive approach to asset pricing research. With its requirement of realism in assumptions, behavioral finance also brings discipline to financial modeling.[12] Some financial economists continue to favor, on an *a priori* basis, models with rational agents only. Fama (1998) and others worry that researchers will arbitrarily pick and choose from a list of psychological biases in order to behavioralize market anomalies. Depending on the anomaly, at least one bias will inevitably fit the facts. I very much share their concern. If carefully defined, however, psychological biases are probably not as slippery a concept as rationality. In principle, laboratory, survey, and market data can falsify the hypothesis at hand.

*Werner De Bondt is a professor of finance, investment, and banking at the University of Wisconsin, Madison. This article is based in part on his previous work. The text borrows ideas from De Bondt (1998, 2000, 2002). The author thanks Robert Chirinko and Bertrand Renaud for their comments and Paul Harrison for useful discussions.

Notes

1. In answer to the question "What did we learn from the [1987] crash?" Fama (1989) replies: "The market moved with breathtaking quickness to its new equilibrium ... its performance during the period of hyperactive trading is to be applauded."

2. Because space is limited, I will not discuss the psychology of choice, for example, prospect theory, loss aversion, procrastination, hyperbolic discounting, self-control, habit formation, and so on. See Warneryd (2001).

3. As early as 1620, in *Novum Organum*, Francis Bacon stated that "The human understanding supposes a greater degree of order and equality in things than it really finds; and although many things in nature be sui generis and most irregular, will yet invest parallels and conjugates and relatives where no such thing is."

4. Many people believe that they can benefit from this enterprise, including individual investors, financial planners, money managers, and executives who manage earnings with an eye towards the firm's stock price. The list even includes central bankers. In the arsenal of monetary policy tools, Federal Reserve Chairman Alan Greenspan's spoken words are arguably among his most powerful weapons. The pragmatic purpose, of course, is to make better decisions. (Modern finance has no comparable agenda since it starts from the premise that investors already know what is best.) Paul Slovic (1972) states it well when he writes: "A full understanding of human limitations will ultimately benefit the decision maker more than will naïve faith in the infallibility of his intellect."

5. "Even when the underlying motive of purchase [of common stocks] is mere speculative greed, human nature desires to conceal this unlovely impulse behind a screen of apparent logic and good sense," (Graham and Dodd, 1940).

6. See, again, Francis Bacon (1620): "Man prefers to believe what he prefers to be true."

7. Even Warren Buffett, not exactly an amateur trader, seems to fall into this trap: "We believe that if you are a know-something investor, able to find five to 10 sensibly priced firms that possess important long-term competitive advantages, then conventional diversification makes no sense for you. It is apt simply to hurt your results and increase your risk. I cannot understand why an investor of that sort elects to put money into a business that is his twentieth favorite rather than simply adding money to his top choices—the businesses he understands the best, and that present the least risk, along with the greatest profit potential," (Berkshire Hathaway Annual Report, 1993).

8. In his *Primer on Political Economy* (1878), William Stanley Jevons also suggests a link between investor psychology and asset pricing—in particular, between herding behavior and the apparent profitability of contrarian investment strategies. He states: "As a general rule, it is foolish to do just what other people are doing, because there are almost sure to be too many people doing the same thing."

9. Alternative, not mutually exclusive, explanations include systematic biases in risk perception and trading that is motivated by what is happening in the market rather than changes in economic fundamentals, for example, program trading and portfolio insurance.

10. One interpretation of this behavior is excessive risk-taking or recklessness. Frank Knight (1921) emphasizes, however, that the risk does "not relate to objective external probabilities, but to the value of judgment and executive powers of the person taking the chance ... Most men have an irrationally high confidence in their own good fortune, and that is doubly true when their personal prowess comes into the reckoning ... To these considerations must be added the stimulus of the competitive situation, constantly exerting pressure to outbid one's rivals ... Another ... factor is the human trait of tenacity ... once committed, ... the general rule is to hold on to the last ditch," (pp. 365–366).

11. Successful wealth management requires a structured and disciplined framework. The rationality of many social systems—either purposefully designed rules and regulations, or spontaneous market mechanisms— transcends individual rationality. The Swiss Henri-Frederic Amiel said it best: "L'experience de chaque home se recommence. Seules les institutions deviennent plus sages." (Translation: "The experience of every person starts anew. Only institutions become wiser.")

12. Consider, for instance, the case of stock market overreaction. The arguments in favor are at three distinct levels. First, in experiments, subjects behave as predicted by the representativeness heuristic. Second, survey and trading data confirm that most investors love past winner stocks and hate past losers. Third, at the market level, price reversals are observed.

References

Angell, Marcia, 1996, *Science on Trial*, New York: W.W. Norton.

Brunnermeier, Markus K., 2001, *Asset Pricing Under Asymmetric Information: Bubbles, Crashes, Technical Analysis and Herding*, Oxford, UK: Oxford University Press.

Chancellor, Edward, 1999, *Devil Take the Hindmost: A History of Financial Speculation*, New York: Farrar-Straus-Giroux.

Dawes, Robyn, 1979, "The Robust Beauty of Improper Linear Models in Decision Making," *American Psychologist*, Vol. 34, pp. 571–582.

De Bondt, Werner F. M., 2002, "Discussion of Competing Theories of Financial Anomalies," *Review of Financial Studies*, Vol. 15, pp. 607–613.

_____, 2000, "The Psychology of Underreaction and Overreaction in World Equity Markets," in *Security Market Imperfections in Worldwide Equity Markets*, D. B. Keim and W. Ziemba, eds., Cambridge, UK: Cambridge University Press.

_____, 1998, "A Portrait of the Individual Investor," *European Economic Review*, Vol. 42, pp. 831–844.

De Bondt, Werner F. M., and William P. Forbes, 1999, "Herding in Analyst Earnings Forecasts: Evidence from the United Kingdom," *European Financial Management*, Vol. 5, pp.143–163.

De Bondt, Werner F. M., and Richard H. Thaler, 1995, "Financial Decision Making in Markets and Firms: A Behavioral Perspective," in *Handbook of Finance*, R. A. Jarrow, V. Maksimovic, and W. T. Ziemba, eds., Amsterdam: Elsevier-North Holland.

_____, 1990, "Do Security Analysts Overreact?" *American Economic Review*, Vol. 80, pp. 52–57.

Fama, Eugene F., 1998, "Market Efficiency, Long-term Returns, and Behavioral Finance," *Journal of Financial Economics*, Vol. 49, pp. 283–306.

_____, 1989, "Perspectives on October 1987, or, What Did We Learn from the Crash?," in *Black Monday and the Future of Financial Markets*, R. W. Kamphuis, Jr. et al., eds., New York: Irwin.

Gilovich, Thomas, 1991, *How We Know What Isn't So: The Fallibility of Human Reason in Everyday Life*, New York: Free Press.

Graham, Benjamin, and David Dodd, 1934, *Security Analysis*, New York: McGraw-Hill, 2nd edition, 1940.

Harrison, Paul, 1998, "Rational Equity Valuation at the Time of the South Sea Bubble," Federal Reserve Board, working paper.

Kahneman, Daniel, Paul Slovic, and Amos Tversky, eds., 1982, *Judgment Under Uncertainty: Heuristics and Biases*, Cambridge, UK: Cambridge University Press.

Keynes, John M., 1936, *The General Theory of Employment, Interest, and Money*, New York: Macmillan.

Kindleberger, Charles, 1978, *Manias, Panics, and Crashes: A History of Financial Crisis*, New York: Basic Books.

Knight, Frank H., 1971, *Risk, Uncertainty, and Profit*, Chicago: University of Chicago Press, first published by Houghton Mifflin, 1921.

Mackay, Charles, 1841, *Extraordinary Popular Delusions and the Madness of Crowds*, New York: Farrar-Straus-Giroux (1932 edition).

Mayshar, Joram, 1983, "On Divergence of Opinion and Imperfections in Capital Markets, *American Economic Review*, Vol. 73, pp. 114–128.

Oskamp, Stuart, 1965, "Overconfidence in Case-Study Judgments," *Journal of Consulting Psychology*, Vol. 29, pp. 261-265.

Russell, Tom, and Richard H. Thaler, 1985, "The Relevance of Quasi-Rationality in Competitive Markets," *American Economic Review*, Vol. 75, pp. 1071-1082.

Shiller, Robert J., 2000, *Irrational Exuberance*, Princeton, NJ: Princeton University Press.

_____, 1989, *Market Volatility*, Boston: MIT Press.

Shleifer, Andrei, and Robert W. Vishny, 1997, "The Limits of Arbitrage," *Journal of Finance*, Vol. 52, pp. 35–55.

Showalter, Elaine, 1997, *Hystories: Hysterical Epidemics and Modern Culture*, New York: Columbia University Press.

Simon, Herbert A., 1983, *Reason in Human Affairs,* Stanford, CA: Stanford University Press.

Slovic, Paul, 1972, "Psychological Study of Human Judgment: Implications for Investment Decision Making," *Journal of Finance,* Vol. 27, pp. 779–799.

Tirole, Jean, 1982, "On the Possibility of Speculation under Rational Expectations," *Econometrica*, Vol. 50, pp. 1163–1181.

Tversky, Amos, and Daniel Kahneman, 1986, "Rational Choice and the Framing of Decisions," *Journal of Business,* Vol. 59, pp. 67–94.

Warneryd, Karl-Erik, 2001, *Stock Market Psychology: How People Value and Trade Stocks*, Cheltenham, UK: Edward Elgar.

White, Eugene N., 1990, *Crashes and Panics: The Lessons from History*, New York: Business One Irwin.

Chapter 14
Bubbles in Real Estate Markets

Richard Herring*
University of Pennsylvania

and

Susan Wachter
University of Pennsylvania

1. Introduction

Real estate bubbles may occur without banking crises. And, banking crises may occur without real estate bubbles. But the two phenomena are correlated in a remarkable number of instances ranging over a wide variety of institutional arrangements, in both advanced industrial nations and emerging economies. The consequences for the real economy depend on the role of banks in the country's financial system. In the United States, where banks hold only about 22 percent of total assets, most borrowers can find substitutes for bank loans and the impact on the general level of economic activity is relatively slight. But in countries where banks play a more dominant role, such as the United States before the Great Depression (where banks held 65 percent of total assets), or present day Japan (where banks hold 79 percent of total assets), or emerging markets (where banks often hold well over 80 percent of total assets), the consequences for the real economy can be much more severe. (Bank for International Settlements, 1995).

In this paper, we develop an explanation of how real estate bubbles and banking crises may be related and why they occur. First we review the determinants of real estate prices and ask why the real estate market is so vulnerable to sustained positive deviations from fundamental prices. We place special emphasis on the role played by the banking system. Increases in the price of real estate may increase the economic value of bank capital to the extent that banks own real estate. Such increases will also increase the value of loans collateralized by real estate and may lead to a decline in the perceived risk of real estate lending. For these reasons, an increase in the price of real estate may increase the supply of credit to the real estate industry, which in turn, is likely to lead to further increases in the price of real estate.

Bank behavior may also play an important role in exacerbating the collapse of real estate prices. A decline in the price of real estate will decrease bank capital directly by reducing the value of the bank's own real estate assets. It will also reduce the value of loans collateralized by real estate and may lead to defaults, which will further reduce capital. Moreover, a decline in the price of real estate is likely to increase the perceived risk in real estate lending. All of these factors are likely to reduce the supply of credit to the real estate industry. In addition, supervisors and regulators may react to the resulting weakening of bank capital positions by increasing capital requirements and instituting stricter rules for classifying and provisioning against real estate assets. These measures will further diminish the supply of credit to the real estate industry and place additional downward pressure on real estate prices.

This conceptual framework of interactions between the real estate market and bank behavior can be used to interpret recent examples of real estate booms linked to banking crises in Japan and other countries affected by the Asian financial crisis. We conclude with a discussion of the policy implications of our analysis emphasizing measures to limit the amplitude of real estate bubbles and ways to insulate the banking system.

2. Bubbles: The Role of Optimists

We begin with a model of land prices developed by Mark Carey (1990). This provides a straightforward explanation of how bubbles may begin in a simple setting where it is plausible to assume that supply is fixed. This is directly relevant to commercial real estate booms, moreover, because the dynamics of land prices undoubtedly drive overall real estate prices and because, in the cases we analyze in which real estate prices rise, construction lags result in supply that is fixed for a lengthy period. We will consider complications introduced by construction lags in the following section.

Carey's model assumes that N potential investors are identical except with regard to their reservation prices for land, P.[1] These differences of opinion may occur because investors make errors in computing the "fundamental value" of land or because investors may have private information about future expected income from land or the appropriate capitalization rate.[2,3] These reservation prices are distributed along a continuum around the "fundamental value" of land according to a distribution function $F(P)$.[4] In most markets, one could argue that sustained deviations *below* the fundamental value are unlikely because sophisticated investors who know the fundamental value will profit by buying until the price rises to the fundamental value. This presumption seems plausible for the market for land. Conversely, it is tempting to assume that if the price is too *high*, sophisticated investors will profit by selling short until the price falls to the fundamental value. But this assumption is *not* plausible in the market for land because of difficulties in selling land short.[5] Moreover, increases in the supply of land cannot be expected to moderate the rise in price because the supply of land is fixed, at least in the short run.[6]

Optimists, those with reservation prices above the fundamental value, will determine the price in this kind of market with no short sales and fixed supply.[7] Indeed, even if their optimism is unfounded by analysis of fundamental value, they are likely to remain in business so long as the upward trend in prices continues. As we shall see, even if they earn substandard returns, they are likely to be able to borrow against their capital gains so long as lenders value their land at market prices when determining its value as collateral.

The price of land in Carey's model is determined by the proportion of investors willing to pay the price, P, which is sufficient to clear the market for the entire supply of land, Z. The demand for land at any arbitrary P' depends on the proportion of investors who have a reservation price, $P \geq P'$, which is $(1 - F(P'))$, times the number of investors N times the resources, L, available to each investor: which is $N(1 - F(P'))L$.[8] In equilibrium, the demand for land must equal the value of the total supply, PZ, and so:

1) $P = [N(1 - F(P))L]/Z$.

For ease of exposition we will make the simplifying assumption that $F(P)$ is a uniform distribution centered on the fundamental price, P^*, with a range equal to $P^* \pm h$, where h is the measure of the heterogeneity of reservation prices among investors. Since $1 - F(P) = (P^* + h - P)/2h$ we can rewrite equation 1 for the special case of a uniform distribution as:

2) $P = [N(P^* + h)L]/[2hZ + NL]$.

Partial differentiation of equation 2 indicates that P will increase with increases in the number of investors (N), the fundamental price (P^*), and the resources available to investors (L). P will also increase in response to increases in the extent of heterogeneity (h), so long as the total resources available to half of the investors exceed the value of land at the fundamental price, P^*.[9,10]

We can transform equation 2 from a static to a dynamic equation by introducing time subscripts for each of the variables. We will first consider P^*_t and broaden the discussion to include commercial real estate.

The demand for the stock of commercial real estate depends on the price and the discounted present value of the expected stream of future rents which, in turn, depends on demographic factors, the expected growth in income, anticipated real interest rates, taxes and the structure of the economy.[11] In the formation of a bubble, it is plausible that the initial increase in real estate prices was a response to an increase in demand. As examples, in some cases the growth of the economy may accelerate, in others the structure of output may shift in favor of the office-intensive service sector, or anticipated real interest rates may decline.

The variable P_t equilibrates the demand and supply for ownership of the stock of real estate structures, while rents equilibrate the demand and supply of the flow of services from the stock of commercial real estate.[12]

When the price for the stock of existing commercial real estate structures rises above the replacement cost, developers have an incentive to initiate new construction that will increase Z_t (now redefined to represent the stock of commercial real estate structures). This will eventually restore long-run equilibrium in which the ratio of the price of the stock of existing commercial real estate to replacement cost equals one. The price at which the stock of existing commercial real estate is equal to the replacement cost is P^*_t, the fundamental price consistent with long-run equilibrium. New construction, however, takes a substantial amount of time—perhaps two to six years—and so the adjustment process is likely to be slow (Malpezzi and Wachter, 2002).

In general the number of potential investors in commercial real estate (N) will not be an important determinant of the dynamics of real estate prices because it does not vary much. But one exception may have been important during the 1980s and 1990s when many countries began to liberalize financial regulation and open their markets to foreign investors. The liberalization of financial regulation may have increased N_t, by increasing the number of institutions that were permitted to invest in real estate directly or by permitting foreigners to invest in real estate, as in several emerging markets.

Finally, the supply of financial resources available to real estate investors, L_t, appears to have been an important factor that increased the boom in real estate prices and extended its duration in all of the cases we analyze. This raises the question, why, despite the evident dangers of heavy concentrations of real estate lending, did banks permit their exposures to real estate become so large?

3. The Role of Banks

A bank's loan-concentration decision can be modeled as the outcome of an expected profit calculation subject to the constraint that the perceived risk of bankruptcy be no greater than some probability γ (Guttentag and Herring, 1985, 1986a). We can express this constraint as:

3) $\Pr(A \leq M) \leq \gamma$,

where A is the value of the bank's portfolio of assets at the end of the period and M the bank's minimum acceptable value of assets which is determined either by internal risk guidelines or the capital ratio required by regulators, whichever is binding. By making use of Tchebysheff's inequality we can rewrite this constraint as:

4) $\gamma (E(A) - M)^2 - \sigma_p^2 \geq 0$,

where σ_p^2 is the variance of the expected return on the bank's portfolio of loans. Using this formulation of the constraint, we can form the Lagrangian expression:

5) $G(L_j, V) = \sum_{j=1}^{n} L_j(r_j - i) + V(\gamma(E(A) - M)^2 - \sigma_p^2)$,

where V is the shadow price of the risk constraint, r_j is the expected return on asset j and i is one plus the opportunity cost of funds. For ease of exposition we will focus on the two-asset case in which the risk constraint is binding ($V > 0$). L_1 is the amount the bank will choose to lend to the real estate sector given L_2, the other assets in the bank's portfolio:

6) $$L_1 = \left[\frac{1 + 2V\gamma(E(A) - M)}{\sigma_1^2 2V} \right] (r_1 - i) - \frac{L_2 \sigma_{12}}{\sigma_1^2}.$$

The concentration of loans to the real estate sector—the amount lent relative to capital—will be greater the higher the expected return relative to the opportunity cost of funds and the lower the perceived covariance of returns with the rest of the portfolio. Differentiation of the first-order conditions (in appendix A, available from authors) shows that the desired concentration *increases* as the promised return *increases* ($\partial L_1/\partial R_1 > 0$); *declines* as the expected probability of a default *increases* ($\partial L_1/\partial \pi_1 < 0$); *declines* as the perceived correlation with the rest of the portfolio *increases* ($\partial L_1/\partial \rho_{12} < 0$ for $\rho_{12} > 0$); *declines* as the capital requirement *increases* ($\partial L_1/\partial M < 0$); and *increases* as the expected value of assets *increases* ($\partial L_1/\partial E(A) > 0$).

This model of bank behavior is nonetheless useful for making inferences about what may motivate banks' decisions to take on increasing concentrations of loans to the real estate sector. First, lending to the real estate sector is attractive when it is expected to be profitable. Promised returns (where R_1 is interpreted to include not just the contractual interest rate but also fees stated in interest-equivalent form) are often higher than rates available on prime corporate loans. Indeed, the initial lending to real estate may occur when banks receive expanded powers intended to increase bank profits and help them to compete more effectively with less heavily regulated financial firms.

Rising real estate prices may also directly encourage greater lending to the real estate sector in two ways. First, to the extent that the bank's own holdings of real estate rise in value, $E(A)$ and the economic value of the bank's capital increases, so would the bank's willingness to hold more real estate loans. Second, to the extent that the market value of collateral on outstanding real estate loans increases, the risk of loss on the existing portfolio of loans declines and it is possible to lend more without increasing the probability of bankruptcy, γ. Increasing real estate prices may also have a more subtle impact on the subjective probability of a default which banks applied to new real estate lending, a possibility we discuss in the next section.

Despite these factors, which increase the attractiveness of real estate lending, it is clear (at least with the benefit of hindsight) that banks often fail to assess risks appropriately. Why do banks underestimate the risks of heavy concentrations of real estate lending? Two hypotheses are plausible: 1) Banks underestimate risks because they are subject to disaster myopia; and 2) Banks ignore risks because of perverse incentives.

4. Disaster Myopia

The ability to estimate the probability of a shock—like a collapse in real estate prices—depends on two key factors. First is the frequency with which the shock occurs relative to the frequency of changes in the underlying causal structure. If the structure changes every time a shock occurs, then events do not generate useful evidence regarding probabilities.

On the other hand, if the shock occurs many times while the structure is stable, probabilities may be estimated with considerable confidence. High-frequency shocks affect many kinds of activities conducted by banks. For example, default rates on credit card receivables and car loans or routine deposit withdrawals can be estimated with considerable confidence. Consequently, high frequency shocks are not a significant source of insolvency exposure for banks. Banks have both the knowledge and the incentive to price high-frequency shocks properly and to make adequate provisions to serve as a buffer against loss.

In contrast, the causal structure underlying low-frequency economic shocks by definition does not remain stable long enough to permit empirical estimation of shock probabilities with much confidence. How do banks make decisions with regard to low-frequency shocks with uncertain probabilities? Specialists in cognitive psychology have found that decisionmakers, even trained statisticians, tend to formulate subjective probabilities on the basis of the "availability heuristic," the ease with which the decisionmaker can imagine that the event will occur (Tversky and Kahnenman, 1982). Since the ease with which an event can be imagined is highly correlated with the frequency that the event occurs, this rule of thumb provides a reasonably accurate estimate of high-frequency events. But ease of recall is also affected by other factors such as the time elapsed since the last occurrence. Under such circumstances the availability heuristic can give rise to an "availability bias."

At some point, this tendency to underestimate shock probabilities is exacerbated by the threshold heuristic (Simon, 1978). This is the rule of thumb by which busy decisionmakers allocate their scarcest resource, managerial attention. When the subjective probability falls below some threshold amount, it is disregarded and treated as if it were zero.

Once this threshold has been reached, behavior seldom changes even in the face of evidence that the actual shock probability has increased as, for example, in the cases discussed in succeeding sections where commercial real estate lending continues despite evidence of rising vacancy rates.

The availability and threshold heuristics together cause "disaster myopia," the tendency over time to underestimate the probability of low-frequency shocks (Guttentag and Herring, 1984, 1986b). To the extent that subjective probabilities (π_t) decline even though actual probabilities remain constant or increase, banks take on greater exposures relative to their capital positions and the banking system becomes more vulnerable to a disaster. This is an insidious process. Disaster myopia can lead banks to become more vulnerable to a disaster without anyone having taken a conscious decision to increase insolvency exposure.

Susceptibility to disaster myopia is often reinforced by several institutional factors. For example, managerial accounting systems may inadvertently favor activities subject to low-frequency shocks. Although standard accounting practices are helpful in monitoring, pricing, and provisioning for high-frequency shocks, they are not useful in controlling exposure to a low-frequency hazard because the shock occurs so infrequently that it will not be captured in the usual reporting period. Indeed, the absence of bad outcomes in the accounting data may intensify pressures to reduce default premiums and reserves. Moreover, in the absence of appropriate provisions for potential losses, an activity subject to low-probability shocks will appear misleadingly profitable. This problem is often compounded by the practice of recognizing fees (which may be considerable in some lines of real estate finance) up front, when the loan is booked, rather than amortizing them over the life of the loan.[13]

The illusion of high profitability creates additional problems. To the extent that salaries and bonuses are based on reported short-term profits without adjustment for reserves against shocks, the line officers who are in the best position to assess such dangers will be rewarded for disregarding them (Pavlov and Wachter, 2002).

In addition, competition may interact with disaster myopia in two related ways to increase vulnerability. First, competitive markets make it impossible for banks that are not disaster myopic to price transactions as if there were a finite probability of a major shock when banks and other competitors who *are* disaster myopic price them as if that probability were zero. Second, if banks are apparently earning returns above the competitive level (disregarding the need for reserves against future shocks), equally myopic banks will be encouraged to enter the market, thus eroding those returns. In response, banks can protect target rates of return on equity for a time by increasing their leverage and rationalizing such actions in terms of the need to maintain target returns in the face of shrinking margins, and in terms of similar actions by other banks. Thus competition, interacting with disaster myopia, may accelerate the process through which banks become increasingly vulnerable to a major shock like a collapse in real estate prices.

Once a shock occurs, disaster myopia turns into disaster magnification. The availability heuristic may exacerbate financial conditions because, just after a shock has occurred, it is all too easy to imagine another sharp decline in real estate prices and the subjective shock probability will rise well above the true shock probability. As Guttentag and Herring (1984) show, this will result in sharply increased tiering of interest rates in financial markets as lenders try to reduce exposures and increase risk premiums in response to sharply higher shock probabilities. The extent of credit rationing is likely to expand for borrowers who cannot offer a credible contractual rate that will compensate for the increase in the perceived risk of default.

The abrupt drop in the flow of credit to the real estate market will put further downward pressure on real estate prices. This is also likely to diminish lending to other sectors of the economy as banks try to rebuild their reserves and capital to cope with the increased risk of default. To the extent that supervisors and regulators are susceptible to disaster myopia, they are also likely to suffer from disaster magnification. In response to the greatly increased subjective probability of a disaster they may seek to protect the banking system by insisting on higher capital ratios and more aggressive provisioning against potential losses.

5. The Role of Perverse Incentives

Commercial real estate is often highly leveraged. Real estate developers usually operate with a minimum of capital in order to shift as much risk as possible to the lender. Banks generally try to protect themselves by requiring low loan-to-value ratios, guarantees, takeout commitments for longer-term financing, and strict loan covenants that will protect them against risky behavior by the developer after the loan is made. But when real estate markets become overheated, underwriting standards may deteriorate.

When disaster myopia sets in, lenders believe that they can accept higher loan-to-value ratios, weaker commitments or guarantees, and looser loan covenants without increasing their risk of loss. Moreover, intensified competition from other disaster myopic lenders may force prudent lenders to accept weaker underwriting standards or withdraw from the market. In this environment real estate developers have increased opportunities for exploiting their creditors by increasing the riskiness of their projects, which are often difficult to monitor.[14] Moreover, when a project is near default, developers may lack incentives to contribute new capital to rescue the project, since most of the benefits would accrue to their creditors (Myers, 1977). Thus, high leverage combined with asymmetric information between bank lenders and real estate investors can give rise to perverse incentives for real estate investors to increase the riskiness of real estate investments. But banks may also be subject to perverse incentives.

Some banks may *ignore* the risk of a disaster because they believe they would be protected if a disaster were to occur. Virtually every country has erected a safety net for depository institutions to guard against a banking disaster that might ignite a financial crisis by disrupting the payments system and interrupting the flow of credit to bank-dependent firms, thereby causing a decline in economic activity.

Banks are structurally vulnerable to a liquidity shock because they finance holdings of opaque, imperfectly marketable assets (like real estate loans) with short-term liabilities, which they promise to redeem at par. Depositors are aware of their informational disadvantage vis-à-vis banks, and they understand that banks are highly leveraged. Thus when a shock, such as a collapse in real estate values, occurs they know that even a relatively small percentage decline in asset values will result in a much larger percentage change in net worth, perhaps rendering the bank insolvent. Depositors may abruptly reduce their estimate of the bank's net worth and run to redeem their deposits, forcing the bank to incur firesale losses to liquidate assets or to borrow at an interest rate sharply higher than its customary rate.

Once begun, runs tend to be self-reinforcing. This vulnerability to runs is a public policy concern (rather than the strictly private concern of an individual bank and its customers) because of the fear that a loss of confidence in the solvency of one bank may lead to a contagious loss of confidence in other banks.

The safety net erected to guard against a contagious collapse, which often includes deposit insurance or other government guarantees and access to an official lender of last resort, tends to insulate banks from potential market discipline. This is especially evident in the case of state-owned banks. All creditors in state-owned banks are likely to believe that they are protected by a state guarantee and thus have virtually no incentive to monitor the riskiness of their bank's lending decisions.

Deposit insurance plays a similar role in privately owned banks, undermining the incentives for insured depositors to monitor and discipline bank-lending decisions. Moreover, uninsured creditors of large banks may believe that they are protected by implicit deposit insurance because of the way in which lender-of-last-resort assistance is usually provided and administrative discretion to terminate a bank is usually exercised. Lenders of last resort routinely lend to banks long after they become insolvent. This permits creditors who are not covered by explicit deposit insurance the opportunity to withdraw their deposits before a bank is terminated. Even then, the authorities usually avoid liquidating the bank and imposing loss on uninsured depositors and creditors, but instead provide assistance while keeping the bank open, or arrange a purchase and assumption transaction in which all liabilities are honored by the acquiring bank.

The protection that the safety net affords gives rise to the classic moral hazard problem in which the existence of insurance may undermine the incentive for depositors to be concerned to prevent the insured risk from occurring. As a consequence bank managers find that if depositors do not demand greater compensation when greater risks are taken, they can increase expected returns to their shareholders by substituting riskier assets, such as commercial real estate loans, for safer assets.

Shareholders will constrain risk exposures to some extent so long as their equity stake is high relative to the potential loss. But as the equity stake falls relative to the potential loss on existing exposures—as in the aftermath of a collapse in property prices, for example—the bank will be tempted to take increasingly greater risks. The reason is that shareholders value a distribution of returns that is truncated at the termination point. They reap all the positive returns above this point, but shift all returns below this point, including negative returns, to the creditors, the deposit insurer, or taxpayers.

Workout loans become especially problematic when potential losses exceed the bank's capacity to bear loss (Herring, 1989). Under these circumstances a bank may be willing to extend a workout loan to a troubled borrower, for example, a real estate developer who cannot pay interest, even when the expected return on the loan is not sufficient to compensate for the opportunity cost of the new funds. Keynes (1931, p. 258) clearly saw this danger when he observed, "Owe your banker £1,000 and you are at his mercy; owe him £1 million and the position is reversed."

Extending a workout loan becomes an especially attractive option for the bank, if it enables the borrower to keep current on interest so that the bank can delay (perhaps indefinitely) the costs of writing down the book value of its outstanding exposure.[15] More generally, the bank has incentives to manipulate its accounts to mask the deterioration in its condition by understating loan losses or by "gains trading" in which assets with market values above book values are sold and those with market values below book are kept at book value.

Perverse incentives may also explain the behavior of supervisory and regulatory authorities in the aftermath of a collapse in real estate prices. Because the safety net tends to shield depository institutions from market discipline, the closure of banks has been converted from a market-driven to an administrative process, with lots of scope for the exercise of administrative discretion. Without the market pressure of a bank run, supervisory authorities are free to engage in forbearance, which opens the possibility of agency problems between supervisory agents and their taxpayer principals.

In the aftermath of a major shock, such as a collapse in commercial real estate values, a long delay usually occurs before insolvencies are recognized and resolved. The supervisory authorities may be simply overwhelmed by the magnitude of the crisis and lack sufficient resources to pay off insured depositors or to make good on implicit guarantees. Because a collapse in real estate prices is often coincident with a decline in aggregate income, the government may be especially reluctant to increase the fiscal deficit to make good on explicit and implicit government guarantees for bank depositors or other creditors.

In addition, the supervisory authorities are usually hesitant to admit the scale of the crisis. On the one hand, supervisors, who are as likely to be subject to cognitive dissonance as bankers, realize that such an admission would raise question about the quality of oversight they had provided. On the other, they may be apprehensive that public acknowledgment of the extent of insolvencies might undermine confidence and increase the risk of igniting a financial crisis.

Finally, the prospect—however remote—that real estate prices might return to levels attained before the collapse provides a rationale for delay in the hope that the passage of time would eliminate the problem. In effect, the supervisory authorities often decide to forbear and gamble that the decline in real estate prices will be reversed.

The reluctance of the authorities to take strong disciplinary action when the banking system is in jeopardy provides another, more cynical motive for herding. A bank knows that if it takes on an idiosyncratic risk exposure and loses, it may face harsh regulatory discipline, including termination. But if it is careful to keep its risk exposures in line with those of other banks, even if a disaster occurs, the regulatory consequences will be much lighter. The supervisory authorities cannot terminate all banks or even discipline them harshly. Indeed, the authorities may be obliged to soften the impact of the shock on individual banks in order to protect the banking system.

In summary, perverse incentives resulting from the combination of high leverage and asymmetric information may lead to riskier real estate projects than if they were financed largely through equity claims. Highly leveraged real estate developers will initiate riskier projects when they can shift most of the downside risk to banks. Like real estate developers, banks are also highly leveraged with opaque assets. Although this would usually impel depositors and other creditors to monitor and discipline bank risk-taking, the official safety net undermines their incentive and so banks will be more willing to undertake risky real estate lending than they would in the absence of the safety net. The supervisory authorities could prevent this by substituting regulatory discipline for market discipline acting as if they were faithful agents for the taxpayers who underwrite the safety net. But, in practice, they often respond by protecting banks from market discipline, rather than protecting the taxpayer principals from bank risk-taking.

6. Concluding Comment

As illustrated by the recent Asian financial crisis, real estate booms often end in banking busts. Because real estate is in fixed supply (at least in the short term), and is difficult to sell short, real estate markets are vulnerable to waves of optimism.

The extent and duration of the resulting rise in prices will be increased so long as banks augment the financial resources of the optimists. The willingness of banks to increase their exposure to real estate lending is likely to increase to the extent that they and their supervisors are subject to disaster myopia.

Moral hazard also plays a critical role, especially when bank shareholders have little to lose and bank depositors believe they will be protected by the safety net. These perverse incentives place a heavy burden on regulators and supervisors, which few have been able to shoulder. When bank capital positions weaken, they often forbear, hoping for the best, and the vulnerability of the banking system to a collapse in real estate prices grows.

When the real estate boom begins to collapse, banks may also hasten the decline in real estate prices. Disaster myopia may turn to disaster magnification leading to a withdrawal of credit. Supervisors may react to the consequent weakening of bank capital by requiring that banks write down nonperforming real estate assets and raise new capital. Or they may choose to forbear, continuing to hope that real estate prices will recover.

Forbearance may also have significant costs. If decapitalized institutions are permitted to operate they may be tempted to gamble for redemption, increasing losses still further. Moreover, even if they do not gamble for redemption, banks which are crippled by large holdings of nonperforming real estate loans will be unable to generate sufficient retained earnings to restore their capital in a timely manner. Instead, they will shed assets, scaling back new lending to all sectors of the economy and declining to roll over outstanding loans when they mature.

In economies where banks are the main source of financing, this can have a devastating impact on investment and economic growth. Moreover, as the Asian financial crisis has made evident, an economy with a decapitalized banking system is highly vulnerable to external shocks such as foreign exchange crises that can severely damage the real economy. Thus the banking sector's importance and link to the real estate sector not only amplifies the real estate bubble but also can have major implications for the overall stability of the economy.

*Richard J. Herring is the Jacob Safra Professor of International Banking Director at The Lauder Institute of The Wharton School and School of Arts and Sciences of the University of Pennsylvania. Susan Wachter is a professor of real estate and finance at The Wharton School at the University of Pennsylvania.

Notes

1. The complete exposition of this model may be found in Carey (1990) Chapter 3, "A Model of the Farm Land Market."

2. The fundamental value of land is the price that is equal to the discounted present value of the net income that can be generated from renting the land. The "fundamental value" is the value consistent with long-term equilibrium. In section 3, the concept is broadened to include commercial real estate and the fundamental price is defined as the price at which the current stock of real estate structures is precisely equal to its replacement cost.

3. As Carey (1990) notes, if investors are permitted to be risk averse, differences in reservation prices may also reflect differences in risk aversion and/or private information regarding the covariance of returns on land and other assets.

4. Carey (1990) shows that the assumption that F is continuously differentiable with a nonzero variance and a symmetric density will yield the key results regarding the impact on P of increases in heterogeneity, the mean and financial resources.

5. Such markets are not inconceivable. Indeed, it may be useful public policy to nurture an organized options market in land. Publicly traded property companies are relatively common, but they do not provide a very efficient means of selling land short.

6. Of course, this is not precisely true. Zoning laws may change freeing up land for commercial use, but generally such measures take a significant amount of time.

7. Krugman (1998) develops a model based on moral hazard that yields similar results in which "Pangloss" values dominate markets for assets in fixed supply.

8. At this stage L represents both the investor's equity and loans available to the investor. In section 3 we shall consider L to be loans. This simplification is useful because land and commercial real estate tend to be highly leveraged investments. Indeed, the extent of leverage gives rise to some difficult principal agent problems, which are discussed below.

9. The sign of $\partial P/\partial h$ will be positive so long as $NL/2 > P^*Z$. If total resources available to half the investors fall short of the value of land at the fundamental price, P will fall below P^*. The optimists will lack sufficient resources to raise the price above P^*.

10. Note also that if opinions are homogeneous ($h = 0$) and centered on the fundamental price, the equilibrium price will not deviate from the fundamental price.

11. Allen and Gale (2000) emphasize that expectations regarding the supply of credit may also play an important role in the dynamics of real estate and equity prices.

12. In the empirical literature, rent adjustment equations are specified with rent change a lagged function of the deviation in the actual vacancy rate from the natural vacancy rate. That is, the expected rate of change in real office market rents is modeled as depending positively on the gap between the actual vacancy rate and the beginning-period vacancy rate. A natural vacancy rate is imbedded in the constant term, which is interpretable as the product of the adaptation coefficient and the natural vacancy rate (see Shilling, Sirmans, and Corgel, 1987, and Wheaton and Torto, 1988).

13. While we focus here on disaster myopia on the part of banks, it clearly impacts optimists' behavior as well.

14. Allen and Gale (2000) emphasize this asset substitution problem in their model of bubbles and financial crises.

15. In the United States, this practice is known as "evergreening." Bank examiners seek to prevent it.

References

Allen, F., and D. Gale, 2000, "Bubbles and Crises," *Economic Journal*, Vol. 110, pp. 236–255.

Bank for International Settlements, 1995, *Annual Reports*, Basel, Switzerland, June.

Carey, Mark S., 1993, "Snacking and Smoothing: Gains Trading of Investment Account Securities by Commercial Banks," Board of Governors of the Federal Reserve, working paper.

_____, 1990, "Feeding the Fad: the Federal Land Banks, Land Market Efficiency, and the Farm Credit Crisis," University of California, Berkeley, Ph.D. dissertation.

Guttentag, Jack M., and Richard J. Herring, 1986a, "Financial Innovations to Stabilize Credit Flows to Developing Countries," *Studies in Banking and Finance*, Vol. 3, pp. 263–304.

_____, 1986b, *Disaster Myopia in International Banking*, Princeton University Essays in International Finance, No. 164, September.

_____, 1985, "Commercial Bank Lending to Developing Countries: From Overlending to Underlending to Structural Reform," in *International Debt and the Developing Countries*, G. Smith and J.Cuddington, eds., Washington, DC: World Bank.

_____, 1984, "Credit Rationing and Financial Disorder," *Journal of Finance*, 39, December, pp. 1359–1382.

Herring, Richard, 1996, "Banking Disasters: Causes and Preventative Measures: Some Extrapolations from Recent U.S. Experience," paper presented at the Foundation for Advanced Information and Research (FAIR)/Wharton Joint Conference on Issues in International Risk: The Japanese Banking System, Tokyo, Japan.

_____, 1989, "The Economics of Workout Lending," *Journal of Money, Credit, and Banking*, Vol. 21, No. 1, February, pp. 1–15.

Herring, Richard J., and Susan Wachter, 1999, "Real Estate Booms and Banking Busts: An International Perspective," Group of Thirty, occasional papers, No. 58.

Keynes, John M., 1931, "The Consequences to the Banks of the Collapse in Money Values," in *Essays in Persuasion, Collected Writings of J. M. Keynes*, Vol. 11, London: Macmillan.

Krugman, Paul, 1998, "What Happened to Asia?," Massachusetts Institute of Technology, working paper, January.

Malpezzi, Stephen, and Susan Wachter, 2002, "The Role of Speculation in Real Estate Cycles," Wharton Real Estate Center, working paper, February.

Myers, Stewart C., 1977, "Determinants of Corporate Borrowing," *Journal of Financial Economics*, Vol. 5, November, pp. 147–175.

Pavlov, Andrey, and Susan Wachter, 2001, "Robbing the Bank: The Option Value of Non-Recourse Lending and Inflated Asset Prices," Wharton Real Estate Center, working paper, December.

Simon, Herbert A., 1978, "Rationality as Process and as Product of Thoughts," *American Economic Review*, Vol. 68, May, pp. 1–16.

Shilling, J., C. F. Sirmans, and J. Corgel, 1987, "Price Adjustment Process for Rental Office Space," *Journal of Urban Economics*, Vol. 22: pp. 90–100.

Tversky, Amos, and Daniel Kahneman, 1982, "Availability: A Heuristic for Judging Frequency and Probability," in *Judgment under Uncertainty: Heuristics and Biases*, D. Kahneman, P. Slovic, and A. Tversky, eds., New York: Cambridge University Press, pp. 163–178.

Wheaton, W. C., and R. G. Torto, 1988, "Vacancy Rates and the Future of Office Market Rents," *Journal of American Real Estate & Urban Economics Association*, Vol. 16, pp. 430–436.

Chapter 15
Comments on: "Stocks as Money ..." and "Bubble Psychology"

Robert S. Chirinko*
Emory University and Center for Economic Studies

What determines stock prices? This fundamental question has been addressed in several of the papers presented at this conference. It has been the subject of intense research activity during the past 40 years. It occupies the attention of professional and individual investors. And, it has a direct bearing on the appropriate stance of public policies toward financial markets.

The papers by John Cochrane and Werner De Bondt nicely describe the major perspectives on asset pricing. In these remarks, I use their papers to draw the battle lines among competing perspectives on asset pricing and confine my discussion to a single question: How do these perspectives explain the significant rise and dramatic fall of the NASDAQ? As shown in Cochrane's figure 8, the total market value of the NASDAQ began to rise (relative to the NYSE index) in the beginning of 1998, doubled within two years, and then lost half of its value. Toward the end of 2001, the NASDAQ had collapsed back to the level of the NYSE. These movements were even more dramatic for the "tech" part of the NASDAQ. How well can these movements be accounted for by the paradigms presented in the Cochrane and De Bondt papers, as well as two additional paradigms—one that holds strongly to the rational investor view and another that recognizes the unique aspects of intangible investments and information technology? Each paradigm offers a compelling interpretation of recent NASDAQ gyrations. Which paradigm is relevant is vitally important for policy conclusions discussed in the concluding section.

1. Battle among Competing Perspectives

In order to compare different perspectives, it will be useful to cast the discussion in terms of a simple asset pricing model. Stocks are long-lived assets whose value is determined by today's payoffs and those expected into the indefinite future. Since the payoffs are uncertain and accrue over time, they need to be discounted appropriately. If we make the convenient assumption that all payoffs are in the form of dividends ($DIVD$) expected to grow at a constant rate (g^e) and that the expected discount rate (r^e) is constant, today's stock price (SP) equals the following growing perpetuity (known as the Gordon model),

1) $SP = DIVD / (r^e - g^e)$.

Note importantly that r^e and g^e are expected values of variables that are unknown currently and extend over a long interval. Equation 1 will prove convenient in interpreting the NASDAQ in terms of the following four paradigms.[1]

2. Rational Behavior without Apology

The efficient markets view reigned as the unquestioned asset pricing paradigm in the 1970s and 1980s.[2] This paradigm holds that stock prices are based on fundamentals, defined as the expectations of discounted future cash flows. In the event that stock prices differ from fundamentals, arbitrage pressure from a subset of rational investors will quickly eliminate any discrepancies.

In this asset pricing model, bubbles cannot exist, and the organizing theme of this conference is open to question. The sharp rise and fall in the NASDAQ can be linked to a change in the expectations of future growth rates. While the excessively optimistic valuations of NASDAQ firms seem apparent today, hindsight is 20/20. Past episodes of purported bubbles, including the famous Dutch tulip mania, are under revision (Garber, 2000; Cochrane, 2001). Most importantly, given the lengthy interval over which stocks are valued, small movements in expected growth rates can have significant changes in stock prices. As documented in the following table (based on equation 1 and $r^e = 7$ percent), if g^e had been 3 percent, and investors lower expectations by 1 percent, stock prices will fall by 20 percent. The NASDAQ situation prevailing in the late 1990s requires a larger base growth rate, and the computations in column 3 are based on an initial g^e of 6 percent. Downward revisions of expected future growth rates result in dramatic declines of 50 percent to 75 percent.

Percentage Change in the Stock Price

Revision in g^e	Initial $g^e = 3$ percent	Initial $g^e = 6$ percent
(1)	(2)	(3)
−1%	−20%	−50%
−2%	−33%	−67%
−3%	−43%	−75%

The efficient markets model would seem to be able to explain the dramatic declines in stock prices witnessed recently on the NASDAQ.[3]

Despite the explanatory power of the efficient markets model, concerns exist about some of its implications for asset prices—the predictability of stock returns in both the short-run (momentum) and the long-run (mean reversion), the closed-end puzzle (a persistent and fluctuating difference between fundamental value and stock market value), and the systematic reaction of stock prices to information that does not affect fundamentals (e.g., inclusion in the Standard & Poor's 500 index). The excess volatility documented by Shiller (1981), the major gyrations in stock prices documented in this volume by Mishkin and White, and the dramatic drop in the Dow Jones Industrial Average on October 19, 1987, without any apparent change in fundamentals suggest that the rational asset pricing model is incomplete. Appeals to time-variation in risk seem an all too convenient deus ex machina, and there is a need for extensions or a wholesale reworking of this model.

3. Rational Behavior with Frictions

John Cochrane's paper provides a simple yet powerful extension of the rational asset pricing model. He considers the role of frictions that may lead to a discrepancy between fundamental and actual values in stock markets. In his model, there exists a convenience yield to holding certain stocks, just like there is a convenience yield to holding currency in macroeconomic models of money. The key assumption is that these stocks, like money, must possess some unique properties. Convenience yields —denoted by δ—have been attributed to other financial assets. The intensively traded 30-year U.S. Treasury bond generates a return that is 1.5 percent lower than the return on a comparable 29-year bond. This differential can be interpreted as a convenience yield. In Japan, a similar convenience yield exists for less actively traded 10-year bonds relative to the benchmark bond; this yield vanishes when the benchmark bond changes.

Cochrane documents the importance of the convenience yield by undertaking a case study of 3Com and its Palm subsidiary, 95 percent of which was owned by 3Com. The key anomalous fact was that, in March 2000, the value of Palm exceeded that of 3Com.[4] Such an outcome clearly violates rational behavior absent any frictions. Cochrane argues that, because of the need of short-sellers, a convenience yield existed for Palm shares. A constant convenience yield is not sufficient to explain the movements in the NASDAQ. Cochrane further argues that the convenience yield depends on the demand for shares and, hence, trading volume will be positively related to price increases. A final persuasive fact is that the price of shares with short-selling constraints falls when the supply of shares available for trading increases.

The implications for asset prices of a positive convenience yield can be seen in terms of the Gordon model,

2) $\quad SP = DIVD / (r^e - g^e - \delta)$.

A positive δ boosts SP. As shown in Cochrane's table 2, the impact on stock prices can be very large for tech firms characterized by large g^es.

This convenience yield insight offers a powerful explanation of the movements in price and volume for Palm. Two outstanding questions remain, however, before we can be comfortable with this explanation of NASDAQ's recent volatility. Did a convenience yield exist for a sufficiently large number of NASDAQ firms so that it can explain the movements in the index, as opposed to the movements in a few high-profile stocks? Are the δ's large enough to explain the movement in the NASDAQ?

The δ of 1.5 percent was derived from an asset with a 30-year horizon. The short-sales constraint that is at the core of the convenience yield model is not expected to exist for extended periods of time. These caveats aside, the story told here is intriguing, and will surely be the basis of future work in asset pricing within the rational asset pricing framework.

4. Behavioral Finance

Recent work in behavioral finance challenges the rational investor assumption that underlies the above two paradigms. This alternative uses descriptive theories that "study financial decisionmaking with the help of concepts borrowed from psychology." The De Bondt paper does a very nice job of relating the core insights from this expansive literature to financial markets. Among other key concepts, decisionmakers use heuristics such as anchoring (first impressions have a disproportionate impact on decisions), framing (employing simple abstractions), availability (immediate information has a substantial influence), and representativeness (stereotypes weigh heavily in decisions). The validity of these behavioral tendencies—collectively referred to as investor sentiment—is supported by an extensive body of psychological experiments.

Investor sentiment has several implications for asset prices. Individual investors will have a tendency to extrapolate current information in a way that violates rationality (as dictated by Bayesian learning), and may lead to overconfidence and "chasing winners." For analysts, investor sentiment will tend to lead to consensus forecasts with large errors and a tendency for herding behavior. In terms of the Gordon model, investor sentiment results in $g^e > g^*$ (the fundamental growth rate) and stock market bubbles. These behavioral effects in which "decision processes shape decision outcomes" can lead to the sharp increase in the NASDAQ.

While a very forceful challenge to the rational investor paradigms, a behavioral finance explanation of NASDAQ faces three unsettled questions. First, herding and excessive optimism by analysts can reflect a highly rational quid pro quo between underwriters searching for business and actual and prospective clients searching for "hype" and higher stock prices, relationships that have caught the attention of regulators and district attorneys. Second, the pervasive psychological biases and the associated "noise trading" persuasively presented by De Bondt do not immediately translate into inefficient market outcomes. One of the traditional guardians of efficient markets is arbitragers who neutralize the adverse effects of noise traders. For noise trading to matter, arbitrage must be costly, and hence limited (Shleifer, 2000, Chap. 1). Is arbitrage so sufficiently costly that the effects of noise trading cannot be eliminated (a question taking us back to the 3Com/Palm situation analyzed by Cochrane)? Third, while overconfidence might explain why NASDAQ prices rose, what forces or additional psychological biases explain the subsequent decline? While reading the behavioral finance literature, one gets the feeling of being in a well-stocked supermarket with a multitude of psychological tendencies waiting to be plucked from the shelf to explain the NASDAQ decline and other financial market outcomes. (This issue is noted in De Bondt's paper.) With a surplus of explanations, it is difficult to know how to evaluate and discriminate among behavioral theories. These concerns notwithstanding, replacing the rational investors by a behaviorally grounded individual generates a wealth of insights that will continue to cause excitement in asset pricing research and elsewhere in economics, as indicated by the awarding of the 2001 John Bates Clark medal to Matthew Rabin for "incorporating well-documented psychological evidence about human behavior into economic models" (American Economic Association).

5. Intangible and Information Technology Capital is Special

Bubbles arise when there is a persistent discrepancy between expected and fundamental growth rates (cf. equation 1). A fourth explanation of the NASDAQ focuses on specific characteristics of NASDAQ firms. D'Avolio, Gildor, and Shleifer (2001) note that NASDAQ firms rely heavily on intangible and information technology (IIT) capital. Relative to traditional plant and equipment, the future returns from IIT capital are difficult to assess. In isolation, this difficulty would result in a wider dispersion of growth forecasts, but not a systematic deviation between g^e and g^*. The authors introduce a second element, noting that firms have a heightened incentive to manipulate earnings. They then provide a tantalizing piece of evidence suggesting that the quality of information has deteriorated. Managers have much greater freedom in determining pro-forma earnings relative to GAAP (generally accepted accounted principles) earnings, and D'Avolio, Gildor, and Shleifer (2001, table 5) observe the number of firms reporting pro-forma earnings has increased tremendously over the past two decades: 1980–9, 1990–64, and 2000–1,066. An uncertain environment and manipulated earnings lead to a systematic deviation between g^e and g^*. This is a very persuasive story about NASDAQ stock prices. As with the other three models discussed here, the question remains whether this appealing qualitative story is sufficiently important to be able to explain the quantitative movements in the NASDAQ.

6. Policy Implications

These four different explanations of the same phenomenon highlight the difficulties in discriminating among competing theories of asset pricing. Which model ultimately prevails will be determined on the academic battlefield (perhaps extended to other countries, other time periods, or other assets). That outcome is of vital interest to policymakers because the different theories have substantially different implications for regulatory policies.

The rational behavior paradigms—either without apology or with frictions—imply a restrained role for policymakers. Regulations that interfere with investors' pursuit of profit opportunities or the flow of information will be detrimental to financial market efficiency. In those models where frictions are identified, such as the supply of shares in Cochrane's analysis, enlightened public policies will attempt to eliminate those frictions by removing restrictions on trading (e.g., lock-ups) and financial innovations.

Behavioral finance and IIT models have substantially different implications. Investors need to be protected from inherent biases that affect financial decisionmaking.

Regulations should be tightened on self-directed retirement plans and the access that "unsophisticated" investors have to sophisticated and risky financial products. Transactions taxes effected to retard speculation would be a radical intervention. Privatizing social security would be a particularly bad policy in the face of the psychological biases preventing efficient financial decisionmaking. If IIT capital provides both the means and motivation for firms to manipulate earnings and lower the quality of information flows, then tighter regulations on accounting and advertising and greater penalties for false reporting would seem warranted.

These competing paradigms raise an intriguing question about the real effects of asset market fluctuations. Some of the conference papers and a few published studies have examined the links between financial market bubbles and consumption and investment spending. The results have been mixed, with some but not all studies finding economically important effects. Does the magnitude of these channels depend on whether the bubble had been generated by short-sellers' demands, investor sentiment, or managerial manipulation? Despite the insights contained in the papers by Cochrane, De Bondt, and others at this conference, open questions remain about the determinants of asset prices, their effects on real behavior, and the appropriate setting of public policies.

*Robert S. Chirinko is a professor of economics at Emory University and a research fellow at the Center for Economic Studies in Munich. The author thanks Huntley Schaller for helpful discussions. All errors, omissions, and conclusions remain the sole responsibility of the author.

Notes

1. Equation 1 is also useful in understanding the "bubble" episodes in Sweden and Japan in the 1980s. Both episodes have been attributed to exceedingly low discount rates due to overly loose monetary policy (Japan) or overly generous tax policy (Sweden). Downward movements of r^e can lead to large increases in SP, especially when r^e is close to g^e.

2. A forceful statement of this position can be found in Fama (1970, 1991). See Shleifer (2000) for an equally forceful counterargument.

3. In an interesting paper that was to have been presented at this conference in October, Siegel (2001) examines stock market returns after the "bubble" episodes of 1929 and 1987, and defines stock market overvaluation as a 30-year return that is two standard deviations (3.6 percent) below the average real return of 7 percent. Based on this metric, the stock market was not overvalued at the 1929 and 1987 peaks.

4. 3Com/Palm is not an isolated incident. Mitchell, Pulvino, and Stafford (2002) uncover 82 cases where the market value of the partly owned subsidiary exceeded that of the parent.

References

Cochrane, John H., 2001, "Book Review: *Famous First Bubbles: Famous First Manias*," *Journal of Political Economy*, Vol. 109, October, pp. 1150–1154.

D'Avolio, Gene, Efi Gildor, and Andrei Shleifer, 2001, "Technology, Information Production, and Market Efficiency," in *Economic Policy for the Information Economy,* Kansas City: Federal Reserve Bank Of Kansas City, pp. 125–160.

Fama, Eugene, 1991, "Efficient Capital Markets II," *Journal Of Finance,* Vol. 46, 1991, pp. 1575–1617.

_____, 1970, "Efficient Capital Markets: A Review of Theory and Empirical Work," *Journal Of Finance,* Vol. 25, pp. 383–417.

Garber, Peter M., 2000, *Famous First Bubbles: Famous First Manias,* Cambridge, MA: MIT Press.

Lamont, Owen, and Richard H. Thaler, 2001, "Can the Market Add and Subtract?: Mispricing in Tech Stock Carve-Outs," University of Chicago, working paper.

Mitchell, Mark, Todd Pulvino, and Erik Stafford, 2002, "Limited Arbitrage in Equity Markets," *Journal Of Finance,* Vol. 57, pp. 551–584.

Shleifer, Andrei, 2000, *Inefficient Markets: An Introduction to Behavioral Finance,* Oxford: Oxford University Press.

Shiller, Robert J., 1981, "Do Stock Prices Move too Much to be Explained by Subsequent Changes in Dividends?," *American Economic Review,* Vol. 71, June, pp. 421–436.

Siegel, Jeremy J., 2001, "What is an Asset Price Bubble? An Operational Definition," Wharton School, manuscript, August.

Chapter 16
Comments on Theory and History of Asset Price Bubbles

Bertrand Renaud*
World Bank Group

This session addresses historical and theoretical developments that can be of value to central banks and financial regulators concerned with the buildup of financial imbalances and their impact on monetary and financial stability. The three papers presented are very different in focus, form, and content. Given my greater familiarity with real estate asset booms and busts, I will comment only briefly on the papers by John Cochrane and Werner De Bondt. I will devote much of my time to the presentation by Richard Herring and Susan Wachter and to the issues they raise.

The paper presented by John Cochrane is a very interesting analysis of a market microstructure. His information-rich and finely crafted paper contrasts sharply with the environment of limited information and inadequate market infrastructure that still characterizes most real estate markets around the world, especially in much of Asia after the 1997 crisis. Cochrane's meticulous use of the dynamics of the Palm and 3Com shares as a means to understand the dynamics of the NASDAQ/tech stock experience is quite effective in showing the rise and fall of tech stocks in the late 1990s. On the other hand, the focus on the existence of a "small convenience yield" seems to go only part of the way in explaining the trading frenzies and the behavior of high frequency traders that typically mark the top of an asset bubble, be it in stocks or in real estate. Are there factors other than this convenience yield at work? A recent paper by Emanuel Derman (2002) adds a very interesting dimension with the argument that perceptions of risk return trade-offs change under high frequency trading. In addition to the usual financial parameters of trading, Derman argues that a high frequency trader's perception of time focuses on "the number of trading opportunities that occur," and not on "the calendar time that passes between them." Derman also argues that traders will expect returns proportional to the "temperature of a stock," which he defines as the product of a stock's volatility by its trading frequency. The Derman paper adds a testable behavioral dimension that is missing from the convenience yield explanation sought by Cochrane. In fact, the two explanations do not appear to be mutually exclusive, but rather complementary.

Not being a researcher of high frequency trading, I will stop my conceptual comments here. However, because this conference is mainly about market monitoring and the difficulty of identifying bubbles in the making, it is worth highlighting that an accelerating change in the frequency and volume of real estate trading is one of the indicators of a potential bubble that can be monitored and acted upon to facilitate a "soft lending" of asset prices. One such case was the accelerating volume and speed of trade in "pre-sales" of housing units in Hong Kong before 1997, which led the Monetary Authority to tighten mortgage lending rules. A similar risk-mitigating policy was followed by Singapore across real estate markets. In contrast, during the numerous real estate booms and busts experienced in the 1980s and 1990s, most financial authorities around the world did not take any mitigating measures for the simple reason that they did not even have adequate monitoring indicators of real estate markets.

Werner De Bondt discusses the emergence of behavioral finance as a positive development in financial economics. This new field adds a welcome analytical dimension to financial analysis that Richard Thaler captures well in the title of a paper about economics in the new millennium "From Homo Economicus to Homo Sapiens." In particular, work on the formation of expectations is expanding. In real estate market analysis, much has happened since the pioneering work by Case and Shiller in the 1980s. By now, it is difficult to conceive of a good model of a real estate cycle that would ignore the formation of expectations. Models of real estate cycles can now draw on various forms of expectations. For instance, in the important case of Japan, Edelstein and Paul (1997) have successfully built an econometric model to show how changing expectations have determined the boom-bust cycle in the Japanese real estate markets.

In Herring and Wachter's paper, they raise three points that are central to the purpose of this conference: the structure of the financial system in which a real estate boom and bust might take place; important developments in our understanding of real estate cycles; and ongoing structural changes in financial markets that can lower the probability of sharp and very costly real estate asset bubbles.

First, the distinction between bank-based and market-based financial systems is a necessary contextual starting point for the discussion of asset bubbles. It is well known that in higher income countries domestic stock markets become important relative to domestic banks. In contrast, most middle and lower income economies are bank-dependent (see Demirgüç-Kunt and Levine, 2001).[1] Curiously, this major structural difference remains unmentioned in most discussions of asset price bubbles. Yet it is obvious that the channels for the development of large financial imbalances and resource misallocation will be quite different in each case. The corollary of a bank-dependent financial structure is that financial vulnerability to real estate bubbles will be much greater than vulnerability to stock market bubbles—even if some analysts of emerging markets make futile attempts to build econometric models of asset bubbles relying on stock market data because such data are more readily available than real estate prices! The more bank-dependent a financial system is, the more closely financial authorities must monitor the dynamics of real estate prices. Such monitoring was more the exception than the rule across Asia before the 1997 crisis—worst of all in Japan but also during the banking crises across Organization for Economic Cooperation and Development countries of the late 1980s.

With their application of the concept of disaster myopia, Herring and Wachter have made a lasting contribution to our understanding of real estate booms and banking busts. However, without begrudging Herring and Wachter their fresh contribution at all, it is significant for today's discussion to recall the context in which the concept of disaster myopia was first developed by Guttentag and Herring (1986). Guttentag and Herring developed the concept of disaster myopia in the aftermath of the commercial banking crises in Latin America in the 1980s. This was a period when capital flows to emerging markets took mostly the form of commercial bank loans. The point was made then that there had been too much debt and not enough equity. In today's discussion of assets bubbles should we really be giving equal emphasis to stock market price bubbles and to real estate price bubbles in terms of financial system risks? Why, then, do we use equity? I would argue that debt-based bubbles built on excess leverage in real estate are considerably more harmful, even in the case of market-based financial systems. Making this point in the case of bank-based systems is, of course, tautological.

Second, Herring and Wachter also make the point that an important structural difference between real estate markets and securities markets is the higher degree of vulnerability of real estate markets to waves of optimism, in part because short sales are very difficult. Their point, with which I agree, presupposes a financial approach to real estate investments decisions that is far from universally used. From the viewpoint of the history of asset bubbles, the real estate finance "revolution" that treats real estate as a special class of assets has been spreading over the last decade. Until now, a very different view of real estate has been commonly held in Asia and other parts of the world. That traditional view is that real estate is for households a special type of investment of unique socioeconomic significance that lies outside the realm of financial and economic criteria. For business firms, real estate is viewed as an asset of strategic significance beyond the services that it provides to business operations, which is diametrically opposed to the basics of modern corporate real estate management. The concept of a short sale is alien to such thinking, especially in a bank-dependent system.

Major progress has been made on two fronts: our understanding of real estate cycles and their interactions with business cycles and, in a related manner, how we differentiate real estate as an asset class from public securities. From the policy viewpoint of financial imbalances and financial vulnerability, it is essential to keep in mind that real estate does not behave as a single sector within the economy. Some classes of real estate assets are much more prone to cyclical behavior than others. A first significant distinction is between housing and "income producing" real estate markets that include offices and retail/commercial and industrial real estate. Housing is a leading sector in business cycles. "Income producing" real estate asset classes lag the business cycle. From a financial stability point of view, during asset bubbles the classes of income-producing assets that have consistently done the most damage are office markets and retail markets because they tend to have strong endogenous cycles, while other classes of real estate assets do not (see Wheaton, 1999). Another reason has been the preferred use of these classes in secured lending. Volatility increases when inadequate regulations and banking practices facilitate highly leveraged financing, as could be seen during the various real estate booms and banking busts that followed banking liberalization in the 1980s around the world.

In market-based financial systems such as in the United States, major structural changes have taken place during the 1990s that lower risks in every real estate subsector. Better banking regulations, supervision, and improved valuation were mandated by the Financial Institutions Reform, Recovery and Enforcement Act in 1989 following the boom and bust of the early 1990s. But, probably the most important and lasting changes have been in the development of the capital market infrastructure for retail mortgage-backed securities (RMBS), commercial mortgage-backed securities (CMBS), and real estate investment trusts (REITs). These new products have stimulated analytical innovations coupled with great progress in the timeliness and accuracy of real estate data across some 70 major markets in the country that are deeply changing the contents of investment decision processes.

Finally, debates about real estate as an inefficient class of assets have recently taken a very interesting and promising turn. It has long been argued that predictable patterns in asset prices are suggestive of market inefficiency. In equities, phenomena of short-term momentum and longer-term reversals have generated much debate between the "Fama" and the "Thaler and Shiller" schools, if such a personalization is considered appropriate. Given the existence of endogenous real estate cycles, Costello et al. (2001) have raised "the key question whether real risk should be defined, measured, and estimated as it has been done in the public securities markets." Because real estate markets are not random in their movements, this creates considerable predictability in both market fundamentals and capital market returns. The empirical challenge is to include this information in forward-looking estimates of risk for a given segment of real estate in each main U.S. market. Such promising development should further improve risk management for investors, for their financiers, and for the financial authorities, themselves, because sector and macroeconomic volatility should be reduced.

*Bertrand Renaud is an international consultant. Until 2001, he was an advisor to the Financial Sector Development Department of the World Bank Group.

Notes

1. To illustrate the difference, Demirgüç-Kunt and Levine report that during the 1980–90s, in the market-dependent U.S. financial system the ratio of bank claims on the private sector to gross domestic product (GDP) was 0.64 while the ratio of market-traded value to GDP was almost equal at 0.62. In contrast, in a bank-dependent system like Japan's, the ratios were 1.17 and 0.28, respectively; in Germany they were 0.94 and 0.28, respectively. In a bank-dependent market of limited depth like Indonesia's, the ratios were much lower, at 0.46 and 0.08, respectively, and the bank bias, stronger (see Demirgüç-Kunt and Levine, table 3.7).

References

Costello, James M., Robert E. Hopkins, Petros S. Sivitanides, Jon A. Southard, Raymond G. Torto, and William C. Wheaton, 2001, "Real Estate Risk: A Forward-Looking Approach," *Real Estate Finance*, Vol. 18, Fall, pp. 20–28.

Demirgüç-Kunt, Asli, and Ross Levine, eds., 2001, *Financial Structure and Economic Growth*, Cambridge, MA: MIT Press.

Derman, Emanuel, 2002, "The Perception of Time, Risk and Return During Periods of Speculation," Goldman, Sachs & Co, working paper, January 10.

Edelstein, Robert, and Michel Paul, 1997, "Are Japanese Land Prices Based on Expectations?," University of California, Berkeley, working paper, December.

Guttentag, Jack, and Richard Herring, 1986, *Disaster Myopia in International Banking*, Princeton University Essays in International Finance, No. 164, September.

Mera, Koichi, and Bertrand Renaud, eds., 2001, *Asia's Financial Crisis and the Role of Real Estate*, Armonk, NY: M.E. Sharpe.

Wheaton, William, 1999, "Real Estate Cycles: Some Fundamentals," *Real Estate Economics*, Vol. 22, pp. 209–230.

PART IV

EMPIRICAL DIMENSIONS OF ASSET PRICE BUBBLES

Chapter 17

Imbalances or "Bubbles?" Implications for Monetary and Financial Stability

Claudio Borio*
Bank for International Settlements

and

Philip Lowe
Bank for International Settlements

1. Introduction

Economic historians will no doubt look back on the last 20 years of the 20th century as those that marked the end of a long inflationary phase in the world economy.[1] Burned by the experience of the 1970s, policymakers had put in place credible institutional safeguards against monetary instability. They had done so by endowing central banks with clear mandates to maintain price stability and with the necessary autonomy to pursue them. And yet, the same decades will in all probability also be remembered as those that saw the emergence of financial instability as a major policy concern, forcing its way to the top of the international agenda. One battlefront had opened up just as another was victoriously being closed. Ostensibly, lower inflation had not *by itself* yielded the hoped-for peace dividend of a more stable financial environment.

Is this confluence of events coincidental? What is the relationship between monetary and financial stability? What is an appropriate policy framework to secure both simultaneously? These are some of the questions that we begin to explore in this paper.

There are many possible routes that can be taken to arrive at the heart of these issues. Given the focus of this conference, we start from asset prices. Medium-term swings in asset prices have historically accompanied episodes of widespread financial instability. And, in recent years the question of whether monetary policy should respond to asset price "bubbles" has been asked with increasing frequency. Opinions on the subject are just as divided as ever.

We would like to make three points.

First, posing the question in terms of the desirability of a monetary response to "bubbles" per se is not the most helpful approach. Widespread financial distress typically arises from the unwinding of financial imbalances that build up disguised by benign economic conditions. Booms and busts in asset prices, whether characterized as "bubbles" or not, are just one of a richer set of symptoms. It is the *combination* of these symptoms that matters. Other common signs include rapid credit expansion and, often, above-average capital accumulation. These developments can, jointly, sow the seeds of future instability. As a result the financial cycle can amplify, and be amplified by, the business cycle.

Second, while not disputing the fact that low and stable inflation promotes financial stability, we stress that financial imbalances can and do build up in periods of disinflation or in a low inflation environment. One reason is the common positive association between favorable supply-side developments, which put downward pressure on prices, on the one hand, and asset price booms, easier access to external finance, and optimistic assessments of risk, on the other. A second is that the credibility of the policymakers' commitment to price stability, by anchoring expectations and, hence, inducing greater stickiness in price and wages, can alleviate, at least for a time, the inflationary pressures normally associated with the unsustainable expansion of aggregate demand. A third reason is that by obviating the need to tighten monetary policy, such conditions can allow the buildup of imbalances to proceed further.

Third, achieving monetary and financial stability requires that appropriate anchors be put in place in both spheres. In a fiat standard, the only constraint in the monetary sphere on the expansion of credit and external finance is the policy rule of the monetary authorities. The process cannot be anchored unless the rule responds, directly or indirectly, to the buildup of financial imbalances. In principle, safeguards in the financial sphere, in the form of prudential regulation and supervision, might be sufficient to prevent financial distress. In practice, however, they may be less than fully satisfactory. If the imbalances are large enough, the end-result could be a severe recession coupled with price *deflation*. While such imbalances can be difficult to identify ex ante, the results presented in this paper provide some evidence that useful measures can be developed. This suggests that, despite the difficulties involved, a monetary policy response to imbalances as they build up may be both possible and appropriate in some circumstances. More generally, cooperation between monetary and prudential authorities is essential.

The outline of the paper is as follows. In section 2 we begin to systematically explore the relationship between financial and real imbalances, on the one hand, and financial instability, on the other. By stressing cumulative processes, we examine to what extent symptoms of financial instability can be detected *ex ante* in a sample of 34 industrial and middle-income emerging market economies. In section 3 we then consider the relationship between monetary and financial stability, laying out the conceptual nexus and drawing on some descriptive empirical evidence. In section 4 we assess the policy implications. Finally, the conclusions highlight some open questions and issues for future research.

2. Asset Prices and Credit: Threats to Financial Stability?

2.1. What Do We Know?

Large swings in asset prices figure prominently in many accounts of financial instability. Indeed, a boom and bust in asset prices is perhaps the most common thread running through narratives of financial crises. This is true for both industrial and emerging market countries alike. Typical examples in recent decades include Latin America in the late 1970s and early 1980s, the Nordic countries in the late 1980s, and East Asia in the mid to late 1990s. These experiences are, of course, not new. In many respects the descriptions of the Australian boom and bust of the 1880–90s, for example, could be used with only limited editing to describe some of the more recent episodes of financial instability. Likewise, while perhaps more controversial, the experience of the United States in the late 1920s and early 1930s also exhibits similar features.[2]

Despite the importance of asset price developments, they have received relatively little attention in the recent empirical literature examining the determinants of banking system crises. To a large extent this reflects the lack of adequate cross-country data for property prices.[3] Formal cross-country econometric tests of the links between asset price cycles and financial stability are severely hampered and at best limited to equity prices.[4]

While asset prices have not generally been considered in these studies, their close cousin—credit—has been subject to considerable empirical investigation. One of the relatively few robust findings to emerge from the literature on leading indicators of banking crisis is that rapid domestic credit growth increases the likelihood of a problem.[5] Typical of the literature is Eichengreen and Arteta's (2000) finding that a one percentage point increase in the rate of growth of domestic credit (evaluated at the mean rate of credit growth) increases the probability of banking crisis in the following year by 0.056 percent. Other studies focus on credit growth lagged two years and find broadly similar effects, at least qualitatively.

Although these results tend to support the notion that booms in credit (and implicitly asset prices) increase the likelihood of financial problems, they provide little, if any, practical guidance about what constellation of outcomes materially increases the potential for instability. This reflects the design of the empirical work as well as the lack of data. Most studies do not take account of cumulative effects, or stocks, instead simply considering the effects of a single year of rapid credit growth, and posit a simple increasing relationship between credit growth in that year and the likelihood of financial problems. Moreover, the interactions between credit, asset prices, and the real economy are typically ignored.

One consequence of this is that the existing literature provides relatively little insight into key questions that are of concern to both central banks and supervisory authorities. These include: 1) When should credit growth be judged as "too fast?," 2) What is the cumulative effect of an extended period of strong credit growth?, and 3) Are lending booms more likely to end in problems if they occur simultaneously with other imbalances, either in the financial system or the real economy?

2.2. Beyond Bubbles

From a practical perspective the issue of interactions between various imbalances is particularly important. Rapid credit growth, *by itself*, may pose little threat to the stability of the financial system. The same could be said for rapid increases in asset prices or an investment boom. Rather, the historical narratives suggest that it is the *combination* of events, in particular the simultaneous occurrence of rapid credit growth, rapid increases in asset prices and, in some cases, high levels of investment—rather than any one of these alone—that increases the likelihood of problems.

For policymakers, therefore, the more relevant issue is not whether a "bubble" exists in a given asset price, but rather what *combination* of events in the financial and real sectors exposes the financial system to a materially increased level of risk. While the bubble question is intrinsically interesting, it is extremely difficult to answer. Moreover, even if the authorities were confident in their judgement, serious political economy problems are likely if policy responses are explicitly conditioned on that judgement. Instead, a more constructive focus is likely to be on an overall assessment of the risks facing the financial system. Knowing the answer to the "bubble question" would obviously be helpful here, although it is by no means crucial.

2.3. A Preliminary Statistical Analysis

Ideally, we would like to construct an accurate index of financial sector vulnerability that takes account of the interactions between all the relevant variables. In practice, this is extremely difficult (and perhaps even impossible) to do. Rather, in this paper our less ambitious goal is to undertake a preliminary investigation into the usefulness of credit, asset prices, and investment as predictors of future problems in the financial system. Our intention is to be as parsimonious as possible and to explore how far a few key variables can take us. We are particularly interested in two questions. First, can useful indicators be constructed using only information available to the policymaker at the time that the policy decision is made? And second, can signals be made more accurate by *jointly* considering asset prices, credit, and investment?

Our approach builds on the work of Kaminsky and Reinhart (1999). In particular, we examine whether the occurrence of a boom in asset prices, credit, or investment provides a useful signal that a financial crisis is imminent. As in Kaminsky and Reinhart, the idea is to define a threshold value for each of the relevant indicator series. When the indicator takes a value that exceeds the threshold value, we define this as a "boom" and it is said to signal an impending crisis. We examine how the usefulness of the signals changes as we change the threshold values.

Our approach, however, differs from Kaminsky and Reinhart's in a number of respects.

1. We focus on *cumulative processes*, rather than growth rates over just one year. Vulnerabilities are generally built up over an extended period, rather than in a single year. To capture this idea, we identify a credit boom as a period in which the ratio of credit to gross domestic product (GDP) deviates from its trend by a specified amount (we refer to this deviation as the "credit gap"). A large gap

could develop through either one year of very rapid credit growth or, alternatively, as the result of a number of years of above trend growth. Similarly, we define asset price and investment booms as periods in which real asset prices and the ratio of investment to GDP, respectively, deviate from their trends by specified amounts. Again, we refer to these deviations as the "asset price gap" and "investment gap," respectively.

2. We use *only ex ante information* in determining whether a boom exists. Our approach is to calculate the various gaps using only information that would have been available to the policymaker at the time that he was making an assessment of whether or not a boom existed. Accordingly, a rolling Hodrick-Prescott filter is used to estimate the gaps; for example, the credit gap for 1985 is estimated only using data up until 1985. One important consequence of this approach is that the threshold values that define the existence of a boom need to be determined without reference to the entire history of the relevant series.[6] To do this, we simply define the thresholds in terms of percentage (or percentage point) gaps. One advantage of this approach is that it leads to threshold values that are easier to interpret than those used by Kaminsky and Reinhart.

3. We consider *combinations of indicators*, rather than just single indicators. In particular, we examine what combinations of the credit, asset price, and investment gaps provide the most useful signals. In contrast, the approach used by Kaminsky and Reinhart to examine multiple indicators involves simply tallying the proportion of indicators that are "on" at any point in time. Our approach allows us to search over various combinations to determine to what degree the optimal threshold values change as we consider multiple indicators.

4. We consider *multiple horizons*. In general, it is extremely difficult to predict the timing of a crisis, even if it is almost certain that one will occur. Accordingly, we consider the usefulness of the indicators in predicting crises within one, two, and three years, respectively.

We intentionally restrict the list of countries that we consider to a relatively homogeneous set given that the factors that underlie financial crises in very poor countries, or those with very repressed financial sectors, might differ from those that cause problems in more wealthy countries with developed financial systems. Accordingly, the list of countries is limited to those that had a ratio of credit to GDP in excess of 35 percent at some point between 1960 and 1999, had GDP per capita in 1995 in excess of US$4,000 (at purchasing power parity exchange rates), and had total GDP in 1995 in excess of US$20 billion. Moreover, only countries with credit data and an equity price series since at least 1980 were considered. All up, our sample consists of 34 countries, including all of the Group of Ten.[7]

Annual data from 1960 to 1999 are used. Where adequate data are available, the first observation for the estimated gaps is 1970. In constructing the asset price gap, we are unfortunately restricted to considering only equity prices (in real terms). This is clearly second best, as we would prefer to use indices of real estate prices, particularly given the central role that real estate plays as collateral for bank loans. However, such indices are available for only a small group of countries and even then do not go back sufficiently far in time to construct meaningful ex ante measures of the asset price gap for most of the years in the 1980s.

In determining the crisis dates we have used Bordo's et al. (2001) dating, rather than specifying the dates ourselves.[8] This has both benefits and costs. On the benefit side, these dates are representative of those used elsewhere in the literature. On the cost side, they exclude episodes characterized by strong financial headwinds, but not significant failures of banks. For example, the early 1990s is not recorded as a crisis episode for the United States, nor is it for the United Kingdom. While these periods of financial headwinds may not fit the narrow definition of a "crisis," they were certainty characterized by significant macroeconomic costs arising from developments in the financial system and arguably should be included as crisis episodes. In future work, we hope to extend our analysis to consider periods of "financial stress" and not just financial crises, since in practice the distinction between the two is often relatively small.

To start with, table 1 reports our basic results for the indicators—i.e., the asset price, credit, and investment gaps—taken *individually*, and using a horizon of one year.[9] For each indicator, the table shows a range of relevant threshold values and the associated noise to signal ratio for each of these values.[10,11] The share of actual crises

Threshold	Noise/signal	% predicted	Threshold	Noise/signal	% predicted
asset price gap			credit gap		
20	.56	53	3	.29	79
30	.44	50	4	.24	79
40	.32	50	5	.25	63
50	.29	45	6	.25	55
60	.29	34	7	.20	55
70	.30	24	8	.20	47
80	.27	21	9	.18	45
90	.43	11	10	.18	37
investment gap			real credit growth		
2	.57	58	7	.54	74
3	.54	55	8	.47	74
4	.50	50	9	.44	68
5	.52	42	10	.39	68
6	.61	32	11	.36	66
7	.55	29	12	.33	66
8	.54	26	13	.30	63
9	.44	26	14	.30	53

Note: The threshold values for the credit gap are defined in terms of the deviation in *percentage points* of the actual credit ratio from the trend ratio. For the other two gaps, the threshold values are expressed as *percentage* deviations from the trend.

Table 1: Performance of Single Indicators at One-Year Horizon

correctly signalled is also reported. For comparative purposes we also report results for a credit boom defined using just the annual rate of real credit growth.

A number of points emerge from the analysis of single indicators.

- Of the indicators examined, the credit gap is clearly the best; it has the lowest noise to signal ratio and correctly predicts the largest number of crises. A threshold value around four percentage points appears to produce the best results. Using this value, almost 80 percent of crises are predicted at a one-year horizon, while false positive signals are issued around 18 percent of the time. Using slightly higher threshold values leads to a noticeable reduction in the share of crises correctly predicted with no, or little reduction, in the noise to signal ratio.

- Taking account of cumulative processes (in this case through the credit gap) yields better indicators than considering just developments over one year. In particular, when comparing the credit gap and the real credit growth indicators, the credit gap produces a lower noise to signal ratio for a given percentage of crises correctly predicted.[12]

- The asset price and investment gaps provide relatively noisy signals. For asset prices a threshold value of 40 or 50 percent appears to produce the best results. Using the 40 percent threshold, half the crises are predicted with a one-year horizon, and false positive signals are issued 15 percent of the time. For the investment gap, small threshold values appear to produce the best results, as increasing the threshold value above 4 or 5 percent does not lead systematically to a reduction in the noise to signal ratio but it does reduce the share of crises successfully predicted. Using a 5 percent threshold, 42 percent of crises are predicted at the one-year horizon and false positive signals are issued 21 percent of the time.

- The performance of the indicators improves considerably as the time horizon is lengthened. This improvement is most noticeable for the asset price and credit gaps. For example, if we extend the horizon from one year to three years and use a four-percentage point threshold for the credit gap, the number of false positive signals falls by around 20 percent. For the asset price gap, the reduction is even larger and the share of crisis predicted also increases as the horizon is lengthened.

Next we examine combinations of indicators. We look at three particular combinations: 1) credit and asset prices; 2) credit and investment; and 3) credit, asset prices, and investment. In each case a crisis is signalled if both (all) gaps are beyond the specified threshold levels. As above, we consider a range of possible threshold values.

Selected results for the one-year horizon for the first two combinations are reported in table 2. In both cases, the noise to signal ratio is lower than when the indicators are considered separately. This is particularly so when credit is combined with asset prices. Overall, we judge that a credit gap of around four percentage points *and* an asset price gap of 40 percent provide the best combined threshold values. For these values the noise to signal ratio is almost 50 percent lower than the ratio when the signal is activated by a credit gap (of 4 percentage points) alone. Furthermore, as can be seen in table 3, the noise to signal ratio falls considerably further when the horizon is lengthened to three years. Again, the decline in the ratio is larger for the combined indicator than for the credit gap alone.

Credit and asset prices				Credit and investment			
Threshold for:				**Threshold for:**			
Credit gap	Asset price gap	Noise/ signal	% predicted	Credit gap	Invest. gap	Noise/ signal	% predicted
4	30	.17	42	4	1	.25	45
4	40	.13	42	4	2	.24	42
4	50	.12	39	4	3	.23	42
5	30	.16	37	5	1	.25	39
5	40	.12	37	5	2	.25	37
5	50	.12	34	5	3	.23	37
6	30	.17	32	6	1	.25	34
6	40	.13	32	6	2	.25	32
6	50	.13	29	6	3	.23	32

Table 2: Performance of Joint Indicators at One-Year Horizon

The reduction in the noise to signal ratio obtained by combining indicators arises from a significant reduction in the number of false positive signals. Using our preferred threshold values the number of false positive signals at the one-year horizon falls by almost 75 percent when asset prices are added to credit (at the three-year horizon the fall is 80 percent). As a result, false positive signals are issued less than 5 percent of the time.

This reduction in noise, however, comes at the cost of a reduction in the share of crises correctly predicted. For example, when we use our combined threshold values of four percentage points and 40 percent, we predict 42 percent of crises, compared to 79 percent when we use credit growth alone. This decline largely comes about because when we combine the indicators we miss a number of the crises in Southeast Asia in the mid/late 1990s and in Latin America in the late 1970s. In these episodes, booming equity markets do not appear to be a central part of the story, although the narratives of these episodes typically attribute an important role to real estate prices. As we have already noted, a lack of data makes it impossible to confirm this in this type of empirical study.

Horizon (years)	Threshold: Credit gap = 4% points		Threshold: Credit gap = 4% points AND asset price gap = 40%	
	Noise/signal	% predicted	Noise/signal	% predicted
1	.24	79	.13	42
2	.21	79	.08	53
3	.20	79	.06	55

Table 3: Performance of Joint Indicators at Different Horizons

We now add investment to the picture so that a crisis is signalled only if the credit, asset price and investment gaps all exceed their threshold values. Selected results are reported in table 4.

The best combination appears to be for a credit gap of four percentage points, an asset price gap of 40 percent, and an investment gap of zero. While adding investment leads to a marginal drop in the noise to signal ratio, it also leads to a reduction in the number of crisis correctly predicted. On balance, we judge that adding investment in this way makes no significant improvement.

Overall, while this empirical exercise is meant as no more than a first step in exploring the factors that increase the vulnerability of the financial system, it does provide reasonably strong circumstantial evidence that useful ex ante indicators of financial vulnerability can be constructed. The results confirm that, at a minimum, indicators of vulnerability should take into account cumulative processes and pay particular attention to the interaction of asset prices and credit. While we would not like to place too much weight on the precise threshold values, the results do suggest that an economy in which the credit gap is above four or five percentage points and asset prices are 40 percent or 50 percent above trend is more than usually vulnerable to problems in the financial system.

One general issue raised by these results is the trade-off between Type I and Type II errors. Ideally, what we are searching for are combinations of indicators that reduce the noisiness of the signal, while at the same time maintain the share of crises actually predicted. In practice, what we find is that by combining indicators we can significantly reduce the noise (i.e., reduce Type II errors), but we miss a larger number of crises (i.e., increase Type I errors). From a policy perspective, a relevant issue is whether it is a bigger error to fail to respond to emerging vulnerabilities or to mistakenly respond to incorrect signs of future problems.

The correct answer inevitably depends upon the particular circumstances and the nature of the policy response. One argument is that, in a relative sense, prudential supervisors might care less about Type II errors than would monetary authorities, particularly those with inflation targets. The reason is partly a political economy one (although as we discuss below there may be economic reasons, as well). If a central bank with an inflation target tightened monetary policy in an effort to contain what it

Threshold for:					Threshold for:				
Credit gap	Asset price gap	Invest. gap	Noise/ signal	% predicted	Credit gap	Asset price gap	Invest. gap	Noise/ signal	% predicted
4	30	0	.15	34	5	30	0	.15	29
4	30	1	.16	32	5	30	1	.17	26
4	30	2	.15	29	5	30	2	.17	24
4	40	0	.12	34	5	40	0	.12	29
4	40	1	.13	32	5	40	1	.13	26
4	40	2	.13	29	5	40	2	.13	24

Table 4: Performance of the Three Indicators Combined

thought were financial imbalances, and it later turned out that no imbalances existed, the bank is likely to come under heavy criticism for deviating from its normal policy approach. If this is the case, it might want to be almost certain before it acted. In contrast, it is arguable that a tightening of prudential standards when in reality none was needed may provoke less criticism, and so prudential authorities might be prepared to act with less strong evidence. As we argue below, however, this situation could change with the adoption of an alternative monetary policy regime under which it was understood that monetary policy had a role to play in preserving financial stability over and above keeping inflation under control in the short run. It is to this issue of the interaction of financial and monetary stability that we now turn.

3. From Monetary Stability to Financial Stability?

In the discussion so far we have not addressed the all-important link between monetary and financial stability. Two broad interrelated questions are of particular interest. First, to what extent does monetary stability—which we interpret here as meaning low and stable inflation—contribute to financial stability? Second, what type of monetary policy regime is likely to deliver the ideal combination of monetary *and* financial stability?[13]

3.1. The Conventional Wisdom

The conventional wisdom on the links between monetary and financial stability is nicely summarized by Bordo et al. (2000) who write "that a monetary regime that produces aggregate price stability will, as a byproduct, tend to promote stability of the financial system," (p. 27).

As a general point, few would disagree with this statement, particularly the idea that volatility in the inflation rate can harm the stability of the financial system. An unexpected decline in inflation increases the real value of outstanding debt, making defaults more likely. Accordingly, periods of declining inflation, particularly if they are associated with restrictive monetary or fiscal policies, are more likely to see stresses in the financial system than are periods with stable inflation. Similarly, the vulnerability of the financial system measured over the horizon of a couple of years tends to rise when inflation is higher than expected, particularly if macroeconomic policies need to be tightened significantly to reduce inflation. Furthermore, high inflation, even if it is relatively stable, can pose a threat to financial stability, particularly if it encourages leveraged asset acquisitions and the misallocation of resources.[14]

There is some empirical work to support these ideas. For example, Hardy and Pazarbasioglu (1999) find that an increase in inflation, followed by a sharp reduction, significantly increases the probability of a financial crisis, while Demirgüç-Kunt and Detragiache (1997) find that countries with high levels of current inflation are more likely to experience a financial crisis. Similarly, Bordo et al. (2000) argue that episodes of financial distress in the United States in the 18th and 19th centuries generally took place in a disinflationary environment following several years of inflation.

3.2. Beyond the Conventional Wisdom

While the empirical evidence is broadly consistent with the idea that monetary instability can cause financial instability, the interpretation of this evidence, and the policy conclusions that follow, are arguably subtler than is sometimes recognized. In particular, the evidence does not mean that either: a) unexpected changes in the inflation rate are by themselves a major source of financial instability, or that b) financial vulnerabilities will not develop in a low and stable inflation environment.

Bordo et al. (2000), for example, interpret the evidence as suggesting that the only contribution that monetary policy can make to financial stability is through avoiding unanticipated changes in prices, and that the cause of any anticipated price change is unimportant.[15] Such a strong conclusion seems difficult to justify. In general, it is not the unanticipated decline in goods and services price inflation *per se* that causes financial problems. Rather, it is the decline in asset prices and the unwinding of financial imbalances built up in previous years that largely explains the onset of a crisis.[16] In many cases the fall in inflation that can occur around the time of the crisis is part of the process of the unwinding of the previous excesses, and is not itself the main cause of the crisis. Moreover, in episodes where inflation has fallen unexpectedly (perhaps due to a positive supply shock) but that have not been characterized by the unwinding of imbalances, the financial system has typically not come under significant strain. The experience of the unexpected decline in inflation in many countries in 1986 and 1987 due to the fall in oil prices is perhaps an example. To reiterate the central point: *It is the unwinding of financial imbalances that is the major source of financial instability, not an unanticipated decline in inflation per se.*[17] Often the two will go together, but they need not!

A corollary of this point is that while low and stable inflation promotes financial stability, financial imbalances can still build up without any noticeable pickup in inflation. This can be seen in figure 1, which shows the evolution of the average inflation in the years prior to, and after, the crises examined in section 2 (also shown is the average inflation rate around the time of lending booms). While, on average, inflation falls immediately after the crisis, there is no evidence that inflation picks up systematically either in the years prior to the crisis or as lending booms are developing.

The best example, at least over recent times, of financial imbalances developing in a low inflation environment is Japan in the late 1980s. In 1986, 1987, and 1988 Consumer Price Index (CPI) inflation was essentially zero (see figure 2). It was not until mid 1989 that evidence of an increase in inflation emerged, and even then inflation measured using the CPI peaked at only 3.9 towards the end of 1990 (measured using the GDP deflator the peak was just 3 percent). In contrast, stock prices nearly tripled between the end of 1985 and mid 1989, with commercial property prices in Tokyo increasing by even more.

While the Japanese experience in the 1980s is unusual, there are other examples of imbalances developing during periods of low or declining inflation. In South Korea, for example, inflation was generally falling throughout the 1990s, declining from a peak of more than 11 percent early in the decade, to less than 4 percent just before the crisis. Elsewhere in Asia, inflation was also relatively low, and tending to decline, prior to the crisis in 1997, yet asset prices and credit were rising strongly.

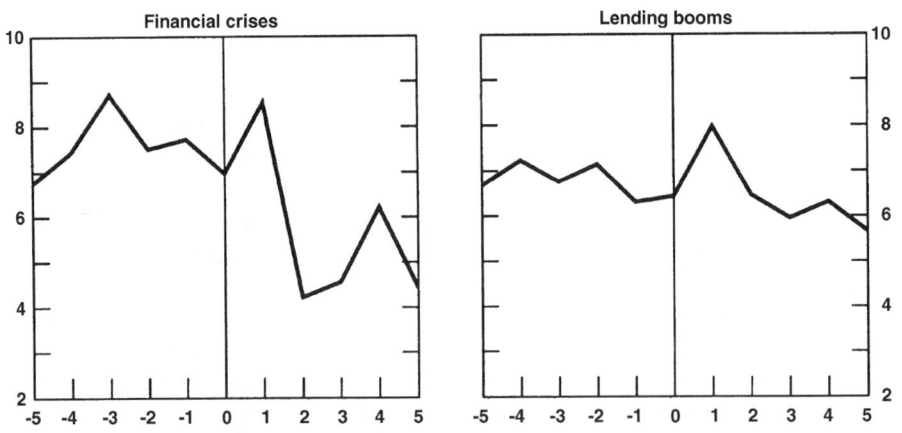

Notes: Simple arithmetic means of annual percentage changes of consumer prices across all countries (except Latin America) are used. Lending booms are defined as year in which the credit/GDP gap (first) exceeds four percentage points; *ex ante* HP filter applied.

Figure 1: Behavior of Inflation around Financial Crises and Lending Booms

These experiences are, of course, not new. In the United States, the CPI actually fell by 10 percent between 1925 and 1930, while credit and stock prices boomed. In the 19th century, too, banking crises often developed in low inflation environments. One example is the Australian banking crisis of 1893, which occurred after a frantic property boom in the 1880s.[18] This boom saw the ratio of bank credit to GDP rise by an estimated two-thirds over the decade prior to 1893. Property prices in Melbourne and Sydney doubled at least over the same period, with particularly large increases recorded in the late 1880s. In contrast, the GDP deflator actually fell over the decade before the crisis, with the largest increase in any single year being less than 5 percent.

The co-existence of an unsustainable boom in credit and asset markets on the one hand, and low and declining inflation on the other, can be explained by a number of factors or events.[19]

The *first* of these is the successful implementation of a stabilization program. This factor has been important in the development of financial imbalances in developing countries, particularly in Latin America in the late 1970s. The implementation of a credible stabilization program that anchors price expectations (through perhaps a controlled deprecation of the exchange rate) can lead to a significant and immediate reduction in inflation. This reduction can generate optimism about future economic prospects, which, together with financial liberalization, can underpin a consumption and lending boom (often financed by inflow of foreign capital). In response, asset prices, particularly real estate prices, typically rise further reinforcing the credit boom. Although inflation remains low, the poor lending decisions made during the credit boom sow the seeds for future problems. These problems can be compounded if the process of disinflation leads to a gradual appreciation of the real exchange rate.[20]

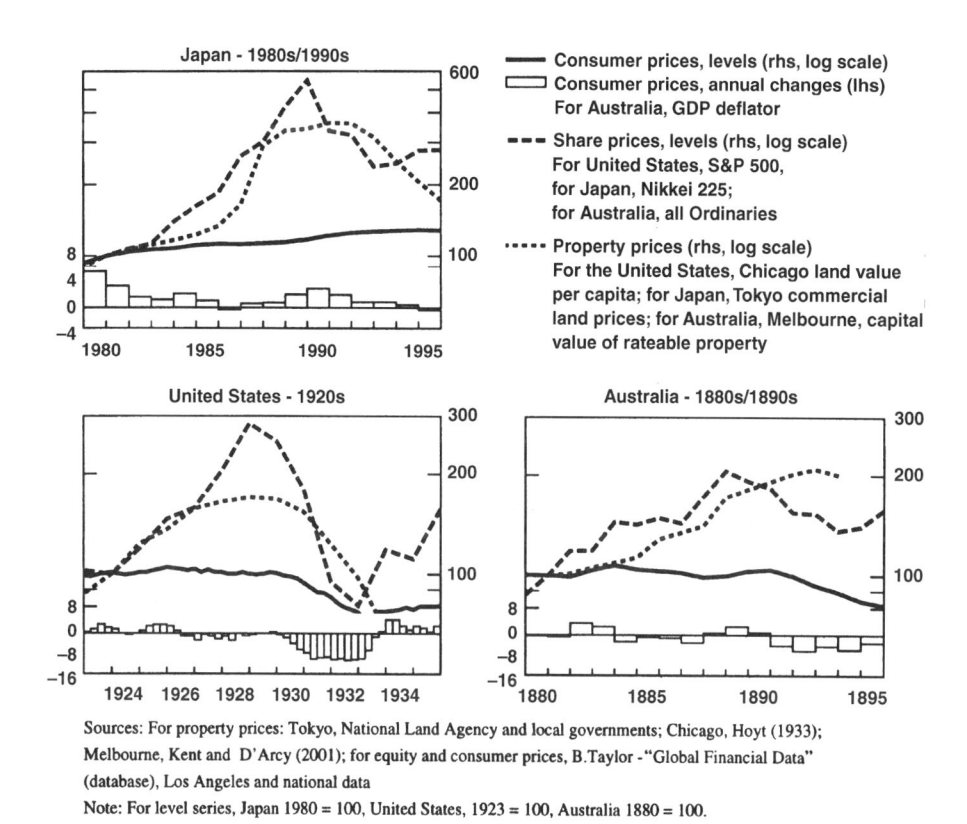

Figure 2: Consumer and Asset Prices for Selected Countries and Periods

Sources: For property prices: Tokyo, National Land Agency and local governments; Chicago, Hoyt (1933); Melbourne, Kent and D'Arcy (2001); for equity and consumer prices, B.Taylor - "Global Financial Data" (database), Los Angeles and national data

Note: For level series, Japan 1980 = 100, United States, 1923 = 100, Australia 1880 = 100.

A *second* factor that can result in subdued inflation and the development of financial imbalances is an improvement in the supply side of the economy—for example, a pickup in the pace of technological advancement or reform of the labor market. Such developments can put upward pressure on asset prices, not only because of their positive effect on current levels of corporate profitability, but also because of the sense of general optimism about the future that they typically generate. Simultaneously, they can put downward pressure on the prices of goods and services, particularly by reducing unit labour costs. The Bank of Japan, for instance, has argued that faster productivity growth and shifts in the structure of the labor market were partly responsible for the low inflation rates of the 1980s. A decade later, a pickup in the rate of productivity growth in a number of countries, most notably in the United States, has also been used to explain the benign inflation outcomes of the late 1990s and the strength of many equity markets.

The combination of rising asset prices, strong economic growth, and low inflation can lead to overly optimistic expectations of the future in a similar vein to the overly optimistic expectation that can follow a stabilization program.[21] In turn, these expectations can generate increases in asset and credit markets significantly beyond those justified by the original improvement in productivity. A self-reinforcing boom can then emerge, with increases in asset prices supporting stronger demand and sustaining, at least for a while, the optimistic expectations of the future. While the stronger demand can put upward pressure on inflation, this pressure can be masked by the improvements to the supply side of the economy.

A *third*, and subtler, factor is the existence of a high degree of monetary policy credibility. Where credibility is high, inflation expectations tend to become well-anchored and long-term price and wage contracting becomes more frequent. These endogenous responses to credible monetary policy may make the inflation rate less sensitive, at least for a period of time, to demand pressures in the economy. During periods of strong demand growth, this cost and price stickiness can boost profits, particularly if firms are operating with excess capacity or under increasing returns to scale. At the same time, highly credible monetary policy can reduce the degree of uncertainty that people feel about the future. In particular, a successful record by the central bank may well reduce the probability that the public assign to the occurrence of a sustained economic downturn. Lower uncertainty can then translate into higher asset prices and an increased willingness of investors to borrow and financial institutions to lend. These responses can ultimately make the financial system more vulnerable to an economic downturn.

The *fourth* and related reason is that low and possibly falling inflation together with a high degree of credibility of monetary policy would give little reason for the authorities to tighten policy if they respond *only* to clear signs of inflationary pressures. Paradoxically, these endogenous responses to credible monetary policy increase the probability that latent inflation pressures manifest themselves in the development of imbalances in the financial system, rather than immediate upward pressure on higher goods and services price inflation. Failure to respond to these imbalances, either using monetary policy or another policy instrument, may ultimately increase the risk of both financial instability and subsequently deflation (during the period in which the imbalances are unwound). The implication of this is that central banks with a high degree of credibility need to remain alert to the possibility that inflationary pressures first become evident in asset markets, rather than goods markets.

4. The Challenge for Monetary Authorities

The possibility of financial vulnerabilities developing during a low inflation period raises interesting issues about the design of monetary policy frameworks.[22] Of particular interest is the question of what type of monetary regime is most likely to deliver the "best" combination of monetary and financial stability. More concretely, is a monetary regime focused exclusively on controlling short-run deviations of inflation around some desired average level likely to deliver the right combination of monetary and financial stability?

This is a difficult question, particularly given the relatively short period over which inflation-targeting regimes have been in operation. While there are solid reasons to believe that such regimes will, as a byproduct, promote financial stability, there are risks as well. Most notably, such regimes might fail to respond in a sufficiently timely manner to emerging threats to the financial system, particularly if these develop during a period of subdued inflation pressures.

If the risk of this occurring is significant, then a slightly modified policy regime, under which the central bank responds not only to short-term inflation pressures but also, at least occasionally, to financial imbalances, may ultimately deliver a better combination of monetary and financial stability. Under such a regime the central bank might opt for higher interest rates than are justified simply on the basis of the short-term inflation outlook if there are clear signs of financial imbalances, such as if credit growth is rapid and asset prices are rising quickly. The justification for doing so could be that the higher interest rates could help contain the financial excesses and, in so doing, reduce the probability of future financial instability and possibly a sustained undershooting of the inflation objective. To the extent that the current and prospective prudential framework may not *by itself* guarantee the desired degree of financial stability, the justification for such a monetary policy response is strengthened.

Three powerful objections have, however, been levied against using monetary policy in this way.[23]

First, the authorities may not be able to identify the financial imbalances sufficiently early and with the required degree of comfort to take remedial action. If so, attempting to respond to financial imbalances could add to the volatility of the economy.

Second, the risk of destabilizing the economy may be compounded by the unpredictability of the effect of the policy response. Calibration may be exceedingly difficult. On the one hand, for instance, small interest rate increases may not be sufficient to contain financial excesses. It has even been argued that, paradoxically, they could be counterproductive if they help to dispel doubts about the central bank's credibility as a guarantor of price stability, thereby possibly fuelling market participants' optimism about the sustainability of the boom.[24] On the other hand, large increases could risk tipping the economy into an unnecessary recession.

Third, even if technically possible, any such response may be too hard to justify to the public. Political economy considerations militate against the use of the instrument. It takes a brave central bank to raise interest rates in the absence of obvious inflationary pressures, given the risk of being perceived as undermining prosperity. Moreover, even if the central bank were successful in containing the imbalances, this would necessarily lead to a slowdown in economic growth. In the absence of any evidence to the contrary, the central bank could come under heavy criticism for undermining what many people would have regarded as a strong and sustainable boom.

Powerful as these objections are, they fall short, in our view, of ruling out a monetary policy response altogether. They arguably overestimate the difficulties in identifying financial imbalances. They may fail to take sufficient account of the asymmetric nature of the costs associated with policy mistakes. And they ultimately stand or fall on the paradigm used to interpret the forces driving the economy. Consider each point in turn.

The difficulties in *identifying financial imbalances* are artificially magnified when the question is put in terms of *asset price bubbles*. The pitfalls in assessing "fundamental values" are well known. Indeed, it is precisely this observational indeterminacy that facilitates the formation of financial imbalances. When framed in these terms, the debate easily strays into almost ideological territory, unnecessarily pitching supporters and skeptics of "market efficiency" against each other.

The identification difficulties, however, look less daunting when the issue is articulated in terms of the *set of conditions* that are likely to generate significant strains in the financial system. As our preliminary empirical analysis suggests, certain regularities do exist. In particular, periods of strong credit growth, booming asset prices, and high levels of investment almost invariably lead to stresses in the financial system. And importantly, as necessary for policy, these regularities can be discerned purely on the basis of ex ante information and pertain to horizons that would not necessarily rule out a monetary response.

Are these regularities sufficiently strong? The statistical analysis in this paper is just a first step in more ways than one. It simply indicates a direction of future work, based on greater attention to conceptual underpinnings (e.g., cumulative vs. marginal processes, specific constellations of conditions vs. individual signals) and to policy requirements (e.g., *ex ante* vs. *ex post* information, appropriate horizons). And, it is only part of a richer set of information on which the authorities can and do rely to form a judgement about vulnerabilities and risks. On balance, we feel that on purely technical grounds these considerations make at least occasional policy responses viable. Moreover, additional work in this area may well strengthen the case further. After all, compared with the sheer volume of analytical and empirical studies about the inflation process, this field is in its infancy.

The *asymmetric nature of the costs of policy errors* arguably strengthens the previous argument. If the economy is indeed robust and the boom is sustainable, actions by the authorities to restrain the boom are unlikely to derail it altogether. By contrast, failure to act could have much more damaging consequences, as the imbalances unravel.

It may well be true, of course, that the threshold degree of comfort is considerably higher for the monetary than the prudential authorities. This reflects the need to trade off their mandated primary objective (price stability) with financial stability and translates into different perceptions of the costs of Type I and Type II errors, as already discussed. Furthermore, these perceived trade-offs underlie the political economy problems faced in deviating from what are now seen as legitimate policy norms.

The point to emphasize is that the *perceived trade-offs* are themselves to a significant degree a function of what we *think we know about the workings of the economy and the role of policy*. This determines views about the consequences of actions and of failures to act by the central bank. Such views change over time, in the light of evolving circumstances. It was, for instance, the recognition of the absence of a long-run trade-off between inflation and unemployment during the global inflationary phase that laid the basis for the adoption of the current mandates and policy rules.

Might not a subtle paradigm shift be worth considering again? As has the one that has taken place since the 1970s, this shift would have implications for our standard conception of the dynamics of the economy with consequences for policy that would, however, be less far-reaching.

If financial imbalances can build up in an environment of low inflation it stands to reason that a monetary policy reaction function that does not respond to these imbalances when they occur can unwittingly accommodate an unsustainable and disruptive boom in the real economy. The result need not take the form of inflation, although latent inflationary pressures would normally exist. Rather, it would be a contraction in economic activity, possibly accompanied by outright deflation, amplified by widespread financial strains. Accordingly, one could argue that the more serious "bubble" was in the real economy itself.

In this scenario, the consequences of failing to act early enough can be serious. If the contraction in economic activity is deep enough and prices actually decline, they can cripple the effectiveness of monetary policy tools and undermine the credibility of institutions. The Japanese experience is very instructive here. Moreover, reaction functions that are seen to imply asymmetric responses, lowering rates or providing ample liquidity when problems materialize but not raising rates as imbalances build up, can be rather insidious in the longer run. They promote a form of moral hazard that can sow the seeds of instability and costly fluctuations in the real economy.

This paradigm sees the financial imbalances as contributing to, but, more importantly, as signalling distortions in the real economy that will at some point have to be unwound. In other words, the behavior of prices of goods and services is not a sufficient statistic for those distortions. This runs contrary to the standard macroeconomic models used nowadays.[25]

From a policy perspective, the modification in policy rules we are suggesting is, in fact, fully consistent with long-cherished central bank values.

For one, it emphasises *long horizons* rather than short-term inflation control. It is precisely in order to maintain sustained price stability over horizons longer than two years, not jeopardized by deflationary pressures, which are harder to control, that a prompt response to financial imbalances would be called for.[26] Financial stability would result as a byproduct. In this sense, the pursuit of price stability, properly defined, would still be the best contribution that monetary policy could make to financial stability.

In addition, the suggested modification highlights *pre-emptive actions*. This has been a perennial concern of central banks. It is precisely one of the purported reasons for the increased focus on monetary aggregates in the 1970s: the fear that waiting to see clear signs of higher inflation would be too risky. In a way, the more explicit focus on financial imbalances harks back to this intellectual tradition. The emphasis, however, is on credit rather than money. And, no automatic responses (strict targets) are being proposed.

5. Conclusions

This paper has argued that financial imbalances can build up in low inflation environments and that in some cases it is appropriate for policy to respond to these imbalances. Indeed, the current configuration of arrangements in the monetary and financial spheres may well have increased the likelihood of low inflation co-existing with the development of imbalances in the financial system. Monetary policy rules that do not take these imbalances into account may unwittingly accommodate their further buildup. The same could be said for prudential policy. Against this background, there is a risk of greater amplitude in financial cycles going hand in hand with more disruptive booms and busts in real economic activity. A policy response worthy of serious consideration would be a strengthening of the systemwide focus in the prudential framework coupled with a greater willingness of monetary authorities to respond to the occasional development of financial imbalances that pose a threat to the ongoing health of the macroeconomy. Greater cooperation between monetary and prudential authorities is important, not just in the management of crises, as well understood today, but also in preventing their emergence.

We are fully aware of the difficult technical and political economy issues that such a policy shift would entail. We believe, however, that it would be unwise to rule it out a priori. A precondition would be a greater consensus than exists at present regarding the nexus between monetary and financial stability and about the role of monetary and prudential policies in influencing the business cycle. To that end, further work appears desirable in at least three areas.

The first is *more and better data*. There is, in particular, a remarkable dearth of data on real estate prices, despite their proven role in the genesis of financial crises and, increasingly, in influencing the business cycle. Data gathering has so far been largely left to the initiative of private firms, which naturally tailor the data to their own requirements. Given the "public good" properties of the data, there seems to be a good case for official authorities to put efforts in this area.

The second is *more and better empirical research* aimed at identifying the set of conditions that increases the likelihood of financial strains. This paper has attempted to take a small step in this direction. Such work should pay greater attention to conceptual paradigms (e.g., cumulative processes, sets of variables) and be more closely tailored to the needs (e.g., horizons, exclusive use of ex ante information, balance between Type I/Type II errors) of policymakers. The definition of the relevant financial strains, not examined here, is another area meriting more attention; for instance, a broader definition of generalized credit and asset price strains may be more appropriate. We believe that there is considerable potential in this field; the corresponding literature is just in its infancy. Moreover, as firms' risk management systems become more sophisticated and financial institutions strengthen disclosure, data availability should greatly improve over time.

The third is *more and better analytical research* into the nature of the interaction between financial and real factors as determinants of business fluctuations. This should aim to clarify the conditions under which unsustainable booms in economic activity show up as financial imbalances rather than as obvious inflationary pressures. The explicit inclusion of the financial sector and a meaningful interaction with the process of capital accumulation would seem to be prerequisites for any such exercise. This line of work could help guide empirical research and provide a sounder basis for the formation of an intellectual and policy consensus.

---

*Claudio Borio is head of research and policy analysis at the Bank of International Settlements (BIS). Philip Lowe is head of the Financial Institutions and Infrastructure Section at the BIS. The authors thank Jeff Amato, Svein Andresen, Kostas Tsatsaronis, and Bill White for helpful comments and Steve Arthur, Philippe Hainaut, and Gert Schnabel for excellent research assistance. The views expressed are those of the authors and are not necessarily those of the BIS.

Notes

1. This paper is a condensed version of Borio and Lowe (2002).

2. For a discussion of the Australian banking crisis of 1893 see Fisher and Kent (1999). See Persons (1930) for a detailed account of the rapid credit growth in the United States in the 1920s.

3. Comparatively good data are limited to industrial countries. See Bank for International Settlements (1993) and Borio et al. (1994) for a discussion of asset price trends (including for commercial and residential property), their link to credit cycles, and financial stability. That analysis is partly based on an aggregate asset price index measure. See Borio and Lowe (2002) for an update of asset price trends.

4. See, for example, Hutchison and McDill (1999) and Kaminsky and Reinhart (1999).

5. See, for example, Demirgüç-Kunt and Detragiache (1997, 1998), Gourinchas, Valdes, and Landerretche (2001), Hardy and Pazarbasioglu (1999), Hutchinson and McDill (1999), Kaminsky (1999), and Kaminsky and Reinhart (2000). Bell and Pain (2000) and Eichengreen and Arteta (2000) provide useful overviews of the literature.

6. Kaminsky and Reinhart define the thresholds relative to the percentile of the distribution of the indicator *over the whole sample period*. The chosen percentiles differ across indicators but are constant across countries.

7. Data are available from the authors upon request.

8. Where the crisis episodes extend over multiple years we consider just the first year. In all there are 38 crisis episodes between 1970 and 1999 spread across 27 of the 34 countries.

9. Results for two- and three-year horizons are available upon request. For the asset price indicator we introduce a lead of two years; i.e., when measuring whether the asset price gap exceeds a particular threshold we use the level of the equity price gap two years earlier. We do this for two reasons. First, previous studies have shown that equity markets provide a reasonable leading indicator of economic activity and financial problems, with the lead generally being around one to two years. Second, in many episodes a boom in property markets follows a boom in the equity market with a lag of a couple of years. In the absence of data on property prices, introducing a lead on the equity prices gap may allow equity prices to serve as a proxy (at least in some cases) for property prices.

10. In all three cases an indicator is judged to successfully signal a crisis if it is "on" also in the year of the crisis. The justification for doing this is that we are using annual data and we cannot distinguish when in the year the crisis occurs and when in the year the indicator goes "on."

11. The noise to signal ratio is defined as the ratio of size of Type II errors (i.e., the percentage of noncrisis periods in which a crisis is incorrectly signalled) to one minus the size of Type I errors (i.e., the percentage of crises that are not correctly predicted). Where an indicator has been "on" prior to (or at the time of) the crisis and remains on after the beginning of the crisis for either one or two years we exclude the signals in the years after the crisis from the "noise" calculation (as they are not really false signals).

12. Moreover, if we define the threshold for real credit growth in terms of the *percentile* of the distribution *over the whole sample* (as do Kaminsky and Reinhart) the noise to signal ratio for a given share of crises predicted is *even higher* than when the threshold is defined in terms of an (arbitrarily high) absolute growth rate. This suggests that what is important is the *absolute* growth rate, not the growth rate relative to historical experience. In other words, if the growth rate in a country were generally moderate, the top percentile would be a poor indicator of strains.

13. Borio and Crockett (2000) and Borio and Lowe (2002) suggest a stylized conceptual framework to understand the relationship between monetary and financial stability across monetary and financial regimes and apply it to historical experience since the gold standard.

14. Schwartz (1995) argues that high inflation contributes to unproductive lending as it exacerbates information asymmetries making it more difficult for lenders to assess the true riskiness of potential borrowers. Furthermore, it could be argued that the demand for real estate tends to increase in high inflation environments given that real estate provides a reasonable hedge against inflation. Moreover, many tax systems contribute to the attractiveness of leveraged asset purchases when inflation is high.

15. Specifically, they write "Similarly, the contribution of aggregate price stability to the stability of the financial system depends neither on the cause of specific price level movements nor on the nature of the monetary regime, except insofar as they affect the extent that changes in aggregate prices are anticipated," (p. 7). In subsequent work, Bordo and Jeanne (2002) argue that there may be grounds to use monetary policy to diffuse an asset price boom in order to prevent a credit crunch.

16. The unwinding could, but need not, be associated with a prior tightening of monetary policy.

17. This is not to deny, of course, as first emphasised by Fisher (1931), that ceteris paribus deflation can contribute to financial instability, by increasing the value of real debts. But the *context* in which that is occurring, i.e., exogenous improvements in productivity and profits versus depressed demand conditions and declines in asset values, is critical. On this, see also Selgin (1997).

18. See Fisher and Kent (1999) and Kent and D'Arcy (2001).

19. One additional factor not discussed below arises from the Modigliani-Cohn (1979) effect. When inflation declines, the change in accounting profits tends to overstate the change in economic profits as the lower nominal interest rates that eventually accompany lower inflation lead to a reduction in interest servicing costs (even if real interest rates remain unchanged). If investors fail to recognize this effect, equity prices are likely to be bid up, and in some circumstances this rise in prices may be the catalyst for an unsustainable boom. On the empirical significance of this, see McCauley et al. (1999).

20. Much of the literature on the ultimate failure of these type of stabilization schemes focuses on the lack of credibility of the stabilization program; see, for example, the discussion in Calvo and Végh (1999). Arguably, however, the imbalances built up in the financial system in the initial phase of the program are driven not by a lack of credibility, but by the combination of deregulation and too much initial confidence that the program will succeed.

21. See Borio et al. (2001) for a detailed discussion of possible reasons why this occurs.

22. The policy dilemmas raised in this section, including those for prudential authorities, are also addressed in BIS (2001), Borio and Crockett (2000), Borio et al. (2001), Borio and

Lowe (2001) and Crockett (2000a), (2000b) and (2001). See also Carmichael and Esho (2001).

23. For skeptical views concerning the use of monetary policy in this way see Bernanke and Gertler (1999), Vickers (1999), and some of the points made in Center for Economic Policy Research/BIS (1998).

24. On this see, in particular, Yamaguchi (1999).

25. As much in economics, this point, of course, is not new. In the interwar years there was a heated debate on this issue. See, for instance, Haberler (1932) and Laidler (1999) for a review and Bernard and Bisignano (2001) for a look at the Austrian School. See also Selgin (1997) for a review of the debate on productivity norms. The notion that responding to inflation will, over time, guarantee appropriate macroeconomic outcomes has been formalized, for instance, in so-called neo-Keynesian models (Rotenberg and Woodford, 1999). More generally, however, it permeates all the mainstream macroeconomic approaches. It is also reflected, for example, in the common prescription that following stronger productivity growth central banks should reduce interest rates if and as inflationary pressures abate (e.g., Taylor, 1999, and Clarida et al., 1999). From a Wicksellian perspective, however, this would normally result in a reduction in the real interest rate precisely at a time when the natural rate would rise. If a lower or constant real interest rate can be kept for long *without* the disequilibria showing up in inflation, then presumably they should emerge elsewhere. Financial imbalances would be obvious candidates. On some of these issues, see Amato (forthcoming).

26. Kent and Lowe (1997) provide a theoretical justification for this view; Shiratsuka (2001) makes a similar point with reference to the notion of "sustainable" price stability. For arguments in favor of raising interest rates on financial stability grounds, see also Borio et al. (1994) and Cecchetti et al. (2000); Okina et al. (2000) do so with reference to the recent Japanese experience. Goodhart (1995) also stresses the need to take the behavior of asset prices into account in the setting of monetary policy. BIS (1998) contains a series of contributions by central bank economists on the appropriate role of asset prices in monetary policy.

References*
*References listed with an * are available online at the BIS website (www.bis.org).

Amato, J., 2001, "Wicksell, New Keynesian Models and The Natural Rate of Interest," Bank For International Settlements, working paper.

Bank for International Settlements, 2001, *71st Annual Report*, June.*

_____, 1998, "The Role of Asset Prices in the Formulation of Monetary Policy," Bank for International Settlements, Conference Paper No. 5, March.

_____, 1993, *63rd Annual Report*, June.

Bell, J., And D. Pain, 2000, "Leading Indicator Models of Banking Crises—A Critical Review," *Financial Stability Review*, Bank of England, December, pp. 113–129.

Bernanke, B. S., and M. Gertler, 1999, "Monetary Policy and Asset Price Volatility," in New Challenges for Monetary Policy, a symposium sponsored by the Federal Reserve Bank Of Kansas City, Jackson Hole, WY, August 26–28.

Bernard, H., and J. Bisignano, 2001, "Bubbles and Crashes: Hayek and Haberler Revisited," *Asset Price Bubbles: Implications for Monetary and Regulatory Policies*, 13, pp. 3–39.

Bordo, M., M. Dueker, and D. Wheelock, 2000, "Aggregate Price Shocks and Financial Instability: An Historical Analysis," National Bureau of Economic Research, working paper, No. 7652.

Bordo, M., B. Eichengreen, D. Klingebiel, and M. S. Martinez-peria, 2001, "Financial Crises: Lessons from the Last 120 Years," *Economic Policy*, April.

Bordo, M., and O. Jeanne, 2002, "Boom-busts in Asset Prices, Economic Instability, and Monetary Policy," mimeo.

Borio, C., and A. D. Crockett, 2000, "In Search of Anchors for Financial and Monetary Stability," *Greek Economic Review*, Vol. 20(2), pp. 1–14.

Borio, C., C. Furfine, and P. Lowe, 2001, "Procyclicality of the Financial System and Financial Stability: Issues and Policy Options," *In Marrying The Macro- and Micro-prudential Dimensions of Financial Stability*, Bank for International Settlements Papers No. 1, pp. 1–57.*

Borio, C., N. Kennedy, and S. Prowse, 1994, "Exploring Aggregate Asset Price Fluctuations Across Countries: Measurement, Determinants and Monetary Policy Implications," Bank for International Settlements Economic Papers No. 40, Basel.

Borio, C., and P. Lowe, 2002, "Asset Prices, Financial and Monetary Stability: Exploring the Nexus," Bank for International Settlements Papers, July.

_____, 2001, "To Provision or Not to Provision," *Quarterly Review*, Bank for International Settlements, June, pp. 36–48.*

Carmichael, J., and N. Esho, 2001, "Asset Price Bubbles and Prudential Regulation," Australian Prudential Regulation Authority.

Center for Economic Policy Research/Bank for International Settlements, 1998, "Asset Prices and Monetary Policy: Four Views."

Cecchetti, S., H. Genberg, J. Lipsky, and S. Wadhwani, 2000, "Asset Prices and Monetary Policy," report prepared for the conference Central Banks and Asset Prices, organized by the International Center for Monetary and Banking Studies, Geneva, May.

Calvo, G., and C. Végh, 1999, "Inflation Stabilization and Bop Crises in Developing Countries," National Bureau of Economic Research, working paper, No. 6925.

Clarida, R., H. Gakf, and N. Gertker, 1999, "The Science of Monetary Policy: A New Keynesian Perspective," *Journal of Economic Literature*, Vol. 37, December, pp. 1661–1707.

Crockett, A.D., 2001, "Monetary Policy and Financial Stability," Bank For International Settlements Speeches, February 13.*

_____, 2000a, "In Search of Anchors for Financial and Monetary Stability," speech to the Société Universitaire Européenne De Recherches Financières Colloquium, Vienna, April 27–29.*

_____, 2000b, "Marrying the Micro- and Macro-prudential Dimensions of Financial Stability," Bank for International Settlements Review, No. 76, September 22.

Demirgüç-Kunt, A., and E. Detragiache, 1998, "Financial Liberalization and Financial Fragility," International Monetary Fund, working paper, No. WP/98/83.3.

_____, 1997, "The Determinants of Banking Crises: Evidence from Developing and Developed Countries," International Monetary Fund, working paper, No. WP/97/106.

Eichengreen, B., and C. Arteta, 2000, "Banking Crises in Emerging Markets: Presumptions and Evidence," Center for International and Development Economics Research, working paper C00-115, August.

Fisher, I., 1932, *Booms and Depressions*, New York: Adelphi Co.

Fisher, C., and C. Kent, 1999, "Two Depressions, One Banking Collapse," Reserve Bank of Australia, research discussion paper, No. 1999-06.

Goodhart, C. A. E., 1995, "Price Stability and Financial Fragility," in *Financial Stability in a Changing Environment*, K. Kawamoto, Z. Nakajima and H. Taguchi, eds., Macmillan: London, Chap. 10, pp. 439–510.

Gourinchas, P., R. Valdes, and O. Landerretche, 2001, "Lending Booms: Latin America and the World," National Bureau of Economic Research, working paper, No. 8249.

Haberler, G., 1932, "Money and the Business Cycle," in *Gold and Monetary Stabilisation*, Q. Wright, ed., Chicago: University of Chicago Press.

Hardy, D., and C. Pazarbasioglu, 1999, "Determinants and Leading Indicators of Banking Crises: Further Evidence," International Monetary Fund, staff papers, 46(3), pp. 247–258.

Hoyt, H., 1933, *One Hundred Years of Land Values in Chicago*, Chicago: University of Chicago Press.

Hutchison, M., and K. McDill, 1999, "Are All Banking Crises Alike? The Japanese Experience in International Comparison," National Bureau of Economic Research, working paper, No. 7253.

Kaminsky, G., 1999, "Currency and Banking Crises: The Early Warnings of Distress," International Monetary Fund, working paper, No. WP/99/178.

Kaminsky, G., and C. Reinhart 1999, "The Twin Crises: The Causes of Banking and Balance-of-Payments Problems," *American Economic Review*, Vol. 89(3), pp. 473–500.

Kent, C., and P. Lowe, 1997, "Asset-Price Bubbles and Monetary Policy," Reserve Bank of Australia, research discussion paper, No. 9709 (see also Bank for International Settlements Conference Paper No. 5, March 1998).

Kent, C., and P. D'Arcy, 2001, "Cyclical prudence—Credit Cycles in Australia," in Marrying the Macro- and Micro-prudential Dimensions of Financial Stability, Bank for International Settlements Papers, No. 1, pp. 58–90.*

Laidler, D., 1999, "Fabricating the Keynesian Revolution," University of St. Gallen, Cambridge University Press.

McCauley, R., J. S. Ruud, and F. Iacono, 1999, *Dodging Bullets: Changing US Corporate Capital Structures in the 1980s and 1990s*, Cambridge, MA: MIT Press.

Modigliani, F., and R. A. Cohn, 1979, "Inflation, Rational Valuation, and the Market," *Financial Analysts Journal*, Vol. 35(2), pp. 24–44.

Okina, K., M. Shirakawa, and S. Shiratsuka, 2000, "Asset Price Bubbles and Monetary Policy: Japan's Experience in the Late 1980s and the Lessons," Institute for Monetary and Economic Studies, Bank of Japan, discussion paper, No. 2000-E-12.

Persons, C., 1930, "Credit Expansion, 1920 to 1929, and its Lessons," *Quarterly Journal of Economics*, November, pp. 94–130.

Rotemberg, J. J., and M. Woodford, 1999, "Interest-rate Rules in an Estimated Sticky Price Model," in *Monetary Policy Rules*, J. B. Taylor, ed., Chicago: University of Chicago Press, pp. 57–119.

Schwartz, A., 1995, "Why Financial Stability Depends on Price Stability," *Economic Affairs*, Autumn, pp. 21–25.

Selgin, G., 1997, "Less than Zero: The Case for a Falling Price Level in a Growing Economy," The Institute of Economic Affairs, Hobart Paper, No. 132, April, London.

Shiratsuka, S., 2001, "Asset Prices, Financial Stability, and Monetary Policy: Based on Japan's Experience of the Asset Price Bubble," Bank for International Settlements Papers, No. 1, Basel.*

Taylor, J. B., 1999, "Monetary Policy Rules," Chicago: University of Chicago Press.

Vickers, J., 1999, "Asset Prices and Monetary Policy," *Bank of England Quarterly Bulletin*, 34, November, pp. 478–435.

Yamaguchi, Y., 1999, "Asset Prices and Monetary Policy: Japan's Experience," in New Challenges for Monetary Policy, a symposium sponsored by the Federal Reserve Bank of Kansas City, Jackson Hole, WY, August 26–28.

Chapter 18
Testing for Stock Market Overvaluation/ Undervaluation

Ellen R. Mcgrattan*
Federal Reserve Bank of Minneapolis and University of Minnesota

and

Edward C. Prescott
University of Minnesota and Federal Reserve Bank of Minneapolis

The purpose of this conference is to discuss the potential role of central banks and regulatory agencies in preventing asset price overvaluations and subsequent financial and real instability. We can imagine the same conference being held in 1929 following the October crash of the U.S. stock market. Our discussion here focuses on 1929 because we believe that there are important lessons to be learned from this historical episode.

Annual reports of the Board of Governors of the Federal Reserve System are clear—open market committee members were alarmed by the dramatic rise in stock prices before the 1929 crash. They viewed investment in stocks as speculative and wanted member banks to cut credit to stock investors. This was done through a policy of "direct pressure," through sharp increases in discount rates, and through discriminatory lending in favor of farmers and businesspeople.[1]

Now that we have the advantage of hindsight and the tools of modern theory, we can ask if there was reason for alarm. This is exactly what we do in McGrattan and Prescott (2001b). In particular, we test Irving Fisher's view that stock values were in line with fundamentals.

Various approaches can be used to estimate the fundamental value of corporate equities. The standard approach is to estimate the present value of dividends net of taxes. Absent transaction costs and other frictions, competitive theory implies that this measure is equal to the market value of corporate equities. The problem with the standard approach is that it requires the set of Arrow-Debreu event-contingent prices and dividends. These elements are not directly observable and must be estimated. It is not surprising, then, that researchers using this method have come to opposite conclusions about the value of the market in 1929. Compare, for example, Shiller (1981, figure 1) and Donaldson and Kamstra (1996, figure 7).

1. Our Approach to Estimating the Fundamental Value of the Stock Market

We adopt a different approach, which we developed in McGrattan and Prescott (2000, 2001a). With our approach, we exploit another implication of competitive theory to estimate the fundamental value of corporate equity: The value of a set of real assets is just the sum of the values of the individual assets in the set. In the public finance literature, this implication is referred to as the q theory of stock market value, where the value of a corporation is just the value of its capital corrected for tax consequences.[2] We take this approach in our research (McGrattan and Prescott, 2001a), but advance it in two respects. First, we do not ignore intangible capital, which, like tangible capital, adds to the value of corporations. Instead, we develop a method for estimating its magnitude using national accounts data. Second, our model economy has capital gains taxed on a realized basis rather than some fraction of capital gains taxed on an accrual basis. Under U.S. tax code, only realized capital gains are taxed. Both of these modifications are quantitatively important in estimating the fundamental value of the stock market.[3]

Our formula for the fundamental value of corporate equities V is:

1) $V = (1 - \tau_d)K'_T + (1 - \tau_d)(1 - \tau_c)K'_I,$

where

τ_d is the tax rate on distributions,
τ_c is the tax rate on corporate income,
K'_T is the end-of-period tangible corporate capital stock, and
K'_I is the end-of-period intangible corporate capital stock.

The reasons for the tax factors are as follows. Corporate earnings significantly exceed corporate investment and, as a result, aggregate corporate distributions are positive. Historically these distributions have been in the form of dividends. Therefore, the cost of a unit of tangible capital on margin is only $1 - \tau_d$ of forgone consumption. In the case of intangible capital, the consumption cost of a unit of capital is even smaller because investments in intangible capital reduce corporate tax liabilities.[4]

We construct measures of tangible capital and corporate tax rates using data from the U.S. Department of Commerce's Bureau of Economic Analysis. We construct measures of tax rates on distributions using data from the Internal Revenue Service's *Statistics of Income*. These measures indicate that tax rates in 1929 were very low and that the reproducible cost of capital was very high relative to postwar levels.

The tricky part of our calculation is constructing a measure of intangible capital. These investments reduce current accounting profits, and they increase future economic profits. The formula for steady-state before-tax accounting profits is:

2) $\pi = \dfrac{i}{1 - \tau_c} K_T + iK_I - gK_I,$

where g is the steady-state growth rate of the economy and i is the steady-state after-tax real interest rate. Note that gK_I is steady-state investment in intangible capital, which reduces accounting profits because it is expensed. The reason that the after-tax and not the before-tax real interest rate is the return on intangible capital is that intangible capital investments are expensed. Note also that all the variables in this formula are reported in the system of national accounts except i and K_I.

2. Our Findings

In McGrattan and Prescott (2001a), we estimate the steady-state after-tax real interest rate using national income data. In particular, we estimate the after-tax return on capital in the noncorporate sector, which has as much capital as the corporate sector. We found that the stock market was neither overvalued nor undervalued in 1962 and 2000. The reason for the low valuation relative to gross national product (GNP) in 1962 and the high valuation relative to GNP in 2000 is that the tax on distributions was much higher in 1962 than it was in 2000.

Unfortunately, data limitations preclude estimating the real after-tax interest rate in 1929 in the same way. Given these limitations, we use equation 2 to determine the implied stock of intangible capital for a range of real interest rates. For real interest rates below 6 percent—an upper bound based on theory and empirical evidence—we find that the stock market was actually *undervalued* in 1929. We were surprised by this result because our priors found that the market was overvalued in 1929. We viewed our exercise as one in which we would quantify the extent of overvaluation. However, we found instead that the quantification was on the extent of undervaluation.

An after-tax real interest rate over 6 percent is not reasonable for many reasons. One is that national income accounts show the rate between 4 and 4.5 percent throughout the postwar period (see McGrattan and Prescott, 2001a). Another reason is that yields on the highest-grade corporate bonds in 1929, a period when prices had been stable and it was reasonable to think that they would continue to be, were near 5 percent. Still, another reason is that this high interest rate, given the rate of growth of consumption, would have implied a curvature parameter larger than that found in other general equilibrium studies of growth and fluctuations.

3. Why Did the Stock Market Crash in 1929?

If the 1929 stock market was not overvalued, why did it crash? It is true that corporate valuation relative to GNP was higher in 1929 than in the preceding four years and that earnings relative to GNP were about the same (see McGrattan and Prescott, 2001b, figures 1 and 3). These facts, however, do not imply that the stock market was overvalued in October of 1929 just before the crash. Indeed, we found that the market was not overvalued.[5]

Our theory is that the crash was due in large part to the Federal Reserve's reaction to the rising stock prices, which it viewed as reducing real investments in the corporate sector. Determined to stem investment in stocks, the Federal Reserve increased short-term interest rates dramatically (see McGrattan and Prescott, 2001b, figures 5 and 6). The short-term interest rates that increased the most were those on brokerage loans, and this was almost surely the result of the Federal Reserve's "direct pressure" policy. This policy entailed the threat to deny member banks that made brokerage loans access to the discount window, which was heavily used in that era.

When prices started to decline and margin calls were made, loan extensions became difficult to get. Stock prices slipped further as investors had to sell. As the Federal Reserve eased credit, the stock market recovered. By the middle of 1930, stocks had recovered much of the ground lost in 1929. Perhaps the crash could have been avoided. This historical episode is strong evidence that Federal Reserve policy can create a stock market crash by disrupting the credit system. If stock market participants are subject to an unexpected credit crunch, a stock market crash is likely.

4. Concluding Comment

We have developed a way to determine whether the stock market is overvalued or undervalued and applied it to the 1929 U.S. stock market. We found that the reason for the 1929 crash was not that the stock market was overvalued relative to fundamentals.

Significant overvaluation of the stock market is reason for concern. If the market is overvalued, the likelihood of a crash is high, and a crash would result in large declines in net worth of people and corporations. A stock market crash would cause state and local pension plans to suffer large declines in the value of their assets, and this would necessitate increases in taxes if promises were to be honored. The same decline would occur for private defined benefit plans, which would further reduce the value of the stock market. People with individual retirement accounts would also suffer losses. In such situations, there is a danger that policies will be adopted that have adverse real economic effects.

Are there any consequences to the stock market being undervalued? Our answer is "Yes." An undervaluation will lead to greater underinvestment in the corporate sector and lower economic efficiency.

Should the Federal Reserve take into consideration the consequences of its policy for the value of the stock market? Our answer is "No." The role of the Federal Reserve is to maintain an efficient payment and credit system, and it should not consider the effect of its policies on the value of the stock market. The central bank should not try to prop up the value of the stock market as it did recently in Hong Kong and Taiwan or depress the stock market as the Federal Reserve did in the United States in 1929.

If not the central bank, then who should deal with stock market overvaluation or undervaluation? Our answer is that economists should convey to the public information about the degree of overvaluation or undervaluation. If the public has this information and acts on it, the problem of incorrect stock market valuation will not arise.

*Ellen R. McGrattan is a senior economist at the Federal Reserve Bank of Minneapolis and Edward C. Prescott is a Regents' Professor at the University of Minnesota and senior advisor to the Federal Reserve Bank of Minneapolis. Edward Prescott acknowledges financial support of the National Science Foundation. The views expressed herein are those of the authors and not necessarily those of any organization, including the Federal Reserve Bank of Minneapolis and the Federal Reserve System.

Notes

1. See Federal Reserve Board of Governors (1930, p. 4).

2. For excellent reviews of this development, see Auerbach (2000) and Poterba (2000).

3. We also found that the transition from a system where almost no corporate equity is held in retirement accounts and as pension fund reserves introduces long transitional dynamics because people cannot shift their equity from nonretirement to retirement accounts without penalty.

4. In fact, formula 1 must be adjusted if economic depreciation and accounting depreciation are not equal and if there is an investment tax credit.

5. The rise in the value of the stock market in the 1925–29 period could very well have been the result of people becoming more confident that the current system would persist into the foreseeable future. A maintained hypothesis in this analysis is that people did not expect the Great Depression in 1929.

References

Auerbach, Alan J., 2000, "Taxation and Corporate Financial Policy," in *Handbook of Public Economics*, Alan Auerbach and Martin Feldstein, eds., Amsterdam: North-Holland.

Donaldson, R. Glen, and Mark Kamstra, 1996, "A New Dividend Forecasting Procedure that Rejects Bubbles in Asset Prices: The Case of 1929's Stock Crash," *Review of Financial Studies*, Vol. 9, Summer, pp. 333–383.

Federal Reserve Board of Governors, 1930, *Sixteenth Annual Report of the Federal Reserve Board for the Year 1929*, Washington, DC: U.S. Government Printing Office.

McGrattan, Ellen R., and Edward C. Prescott, 2001a, "Taxes, Regulations, and Asset Prices," Federal Reserve Bank of Minneapolis, working paper, No. 610, revised July 2001.

_____, 2001b, "The Stock Market Crash of 1929: Irving Fisher was Right!," Federal Reserve Bank of Minneapolis, staff report, No. 294, revised December 2001.

_____, 2000, "Is the Stock Market Overvalued?," *Federal Reserve Bank of Minneapolis Quarterly Review*, Vol. 24, Fall, pp. 20–40.

Poterba, James M., 2000, "Taxation, Risk-taking, and Household Portfolio Behavior," in *Handbook of Public Economics*, Alan Auerbach and Martin Feldstein, eds., Amsterdam, North-Holland.

Shiller, Robert J., 1981, "Do Stock Prices Move too Much to be Justified by Subsequent Changes in Dividends?," *American Economic Review*, Vol. 71, June, pp. 421–436.

Chapter 19
A Stochastic Index of the Cost of Life: An Application to Recent and Historical Asset Price Fluctuations

Michael F. Bryan*
Federal Reserve Bank of Cleveland

Stephen G. Cecchetti
Ohio State University and National Bureau of Economic Research

and

Róisín O'Sullivan
Ohio State University and Smith College

1. Introduction

This paper considers the role of asset prices in the construction of measures of inflation. Following work begun in Bryan, Cecchetti, and O'Sullivan (2001), we examine the potential bias in aggregate price statistics that can arise in measures that focus solely on the price of current consumption. If the role of the central bank is to eliminate changes in the overall price level, then the appropriate price index should capture the current cost of purchasing claims to future as well as current consumption. One interpretation of this is that policymakers should be concerned with the current cost of expected lifetime consumption rather than the more conventional measures that focus exclusively on the current cost of current consumption. The simplest way to think about this is that changes in the real interest rate affect the current price of future consumption. When the real interest rate falls, the cost of lifetime consumption rises, and this is inflationary. Ignoring future consumption in the computation of inflation is analogous to leaving out a good that belongs in the index and creates the potential for what we will call "intertemporal substitution bias." Since asset prices measure the current cost of future consumption, including them in a measure of inflation potentially allows for this real interest rate impact and eliminates this bias. We call this a "cost-of-life index."

Following the methodology in our earlier work, we are able to introduce a number of candidate asset prices into our cost-of-life index. This allows us to estimate the size of the intertemporal substitution bias, both on a year-by-year basis and on average over decades. We find that the bias from omitting asset prices in the measurement of inflation is roughly the same size as that associated with other well-known biases, including those that arise from commodity substitution and the like. We also show that this bias is time-varying and over periods of several years may significantly distort the magnitude and timing of how the central bank perceives inflation. Specifically, intertemporal substitution bias between current consumption and future consumption tended to understate the inflation being recorded by current-consumption price statistics such as the Consumer Price Index (CPI) during the latter half of the 1990s. This reversed the upward bias to the retail price measure that existed over much of the 1977 to 1995 period.

During some periods this bias can be extreme. Such appears to have been the case between the two world wars of the last century when the relatively low real interest rate in the mid 1920s suddenly rose. Our measure of inflation is between one percentage point and two percentage points higher than conventional (consumption-based) indicators suggested during the 1920s—and, similarly, more deflationary during the early years of the 1930s.

The organization of this paper is as follows. Section 2 describes how it is that ignoring asset prices introduces a bias into aggregate price statistics. In section 3, we introduce the weighting methodology used to incorporate "excessively noisy" asset prices so as to produce a price index for the current "cost of life" that eliminates the intertemporal substitution bias. Section 4 reports on the behavior of this index relative to the more common cost-of-living statistics used by economists and policymakers. In section 5 we show how such a price measure would have changed our interpretation of price movements during the great deflation between the two world wars. In section 6, we conclude.

2. Asset Prices and the Cost of Life: A Case of Missing Goods Bias

Which goods should be used in the computation of a price statistic? This is one of the oldest questions in quantitative macroeconomics and, not surprisingly, the answer depends on the question the statistic is intended to answer. Whether or not to include asset prices in the computation of aggregate inflation depends on what relevant information they contain for the question at hand. Asset prices are essential in any calculation that incorporates intertemporal consumption decisions since they measure today's cost of future consumption. Households allocate current income to both current and future consumption. In fact, theory suggests that current decisions by economic agents attempt to ensure a particular level of lifetime consumption. This means that the appropriate price statistic—both for households' decisions and policymakers—must take account of changes in the cost of current relative to future consumption. Ignoring changes in this relative price (changes in the real interest rate) will create a bias in price measurement that is exactly analogous to what is commonly called "omitted goods bias."

This issue is especially important to a central bank that has among its objectives the management of inflation. The link connecting central bank policy to inflation is often presumed to be "long and variable," as changes in target interest rates and central bank money affect prices slowly and unpredictably. Since these policies alter the real interest rate, causing intertemporal substitution in consumption, the central bank may be missing an important part of the inflationary process by focusing exclusively on the drift in current retail (consumption) prices.

Following the arguments first set out by Alchain and Klein (1973), this leads us to consider a price statistic that is designed to gauge the current (intertemporal) cost of life—that is—a measure that takes account of the current cost of both current and future consumption. The cost of life is distinct from the current cost of living that provides the conceptual basis for statistics such as the CPI or the deflator for personal consumption expenditures. Those measures are designed to capture the cost of current consumption and intentionally omit current prices of future consumption. Therefore, there exists a relative price change such that its exclusion from the set of prices distorts the aggregate so that it no longer gives an accurate answer to the question under consideration.

To illustrate this point, we can think of price changes for all goods, services, and assets today as having a common and idiosyncratic component. We write this as

1) $\pi_{it} = \pi_t + x_{it}$,

where i indicates the set of goods, services, or assets, and t is time, and so π_{it} is the inflation of individual good i at time t, π_t is the common trend in inflation that we are trying to measure, and is the deviation of good i inflation at time t from this trend. An inflation index is constructed by weighting together these individual inflation measures. That is,

2) $\dot{P}_t = \sum_i w_{it} \pi_{it}$,

where the weights (w_{it}) can change over time, but have the property that they sum to one. That is

3) $\sum_i w_{it} = 1 \forall t$.

Using this fact, we can now rewrite the aggregate price change as

4) $\dot{P}_t = \pi_{it} + \sum_i w_{it} \pi_{it}$.

Our goal is the measurement of the common trend in all prices (inflation), π_t. To do this we need to find a set of goods, services, and assets where the (weighted) relative changes, the x_{it}s, cancel out. But the weighted sum of these relative inflation measures will only cancel out if we have a complete set of prices. If a good with a non-zero relative price disturbance (x_{it}) is left out, then the sum of the weighted price adjustments will not sum to zero, and so the index $\dot{P}_t$ will not equal π_t, the common inflation trend we are trying to measure. If asset prices are excluded from the cost-of-life statistic, any intertemporal substitution between current and future consumption originating from a change in the real interest rate will create a bias in the resulting measure of inflation. Specifically, during periods when the real interest rate is declining, prices of current consumption fall relative to current claims on future consumption, causing any aggregate price measure based only on current consumption prices to be too low. (The opposite would be true in situations when the real interest rate has risen.)

3. Estimating Changes in the Cost of Life

Using consumer theory, Pollack (1975) and Shibuya (1992) derive and implement a cost-of-life index that weights traditional consumer prices together with various asset price measures. We have argued elsewhere that such a methodology yields price measures that are implausibly volatile over short horizons.[1] In order to create an index that is potentially useful in a high-frequency decisionmaking environment such as setting monetary policy, we follow the methodology first proposed in Bryan and Cecchetti (1993). In that work, we utilize the joint statistical properties of the individual price series in order to construct a dynamic factor index (DFI). The DFI exploits the fact that the information contained in individual π_{it}s about the common trend π_t differs—that is the "signal-to-noise" ratio varies across different sets of goods, services, and assets. In particular, asset prices tend to be quite noisy, and so may not be very important in constructing the DFI. As in Bryan and Cecchetti (1993), we write the model as

5) $\dot{p}_{it} = \dot{\pi}_t + \dot{x}_{it}$

6) $\psi(L)\dot{\pi}_t = \delta + \xi_t$

7) $\theta_i(L) \dot{x}_{it} = \eta_{it}$,

where $\dot{p}_{it}$, $\dot{\pi}_t$, and $\dot{x}^{it}$ are the first differences of the logs of the observed variables, the common unobserved component representing inflation and the idiosyncratic relative price movement in the ith series, respectively. $\psi(L)$ and $\theta_i(L)$ are vectors of lag polynomials and ξ_t and η_t are i.i.d. (independent and identically distributed) random variables. Throughout, it is assumed that both the common element, $\dot{\pi}_t$, and the idiosyncratic components, $\dot{x}_{it}$ can be modeled as AR(2) processes.

The main identifying assumption of the model is that the common component and the idiosyncratic components are mutually uncorrelated at all leads and lags. This is achieved by assuming that $\theta(L)$ is diagonal and that all the error terms in the model are mutually uncorrelated. This is consistent with the notion that the common component captures all the comovement in the observed series, leaving $\dot{x}^{it}$ to reflect only idiosyncratic movements. To set the scale of π_{it}, the variance of ξ_t is normalized to one. The parameters of the model are then estimated via maximum likelihood using the Kalman filter. As a byproduct, the Kalman filter recursively constructs mimimum mean squared error estimates of the unobserved components $\hat{\pi}_t$ and $\hat{x}_{it}$ given observations of $\dot{p}_{it}$. The common index can be written as a linear component of current and past values of the observed series

8) $\quad \hat{\pi}_t = \sum_i \hat{w}_i(L) \dot{p}_{it}.$

These are the (implicit) weights used to construct the common inflation component.

In an alternative approach to this "signal-extraction" problem, Wynne (2000) describes the implementation of a simple variance-weighted price index where the weights,

9) $\quad w_i = \dfrac{\dfrac{1}{\sigma_i^2}}{\sum_{i=1}^{N} \dfrac{1}{\sigma_i^2}},$

are based on the variance of the rate of change in the price of each good i, σ_i^2.

A simple variance-weighting scheme of this type is a good indicator of the likely importance of a particular series in the construction of more complex (and difficult to compute) dynamic factor indices. To see why, note that the variance of the "common" element in any scheme, similar to that describe in equation 9 above, will have the property that the estimated inflation index will have variance equal to or less than the variance of the least volatile component used.[2] In the analysis that follows in sections 4 and 5, we also report the variance weights for comparison to the weights used in our dynamic factor index.

4. Comparing the Cost-of-Living to the Cost-of-Life

Using nine sub-indices of the current CPI, together with prices of six major assets, we estimate a cost of life index for 1977 to 2001. The assets include housing, stocks, bonds, commodities, money, and gold.

Table 1 displays the implied weights for the data set using the alternative methodologies. In the first three columns of the table we report results for the cost-of-living approach—that is, retail prices excluding asset prices. The remaining columns incorporate asset prices and so are the weights for similarly constructed cost-of-life indices. The first observation we make is that even on a conceptually similar basis, dynamic factor weights are significantly different from the expenditure weights used in the official CPI. This is because the Kalman filter technology tends to reduce the weight assigned to price series with a relative high time-series variance, giving more weight to those series that provide a better signal of the common element (the DFI). These weights are oblivious to the relative importance of the good in the typical consumer market basket. The result is an index similar in spirit to a "core" inflation statistic like the CPI excluding food and energy, where the market basket is altered to adjust for transitory fluctuations in the data that are not believed to be part of a more generalized inflation process. Note that the DFI cost-of-living weights (those weights based

	Cost-of-Living Weights (CPI Components only)			Cost-of-Life Weights (CPI components with asset prices)	
	Expenditure	DFI	Variance	DFI	Variance
Food/Beverages	16.7	7.7	11.1	8.5	9.9
Housing	40.7	15.5	20.5	10.3	18.2
Apparel	4.8	8.0	5.0	10.5	4.5
Transportation	18.1	3.8	1.7	4.8	1.5
Medical Care	5.9	11.1	22.1	8.3	19.7
Entertainment	6.3	22.2	19.1	14.5	17.0
Education	2.6	9.2	6.5	11.5	5.8
Tobacco	1.3	1.0	0.4	2.0	0.4
Personal Care	3.6	21.5	13.8	14.5	12.3
Houses	—	—	—	2.3	0.1
Stocks	—	—	—	0.8	0.1
Bonds	—	—	—	0.4	0.0
Commodities	—	—	—	5.6	2.3
Money Supply	—	—	—	5.3	8.3
Gold	—	—	—	0.7	0.0
Sum of Weights	100	**100**	100	**100**	100

Table 1: Alternative Weights for the Recent Era (1977–2001)

on CPI component series only) are more closely aligned with the conceptually similar cost-of-living variance weights. That is, food, transportation, and housing are given a substantially smaller share of the overall price index compared with the ordinary expenditure-weighted CPI, while medical care, personal care, and education get larger weights in these reduced-noise price statistics.

Using the DFI procedure, we constructed a cost-of-life index that includes six asset price series along with nine retail price series. We find that stocks (0.8 percent), bonds (0.4 percent), and gold (0.7 percent) are assigned very small weights in the computation of the cost-of-life index. This reflects the extreme volatility of these series at a monthly frequency (also evidenced by the near zero weight these assets are given on the basis of the variance weighting criteria.) Nevertheless, some assets are assigned a relatively large share of the "market basket," like new homes (2.3 percent), commodities (5.6 percent) and the money supply (5.3 percent).

Turning to the estimated price indices themselves, figure 1 shows the 12-month growth rates of the three key inflation statistics for the recent era, the CPI, the cost-of-living dynamic factor index (DFI cost-of-living) and the cost-of-life dynamic factor index (DFI cost-of-life). First, as we expect, the two DFI series are considerably smoother than the expenditure-weighted CPI. More importantly for the purposes of this paper, there are persistent differences between the DFI cost-of-living measure and the DFI cost-of-life measure. This is the "bias" between these two conceptually different approaches. Specifically, while the price series including asset prices tended to track below the consumption-only price measure during the 1980–94 period, it tended

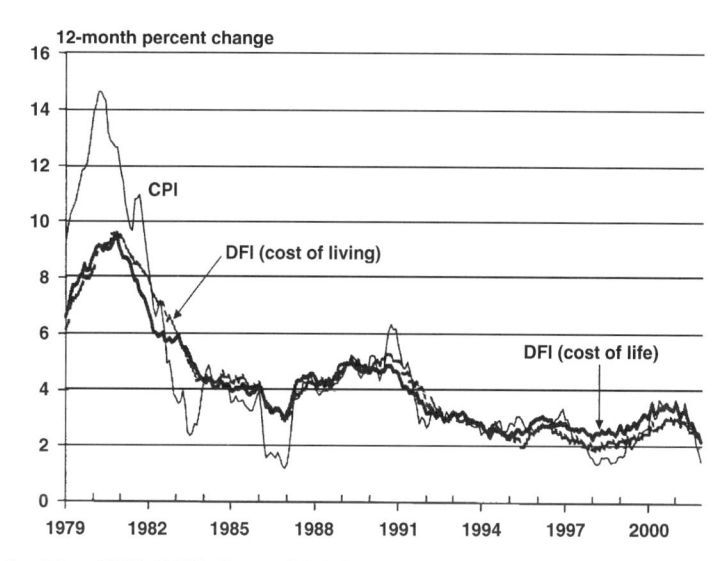

Figure 1: The CPI, DFI Cost-of-Living, and DFI Cost-of-Life

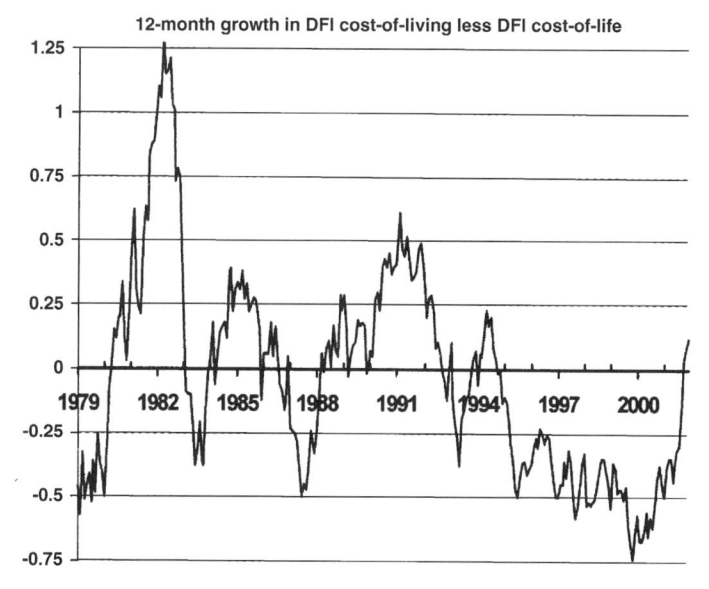

Figure 1a: The Intertemporal Substitution Bias

to be higher between 1995 and 2000, and only very recently have the two measures converged.

The significance of this observation is that a real interest rate drop in the mid-1990s appears to have been responsible for an intertemporal substitution between current consumption and future consumption.[3] This suggests that the CPI (or other similarly conceptualized retail price measures) were biased downward by one-quarter to one-half percentage point per year as measures of inflation compared with the rise in prices recorded by current claims to current and future consumption.

Since 1995, the bias we have identified has worked in the opposite direction to the more commonly discussed biases in retail price measures that come from other (but related) sources. But in the first half of our sample, this bias worked to reinforce the belief that measurement biases lead to the overestimation of inflation by conventional indices. Furthermore, the tendency of the intertemporal substitution bias to fluctuate suggests that measures of real interest rates and other nominal, intertemporal phenomena can, at times, be significantly over- or under-stated if the price deflator does not include the price of current purchases of future consumption—assets.

5. A Retrospective of the Inter-War Deflation

We have demonstrated that the failure to include asset prices when calculating a "cost of life" index can create an intertemporal substitution bias in the cost-of-life statistic and that this exclusion may influence one's interpretation of inflation. In this section, we ask if correcting this bias might lead to a reinterpretation of the events during the 1920s and 1930s—the period between the two world wars—and one of the great deflations in U.S. history.

The extreme movements in stock prices and the historical fall in the price level during this period are well documented, and figure 2 illustrates the movements in consumer and stock prices between 1920 and 1937.[4] We computed our DFI measures, with and without asset prices using data series that closely match those used in the previous section.[5] Consumer prices were obtained from Sayre (1948), where series on the prices of food, housing, clothing, fuel, and house furnishings and sundries were available along with the overall CPI index. Stock and bond prices and money stock data were taken from the NBER macro history database while the commodity price index was available from the BLS.

Two series used in the modern analysis could not be included directly. The first of these—house prices—are simply not available on a monthly basis. As a compromise, we used an index of building materials costs instead. The second series that presented a problem was gold prices. While price data are available, the behavior of gold prices was dictated by the central bank's gold standard and therefore are not suitable for our purpose. From 1920 to 1934 we were able to substitute the price of silver for the price of gold. After 1934, these data become unusable because of the Silver Purchase Act of 1934, which resulted in significant government intervention in the market for silver.

Table 2 summarizes the weights obtained when the DFI technique is applied to various combinations of the historical series. Variance-based weights and expenditure weights for the components of the CPI are included for comparison purposes.[6]

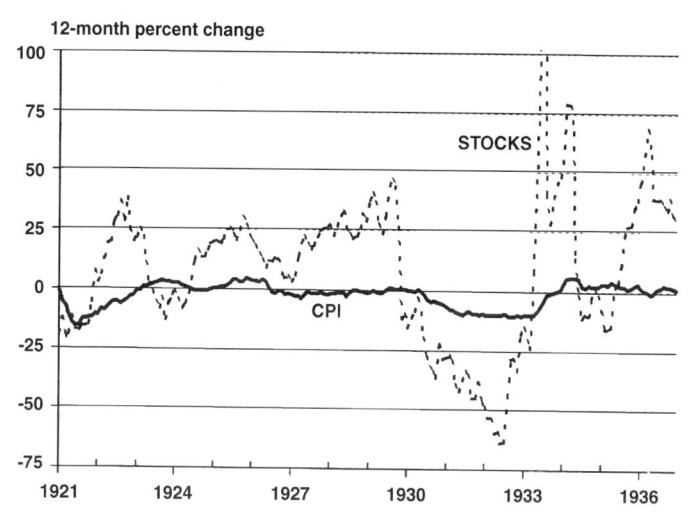

Figure 2: Consumer Prices and Stock Prices in the Interwar Period

Looking first at the constituent series of the CPI, we see that the category with the largest expenditure weight—food—attracted a significantly smaller weight when both the DFI and variance-based signal extraction techniques were used. In contrast, the relatively stable house furnishings and sundries category, which includes costs associated with such items as medical care, personal care, and transportation, was attributed DFI and variance-based weights more than double its expenditure share.

Looking more closely at the DFI cost-of-life index we see that the building costs index—included here as a proxy for house prices—attracted the largest weight among

	Cost-of-Living Weights (CPI Components only)			Cost-of-Life Weights (CPI components with asset prices)	
	Expenditure	DFI	Variance	DFI	Variance
Food	33.00	**6.59**	3.56	**8.80**	2.88
Housing	19.00	**10.68**	18.16	**8.28**	14.70
Clothing	10.00	**4.79**	3.75	**6.74**	3.04
Fuel	6.00	**8.17**	10.21	**5.63**	8.26
House Furnishings and Sundries	32.00	**69.78**	64.33	**37.31**	52.06
Building Costs	—	—	—	**7.03**	3.98
Stock Prices	—	—	—	**2.35**	0.27
Bond Prices	—	—	—	**5.75**	4.50
Commodity Prices	—	—	—	**6.49**	3.49
Money Supply	—	—	—	**11.62**	6.83
Sum of Weights	100	**100**	100	**100**	100

Table 2: Alternative Weights for the Historical Series (1920–37)

the non-CPI series. This may overstate the strength of the common price signal in house prices, as they tend to be more volatile than building costs in the short run. It is also worth noting that the unprecedented developments in the stock market during this time period resulted in a higher weight being given to bond prices than stock prices. This is in contrast to the outcome obtained using the modern data. Indeed, according to the variance-weighted approach, the stock price series contains virtually no information at all about the common trend in prices.

Still, despite the volatility experienced in asset markets during this period, the DFI approach attributes almost one third of the weight to the non-CPI component series.[7] The 33 percent share of DFI weights attributed to asset prices is about twice the share assigned by a variance-weighting approach. In other words, these asset data, though volatile, appear to have an important common signal embedded in their movement, suggesting that their exclusion would have biased the cost-of-life measure compared with the conventional cost-of-living statistic.

Turning to the growth rates of the various inflation series, figure 3 plots the year-to-year growth rates for the headline CPI, the DFI series based on CPI components only (DFI cost-of-living), and the DFI including all 10 series (DFI cost-of-life). The growth in the cost-of-living based DFI series is obviously smoother than the headline CPI rate over the period, with this series recording deflation rates in the early 1930s of about half those obtained using the headline CPI rate. When asset prices are included, however, the deflation was higher than that calculated from the headline rate, while the rebound in the 1930s was also more pronounced. That is, the DFI cost-of-life index shows more extreme movements than the conventional cost-of-living index.

As noted for the modern period, the gap between the DFI cost-of-living and the DFI cost-of-life (all assets) series can be interpreted as reflecting movements in the

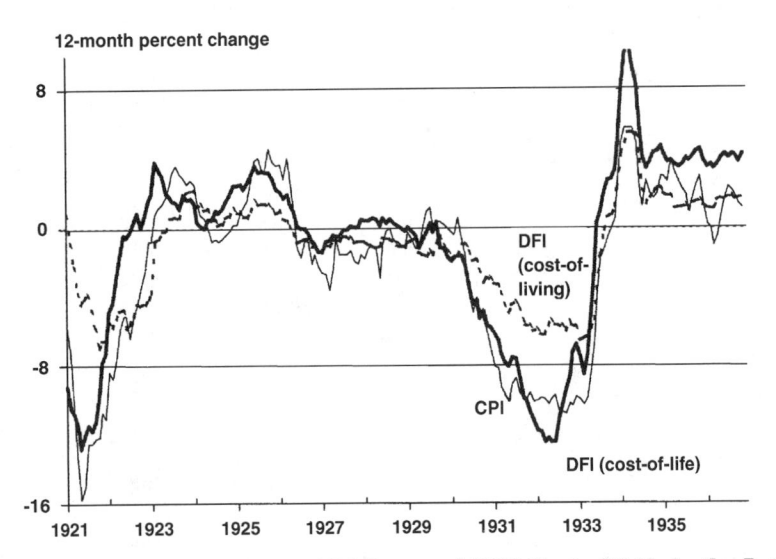

Figure 3: The CPI, DFI Cost-of-Living, and DFI Cost-of-Life in the Interwar Period

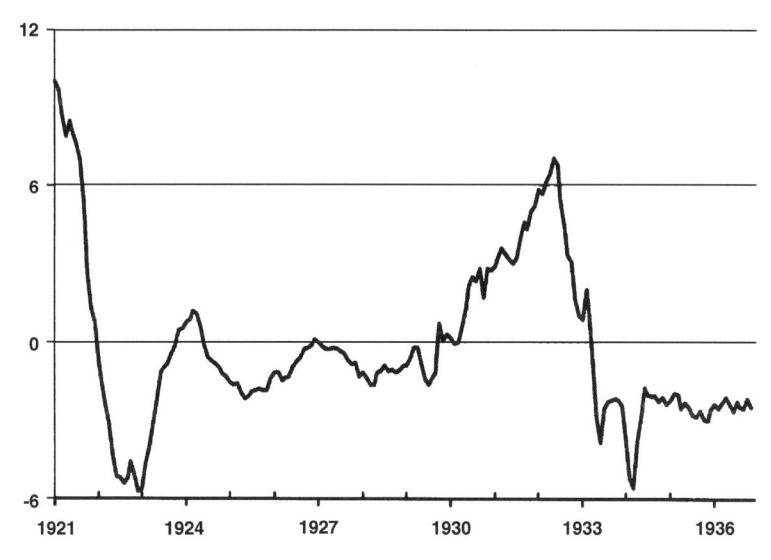

Figure 3a: The Intertemporal Substitution Bias

real interest rate. The correlation between the change in the ex ante real interest rate taken from Cecchetti (1992) and the difference between the two DFI series is significantly positive—the correlation coefficient is 0.16 with a robust t-ratio of 2.05. In particular, the greater fall in the cost-of-life DFI series compared with the DFI series without asset prices during the early 1930s reflected the relatively steep drop in stock prices at that time. Our interpretation is that this fall in asset prices reflected a higher discount rate or real interest rate at a time when nominal interest rates were falling quite dramatically. But more fundamentally, it suggests a strong intertemporal substitution bias in the conventional retail price measure of a rather extreme level (peaking at around six percentage points in mid 1932) that substantially alters the inflation pattern we record for the period compared with what is shown by the CPI.

6. Conclusion

This paper considers a particular problem associated with the failure to include asset prices in an aggregate price statistic. If the statistic is intended to gauge inflation, meaning a persistent change in the cost of life as distinct from the current cost of living, then the failure to include asset prices in the aggregate price measure can bias your inflation estimate. Using a modified Kalman filter—a dynamic factor index—we compute an aggregate cost-of-life index and compare it with both the CPI (an expenditure-weighted cost-of-living measure) and a methodologically similar dynamic factor index that also measures only the cost-of-living. Over time, we find the differences between these statistics to be somewhat small, often less than one-quarter percentage point per year. However, over some periods, namely, periods when the real interest rate fluctuates, we find that the exclusion of asset prices can significantly distort one's reading of monetary inflation common to all goods. Such appears to have been the case during the great deflation in the early 1930s, and also in the latter half of the last decade.

*Michael F. Bryan is a vice president and economist in the Research Deparment at the Federal Reserve Bank of Cleveland. Stephen G. Cecchetti is a professor of economics at Ohio State University and a research associate at the NBER. Róisín O'Sullivan was a Ph.D. candidate at Ohio State University at the time of the conference and is member of the economics department faculty at Smith College. The views expressed in this paper do not necessarily reflect the views of the Federal Reserve Bank of Cleveland, the Federal Reserve System, or the NBER.

Notes

1. See Bryan, Cecchetti, and O'Sullivan (2001).

2. This is strictly true in the DFI model we use given the identification assumptions employed. In the variance weighting case, certain restrictions are necessary on the covariances between the constituent series.

3. In fact, the difference between the DFI cost-of-living and the DFI cost-of-life is an estimate of the change in the ex ante real interest rate. This is supported by the fact that this difference and the change in the ex post real interest rate, computed from the three-month U.S. Treasury bill rate and headline CPI inflation, are significantly positively correlated with a correlation coefficient of 0.13 and a robust t-statistic of (2.1).

4. See, for example, Friedman and Schwartz (1963).

5. Reasonable data on bond prices were not available for the period between 1937 and 1940 and so only data up to January 1937 were used. Results based on series excluding bonds showed little difference when the additional four years of data were included.

6. When silver prices were added for the period up to 1934, the series attracted a small weight (3.37)—the second smallest after stocks.

7. To examine the robustness of the weighting methodology during this turbulent time, DFI and variance-based weights were also calculated for rolling 10-year windows, beginning with 1920–30 and ending with 1927–37. The weights assigned to the various series were relatively stable across the time period windows, with a fall in the weight attached to the money stock reflected mainly in an increase in the house furnishings and sundries weight. That is, the DFI weights appear to be robust throughout this sample.

References

Alchian, A. A., and B. Klein, 1973, "On a Correct Measure of Inflation," *Journal of Money, Credit, and Banking*, 5(1), February, part 1, pp. 173–191.

Blank, David M., 1954, "Relationship Between an Index of House Prices and Building Costs," *Journal of the American Statistical Association*, Vol. 49, No. 265, March, pp. 67–78.

Bryan, M., and S. Cecchetti, 1993, "The Consumer Price Index as a Measure of Inflation," *Economic Review*, Federal Reserve Bank of Cleveland, Vol. 29, No. 4, pp. 15–24.

Bryan, M., S. Cecchetti, and R. O'Sullivan, 2001, "Asset Prices in the Measurement of Inflation," *De Economist*, Vol. 149, No. 4, pp. 405–431.

Bureau of Labor Statistics, 1997, *Handbook of Methods*, Chapter 17.

_____, *Detailed Report*, various issues.

Cecchetti, S., 1992, "Prices During the Great Depression: Was the Deflation of 1930–32 Really Unanticipated?" *American Economic Review*, Vol. 82, March, pp. 141–156.

Friedman, M., and A. Schwartz, 1970, "*Monetary Statistics of the United States*," NBER.

_____, 1963, "The Great Contraction," in *A Monetary History of the United States*, Princeton: Princeton University Press.

Leavens, D., 1946, "Bullion Prices and the Gold-Silver Ratio 1929–45," *The Review of Economics and Statistics*, Vol. 28, No. 3, August, pp. 160–164.

Reed, S., and K. Stewart, 1999, "Consumer Price Index Research Series using current methods, 1978–98," *Monthly Labor Review*, June.

Pollack, Robert A., 1975, "The Intertemporal Cost-of-Living Index," *Annuals of Economic and Social Measurement*, 4(1), Winter, pp. 179–195.

Sayre, R., 1948, *Consumers' Prices 1914–1948*, New York: National Industrial Conference Board Inc.

Shibuya, Hiroshi, 1992, "Dynamic Equilibrium Price Index: Asset Price and Inflation," Bank of Japan, Monetary and Economic Studies, paper.

Stock, J., and M. Watson, 1991, "A Probability Model of the Coincident Economic Indicators," in *Leading Economic Indicators, New Approaches and Forecasting Records*, K. Lahiri and G. H. Moore, eds., Cambridge: Cambridge University Press, pp. 63–89.

Warren, G. E., and F. A. Pearson, 1935, *Gold and Prices*, New York: Wiley & Sons.

Wynne, M., 2000, "Core Inflation: A Review of Some Conceptual Issues," unpublished manuscript.

Chapter 20
Comments on Empirical Dimensions of Asset Price Bubbles

Andrew J. Filardo*
*Council of Economic Advisers
and Federal Reserve Bank of Kansas City*

In the past two decades, corporate equity and housing markets have experienced spectacular swings in asset prices. While there is little doubt that these swings have been significant and have led to a misallocation of resources, economists have had limited success in establishing that such asset price movements represent the inflation and collapse of asset price bubbles. For some economists, the term asset price bubble is a rhetorical device used to describe the size of asset price movements: Small movements are called fluctuations, and large persistent movements that end with a precipitous decline are called asset price bubbles. For others, however, the term "asset price bubble" has a more significant implication, especially for policymaking. According to this view, asset price bubbles represent periods of turbulent economic times that may be avoidable—especially if monetary and banking policies are well designed.

Despite skepticism in the economics profession about the existence of asset price bubbles, the fact that asset prices can swing dramatically and destabilize the economy indicates that this issue deserves further examination. The papers by Bryan, Cecchetti, and O'Sullivan, McGrattan and Prescott, and Borio and Lowe do just that and provide important insights into the empirical relevance of asset price bubbles and the implications for policymaking.

1. Asset Prices and the Stochastic Index of the Cost of Life
Bryan, Cecchetti, and O'Sullivan (2002) give a nice empirical contribution to an old literature that I have always associated with Alchian and Klein (1973) on the cost of life index. Alchian and Klein argue that the standard Consumer Price Index (CPI) was

a biased measure of the cost of life because forward-looking consumers care not only about current prices but also about future prices in calculating what they can afford. I (Filardo, 2000) illustrate how to interpret this price index as an intertemporal extension of the standard index theory behind the construction of the CPI. The problem then, as now, was how best to incorporate observed future prices into a standard price index.

Alchian and Klein argue that if one had access to futures prices from financial markets, a statistical agency such as the Bureau of Labor Statistics could simply construct the cost of life index. However, such detailed futures prices are not readily available for every good and service that a consumer would want to purchase today and in the future. For example, there is not a market that reports the future price of a Chicago-style hot dog in one, five, and 10 years. Alchian and Klein solve this problem by constructing a hypothetical asset price that would be observationally equivalent to having the full set of futures prices. Of course, such a hypothetical asset does not exist, but Alchian and Klein conjecture that there might be some reasonable empirical proxies, such as the value of the stock market or housing equity. Bryan, Cecchetti, and O'Sullivan propose an interesting method to try to approximate the Alchian and Klein hypothetical asset price by using a dynamic factor model. The key question is whether the new method produces a good approximation both empirically and with respect to policymaking.

The results of Bryan, Cecchetti, and O'Sullivan are at odds with past theoretical findings about the implied weights used to construct the Alchian and Klein cost of life index. For example, Shibuya (1992) shows that the Alchian and Klein inflation measure can be interpreted as a weighted average of asset price inflation and standard CPI inflation. Theory suggests that most of the weight (e.g., 95 percent) would be placed on asset price inflation and a small weight on CPI inflation. In contrast to this theoretical result, Bryan, Cecchetti, and O'Sullivan find that most of the weight is on the components that comprise CPI inflation. This empirical difference with the theoretical Alchian and Klein inflation measure raises doubts about the usefulness of the Bryan, Cecchetti, and O'Sullivan version of cost of life inflation measure.

The key policy implication of Bryan, Cecchetti, and O'Sullivan is that their new measure of inflation is higher than CPI inflation in the late 1990s, reflecting the rapid increase in asset price inflation. This leads to the obvious empirical counterfactual thought experiment: Would this new inflation measure have been a good monetary policy guide? It depends. The accuracy of this policy guide depends on the source of the asset price increase. In the late 1990s, the run-up in asset prices could have been due to an increase in futures prices (and possibly the discount factor), to higher productivity (and therefore dividends), or to a bubble. If the increase in asset prices was due to higher expected goods prices, then the Bryan, Cecchetti, and O'Sullivan method would lead the monetary authority to tighten monetary policy and reduce the inflationary pressures. If, however, the increase in asset prices was due to an asset price bubble, then the Bryan, Cecchetti, and O'Sullivan method would generate an upward bias in their cost of life inflation measure and cause the monetary authority to pursue an unnecessarily tighter monetary policy, which could have scuttled the expansion and deepened the 2001 recession.

The authors have made a useful extension of the empirical methods to examine Alchian and Klein's cost of life inflation measure but have fallen short in showing how to resolve the bias induced by asset price bubbles. The authors might want to construct a more unbiased estimator of the Alchian and Klein inflation estimate by trying to extract future price information with modern finance methods or by empirically controlling for asset price bubbles—which, admittedly, is not particularly straightforward or easy.

2. The Stock Market Crash of 1929

McGrattan and Prescott (2002) provide an excellent and thought-provoking investigation of the empirical literature on asset price bubbles. It surely is likely to be one of the formable indictments of those who take a view that I call the "Justice Potter Stewart view" of asset prices: Justice Stewart (1964) wrote "It has been said of that definition [of obscenity], 'I could never succeed in [defining it] intelligibly, but I know it when I see it.'" Many economists and policymakers often express this same sentiment about asset price bubbles—while they cannot formally define it, they assert that they know it when they see it.

The key contribution of this paper is to raise fundamental questions about the ability of economists to identify asset price bubbles, *ex ante* in the case of Irving Fisher or *ex post* in the case of McGrattan and Prescott. The findings in the paper are so stark because the authors take on the "granddaddy" of asset price bubbles—the 1929 U.S. stock market crash.

This paper is also important for the methodological treatment of asset price bubbles. The standard textbook approach to estimating rational bubbles is to write asset prices as being comprised of two parts: a fundamental component that is typically estimated as the present discounted value of future dividends and a bubble component. As the authors point out, empirical modelers using this approach have to make an assumption about how to measure the expectations of future dividends. In contrast, McGrattan and Prescott skirt this issue by exploiting a set of first-order conditions that indicate that the value of a firm can be estimated from the after-tax value of tangible and intangible capital.

Empirically, the strength of the paper—the novel approach to valuing corporate equity—is also a source of weakness. To assess the value of corporate America, the authors use estimates of the capital stock, which are notoriously imprecisely measured. In addition, as McGrattan and Prescott indicate, the estimates are quite sensitive to tax rates, which in macroeconomic terms are derived from a distillation of the federal and state tax codes into a set of effective tax rates. To overcome the inherent imprecision of the estimates, McGrattan and Prescott perform a robustness analysis—not in a formal statistical sense but a "back of the envelope"-type approach. The authors' robustness analysis provides a fairly compelling case that the lower bound of corporate capital was greater than the upper bound of the stock market valuation of corporations in 1929. Hence, they conclude that the corporate equity market does not appear to have been overvalued in 1929. This finding is provocative because it raises questions not only about the existence of asset price bubbles generally and in 1929 specifically, but also about the accuracy of using the standard dividend model of asset pricing to identify bubbles.

McGrattan and Prescott, however, do not go on to answer what seems to be the obvious follow-up question: If there was no bubble in September 1929, was there a negative asset price bubble after the stock market crashed in October 1929? The answer to this question would be interesting for several reasons. First, if the answer were "Yes," the identification of a negative bubble would provide evidence that asset price bubbles do exist. Moreover, since policymakers are generally concerned about positive asset price bubbles, policymakers may need to reorient their thinking about the relevant types of bubbles and the various policy options to address the concern. Second, if the new approach of McGrattan and Prescott fails to identify a negative bubble after the 1929 crash, then there may be legitimate empirical questions about whether the McGrattan and Prescott methods for identifying bubbles have sufficient statistical power to distinguish asset price bubbles from random fluctuations in asset prices. A more formal statistical evaluation (i.e., formal hypothesis testing) of the statistical measures of McGrattan and Prescott is also needed.

Finally, McGrattan and Prescott offer an intriguing conjecture about how monetary policy might have precipitated the sharp decline in asset prices in 1929, a conjecture that may provide a benchmark for future empirical research on asset price bubbles and monetary policy. The authors argue that, "The historical evidence suggests that the stock market crashed because the Federal Reserve severely tightened credit to stock investors, not because they were overvalued." Their interpretation is strengthened by evidence from the Federal Reserve's public record of 1929: The Federal Reserve noted that, "The unprecedented rise in security prices gave unmistakable evidence ... of speculative ... operations." This suggests that the Federal Reserve may have pursued a tighter monetary policy than it otherwise would have in order to rein in speculation that had been feeding what it thought of as an asset price bubble. If McGrattan and Prescott's empirical analysis is correct in finding that there was no asset price bubble at the height of the market, then the 1929 crash and its aftermath is a good example of the costs of fighting an asset price bubble when a bubble is not really present. Such estimates can be used to calibrate models in which this type of cost is a parameter. Overall, the McGrattan and Prescott paper, along with their earlier research on asset price valuation, suggests that policymakers should be skeptical about reacting to asset price movements that look like—for lack of a better word— bubbles.

3. Asset Prices and Financial and Monetary Stability

Borio and Lowe (2002) offer an impressive study of the practical policy implications of wide swings of asset prices for monetary and bank regulatory policy. Borio and Lowe in a sense burst any bubble of complacency that suggests the central banking world can rest on its laurels now that most major central banks have achieved success in pursuing low and stable inflation regimes. One only has to look to Japan in the late 1980s as stark reminder of what is possible.

Borio and Lowe paint a picture of a very risky policy environment where financial instability is omnipresent and a natural consequence of economic success. This view reflects a long tradition in macroeconomics—a view I often associate with the research of Minsky (1982). Even though this endogenous business cycle view is at odds with standard macroeconomic models of the business cycle, it may nonetheless do a better job accounting for economic developments in the United States and abroad during the 1980s and 1990s. And, if the endogenous business cycle view is correct, the policy trade-offs for central bankers is much more complex than standard textbook models suggest.

Despite the importance of wide swings in asset prices, Borio and Lowe do not cast their policy concerns as an asset price bubble problem *per se*, but as a complex interrelationship between credit provision, asset prices, and endogenous risk assessments by the private sector. By avoiding the inherent difficulties of identifying and measuring bubbles, their case for monetary and regulatory vigilance in preventing the unhealthy buildup in financial imbalances does not depend on proving the existence and measurement of asset prices bubbles—which may be important, given the state of the empirical literature on asset price bubbles. For Borio and Lowe, wide swings in asset prices simply reflect that the factors driving endogenous business cycles are important.

But, one has to wonder, if asset price bubbles are really at the heart of the problem, would not explicit treatment of asset price bubbles provide additional insights about trade-offs facing policymaking? For example, the recent empirical literature on monetary policymaking in the presence of asset price bubbles does this by explicitly accounting for bubbles and examining the policy implications (see Filardo, 2001). Asset price bubbles have presumably different empirical properties than asset price fluctuations driven by fundamentals, and, therefore, present different challenges to policymakers.

One of the important contributions of the paper is its successful use of the narrative approach to address practical policy issues. Borio and Lowe document wide and persistent swings in credit aggregates and asset prices and show that these aggregates and asset prices are prone to sharp declines, or busts. Moreover, the busts are often associated—across countries and across time—with financial crises. This empirical approach is quite suggestive but one has to wonder, if the McGrattan and Prescott methods were applied to each episode would the problem look as severe? And, even the indicator model of financial crisis that builds on Kaminsky (1999) begs the question about the theoretical foundations for the analysis. Of course, correlations do not imply causation. But, is there a deeper causal relationship between the indicators of financial crises and the crises themselves? Further theoretical and empirical research is warranted.

Borio and Lowe are not reticent about putting forth their own policy prescriptions, taking to heart their own view that "the consequences of failing to act early enough can be serious." Their conclusions about the importance of discretionary policymaking are thought provoking. Borio and Lowe suggest that a "leaning against the wind" approach to policymaking may be the best policy. Further empirical research into the robustness of their policy recommendations under alternative economic environments deserves attention. Certainly, the McGrattan and Prescott interpretation of 1929 should be a cautionary tale for any monetary policy approach that stresses a "leaning against the wind policy" during a run-up in asset prices.

In addition, further investigation into bank regulation may uncover some unintended adverse consequences of some of the authors' policy recommendations. For example, the authors offer a recommendation that regulators use tighter capital standards during an expansion in order to rein in unwarranted optimism. However, in such a situation, financial funds would flow out of the regulated banking sector into the relatively unregulated nonbank financial markets. Not only would this artificially reduce the beneficial role that banks play in the provision of loanable funds, but it also would boost the size of the unregulated nonbank financial sector, which would presumably fuel further unwarranted optimism and asset price appreciation. Hence, in this case, a "leaning against the wind" policy may have the opposite effect on financial stability than policymakers would expect.

A major contribution of Borio and Lowe is the recommendation of an ambitious research program to further address the role of asset prices and policymaking, including constructing better datasets to test their view of asset price fluctuations, putting more effort into identifying the key empirical forces that Granger "cause" asset price buildups and corrections, and investigating further the policy options facing central banks. I agree that there is more basic research that needs to be done before their built-in financial stabilizer approach to regulatory and monetary policies should be embraced, but the authors certainly have thrown down the gauntlet.

4. Conclusion

Are we any closer to knowing empirically whether asset prices bubbles matter? Those looking for a dogmatic "yes" or "no" may be out of luck. There still is considerable uncertainty about how to measure bubbles, if they exist at all. Moreover, it may be reasonable to conclude that despite the fact that economists have had a long fascination with asset price bubbles, the state of the empirical asset price bubble research is still in its infancy.

The three papers under review—while not answering the fundamental question about the existence of bubbles—have nonetheless provided valuable insights into the empirical dimensions of asset price bubbles. Such information might be useful to policymakers because the empirical findings help to characterize the uncertainty associated with interpreting asset price movements. I (Filardo, 2001), for example, show how knowledge about the uncertainty of the macroeconomic significance of asset price movements can shed light on the trade-offs facing policymakers. Such an approach calls for specifying an econometric model with a role for asset prices, defining conditions when asset prices matter and do not matter, modeling the objective function of the policymaker, and tabulating the expected benefits of responding to asset prices. While the economics profession tries to answer the fundamental question of whether asset prices and, in particular, asset price bubbles matter, progress on the policy front can still be made by exploring the empirical properties of asset prices and decisionmaking under uncertainty.

*Andrew J. Filardo is on staff of the President's Council of Economic Advisors and is also currently on leave as assistant vice president and economist in the Research Department at the Federal Reserve Bank of Kansas City.

References

Alchian, A., and B. Klein, 1973, "On the Correct Measure of Inflation," *Journal of Money, Credit, and Banking*, February.

Borio, C., and P. Lowe, 2002, "Imbalances or 'Bubbles?' Implications for Monetary and Financial Stability," *Asset Price Bubbles: The Implications for Monetary, Regulatory, and International Policies,* William C. Hunter, George G. Kaufman, and Michael Pomerleano, eds., Boston: The MIT Press.

Bryan, M., S. Cecchetti, and R. O'Sullivan, 2002, "A Stochastic Index of the Cost of Life: An Application to Recent and Historical Asset Price Fluctuations," *Asset Price Bubbles: The Implications for Monetary, Regulatory, and International Policies,* William C. Hunter, George G. Kaufman, and Michael Pomerleano, eds., Boston: The MIT Press.

Filardo, A., 2001, "Should Monetary Policy Respond to Asset Price Bubbles? Some Experimental Results," in *Asset Price Bubbles: Implications for Monetary and Regulatory Policies,* G. Kaufman, ed., Vol. 13 of *Research in Financial Services: Private and Public Policy*, Oxford: Elsevier Science.

_____, 2000, "Asset Prices and Monetary Policy," Federal Reserve Bank of Kansas City, *Economic Review*, 3rd Quarter.

Kaminsky, G., 1999, "Currency and Banking Crises: The Early Warnings of Distress," International Monetary Fund, working paper, No. WP/99/178.

McGrattan, E., and E. Prescott, 2002, "Testing for Stock Market Overvaluation/Undervaluation," *Asset Price Bubbles: The Implications for Monetary, Regulatory, and International Policies,* William C. Hunter, George G. Kaufman, and Michael Pomerleano, eds., Boston: The MIT Press.

Minsky, H., 1982, *Can "It" Happen Again? Essays on Instability and Finance,* New York: M.E. Sharpe, Inc.

Shibuya, H., 1992, "Dynamic Equilibrium Price Index: Asset Price and Inflation," *Bank of Japan Monetary and Economic Studies*, February.

Stewart, P., 1964, *Jacobellis v. Ohio,* 378 U.S. 184.

Chapter 21
Bubbles, Inflation, and the Big One: Comments on "A Stochastic Index of the Cost of Life ..." and "Testing for Stock Market Overvaluation/Undervaluation"

Bruce Lehmann*
University of California, San Diego

1. Bryan, Cecchetti, and O'Sullivan

Inflation appears to be like liquidity and pornography: Everybody seems to know what it is when they see it, but no one seems to have the ability to define it precisely. Sometimes this inability arises because of the competing demands placed on price indices such as the measurement of the cost of a basket of goods at a point in time as opposed to the variable targeted by a monetary authority. Sometimes there are conceptual issues associated with the appropriate basket of goods, the appropriate weights to place on them, and the inclusion of estimates of future goods prices.

In a series of papers involving different convex combinations of the authors, Bryan, Cecchetti, and O'Sullivan have examined both kinds of issues. In this paper, they concentrate on the latter class, although the former set figures prominently in the choice of statistical tools they employ. In what follows, I will examine the assumptions underlying the statistical model first and some of the conceptual issues associated with intertemporal cost-of-living indices second.

The statistical model employed in the paper is the dynamic factor model that has enjoyed some popularity in macroeconomics. In their formulation, Bryan, Cecchetti, and O'Sullivan assume that actual percentage changes in the price of good, service, or asset π_{it} is the sum of two unobserved components:

$$\pi_{it} = \pi_t + x_{it},$$

where π_t is the presumably common inflation component and x_{it} is the percentage change in i's price relative to π_t. There are several identifying assumptions that have economic consequences, the main ones being that π_t and x_{it} are uncorrelated at all leads and lags, that x_{it} and x_{jt} are uncorrelated at all leads and lags for all $i \neq j$, and that π_{it}, π_t, and x_{it} are all covariance stationary.

This model suggests an easy strategy for constructing an index perfectly correlated with π_t: Simply take an average of a large number of price series. A weak law of large numbers applies to the serially correlated but mutually uncorrelated random variables x_{it} and so:

$$\frac{1}{N}\Sigma_i \pi_{it} = \pi_t + \frac{1}{N}\Sigma_i x_{it} \to \pi_t + \bar{\mu}; \quad \bar{\mu} = \lim_{N\to\infty} \frac{1}{N}\Sigma_i \mu_i,$$

where μ_i is the unconditional mean of x_{it}. More generally, any set of weights of the form:

$$\Sigma_i w_i \pi_{it} = \pi_t + \Sigma_i w_i x_{it} \to \pi_t + \mu_w; \quad \mu_w = \lim_{N\to\infty} \Sigma_i w_i \mu_i \ \forall \ \{w_i: \Sigma_i w_i = 1; \ \Sigma_i w_i^2 \to 0\}$$

yields an inflation index perfectly correlated with π_t; the variance-weighted index of Wynne (2000) examined in this paper is of this form. In order to have a forward looking index, a well-diversified portfolio of many assets will contain negligible idiosyncratic risk due to the obvious effects of diversification when the portfolio weights are of order one over the number of assets. The constants μ_w—constants that arise because of weighting or omitted goods biases—will differ across indices, but they must be dealt with in their more complicated model, as well.

It would appear that the best way to implement this method is to find many price series and attribute the commonality among them to the inflation factor. However, I do not think that Bryan, Cecchetti, and O'Sullivan would consider using an equally-weighted portfolio of a few thousand stocks, bonds, and derivatives in place of π_t. Similarly, I do not think that an empirical investigation of fixed weight indices with weights of order $1/N$ will yield perfectly correlated inflation indices. Accordingly, allowance must be made for other common factors among asset returns and the inflation rates of goods and services. Such a modification would require additional assumptions to sort observed price changes into inflation-related and noninflation-related unobserved components.

Now consider the link between the statistical model and intertemporal cost-of-living indices. There are two issues associated with the difference between the two. First, the authors made a distinction in previous papers between cost-of-living indices, which are index numbers that make deflated nominal prices and quantities comparable, and the common trend in prices that we generally think of as inflation. Second, it may be that households care about trends in the growth rate of the price of consumption plans—that is, something like permanent consumption or real consumption annuities—as opposed to the price of a unit of consumption at a point in time. I will discuss these issues in turn.

It seems to me that these distinctions largely disappear if one thinks through the intertemporal decision problem confronting households. In particular, the continuous time analysis of Breeden (1979) illustrates why conventional expenditure weighting is likely to be the correct index at a point in time, suggesting that real annuity prices should be calculated on the basis of expected future indices, not from asset returns. That analysis presumes that nominal goods and asset prices all follow diffusion processes along with the consumption rates of goods and services and that there are no omitted goods. In section 7 of his paper, Breeden showed that the appropriate real consumption index in this setting is aggregate nominal consumption expenditures scaled by the price index created by weighting each good price by its budget share—that is, its share in aggregate expenditure. Homotheticity of preferences is not required because of the local linearity of marginal utility when consumption rates follow diffusion processes. Local linearity also facilitates aggregation across households.

Accordingly, the price of permanent income or a real consumption or other annuity can be computed via the appropriate present value calculation, taking account of the drift in aggregate budget shares. Asset prices do not appear directly in this calculation, which depends on the future price of real consumption, but show up in precisely the right place: as inputs into the measurement of the appropriate discount factors. This need not be a simple matter, but it is one made easier by appropriate modeling. As noted above, a one-factor structure makes the computation easy to do so, but it appears to make it too easy. The household decision problem has an enormous amount of implicit separability built into it under the assumptions made in this paper.

Of course, the volatility of a cost-of-life index depends on the nature of the life being financed. Growing annuities with stochastic growth rates will experience larger fluctuations than those for a prespecified number of units of aggregate consumption on different dates. A *pro rata* share of the social dividend—that is, aggregate consumption—is an equity-like security or, more precisely, an equity-plus-debt-like asset that is a claim on private sector output and, hence, will and should have equity-like volatility. A real annuity can be priced as a claim on a portfolio of real bonds, the prices of which are observed in the case of index-linked bonds like Treasury Inflation Protected Securities or can be inferred from models of the real term structure, and should experience bond-like volatility. A reduced-form cost-of-life index like that constructed in this paper can approximate these calculations by appropriate weighting of different assets, but the weights are likely to differ considerably across these broad classes of consumption plans. Accordingly, I think this approach can be improved upon substantially by thinking systematically about the economic life whose cost we wish to measure.

2. McGrattan and Prescott

Intangible assets have long played an important role in accounting, finance, and macroeconomics. They are often called "good will" in accounting, the "present value of growth opportunities" in finance, "franchise value" in security analysis, and Tobin's q in macroeconomics. Not surprisingly, the measurement of intangible asset values or their returns is fraught with hazard. It is also of considerable economic importance.

The present paper is one of a series by McGrattan and Prescott, who boldly parameterize an equilibrium model that permits them to infer intangible capital estimates from the National Income and Product Accounts (NIPA). They show that personal income taxes do not incrementally distort the relative returns to tangible and intangible capital beyond that engendered by the taxation of corporate profits, a result reminiscent of Miller's (1977) analysis debt, taxes, and capital structure in the presence of personal and corporate taxes. This observation greatly simplifies the measurement of the value of both kinds of capital without using market value in any direct way.

The task that McGrattan and Prescott set for themselves is a deceptively simple one. The stock of *any* asset k_{it} subject to economic depreciation d_{it}—that is, depreciation inclusive of any capital gains or losses at market values—accumulates according to:

$$k_{it+1} = (1 - d_{it}) k_{it} + x_{it} = k_{it} + x_{it} - d_{it} k_{it},$$

where x_{it} is gross investment in capital stock i. Hence, measurement of the market value of capital at any time requires only observations on net investment $x_{it} - d_{it} k_{it}$.

The measurement of gross investment in intangible capital is straightforward given one simplifying assumption: All components of the NIPA, save for gross investment in intangible capital, are observed without error. Then the usual national income equals expenditure identity yields:

$$c_t + x_{mt} + x_{ut} + g_t + im_t = y_t \Rightarrow x_{ut} = y_t - c_t - x_{mt} - g_t - im_t,$$

where y_t is expenditure, c_t is consumption, g_t is government expenditure (that is, public consumption), im_t is net imports, and x_{mt} and x_{ut} are gross tangible (that is, measured) and intangible (that is, unmeasured) capital investment, respectively. Since gross intangible capital investment is being measured as a residual, any measurement error in the components of national income will infect estimates of x_{ut}. This source of measurement error will not have a permanent impact on measured capital stocks so long as economic depreciation eventually (i.e., asymptotically) diminishes the value of the capital stock.

Hence, "only" the absence of observations on the (potentially time-varying) rates of economic depreciation d_{mt} and d_{ut} of tangible and intangible capital, respectively, prevents us from imputing the corresponding capital stock from the NIPA via:

$$k_{mt+1} = (1 - d_{mt}) k_{mt} + x_{mt}$$

$$k_{ut+1} = (1 - d_{ut}) k_{ut} + x_{ut},$$

where k_{mt} and k_{ut} are the stocks of tangible and intangible capital, respectively, so long as we observe y_t, c_t, g_t, im_t, and x_{mt} without error. Now economic depreciation is the all-in change in the present value of the after-tax cash flows attributable to a given capital asset. It includes the usual notion of wear-and-tear that causes capital to be less productive in the future or to require incremental maintenance, the costs of which reduce its after-tax cash flows. However, economic depreciation is a much broader concept because the value of the marginal product of a capital asset can rise or fall for a number of reasons, including changes in product market competition that affect the rents accruing to intangible assets like brand names or intellectual property and in factor market competition from close substitutes in production.

This is why McGrattan and Prescott build an explicit, two sector general equilibrium model including two types of capital and two types of goods along with a government that taxes income and capital that it uses to transfer income among households. They seek to directly estimate fundamental capital asset values and so they look to relations among measured output, corporate profits, and implied net returns to tangible and intangible assets to provide the required estimates of economic depreciation. If they can do so in a way that eliminates the need to estimate the expected present value of future dividends, they can compare their fundamental value estimates with observed market valuations to see if the market was undervalued or overvalued at any time.

It is illuminating to study intangible asset valuation via the present value calculations that McGrattan and Prescott sidestep by implicitly using the capital accumulation equation in conjunction with a model-based estimate of the economic depreciation rate of intangible capital. Accordingly, suppose that the value of an asset V_t to an investor with a constant marginal tax rate t_p is the present value of its future after-tax dividend stream $\{(1-t_p)d_{t+j}, j > 0\}$:

$$V_t = (1 - \tau_p)\sum_{j=1}^{\infty} \frac{E_3[d_{t+j}|\wedge_t]}{(1 + r_{t,j})^j} \; ; \; \frac{1}{(1 + r_{t,j})^j} = 1 + \text{cov}_3\left[\frac{d_{t+j}}{E_3[d_{t+j}|\wedge_t]}, m_{t+j}|\wedge_t\right],$$

where the expectations $E_3[\bullet|\wedge_t]$ and $\text{cov}_3[\bullet|\wedge_t]$ are based on investor probability beliefs 3 and time t information $\wedge_t$ while $r_{t,j}$ is the discount factor at time t appropriate for discounting time $t + j$ cash flows based on $\text{cov}_3[d_{t+j}, m_{t+j}|\wedge_t]$. In general, m_{t+j} is the state price per unit probability, which is the intertemporal marginal of substitution of inframarginal investors in equilibrium models like that of McGrattan and Prescott.

Note that there is no presumption that the probability beliefs implicit in 3 are rational or that price equals fundamental value. For example, this asset will be overvalued if expectations are excessively optimistic even if the discount factors are "correct." Similarly, overvaluation obtains if discount factors are "too low"—that is, when the perceived covariance between d_{t+j} and m_{t+j} is smaller than would obtain under rational expectations—even if the expectations of future dividends are rational.

Of course, dividends represent the use of funds not the source of funds, the corporate profits that devolve from the earning power of the firm. The transformation of the present value relation for dividends into one for earnings requires only a simple adjustment for the arithmetic of stocks and flows. Let x_t be any flow and let X_t be its associated stock that satisfies the so-called clean surplus relation:

$$x_t - d_t = X_t - X_{t-1}; \quad \lim_{T\to\infty} \frac{E_3[X_{t+T}|\wedge_t]}{(1 + r_{t,T})^T} = 0,$$

where the transversality condition places only mild growth restrictions on x_t relative to d_t. In Lehmann (1992), I show that the substitution of this stock/flow relation into the present value formula yields:

$$V_t = (1-\tau_p)X_t + (1-\tau_p)\sum_{j=1}^{\infty}\frac{E_3[X_{t+j} - \lambda_{t,j}X_{t+j-1}|^\wedge{}_t]}{(1+r_{t,j})^j} \quad ; \quad \lambda_{t,j} = \frac{(1+r_{t,j})^j}{(1+r_{t,j-1})^{j-1}},$$

where $l_{t,j}$ is a risk-adjusted analogue of a forward rate. Note that there is no economics in this translation of the present value relation save for the mild restrictions implicit in the transversality condition; it is a purely mechanical consequence of the arithmetic of stocks and flows.

In the NIPA, after-tax corporate profits p_t and tangible capital k_{mt} satisfy:

$$p_t - d_t = k_{mt} - k_{mt-1},$$

since after-tax profits include historical or measured depreciation. Unsurprisingly, the revised present value relation:

$$V_t = (1-\tau_p)k_{mt} + (1-\tau_p)\sum_{j=1}^{\infty}\frac{E_3[\pi_{t+j} - \lambda_{t,j}k_{m+j-1}|^\wedge{}_t]}{(1+r_{t,j})^j},$$

reflects intangible capital in the present value of growth opportunities since:

$$V_t = (1-\tau_p)[k_{mt} + (1-\tau_c)k_{ut}] \Rightarrow (1-\tau_c)k_{ut} = \sum_{j=1}^{\infty}\frac{E_3[\pi_{t+j} - \lambda_{t,j}k_{m+j-1}|^\wedge{}_t]}{(1+r_{t,j})^j},$$

where t_c is the corporate tax rate. The excess payoff to tangible capital $p_{t+j} - l_{t,j}k_{mt+j-1}$ is known as residual income in managerial accounting, where it is used for performance-based management compensation. In the present setting, it represents the earning power of the intangible assets of the firm.

McGrattan and Prescott make three assumptions that facilitate the evaluation of the present value of measured residual income. The first is that NIPA after-tax corporate profits represent economic profits or, more precisely, that measured depreciation of tangible capital is actual economic depreciation, the market value of any capital gains or losses. The second is that the net after-tax opportunity costs of tangible and intangible capital are both equal to a constant real interest rate i. The third is that the expected growth rate of both earnings and dividends is a constant g. There are other assumptions, like the assumed constancy of prospective tax rates, but they strike me as less important or, at least, tangential to my main concerns.

Under these assumptions, the value of intangible capital is equal to:

$$(1-\tau_c)k_{ut} = \sum_{j=1}^{\infty}\frac{E_3[\pi_{t+j} - ik_{mt+j-1}|^\wedge{}_t]}{(1+i)^j} = \frac{\pi_t - ik_{mt-1}}{i-g}.$$

Thus the present value calculation under the arbitrary beliefs $E_3[\bullet|^\wedge{}_t]$ regarding growth opportunities and discount factors delivers the McGrattan and Prescott estimate of the value of intangible capital with no assumptions about market participants' expectations. The two calculations are opposite sides of the same coin or, more precisely, of the same equation.

That these assumptions simplify the calculations is evident, but what is much less obvious is their plausibility in the 1920s (or, for that matter, in the various subperiods in the last half century they examine elsewhere). McGrattan and Prescott provide reasoned arguments for the choices that make them conclude that the stock market was overvalued or, at least, not undervalued at its peak in 1929. Nevertheless, it is also reasonable to be skeptical about their assumptions, and small changes in them can produce large changes in fundamental value estimates. The simple fact is that present value calculations are very sensitive to their inputs, the basic source of the inability of practitioners and academics alike to agree on whether or not market prices equal their underlying intrinsic values.

Much is often made about the difference between the book and market values of capital assets. Any such differences are magnified during times of rapid technological change and, especially, for intangible assets that are expected to affect the production of more and different goods and services a few years down the road. In these circumstances, it is commonplace for tangible capital to depreciate rapidly in price/performance terms due to obsolescence, not to deterioration—computers are a perfect recent example. Intangible assets that represent bets on tastes and technology beyond the immediate future can succeed spectacularly or fail miserably, resulting in nontrivial changes in expected rates of economic appreciation or depreciation that is missed by the assumption of geometric decay at a constant rate.

There are several potential problems associated with the assumptions regarding *ex ante* real rates and net rental rates of tangible and intangible capital. On the one hand, *ex ante* real rates were probably below 5 percent at the end of the 1920s, and the combination of a real interest rate below 5 percent and a growth rate of 3.64 percent implies a price/dividend ratio in excess of 75, casting doubt on the model's validity, not on the market's valuation. On the other hand, it is implausible that the net rental rates of tangible and intangible capital were equal to each other and to the *ex ante* real interest rate. We would typically expect tangible capital and intangible capital related to process innovation to earn risk premiums, although McGrattan and Prescott (2000) argue that such premiums are likely to be small. More importantly, intangible capital related to nontrivial technological or market innovations would typically earn a substantial risk premium. If they are right that intangible capital is a nontrivial fraction of overall capital, the weighted average opportunity cost of tangible and intangible capital might well have been above 6 percent, the threshold at which the market becomes overvalued in their analysis.

McGrattan and Prescott treat the *ex post* average growth rate for 1925–29 of 3.64 percent as the *ex ante* expectations that were in the minds of market participants. There are two dimensions in which this estimate is suspect. First, it is likely that *ex ante* expectations of long run growth rates were below 3.64 percent on the hypothesis that growth rates in the late 1920s were quite high by historical standards. Any such overestimate is empirically relevant; For example, valuation assuming a 3.64 percent growth rate is almost 50 percent higher than one assuming 3 percent if the real interest rate is 5 percent. The second, more subtle, point is that it is likely that investors thought that there would be a period of higher than normal growth followed by a return to normal growth. Security analysts who value growing firms with earnings or dividend discount models typically allow for two or three phases of growth corresponding to a period of high growth followed by one of stable growth, often with an intervening transition period. Omitting such effects is empirically relevant as well; for example, valuation assuming a 3.64 percent growth rate forever is almost 40 percent higher than one assuming a 3.64 percent growth rate for 10 years followed by 3 percent growth forever if the real interest rate is 5 percent. Hence, reasonable alternative assumptions regarding growth prospects in 1929 are compatible with the market being overvalued, a consequence of the extreme sensitivity of present value calculations to modest changes in prospective growth rates.

In this paper, McGrattan and Prescott provide a provocative analysis of the value of tangible and intangible capital in the United States just prior to the stock market crash—*the* crash—of 1929 that complements their earlier work on the asset pricing effects of tax changes in the last 50 years and the so-called Internet bubble that peaked in March 2000. The analysis can be made more persuasive with more direct evidence on measured versus economic depreciation, net rental rates of capital, and expected earnings growth rates. McGrattan and Prescott will doubtless apply these tools to other episodes and adduce additional evidence regarding differences between market and fundamental asset values. That said, I fear that evidence will not settle outstanding questions regarding such differences, in large measure because the present values of long-lived assets change so much with such small changes in their inputs. However, this is a conclusion to be drawn after the evaluation of said evidence, which might prove to be persuasive in the end. This is the hope implicit in this research program.

*Bruce Lehmann is a professor in the Graduate School of International Relations and Pacific Studies at the University of California, San Diego.

References

Breeden, Douglas T., 1979, "An Intertemporal Asset Pricing Model with Stochastic Consumption and Investment Opportunities," *Journal of Financial Economics*, Vol. 7, pp. 265–296.

Bryan, Michael F., and Stephen G. Cecchetti, 1993, "The Consumer Price Index as a Measure of Inflation," *Economic Review*, Federal Reserve Bank of Cleveland, Vol. 29, pp. 15–24.

Bryan, Michael F., Stephen G. Cecchetti, and Roisin O' Sullivan, 2001, "Asset Prices in the Measurement of Inflation," *Economist*, Vol. 149, pp. 405–431.

Lehmann, Bruce N., 1993, "Earnings, Dividend Policy, and Present Value Relations: Building Blocks of Dividend Policy Invariant Cash Flows," *Review of Quantitative Finance and Accounting*, Vol. 3, pp. 263–282.

McGrattan, Ellen R., and Edward C. Prescott, 2001, "Taxes, Regulations, and Asset Prices," Federal Reserve Bank of Minneapolis, unpublished manuscript.

_____, 2000, "Is the Stock Market Overvalued?," *Quarterly Review*, Federal Reserve Bank of Minneapolis, Vol. 24, pp. 20–40.

Miller, Merton H., 1977, "Debt and taxes," *Journal of Finance*, Vol. 32, pp. 261–275.

PART V

INTERNATIONAL TRANSMISSION OF FINANCIAL SHOCKS

Chapter 22
Globalization and Changing Patterns in Crisis Transmission

Michael D. Bordo*
Rutgers University and National Bureau of Economic Research

and

Antu Panini Murshid
University of Wisconsin, Milwaukee

1. Introduction

This paper examines the pattern in crisis-transmission, in particular, currency crises, under the pre-World War I classical gold standard, between 1880 and 1914, and contrasts this evidence with more recent experience in the post-Bretton Woods era, between 1975 and 2000.

International financial crises are not new (Kindleberger, 1978), but the scope of these crises and the manner in which they have been internationally transmitted has changed. This may reflect among other factors, differences in the exchange rate regime, the extent of financial integration, and the development of financial institutions. Thus a contrast of the scope of crises and the pattern in their transmission then versus now helps us understand the consequences of these changes in the international monetary system.[1]

We compare the recent period to the pre-1914 era because it was the previous era of international financial globalization. The extent of international financial integration before World War I according to several metrics was comparable to today (Bordo, 2003; Obstfeld and Taylor, 2002). Moreover, along with globalization, the incidence of financial crises, especially currency crises involving emerging countries, was comparable to today (Bordo et al., 2001).

Although there were similarities in the economic environments of the two eras of globalization there were also several key differences that could explain the differences in the patterns of transmission of crises that we find in this study.

First, most countries pre-1914 adhered to the fixed exchange rates of the classical gold standard. In the absence of gold flows, in today's era of managed floating and soft pegs, transmission would occur via other channels.

Second, before World War I, the commercial and financial centers of the world were concentrated in a few countries in Western Europe, while the "emergers" consisted primarily of countries of new settlement (the United States, Canada, Australia, and Argentina) and the European periphery. This implied that there were naturally strong ties between these satellite countries and the center. Today a more diverse group of countries spanning several regions constitute the advanced countries. Similarly diverse are the emerging countries. Consequently, today's emerging counties are subject to varied influences from a more diverse set of advanced countries. The center-periphery relationships that existed in the pre-1914 era can be thought of in terms of a model of an atom: a *single* nucleus with orbiting electrons. It is less clear that such an analogy could be extended to describe the relationships between today's advanced and emerging countries.

Finally, the pre-1914 advanced countries had not completely developed the tools to provide financial stability, such as an effective lender of last resort, moreover adherence to gold convertibility, and the attendant imperative to protect gold reserves dominated all other objectives (Eichengreen, 1992). Consequently, shocks in the past had harsher repercussions (Bordo et al., 2001). The severity of the downturns that accompanied the negative shocks to financial markets amplified their cross-border impact. Today, better policies and improved financial systems limit the severity of shocks and minimize their international impact.

Our analysis is divided into three parts. First, we examine the international co-movement in exchange market pressure (EMP) indices.[2] Second, we develop a global crisis index and use extreme value methods to estimate the incidence of global crises. Finally, we use impulse response functions from Values-at-Risk (VaRs) estimated using weekly data to identify the direction and impact of financial shocks between individual countries.

Our principal findings are the following.[3]

- The degree of co-movement in EMP indices across all countries is greater for the pre-1914 era. In contrast, today there is tight co-movement within the advanced countries, and within the emerging countries the pattern of dependence is regional.

- The likelihood of a global crisis was higher in the pre-1914 era, although the probability of international crises within the advanced countries is about as high today as it was in the past.

- Before 1914, financial shocks were communicated from the core countries of Europe (especially the United Kingdom) to the periphery, but in general this channel did not operate in reverse. Today, strong interlinkages exist between advanced countries and shocks are transmitted within this group; however, generally these shocks are not communicated to the emerging countries (see also evidence in Hartmann et al., 2002). Within the emerging countries, to a limited extent, shocks are communicated regionally, but not globally.

Globalization and Changing Patterns in Crisis Transmission 311

A number of implications follow from our results. First, the world is generally a more stable place today; crises are less likely to have global reach relative to the pre-1914 era. This is, perhaps, not a surprising finding. The pre-1914 gold standard was characterized by a system of fixed exchange rates, a concentration of financial and commercial power in a handful of European countries, and relatively weak financial markets even in the advanced countries. Hence, countries were neither insulated from shocks nor capable of accommodating these shocks.

Second, although today's advanced countries have developed the tools to provide greater financial stability, shocks have still been communicated through the fixed exchange rates of the European Monetary System and other channels. Thus, speculative attacks on currencies have not been avoided; however, we posit that today's advanced countries are better able to accommodate these shocks; consequently, the output effect of these crises have been smaller (Bordo et al., 2001). In contrast, in the pre-1914 era, banking and currency crises often gave rise to virulent twin crises. These sharp negative shocks to the center then sent impulses through the gold standard world wreaking havoc at the periphery.

Third, the regional pattern of crisis-transmission within the emerging countries seems to suggest the importance of trade channels (Glick and Rose, 1999); however, it also underscores the vulnerability of emerging countries to financial shocks. This inability of emerging countries to insulate their economies from negative shocks reflects not just the failure of macro-policies, but weaknesses in the banking and financial structure. Yet, while financial distress exhibits a global pattern across emerging countries (Bordo and Murshid, 2002; Mauro et al., 2002), emerging-country crises are overwhelmingly regional. An explanation may be that when international capital markets tighten, as measured by the volume, cost, and maturity of funds, their impact is most acute in the region in which the crisis originates (Eichengreen et al., 2001); consequently, whether or not strong intraregional dependencies across emerging countries can be identified, crises are likely to be regional.

The remainder of this chapter is organized as follows. In the next section we briefly discuss our data. We then present evidence on the cross-country co-movement in exchange market pressure indices. Next, we present estimates on the likelihood of a global currency crisis, followed by a summary of our results from a number of vector autoregressions, which we estimate to trace the impact of innovations in interest rates in one country on another. Finally, we provide some conclusions.

2. Data

We utilize monthly data on short-term interest rates, long-term government bond yields, as well as data on exchange rates and reserves, to construct our indices of exchange market pressure. Our EMP indices are simply a weighted average of changes in exchange rates, short-term interest rates (if available, otherwise long-term government bond yields), and foreign exchange reserves (if available).[4] In addition, we use weekly short-term interest rate data to estimate a number of VaRs.

For the pre-World War I period, our sample consists of 13 countries, including five advanced countries—Belgium, France, Germany, the Netherlands, and the United

Kingdom—and eight emerging countries—Argentina, Austria, Brazil, Chile, Denmark, Italy, Japan, and the United States[5]—spanning a 34-year period from 1880 to 1914. With the exception of reserves, our monthly data provide relatively complete coverage. Our weekly interest rate data, however, are only available for the European countries and the United States.[6]

For the post-Bretton Woods period our sample includes 21 countries. This includes five of the Group of Seven countries—France, Germany, Japan, the United Kingdom, and the United States—as well as Greece, Portugal, Spain, and 13 emerging countries—Argentina, Brazil, the Czech Republic, Chile, Hungary, Hong Kong, Indonesia, Korea, Malaysia, México, Singapore, the Slovak Republic, and Thailand.

With some exceptions, data on exchange rates, short-term interest rates (called money rates where available, discount rates otherwise) and reserves, observed at a monthly frequency, are available from 1975 to 2000.[7] However, our weekly data on short-term interest rates are typically available only for the 1990s.[8]

3. Patterns in Crisis Transmission: Co-Movement in EMP Indices

In this section, we apply principal components analysis to examine the extent of cross-country dependence in proxies for currency crises, observed at a monthly frequency. We present our results in two sets of figures that reveal the scope of, and patterns in, cross-country dependence.

The first set of figures is simply a plot of the variance attributed to the first three principal components. This provides an indication of the degree of co-movement in our sample. The second set of figures plot the factor loadings corresponding to the first three principal component vectors. These are simply the correlations between the variables and the principal components. A graph of these factor loadings can highlight patterns in correlations, thus revealing subsets of countries differentiated from each other in the pattern of their dependence. This categorization of countries into separate groups is done by employing a clustering algorithm.[9]

3.1 Main Findings

Our pre-1914 sample includes four advanced countries—Belgium, France, Germany, and the Netherlands—and six emerging countries—Austria, Argentina, Brazil, Chile, Japan, and the United States. The corresponding analysis for the post-Bretton Woods era was carried out using a sample also comprised of four advanced countries—France, Germany, Japan, and the United Kingdom—and six emerging countries—Argentina, Brazil, Mexico, Indonesia, Malaysia, and Thailand.

- The degree of international co-movement in our EMP indices is greater in the pre-1914 data (see figure 1).
- During both periods the pattern of co-movement varies across advanced and emerging countries. In the pre-1914 era, a plot of the factor loadings separates the two groups (figure 2A). But we need to be careful as to what distinguishes the group of advanced countries from the group of emerging countries. Importantly, both advanced and emerging countries exhibit strong correlations with the first

Globalization and Changing Patterns in Crisis Transmission 313

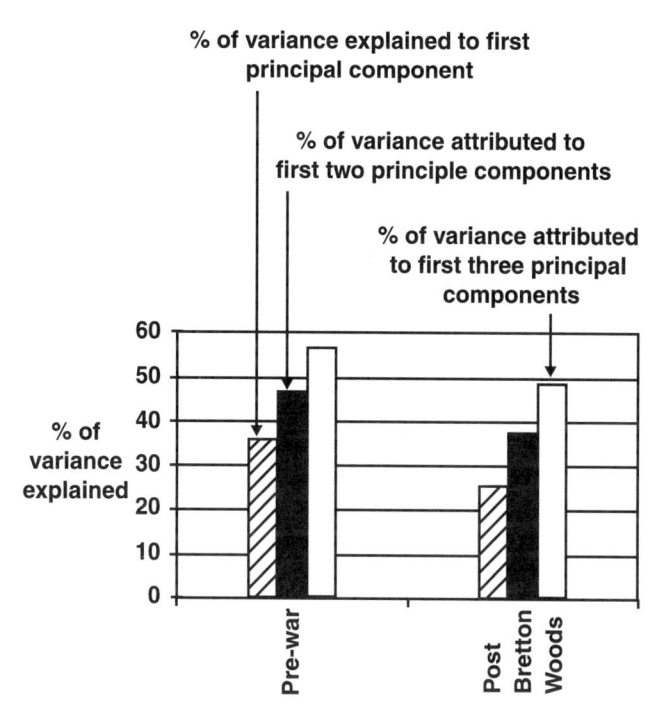

Figure 1: Overall Co-Movement in EMP: 1880–1914 and 1975–2000

principal component, which, in turn, implies positive correlations across these groups. The distinguishing characteristic between them is that the group of emerging countries is negatively correlated with the second principal component, which, with the exception of the Netherlands, is not a trait shared by the advanced countries. This could be picking up the effect of crises within emerging countries that did not filter through to the core countries of Europe.

- The evidence for the recent period suggests a more pronounced pattern of separation between advanced and emerging countries. The key characteristic of the advanced group is its strong positive correlation with the first principal component, which indicates not only that there was strong co-movement within this group, but that, overall, a larger proportion of the variance in the EMP indices can be attributed to the advanced countries than to any other group. However, advanced-emerging country associations are not completely absent. In particular, the Asian countries exhibit weak, but positive, correlations with the first principal component (figure 2B). Hence there is some evidence to indicate that crises affecting the advanced countries may have had repercussions for the Asian countries. In contrast, however, there is little indication of a pattern of dependence between the advanced countries and the Latin American countries.

- In addition, the pattern of dependence within today's emergers suggests intraregional co-movement (figure 2B, see also evidence in Hartmann et al., 2002).

314   Chapter 22

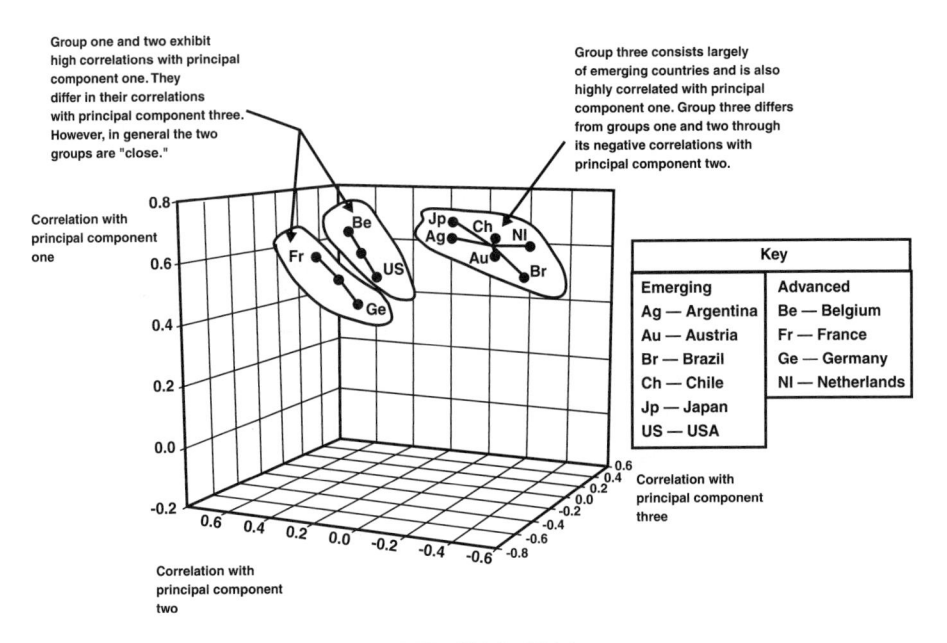

Group one and two exhibit high correlations with principal component one. They differ in their correlations with principal component three. However, in general the two groups are "close."

Group three consists largely of emerging countries and is also highly correlated with principal component one. Group three differs from groups one and two through its negative correlations with principal component two.

Key

Emerging	Advanced
Ag — Argentina	Be — Belgium
Au — Austria	Fr — France
Br — Brazil	Ge — Germany
Ch — Chile	Nl — Netherlands
Jp — Japan	
US — USA	

Figure 2A: Factor Loadings, EMP, 1880–1914

Group three co-movement within Latin American countries captured by third principal component

Group one and two: Advanced and Asian countries exhibit high correlations with principal component one.

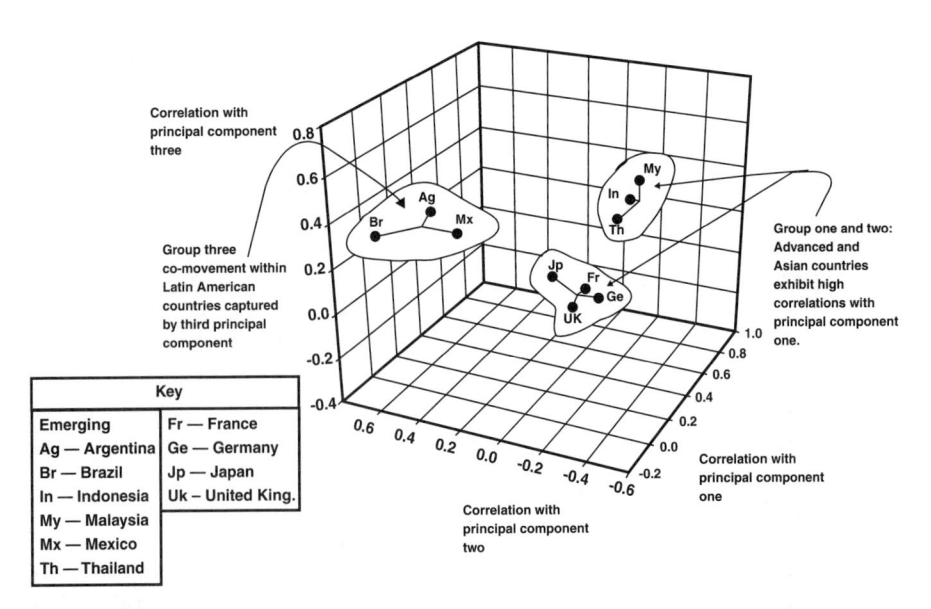

Key

Emerging	Fr — France
Ag — Argentina	Ge — Germany
Br — Brazil	Jp — Japan
In — Indonesia	Uk – United King.
My — Malaysia	
Mx — Mexico	
Th — Thailand	

Figure 2B: Factor Loadings, EMP, 1975–2000

3.2 Summary

Of the two eras, the extent of crisis transmission has been somewhat greater in the pre-1914 era than more recently. It is not difficult to see why. Despite some differences in their patterns of dependence, the co-movement of advanced and emerging country EMP indices suggests the presence of interlinkages across these two groups. The underlying theme seems to have been one of "muted" global co-movement across countries. In contrast, the association between advanced and emerging countries in recent years has been far weaker. Moreover, emerging market crises have rarely been global and, instead, follow a more pronounced regional pattern.

4. Incidence of Global Crises

In this section, as a complement to our earlier analysis, we examine the incidence of global currency crises in the two periods. In addition, we group countries into advanced and emerging and examine the incidence of international crises within these groups.

We use a global-crisis index to estimate the probability of these events over any six-month period. Our (global) crisis-index, which is simply the first principal component of the EMP data,[10] aims to capture the common or shared-element in exchange market pressure across the countries in our sample.[11] To examine the incidence of shared or common crises within particular groups of countries, we construct, in a similar fashion, a crisis-index for each group.

Global crises were defined in terms of our global-crisis index. Specifically, values in excess of 10—the total variance in our sample—were defined as global crises. For the purposes of comparison across regimes, however, the actual value of the threshold is unimportant, and we continue to use 10 as our crisis-threshold for the smaller samples.[12] The incidence of global crises was then obtained as simply a frequency of "exceedances" above this crisis-threshold. Additionally, we used extreme value methods to fit the appropriate distribution to the right tail of our global-crisis index (see Murshid, 2001, for details).

The results are presented in two tables. Table 1 reports the incidence of global crises for both periods, while table 2 reports the incidence of international crises within each of the sets of advanced and emerging countries.

4.1 Main Findings

- The probability of a global crisis in recent years has been considerably lower than the probability during the earlier period. Over any six-month period, during the prewar era, the likelihood of a global crisis was more than three times as high as the likelihood of such an event today (table 1).

- However, this aggregate result masks significant differences across the advanced and emerging countries. From table 2, we find that the likelihood of observing an international crisis in the advanced countries, which consist largely of countries from Western Europe, is just as great today as it was in the past. The key difference across the two periods is in the incidence of crises across the set of emerging countries, which has been significantly lower in the recent period.

Prewar		Post Bretton Woods	
(1)	(2)	(3)	(4)
Frequency	EVM[a]	Frequency	EVM[a]
0.12	0.09	0.02	0.02

[a]Probability estimates were obtained by fitting a generalized extreme value distribution to the semiannual maxima of the global crisis index.

Table 1: Incidence of Global Crises over a Six-Month Period, 1880–1913 and 1975–2000

Prewar				Post Bretton Woods			
Advanced		Emerging		Advanced		Emerging	
(1)	(2)	(3)	(4)	(5)	(6)	(7)	(8)
Freq.	EVM[a]	Freq.	EVM[a]	Freq.	EVM[a]	Freq.	EVM[a]
0.21	0.18	0.10	0.14	0.23	0.24	0.02	0.03

[a]Probability estimates were obtained by fitting a generalized extreme value distribution to the semiannual maxima of the global crisis index.

Table 2: Incidence of International Crises over a Six-Month Period, within the Set of Advanced Countries and within the Set of Emerging Countries, 1880–1913 and 1975–2000

4.2 Interpretations

The high incidence of international crises within the four pre-1914 European advanced countries is what we might expect, given their strong ties through a system of fixed exchange rates and possibly linkages through commerce. By similar reasoning the high incidence of international crises within today's advanced countries should not be surprising, since our sample is comprised mainly of European countries, which over much of the post-Bretton Woods period practiced various forms of exchange rate targeting.

Separating the pre-1914 era from today is the higher incidence of international crises within the pre-1914 emergers. The implication of this might be that there were strong linkages between these countries, either directly through their ties to gold, or indirectly through their ties to the center countries of Europe. The latter interpretation is supported by the results in table 1, namely that there was a high incidence of global crises across the entire sample of pre-1914 countries. In contrast, a significantly lower incidence of global crises in recent years, whether we examine the sample as a whole or restrict our attention to the emergers, has two very different implications for the pattern of crisis-transmission today in comparison with the earlier era.

First, the interlinkages between the emerging countries as a whole are weak. This reflects the mixed composition of our sample, which spans two regions. Thus, while crises may be regional, affecting either just the Asian countries or just the Latin American countries, they are rarely interregional.[13] Second, unlike the pre-1914 era, the interlinkages between advanced and emerging countries seem to have been weaker in recent years. This is suggested by both the low incidence of international crises within the set of emerging countries, as well as across the full sample of countries.

Thus, our findings in this section have implications for the role of advanced countries in transmitting crises in the past, in comparison to the role they play today. To get at this issue, in the next section we attempt to isolate the interlinkages of shocks between various countries.

5. Interlinkages between Advanced and Emerging Countries: Evidence from VaR Analysis

Our earlier analysis suggested that the relationship between the advanced and emerging countries has changed between the first era of globalization before 1914 and today. Perhaps not unrelated to this, we observe a change in the pattern of crisis-transmission: Crises today are less likely to be global and, instead, more likely to be regional. These distinct patterns of behavior give rise to a number of questions. How have the interlinkages that existed under the classical gold standard, between the industrialized core and the nonindustrialized periphery, changed between the two eras of globalization? What are the interrelationships across countries from the same region? In particular, do they explain the recent patterns in crisis-transmission?

To this end, we estimate a number of vector autoregressions using weekly data on interest rates. For the prewar period we examine a sample of six European countries, consisting of three advanced—France, Germany, and the United Kingdom—and three emerging countries—Austria, Denmark, and Italy—observed over a 34-year period from 1880 to 1914. As the United States was the only non-European country for which we were able to obtain high frequency data, it would be difficult to draw any conclusions as to the importance of interregional linkages, hence our focus on the European countries.

In contrast, the time series for the recent period, while relatively short, covered countries from several regions. For the recent period, we estimate three separate systems.

First we estimate a VaR comprised of six European countries with an even split between advanced—France, Germany, and the United Kingdom—and emerging—the Czech Republic, Hungary, and the Slovak Republic—thus, approximating our pre-1914 sample of countries. Our analysis is carried out over a six-year period from 1995 to 2001.

A characteristic distinguishing the countries from the prewar era was their ties to gold and, hence, their adherence to fixed exchange rates. To better understand the role of fixed exchange rates in communicating shocks, we examine the relationships between member nations of the European Union over a seven-year period beginning in 1994. While the sample could no longer be split into advanced and emerging, the countries were chosen so as to emphasize differences in per capita income. Thus at one end of the spectrum we have France, Germany, and the United Kingdom, and at the other end we have Greece, Portugal, and Spain.[14]

Finally, we examine the scope of interlinkages within the class of Asian emerging countries as well as the impact of the United States and Japan on these countries. Specifically, we estimate a VaR for the United States, Japan, Hong Kong, Korea, Singapore, and Thailand. Our data covers a period from 1994 to 2002.

Due to space considerations, the output from the VaR analysis is not presented here (see appendix in Bordo and Murshid, 2002). Below, we summarize the main findings.

5.1 Main Findings

- **Interlinkages between advanced countries**—Both in the past and more recently, interlinkages within the advanced countries have been evident. Consistent with the evidence in Lindert (1969), we find that the United Kingdom was the dominant country through which shocks were communicated under the pre-1914 gold standard, although the relationship was mutually reinforcing, as shocks to Germany also impacted on the United Kingdom.[15] Today, we observe a similar pattern of interlinkages within the advanced countries of Europe; we also observe evidence of transmission from the United States to Japan.

- **Interlinkages between emerging countries**—The evidence of spillovers within the class of emerging countries is weaker than what we observe for the advanced countries, although not completely absent. In particular, in the pre-1914 era, shocks originating in Austria appear to have spilled over, affecting advanced and emerging countries alike. More recently, cross-border transmission within the transitional countries of Europe is also evident.

- **Interlinkages between advanced and emerging countries**—The evidence of interlinkages between advanced and emerging countries is mixed and needs to be qualified. In the first instance, the relationships between advanced and emerging countries are often unidirectional. Thus, in the pre-1914 era, a shock to the United Kingdom had a ripple effect on all the other countries in our sample; however, the United Kingdom was insulated from shocks in emerging countries. While in recent years, shocks to Germany have had a similar effect on the European Union, shocks to the smaller European nations have not had a significant influence on Germany.

  Second, evidence of interrelationships between the advanced and emerging countries is weaker outside of the European Union. While there is some evidence of cross-border transmission from the United States to the Asian countries that maintained pegs with the dollar, this evidence is weak. Moreover, there is no evidence of transmission from Japan to the Asian countries.

- **Interlinkages within regions**—Our analysis of the pre-1914 European nations suggests that regional transmission may have been an important factor through which financial shocks were communicated. However, it is difficult to separate the importance of regional ties, over other influences, such as the exchange rate regime. We will, however, note that in a system that includes the United States, there was evidence of transmission from the United Kingdom to the United States, suggesting that cross-regional transmission, possibly through the exchange rate regime, may have been important.

In the recent period, we do find evidence of regional transmission within Europe and Asia. Again, it is difficult to isolate the importance of regional ties. However, within the Asian emergers, the evidence of regional patterns is far weaker.

6. Conclusions

The three most important results that emerge from this paper are:
1. The incidence of global crises in the pre-1914 era was higher than what we observe today.
2. The incidence of international crises within today's advanced countries has been just as high as in the past.
3. Within the emerging countries, crises have tended to be regional.

How can we explain these results? There were a number of important factors that helped to define the nature of crises in the past. First, shocks and crises were communicated through gold flows. Second, adherence to gold convertibility implied subordinating all other policy objectives. The peg to gold, therefore, acted like "golden fetters" amplifying the effects of a negative shock (Eichengreen, 1992). Moreover, even the advanced countries from that era had not completely developed the tools to provide financial stability. Third, prior to World War I, financial power was concentrated in a handful of Western European countries, which were the major creditors of that era. In addition to exporting capital, these countries also provided export markets to the emergers. A crisis at the center, therefore, exposed the periphery to reinforcing shocks on the current and capital accounts (Eichengreen, 1996). In contrast, today a large, diverse group of countries now constitute the center. Consequently, emerging markets are subject to various influences and are less prone to disturbances in any one part of the center.

The high incidence of crises within today's advanced countries reflects, in part, the composition of countries in our sample, which includes primarily member countries of the European Union. Our analysis of short-term interest rates using VaRs has suggested the presence of strong interlinkages between these countries; in particular, shocks to Germany are communicated strongly throughout Europe. The pattern is weaker for advanced countries in general, but is not inconsistent with the possibility of a tight correspondence in macroeconomic fundamentals associated with an international business cycle. Clearly, advanced countries, in particular countries of the European Union, have not been immune to speculative attacks; however, today's advanced-country crises have had a more limited effect on output relative to earlier crises (Bordo et al., 2002). Consequently, their propensity to spill over into global crises has diminished.

Within today's emerging countries, crises have suggested an overwhelmingly regional pattern (see also evidence in Glick and Rose, 1999; Hartmann et al., 2002). Perhaps this is indicative of trade linkages (Glick and Rose, 1999). However, as was implied from our VaR analysis, the evidence of a tight intraregional correspondence in fundamentals between emerging countries is somewhat weaker than for advanced countries. What then explains the pattern of emerging-market crises? Weaknesses in financial systems and a lack of transparency in emerging financial markets has possibly heightened their vulnerability to shocks and increased the possibility of contagion. The regional pattern in emerging-market crises then simply corresponds to an unbalanced pattern in financial distress. Recent experience suggests that the reversal of capital flows that accompany crises is often most acute in the region where the crisis originates (Eichengreen et al., 2001). For other countries, the crisis typically represents only a discrete interruption in capital-market access. Hence, a cross-regional pattern in crisis-transmission is typically not observed.

Our evidence cannot provide definitive answers as to what underlies the greater stability across financial markets in the last few decades relative to the previous era of globalization. However, severing the links to gold, the adoption of a managed floating regime, the growing financial maturity of advanced countries, and the widening of the center could be key to understanding the reduced incidence of global crises.

*Michael D. Bordo is a professor of economics at Rutgers University and an associate at the National Bureau of Economic Research. Antu Panini Murshid is an assistant professor in the Department of Economics at the University of Wisconsin, Milwaukee. The authors are indebted to Marc Weidenmier for providing much of the data covering the pre-World War I era and for comments on an earlier paper, on which this paper builds. The authors are also indebted to the conference participants and, in particular, Ashoka Mody, for comments and suggestions. In addition, the authors would like to thank Eugene White and Hugh Rockoff for comments on earlier related research.

Notes

1. Recently a number of studies have attempted to develop these contrasts. See, for instance, Bordo et al. (2001), Mauro et al. (2002), Murshid (2001), and Neal and Weidenmier (2003).

2. Exchange market pressure indices are often used as a measure of currency crises (see, for instance, Eichengreen et al., 1996 and Kaminsky and Reinhart, 1999).

3. We also examined the co-movement of long-term bond yield spreads as an indicator of financial stress. The patterns of transmission observed complemented the results reported here. Because of space limitations we omit these results but report them in Bordo and Murshid (2002).

4. See Bordo and Murshid (2002) for details.

5. We follow Bordo et al. (2001) and classify the United States as an emerging country; however, this classification is borderline at best. By the turn of the century, the United States had become a net creditor; moreover, financial markets in the United States were highly developed for the time. However, for our purposes it does not matter whether we treat the United States as an advanced or emerging country, inasmuch as our results are qualitatively unaffected.

6. Short-term interest rates are open market rates on three-month bills. These data were obtained from Neal and Weidenmier (2003). Our data on long-term government bond yields were obtained from Neal and Weidenmier (2003) and Global Financial Data: http://www.globalfindata.com. Exchange rate data was obtained from Global Financial Data. The source of the reserves data, which are available for six countries, is the *The Economist* magazine and the National Bureau of Economic Research Macro-History Database: http:/www.nber.org.

7. These data were taken from *International Financial Statistics*, CD ROM version.

8. These data, which are available from Global Financial Data: http:www.globalfindata.com, are domestic interbank Eurocurrency rates with a maturity of one to three months.

9. Note that k-means clustering requires that the number of clusters be defined *a priori*. In the present context countries were always divided into three separate clusters.

10. Several software packages report standardized principal components. Within the current context, however, standardizing the principal components would not be particularly useful.

11. We continue to use the same sets of countries as in the previous section.

12. A comparison across groups comprised of differing numbers of countries is complicated by the fact that the overall variance in the larger sample is greater. Hence, all else equal, the variance of the crisis index for the larger sample will also be greater. To allow a better comparison across groups, the global crisis indices were appropriately re-scaled.

13. See the evidence in the previous section and in Murshid (2001), which examines the incidence of crises within regional groups.

14. With the exception of the United Kingdom the countries in our sample explicitly targeted the exchange rate. However, our data starts in 1994, by which point the exchange rate bands had been widened to +/− 15 percent. The exchange rate arrangements subsequently went through a change in January 1999, which effectively amounted to a hardening of the exchange rate pegs. This, undoubtedly, had implications for the manner in which shocks were communicated to these countries; however, this is not an avenue that we explore.

15. Also see Tullio and Wolters (1996).

References

Bordo, Michael D., 2003, "The Globalization of International Financial Markets: What can history teach us?," in *International Financial Markets*, Leonardo Auernheimer, ed., Chicago: University of Chicago Press, forthcoming.

Bordo, Michael D., Barry Eichengreen, Daniela Klingebiel, and Maria Soledad Martinez-Peria, 2001, "Is the Crisis Problem Growing More Severe?," *Economic Policy*, Vol. 32, April, pp. 51–75.

Bordo, Michael D., and Antu P. Murshid, 2002, "Globalization and Changing Patterns in the Transmission of Shocks in Financial Markets," National Bureau of Economic Research, working paper, June.

_____, 2001, "Are Financial Crises Becoming Increasingly More Contagious? What is the Historical Evidence?," in *International Financial Contagion*, Stijn Claessens and Kristin Forbes, eds., London: Kluwer Academic Publishers, pp. 367–406.

Eichengreen, Barry, 1996, *Globalizing Capital: A History of the International Monetary System*, Princeton: Princeton University Press.

_____, 1992, *Golden Fetters: The Gold Standard and the Great Depression, 1929–1933*, New York: Oxford University Press.

Eichengreen, Barry, Andrew Rose, and Charles Wyplosz, 1996. "Contagious Currency Crises," *Scandinavian Journal of Economics*, Vol. 98, December, pp. 463–84.

Eichengreen, Barry, Galina Hale, and Ashoka Mody, 2001, "Flight to Quality: Investor Risk Tolerance and the Spread of Emerging Market Crises," in *International Financial Contagion*, Stijn Claessens and Kristin Forbes, eds., London: Kluwer Academic Publishers, pp. 129–56.

Glick, Reuven, and Andrew K. Rose, 1999, "Contagion and Trade: Why Are Currency Crises Regional?," *Journal of International Money & Finance*, Vol. 18, August, pp. 603–17.

Hartmann, Philipp, Stefan Straetmans, and Casper G. de Vries, 2002, "Extreme Currency Linkages," in *Asset Price Bubbles: The Implications for Monetary, Regulatory and International Policies*, William C. Hunter, George G. Kaufman, and Michael Pomerleano, eds., Boston: The MIT Press.

Kaminsky, Graciela, and Carmen Rienhart, 1999, "The Twin Crises: The Causes of Banking and Balance of Payments Problems," *American Economic Review*, Vol. 89, June, pp. 473–500.

Kindleberger, Charles P., 1978, *Manias, Panics and Crashes: A History of Financial Crises*, New York: John Wiley and Sons.

Lindert, Peter H., 1969, "Key Currencies and Gold, 1900–1913," *Princeton Studies in International Finance*, No. 24, Princeton: Princeton University Press.

Mauro, Paolo, Nathan Sussman, and Yishay Yafeh, 2002, "Emerging Market Spreads: Then Versus Now," *Quarterly Journal of Economics*, Vol. 117, May, pp. 695–733.

Murshid, Antu P., 2001, "Echoes from the Past: Are Global Financial Crises Reasserting Themselves?," Rutgers University, Ph.D. dissertation.

Neal, Larry, and Marc Weidenmier, 2003, "Crises in the Global Economy from Tulips to Today: Contagion and Consequences," in *Globalization in Historical Perspective*, Michael D. Bordo, Alan M. Taylor, and Jeffrey G. Williamson, eds., Chicago: University of Chicago Press, forthcoming.

Obstfeld, Maurice, and Alan Taylor, 2002, "Globalization and Capital Markets," National Bureau of Economic Research, working paper, No. 8846, March.

Tullio, Giuseppe, and Jurgen Wolters, 1996, "Was London the Conductor of the International Orchestra or Just the Triangle Player? An Empirical Analysis of Asymmetries in Interest Behavior During the Classical Gold Standard, 1876–1913," *Scottish Journal of Political Economy*, Vol. 43, September, pp. 419–443.

Chapter 23
Asset Price Bubbles and Stock Market Interlinkages

Franklin Allen*
University of Pennsylvania

and

Douglas Gale
New York University

1. Introduction

Stock market interlinkages have played an important role in the formation and collapse of bubbles from early times. For example, Carswell (1960) describes the links between the 1719 bubble in the stock of the Mississippi Company in Paris and the 1720 bubble in the stock of the South Sea Company in London. There were significant flows between the financial centers as these bubbles inflated and burst. Similarly, there were also flows between London and Paris and other financial centers in Europe such as Amsterdam, and asset price movements were interdependent.

In more recent times, stock market interlinkages also appear to play an important role in asset price bubbles. Higgins and Osler (1997) consider 18 Organization for Economic Cooperation and Development (OECD) countries and document a significant simultaneous rise in real estate and stock prices during the period 1984–89. These prices subsequently fell during the period 1989–93. Regression results indicate a 10 percent increase in real residential real estate prices above the OECD average in 1984–89 was associated with an 8 percent steeper fall than average in 1989–93. Similarly, for equities a 10 percent increase above the average in the earlier period is associated with a 5 percent steeper fall in the later period. Higgins and Osler interpret this as suggestive of the existence of bubbles. Investment and real activity were also sharply curtailed during the latter period. The fact that the rises and falls occurred during the same period suggests interlinkages may play a significant role.

The purpose of this paper is to investigate the effect of stock market interlinkages on asset price bubbles. The theory of bubbles the analysis is based on was developed in Allen and Gale (2000, 2003). Standard theories of asset pricing assume that investors purchase assets with their own wealth. In most financial systems, this is not the whole story. Intermediation is important. Many of the buyers of real estate, stocks, and other assets do so with other people's money. This can lead to agency problems that cause bubbles in asset prices.

The type of agency problems that arise can be illustrated by the case of real estate investments. These are usually debt financed. If an investment is successful, the borrower repays the loan and retains the difference between the value of the asset and the principal and interest. If the investment is unsuccessful, the borrower has limited liability and the lender bears the shortfall. When the lender is unable to fully control the risk of the investment made by the borrower this payoff structure leads to a risk-shifting problem. By taking on more risk so there is a higher probability of both large profits and large losses, the borrower can increase his payoff in the good states while the lender bears the losses in the bad states. If many investors are using borrowed funds, asset prices of risky assets can be bid up above their fundamental as a result of this risk-shifting.

Debt is not the only reason for the existence of an agency problem. Mutual funds, pension funds, and insurance companies hold large amounts of stocks. In certain circumstances, managers of these funds also have incentives to take risk. If their investments have high payoffs they will attract new investors in the future. Because they receive management fees in proportion to the assets under their control, they will be significantly better off. If the investment strategy is unsuccessful, there is a limit to the downside risk that the manager bears. In the worst case, she will be fired so her liability is effectively limited.

The agency problem of excessive risk-taking associated with delegated investment decisions is crucial for the analysis presented below. If the penalties for default on debt or the reputational loss from being fired from an intermediary are sufficiently high then there will not be an incentive to take risks. Hence the theory can be thought of as applying to cases where these factors are not sufficient to prevent risk-taking.

The existence of an agency problem leads to the prices of risky assets being bid up above their fundamental values and there is a bubble. The more risky the asset the greater is the amount that can be shifted and the larger is the bubble. This risk can come from two sources. The first is asset return risk. The second is financial risk. This is the risk associated with future financial conditions such as the amount of credit that will be available.

It is shown that stock market interlinkages can play an important role in the evolution of these bubbles. The effect depends on the source of the risk that underlies the bubble. Suppose two countries with differing amounts of financial risk are linked together. The impact of the interlinkage is to reduce the bubble in the country with the larger degree of uncertainty and the higher asset prices. In the country with less uncertainty and lower asset prices, the effect is to increase the bubble. The effect of the stock market interlinkages is thus to reduce the dispersion of asset prices. However, when the difference is due to riskiness in asset payoffs the effect of introducing the interlinkage is the opposite. In this case the high asset price is increased further and the low asset price is reduced. Thus links can ameliorate or exacerbate the extent of asset price bubbles.

2. Bubbles and Agency Problems

In many recent cases where asset prices have risen and then collapsed dramatically, an expansion in credit following financial liberalization appears to have been an important factor. Perhaps the best-known example of this type of phenomenon is the dramatic rise in real estate and stock prices that occurred in Japan in the late 1980s and their subsequent collapse in 1990.

Financial liberalization throughout the 1980s and the desire to support the United States dollar in the latter part of the decade led to an expansion in credit. During most of the 1980s asset prices rose steadily, eventually reaching very high levels. For example, the Nikkei 225 index was around 10,000 in 1985. On December 19, 1989, it reached a peak of 38,916. A new governor of the Bank of Japan, less concerned with supporting the U.S. dollar and more concerned with fighting inflation, tightened monetary policy and this led to a sharp increase in interest rates in early 1990 (Frankel, 1993; Tschoegl, 1993). The bubble burst. The Nikkei 225 fell sharply during the first part of the year and by October 1, 1990, it had sunk to 20,222. Real estate prices followed a similar pattern. The next few years were marked by defaults and retrenchment in the financial system. The real economy was adversely affected by the aftermath of the bubble and growth rates during the 1990s have mostly been low or negative, in contrast to most of the postwar period when they were much higher. Similar events occurred in Norway, Finland, and Sweden in the 1980s (Heiskanen, 1993; Drees and Pazarbasioglu, 1995). Mexico provides a dramatic illustration of an emerging economy affected by this type of problem (Mishkin, 1997).

How can bubbles and ensuing crashes such as those in Japan, Scandinavia, and Mexico be understood? The typical sequence of events in such crises is as follows. There is initially a financial liberalization of some sort and this leads to a significant expansion in credit. Bank lending increases by a significant amount. Some of this lending finances new investment but much of it is used to buy assets in fixed supply such as real estate and stocks. Since the supply of these assets is fixed the prices rise above their fundamentals. Practical problems in short selling such assets prevent prices from being bid down as standard theory suggests. The process continues until there is some real event that means payoffs on the assets will be low in the future. Another possibility is that the central bank is forced to restrict credit because of fears of "overheating" and inflation. The result of one or both of these events is that the prices of real estate and stocks collapse. A banking crisis results because assets valued at bubble prices were used as collateral. There may be a foreign exchange crisis as investors pull out their funds and the central bank chooses between trying to ease the banking crisis or protect the exchange rate. The crises spill over to the real economy and there is a recession.

In the popular press and academic papers, these bubbles and crises are often related to the particular features of the country involved. However, the fact that a similar sequence of events can occur in such widely differing countries as Japan, Norway, Finland, Sweden, and México suggest such bubbles and crashes are a general phenomenon.

How can this phenomenon be understood? The crucial issues we will focus on below are:

1) What initiates a bubble?
2) What is the role of the banking system?
3) What causes a bubble to burst?

3. The Risk-Shifting Problem

A simple example is developed to illustrate the model in Allen and Gale (2000).[1] We develop a theory based on rational behavior to try and provide some insight into these issues. Standard models of asset pricing assume people invest with their own money. We identify the price of an asset in this benchmark case as the fundamental. A bubble is said to occur when the price of an asset rises above this benchmark.[2] If the people making investment decisions borrow money, then because of default they are only interested in the upper part of the distribution of payoffs of the risky asset. As a result, there is a risk-shifting problem and the price of the risky asset is bid up above the benchmark so there is a bubble.

In the example presented the people who make investment decisions do so with borrowed money. If they default there is limited liability. Lenders cannot observe the riskiness of the projects invested in so there is an agency problem. For the case of real estate, this representation of the agency problem is directly applicable. For the case of stocks, there are margin limits that prevent people directly borrowing and investing in the asset. However, a more appropriate interpretation for the case of stocks is that it is institutional investors making the investment decisions. This group constitutes a large part of the market in many countries. As explained in the introduction, the agency problem that occurs is similar to that with a debt contract. First, the people that supply the funds do not have full control over how they are invested. Second, the reward structure is similar to what happens with a debt contract. If the assets the fund managers invest in do well, the managers attract more funds in the future and receive higher payments as a result. If the assets do badly, there is a limit to the penalty that is imposed on the managers. The worse that can happen is that they are fired. This is analogous to limited liability (Allen and Gorton, 1993). Hence, similar results to those below could be obtained for stocks.

Initially there are two dates $t = 1, 2$. There are two assets in the example. The first is a safe asset in variable supply. For each 1 unit invested in this asset at date 1 the output is 1.5 at date 2. The second is a risky asset in fixed supply that can be thought of as real estate. There is 1 unit of this risky asset. For each unit purchased at price P at date 1 the output is 6 with prob. 0.25 and 1 with prob. 0.75 at date 2 so the expected payoff is 2.25. The details of the two assets are given in table 1.

Asset	Supply	Investment at date 1	Payoff at date 2
Safe	Variable	1	1.5
Risky	1	P	$R = 6$ with prob. 0.25 $= 1$ with prob. 0.75 $ER = 2.25$

Table 1: The Basic Example

All agents in the model are assumed to be risk neutral.

3.1 The Fundamental

Suppose each investor has wealth 1 initially and invests her own wealth directly. Since everybody is risk neutral the marginal returns on the two assets must be equated.

$$\frac{2.25}{P_F} = \frac{1.5}{1}$$

or

$$P_F = \frac{2.25}{2.5} = 1.5.$$

The value of the asset is simply the discounted present value of the payoff where the discount rate is the opportunity cost of the investor. This is the classic definition of the fundamental. The benchmark value of the asset is thus 1.5, and any price above this is termed a bubble.

3.2 Intermediated Case

Suppose next that investors have no wealth of their own. They can borrow to buy assets at a rate of 33 percent. The most they can borrow is 1. If they borrow 1 they repay 1.33 if they are able to. If they are unable to pay this much the lender can claim whatever they have. As explained, lenders can't observe how loans are invested and this causes an agency problem.

The first issue is can $P = 1.5$ be the equilibrium price? Consider what happens if an investor borrows 1 and invests in the safe asset.

Marginal return safe asset = $1.5 - 1.33 = 0.17$.

Suppose instead that she borrows 1 and invests in the risky asset. She purchases 1/1.5 units. When the payoff is 6 she repays the principal and interest of 1.33 and keeps what remains. When it is 1 she defaults and the entire payoff goes to the lender so she receives 0.

Marginal return risky asset = $0.25 \, (1/1.5 \times 6 - 1.33) + 0.75 \times 0 = 0.67$.

The risky asset is clearly preferred when $P = 1.5$ since $0.67 > 0.17$. The expected payoff of 1.5 on the investment in 1 unit of the safe asset is the same as on the investment of 1/1.5 units of the risky asset. The risky asset is more attractive to the borrower though. With the safe asset the borrower obtains 0.17 and the lender obtains 1.33. With the risky asset the borrower obtains 0.67 while the lender obtains $0.25 \times 1.33 + 0.75 \times 1 \times (1/1.5) = 1.5 - 0.67 = 0.83$. The risk of default allows 0.5 in expected value to be shifted from the lender to the borrower. This is the risk-shifting problem. If the lender could prevent the borrower from investing in the risky asset he would do so but he cannot since this is unobservable.

What is the equilibrium price of the risky asset given this agency problem? In an equilibrium where the safe asset is used, the price of the risky asset, P, will be bid up since it is in fixed supply, until the expected profit of borrowers is the same for both the risky and the safe asset:

$$0.25 \,(1/P \times 6 - 1.33) + 0.75 \times 0 = 1.5 - 1.33$$

so

$$P = 3.$$

There is a bubble with the price of the risky asset above the benchmark of 1.5.

The idea that there is a risk-shifting problem when the lender is unable to observe how the borrower invests the funds is not new (see, for example, Jensen and Meckling, 1976, and Stiglitz and Weiss, 1981). However, it has not been widely applied in the asset pricing literature. Instead of the standard result in corporate finance textbooks that debt-financed firms are willing to accept negative net present value investments, the manifestation of the agency problem here is that the debt-financed investors are willing to invest in assets priced above their fundamental.

The amount of risk that is shifted depends on how risky the asset is. The greater the risk the greater the potential to shift risk and hence the higher the price will be. To illustrate this consider the previous example but suppose the payoff on the risky asset is a mean-preserving spread of the original payoffs as shown in table 2.

Asset	Supply	Investment at date 1	Payoff at date 2
Safe	Variable	1	1.5
Risky	1	P	$R = 9$ with prob. 0.25
			$= 0$ with prob. 0.75
			$ER = 2.25$

Table 2: A Mean-Preserving Spread of the Basic Example

Now the price of the risky asset is given by

$$0.25 \,(1/P \times 9 - 1.33) + 0.75 \times 0 = 1.5 - 1.33$$

so

$$P = 4.5.$$

More risk is shifted and as a result the price of the risky asset is bid up to an even higher level.

It is interesting to note that in both the stock market boom of the 1920s and the one in the 1990s the stocks that did best were "high-tech" stocks. In the 1920s it was radio stocks and utilities that were the star performers (White, 1990). In the 1990s it was telecommunications, media and entertainment, and technology stocks that did the best. It is precisely these stocks which have the most uncertain payoffs because of the nature of the business they are in.

One of the crucial issues is why the banks are willing to lend to the investors given the chance of default. To see this consider again the case where the payoffs on the risky asset are those in table 1 and $P = 3$. In this case the quantity of the risky asset purchased when somebody borrows 1 is $1/P = 1/3$. In the equilibria considered above the investors are indifferent between investing in the safe and risky asset. Suppose for the sake of illustration the fixed supply of the risky asset is 1. The amount of funds depositors have is 10 and the number of borrowers is 10. In the equilibrium where $P = 3$, 3 of the borrowers invest in the risky asset and 7 in the safe in order for the fixed supply of 1 unit of the risky asset to be taken up. In this case, 30 percent of borrowers are in risky assets and 70 percent are in safe assets. A bank's expected payoff from lending one unit is then given by the following expression.

Bank's expected payoff = $0.3[0.25 \times 1.33 + 0.75 \times (1/3) \times 1] + 0.7[1.33] = 1.11$.

The first term is the payoff to the bank from the 30 percent of investors in the risky asset. If the payoff is 6, which occurs with probability 0.25, the loan and interest is repaid in full. If the payoff is 1, which occurs with probability 0.75, the borrower defaults and the bank receives the entire proceeds from the 1/3 unit owned by the borrower. The payoff is thus $(1/3) \times 1$. The 70 percent of investors in the safe asset are able to pay off their loan and interest of 1.33 in full.

If the banking sector is competitive the receipts from lending, 1.11, will be paid out to depositors. In this case it is the depositors that bear the cost of the agency problem. In order for this allocation to be feasible markets must be segmented. The depositors and the banks must not have access to the assets that the investors who borrow invest in. Clearly if they did they would be better off to just invest in the safe asset rather than put their money in the bank.

4. Credit and Interest Rate Determination

The quantity of credit and the interest rate have so far been taken as exogenous. These factors are incorporated in the example next to illustrate the relationship between the amount of credit and the level of interest rates. We start with the simplest case where the central bank determines the aggregate amount of credit B available to banks. It does this by setting reserve requirements and determining the amount of assets available for use as reserves. For ease of exposition we do not fully model this process and simply assume the central bank sets B. The banking sector is competitive. The number of banks is normalized at 1 and the number of investors is also normalized to 1. Each investor will therefore be able to borrow B from each bank. The safe asset pays a fixed return r to the investor: If x is invested in the safe asset at date 1 the return is rx at date 2. The safe asset can be interpreted in a number of ways. One possibility is that it is debt issued by the corporate sector. Another possibility is that it is capital goods, which are leased to the corporate sector. The investors treat the rate of return as fixed because they are small relative to the size of the corporate sector.

In equilibrium, competition will ensure that the rate of return on the safe asset is equal to the marginal product of capital in the economy. This in turn depends on the amount of the consumption good x that is invested at date 1 in the economy's productive technology to produce $f(x)$ units at date 2. The total amount that can be invested is B and the amount that is invested at date 1 in the risky asset since there is 1 unit is P. Hence the date 1 budget constraint implies that $x = B - P$. It is assumed

1) $f(x) = 3(B - P)^{0.5}$.

Provided the market for loans is competitive, the interest rate r will be bid up by investors until

2) $r = f'(B - P) = 1.5(B - P)^{-0.5}$.

At this level the safe asset will not yield any profits for investors. If it were lower than this there would be an infinite demand for the safe asset and if it was higher than this there would be zero demand.

The amount the investors will be prepared to pay for the risky asset assuming its payoffs are as in table 1 is then given by

$0.25(1/P \times 6 - r) + 0.75 \times 0 = 0$.

Using equation 2 in this,

$P = 4(B - P)^{0.5}$.

Solving for P gives

3) $P = 8(-1 + \sqrt{1 + 0.25B})$.

When $B = 5$ then $P = 4$ and $r = 1.5$. The solid line in figure 1 shows the relationship between P and B. By controlling the amount of credit the central bank controls the level of interest rates and the level of asset prices. Note that this relationship is different from that in the standard asset pricing model when the price of the risky asset is the discounted expected payoff

$P_F = 2.25/r$.

This case is illustrated by the dotted line in figure 1. A comparison of the two cases shows that the fundamental is relatively insensitive to the amount of credit compared to the case where there is an agency problem. Changes in aggregate credit can cause relatively large changes in asset prices when there is an agency problem.

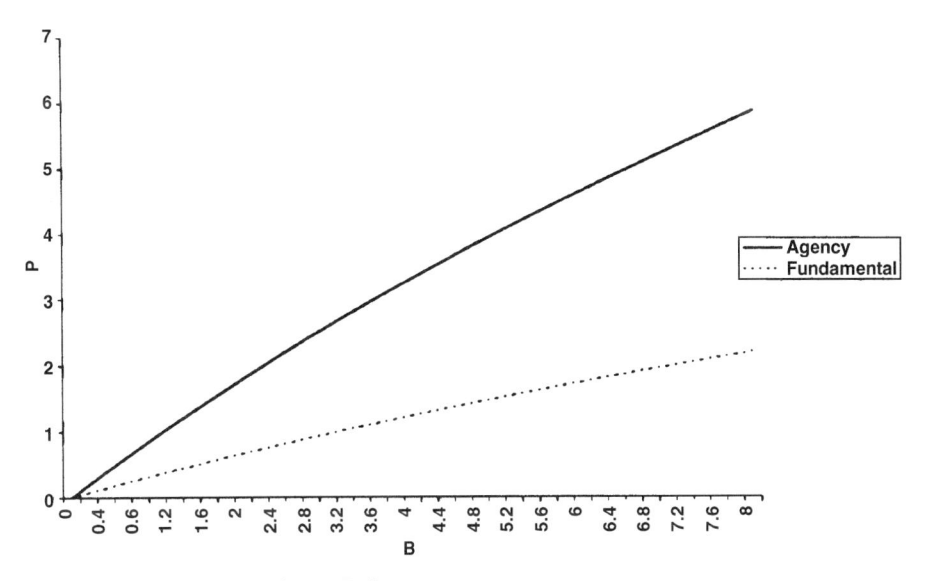

Figure 1: Credit and Asset Prices

5. Financial Risk

The previous section assumed that the central bank could determine the amount of credit B. In practice the central bank has limited ability to control the amount of credit, and this means B is random. In addition there may be changes of policy preferences, changes of administration, and changes in the external environment, which create further uncertainty about the level of B. This uncertainty is particularly great in countries undergoing financial liberalization. In order to investigate the effect of this uncertainty an extra period is added to the model. Between dates 1 and 2 everything is the same as before. Between dates 0 and 1 the only uncertainty that is resolved is about the level of B at date 1. Thus between dates 0 and 1 there is financial uncertainty. The uncertainty about aggregate credit B at date 1 causes uncertainty about P at date 1. Given that investors are borrowing from banks at date 0 as before this price uncertainty again leads to an agency problem and risk shifting. The price of the risky asset at date 0 will reflect this price uncertainty and can lead the asset price to be even higher than at date 1.

Suppose that there is a 0.5 probability that $B = 5$ and a 0.5 probability that $B = 7$ at date 1. Then using equations 2 and 3 the prices and interest rates are as shown in table 3.

Probability	B	P	r
0.5	5	4	1.5
0.5	7	5.27	1.14

Table 3: The Basic Example Extended to Include Financial Risk

The pricing equation at date 0 is

$$0.5\,(1/P_0 \times 5.27 - r_0) + 0.5 \times 0 = 0,$$

where r_0, the date 0 interest rate, is given by equation 2 with B and P replaced by B_0 and P_0. Substituting for r_0 and simplifying

$$P_0 = 5.27/(1.5(B_0 - P_0)^{-0.5}).$$

Taking $B_0 = 6$ and solving for r_0 and P_0 gives

$$r_0 = 1.19, \quad P_0 = 4.42.$$

As when the uncertainty is due to variations in asset payoffs, the greater the financial uncertainty the greater is P_0. Consider a mean preserving spread on the financial uncertainty so that table 4 replaces table 3.

Probability	B	P	r
0.5	4	3.14	1.81
0.5	8	5.86	1.03

Table 4: A Mean-Preserving Spread of the Example with Financial Risk

In this case it can be shown

$$r_0 = 1.27, \quad P_0 = 4.61.$$

The risk shifting effect operates for financial risk in the same way as it does for asset payoff risk. Although the expected payoff at date 2 is only 2.25 the price of the risky asset at date 1 in this last case is 4.61. The possibility of credit expansion over a period of years may create a great deal of uncertainty about how high the bubble may go and when it may collapse. This is particularly the case when economies are undergoing financial liberalization. As more periods are added it is possible for the bubble to become very large. The market price can be much greater than the fundamental.

6. Stock Market Interlinkages

So far we have considered what happens in single countries. We next turn to the case where there are multiple stock markets and interlinkages between them. Initially, we start by investigating the effect of interlinkages between countries with different levels of financial risk and then go on to the case where the countries have different variability in asset payoffs. It turns out that the interlinkages have quite different effects in the two situations.

6.1 Different Levels of Financial Risk

The case considered is where the interest rate is endogenously determined as above and there is financial risk due to uncertain levels of credit.

Suppose there are two countries, X and Y. Countries X and Y have the same parameters as those analyzed in tables 3 and 4, respectively. Country X has a 0.5

probability that $B = 5$ and a 0.5 probability that $B = 7$. Country Y has a 0.5 probability that $B = 4$ and a 0.5 probability $B = 8$. Country X thus has lower financial risk than Country Y. The realizations of the amounts of credit in each country are assumed to be independent. The interest rates and prices when the countries are autarchic are as in the previous section. At date 0, they are $r_{X0} = 1.19$ and $P_{X0} = 4.42$ in Country X, and $r_{Y0} = 1.27$ and $P_{Y0} = 4.61$ in Country Y. The low risk country has a lower interest rate and asset price than the high-risk country.

If the two countries have links between the stock markets so they are effectively like one market then interest rates must be equalized. Since both risky assets have the same distribution of payoffs at date 2 they will have the same price as well. The total credit available will be split equally between the countries. Table 5 shows the four possible outcomes at date 1 for prices and interest rates.

Probability	B_X	B_Y	$(B_X + B_Y)$	$(B_X + B_Y)/2$	P	r
0.25	5	4	9	4.5	3.66	1.64
0.25	7	4	11	5.5	4.33	1.39
0.25	5	8	13	6.5	4.96	1.21
0.25	7	8	15	7.5	5.57	1.08

Table 5: The Effect of Stock Market Linkages When Countries Have Different Levels of Financial Risk

It can be shown in the usual way that if $B_0 = 6$ in each country then $r_0 = 1.23$, $P_0 = 4.52$.

The effect of the interlinkages here is that Country X experiences a higher asset price and interest rate and Country Y a lower asset price and interest rate than before. The effect of interlinkages is to moderate the bubbles. Asset prices lie between those that would occur without the interlinkages. This is due to the fact that the variations in credit across countries are smoothed.

6.2 Differences in Asset Payoffs

Next suppose that Country X is as before. Country Y has the same credit distribution as Country X. Both have a 0.5 probability that $B = 5$ and a 0.5 probability that $B = 7$. The realizations of the level of credit in each country at date 1 are independent. The difference between the countries is now that in Country Y the risky asset payoff at date 2 is given by table 2 rather than table 1. The payoff on Country Y's asset is more risky than the payoff on Country X's asset. When Country Y is autarchic it can be shown in the usual way that the price distribution at date 1 is

Probability	B	P	r
0.5	5	4.45	2.02
0.5	7	6	1.5

Table 6: The Date 1 Equilibrium in Country Y When It Is Autarchic

and at date 0

$r_{Y0} = 1.29$, $P_{Y0} = 4.64$.

This contrasts with Country X where $r_{X0} = 1.19$ and $P_{X0} = 4.42$. Since the payoffs in Country Y are more variable than in Country X the price of the risky asset is higher. Given $r = f'(B - P)$ if the price is higher the interest rate is also higher since $f' < 0$.

When stock market interlinkages are introduced the effect is rather different in this case than in the previous example. Table 7 shows the four possible outcomes at date 1 for prices and interest rates.

Probability	B_X	B_Y	$(B_X + B_Y)/2$	P_X	P_Y	r
0.25	5	5	5	3.42	5.12	1.76
0.25	5	7	6	4	6	1.5
0.25	7	5	6	4	6	1.5
0.25	7	7	7	4.56	6.84	1.31

Table 7: The Effect of Stock Market Interlinkages When Countries Have Different Levels of Asset Returns

At date 0

$r_0 = 1.25$, $P_{X0} = 3.65$, $P_{Y0} = 5.47$.

Here the effect of introducing stock market interlinkages is to exacerbate the bubble in the country with the high autarchic asset price and reduce it in the other country. At date 1, the higher price in Country Y drives up the interest rate relative to Country X's autarchic allocation and this drives down the price of the risky asset in Country X. Relative to Country Y's autarchic case the interest rate is lower and this drives up the price of the risky asset for Country Y. At date 0 interest rates are again higher for Country X and lower for Country Y and this reinforces the fall in the price of Country X's risky asset and the increase in the price of Country Y's risky asset. In contrast to the case with differing levels of credit risk the bubble in the country with the highest risky asset price is increased.

7. Concluding Remarks

This paper has suggested that one basic reason for the existence of bubbles is an agency problem. Many decisionmakers in real estate and stock markets obtain their investment funds from external sources. If the providers of funds are unable to observe the characteristics of the investment, there is a classic risk-shifting problem. Risk-shifting increases the return to investment in risky assets and causes investors to bid up prices above their fundamental values. A crucial determinant of asset prices is then the amount of credit that is provided for speculative investment. Financial liberalization, by expanding the volume of credit for speculative investments and creating uncertainty about the future path of credit expansion, can interact with the agency problem and lead to a bubble in asset prices. In addition it was shown that stock market interlinkages can have a significant effect on asset price bubbles that arise from agency problems. Depending on the form of risk that leads to risk-shifting, introducing interlinkages can either reduce or increase the extent of bubbles.

*Franklin Allen is the Nippon Life Professor of Finance, a professor of economics, and co-director of the Financial Institutions Center at The Wharton School of the University of Pennsylvania. Douglas Gale is a professor and chair of the Economics Department at New York University. The authors thank their discussants, Ashoka Mody and especially Anna Schwartz, for their helpful comments.

Notes

1. For ease of exposition, the example is slightly different from the model presented in that paper.

2. See Allen, Morris, and Postlewaite (1993) for a discussion of the definition of fundamental and bubble.

References

Allen, F., and D. Gale, 2003, "Asset Price Bubbles And Monetary Policy," in *Financial Crises and Global Governance*, proceedings of a conference held at the London School of Economics, October 13 and 14, 2000, forthcoming.

―――, 2000, "Bubbles and Crises," *Economic Journal*, Vol. 110, pp. 236–255.

Allen, F., and G. Gorton, 1993, "Churning Bubbles," *Review of Economic Studies*, Vol. 60, pp. 813–836.

Allen, F., S. Morris, and A. Postlewaite, 1993, "Finite Bubbles with Short Sale Constraints and Asymmetric Information," *Journal of Economic Theory*, Vol. 61, pp. 206–229.

Carswell, J., 1960, *The South Sea Bubble*, Stanford, CA: Stanford University Press.

Drees, B., and C. Pazarbasioglu, 1995, "The Nordic Banking Crises: Pitfalls in Financial Liberalization?," International Monetary Fund, working paper, No. 95/61.

Frankel, J., 1993, "The Japanese Financial System and the Cost of Capital," in *Japanese Capital Markets: New Developments in Regulations and Institutions*, S. Takagi, ed., Oxford: Blackwell, pp. 21–77.

Heiskanen, R., 1993, "The Banking Crisis in the Nordic Countries," *Kansallis Economic Review*, Vol. 2, pp. 13–19.

Higgins, M., and C. Osler, 1997, "Asset Market Hangovers and Economic Growth: The OECD during 1984–93," *Oxford Review of Economic Policy*, Vol. 13, pp. 110–134.

Jensen, M., and W. Meckling, 1976, "Theory of the Firm: Managerial Behavior, Agency Cost and Ownership Structure," *Journal of Financial Economics*, Vol. 3, pp. 305–360.

Stiglitz, J., and A. Weiss, 1981, "Credit Rationing in Markets with Imperfect Information," *American Economic Review*, Vol. 71, pp. 393–410.

Tschoegl, A., 1993, "Modeling the Behavior of Japanese Stock Indices," in *Japanese Capital Markets: New Developments in Regulations and Institutions*, S. Takagi, ed., Oxford: Blackwell, pp. 371–400.

White, E., 1990, *Crashes and Panics: The Lessons from History,* Homewood, IL: Dow Jones Irwin.

Chapter 24

Banking Policy and Macroeconomic Stability: An Exploration

Gerard Caprio, Jr.*
World Bank Group

and

Patrick Honohan
World Bank Group

1. Introduction

In view of the depressing record of the last two decades with banking crises around the world and, in particular, in emerging markets, it is understandable that authorities are interested in whether (and when) banking serves to stabilize the economy. Evidently, a crisis of bank insolvency has the potential to push the economy into a slump, in what is the most extreme form of credit-driven macroeconomic cycle. This is an example of bad banking worsening macroeconomic performance, and episodes in which banks are alleged to contribute to booms or asset bubbles are not difficult to find, as well. But could some forms of "good" banking also have a destabilizing role?

For example, worsening creditworthiness conditions as a slump gets under way can lead a cautiously managed bank to raise its credit quality thresholds and shift to safe assets such as government bonds; the ensuing credit crunch can exacerbate a downturn (Bernanke, 1983; Bernanke-Lown, 1991; Greenwald-Stiglitz, 1993). In an upturn the opposite can be the case, with increasing confidence triggering a relaxation of credit standards and a surge of credit driving the economy even higher—and amplifying credit cycles. Some authors have noted that the tightness of supervisory guidelines can act in the same procyclical way (Berger et al., 2001).

Unfortunately, in assessing the importance of each of these models in practice, the econometrician is faced with difficult problems. While banking crises can contribute to a subsequent output dip, it is equally true that adverse output shocks can trigger a banking crisis (IMF, 1998; Hoggarth et al., 2002). Disentangling cause and effect is very difficult in practice. Likewise, it is usually hard to determine whether a particular decline in credit can be attributed to demand or supply shocks. The relevant structural equations are usually not well determined, as evidenced from the large literature on the East Asia crisis and the potential role of a credit crunch there (Agenor et al., 2000; Ding et al., 1998).

An alternative approach to addressing the question of good banking and macro stability is to look at some instruments for banking quality and examine the macroperformance of economies by reference to these instruments. The advantage of this approach is that it can provide guidance as to the type of banking system that government officials could expect to maximize stabilizing influences. Two distinct types of instruments on which some data are available are 1) the nature of bank regulation and 2) presence of, or openness to, foreign bank ownership.[1]

Already there is a literature on the cross-country contribution of financial depth to macroeconomic stability (Easterly, Islam, Stiglitz, 2000; Beck, Lundberg, Majnoni, 2001). It concludes that deeper financial systems—at least up to a certain point—do seem to be able to insulate economies against certain types of shock. The question posed in this paper can be seen as addressing the same question but along different dimensions of banking sector quality.

While the presence of reputable foreign banks is usually held to contribute to the institutional strength of the banking system (Levine, 1996), heavy reliance on foreign banks could be destabilizing if they introduce or transmit foreign shocks to a greater extent than they absorb shocks of domestic origin.

Schematically we can see the banking system as a filter through which foreign and domestic shocks feed through to the domestic economy. The filter can dampen or amplify the shocks, through various credit market channels including credit growth, import of foreign capital, and, possibly, interest rates. Our question is whether the prudential quality of banking, as proxied by measures of regulatory quality and of openness to foreign banking, amplify or dampen these shocks. Barth, Caprio, and Levine (2001b) find that some aspects of the regulatory environment can help stimulate increased financial depth as well as reduce the likelihood of financial crises, and here we look at whether the same or other features of the regulatory environment can dampen short-term macroeconomic volatility.

Although it is hard to identify a statistically clear role for different aspects of the regulatory environment among the many factors influencing overall macroeconomic volatility, when we look at the way in which banking system balance sheets evolve in response to shocks, we do find systematic patterns. In general, many of the regulatory characteristics that have been found to deepen a financial system and make it more robust to crises—notably those that empower the private sector—also appear to reduce the sector's ability to provide short-term insulation to the macroeconomy. It is as if prudent bankers are reluctant to absorb short-term risks that might cause solvency and growth problems in the longer run. But this apparent trade-off can be avoided: Banking systems that have a higher share of foreign-owned banks, already a feature associated with financial deepening and lowered risk of crisis, also seem to score well in terms of short-term macroeconomic insulation.

In the next section, we review some of the earlier efforts to address these issues. Section 3 follows with new empirical work, and section 4 concludes with advice for policymakers.

2. Banking on Stability: What Do We Know?

...no degree of regulatory wisdom could, or should, have made the 1920s a profitable time for banks in agricultural regions affected by drastic declines in prices and land values ... What regulation could have done, but did not do, was make the system as a whole less susceptible to shocks and more resilient in its response to failures.

Calomiris, 1989

There has been little disagreement that one of the important goals of banking and, more generally, finance is to help individuals and society cope with changing economic circumstances (Levine, 1997). One of the most basic functions of finance, namely the mobilization of savings, itself, represents a way for individuals to protect themselves from economic downturns. And, from the (small business) man on the street looking for a loan to the sophisticated consumer of derivative products, the function of transforming risk (reducing it through aggregation and enabling it to be carried by those better able to bear it) also is a key way to deal with economic volatility (World Bank, 2001).

But is banking a source of stability? Although they note that the distinction can be overdrawn, Allen and Gale (2000) suggest that markets tend to be destabilizing, whereas banks and other intermediaries, by virtue of being able to re-contract more seamlessly, help to stabilize economies. And, at least theoretically, banks should be forward-looking in their decisions. They should hold a well-diversified portfolio, taking provisions and holding capital in order to ensure their survival. Banking and the building of special relationships does not fit with the perfectly competitive model, and bank charters have a value, which bankers can capture by making sure that they survive. Failure in banking, as in other industries, can send valuable signals and should be permitted, but there is a reduction in information capital when banks shut down so that society suffers some loss. "Bad" banks are those that risk failure either deliberately or through myopic decisions on risk-taking, but at least in this theoretical approach, good banks will outweigh the bad.

Nevertheless, it is not without some irony that in many banking crises—as in the 1920s and 1930s, among other episodes—it has been noted that the banking sector itself appears to have acted to amplify risks rather than to help mitigate them. What could cause such amplification?

Some have argued that regulators are to blame: By tightening capital regulations or raising provisioning standards after a boom is already well under way, or indeed after one has begun collapsing, banks may be induced to vary their lending in a procyclical fashion (Berger et al., 2001). And, some features of the 1988 Basel Accord, such as the lower risk weight for short-term credit, may individually be sensible for banks but collectively can induce an increased ratio of short-term to total debt and, therefore, greater financial fragility, meaning more economic volatility.

Others claim that the rating agencies are the culprits: By downgrading companies or countries after a slowdown has already begun, an application of existing capital standards in most countries would automatically lead to a tightening of credit conditions. Although the evidence suggests that rating agencies do a respectable job of anticipating companies' misfortunes, they appear to perform less well when it comes to country risk (Ferri, Liu, and Majnoni, 2001).

And, still others argue that it is the bankers themselves exhibiting lemming-like behavior. This behavior could be entirely rational. Errors in judgment may be punished more severely, both by the market and by internal compensation schemes: When the bank or the analyst makes a mistake in isolation, adverse consequences may be more significant than one made in good company. Alternatively, the manner in which bank executives are compensated could more actively lead to potential procyclical lending: If compensation is based on the short-run performance of bank stock prices, the mercurial tendency of markets will be transmitted directly to banks (John, Saunders, and Senbet, 2002).

Volatility, regardless of its source, is a legitimate source of concern in a world of less than complete markets, because individuals cannot costlessly enter into contracts for all conceivable states of the world. This statement holds with particular force in emerging market countries where the variety of financial services available tends to be more limited than in more advanced countries. Moreover, real, nominal, and financial volatility all are greater in emerging markets due to their smaller size and typically greater economic concentration (Caprio and Honohan, 1999; World Bank, 2001), so if volatility matters in high-income economies, it must have been an even greater source of concern for developing countries.

Bernanke and Gertler (1989) and Gertler and Rose (1994) note that shocks to net worth can translate into a greater real volatility in the presence of credit market imperfections. The more significant information problems are, the more bankers will rely on the collateralizable net worth of borrowers, changes in which can lead to simultaneous expansion or shrinkage of bank balance sheets, leading to greater volatility of real income and inflation, and, thus, affecting economic welfare. Kiyotaki and Moore (1997) also note that such imperfections can increase the effects of temporary shocks and contribute to their persistence. The assumption that these imperfections are more pronounced in developing countries, consistent with the well-known lack of financial development there, makes it all the more likely than emerging markets will be particularly affected by greater volatility. Banking is also important because for most countries it is the primary channel to break the link between domestic investment and savings, thereby permitting a more efficient allocation of capital worldwide.

So how can countries achieve a banking sector—more "good" banks and fewer bad ones—that mitigates rather than magnifies economic volatility? Here the answers are thought to be well known: Adopt international best practices for everything from accounting and corporate governance to bank regulation and supervision. In addition to suffering from some circularity (essentially telling developing countries that they would become richer if only they adopted the institutional framework that advanced countries evolved over many generations), these recommendations for best practices are based exclusively on "armchair empiricism."

One answer might be to become more developed financially. Beck, Lundberg, and Majnoni (2001) find that although real sector shocks are dampened as financial systems develop, monetary shocks are amplified: Firms depend more on external resources with significant financial sector development, which exposes them more to monetary or financial shocks.[2] But this still begs the question of whether countries with deep financial systems are equally capable of dampening even some forms of volatility. Are some types of deep financial systems more effective in this respect than others?

To fill this void, Barth, Caprio, and Levine (2001b) collect data on regulatory and supervisory practices around the world and find that numerous regulatory features, such as regulatory barriers to bank entry, regulatory restrictions on bank activities, greater supervisory power, and government ownership of banks are positively associated with government corruption except when political openness is pronounced; for most countries, greater supervisory powers go with greater corruption and *worse* outcomes for bank development and stability. More positively, they find that regulatory and supervisory strategies that focus on empowering the private sector (improving transparency and disclosure) and limiting the adverse incentive effects from generous deposit insurance work best to promote bank performance and stability. An additional feature of the regulatory environment that helps bank stability is found in their analysis to be the ability of foreign banks to enter the local market. In Barth, Caprio, and Levine (2001b), the dimension in which stability is measured refers to banking crises. But even if no crisis occurs, banking can perform an insulating function, as is examined further below.

Most other approaches to this question focus on individual cases, and even individual features of the regulatory environment. Jordan, Peek, and Rosengren (2000) find that U.S. banks that disclose less information then encountered more severe market reaction on eventual announcement and that this reaction was potentially contagious. In other words, better disclosure was at least consistent with lower volatility in the stock market prices of these banks. An earlier effort by Peek and Rosengren (1995) found that banks holding low capital ratios were forced to cut back more on their real estate portfolio in bad times, suggesting that bad banking can indeed exacerbate real volatility through credit decisions.

Other research has examined the impact of foreign banks, either in their offshore activities or onshore in industrial and emerging markets. Goldberg (2001) uses bank-specific data on U.S. bank lending to foreign countries and finds that, while in general these are not sensitive to local output and interest rate conditions in emerging markets, the volume of U.S. bank claims on foreign countries is quite sensitive to changes in U.S. conditions. This finding echoes that of Peek and Rosengren (2000), who established how Japanese banks pulled back from U.S. lending in the 1990s and that the retrenchment had real economic effects in select U.S. real estate markets. This suggests that foreign banks may help mitigate the effect of domestic shocks but could amplify the impact of foreign shocks. Those results were strongly driven by cross-border banking activities; in contrast, local operations of foreign-owned banks may be less ambiguous in their contribution to stability. For example, Crystal, Dages, and Goldberg (2001) find that in Argentina, Chile, and Columbia, foreign-owned banks showed not only high but more stable loan growth and higher capital asset ratios. This important finding strongly suggests that foreign-owned banks provide stability and do so as a result of their greater financial strength and, perhaps, because they are better regulated (Berger et al., 2000) and/or are less myopic, as well.[3]

To summarize then, the literature provides some hope that certain aspects of the banking environment can help reduce volatility in emerging markets. In the next section we look at data on bank lending behavior in a wide cross section of countries to see what light it throws on this issue.

3. Using Aggregate Balance Sheet Data to Assess the Insulating Potential of the Banking System

If a banking system acts to stabilize or destabilize macroeconomic aggregates, this should become evident in the way in which the size and composition of its balance sheet evolves in response to shocks. In this section we look at the short-term dynamics of banking-system balance sheets as they change from quarter to quarter. In contrast to previous work examining the probability of crises—relatively rare events occurring perhaps one or twice in a quarter-century—our goal is to examine the ability of banking systems to insulate high-frequency disturbances.

This goal requires linking two distinct sources of data, namely quarterly balance sheet aggregates and information on structural characteristics of the banking systems. For the latter, we use the database of Barth, Caprio, and Levine (2001a), which defines the outer margins of our sample of countries. For the former, we turn to *International Financial Statistics* (*IFS*).

3.1 Simplified Banking System Balance Sheets

Drawn upon what is, in principle, a common set of definitions, *IFS* contains monetary survey data on well over 100 countries, including almost all of the countries for which we have banking quality data. Our focus is on the component data for deposit-money banks, not including the monetary authorities. But the balance sheet classifications of the monetary survey are too numerous to allow for a cross-country study without considerable consolidation and rationalization. A total of 44 distinct balance sheet category codes are included in the monetary survey, though any given country only has entries against a subset of these, typically fewer than 20. Even 20 classifications is much too detailed a breakdown for the purpose at hand, namely to understand the influences on the broad allocation of different sources of funds to different uses in the balance sheet.

Therefore, we have simplified and consolidated the data into a simple format, the same for all countries, distinguishing between just six broad categories with convenient notation as follows:

Assets	Liabilities
a loans and advances	*c* capital
b bills and other liquid investments (net)	*d* deposits and deposit-type instruments
	e net other liabilities
	f net foreign liabilities

Here *a* ("advances"—though we use the term interchangeably with loans) equals total domestic credit, including claims on central, state, and local governments (these expressed net of deposits), public enterprises, nonmonetary financial institutions, and the private sector. The remaining asset-side item *b*, "bills," includes bank reserves net of credit to banks from the monetary authorities. The item *c*, "capital," is the entry under capital accounts in *IFS*; it does not in all cases correspond to regulatory capital under the Basel conventions. The major item under liabilities is *d*, "deposits," which includes not only demand and time deposits (other than the public sector deposits already netted out of *a*) but also money market and other liquid liabilities. The residual item *e* also includes bonds issued by banks. Net foreign liabilities *f* is self-explanatory.[4]

Over time, each of the elements of the balance sheet evolve, but at any given moment, the balance sheet identity is satisfied by the data for each country:

$$a + b = c + d + e + f.$$

This identity reflects not only the nature of banking *transactions* but also the fact that *valuation changes* (such as changes in loan-loss provisioning) give rise to offsetting changes in the net residual, capital.

In order to look at the evolution of the typical balance sheet structure in our data set, we express each element as a percentage of the sum of the two asset items $a + b$ (advances plus bills). In interpreting the resulting ratios, note that this denominator is not the same as the balance sheet total. For one thing, borrowing from the central bank is netted out of "bills." Also, foreign assets are netted from the liability figure "foreign liabilities." With this caveat, we see from figure 1 that deposits dominate the liabilities and advances, the assets side of the mean portfolio structure.[5] The other four elements are, on average, rather small. Nevertheless, when we look at the variation both between countries and over time (1990–2000), we discover that each of the six elements contributes approximately the same amount (figures 2a and 2b). This confirms that none of the elements of the chosen grouping of balance sheet items can be ignored in understanding the portfolio dynamics.

Over time, there has been a trend towards declining relative importance of the two large items, advances and deposits, as shown in figure 3a, which shows the value for the median country at each date. Each of deposits and advances has trended downwards at a rate of between 0.5 and 0.7 percent points per annum. The slack has been taken up by an increase in net liquidity on the asset side and mainly by capital items on the liability side (figure 3b). These trends presumably reflect increased regulatory emphasis on capital and liquidity, as well as a shift away from the use of discount lending by central banks.

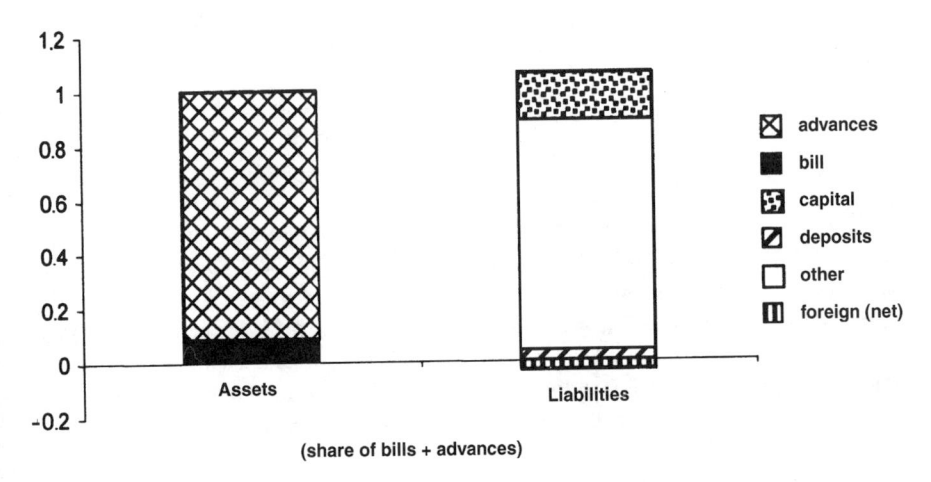

Figure 1: Mean Balance Sheet Structure

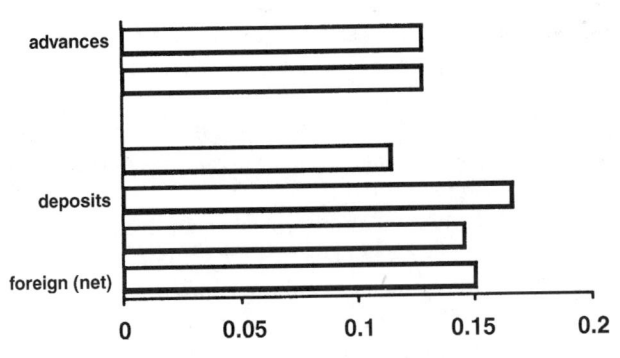

Figure 2a: Standard Deviation of Elements of Balance Sheet (Across Countries)

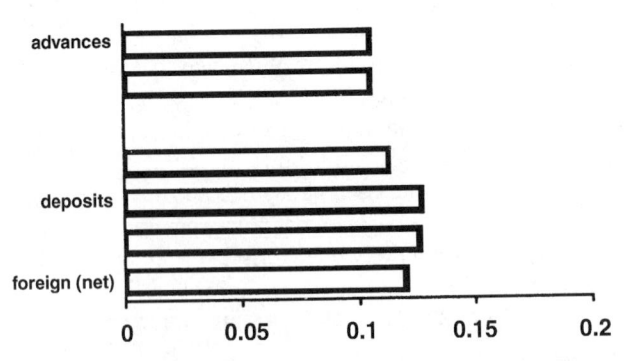

Figure 2b: Standard Deviation of Elements of Balance Sheet (Across Dates)

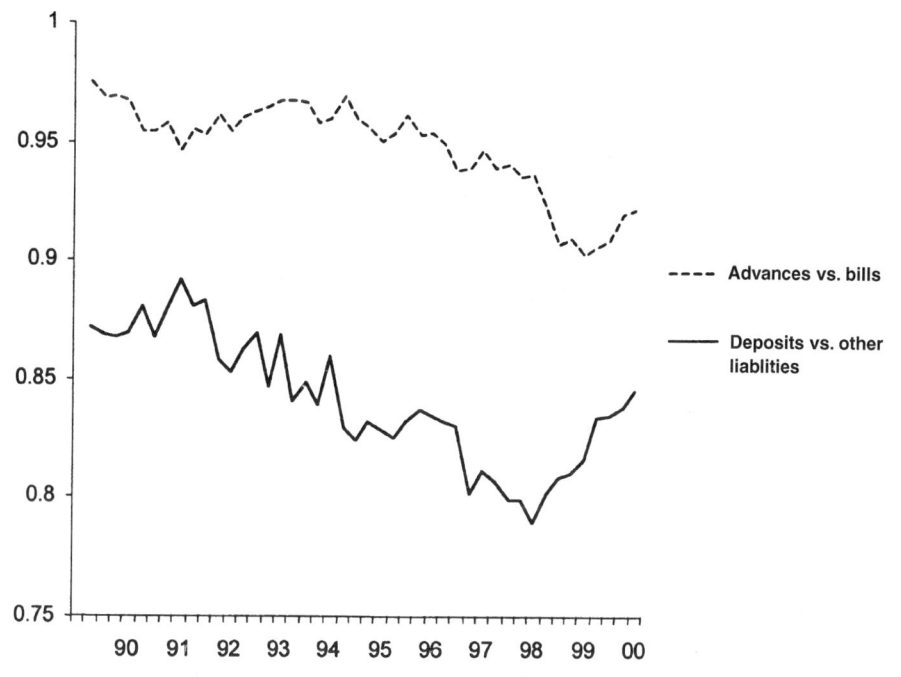

Figure 3a: Trend in Balance Sheet Composition Main Items

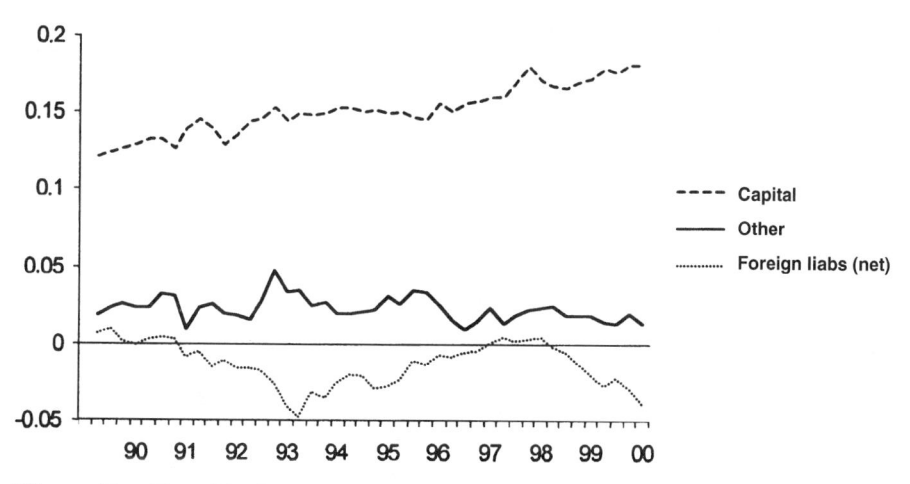

Figure 3b: Trend in Balance Sheet Composition—Other Liabilities

We also notice that fluctuations in the balance sheet aggregates are sizable: movements of several percentage points even for the median of more than 70 countries. Individual countries experienced much more volatility.

So what are the drivers of this volatility, and how do they vary between different types of banking system?

3.2 Using the Monetary Survey Data to Assess the Banking System's Absorptive Capacity

Deposit shocks can be severe; witness the dramatic experiences in Argentina in 1994–95 and again during 2001, when deposits fell by more than 20 percent and 10 percent, respectively, or in Turkey in 1994. The heightened depositor uncertainty that they typically imply can also reflect heightened lender uncertainty; but, even if the bank lenders do not have a heightened sense of lending risk, they will have to find alternative sources of funding if they are not to shrink their loan portfolio in response to a withdrawal of deposits. Fluctuations in loans, in turn, can drive macroeconomic fluctuations. So we want to know whether the banking system does, in fact, act to insulate the volume of loans from exogenous shocks in deposits, with the presumption that such insulation is socially beneficial.

Even if deposits remain stable, disturbances in loan-loss experience can affect the banks' capitalization. This in turn will lead to other portfolio adjustments including fluctuations in lending impacting the macroeconomy. Here, again, we want to know if the banks are prone to cutting back on new loans simply because of loan-losses (as distinct from cutting back in a prudent response to heightened risk). If they do so, this is likely to exacerbate an economic downturn and, as such, be socially undesirable.

In the case both of shocks to deposits and to capital, it is evident that simultaneity and feedback will be a crucial issue. For example, a poor harvest will tend to affect both credit demand and deposits, without there being any causality from the latter to the former. In what follows we use standard econometric techniques to correct for this problem.

Before attempting to capture the magnitude of these effects and how they may differ between different types of countries, it may be convenient to sketch the formal framework that could underlie our generally intuitive approach to the econometric modeling.

3.2.1 A Modeling Framework

Let us denote the vector of balance sheet items as $x = (a,b,c,d,e,f)'$. In a competitive environment, each bank can be thought of as choosing a value x^* to optimize an expected profit function $\pi_t(x,r)$ in response to an exogenous expected vector of returns r (and subject to the adding-up condition $x'l = 1$, where l is the unit vector). More generally, in a noncompetitive environment, the banks may choose an optimal point (x^*, r^*) along a demand surface $\Delta_t(x,r) = 0$. Finally, banks may be quantity-takers as well as price-takers for some of the elements of the balance sheet, in that they may, for example, be required to accept all deposits presented to them at a parametric rate of return. If so, the optimal portfolio will be conditional on the actual value of the deposits received. In practice, there may also be adjustment costs, so that the actual value of

x may deviate from the optimized value, notably if there is some shock to the exogenous rates of return and/or the given flow of deposits.

If we only have data on the quantities and not on the rates of return, we cannot hope to estimate the profit function or the demand surfaces. But, with some further assumptions, we can draw some inferences as to the role of the banking system in contributing to macroeconomic stability.

For example, if banks are quantity-takers for deposits, then shocks to aggregate deposits d must be absorbed by some or all of the other elements of the balance sheet. (There may also be price adjustments.) If the adjustment is through a change in the net foreign liability f, with no change in the level of advances a, then the banking system is completely insulating the level of advances from shocks to the level of deposits.

According to the credit view of monetary transmission, it is through changes in loans and advances that the banking system has its biggest short-run[6] impact on the macroeconomy. If so, it is of interest to compare the degree to which deposit shocks are passed through to advances, or whether the banking system acts to insulate advances. In practice, of course, much of the dollar value of shifts in deposits typically passes through to advances, which are normally the largest element of the asset side of the balance sheet. Are there systematic variations in the extent of pass-through, and are these correlated with banking quality variables?

3.2.2 Response of Loans and Advances to Fluctuations in Deposits

Naturally, being the largest balance sheet elements, deposit and loan fluctuations tend to be highly correlated over time and across countries. We regressed the quarterly logarithmic change in a on the contemporaneous change in d for our panel of 74 countries, 1990–2000. A simple ordinary least squares (OLS) regression a coefficient of 0.78 with a standard error of a little over 0.01 (table 1a, equation 1.1). Of course, simultaneity bias may be present, and we look at this momentarily.

Taking this estimate at face value suggests that a fall in deposits of 10 percent will pass through to advances to the extent of 7.8 percent. This is the average over all countries. The next question is whether this pass-through is affected by the nature and quality of bank regulation and by the presence of foreign banks.

However, when we allow the coefficient on d to vary depending on the value of the banking quality variables by adding cross-product terms one-by-one to the equation, we find significant effects, many of them positive, suggesting that banking system quality does influence the pass-through and can actually tend to *destabilize* loans and advances in the short-run.[7] An exception is foreign ownership, which tends to insulate advances from deposit shocks.

In order to interpret these regressions, we take our cue from Barth, Caprio, and Levine (2001b), though with a slightly different perspective given the different concerns at hand. Our conjecture is that banking systems that are subject to effective monitoring by market forces or by nondiscretionary official bodies are more likely to adjust their lending in response to deposit fluctuations for fear of falling foul of the oversight. Although shareholders may have different views about increasing the leverage of their bank (which would occur if a fall in deposits were made up at the expense of the quantity or quality of capital), those who are creditors to the bank will prefer to

Equation no:	1.1	1.2	1.3	1.4	1.5	1.6	1.7	1.8	1.9	1.10
Level effect	0.78 (67.5)	0.69 (34.3)	0.66 (46.2)	0.76 (62.2)	0.76 (61.3)	0.79 (67.2)	0.78 (67.5)	0.66 (47.4)	0.78 (67.6)	0.83 (47.1)
Capital rules (−)		−0.02 (1.5)	−0.04 (2.8)	−0.09 (7.2)						
Official regulatory powers (−)		−0.04 (2.5)	−0.06 (3.9)		0.07 (6.6)					
Private monitoring (+)		−0.02 (1.4)	−0.01 (0.9)			−0.01 (0.7)				
Entry standards (+)		0.02 (1.8)	0.03 (2.2)				0.04 (4.5)			
Prompt corrective action (+)		0.25 (12.2)	0.24 (12.2)					0.22 (14.7)		
Line of business restrictions (+)		−0.01 (0.6)	−0.02 (1.2)						−0.04 (3.6)	
Foreign ownership (−)		−0.24 (3.6)								−0.25 (3.7)
R-squared/DW	0.616 2.10	0.660 2.02	0.647 2.01	0.623 2.08	0.622 2.09	0.616 2.10	0.619 2.09	0.643 2.04	0.618 2.08	0.62 2.12

Sample: *Pool74*: 74 countries; quarterly data 1990Q1-2000Q4; method: pooled least squares
The estimated equation is $\Delta\ln(a_t - a_{t-1}) = \alpha + \beta \Delta\ln(d_t - d_{t-1}) + \Sigma_j \gamma_j \Delta\ln(d_t - d_{t-1}) * z_j$. The "level effect" is the coefficient α.
The explanatory variables z_j are *Capindexpc, Officialpc, Privepc, Entrypc, Promptpc, Restrictpc,* and *Foreignown*. Expected sign shown in parenthesis in first column.

Table 1: Sensitivity of Lending to Changes in Deposits: OLS Regressions

see the lending portfolio shrink because they otherwise would be more exposed to loss and enjoy no upside gain from increased risk.

In contrast, banking systems subject mainly to discretionary oversight by official regulators (even if this involves high capital requirements) will be more likely or better able to smooth the impact of deposit fluctuations on loans in order to maintain the comfortable borrowing relationship and steady flow of profits. albeit at the risk of violating regulatory norms.

Banking systems restricted from a wider range of lines of business may also be in a weaker position to insulate their borrowers from deposit fluctuations (e.g., by being unable to switch resources from the other lines). Finally, banking systems with foreign ownership may be better placed to intermediate or raise capital from abroad, thereby insulating the domestic borrowers from domestic deposit shocks.

This gives us predicted signs for each group of variables as shown in the first column of table 1. The regression strategy for the equations reported in this table is a very simple one (and may need to be refined in future work). We simply include any or all of the structural variables as slope-shift (interaction) terms with the (logarithmic) change in deposits d. These structural explanatory variables are drawn from Barth, Caprio, and Levine and are constant for each country.

In general the results are broadly consistent with the expected pattern. We note an especially large and statistically significant effect for the prompt corrective action variable: In regression 1.2 this amplifies the pass-through effect by more than one-third; this suggests that such action may tend to induce a regulatory credit-crunch. The effect of foreign ownership—a kind of buffer that reduces the pass-through from deposits to loans again by more than a third, is also highly significant whether included with the other variables (regression 1.2) or on its own[8] (regression 1.10). Otherwise, the only deviations from predicted signs are in respect of private monitoring (unexpected sign, but anyway insignificant), the official regulatory powers variable that has the expected sign in the multivariate regression, but changes sign when included on its own (regression 1.5), and the line of business restrictions variable, insignificant in the multivariate specifications, but with an unexpected sign when included on its own.

These OLS results need to be subjected to robustness tests of various sorts. One essential is to correct for simultaneity bias, which we do by instrumenting for the change in deposits (the list of instruments are shown in the notes to table 2). When only the instrumented change in deposits is included (regression 2.1) the coefficient is now higher, suggesting approximately 1 for 1 pass-through. Once again, when the other explanatory variables are added, the pattern of signs is broadly in line with expectations—in fact more so, inasmuch as the unexpected sign on official powers in regression 2.5 is now wholly insignificant. The line of business restrictions are now significant in the multivariate regressions with the expected sign. The index of private monitoring also now enters significantly with the expected sign.[9] The estimated effect of prompt corrective action remains significant, though smaller in sign. The impact of foreign ownership is also smaller and is now insignificant in the multivariate specification, though it remains significant on its own in regression 2.10.

Evidently, the econometric model is a very simple one, and the results obtained could be fragile to variations in specification, and in particular to omitted variables

Equation no:	2.1	2.2	2.3	2.4	2.5	2.6	2.7	2.8	2.9	2.10
Level effect	1.04 (44.8)	0.95 (22.8)	0.91 (26.2)	0.98 (36.2)	1.03 (38.6)	1.00 (41.3)	1.02 (41.2)	0.96 (29.7)	1.02 (42.0)	1.09 (34.4)
Capital rules (−)		−0.03 (1.2)	−0.04 (1.5)							
Official regulatory powers (−)		−0.08 (2.6)	−0.08 (3.0)	−0.08 (3.5)	0.01 (0.3)					
Private monitoring (+)		0.10 (4.5)	0.09 (4.9)			0.08 (4.5)				
Entry standards (+)		0.04 (1.6)	0.03 (1.3)				0.02 (1.0)			
Prompt corrective action (+)		0.12 (2.9)	0.13 (3.5)					0.09 (3.0)		
Line of business restrictions (+)		0.07 (2.6)	0.08 (3.1)						0.03 (1.1)	
Foreign ownership (−)		−0.09 (0.7)								−0.23 (2.1)
R-squared/DW	0.455 2.06	0.496 2.05	0.466 2.05	0.438 2.10	0.435 2.12	0.440 2.13	0.435 2.12	0.437 2.09	0.436 2.12	0.463 2.12

Sample: *Pool71*: 71 countries; quarterly data 1990Q1-2000Q4; method: pooled least squares
The estimated equation is as in Table 1, except that $\Delta \ln(d_t - d_{t-1})$ is replaced with its predicted value from a regression of $\Delta \ln(d_t - d_{t-1})$ on four lags of $\Delta \ln(a_t - a_{t-1})$; $\Delta \ln(d_t - d_{t-1})$ and $\Delta \ln(f_t - f_{t-1})$ and the values of *Capindex*, *Entrytest*, *Officindex*, *Priviindex*, *Restrict*, and *Prompt*.
The explanatory variables z_i are *Capindexpc*, *Officialpc*, *Privtepc*, *Entrypc*, *Promptpc*, *Restrictpc*, and *Foreignown*. Expected sign shown in parenthesis in first column.

Table 2: Sensitivity of Lending to Changes in Deposits: 2SLS Regressions

bias. Nevertheless, the results seems to confirm the fear of some authors that excessive caution in banking could result in a worsening of the capacity of the banking system to absorb deposit shocks from passing through to loans and advances in the short run. Thus, somewhat paradoxically, the type of regulation that has been shown to be relatively ineffective in protecting banking systems from failure and in helping to develop the banking system long term could help provide some short-term stability.

Foreign ownership is an important exception. Found by others to be good for prudential considerations, it is also a stabilizer in the present context, likely because it brings a benefit, greater diversification, that adds to stability in the short and long term.

3.2.3 Capital Shocks and Loan Growth

How is loan growth affected by shocks to banking confidence? The most obvious way in which our balance sheet data can be used to throw light on this question is by examining what happens to loans after a decline in bank capital. Do banks raise their credit standards, thereby slowing loan growth? Timing is important here. A revaluation of the loan portfolio following recognition of loan losses is a major source of variation in bank capital. This is a mechanical accounting effect, and not one that we wish to confuse with a behavioral response of lending to heightened portfolio risk and reduced capitalization. Therefore, in contrast to the deposit effect, which we allowed in the previous section to be simultaneous within the same quarter, we need to examine changes in a which follow changes in c. Capital can also change for other reasons, including new issues, retained earnings, etc. So it is at best a very noisy indicator of confidence based on recent loan-loss experience (and one could do a lot better with more detailed income statement data) but it is the closest thing in the dataset we are using here.

Assuming that the confidence impact changes occur mainly in the year following a change in capital, we adopt the change in capital over the four previous quarters as our main explanatory variable. Various functional forms could be employed. In this preliminary effort, we have chosen to restrict the impact to be the same for each of the four quarters (relaxing the restriction risks increasing omitted variables bias in these lightly specified equations). Also, instead of the logarithmic rate of change, we express the change in capital c as a ratio of the contemporaneous loan stock a. Finally, we report regressions corrected for first-order autocorrelation.

The results are in table 3. The patterns obtained confirm those of the previous section. Foreign ownership is again a stabilizing factor, perhaps in this case also reflecting a greater ability by foreign-owned banks to access capital. Also stabilizing (to a lesser extent) is reliance on official prudential regulation. In contrast, the measures of private prudential strength tend to be associated with a higher pass-through of capital changes to lending, as are restrictions on line of business.

3.2.4 Bank Foreign Borrowing and Deposit Shocks

One way of insulating a national banking system from shocks is to offset these shocks by trading in the international capital market. Deposit withdrawals can be replaced, by healthy banks, with funds drawn from the international money market. Likewise, a

Equation no:	3.1	3.2	3.3	3.4	3.5	3.6	3.7	3.8	3.9	3.10
Level effect	0.59 (24.0)	0.53 (12.2)	0.40 (15.0)	0.53 (21.1)	0.55 (22.1)	0.55 (23.0)	0.58 (23.4)	0.46 (17.4)	0.59 (23.8)	0.76 (21.6)
Capital rules (−)		−0.05 (1.7)	−0.08 (2.8)							
Official regulatory powers (−)		−0.04 (1.1)	−0.09 (2.7)	−0.18 (6.4)						
Private monitoring (+)		0.10 (4.2)	0.14 (6.5)			0.13 (6.1)				
Entry standards (+)		0.02 (0.8)	0.01 (0.3)				0.01 (0.6)			
Prompt corrective action (+)		0.28 (6.3)	0.31 (7.6)					0.29 (9.3)		
Line of business restrictions (+)		0.10 (3.3)	0.10 (3.9)						0.00 (0.0)	
Foreign ownership (−)		−0.47 (3.3)			0.12 (4.9)					−0.66 (5.8)
AR(1)	0.35 (17.5)	0.28 (12.8)	0.28 (13.3)	0.33 (16.7)	0.34 (17.3)	0.32 (15.8)	0.35 (17.5)	0.32 (16.1)	0.35 (17.5)	0.34 (16.0)
R-squared/DW	0.434 2.17	0.492 2.13	0.470 2.12	0.444 2.17	0.440 2.19	0.443 2.14	0.434 2.17	0.456 2.18	0.434 2.17	0.465 2.17

Sample: *Pool71*: 71 countries; quarterly data 1990Q1-2000Q4; method: autoregressive pooled least squares (eviews)

The estimated equation is $\Delta \ln(a_t - a_{t-1}) = \alpha + \beta \, \Sigma_{\tau=1,4} \Delta\ln(c_{t-\tau} - c_{t-\tau-1})/a_{t-\tau} + \Sigma_j \gamma_j \{\Sigma_{\tau=1,4} \Delta\ln(c_{t-\tau} - c_{t-\tau-1})/a_{t-\tau}\} *z_j$. The "level effect" is the coefficient α.

The explanatory variables z_j are *Capindexpc, Officialpc, Priviepc, Entrypc, Promptpc, Restrictpc,* and *Foreignown*. Expected sign shown in parenthesis in first column.

Table 3: Sensitivity of Lending to Previous Changes in Capital: OLS Regressions

surplus of deposit funds can be placed in the international market. This is a potentially important form of insulation provided by a banking system that is well integrated with the world financial markets. Using our data, a small modification of the method already applied throws light on the extent to which foreign borrowing has in practice been used in this way.

The regressions reported in tables 4 and 5 explain changes in net foreign liabilities of the banking system (the change normalized, as in the figures above, as a share of the total of $a + b$) as a function of the logarithmic change in deposits. The same explanatory variables (slope-shifts) are used as before. A banking system that offsets deposit outflows with foreign borrowing will have a negative coefficient on the change in deposits (level effect). Slope-shift factors that increase the insulation will show up with negative coefficients.

Table 4 shows the OLS results. Once again the pattern is generally as expected from the framework discussed above. On average, additional foreign borrowing as a share of the balance sheet pseudo-total $a + b$ is about 11 percent of the logarithmic change in deposits, implying that about 15 percent of the deposit shock is insulated on average (regression 4.1). The multivariate regression 4.2 has the expected values for all of the coefficients, and displays a very strong insulating effect from foreign ownership.

However, turning to table 5, a caveat is indicated, as the results do not come through as clearly for the two-stages least squares (2SLS) estimates. The signs are mostly the same, but size and significance have fallen. (The line-of-business restrictions variable is significant but with an unexpected sign). Also the R-squared values are low—some of them, not even statistically significant using F-tests. This suggests that the instruments have not been strong enough to identify the actual effects reliably.

Nevertheless, the main conclusion is that foreign ownership is a stabilizing force, while other regime features known to be good for long-term prudential and financial development goals are not.

4. Concluding Remarks

Previous work on prudential banking policy has rightly emphasized the importance of placing a great deal of reliance on the risk management capacity and incentive of informed market participants. That is the way to reduced risk of crisis and to long-term financial deepening.

At the same time, there remains a nagging concern that tightly managed banking systems could underperform in terms of insulating the macroeconomy from short-term volatility. Our analysis of quarterly aggregate banking balance sheet data from more than 70 countries suggests that these concerns are not altogether without foundation. The seeming paradox between the short-term and long-term effects of some features of the regulatory environment can be readily dispelled, as it likely is that by forcing greater adjustment to short-term changes, private monitoring may be better at preventing the buildup of large losses. Unless either markets or officials become able to forecast accurately which shocks are permanent and which are transitory, a policy of quicker adjustment of loans to deposits appears to be the better way to ensure the

Equation no:	4.1	4.2	4.3	4.4	4.5	4.6	4.7	4.8	4.9	4.10
Level effect	−0.11 (14.7)	−0.15 (11.7)	−0.03 (1.4)	−0.15 (19.6)	−0.13 (16.7)	−0.11 (15.3)	−0.11 (15.0)	−0.19 (20.4)	0.11 (14.8)	−0.05 (4.8)
Capital rules (−)		−0.07 (7.4)	−0.04 (2.8)							
Official regulatory powers (−)		−0.02 (2.1)	−0.01 (0.8)	−0.12 (14.5)	0.05 (7.9)					
Private monitoring (+)			0.04 (3.2)			0.04 (6.8)				
Entry standards (+)		0.03 (3.8)	−0.01 (0.5)							
		0.04 (5.6)								
Prompt corrective action (+)		0.10 (7.7)	0.03 (1.3)				0.03 (5.1)			
Line of business restrictions (+)		−0.04 (3.8)	−0.04 (2.8)					0.13 (13.8)		
Foreign ownership (−)		−0.26 (5.5)							−0.06 (8.3)	−0.33 (7.6)
R-squared/DW	0.073 1.87	0.21 1.90	0.022 2.08	0.138 1.90	0.093 1.88	0.088 1.92	0.081 1.88	0.132 1.87	0.095 1.85	0.097 1.90

Sample: *Pool71*: 71 countries; quarterly data 1990Q1–2000Q4; method: pooled least squares
The estimated equation is $\Delta \ln(f_t - f_{t-1})/(a_t + b_t) = \alpha + \beta \Delta \ln(d_t - d_{t-1}) + \Sigma_j \gamma_j \Delta \ln(d_t - d_{t-1})^* z_j$. The "level effect" is the coefficient α.
The explanatory variables z_j are *Capindexpc, Officialpc, Priviepc, Entrypc, Promptpc, Restrictpc,* and *Foreignown.* Expected sign shown in parenthesis in first column.

Table 4: Response of Bank Foreign Borrowing to Deposit Changes: OLS Regressions

Equation no:	5.1	5.2	5.3	5.4	5.5	5.6	5.7	5.8	5.9	5.10
Level effect	0.01 (0.7)	0.01 (0.3)	-0.03 (1.4)	-0.03 (1.9)	-0.06 (0.4)	-0.01 (0.6)	0.01 (1.0)	-0.03 (1.8)	0.02 (1.8)	0.01 (0.6)
Capital rules (−)		-0.03 (2.1)	-0.04 (2.8)							
Official regulatory powers (−)		-0.00 (0.1)	-0.01 (0.8)	-0.07 (5.1)	0.03 (2.2)					
Private monitoring (+)						0.05 (5.2)				
Entry standards (+)		0.03 (2.2)	0.04 (3.2)							
		-0.00 (0.2)	-0.01 (0.5)							
Prompt corrective action (+)		0.03 (1.2)	0.03 (1.3)				-0.02 (1.2)	0.06 (3.4)		
Line of business restrictions (+)		-0.04 (2.2)	-0.04 (2.8)						-0.07 (4.9)	
Foreign ownership (−)		-0.14 (1.8)								-0.01 (2.9)
R-squared/DW	0.000 2.02	0.02 2.09	0.022 2.08	0.011 2.04	0.002 2.08	0.011 2.04	0.001 2.02	0.005 2.03	0.010 2.05	0.004 2.03

Sample: *Pool71*: 71 countries; quarterly data 1990Q1-2000Q4; method: pooled least squares
The estimated equation is as in table 4, except that $\Delta \ln(d_t - d_{t-1})$ is replaced with its predicted value from a regression of $\Delta \ln(d_t - d_{t-1})$ on four lags of $\Delta \ln(a_t - a_{t-1})$, $\Delta \ln(d_t - d_{t-1})$, and $\Delta \ln(f_t - f_{t-1})$ and the values of *Capindex, Entrytest, Officindex, Privtindex, Restrict,* and *Prompt.*

Table 5: Response of Bank Foreign Borrowing to Deposit Changes: 2SLS Regressions

medium-term stability of the economy and the banking system, admittedly at the expense of the short-term stability of the former.

Fortunately, there appears to be one tool that authorities can use to improve both short-term and long-term stability, and that is greater reliance on foreign ownership. Greater foreign ownership appears to add diversification to all economies, large and small, but is especially important to the many small economies around the world. Although foreign entry is never popular with the current owners of the banking system, as noted in a recent report (World Bank, 2001), authorities need to recall that what matters for growth and development is access to good quality financial services, not who provides them.

*Gerard Caprio, Jr., holds the joint appointment of director, Financial Policy and Strategy Group, in the World Bank's Financial Sector Operations Vice Presidency, and manager, Financial Sector Research, in the bank's Development Research Group. Patrick Honohan is a lead economist in the World Bank's Development Research Group and adviser in the bank's Financial Sector Strategy and Policy Department. This research could not have been completed without the help of Xin Chen and Anqing Shi, both of whom provided extraordinary research assistance. The authors are also grateful to Ross Levine for helpful comments. The findings do not necessarily represent the opinions of the World Bank, its management, the executive directors, or the countries they represent.

Notes

1. The major source of most of this data is the World Bank's survey of regulation (Barth, Caprio, and Levine, 2001a).

2. Easterly, Islam, and Stiglitz, (2000) found that volatility decreased with financial sector development until very high levels of development are reached when volatility appears to grow.

3. Clarke, Cull, and Martinez-Peria (2001) also show that access to credit by small- and medium-scale enterprises is greater with a higher foreign banking presence. Since many countries have resorted to expensive directing credit programs to solve this access problem, this finding would also suggest that foreign bank entry improves long-term stability, as well.

4. Detailed definitions are available from the authors.

5. The figure shows the mean over 71 countries for each country's mean on quarterly data during 1990Q1–2000Q4.

6. And, according to the finance and growth literature, loans and advances are the key channel from finance to growth.

7. This finding relates to high-frequency fluctuations and does not contradict previous evidence that the odds of a banking crisis are lower in such systems.

8. By "on its own" we mean that the variable is included as the only slope-shift (interaction) term with the logarithmic change in deposits. A single constant term is included but not reported in all the regressions of tables 1 and 2.

9. One of the components of this index captures the role of rating agencies, often thought to induce a procyclical tendency.

References

Agenor, Pierre-Richard, Joshua Aizenman, and Alex Hoffmaister, 2000, "The Credit Crunch in East Asia: What Can Bank Excess Liquid Assets Tell Us?," National Bureau of Economic Research, working paper, No. 7951.

Allen, Franklin, and Douglas Gale, 2000, *Comparing Financial Systems*, Boston: MIT Press.

Barth, James, R., Gerard Caprio, Jr., and Ross Levine, 2001a, "The Regulation and Supervision of Banks Around the World: A New Database," in *Integrating Emerging Market Countries into the Global Financial System, Brookings-Wharton Papers on Financial Services*, Robert E. Litan and Richard Herring, eds., Washington, DC: Brookings Institution Press.

_____, 2001b, "Bank Regulation and Supervision: What Works Best," World Bank, Policy Research, mimeo, working paper, No. 2725.

Beck, Thorsten, Mattias Lundberg, and Giovanni Majnoni, 2001, "Financial Intermediary Development and Economic Volatility: Do Intermediaries Dampen or Magnify Shocks?," World Bank Policy Research, working paper, No. 2707.

Berger, Allen N., Margaret K. Kyle, and Joseph M. Scalise, 2001, "Did U.S. Bank Supervisors Get Tougher During the Credit Crunch? Did They Get Easier During the Banking Boom? Did It Matter to Bank Lending?," in *Prudential Supervision: What Works and What Doesn't*, Frederic S. Mishkin, ed., Cambridge, MA: National Bureau of Economic Research.

Berger, Allen, Robert DeYoung, Hesna Genay, and Gregory F. Udell, 2000, "Globalization of Financial Institutions: Evidence from Cross-Border Banking Performance," in *Brookings-Wharton Papers on Financial Services*, Vol. 3, Robert E. Litan and Anthony M. Santomero, eds., Washington, DC: Brookings Institution Press.

Bernanke, Ben, 1983, "Nonmonetary Effects of the Financial Crisis in the Propagation of the Great Depression," *American Economic Review*, Vol. 73, No. 3, pp. 257–276.

Bernanke, Ben, and Mark Gertler, 1989, "Agency Costs, Net Worth, and Business Fluctuations," *American Economic Review*, Vol. 79, No. 1, pp. 14–31.

Bernanke, Ben, and Cara Lown, 1991, "The Credit Crunch," *Brookings Papers on Economic Activity*, No. 2, pp. 205–248.

Calomiris, Charles W., 1989, "Do 'Vulnerable' Economies Need Deposit Insurance?: Lessons from the U.S. Agricultural Boom and Bust of the 1920s," Federal Reserve Bank of Chicago, working paper, No. WP-89-18, October.

Caprio, Gerard, and Patrick Honohan, 1999, "Beyond Capital Ideals: Restoring Banking Stability," *Journal of Economic Perspectives*, Vol. 13, No. 4, pp. 43–64.

Clarke, George, Robert Cull, and Maria Soledad Martinez Peria, 2001, "Does Foreign Bank Penetration Reduce Access to Credit in Developing Countries? Evidence from Asking Borrowers," World Bank, Policy Research, working paper, No. 2716.

Crystal, Jennifer, Gerard Dages, and Linda Goldberg, 2001, "Does Foreign Ownership Contribute to Sounder Banks in Emerging Markets? The Latin American Experience," Federal Reserve Bank of New York, staff report, No. 137.

Demirgüç-Kunt, Asli, Ross Levine, and Hong-Ghi Min, 1998, "Opening to Foreign Banks: Issues of Stability, Efficiency and Growth," in *The Implications of Globalization of World Financial Markets*, Alan Meltzer, ed., Seoul: Bank of Korea.

Goldberg, Linda, 2001, "When Is U.S. Bank Lending to Emerging Markets Volatile?," Federal Reserve Bank of New York, staff report, No. 119.

Easterly, William, Roumeen Islam, and Joseph E. Stiglitz, 2001, "Shaken and Stirred: Explaining Growth Volatility," in *Annual Bank Conference on Development Economics, 2000*, Bruno Pleskovic and Joseph Stiglitz, eds., Washington, DC: World Bank.

Ding, Wei, Ilker Domac, and Giovanni Ferri, 1998, "Is There a Credit Crunch in East Asia?," World Bank, Policy Research, working paper, No. 1959.

Ferri, Giovanni, Li-Gang Liu, and Giovanni Majnoni, 2001, "The Role of Rating Agency Assessments in Less Developed Countries: Impact of the Proposed Basel Guidelines," *Journal of Banking and Finance*, Vol. 25, No. 1, pp. 115–148.

Gertler, Mark, and Andrew Rose, 1994, "Finance, Public Policy and Growth," in *Financial Reform: Theory and Experience*, Gerard Caprio, Izak Atiyas, and James A. Hanson, eds., Cambridge, UK: Cambridge University Press.

Greenwald, Bruce C., and Joseph E. Stiglitz, 1993, "Financial Market Imperfections and Business Cycles," *Quarterly Journal of Economics*, Vol. 108, No. 1, pp. 77–114.

Hoggarth, Glenn, Ricardo Reis, and Victoria Saporta, 2002, "Cost of Bank Instability: Some Empirical Evidence," *Journal of Banking and Finance*, Vol. 26, No. 5, pp. 825–855.

International Monetary Fund (IMF), 1998, *World Economic Outlook*, Washington, DC: IMF, May.

John, Kose, Anthony Saunders, and Lemma Senbet, 2000, "A Theory of Bank Regulation and Management Compensation," *Review of Financial Studies*, Vol. 13, pp. 95–125.

Jordan, John, Joe Peek, and Eric Rosengren, 2000, "The Market Reaction to the Disclosure of Supervisory Actions: Implications for Bank Transparency," *Journal of Financial Intermediation*, Vol. 9, No. 3, pp. 298–319.

Kiyotaki, Nobuhiro, and John H. Moore, 1997, "Credit Cycles," *Journal of Political Economy*, Vol. 105, No. 2, pp. 211–248.

Levine, Ross, 1997, "Financial Development and Economic Growth: Views and Agenda," *Journal of Economic Literature*, Vol. 35, pp. 688–726.

_____, 1996, "Foreign Banks, Financial Development and Economic Growth," in *International Financial Markets: Harmonization versus Competition*, Claude E. Barfield, ed., Washington, DC: AEI Press.

Peek, Joe, and Eric Rosengren, 2000, "Collateral Damage: Effects of the Japanese Bank Crisis on Real Activity in the United States," *American Economic Review*, Vol. 90, No. 1, pp. 30–45.

_____, 1995, "Bank Regulatory Agreements and Real Estate Lending," *Real Estate Economics*, Vol. 24, No. 1, pp. 55–73.

World Bank, 2001, *Finance for Growth: Policy Choices in a Volatile World,* Washington, DC: World Bank.

Chapter 25
A Global Perspective on Extreme Currency Linkages

Philipp Hartmann*
European Central Bank and Center for Economic Policy Research

Stefan Straetmans
Maastricht University

and

Casper de Vries
Erasmus University Rotterdam

1. Introduction

Various financial crises during the 1990s have led policymakers, market participants, and academic scholars to make special efforts to better understand the spreading of instability across international capital markets and take precautions against widespread collapse. On the policy side the international financial institutions (International Monetary Fund (IMF), The World Bank Group, Bank for International Settlements, Financial Stability Forum, etc. ...), central banks, and national supervisory bodies spent extra efforts to improve macro-prudential surveillance and regulations of financial institutions (see, e.g., Hunter, Kaufman, and Krueger, 1999). On the market side, new portfolio risk management and hedging tools were developed and new institutions were built to ensure safer cross-border settlement procedures (see, e.g., the Continuous Linked Settlement Bank for foreign exchange transactions). Finally, a new theoretical and empirical literature on systemic risk and contagion has emerged in academia and policy research departments that covers the breadth, underlying causes, and propagation mechanisms of financial crises (see De Bandt and Hartmann, 2000, for a recent survey).

Almost by definition foreign exchange markets are a primary locus of the international transmission of shocks and financial crises. Foreign exchange spot and derivatives markets are the largest financial markets in the world. For the international investor, these markets connect money, bond, and stock markets of different countries. Investors' benchmark performance in their respective home currency can change dramatically even if a foreign investment's local performance does not. Even market-oriented economists observe occasionally long-term misalignments of exchange rates, biasing project performance from the perspective of an outside investor. Moreover, the occasional sudden jumps in exchange rates cause heavy (short-term) losses to financial institutions caught on the wrong side of the market. At least the former can also have important macroeconomic implications for open economies. For these reasons we want to focus on extreme movements observed in global currency markets and particularly the co-movements of extreme exchange rate returns in this paper. We ask the question whether certain currencies are more prone to crashes than other currencies and whether certain currency pairs crash together more frequently than others. We quantify the likelihood of extreme currency crashes and co-crashes for a sample of four major industrial countries and 10 nonindustrial countries, covering four continents. The sample that we use covers almost 22 years of weekly exchange rate returns, extending from 1980 to 2001.

Our methodological approach is extreme value analysis (EVA), the statistical technique for studying the tail behavior of distributions. This technique is particularly well designed to address the occurrence of financial market crises, which are rare events located far out in the tails of empirical return distributions. In a univariate setting this approach has been used to study the frequency of currency market (Koedijk, Schafgans, and de Vries, 1990; Hols and de Vries, 1991), stock market (Jansen and de Vries, 1991; Longin, 1996), and bond market crashes (Hartmann, Straetmans, and de Vries, 2001) in industrial countries. Koedijk, Stork, and de Vries (1992) study the tail behavior of 12 South American black market exchange rates. In this paper we also provide a univariate analysis of the fatness of exchange rate tails and the likelihood of currency market crashes. In contrast to the previous literature, however, we also include currencies from Asia and Africa and use a more recent sample period. More importantly, we extend the analysis of extreme exchange rate fluctuations by a bivariate perspective, measuring the co-occurrence of currency market crashes (and booms).

We apply the conditional co-crash measure presented in Straetmans (2000), Embrechts, de Haan, and Huang (2000) and Hartmann, Straetmans, and de Vries (2001) to industrial country and emerging market exchange rates. This measure specifies, for example, how likely it is that the yen and the mark simultaneously depreciate by more than 10 percent against the dollar, given that at least one of the two is falling by this magnitude. An advantage of the semi-parametric estimator we use for our co-crash measure is that we do not have to assume a uniform probability law for the very diverse emerging market currency returns. Moreover, the measure easily captures non-normal type of dependencies, in contrast for example to traditional correlation based analysis. The former aspect may be particularly valuable when many markets are studied and compared, in particular for emerging market currencies, as is the case in the present paper. The latter aspect is of course particularly relevant for crisis situations, since extreme dependency may be different from the dependency observed in the center of return distributions.

Bivariate extreme value analysis has recently been applied to stock market returns by Straetmans (2000) and by Longin and Solnik (2001) parametrically. Ramchand and Susmel (1998) identify large and small stock market spillovers using a bivariate regime-switching autoregressive conditional heteroscedasticity (ARCH) model. Bae, Karolyi, and Stulz (2001) again follow a different line by applying a multinomial logistic regression model to a sample of 17 emerging market stock indices. Hartmann et al. (2001) apply bivariate nonparametric EVA to stock and government bond markets to also study crises cutting across different asset classes and the "flight to quality" phenomenon.[1]

Our work is also related to the literature on the co-occurrence of speculative currency attacks. Eichengreen, Rose, and Wyplosz (1996) estimate a binary probit model for a panel of 20 industrial country currencies to test whether the occurrence of a speculative attack in one country increases the probability of a speculative attack in other countries. An important difference between our approach and theirs is that we consider only effective depreciations, whereas their approach also considers unsuccessful currency attacks, by combining exchange rate returns with interest rate differentials and reserve sales in one index of currency crises. They argue that currency crises, defined as an index value of 1.5 standard deviations or more above the sample mean, explain other currency crises beyond macroeconomic fundamentals. Sachs, Tornell, and Velasco (1996), however, argue that most of the 1994–95 Latin American "tequila" currency crises can be explained by domestic fundamentals. Studying five major currency crisis episodes, Glick and Rose (1999) find that currency crises tend to remain regional in scope. They explain this feature with the importance of real trade linkages for the propagation of such crises. Kaminsky and Reinhart (2000) also find that currency crises somewhere in the world have explanatory power for other crises beyond macroeconomic fundamentals, but they pay more attention to extreme outcomes of their crisis index (an outcome three standard deviations above the sample mean is regarded as a crisis). Moreover, they add that international financial linkages may be more important for the propagation of crises than trade linkages. Van Rijckeghem and Weder (2001) provide a refined analysis of the role of financial linkages in joint currency crises, in particular looking at common creditor country effects.

Finally, our analysis is related to theoretical models explaining why greater macroeconomic fluctuations and boom-bust cycles are more frequent in emerging market countries with an intermediate degree of financial development (Aghion, Bacchetta, and Banerjee, 1999) and to "third generation" currency crisis models that explain the propagation of currency crises across countries with exposures in multi-currency fixed exchange rate systems (Buiter, Corsetti, and Pesenti, 1997), with asymmetric information (Drazen, 1998) or with multiple equilibria and self-fulfilling expectations (Masson, 1999).

We proceed as follows. The next section briefly recalls the construction of the co-crash indicator and the estimation techniques. We then address the univariate properties of currency returns, inter alia comparing the tail behavior of emerging market currencies with that of industrial country currencies. Section 4 discusses the joint occurrence of exchange rate crashes (and booms) among industrial countries, and section 5 discusses such occurrences among emerging market countries. Section 6 addresses the extreme linkages between industrial country and emerging market currencies. The final section concludes.

2. A Measure and Estimator of Extreme Currency Linkages

Let us define the nominal bilateral exchange rate e as the number of units of the home currency one has to pay for one unit of some foreign numraire currency. Thus, a home currency depreciation (or devaluation) implies a rise in e, whereas for an appreciation (revaluation) e falls. In order to assess the "systemic" breadth of dramatic depreciations (or appreciations) in foreign exchange markets, we are interested in the probability that an exchange rate e_i changes by a large amount, given that another exchange rate e_j has changed by a large amount. At this stage, we take this conditional probability of a joint currency crisis to be symmetric, i.e., independent of the conditioning and the conditioned currency. Denoting the log first differences of the exchange rates as random variables R_i and R_j and some large conditioning quantile as r this *conditional "co-crash" probability* can be derived from the standard definition of conditional probability as:

1) $P\{R_i > r \text{ and } R_j > r | R_i > r \text{ or } R_j > r\} =$

$$\frac{P\{R_i > r \text{ and } R_j > r\}}{P\{R_i > r \text{ or } R_j > r\}}$$

$$\frac{P\{R_i > r\} + P\{R_j > r\} - P\{R_i > r \text{ or } R_j > r\}}{P\{R_i > r \text{ or } R_j > r\}} =$$

$$\frac{P\{R_i > r\} + P\{R_j > r\}}{1 - P\{R_i \leq r, R_j \leq r\}} - 1.$$

Depending on the type of exchange rate regime one could also speak of an "extreme co-devaluation" or "extreme co-depreciation."

A closely related linkage measure is the *conditional expected number of currency crashes* given that there has been at least one crash. Let 8 stand for the number of currencies that exhibit simultaneous extreme returns beyond ($\kappa = \Sigma_{i=1}^{2} I(R_i > r)$, where I is the indicator function). The expected number of simultaneous currency crashes is given by the conditional expectation:

2) $E[\kappa | \kappa \geq 1, \kappa \in \{1, 2\}] =$

$$\frac{P\{R_i > r \text{ and } R_j \leq r\} + P\{R_i \leq r \text{ and } R_j > r\} + 2P\{R_i > r \text{ and } R_j > r\}}{P\{R_i > r \text{ or } Y > r\}} =$$

$$\frac{P\{R_i > r\} + P\{R_j > r\}}{1 - P\{R_i \leq r \text{ and } R_j \leq r\}}.$$

Trivially, the two extreme linkage measures (1) and (2) are closely related because $E[\kappa|\kappa \geq 1, \kappa \in \{1, 2\}] = P\{\kappa = 2|\kappa \geq 1, \kappa \in \{1, 2\}\} + 1$.

Hence, an alternative interpretation of the extreme linkage indicator (2) is in terms of (1 plus) the conditional probability that both currencies crash given that at least one currency crashes. We report the estimates of the latter measure in this paper. It can be easily generalized to the multivariate case $\kappa > 2$.[2]

The question is how to estimate (2).[3] Since we want to avoid any strong distributional assumptions regarding the tail interdependency of exchange rate returns (for the reasons explained in the introduction), we rely on asymptotic versions of (2). This requires that the conditioning quantile r is taken very far out in the tails. It turns out that our asymptotic extreme linkage measure E_{ij} (for two exchange rates i and j) can be derived from the two marginal crash probabilities ($p_i = P\{R_i > r\}$, $p_j = P\{R_j > r\}$) and the bivariate probability that one or the other market crashes ($p_{ij} = 1 - P\{R_i \leq r$ and $R_j \leq r\}$).

3) $E_{ij} = \dfrac{p_i + p_j}{p_{ij}}$.

In fact, if the joint return distribution of two markets is in the domain of attraction of a bivariate extreme value distribution, then the denominator follows a well-defined limiting function L. The two marginal probabilities are the arguments of this function $p_{ij} = L(p_i, p_j)$. Therefore E_{ij} is estimated in a univariate step ($\hat{p}_i$, $\hat{p}_j$) and a bivariate step ($\hat{p}_{ij}$). Following standard procedure in the literature applying extreme value theory to financial data, we estimate the *univariate* excess probabilities semi-parametrically by inserting the Hill (1975) estimator of the tail index α_i:

4) $\hat{\alpha}_i = \left[\dfrac{1}{m_i} \sum_{M_i=0}^{m_i-1} \ln\left(\dfrac{R_i^{n-M_i, n}}{R_i^{n-m_i, n}}\right)\right]^{-1}$,

in the semi-parametric probability estimator of de Haan, Jansen, Koedijk, and de Vries (1994):

5) $\hat{p}_i = \dfrac{m_i}{n}\left(\dfrac{R_i^{n-m_i, n}}{r}\right)^{\hat{\alpha}_i}$.[4]

Here n stands for the sample size and $R_i^{n-m_i, n}$ is the m_i-th largest depreciation in the spot market i. The number of extreme exchange rate returns m_i that enters the estimation is determined optimally by trading off bias against variance (see, e.g., Embrechts et al., 1997). The lower the tail index α the fatter the tail of the distribution and, therefore, the higher the probability of extreme exchange rate returns.

We estimate the *bivariate* excess probabilities nonparametrically, using Huang's (1992) polar transform. This amounts to counting the instances at which one or both markets experience an extreme return. Technically the estimator reads:

6) $\hat{p}_{ij} \approx \frac{1}{k_{ij}} \hat{d}_{ij} \sum_{l=1}^{n} I(R_i^l > R_i^{n[k_{ij}\cos\hat{\theta}_{ij}],n}$ or $R_i^l > R_i^{n-[k_{ij}\sin\hat{\theta}_{ij}],n})$,

where the angle θ_{ij} and corresponding radius d_{ij} can be consistently estimated as

$\hat{\theta}_{ij}$ = arctan $(\hat{p}_i / \hat{p}_j)$ and $\hat{d}_{ij} = \sqrt{\hat{p}_i^2 + \hat{p}_j^2}$.

Note that $[k_{ij} \sin\hat{\theta}_{ij}]$ is the integer value of $k_{ij} \sin\hat{\theta}_{ij}$ and I denotes the indicator function. Analogous to m_i and m_j in the univariate step, k_{ij} determines the optimal number of extreme observations that enter the bivariate step (trading off bias and variability).

3. Extreme Currency Movements

We discuss first the univariate properties of extreme currency movements, looking at the largest positive and negative returns, the size of estimated left and right tail indices α, and the univariate probabilities of extreme currency returns. We use weekly log returns of nominal exchange rates for six bilateral spot markets of industrial country currencies and 10 bilateral spot markets of emerging market currencies against the U.S. dollar. The sample extends from early 1980 to mid 2001, giving about 1,100 observations.[5] Industrial country currencies were chosen with an eye on their size in global foreign exchange trading, including the U.S. dollar (USD), the German mark (DEM), the Japanese yen (JPY) and the British pound (GBP).[6] The choice of emerging market currencies covered was determined by geographical coverage, data availability, and data reliability. From South America the Chilean peso (CLP), the Colombian peso (COP), and the Venezuelan bolivar (VEB) are covered and from Africa, the South African rand (ZAR).[7] Asia is represented by the Indonesian rupiah (IDR), the Indian rupee (INR), the Thailand baht (THB), the Philippine peso (PHP), the Malaysian ringgit (MYR), and the Pakistan rupee (PKR). We are particularly interested in the comparison of the size and likelihood of extreme exchange rate returns in industrial country currency markets as compared to emerging market country currency markets.

Table 1 displays the three largest positive and negative exchange rate returns for all markets considered. We first concentrate on the historical minima ($R^{l,n}$) and maxima ($R^{n,n}$) across exchange rates. The largest weekly industrial country returns vary between 4.8 percent (the largest appreciation of the pound against the mark in the last 22 years, occurring in October 1992) and 13.7 percent (the largest appreciation of the yen against the mark, happening in October 1998). The former event relates to the pound's rebound after it had been forced out of the European Monetary System (EMS) in September 1992 and the latter to the extreme financial market volatility observed in the aftermath of the Russian and Long-Term Capital Management (LTCM) crises in fall 1998. Our data show very clearly that the dramatic yen appreciation during this episode was a very broad foreign exchange market phenomenon. The three largest industrial country currency returns in our sample all occurred during that week as yen appreciations (against USD, DEM, and GBP). Emerging market extremes range from 6.1 percent for the Indian rupee to 109.9 percent for the Venezuelan bolivar. Whereas

	Extreme currency returns						
	Highest			Lowest		
Rates	$R^{n,n}$	$R^{n-1,n}$	$R^{n-2,n}$	$R^{1,n}$	$R^{2,n}$	$R^{3,n}$
(Cross)	Panel A: Industrial country currencies}					
GBP/USD	10.02	7.04	5.85	−6.35	−6.07	−5.71
	(21/9/92)	(1/2/93)	(8/6/81)}	(15/4/85)	(23/9/85)	(25/3/85)
JPY/USD	5.57	5.44	4.71	−12.80	−6.97	−6.84
	(21/6/93)	(9/11/98)	(12/6/89)	(12/10/98)	(7/9/98)	(30/9/85)
DEM/USD	5.84	5.80	5.32	−6.77	−6.11	−5.42
	(15/5/95)	(14/9/92)	(22/4/91)	(21/9/81)	(23/2/81)	(23/9/85)
JPY/DEM	6.62	5.13	5.00	−13.69	−6.06	−5.7
	(23/2/81)	(4/12/00)	(18/1/99)	(12/10/98)	(10/4/95)	(10/8/81)
GBP/DEM	10.29	6.62	5.33	-4.79	−4.17	−3.77
	(21/9/92)	(23/2/81)	(22/11/82)	(12/10/92)	(30/5/83)	(20/10/80)
JPY/GBP	5.16	4.93	4.82	−12.62	−10.42	−8.11
	(18/1/99)	(9/11/98)	(15/4/85)	(12/10/98)	(21/9/92)	(30/9/85)
(Dollar)	Panel B: Emerging market currencies (USD numeraire)					
Chile	28.18	22.49	22.30	−14.06	−12.81	−12.73
	(16/8/82)	(19/5/80)	(24/9/84)	(24/3/80)	(3/3/80)	(2/6/80)
Colombia	25.10	9.83	9.59	−9.86	−8.57	−8.32
	(30/11/92)	(5/12/88)	(16/12/91)	(23/12/91)	(28/11/88)	(28/10/91)
Venezuela	109.90	67.01	16.05	−19.10	−16.46	−14.36
	(10/10/83)	(4/12/95)	(30/5/94)	(23/6/86)	(15/12/86)	(11/7/94)
South Africa	15.54	14.30	12.04	−13.10	−7.76	−7.70
	(9/9/85)	(19/8/85)	(25/2/85)	(2/9/85)	(13/1/86)	(28/1/85)
Indonesia	37.34	35.62	33.11	−35.37	−16.64	−13.87
	(15/9/86)	(26/1/98)	(15/12/97)	(2/2/98)	(12/10/98)	(25/5/98)
India	17.66	6.31	6.19	−6.14	−5.94	−5.23
	(8/7/91)	(1/3/93)	(1/8/88)	(8/8/88)	(10/7/89)	(29/5/89)
Thailand	15.58	13.41	12.77	−10.49	−9.24	−7.10
	(5/11/84)	(15/12/97)	(12/1/98)	(16/3/98)	(10/11/97)	(2/2/98)
Philippines	24.98	24.33	12.94	−9.48	−7.96	−7.55
	(10/10/83)	(11/6/84)	(15/12/97)	(16/6/86)	(6/7/87)	(10/3/86)
Malaysia	35.69	11.25	10.27	−13.38	−11.83	−11.08
	(2/11/98)	(12/1/98)	(9/3/98)	(5/4/99)	(31/5/99)	(19/1/98)
Pakistan	11.07	8.35	8.18	−10.24	−6.19	−6.11
	(27/7/92)	(20/10/97)	(28/10/96)	(29/6/92)	(18/5/92)	(6/7/87)

Table 1: Historical Extremes of Weekly Industrial Country and Emerging Market Currency Returns, 1980 to 2001

"on average" the minimum emerging market returns (largest appreciations against the dollar) do not seem to be very far out of line with industrial country currency returns, the maximum returns (largest depreciations against the dollar) are (with the exception of Pakistan) strictly larger than extreme industrial country returns. This is evidence that speculative attacks and currency crises are more severe for emerging market currencies than for industrial country currencies.

Generally, one may observe that only a few of the minimal and maximal currency returns occurred at the dates of one of the recent well-known financial crises. Two or three extremes occurred in the fall of 1998 (Russia, LTCM) and another two or three in September 1992 (EMS crisis). At this stage of the analysis it seems that extreme currency returns do not necessarily cluster massively around the well-known recent crisis times. In particular, none of the most extreme emerging market currency returns occurred during the Asian financial crisis of 1997.

The second and third largest currency returns, also shown in table 1, somewhat qualify the impression from the pure maxima and minima, since a few more extremes fall into the well-known crisis times. For example, during the 1998 Russia-LTCM turmoil the Japanese yen experienced its second largest depreciation both against the dollar and against the pound, but the yen also experienced its second largest appreciation against the dollar, illustrating the volatile character of this episode. However, among the emerging market currencies only the Indonesian rupiah experienced its second largest appreciation during this time. The 1997 Asian financial crisis is also more visible from these secondary extremes. Between October and December 1997 the Thai baht experienced its second largest appreciation and depreciation against the dollar over the last 20 years. The Pakistan rupee exhibited its second largest depreciation and the Indonesian rupiah and the Philippine peso, their third largest depreciation. During the 1992 EMS crisis the mark showed its second largest depreciation against the dollar and the Japanese yen showed its second largest appreciation against the pound sterling. We can also observe that many extremes occurred during 1985, the year in which the dollar reached a historical high and then started a long slide against most other industrial country currencies. In particular, around September 1985 the dollar showed extreme downward corrections against the pound, the yen, and the mark. (Among the emerging market currencies, only the rand showed extreme—two-sided —volatility during this year.) Finally, several very large exchange rate fluctuations happened in relation to the international debt crises of the early 1980s.

Looking at the tail indices (α) introduced in the previous section in (4), gives a broader picture than just looking at the few largest extremes. From table 2 it turns out that all emerging market currency tail indices (ranging from 1.2 for Indonesian rupiah depreciations to 2.9 for Pakistan rupee depreciations, as shown in panel B) are smaller than the industrial country currency tail indices (ranging from 3.0 for yen appreciations against the dollar to 5.2 for yen depreciations against the mark, see panel A). In other words, when the whole left and right tails of the return distributions are considered, extreme appreciations as well as extreme depreciations tend to be more frequent in emerging markets. Therefore, our univariate analysis confirms the conventional wisdom that emerging market currencies are much more risky than industrial country currencies.[8]

Panel A: Industrial country currencies

Exchange rate	$\hat{\alpha}$	Left tail $\hat{p} = \hat{P}\{R_i < r\}$ r = −5%	r = −10%	$\hat{\alpha}$	Right tail $\hat{p} = \hat{P}\{R_i > r\}$ r = 5%	R = 10%
GBP/USD	4.39	0.13540	0.00648	3.59	0.23660	0.019670
JPY/USD	4.12	0.41160	0.02367	3.21	0.20690	0.022360
DEM/USD	4.23	0.22430	0.01194	5.00	0.14920	0.004678
JPY/DEM	4.07	0.35390	0.02104	5.22	0.08058	0.002156
GBP/DEM	3.77	0.04949	0.00362	3.28	0.15600	0.016090
JPY/USD	2.96	0.56553	0.07288	4.04	0.15737	0.009550

Panel B: Emerging market currencies

	$\hat{\alpha}$	Left tail $\hat{p} = \hat{P}\{R_i < r\}$ r = 10%	r = −20%	$\hat{\alpha}$	Right tail $\hat{p} = \hat{P}\{R_i > r\}$ r = 10%	R = 20%
Chile	1.61	0.10807	0.03540	1.40	0.29091	0.11022
Colombia	1.70	0.07199	0.02221	2.21	0.09573	0.02069
Venezuela	1.67	0.22622	0.07108	2.11	0.43866	0.10169
South Africa	1.56	0.20264	0.06854	2.20	0.15552	0.03385
Indonesia	1.27	0.38337	0.15875	1.16	0.61049	0.27271
India	2.78	0.02069	0.00301	2.40	0.05305	0.01005
Thailand	2.28	0.05875	0.01206	1.75	0.13524	0.04010
Philippines	2.30	0.08497	0.01723	2.08	0.17106	0.04053
Malaysia	1.37	0.14229	0.05503	1.48	0.13698	0.04894
Pakistan	1.99	0.09229	0.02328	2.92	0.06158	0.00811

Table 2: Univariate Tail Index and Crash Probability Estimates for Weekly Industrial Country and Emerging Market Currency Returns

Our emerging market tail indices are fairly similar to those found by Koedijk, Stork, and de Vries (1992) for monthly returns of a partly overlapping sample of South and Central American currencies. The authors explained the thinner tails of industrial country currency return distributions with stabilizing market forces under floating exchange rates. Maybe a different way to make a similar point is to infer that fixed (but adjustable) exchange rates or exchange rate bands are associated with occasional attacks and currency crises that apparently lead to larger *extreme* exchange rate fluctuations than in the case of floating rates. This point is also underlined by Koedijk et al.'s tables 3 and 4, which show that EMS tail indices indicate higher extreme returns than floating industrial country currency indices. Notice that this property of many fixed exchange rate regimes does not mean that currency volatility is generally higher. Usually extreme volatility is somewhat higher, due to occasional crises and realignments, but regular volatility—towards the interior of the return distribution—is lower.

There are other, potentially related, explanations for the higher frequency of extreme exchange rate returns observed for emerging market currencies. First, these countries tend to be more frequently affected by political instability. Second, many of them also experience more often difficulties in domestic macroeconomic management, such as monetary or budget policies. Third, Aghion et al. (1999) advance a macroeconomic argument explaining boom-bust cycles in emerging market countries with their intermediate degree of financial development. Finally, most of these countries are relatively small compared to the size of international capital flows, so that changes in market expectations may have more dramatic effects on their exchange rates.

Table 2 also provides the (annualized) probabilities associated with the univariate tail behavior for different extreme quantiles (5 percent and 10 percent for industrial country currency returns in panel A and 10 percent and 20 percent for emerging market currency returns in panel B). For example, we find a 0.5 percent probability that a 10 percent weekly depreciation of the mark against the dollar happens over a one-year time horizon (row DEM/USD, column right tail, $r = 10$ percent). In contrast, for emerging market currencies this probability varies between 5.3 percent (Indian rupee) and 61 percent (Indonesian rupiah). By inverting the figures in the table, we can derive the number of years it takes on average to experience a currency crash (or boom) of a given extreme size. For example, a 10 percent slump of the mark against the dollar is expected to happen once every 214 years ($\approx 1/0.004678$), whereas to the yen that would happen on average once every 45 years ($\approx 1/0.02236$). In contrast, such currency crashes are much more regular for emerging markets: They occur on average once every $3^{1}/_{2}$ years for the Chilean peso, every seven years for the Thai baht and every 15 years for the Pakistan rupee (the emerging market currency with the lowest crash probability at the 10 percent return level). Hence, table 2 illustrates more forcefully that extreme currency returns are much more frequent among emerging market currencies than among industrial country currencies, particularly regarding extreme depreciations against the dollar. Compare these estimates to a normal distribution based estimate that predicts weekly depreciations in, for example, the Chilean peso against the dollar of 10 percent or more to happen only once per 7.58×10^{16} years! Needless to say, a normal distribution based analysis would, as for other financial markets, dramatically underestimate the likelihood of extreme currency returns.

4. Extreme Linkages between Industrial Country Currencies

We now turn to the bivariate results for extreme co-movements between currencies. In this section we concentrate on the co-movements between industrial country currencies and in the next section on the co-movements between emerging market currencies. Finally, section 6 looks at the co-movements between industrial countries and emerging market currencies.

We first want to use our extreme currency linkage indicator E_{ij} to estimate the probability that for any two bilateral foreign exchange markets between industrial country currencies both exchange rates exhibit an extreme positive return, given that one of the two exhibits an extreme positive return (first quadrant). Table 3 displays our results for 10 percent and 20 percent conditioning quantiles. Exchange rate returns are calculated as log first differences of the exchange rates indicated, where the exchange

Exchange rate pairs	k	$\hat{\rho}$	$\hat{E}$ r = 10%	$\hat{E}$ r = 20%
		USD numéraire		
DEM/USD-JPY/USD	200	0.536	1.111	1.033
DEM/USD-GBP/USD	150	0.711	1.212	1.085
JPY/USD-GBP/USD	100	0.412	1.138	1.129
		DEM numéraire		
USD/DEM-JPY/DEM	200	0.451	1.112	1.065
USD/DEM-GBP/DEM	300	0.46	1.291	1.215
JPY/DEM-GBP/DEM	125	0.249	1.048	1.026
		JPY numéraire		
USD/JPY-DEM/JPY	200	0.512	1.313	1.314
USD/JPY-GBP/JPY	180	0.612	1.200	1.121
DEM/JPY-GBP/JPY	200	0.746	1.238	1.135
		GBP numéraire		
USD/GBP-DEM/GBP	150	0.298	1.092	1.102
USD/GBP-JPY/GBP	150	0.468	1.170	1.173
DEM/GBP-JPY/GBP	150	0.459	1.118	1.135
		Mixed pairs		
DEM/USD-JPY/GBP	175	−0.096	1.031	1.035
GBP/USD-JPY/DEM	150	−0.287	1.003	1.008
JPY/USD-GBP/DEM	150	−0.207	1.031	1.032

Table 3: Extreme Linkages between Industrial Country Currencies (1st Quadrant)

rates are expressed as the number of units in the first currency one has to pay for one unit of the second currency. In other words, a positive return corresponds to a depreciation of the first currency with respect to the second. Hence, the estimates in the table refer to the conditional probabilities of joint depreciations of the first currencies in the two exchange rate pairs. It also contains the regular correlation coefficient ρ (for the whole return distribution) and the value of k, determining how many observations entered the estimator E_{ij}. The table is organized in five panels, where in each of the first four one currency is the common denominator, whereas the last panel covers mixed pairs.

The first observation from table 3 is that extreme co-movements between industrial country currencies can be quite different depending on which currency pair one is looking at and which base currency is used. For example, every third crash of the dollar or the mark against the yen is a joint crash, whereas less than every 20th crash of the yen or the pound against the mark is a joint crash. Overall, however, co-crash probabilities among industrial countries are quite high, varying for most currency pairs and base currencies between 10 percent and 30 percent (almost irrespective of the conditioning quantile). These orders of magnitude are reminiscent of the conditional probabilities of joint crashes in Group of Five stock markets, as found in Hartmann,

Straetmans, and de Vries (2001), but larger than for joint government bond market crashes or joint stock-bond crashes. We can also see that extreme co-movements are quite different for different base currencies. This leads us to the following interpretations of the results from a risk management perspective: For a yen-based investor, holding a portfolio of dollar and mark/euro positions is extremely risky, providing hardly any diversification benefits in a crisis situation. Perhaps less surprisingly, the same applies to joint positions in dollar and pound for mark-based (or euro-based) investors. Naturally, the probabilities are lower and also more difficult to interpret for the mixed exchange rate pairs, where the number of country factors is increased from three to four.

Table 4 contains the same information for the third quadrant, i.e. for joint extreme appreciations of the first currencies vis-à-vis the respective base currency. The table confirms that conditional co-boom probabilities vary a lot across currency pairs but most tend to be quite high and that base currencies tend to matter a lot. The interesting new information in table 4 is that whereas in some cases the left-tail joint probabilities and the right-tail joint probabilities are quite similar, there are several important cases in which they differ substantially. For example, whereas the probability of a joint extreme depreciation of dollar and mark against the yen is large (about one-third), the

Exchange rate pairs	k	$\hat{E}$ $r = -10\%$	$\hat{E}$ $r = -20\%$
		USD numéraire	
DEM/USD-JPY/USD	300	1.308	1.282
DEM/USD-GBP/USD	300	1.365	1.346
JPY/USD-GBP/USD	100	1.087	1.078
		DEM numéraire	
USD/DEM-JPY/DEM	50	1.147	1.088
USD/DEM-GBP/DEM	150	1.176	1.152
JPY/DEM-GBP/DEM	120	1.058	1.069
		JPY numéraire	
USD/JPY-DEM/JPY	120	1.039	1.015
USD/JPY-GBP/JPY	150	1.193	1.137
DEM/JPY-GBP/JPY	100	1.161	1.073
		GBP numéraire	
USD/GBP-DEM/GBP	140	1.176	1.184
USD/GBP-JPY/GBP	250	1.171	1.126
DEM/GBP-JPY/GBP	200	1.141	1.119
		Mixed pairs	
DEM/USD-JPY/GBP	100	1.017	1.014
GBP/USD-JPY/DEM	100	1.024	1.017
JPY/USD-GBP/DEM	50	1.028	1.029

Table 4: Extreme Linkages between Industrial Country Currencies (3rd Quadrant)

probability of a joint extreme appreciation of dollar and mark against the yen is markedly lower (2 percent to 4 percent). The reversed phenomenon occurs for the mark and yen against the dollar. In other words, in contrast to the univariate exchange rate tails described in table 2, bivariate exchange rate tail behavior can exhibit asymmetries. This suggests that the importance of country factors in extreme exchange rate returns is not uniform.

The relevance of extreme co-movements in industrial country currency markets is further underlined by the simple observation that the conditional probability of experiencing an extreme exchange rate appreciation or depreciation in one market, given that there was one in another market, is substantially larger than the univariate (unconditional) probability of having such an extreme return in the former market. Moreover, similar as for univariate extreme quantile probabilities, an assessment of extreme co-movements on the basis of the bivariate normal distribution (using the sample means, variances, and covariances) would lead to a tremendous underestimation of spillover probabilities.[9] Note that this is, however, a distinct point from the better known observation that financial market return distributions have fat tails, since the statistical concepts of tail dependence and tail fatness are unrelated (even though financial data both are heavy tailed and display asymptotic dependence). Finally, tables 3 and 4 make clear that simple correlations are unreliable measures of the degree of dependence in the tails of exchange rate return distributions. These three points are qualitatively quite similar to the results we found earlier for stock and government bond markets.

We also calculated similar tables for the second and fourth quadrants of extreme exchange rate returns, which describe extreme opposite movements in different currencies and may, therefore, be indicative of flight movements from one currency to another. We only report here that the related probabilities turned out to be much lower than the joined booms or crashes discussed before. For most currency pairs and base currencies the probabilities were 1 percent to 2 percent or even much lower. Apparently, contagion phenomena and joint crashes are much more frequent during crises within foreign exchange markets than flight phenomena from one currency to another.[10] For interested readers, the detailed results are available from the authors on request.

Summing up this section, it can be concluded that, despite differences across currencies, there are quite some co-movements among industrial country spot foreign exchange markets in critical times. For many exchange rates these are comparable to the extreme dependence among industrial country stock markets. These findings complement the univariate results of the preceding section, which already indicated currencies as a relatively risky asset class.

5. Extreme Linkages between Emerging Market Currencies

We now come to the results for emerging market currencies and compare them to the results for industrial country currencies discussed above. Table 5 shows our extreme linkage indicator estimates for the 10 emerging market countries and three conditioning quantiles (20 percent and 30 percent), as well as regular correlation coefficients

Exchange rate pairs	k	$\hat{\rho}$	$\hat{E}$ r = 20%	$\hat{E}$ r = 30%
Chile-Colombia	150	0.053	1.061	1.035
Chile-Venezuela	150	0.015	1.071	1.070
Chile-South Africa	150	0.027	1.053	1.059
Chile-Indonesia	200	0.030	1.085	1.078
Chile-India	200	0.019	1.025	1.008
Chile-Thailand	125	0.066	1.061	1.045
Chile-Philippines	40	0.047	1.027	1.027
Chile-Malaysia	200	0.057	1.082	1.085
Chile-Pakistan	300	0.058	1.036	1.022
Colombia-Venezuela	250	0.034	1.057	1.055
Colombia-South Africa	120	0.024	1.058	1.057
Colombia-Indonesia	180	0.045	1.016	1.020
Colombia-India	90	0.042	1.019	1.017
Colombia-Thailand	225	0.096	1.102	1.098
Colombia-Philippines	30	0.032	1.035	1.002
Colombia-Malaysia	70	0.004	1.019	1.021
Colombia-Pakistan	100	0.046	1.037	1.052
Venezuela-South Africa	175	−0.003	1.059	1.063
Venezuela-Indonesia	250	0.012	1.051	1.044
Venezuela-India	250	−0.000	1.036	1.026
Venezuela-Thailand	60	0.034	1.024	1.032
Venezuela-Philippines	225	0.278	1.071	1.073
Venezuela-Malaysia	250	0.002	1.076	1.089
Venezuela-Pakistan	25	0.019	1.076	1.056
South Africa-Indonesia	150	0.038	1.027	1.017
South Africa-India	75	0.153	1.036	1.035
South Africa-Thailand	200	0.091	1.132	1.133
South Africa-Philippines	175	0.061	1.081	1.083
South Africa-Malaysia	40	0.117	1.070	1.057
South Africa-Pakistan	80	0.106	1.048	1.020
Indonesia-India	70	0.033	1.022	1.022
Indonesia-Thailand	250	0.362	1.071	1.054
Indonesia-Philippines	140	0.241	1.053	1.038
Indonesia-Malaysia	120	0.365	1.151	1.134
Indonesia-Pakistan	300	0.035	1.022	1.008
India-Thailand	175	0.158	1.072	1.046
India-Philippines	200	0.181	1.106	1.092
India-Malaysia	250	0.081	1.070	1.039
India-Pakistan	280	0.304	1.270	1.262
Thailand-Philippines	190	0.319	1.210	1.203
Thailand-Malaysia	150	0.263	1.179	1.178
Thailand-Pakistan	250	0.147	1.052	1.038
Philippines-Malaysia	250	0.154	1.158	1.157
Philippines-Pakistan	250	0.235	1.074	1.063
Malaysia-Pakistan	250	0.064	1.038	1.026

Table 5: Extreme Linkages between Emerging Market Currencies

and the parameter k. The upper part of the table concentrates on the co-movements between South American dollar rates and between those and the other Asian and African dollar rates. The lower part focuses on the remaining pairs between Asian and African currencies against the dollar.

The first and perhaps most important observation from table 5 compared to table 3 is that emerging market currency extreme co-movements are not more pronounced than industrial country currency extreme co-movements. Actually, many of the non-East Asian currency pairs rather tend to be less interlinked in critical situations like 20 percent weekly depreciations than industrial country currencies.

The second important observation from comparing the upper part of the table with the lower part is that emerging market currency extreme co-movements within South America seem rather weak, the probability of experiencing a joint crash between any two pairs of the three South American currencies given that one experienced a crash varies between 3.5 percent and 7 percent. The same figures for the four East Asian currencies (INR, MYR, PHP, THB) range between 4 percent and 27 percent, with most being above 13 percent. Hence, with few exceptions currency crisis linkages between the countries most affected by the Asian crisis of 1997 seem to be much stronger than the crisis linkages between Latin American countries. The Asian "flu" seems to be much more severe and recurrent than "tequila" effects. For example, already Sachs, Tornell, and Velasco (1996) observed that most events around the 1994–95 Mexican crisis could be explained with domestic macroeconomic fundamentals of Latin American countries. It is interesting to remark in this context that in a recent IMF working paper Loayza, Lopez, and Ubide (1999) observed that regular (noncrisis) fluctuations in real value-added gross domestic product in Latin America between 1970 and 1994 was mainly characterized by country specific components, whereas in East Asia common factors (or rapid cross-country propagation) were much more important, potentially related to a more homogenous industrial structure in these countries. Our data (which do not cover exactly the same sample period) suggest that a similar pattern also characterizes the two regions' respective currency returns during crisis situations.

Cross-continental extreme currency linkages between South America, South Africa, and Asia seem to be of a weaker nature (with few exceptions, such as the extreme linkages of the Thai baht with both the South African rand and the Colombian peso).

The conclusion is that whereas emerging market currencies have fatter tails and, therefore, a higher likelihood of individual crashes and currency attacks than industrial country currencies, the evidence does not allow for a generalization of this result to the multivariate case. Excluding East Asian currencies, the degree of crisis co-movements among emerging market currencies may well be lower than among industrial country currencies. This means that whereas currency crashes of a given extreme size are less frequent in industrial countries than in emerging markets, once an extreme movement has occurred in an exchange rate, the occurrence of further extreme movements cannot be expected to be less likely across industrial countries. Or in other words, once a currency crisis has struck there is no systematic difference between their breadth in emerging and industrial countries.

One type of explanation for this finding is that the industrial countries considered could be more economically and financially integrated among each other than many of the emerging market countries. Another interpretation is that whereas currency crises are more frequent and more severe for emerging markets than for industrial countries, for the reasons discussed above, their propagation mechanisms can be quite similar, irrespective of the precise characteristics of the underlying economy. So crisis behavior, such as cross-country "panic selling" of assets, is not worse for emerging market countries.

6. Extreme Linkages between Industrial Country and Emerging Market Currencies

Finally, we also take a short look at the extreme currency linkages between industrial and emerging market countries. The results are summarized in table 6. It turns out that industrial country-emerging market currency linkages are generally very low. A few exceptions include pound sterling/Indian rupe, perhaps not too surprisingly for the political and economic links between the UK and India, or Japanese yen/Indian rupee. This suggests that during our sample period and across our country cross section only very little currency contagion seems to have taken place either from the industrial country currencies to the emerging market currencies or vice versa. This may not be too surprising, since in an emerging market crisis the "hot money" will usually flow back from the currencies in crisis to the industrial country currencies.

7. Conclusions

Extreme exchange rate depreciations and appreciations can be an important element in international financial instability. They are one primary locus of the international transmission of financial shocks and in the form of currency crises they are often related to severe domestic macroeconomic instability. In this article we try to advance by not only addressing the historical frequency of extreme currency returns but also by assessing the breadth of extremely large exchange rate fluctuations across the foreign exchange market. Applying newly available techniques of multivariate extreme value theory to a broad data set of industrial country and emerging market currencies, we first discuss the size and probability of critically large exchange rate movements univariately and then we address the likelihood of extreme exchange rate spillovers among industrial country currencies, among emerging market currencies, and between industrial country and emerging market currencies.

Our most important result, and perhaps also the most surprising one, is that the likelihood of extreme co-movements between industrial country exchange rates is not lower than the likelihood for emerging market exchange rates. For example for most industrial country currency pairs and for most base currencies the probability of having an extreme currency depreciation in two spot markets, given there was one in at least one of the two, varies between 10 percent and 30 percent. This spillover likelihood is comparable in magnitude to the one historically observed for industrial country stock markets. Further, we observe some asymmetry in bivariate extreme

Exchange rate pairs	k	$\hat{\rho}$	$\hat{E}$ r = 20%	$\hat{E}$ r = 30%
GBP/USD, Colombia	150	0.041	1.021	1.024
GBP/USD, Venezuela	150	−0.011	1.016	1.009
GBP/USD, S. Africa	100	0.379	1.037	1.017
GBP/USD, Indonesia	150	0.056	1.013	1.009
GBP/USD, India	100	0.299	1.072	1.063
GBP/USD, Malaysia	150	0.164	1.026	1.014
GBP/USD, Philippines	150	0.011	1.012	1.008
GBP/USD, Thailand	100	0.151	1.020	1.019
GBP/USD, Chile	70	0.043	1.015	1.021
GBP/USD, Pakistan	150	0.071	1.033	1.031
JPY/USD, Colombia	80	0.026	1.020	1.023
JPY/USD, Venezuela	100	−0.016	1.013	1.015
JPY/USD, S. Africa	50	0.259	1.048	1.026
JPY/USD, Indonesia	150	0.124	1.016	1.011
JPY/USD, India	125	0.203	1.062	1.047
JPY/USD, Malaysia	150	0.168	1.034	1.024
JPY/USD, Philippines	100	0.067	1.017	1.017
JPY/USD, Thailand	100	0.206	1.008	1.013
JPY/USD, Chile	70	0.048	1.036	1.025
JPY/USD, Pakistan	100	0.093	1.020	1.011
DEM/USD, Colombia	150	−0.006	1.007	1.009
DEM/USD, Venezuela	150	−0.018	1.008	1.007
DEM/USD, S. Africa	140	0.371	1.012	1.009
DEM/USD, Indonesia	125	0.019	1.009	1.008
DEM/USD, India	80	0.247	1.014	1.018
DEM/USD, Malaysia	250	0.154	1.007	1.005
DEM/USD, Philippines	110	0.020	1.013	1.010
DEM/USD, Thailand	70	0.133	1.018	1.015
DEM/USD, Chile	150	0.010	1.008	1.007
DEM/USD, Pakistan	190	0.081	1.013	1.008
JPY/DEM, Colombia	100	0.034	1.013	1.001
JPY/DEM, Venezuela	100	0.002	1.001	1.010
JPY/DEM, S. Africa	50	−0.103	1.022	1.021
JPY/DEM, Indonesia	150	0.112	1.007	1.007
JPY/DEM, India	100	−0.036	1.016	1.012
JPY/DEM, Malaysia	100	0.021	1.011	1.010
JPY/DEM, Philippines	100	0.050	1.012	1.011
JPY/DEM, Thailand	150	0.082	1.008	1.007
JPY/DEM, Chile	125	0.041	1.009	1.008
JPY/DEM, Pakistan	70	0.016	1.022	1.017
GBP/DEM, Colombia	150	0.060	1.029	1.030
GBP/DEM, Venezuela	70	0.011	1.016	1.025

Table 6: Extreme Linkages between Industrial Country and Emerging Market Currencies

Exchange rate pairs	k	$\hat{\rho}$	$\hat{\mathrm{E}}$ r = 20%	$\hat{\mathrm{E}}$ r = 30%
GBP/DEM, S. Africa	90	–0.025	1.014	1.020
GBP/DEM, Indonesia	70	0.046	1.021	1.017
GBP/DEM, India	100	0.042	1.045	1.026
GBP/DEM, Malaysia	150	–0.002	1.006	1.010
GBP/DEM, Philippines	160	–0.014	1.009	1.006
GBP/DEM, Thailand	150	0.010	1.020	1.015
GBP/DEM, Chile	100	0.041	1.025	1.017
GBP/DEM, Pakistan	100	–0.019	1.035	1.017

Table 6 (*continued*): Extreme Linkages between Industrial Country and Emerging Market Currencies

co-movements between currencies in that the probability of joint extreme appreciations of two currencies may be quite different from the probability of joint extreme depreciations of the same currencies.

For emerging market exchange rates we find some regional differences in that currency co-crashes tend to be more likely among East Asian currencies than among Latin American currencies. Since East Asia seems also characterized by stronger macroeconomic interdependence in normal times, the reasons for these more pronounced crisis linkages may also be related to greater integration and more similar industrial structures in this region compared to Latin America. However, we generally find cross-continental emerging market currency linkages to be relatively weak. Similarly, we find hardly any evidence of significant currency crisis spillovers between emerging market currencies and industrial country currencies.

Going back to the univariate probabilities of exchange rate returns, we confirm the conventional wisdom that emerging market exchange rates experience more frequent and more dramatic extreme movements. This somewhat qualifies the high crisis linkages between industrial country currencies mentioned above, since crises as such are much less frequent among those countries. However, the general relevance of contagion and joint crash phenomena is underlined by the fact that these univariate (unconditional) probabilities are much lower than the conditional probabilities of spillovers. This also corresponds to results we found in earlier work on extreme co-movements in stock and government bond markets. So, joint crises or contagion are relevant phenomena in international financial markets, in particular within the same asset class. Whereas it is well known that the frequency of market crises is greatly underestimated when applying the univariate normal distribution, we make the distinct point that the application of the multivariate normal distribution to financial market returns also involves a dramatic underestimation of crisis co-movements far out in the tails. Another interesting finding of the univariate analysis is that several of the most extreme exchange rate movements in our sample do not seem to be directly associated with any of the widely publicized major crises.

Our results have implications for policies to preserve the stability of the international financial system and for the management of currency portfolio risk. The results locate the historical "hot spots" of extreme exchange rate volatility, and they describe the propensity of currency crises and attacks to propagate across markets. Although the probabilities of joint crises and contagion are not very large in absolute terms, they do not suggest that current efforts to reform the international financial architecture currency relationships between industrial countries are a completely benign issue for financial stability. As regards risk management implications, we can conclude somewhat surprisingly—at least on the basis of the available historical experience—that portfolios composed of a larger number of emerging market currencies (outside East Asia) should be fairly well diversified in a crisis situation. Portfolios concentrated in industrial country currency exposures or in East Asian currency exposures, however, should carry a relatively large Value-at-Risk.

*Philipp Hartmann is the principal of the economic and financial research unit in the Directorate Genena/Research of the European Central Bank in Frankfurt and an affiliate to the Center for Economic Policy Research. Stefan Straetmans is an assistant professor of finance at the Limburg Institute of Financial Economics of Maastricht University. Casper de Vries is a professor in the Department of Economics at Erasmus University Rotterdam. The authors thank Fabio Canova for a stimulating discussion on international return and volatility spillovers and Paul Embrechts for his encouragement and methodological suggestions. They also appreciated comments from Andreas Pick and from participants of the Chicago Fed/World Bank Group "Asset Price Bubbles" conference, the Verein für Socialpolitik Annual Meetings, in particular our discussant Beatrice Weder, and seminars at Arizona State University, the University of Zurich, the European Central Bank (ECB), and the Bank of Spain. In addition, the authors thank Sandrine Corvoisier for data assistance and Sabine Wiedemann for editorial help. Any views expressed are those of the authors and not necessarily those of the ECB or the Eurosystem. Contacts: philipp.hartmann@ecb.int, s.straetmans@berfin.unimaas.nl, cdevries@few.eur.nl.

Notes

1. Following the early article by King and Wadhwani (1990), there is a small literature addressing financial market contagion phenomena from a micro-theoretical perspective. See, for example, Calvo and Mendoza (2000), Kodres and Prittsker (2002), and Kyle and Xiong (2001). However, these theoretical papers do not explicitly identify crisis situations with very extreme market returns as we do in the present paper (from an empirical perspective).

2. Note that $E[\kappa|\kappa \geq 1, \kappa \in \{1, 2, 3, \ldots, N\}]$ is still equal to the ratio of the sum of the marginal excess probabilities and the joint failure probability. The measure $P\{\kappa = 2|\kappa \geq 1\}$ is, however, not easily extended to higher dimensions than 2.

3. We provide only an abridged description of the estimation techniques here. For a full discussion of the asymptotic arguments and derivations of estimators and test statistics, see, for example, our previous paper (Hartmann, Straetmans, and de Vries, 2001). Within the frame-

work of a parametric probability law, the calculation of (2) would be easy, because it solely required estimating the distributional parameters by maximum likelihood optimization. In this paper we do not make very specific distributional assumptions for currency returns. If one estimated the linkage measure (2) using the wrong distributional assumptions, the estimates may be biased due to misspecification. Indeed, model risk can be expected to be high because of the large heterogeneity in exchange rate regimes and accompanying shock propagation mechanisms within and between the industrial and emerging market currency blocks. For example, the empirical analysis below underlines that the multivariate normal dramatically underestimates the likelihood of extremal currency spillovers regardless of the forex regime or the currency block considered.

4. So the only (weak) structural assumption we are making is that the tails of exchange rate return distributions exhibit the property of "regular variation at infinity." This means that, up to a first order approximation, the rate of decline of the distributions towards the left and right extremes follows a power law. In other words, we are constraining the picture to Frechet laws, a large class of distributions exhibiting "fat tails."

5. All the data were downloaded from Datastream, daily WM/Reuters exchange rate series. Weekly returns are calculated Monday to Monday.

6. After January 1, 1999, the DEM, as all the other European currencies joining the third stage of Economic and Monetary Union, is completely fixed to the euro (EUR). Therefore, from that date on extreme DEM and EUR returns are identical.

7. Unfortunately, the Argentinean and Brazilian currencies are not included. Data quality for the exchange rates of the currencies for the two largest South American economies was so low that we had to eliminate them from our sample. Also, the Argentinean currency board made the peso exchange rate virtually constant against the dollar for an extended period of time.

8. We should caution, however, that the differences in tail indices are in many cases not statistically significant at the usual levels.

9. This is not too surprising knowing that the multivariate normal distribution by construction exhibits asymptotic independence far out in the tails, even if $p \neq 0$.

10. On the surface that may be read as a difference to the relatively high likelihood for flight to quality from stocks into government bonds that we documented in our earlier paper (Hartmann et al., 2001, table 4). In that paper we found flight to quality was not less frequent than joint crashes between stocks and bonds. However, the two analyses are not really comparable, since here we are looking at flight phenomena within the same asset class, whereas in the other paper we stressed flight phenomena across different asset classes.

References

Aghion, P., P. Bacchetta, and A. Banerjee, 1999, "Capital Markets and the Instability of Open Economies," in *The Asian Financial Crisis: Causes, Contagion and Consequences*, P. R. Agénor, et al., eds., London: Cambridge University Press.

Bae, K., G. A. Karolyi, and R. M. Stulz, 2001, "A New Approach to Measuring Financial Contagion," paper presented at the Federal Reserve Bank of Chicago conference on Bank Structure and Competition, Chicago, May.

Bank for International Settlements, 2002, "Triennial Central Bank Survey of Foreign Exchange and Derivatives Market Activity," Basel, March.

Buiter, W., G. Corsetti, and P. Pesenti, 1997, *Financial Markets and European Monetary Cooperation: The Lessons of the 1992–93 Exchange Rate Mechanism Crisis*, London: Cambridge University Press.

Calvo, G. A., and E. G. Mendoza, 2000, "Rational Contagion and the Globalization of Securities Markets," *Journal of International Economics*, Vol. 51, pp. 79–113.

De Bandt, O., and P. Hartmann, 2000, "Systemic Risk: A Survey," European Central Bank working paper, No. 35, Frankfurt, November.

Drazen, A., 1998, "Political Contagion in Currency Crises," paper presented at the National Bureau of Economic Research conference on currency crises, Cambridge, MA, February.

Eichengreen, B., A. Rose, and C. Wyplosz, 1996, "Contagious Currency Crises: First Tests," *Scandinavian Journal of Economics*, Vol. 98, pp. 463–484.

Embrechts, P., C. Klüppelberg, and T. Mikosch, 1997, *Modelling Extremal Events*, Berlin: Springer.

Embrechts, P., L. de Haan, and X. Huang, 2000, "Modelling Multivariate Extremes," in *Extremes and Integrated Risk Management*, P. Embrechts, ed., London: Risk Books, pp. 59–67.

Glick, R., and A. R. Rose, 1999, "Contagion and Trade: Why are Currency Crises Regional?," *Journal of International Money and Finance*, Vol. 18, pp. 603–618.

Haan, L. de, D. W. Jansen, K. Koedijk, and C. G. de Vries, 1994, "Safety First Portfolio Selection, Extreme Value Theory and Long Run Asset Risks," in proceedings from a conference on Extreme Value Theory and Applications, J. Galambos, ed., Bosten: Kluwer Press, pp. 471–487.

Haan, L. de, and J. de Ronde, 1998, "Sea and Wind: Multivariate Extremes at Work," *Extremes*, Vol. 1, pp. 7–45.

Hartmann, P., S. Straetmans, and C. G. de Vries, 2001, "Asset market linkages in crisis periods," European Central Bank, working paper, No. 71, Frankfurt, July (http://www.ecb.int/pub/wp/ecbwp071.pdf).

Hill, B. M., 1975, "A Simple General Approach to Inference about the Tail of a Distribution," *The Annals of Statistics*, Vol. 3, pp. 1163–1173.

Hols, M., and C. G. de Vries, 1991, "The Limiting Distribution of Extremal Exchange Rate Yields," *Journal of Applied Econometrics*, Vol. 6, pp. 287–302.

Huang, Xin, 1992, "Statistics of Bivariate Extreme Values," Tinbergen Institute Research Series, Erasmus University Rotterdam, Ph.D. thesis, No. 22.

Hunter, W. C., G. G. Kaufman, and T. H. Krueger, eds., 1999, *The Asian Financial Crisis: Origins, Implications and Solutions*, Boston: Kluwer Academic Publishers.

Jansen, D. W., and C. G. de Vries, 1991, "On the Frequency of Large Stock Returns: Putting Booms and Busts into Perspective," *Review of Economics and Statistics*, Vol. 73, pp. 19–24.

Kaminsky, G. I., and C. M. Reinhart, 2000, "On Crises, Contagion and Confusion," *Journal of International Economics*, Vol. 51, pp. 145–168.

Kaufman, G. G., 1999, "Banking and Currency Crises and Systemic Risk: A Taxonomy and Review," Federal Reserve Bank of Chicago, working paper, No. WP-99-12, December.

King, M., and S. Wadhwani, 1990, "Transmission of Volatility between Stock Markets," *Review of Financial Studies*, Vol. 3, pp. 5–33.

Kodres, L. E., and M. Pritsker, 2002, "A Rational Expectations Model of Financial Contagion," *Journal of Finance,* Vol. 57, April.

Koedijk, K. G., M. Schafgans, and C. G. de Vries, 1990, "The Tail Index of Exchange Rates," *Journal of International Economics*, Vol. 2(1-2), pp. 93–108.

Koedijk, K. G., P. A. Stork, and C. G. de Vries, 1992, "Differences between Foreign Exchange Rate Regimes: The View from the Tails," *Journal of International Money and Finance*, Vol. 11(5), pp. 462–473.

Kyle, A. S., and W. Xiong, 2001, "Contagion as a Wealth Effect," *Journal of Finance (Papers and Proceedings),* Vol. 56, August.

Loayza, N., H. Lopez, and A. Ubide, 1999, "Sectorial Macroeconomic Interdepencies: Evidence for Latin America, East Asia and Europe," International Monetary Fund, working paper, No. 99/11, Washington, DC, January.

Longin, F., 1996, "The Asymptotic Distribution of Extreme Stock Market Returns," *Journal of Business*, Vol. 69, pp. 383–408.

Longin, F., and B. Solnik, 2001, "Extreme Correlation of International Equity Markets," *Journal of Finance*, Vol. 56, pp. 649–676.

Masson, P., 1999, "Contagion: Macroeconomic Models with Multiple Equilibria," *Journal of International Money and Finance*, Vol. 18, pp. 587–602.

Poon, S. H., Rockinger, M., and J. Tawn, 2001, "New Extreme-Value Dependence Measures and Finance Applications," Center for Economic Policy Research, discussion paper, No. 2762, London, April.

Ramchand, L., and R. Susmel, 1998, "Volatility and Cross Correlation across Major Stock Markets," *Journal of Empirical Finance*, Vol. 5, pp. 397–416.

Sachs, J., A. Tornell, and A. Velasco, 1996, "Financial Crises in Emerging Markets: The Lessons from 1995," *Brookings Papers on Economic Activity*, Vol. 1, pp. 147–198.

Starica, C., 1999, "Multivariate Extremes for Models with Constant Conditional Correlations," *Journal of Empirical Finance*, Vol. 6, pp. 515–553.

Straetmans, S., 2000, "Extremal Spill-Overs in Equity Markets," in *Extremes and Integrated Risk Management*, P. Embrechts, ed., London: Risk Books, pp. 187–204.

Van Rijckeghem, C., and B. Weder, 2001, "Sources of Contagion: Is It Finance or Trade?," *Journal of International Economics,* Vol. 54, No. 2.

Chapter 26
Comments: Shifting the Risk after Shifting the Focus

Anna J. Schwartz*
National Bureau of Economic Research

Of the eight sessions at this conference on asset price bubbles, the fourth session covers a topic that I regard as unrelated to the subject of asset price bubbles. The title of this session is "International Transmission of Financial Shocks." Did the organizers have in mind papers examining international transmission of bubbles? Of the four papers prepared for this session, only the paper by Allen and Gale deals with stock market linkages, and specifically bubble linkages. So it is a puzzle for me what the remaining three papers, which have nothing to say about asset price bubbles, contribute to our understanding of the central concern of this conference.

I do not fault the authors of the three papers for discussing topics that have no connection with asset price bubbles. They have written on the subjects the organizers proposed. The fault is that of the organizers. I see no point, however, in commenting on papers that would make a fine contribution to a different conference on international transmission of financial shocks, instead of one on asset price bubbles. It would compound the error of the organizers to devote attention to such extraneous matters. So I shall restrict my comments to the one paper for this session that is on the conference subject.

The authors of the remaining papers have discussed subjects extraneous to this conference. So I finally come to the paper by Allen and Gale that is relevant to the conference topic. They pose three questions: What initiates a bubble? What is the role of the banking system? What causes a bubble to burst? A final subject the authors cover is interlinkages among stock markets. I shall first lay out the authors' response to each question and then offer my comments, which test their theories against experience with 20th century stock market booms that have been described as bubbles.

1. What Initiates a Bubble?

To answer the question of what initiates a bubble, the authors distinguish the price of an asset purchased by an investor with his own money from the price of an asset purchased with borrowed money. The price of an asset purchased with an investor's own money is said to be "fundamental." A bubble occurs when the price rises above the fundamental. For those who invest with borrowed money, there is limited liability if they default, which the authors describe as an agency problem between banks and the people to whom they lend money. Banks cannot observe how the funds are invested. This causes a shift of risks from investors to banks. This leads investors to bid up the prices of risky assets above their fundamental values, and there is a bubble. The risk comes from two sources: asset return risk and financial risk associated with the amount of credit that will be available in the future. The authors first analyze asset return risk, assuming the probabilities of various payoffs less an assumed interest rate. They distinguish between a safe asset that pays a fixed rate of return determined by the marginal product of capital in the economy, and a risky asset.

Here are some questions the authors' propositions raise in my mind. Is it plausible that only when using his own funds will an investor pay for an asset no more than its fundamental value, and that when using borrowed funds he will ignore the fundamental value and pay whatever increment over that value the market requires? This is crucial for the authors' proposition that because of asymmetric information, the investor knows more than the lender about the investment, so the investor can shift risk to the lender. Now it may be that, if the investor borrows to finance a project, he may know more about the true prospects of the project than he reveals to the lender, although I have my doubts that an adversarial relationship between borrower and lender is the general case, but if the loan is to be used to buy an existing asset, why should the borrower know better than the lender the true value of the asset?

In addition, if the borrower is ready to stiff the lender, how many times can this happen before the lender will quit funding the investor? Indeed, the authors ask why banks are willing to lend to investors given the chance of default. They illustrate their answer with the case of banks' expected payoff when the risky asset is acquired by 40 percent of investors and the safe asset by 60 percent. The risky asset may have a high payoff with a low probability, in which case investors repay the loan and interest in full; alternatively, the risky asset may have a low payoff with a high probability, so investors default, and the bank collects only the low price of the asset. The 60 percent of investors in the safe asset repay their loan and interest in full. The lesson appears to be that if lending to investors in risky assets is limited, even if they default, the banks will come out ahead. So banks must be able to differentiate between risky stocks with high and low payoffs, and lend accordingly. That hardly makes them dupes of investors.

Of course, it isn't only individual investors who acquire stocks. Hundreds of managers of hedge funds, mutual funds, investment funds, and pension funds buy stocks. Which class of buyers plays a bigger role in the price escalation? In any event, managers of funds don't fit the model's depiction of agency problems between lenders and borrowers driving the bubble.

To turn to our recent experience with a bubble, if U.S. investors borrowed to buy stocks in the 1990s and, in the authors' view, shifted risks to the banks, how is it that investors have lost an estimated $3 trillion since the crash in March 2000 and, if there were defaults, the U.S. banks have emerged sound and well-capitalized? The authors state that in a competitive banking sector, the receipts from lending will be paid out to depositors. In this case, depositors bear the cost of the agency problem, the authors say. In the presence of deposit insurance, U.S. bank depositors have borne no cost. If there had been a cost, U.S. taxpayers would have borne it. Was there a cost following the stock market meltdown other than the losses incurred by investors?

Perhaps the risk-shifting paradigm fits the Japanese 1980s stock market and property market bubbles better than the U.S. case, but then the authors would have to specify why the two examples differ. Japanese banks made loans backed by stock and property collateral, the value of which the bust deflated, and their portfolios to this day are crammed with nonperforming loans. But is this debacle the result of asymmetric information? The lenders as much as the borrowers were caught up in the euphoria of the boom in stock and property prices.

2. Role of Banks

I now turn to the authors' answer to the second question they consider, namely, the role of banks. Thanks to bank lending, investment in assets, they say, depends on the aggregate amount of credit available to the banks. To begin with, the authors assume that the central bank is able to control that amount. In that event, the amount invested in the risky asset is the difference between the total amount of credit and the amount invested in the safe asset. In a competitive system, the interest rate that has to be paid to banks will be bid up by investors until the safe asset yields them no profits. The amount investors will be willing to pay for the risky asset depends on the amount of credit the central bank provides. When the central bank controls the amount of credit, it also controls the level of interest rates, and the level of asset prices. The fundamental value of risky assets, however, is insensitive to the amount of credit compared to the case where there is an agency problem. Changes in aggregate credit can cause relatively large changes in asset prices when there is an agency problem, according to the authors,

The authors next assume that the central bank has limited ability to control the amount of credit and this means aggregate credit is random, so there is uncertainty about the level of credit, which is particularly great in countries undergoing financial liberalization. To deal with financial risk, the authors define three periods at dates 0, 1, and 2. Date 1 marks the investment, date 2 the payoff. Between dates 0 and 1 there is financial uncertainty about aggregate credit at date 1 that causes uncertainty about prices at date 1. This leads to an agency problem again when investors borrow from banks at date 0. The price of the risky asset at date 0 will reflect this price uncertainty, and can lead the asset price to be higher at date 0. The greater the financial uncertainty, the greater the price of the risky asset at date 0. Financial uncertainty adds to uncertainty due to variations in asset returns.

The authors say that what is important in determining the risky asset's price at date 0 is expectations about aggregate credit at date 1. A rise in aggregate credit will lead to high asset prices and enable investors to avoid default. A fall in aggregate credit will lead to low asset prices and to default. Expectations of credit expansion influence the amount of borrowings and how much to pay for the risky asset. Even if credit is always expanding, according to the authors, there may still be default.

Here are my comments on the authors' views about the role of banks. I dispute their statement that in practice central banks have limited ability to control the amount of credit. A central bank need only raise its interest rate instrument enough to limit the amount of credit the banks can provide, and reduce its interest rate instrument to flood the economy with credit. Former Federal Reserve Chairman Paul Volcker showed what raising interest rates and current Federal Reserve Chairman Alan Greenspan showed what lowering them will do to credit. I don't doubt that ample credit can contribute to an asset price bubble, but I also believe that a bubble can develop in the absence of lax monetary policy. In the U.S. stock market boom from the end of 1924 to the peak in September 1929, it was not an increase in the aggregate supply of bank credit, but a reallocation of their loan portfolios by banks in favor of loans on securities that supported rising stock prices.

In the authors' view, widespread default is almost inevitable when credit expansion is less than anticipated. That may be an accurate account of U.S. bank losses in the 1930s, but it does not seem to describe the aftermath of the Japanese boom in the 1990s or the U.S. boom in the 2000s. The authors should explain the difference.

3. What Causes a Bubble to Burst?

The end of a bubble, according to the authors, results from disappointed expectations about aggregate bank credit available for investment in stocks. Does this scenario describe the collapse of prices of high-tech stocks in the United States in March 2000? Or was it irrational exuberance that collapsed?

4. Stock Market Interlinkages

The authors finally address the effect of interlinkages between stock markets in different countries with different levels of financial risk and different variability in asset returns. A country with low financial risk has lower interest rates and prices than a high-risk country. If there are links between the stock markets, the countries constitute one market, with the same interest rate and the same price. Total credit will be split equally between the countries. Interlinkages raise asset prices and interest rates in the initially low-risk country, and lower them in the initially high-risk country. When the countries differ in variability of asset returns, introducing stock market interlinkages, exacerbates the bubble in countries with initially high asset prices and reduces them in countries with initially low asset prices. The same result applies to initial interest rates in the two countries.

My question to the authors is why the bubbles that have been known in our time have not been transmitted from one country to another. They note that stock market interlinkages were important in the formation and collapse of bubbles in earlier times. Why not in the 20th century? There are clearly negative linkages in our day between stock markets when capital flows from one market to another one with appreciating asset prices. Why are there no examples of transmission of an asset boom in one country to another in our time?

5. Conclusion

The elements in the Allen-Gale model of the formation of bubbles and their extinction are not applicable as a generalization of 20th century experience. The agency problem that they posit is not confirmed by the U.S. stock market booms in the 1920s and 1990s. Perhaps it has some relevance to the Japanese experience in the 1980s, although the incidence of default is not as pronounced as the authors presume, even there. I believe the assumption that lenders cannot observe the characteristics of investment in securities so risk is shifted by borrowers to lenders is a misrepresentation of the borrower-lender relationship in this market. Borrowers may be able to fool lenders when they initiate a project concerning which they are better informed than lenders. This is not true when the purchase of stocks is the investment. The borrower is not better informed than the lender in this case. I agree with the authors that the role of credit is a crucial determinant of asset prices, but there may be no increase in aggregate credit, but a reallocation of loans in bank portfolios in favor of loans backed by stocks.

*Anna J. Schwartz is a member of the research staff of the National Bureau of Economic Research and a distinguished fellow of the American Economic Association.

PART VI

TECHNOLOGY, THE NEW ECONOMY, AND ASSET PRICE BUBBLES

Chapter 27
Valuation and New Economy Firms

Steven N. Kaplan*
University of Chicago
and National Bureau of Economic Research

1. Introduction

Unlike many of the speakers at this conference, my research does not focus on asset pricing movements and puzzles. So why am I here? I am both a finance professor and the faculty director of my school's entrepreneurship program. In my capacity as a researcher, I have studied venture capitalists and the micro-foundations of business-to-business e-commerce. As a teacher and advisor, I have viewed the ups and downs of many new economy companies directly. This talk, then, is based on both my research and on my experience.

The talk is motivated by the fact that in 1999 and early 2000, the valuations of Internet-related companies reached levels that were extraordinary by most standards. For example, Ofek and Richardson (2001) show that in the aggregate, Internet firms traded at roughly 35 times revenue at the end of 1999. In the two years since then, those valuations have declined precipitously. In this paper, I attempt to explain these patterns and discuss the effects those patterns have had.

The paper proceeds as follows. Section 2 presents a framework that I use to evaluate new economy businesses. Section 3 applies the framework to discuss why valuations might have been so high and to understand why they are now so low. This section also includes a discussion of the implications of the rise and fall of valuations. Section 4 discusses the effects of those changes in market valuation/sentiment on individual companies. Section 5 presents my opinion of what the long-term real effects of the Internet/new economy are likely to be.

2. A Framework for Thinking about the New Economy

The framework begins with a key question: Does the new economy/Internet do things that the old economy—phone, fax, EDI (electronic data interchange)—cannot?[1] Or, in other words, does the new economy/Internet reduce transaction costs relative to the old economy?

The key effect of the Internet and other new economy innovations is to change the costs (and benefits) of transacting. There are five ways that the Internet potentially changes transaction costs: 1) changes/improves processes; 2) changes the nature of the marketplace; 3) changes decisions; 4) changes the degree of information incompleteness/asymmetry; and 5) changes the ability to commit. The choice between an Internet-based transaction or marketplace and a physical one comes down to the relative transaction costs of the two alternatives. Garicano and Kaplan (2001) discuss these in much greater detail.

Changes in processes: The Internet can improve efficiencies by reducing the costs involved in an existing business process.

Changes in the marketplace: The Internet can reduce transaction costs by making a marketplace more efficient. These reduced transaction costs or, equivalently, marketplace benefits, can come from reducing a buyer's or seller's cost of finding trading partners and information about those partners.

Changes in decisions (or indirect effects of transaction cost reductions): Clearly, any reduction in transaction costs results in direct economic gains through a reduction in the cost of undertaking these transactions. It is possible, however, that other indirect benefits also will arise.

Changes in informational incompleteness and asymmetries: Buyers and sellers typically do not have the same information about a particular transaction. As a result, one party (or both) may be at a disadvantage to the other in evaluating the desirability of a transaction. The Internet potentially changes the informational positions of buyers and sellers.

Changes in the ability to commit: The Internet has the potential to increase or decrease the ability of buyers and sellers to commit to transactions. First, by standardizing processes and by leaving an electronic trail, the Internet has the potential to increase the ability to commit (and, therefore, reduce the costs of imperfect commitment). Alternatively, a buyer may avoid intermediary fees by viewing the product over the Internet, but contacting the seller directly.

Who will capture the transaction cost reductions? After applying the framework, it should be possible to understand the effect of a new technology or process on transaction costs. If the technology does reduce transaction costs, it is potentially viable/valuable. The question then becomes who will capture the reduction in transaction costs. If the technology is unique or difficult to imitate, the innovator should be able to capture some of the improvements and become valuable. On the other hand, if the technology can be easily imitated by competitors, the customers will capture most of the benefits.

3. Why Are Valuations that Were So High, Now So Low?

It is well known that publicly traded Internet firms achieved levels that were extraordinary by most standards. For example, Ofek and Richardson (2001) show that in the aggregate, Internet firms traded at roughly 35 times revenue at the end of 1999. If those firms had achieved industry-average net income margins at the time, they would have had price-earnings (P/E) ratios of 605. Ofek and Richardson (2001) also estimate the growth rates that would have been required to justify such high P/E ratios and find that such rates are extremely high by historical standards.

In the two years since the end of 1999, Internet valuations have declined precipitously. From February 2000 to December 2000, Ofek and Richardson report that the value of these firms declined by an average of 80 percent. That decline has continued in the subsequent months.

In this section, I discuss what the market appears to have believed when Internet valuations peaked. I then use the framework of the previous section to discuss why those beliefs turned out to be wrong. I distinguish between businesses focused on the consumer—business to consumer, or B2C—and those focused on other businesses—business to business, or B2B.

3.1 Valuations So High

B2C: Valuations of B2C businesses were based on aggressive growth assumptions. They also were based on nonfinancial measures like Web traffic. Demers and Lev (2000), Hand (2000), Rajgopal et al. (2000), Trueman et al. (2001), and particularly, Jorion and Talmor (2001) present evidence that valuations were based on Web traffic, gross profit, and short-term growth.

The rational story here is that investors believed that B2Cs would grow significantly and would transform traffic into revenues and profits. Negative margins would somehow turn positive. There also was an implicit assumption that competition would be weak, possibly because of network effects.

B2B: Valuations of B2B e-commerce were similarly based on very aggressive growth assumptions. One B2B e-commerce firm, Chemdex, attained a market capitalization of $11 billion with $2 million of true revenues. Rajgopal et al. (2000) also find that B2B valuations related to alliances, acquisitions, and customer acquisition, but not to earnings.

The rational story for these companies is that investors assumed that 1) the businesses delivered large reductions in transaction costs; 2) business customers would adopt quickly, that is, a large volume of activity would move to the Internet; 3) competition would be slow and network effects would emerge; and 4) the B2Bs would be able to capture a meaningful portion of transaction cost savings.

Other: Other areas that also obtained extremely high valuations included Internet consulting businesses—Lante, Viant, etc ...—and Internet infrastructure companies—Kana, Vignette, etc. One might also add telecommunications infrastructure companies—Global Crossing, Qwest, etc. The rational story for these companies is similar to that for the B2Bs.

3.2 Why Are They So Low Now?

Why have the valuations of Internet companies decline so precipitously since March 2000? Clearly, the market's expectations of growth have declined a great deal. Demers and Lev (2001), Keating et al. (2001), and Jorion and Talmor (2001) also tend to find that financial measures of performance—revenue and cash flow—are more important while nonfinancial measures like traffic are less important. Ofek and Richardson (2001) argue that part of the reason for the decline was an increase in the number of selling shareholders driven by expiring lock-up agreements. In this section, I present some additional thoughts concerning the downward revisions in growth expectations for B2C and B2B companies.

B2C: The market greatly reduced its expectations of (some combination of) future growth, the extent to which traffic could be transformed into revenues, the ability to take advantage of network effects, and the extent of competition. Even for successes like Amazon and Yahoo!, the stock prices in March of 2002 were 13 percent and 8 percent of their peak valuations. Is the change in the market's expectations for B2C companies surprising?

It is worth considering the framework from section 2. Many B2C companies are simply improved catalogs. Such businesses reduce transaction costs for individual consumers—the Internet can make it easier to find items (like books) and easier to order them (books and stocks)—and for the cataloger—order-taking and order fulfillment are less costly. However, this is not an earth shattering change. The introduction of catalogs brought with them transaction cost reductions, but not extraordinary valuations. Catalogs (and brokerage firms) also regularly face competition. It is hard to imagine a rational story for such high valuations for these companies.

Portals like Yahoo! also have seen their valuations decline substantially. They, too, have not been able to obtain the growth expected of them nor have they been very successful in converting traffic into revenue. It is not clear how much portals reduce transaction costs. It also is clear that portals face competition.

One exception is a company like eBay. EBay does provide a service that is not available offline. It also benefits from network effects because it connects many buyers to many sellers. Sellers know they are more likely to find buyers at eBay. That attracts more sellers. Buyers know they are more likely to find sellers at eBay. This attracts more buyers. Buyers and sellers are less likely to make good matches through other companies. As more buyers and sellers use eBay, the advantage of eBay over other companies increases.[2] Consistent with this, eBay's value has only declined by slightly more than 50 percent of its peak value.

B2B: As with B2C companies, the market greatly reduced its expectations of (some combination of) the effect of B2B on the extent of transaction cost reductions, the ability to capture those reductions, the speed of adoption, the extent of network effects, and the extent to which competition would be weak. Is the change in the market's expectations for B2B companies surprising?

The extent of the decline in B2B was more of a surprise (at least to me). It was not surprising to see some decline. It was surprising to see a large fraction of these companies fail. Based on the framework, it was more plausible that B2B companies reduced transaction costs substantially. B2B business models also were more likely (than B2C models) to rely on business models that used network effects, matching buyers to sellers in the way eBay does.

What went wrong? In some markets, companies have obtained transaction cost reductions, but B2B companies have not been able to capture much of this reduction because of competition. This is arguably true in the procurement area where a number of companies have been able to provide software and procurement processes that are not largely differentiated from each other. Network effects have not materialized in those markets.

There also was a belief in a number of markets that B2B companies would be able to charge a percentage of the transaction value, rather than a fixed transaction fee. This reflected a misunderstanding of the nature of the transaction cost savings. In many cases, the transaction cost savings is a fixed amount—time spent punching in data—rather than a percentage of the transaction value.

Finally, in some markets, companies just have not adopted the new technologies. This occurred for two reasons. First, some companies, particularly suppliers, were not interested in using Internet marketplaces because they did not want to put an intermediary between their customers and themselves. Second, companies have been able to use the Internet without having to commit, that is, it is possible to use the Internet to get price information, but then go to traditional suppliers for execution.

Other: Internet consulting and infrastructure companies all suffered from a combination of excessive competition and demand that failed to materialize. Most of these companies have declined substantially in value and many have failed. Is this surprising?

In the case of Internet consulting, the declines seem unsurprising and the high valuations were particularly strange. It was difficult to understand how those businesses would scale quickly enough to sustain their market capitalizations.

3.3 Did Sophisticated Investors "Know" Prices Were Too High?

Answering whether people knew prices were too high is, of course, very difficult. Ofek and Richardson present evidence and argue that the decline in Internet stocks is related to short sales constraints and the expiration of initial public offering (IPO) lock-ups. They argue that the rise and fall of Internet stocks can be explained by an initial relative oversupply of optimistic investors who drove prices up followed by the arrival of more pessimistic investors—insiders—who drove prices down.

The Ofek and Richardson story suggests that sophisticated investors—like venture capitalists (VCs)—believed a bubble existed. While this story is plausible, there are a number of pieces of evidence that are not consistent with this explanation.

At the same time that venture capitalists were among some of the insiders who sold shares after lock-ups expired, these venture capitalists also sharply increased the amount of money they raised and the pace of their investments in new Internet and technology related start-ups. Figure 1 shows the large increase in funds committed to VC funds while figure 2 shows the huge increase in investments by VCs in 1999 and 2000. Much of this investment went into new economy investments. Hendershott (2001) documents a similar pattern for pure Internet investments.

Presumably the VCs who made these investments believed that the investments would be profitable on average. To believe the investments would be profitable, many VCs must have believed that many of the companies they invested in would be viable and valuable. In other words, such a large increase in investment seems inconsistent with a pessimistic view of the new economy companies. Furthermore, the VCs received most of their capital commitments from large institutional investors—pension funds, endowments, etc.—who also must have been optimistic about these investments.

One might argue that the VCs and institutional investors made these investments with the expectation of flipping their private investments to irrational public investors. This argument, however, would require the VCs to have believed that stock prices

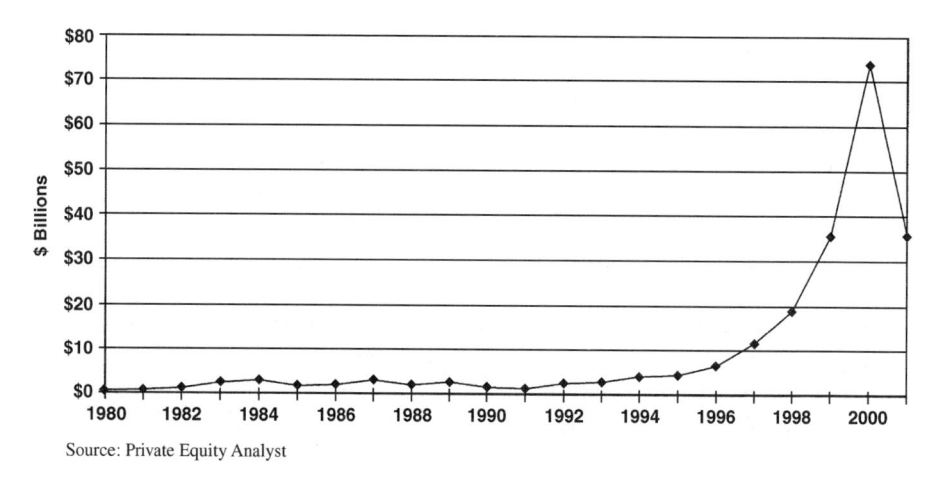

Figure 1: Fundraising by Venture Capital Partnerships, 1980–2001

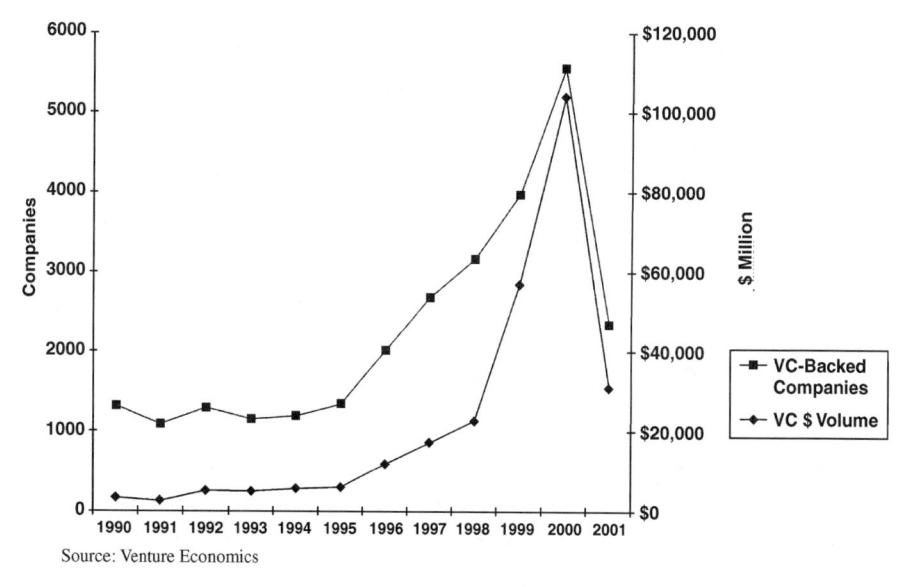

Source: Private Equity Analyst

Figure 2: Venture Capital Financing, 1990–2001

Source: Venture Economics

would remain irrationally high for at least two years—that is, even under optimistic conditions, it still would take that amount of time for the VC to invest in an early stage company, take it public, wait for the lock-up period to end, and then sell the shares. This argument also runs into difficulty in that it assumes that the investors in public securities would be irrational. Yet, a substantial number of investors in public securities were the same institutions that invested in the VC funds.

Figure 3 sheds some light on this. Figure 3 presents a time series of VC-backed IPOs and first VC round investments (based on data from Venture Economics). First

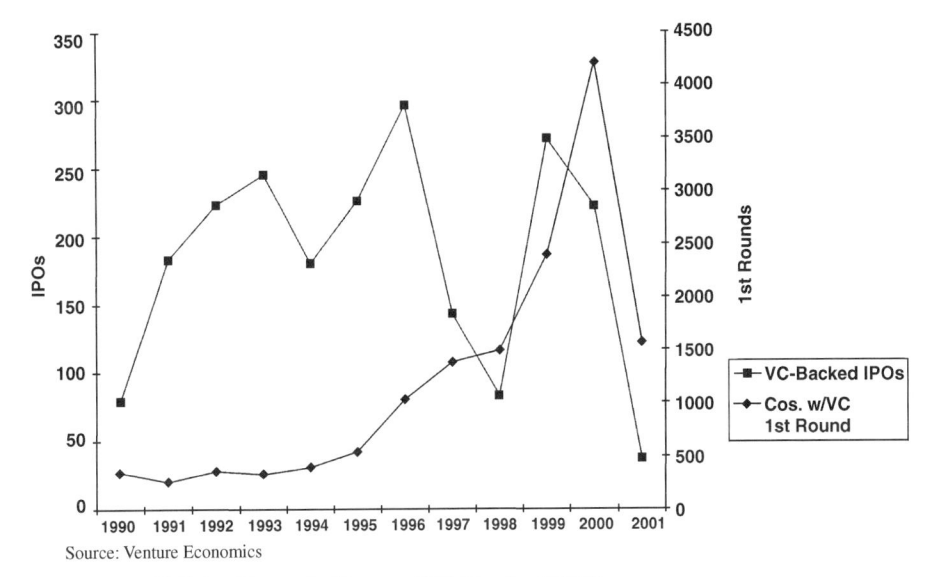

Figure 3: VC 1st Rounds Versus VC-Backed IPOs

VC round investments provide a measure of the number of new companies backed by VCs. Venture capitalists-backed IPOs provide a measure of the number of VC companies that succeed.[3] Figure 3 shows that it was reasonable for VCs to assume there would be 0 to 250 VC-backed IPOs per year. At the same time, figure 3 shows an incredible increase in VC-funded first rounds in 1999 and, particularly, 2000. The large increase in VC investments without a concomitant increase in the number of IPOs is certainly consistent with VCs and institutional investors believing that stock prices would remain high.

Figure 3 also leaves us with a puzzle. The huge increase in the number of companies funded suggests that competition would be a huge problem. Yet it is difficult to justify the high valuations in 1999 and early 2000 without assuming that competition would be modest.

Another relevant observation is the high profile investments by buyout investors in telecommunications companies. Forstmann Little, Hicks Muse, and KKR, among others, invested and subsequently lost billions of dollars in such companies. These sophisticated buyout investors must have believed that the investments had a positive expected value at the time.

A final point (provided by John Cochrane) is that technology/Internet-related companies like Cisco and Lucent also rose and then declined precipitously. The stocks of these companies were widely held and very liquid.

I draw the following conclusion from these observations. Insiders and sophisticated investors—like VCs and some buyout investors—may have believed that some of their individual stocks were overvalued when Internet valuations were high. As a result, they sold shares. At the same, however, those same investors believed that the new economy companies were viable entities and that there were opportunities to create more new economy companies. Furthermore, some of these sophisticated investors believed that some of these companies were undervalued—particularly the buyout investors who invested in telecommunications.

3.4 Summary

To summarize, investors clearly made mistakes in overvaluing Internet and new economy companies in 1999 and 2000. The mistakes seem hardest to explain in B2C investments and in consulting services. It seems likely that investors underestimated the extent of competition in all areas.

At the same time, many sophisticated investors behaved as if they believed that Internet and new economy companies would be much more successful than they have been.

4. What Effects Do the Changes in Market Sentiment Have on Individual Companies?

Here, I am going to talk from my experience advising start-ups and talking to VCs. While this section can be viewed as idiosyncratic to that experience, my sense from talking to others and reading the popular press is that this section is representative.

As noted above, in 1999 and early 2000, the stock market appeared to value many new economy companies as a function of revenues or even potential without much regard for profitability/cash flow. Companies went public at an earlier stage in their life cycles than ever before. This changed substantially in the spring of 2000.

In the second half of 2000 and the first half of 2001, the stock market soured on these companies and valuations declined substantially. The market appeared to have resumed valuing companies on cash flows.

The market conditions clearly had an effect on company behavior. Before mid 2000, the private, VC-funded companies tended to push for additional revenues at the expense of profitability/cash flow. After mid 2000, as stock market values declined, those companies became increasingly focused on profitability/cash flow. It is worth noting, however, that even before mid 2000, the companies and their investors expected to achieve positive cash flows at some future point and believed that those expectations would be borne out.

5. What Are the Real Effects of the Internet/New Economy Likely to Be?

We have seen a boom and bust in new economy/technology valuations. Stock market investors obtained terrific returns and then horrific ones. At present, in April 2002, the Standard & Poor's 500 stands at roughly 1,100 while the NASDAQ Composite rests at roughly 1,750. These are the same levels these indices registered in early 1998. In other words, the stock market has roughly stood still (ignoring modest dividends) overall in the last four years. The results in Hendershott (2001) suggest that the overall return on investment in Internet companies also was roughly breakeven.

The question, then, is whether the investments in the new economy and technology had a similar negligible effect on the overall economy. It is here that the real effects on the economy need not be the same as the effects on the stock market. It is my sense that the information technology, the Internet, and other related technology have generated and will continue to generate substantial improvements in productivity. The favorable productivity numbers since the mid 1990s, and continuing in the recent downturn, certainly are consistent with this.

The Internet and low cost telecommunication costs allow companies to substantially alter many of the processes by which they do business. For example, new economy technology allows large reductions in transaction costs in areas like procurement, accounts payable, and human resources. Many of these are labor-intensive functions that can be outsourced or automated. Consistent with this, an increasing number of companies move tasks and processes like data entry, simple programming, and call center services from the United States to India and other lower wage countries. Much of this would not be possible without the new economy investments and technologies.

General Electric (GE) provides an interesting example. In the late 1990s, former GE Chairman and Chief Executive Officer Jack Welch challenged his employees to move everything they could to the Internet. They found that while they could not move transactions so quickly to the Internet, they could move a large number of internal and support processes. And, they could do so with "simple Web application [software] supported by email."[4] General Electric expects that transactions will gradually move to the Internet as software evolves and other companies move more toward the Internet. General Electric also expects to develop Web-based customer systems that monitor how GE equipment is performing and, therefore, improve the performance of that equipment.

I have not tried to estimate the overall or macro implications of this. Casual empiricism suggests that there are still a large number of existing processes for which new economy technology can reduce transaction costs substantially. The implementation of these transaction cost reductions will be gradual, as they require some upfront investment and adjustment costs.

It is possible, therefore, that the new economy technology can generate strong productivity increases at the same time that the companies and technologies that enable them do not earn much profit and the corporations that implement them do not earn much additional profit. Competition and the ability to copy drive profits down for the enablers. Competition among the companies that implement the improvements drives prices down for end users. In the end, the end user/consumer benefit as measured by the productivity increases despite the fact that the stock market does not.

6. Summary and Conclusions

In this paper, I have presented a framework to evaluate Internet/new economy businesses. The framework focuses on changes in transaction costs.

I used that framework to help discuss why Internet valuations were so high at the end of 1999 and why they have declined so precipitously since then. High valuations were fueled by beliefs that B2Cs would grow significantly and would transform traffic into revenues and profits while B2Bs and infrastructure companies would deliver larger reductions in transaction costs. In both areas, there also was an implicit assumption that competition would be weak, possibly because of network effects.

Valuations fell as the market began to realize that those beliefs and assumptions would not be validated.

I then discussed the implications of the rise and fall of valuations. It is simplistic to argue that smart, informed individuals took advantage of naïve public investors. Sophisticated and previously successful venture capital and buyout investors behaved as if they believed that Internet and new economy companies would be much more successful than they have been.

I then considered the effects of the large swings in market valuation/sentiment on individual companies. The market conditions clearly had a large effect on company actions. Before mid 2000, the private, VC-funded companies tended to push for additional revenues at the expense of profitability/cash flow. After mid 2000, as stock market values declined, those companies became increasingly focused on cash flows.

Finally, I speculated on the long-term real effects of the Internet/new economy. I think it is likely that information technology, the Internet, and other related technology have generated and will continue to generate substantial improvements in productivity. The favorable productivity numbers that have continued since the mid 1990s even into the recent downturn certainly are consistent with this. What is more ambiguous is whether those productivity improvements will contribute to increased corporate profits and favorable stock market performance or, instead, be captured by end users and consumers.

*Steven N. Kaplan is the Neubauer Family Professor of Entrepreneurship and Finance at the University of Chicago and a fellow at the National Bureau of Economic Research.

Notes

1. This section uses the framework described in more detail in Garicano and Kaplan (2001).

2. See Sawhney and Kaplan (1999).

3. The IPO measure is not perfect in that it does not include successful investments that are exited by acquisition. Nevertheless, the patterns in figure 3 are very suggestive.

4. The quote and the information in this paragraph are taken from *The Wall Street Journal*, May 8, 2001, p. A1.

References

Demers, A., and C. Lev, 2000, "A Rude Awakening: Internet Shakeout in 2000," New York University, working paper.

Garicano, Luis, and Steven Kaplan, 2001, "The Effects of Business-to-Business E-Commerce on Transaction Costs," *Journal of Industrial Economics*, December.

Hand, John R. M., 2000, "The Role of Economic Fundamentals, Web Traffic, and Supply and Demand in the Pricing of U.S. Internet Stocks," University of North Carolina, working paper.

Hendershott, Robert, 2001, "Net Value: Wealth Creation (and Destruction) during the Internet Boom," Leavy School, Santa Clara University, working paper.

Jorion, Philippe, and Eli Talmor, 2001, "Value Relevance of Financial and Non Financial Information in Emerging Industries: The Changing Role of Web Traffic Data," University of California, Irvine, working paper.

Ofek, Eli, and Matthew Richardson, 2001, "DotCom Mania: The Rise and Fall of Internet Stock Prices," National Bureau of Economic Research, working paper, No. 8630.

Rajgopal S., S. Kotha, and M. Venkatachalam, 2000, "The Relevance of Web Traffic for Internet Stock Prices," University of Washington, working paper.

Sawhney, Mohan, and Steven Kaplan, 1999, "Let's Get Vertical," *Business 2.0*, September.

Trueman, B., M. H. Wong, and X. Zhang, 2001, "The Eyeballs Have it: Searching for the Value in Internet Stocks," University of California, Berkeley, working paper.

Chapter 28
Home Bias, Transactions Costs, and Prospects for the Euro

Catherine L. Mann*
Institute for International Economics

and

Ellen E. Meade
London School of Economics

1. Overview

This paper brings together two strands of the international finance literature: Home bias and transactions costs and international portfolio flows and exchange rate movements. Each strand of the literature has substantial depth, and the questions that researchers investigate within each strand are not answered unequivocally. Consequently, our goal is to synthesize only some of the research and consider one general and one specific question: Would the U.S. dollar depreciate if the transactions costs associated with trading equities in non-U.S. markets were to fall to the level of transactions costs on U.S. exchanges? More specifically, given the interest in Europe on the development of a single market—including a pan-European financial market—is the current value of the euro low relative to the dollar because of higher transactions costs in European equity markets?

Answering these questions takes several steps:
- First, we need to understand better the nature of transactions costs and their implications for investment strategies in international assets.
- Second, we need to consider the evidence that a change in international portfolio flows can affect the exchange value of a currency.
- Only then can we consider the sensitivity of the links between transactions costs, international portfolio allocations and net capital flows, and the exchange rate.

The conceptual exercise we embark on is rather extensive, and only several elements will be treated in this paper, with others to be examined in future work. We focus on equity markets and the global portfolio behavior of U.S. and European investors, rather than the universe of assets (currency, official securities, corporate bonds) or investors. Equity markets have grown very rapidly in recent years as countries have deregulated financial markets, and the U.S. and European equity markets account for about three-quarters of world market capitalization.

To examine the behavior of the U.S. investor, we use the 1997 benchmark survey of U.S. holdings of foreign equities. United States invested wealth is large, but the share of U.S. equity wealth invested abroad is quite small (about 12 percent). If transactions costs are an important determinant of this allocation, then the effect of a change in transactions costs on U.S. portfolio allocations and cross-border equity flows could be large, with implications for the dollar.

To investigate the behavior of the European investor, we examine the allocations over time of equity portfolios of a set of largely European global investors using the *Economist* portfolio poll. This is a previously unexamined survey data set, which may offer insight into how home bias has changed for European investors with the introduction of the euro.

Using cross-section regression analysis of the 1997 U.S. Survey Benchmark data, we find that transactions costs, as distinct from information asymmetries, are significant in explaining portfolio allocations. The bias in equity allocations is measured using shares in actual holdings and shares of market capitalization available for purchase.

Using new survey data on firm-level equity holdings from the *Economist* magazine, we confirm that European firms show home bias in their holdings of European equities. From the start of the European Monetary Union (EMU) convergence period in 1997, the home bias of European firms falls as their holdings of U.S. equities rises. We are unable to find evidence of home bias for the U.S. firms in this sample.

The next two sections selectively summarize the research in the two strands of the literature that we are weaving together. Following that, we consider the U.S. investor and the European investor, respectively. Finally, we review implications of these results for the euro/dollar exchange rate, discuss financial market integration in Europe, and lay out plans for future work.

2. Portfolio Allocations and Transactions Costs

The extensive literature on "home bias" is the starting point for surveying the relationship between transactions costs and portfolio allocations. If U.S., European, and global investors more generally already hold the optimal portfolio, then looking for how allocations might change under different transactions cost scenarios holds little interest. The literature suggests that portfolios are not optimal and that the cost in terms of lower return and higher risk is large.

Lewis (1999) uses returns from the Standard & Poor's 500 synthetic fund (representing U.S. assets) and Morgan Stanley EAFE (representing the non-U.S. global fund) over the period January 1970 through December 1996 to show that the minimum variance portfolio for the U.S. investor allocates about 40 percent of the portfolio to non-U.S. assets, rather than the 10 percent that is actually invested in non-U.S. equity. By not following this minimum variance allocation strategy, the U.S. investor gives up about 50 basis points per year in return (while also decreasing risk), or 80 basis points per year with no change in risk.

Schröder (2002) considers various equity portfolios for European investors, examining risk and return over the period January 1978 to June 2001. The results for some investors are as dramatic as in Lewis' paper, but for other investors, less so. For a British investor, holding her optimal portfolio of 80 percent nondomestic assets instead of a portfolio of 20 percent nondomestic assets would yield an excess return of 2.2 percent per year. For a German investor, holding his optimal portfolio (which is 100 percent the global allocation) instead of about 20 percent in foreign assets yields an excess return of 3 percent per year. On the other hand, for a French investor, the optimal portfolio is near to her current portfolio allocation of 70 percent domestic French equities, so the gain from additional diversification is small.

The very large gains in terms of return on a portfolio that is diversified internationally suggest that the portfolio allocation strategies of most investors deviate substantially from the optimal allocation. Why is this so in a world of high finance and sophisticated advisors? Some researchers have investigated U.S. data on holdings of assets to determine causes of home bias. Along the way, they investigate whether the stylized fact of home bias of U.S. investors is accurate and whether the portfolio stock data are correct. If the underlying holdings data do not represent the portfolio that investors actually hold, then the huge gains to international diversification would be based on "straw-men" ultimate and initial allocations. (We discuss this further below.)

Transactions costs appear in the literature in a number of places, with differing conclusions. From a theoretical perspective, Lewis (1999) argues that no reasonable transactions costs in financial markets (including information costs as well as the costs of consummating a financial trade) could account for the home bias observed for U.S. investors. On the other hand, the influential work of Obstfeld and Rogoff (2000) explores how costs of engaging in trade in goods is reflected in the investment portfolio, finding that it is not too hard to get reasonable transactions costs in the real world to yield the home bias that is observed in the financial world.

The empirical work follows this theoretical division. Portes and Rey (1999) use the traditional "gravity model" of international trade augmented with information variables such as telephone traffic and number of bank branches to explain bilateral portfolio investment flows, with good results. Explaining the flows goes part of the way toward explaining the puzzles about the stock of holdings. In the empirical work on asset allocation, transactions costs were initially thought to be an unreasonable explanation for U.S. home bias. Tesar and Werner (1995) found that turnover of foreign equities in U.S. portfolios was greater than turnover of domestic equities. Presumably, if transactions costs were higher abroad, U.S. investors would not churn this part of their portfolio more frequently. However, Warnock (2002) using benchmark survey data not available to Tesar and Werner shows that their results are due in part to use of inaccurate data on portfolio holdings.

Warnock (2002) suggests that high transactions costs on foreign stock exchanges might increase indirectly the incentive for foreign firms to list on U.S. exchanges, which does help to explain U.S. home bias. Indeed, Pagano, Randl, Roell, and Zechner (2000) and Pagano, Roell, and Zechner (2002) show that small, fragmented, less liquid, and more costly European exchanges receive fewer cross-listings, and that European firms choosing exchanges on which to list consider the size of transactions costs among other things (including accounting standards and corporate governance rules).

A different strand of the financial research focuses on transactions costs and the rate of return or cost of capital with follow-on implications for portfolio allocations. Domowitz and Steil (2001) and Domowitz, Glen, and Madhaven (2000) using data from Elkins/McSherry LLC (discussed below) calculate that actual trading costs have declined about $2^1\!/_2$ times more in the U.S. than in Europe (1996–98). With an assumed portfolio turnover of two times per year and the U.S. Treasury security as the riskless asset, the U.S. investor should put 17 percent into North American assets rather than 27 percent, and 37 percent into French, German, and UK assets instead of 32 percent, with smaller changes in the portfolio shares for other regions (see table 7 in Domowitz, Glen, and Madhavan, 2002).

In sum, the recent literature suggests that transactions costs are important, not irrelevant, and go part of the way towards explaining the home bias of the U.S. investor.

3. Portfolio Allocations and Exchange Rates

The relationship between international portfolio allocations and exchange rates has a long and rich theoretical history with an abysmal empirical track record, at least until quite recently. Branson and Henderson (1985) review the portfolio balance theory of exchange rates. Frenkel and Mussa (1985) address the relationship in the context of the current account-exchange rate link. Levich (1985) reports on the general failure to find much of a relationship between portfolio allocations and exchange rates.

Despite the empirical failure in the 1980s, the increasing importance of portfolio flows in international capital markets, the clear relationship between portfolio flows and exchange rates in the context of financial crises in the 1990s (the exchange rate mechanism crisis 10 years ago, subsequent crises in Mexico, Asia, Russia, Brazil, and most recently, Turkey and Argentina), and the apparently puzzling depreciation of the euro since its inception, all have turned researchers back to these portfolio balance models in one form or another.

While few authors depend solely on portfolio stocks or flows to explain exchange rate movements, there is some evidence that portfolio flows themselves are statistically relevant for the determination of exchange rates—or at least the euro/dollar rate— above and beyond other factors such as return or productivity differentials (Tille, Stoffels, and Gorbachev, 2001, Alquist and Chin, 2002). Sinn and Westermann (2001) find a role for portfolio flows owing to the changing use of the German mark in advance of the euro. Brooks, Edison, Kumar, and Sløk (2001) find that net equity flows are statistically significant even after accounting for rates of return (as measured by interest rates) and stock market valuation changes, although Warnock and Cleaver

(2002) find evidence of measurement error in net portfolio flows between the U.S. and Europe. Meredith (2001) focuses on the U.S. productivity shock that affected U.S. stock market capitalization relatively more than European markets, as well as a relatively large increase in issuance of euro-denominated debt, both yielding a dollar appreciation. Fender and Galati (2001) argue that European purchases of U.S. firms is a statistically significant determinant of the euro's depreciation against the dollar.

In sum, notwithstanding the well-known result of Meese and Rogoff (1983), differential rates of return are relevant for explaining exchange rate movements, and so may be cross-border portfolio flows. If transactions costs are important for portfolio allocations and/or rates of return, then they could be important for exchange rate determination as well.

4. The U.S. Investor

That the U.S. investor exhibits home bias is not controversial; the questions are why and how much. In our focus on the U.S. investor, we extend the work of two prior studies to explicitly consider transactions costs.

Ahearne, Griever, and Warnock (2001, henceforth AGW) postulate that cross-listing of foreign equities on U.S. exchanges according to U.S. placement rules is one way to offer the same type of information on the foreign firm as for a U.S. firm, and to offer a transactions cost identical to the purchase or sale of a U.S. stock. Using data from the 1997 benchmark survey of U.S. portfolio holdings in a cross-section regression of about 40 countries, they find that the home bias of the U.S. investor against foreign stocks is reduced the greater is the share of the foreign market that is publicly listed in the U.S. (their U.S.LISTED variable). The increase in demand for foreign equities coming from the information contained in cross-listing reduces the share of U.S. assets in U.S. investor portfolios from 90 percent to 75 percent, a substantial move toward the market-capitalization neutral share of about 50 percent.

Pinkowitz, Stulz, and Williamson (2001, henceforth PSW) postulate that not all foreign listed shares actually are available for purchase, since, according to La Porta, Lopez-de-Silanes, Shleifer, and Vishny (1998), firms located outside the United States often are controlled by a large shareholder. Using the 1997 U.S. benchmark survey data in a cross-section regression, PSW find that the share of closely held stocks in a country's markets helps to explain the portfolio allocation of U.S. equity investors and reduces measured home bias. Once closely held stocks are accounted for, the market-capitalization neutral for the United States rises from 50 percent (the U.S. share in world market capitalization) to 58 percent.

Taking into account AGW's increased demand for foreign assets and PSW's reduced supply of foreign assets, a good part of the puzzle of U.S. home bias can be explained. Can transactions costs explain more?

4.1 Transactions Costs

For transactions costs, we use data supplied by the firm Elkins/McSherry LLC (E/M), a firm whose business it is to survey costs of engaging in equity transactions so as to assist other firms in reducing their own transactions costs. The most detailed E/M data track every trade from 1,000 investment managers, 1,700 global brokers, and 208 exchanges in 42 countries. We use less detailed averages for 41 countries; these cost data break down transactions costs into fees, commissions, and "market impact," where the latter measure attempts to capture the degree to which an individual trade moves the market price.[1]

Most other researchers using the E/M data proxy transactions costs with the sum of the three components (fees, commissions, and market impact). However, as noted by Domowitz, Glen, and Madhavan (2000), doing so confounds direct costs (fees and commissions) with indirect costs (market impact). Since we are interested in transactions costs arising from a change in the *intermediation process* from seller to buyer as distinct from the liquidity of the *financial exchange* on which the transaction takes place, we use the E/M data in disaggregated form.

4.2 Empirical Method and Results

In order to gauge the importance of transactions costs in U.S. equity portfolio holdings, we estimated cross-section regressions for 1997 using data for 41 countries from the U.S. benchmark survey and from E/M. First, we report regressions in which the dependent variable is a measure of bias, similar to AGW (henceforth "bias regressions"). Second, we report regressions in which the dependent variable is the actual share in U.S. equity portfolio holdings, similar to PSW (henceforth "share regressions").

In the bias regressions, the dependent variable is defined as BIAS for country x = 1 – (share of country x in actual portfolios of U.S. S investors) / (country x's share of world floating market capitalization), where floating market capitalization is capitalization less capitalization of closely held shares. This measure of bias was proposed in AGW using actual market capitalization and redefined in PSW to exclude that portion of market capitalization controlled by large shareholders.

Figure 1 plots the PSW and AGW bias measures for each of the 41 developed and emerging markets in our dataset. As discussed above, the PSW bias is smaller than the AGW bias because it corrects for the portion of market capitalization that is closely held. In most cases, the PSW bias reduces the extent to which U.S. investors are underweight a particular country in their portfolios relative to the AGW bias measure. With respect to U.S. assets, however, the PSW bias reduces the extent to which U.S. investors are overweight U.S. assets relative to the market neutral portfolio.

We used BIAS as the dependent variable in cross-section regressions for 41 countries;[2] results are shown in table 1. The explanatory variables included (variable names in parentheses): the portion of transactions costs representing fees and commissions (TCFC), the portion of transactions costs representing market impact (TCMI), the share of bank assets relative to gross domestic product (GDP) as a proxy for the importance of bank intermediated finance in a country (BKASSETS), and the portion of the foreign market listed on U.S. exchanges (USLISTED). Each equation included a dummy variable for the home location (HOME equal to 1 for the United States, and 0 otherwise) and a constant term.[3]

To summarize the estimation results, transactions costs are not statistically important in explaining investor *bias*. The positive, significant coefficient on BKASSETS suggests that financial diversity of a country has some bearing on the portfolio

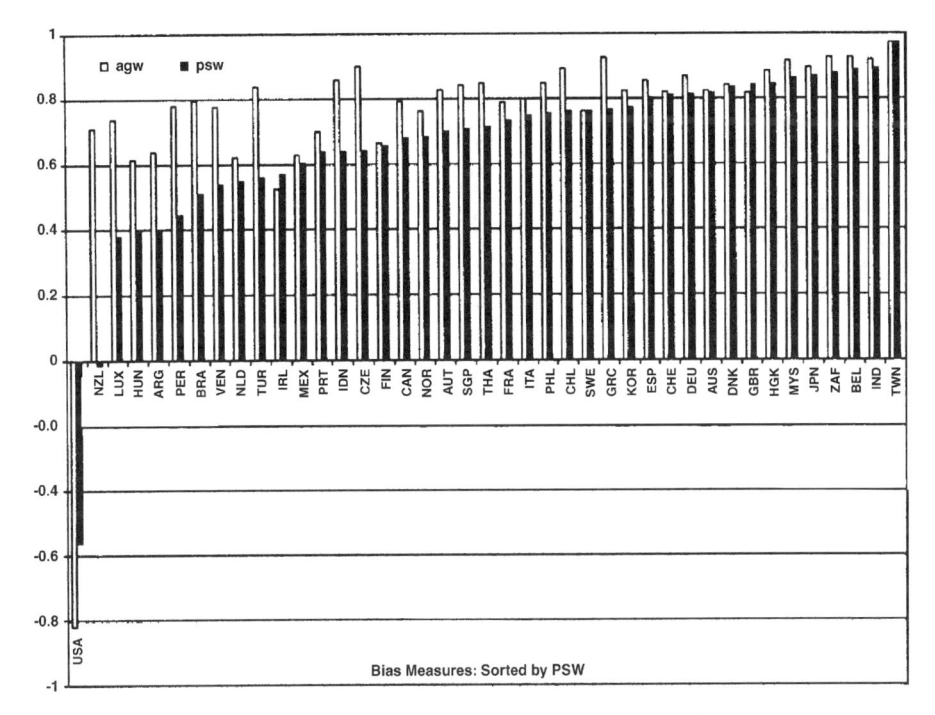

Figure 1: Bias Measures for 41 Developed and Emerging Markets

decisions of U.S. investors over and above what should already be reflected in market capitalization. A lower degree of financial diversity (a higher share of bank assets in GDP) is associated with higher PSW bias. The negative, significant coefficient on USLISTED suggests that underweighting of foreign equities in U.S. portfolios is lower the greater the share of the foreign market that is cross-listed on U.S. exchanges. This finding is similar to the result of Ahearne, Griever, and Warnock (2001), despite a different set of explanatory variables.

In the share regressions, the dependent variable is the actual share of a country's equities in total holdings of U.S. investors. The explanatory variables in the share regressions are identical to those in the bias regressions, except that the country's share in floating market capitalization (FLTSHR) is included as an additional regressor. Results also are reported in table 1. In summary, transactions costs are significant and negative, indicating that higher transactions costs are associated with holding a lower *actual* portfolio share. The fees and commissions component is statistically more important than the market impact component. A higher fraction of cross-listing in the U.S. market is associated with a statistically significantly higher actual portfolio share. The estimated coefficients are very small in magnitude. In essence, the HOME dummy explains 83 percent of actual holdings, floating market capitalization another 15 percent, with the remaining 2 percent of holdings attributable to other factors. These results indicate that, although transactions costs are statistically important, researchers have a long way to go in explaining actual portfolio holdings.

	Dependent Variable			
	BIAS		ACTSHR	
Variable:	(1)	(2)	(3)	(4)
FLTSHR			0.15**	0.14**
			(13.22)	(14.12)
TCFC	0.00	−0.08	−0.001*	−0.001*
	(0.01)	(−1.37)	(−2.41)	(−2.47)
TCMI	−0.03	−0.14	−0.001	−0.001
	(−0.16)	(−0.66)	(−1.66)	(−1.67)
BKASSETS	0.16**		−0.000	
	(3.25)		(−1.00)	
USLISTED		−0.004**		0.000*
		(−3.35)		(2.40)
HOME	−1.23**	−1.00**	0.83**	0.83**
	(−20.20)	(−9.26)	(125.87)	(144.11)
Adjusted R^2	0.60	0.62	0.99	1.00

Note: T-ratios computed using White standard errors. Significance at the 1 (5) percent level indicated by ** (*). Constants included but not reported. See text for variable definitions. See Mann and Meade (June 2002) for further discussion and estimation with additional variables.

Table 1: Estimation Results for Regressions

5. The European Investor

The development of the European capital markets into a pan-European market has been somewhat uneven and, on balance, slower than expected. Policy institutions and researchers have been trying to understand better what stands in the way of developing a pan-European market—what will develop naturally as the market matures, and what role can be played by policy initiatives. The International Monetary Fund's International Capital Market Report (2001) notes that some pan-European markets have developed (unsecured interbank money market) and others are developing (corporate debt). Before looking at the integration of European equity markets, we want to understand the extent to which European investors exhibit home bias, and whether home bias is as large for the European investor as it is for the U.S. investor. We examine this using data from a quarterly portfolio poll published in the *Economist*.

5.1 Economist Portfolio Poll

In a quarterly survey, the *Economist* asks international portfolio managers about the consolidated holdings of their firm by instrument (shares of bonds, equities, and cash) and provides a breakdown of equity holdings by area and bond holdings by currency. Each quarterly poll provides information on about 10 firms. Our sample runs from the first quarter of 1992 and ends in the fourth quarter of 2001 and includes 338 equity portfolio allocations by area reported by 10 firms. While the *Economist* provides information on the totality of a firm's portfolio in terms of equity shares invested in the United States, Japan, continental Europe, the UK, other Americas, and other Asia, we exclude the latter two areas from our analysis.[4]

For each firm in every time period, we computed AGW's measure of bias for the firm's reported holdings of U.S., continental European, UK, and Japanese equities. AGW bias is one minus the share in the actual portfolio relative to the share in the neutral-weighted portfolio (as measured by Morgan Stanley Capital International (MSCI), also reported in the *Economist* survey). If a firm holds the neutral-weighted portfolio, then AGW bias is equal to zero. If a firm holds a greater share of a particular region's equities than the neutral-weighted portfolio would suggest, then the portfolio is "overweight" and the AGW bias measure is negative. Conversely, if a firm holds less than the neutral-weighted portfolio, AGW bias is positive and the portfolio is "underweight."

Using the location of the firm's headquarters, we assigned home locations to each firm. Table 2 identifies the firms in the sample, their home locations, and the number of quarters for which we have information on their equity holdings by area.

Figures 2 and 3 plot the time series for Robeco Group Asset Management, Bank Julius Baer, Commerz International Capital Management, and Credit Suisse Asset Management—four of the six European firms in our dataset—with respect to shares of U.S. (figure 2) and European (figure 3) equities. The solid line in each chart is the MSCI neutral-weighted portfolio allocation. The charts indicate that European firms are overweight European equities (thus evidencing home bias) and underweight U.S. equities, relative to the MSCI neutral-weighted portfolio.

We used simple hypothesis tests to examine whether the mean AGW bias for the four European firms was statistically significantly different from zero. The results of this exercise are shown in table 3. In each case, a t-test of the mean AGW bias indicated that the null hypothesis of a zero mean could be rejected at the 5 percent significance level. Each of the four European firms exhibits "home" bias—that is, each firm is overweight European equities relative to the neutral portfolio (with Credit Suisse Asset Management the most overweight). In addition, the four European firms are underweight U.S. assets relative to the neutral portfolio.

Firm	# Obs	Home
Merrill Lynch	24	U.S.
Lehman Brothers	36	U.S.
Nikko Securities	27	J
Daiwa	36	J
Credit Agricole/Indocam	28	E
Robeco Group Asset Management	40	E
Bank Julius Baer	40	E
Phillips & Drew/ UBS	29	E
Commerz International	40	E
Credit Suisse Asset Management	38	E

U.S.=United States; J=Japan; E=continental Europe

Table 2: Portfolio Poll Firms and Home Locations

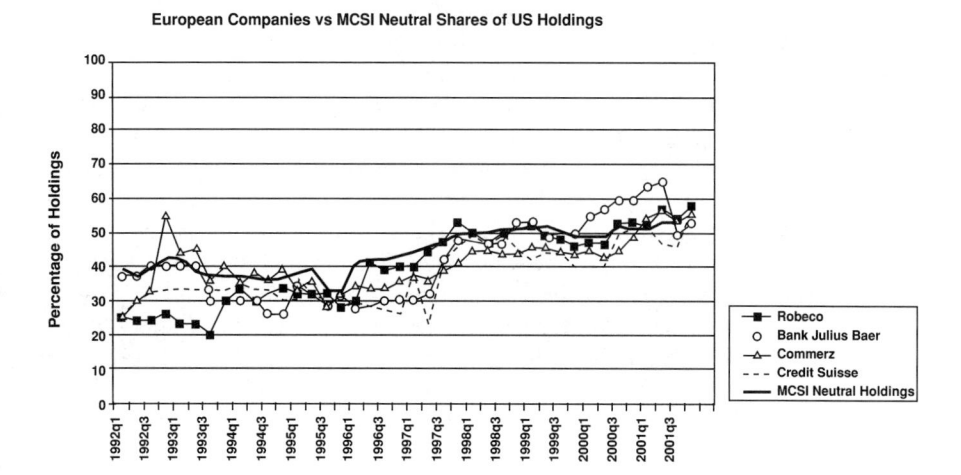

Figure 2: *Economist* Portfolio Poll Data for U.S. Firms

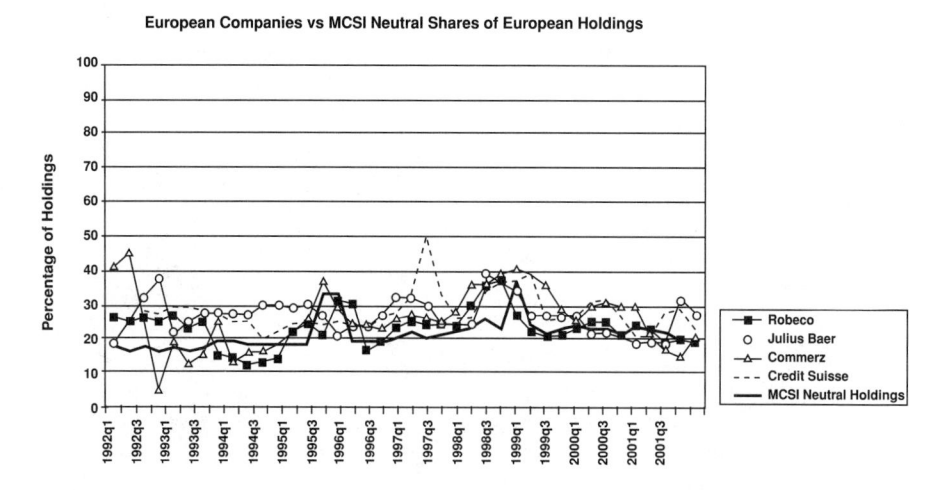

Figure 3: *Economist* Portfolio Poll Data for European Firms

	Mean bias for equity holdings of:	
Firm:	U.S.	Europe
Robeco Group Asset Management	0.1	–0.1
Bank Julius Baer	0.1	–0.3
Commerz International	0.1	–0.3
Credit Suisse Asset Management	0.1	–0.4

Table 3: T-tests for Bias, Individual European Firms

Next, we grouped firms by the location of their home, then used simple hypothesis tests to examine whether the mean of the asset holdings of the firms from a particular "home" location evidences home bias. In addition, because we have information on the firm's entire portfolio, we are able to examine mean holdings of firms in a given location with respect to "foreign" assets of different countries or regions. We test whether the AGW bias differs significantly from zero, and relatedly, whether AGW bias differs significantly from one home location to another. We look at the entire sample period, as well as two subperiods: before EMU convergence (1992Q1–1996Q4) and EMU convergence (1997Q1–2001Q4).

Table 4 shows the mean AGW bias for firms grouped by home location over the entire sample from 1992 through 2001. When a t-test of the mean has indicated that the null hypothesis of a zero mean cannot be rejected (at the 5 percent significance level), a "0" is shown for the mean bias. Bolded entries on the diagonal give the result for "home" bias.

Does the average holding of European firms exhibit home bias? Yes, European firms are significantly overweight holdings of European equities (–0.3), and underweight holdings of U.S. and Japanese equities relative to the neutral-weighted portfolio (0.1 and 0.1, respectively). Firms in the United States do not exhibit home bias (in contrast to the literature discussed above), are underweight Japan (0.2), and exhibit no bias with respect to European or UK equities. Japanese firms do exhibit home bias

	Mean bias for equity holdings of:			
Home:	U.S.	Japan	Europe	UK
U.S.	**0.0**	0.2	0.0	0.0
Japan	0.2	**–0.2**	0.0	0.0
Europe	0.1	0.1	**–0.3**	0.0

	1992Q1–1996Q4		1997Q1–2001Q4	
Home:	U.S.	Europe	U.S.	Europe
U.S.	**0.0**	0.0	0.1	–0.1
Europe	0.2	**–0.4**	0.1	**–0.2**

Table 4: T-tests for Bias, Firms Grouped by Home Location

(–0.2), are underweight U.S. assets (0.2), and are neutral with respect to European and UK equities.

Table 4 also shows the results for the average holding of U.S. firms and European firms for the two sample subperiods. Has the home bias of European firms changed between the period before convergence and the convergence period? Our results indicate that European home bias has declined, indicating diversification out of European assets. European firms have increased their holdings of U.S. equities, although not enough to move fully to the neutral-weighted portfolio. Firms in the United States moved from a neutral position with respect to U.S. and European equities in the early period to acquire a greater share of European equities in the later period.

There are several hypotheses for why the EMU convergence period might have yielded these allocations. Eliminating exchange rate risk no doubt alters the diversification strategy. Perhaps consolidation of financial markets in Europe is leading to a higher covariance among European stocks, thus reducing the value of diversification coming from buying into the various domestic markets. Unfortunately, it is too early to tell whether intra-European diversification is increasing (with diversification achieved through a broader array of stocks exhibiting sectoral variation) as found by Adjaouté and Danthine (2001b) or decreasing, with incomplete consolidation of the financial markets within Europe leaving sectoral variation quite small and national correlations quite high (as found by Adjaouté and Danthine (2001a) and Fratzscher (2001)).

6. Implications for the Euro/Dollar Exchange Rate

From the cross-section analysis, we determined that transactions costs influence the degree of home bias (as adjusted by the portion of market capitalization that is available for purchase). In particular, we find that the fees and commissions component of the E/M data on transactions costs, rather than the market impact component, is statistically significant. Since 1997, there has been a convergence in commissions in Europe (not shown in the charts) that is consistent with the reduction in U.S. investor bias against holdings of European assets observed in the portfolio poll analysis. This finding taken in isolation would tend to raise the value of the euro against the dollar.

The portfolio poll data allow inferences on trans-Atlantic capital flows both ways. If European investors diversified out of European assets to a greater extent than U.S. investors diversified into European assets, then the net equity capital flows would tend to favor the dollar. Are there data to check this hypothesis? Not yet.

For U.S. outbound trans-Atlantic flows, the U.S. data on portfolio flows (the Treasury International Capital, or TIC data) are suspect because the flow data are classified by transactor, not ultimate beneficiary or obligor. Moreover, as detailed in Warnock and Cleaver (2002), the accumulated and valuation-adjusted flow data yield significantly flawed assessments of the bilateral portfolio holdings for dates between survey benchmarks. Warnock and Cleaver document that the portfolio flow data underestimate U.S. holdings of euro area equities over a four-year period by some 30 percent, even as flows and holdings of U.S. equities by European investors seem to be adequately accounted for. We would expect foreign exchange markets to see through any statistical quirks, even if empirical researchers cannot.

To be provocative, we would like to quantify the potential effect of a change in transactions costs on the euro/dollar exchange rate. Suppose a truly pan-European equity market develops, one where intra-European equity markets are linked such that an investor can buy any European asset from any exchange for a single transaction cost. In that scenario, transaction costs in Europe would decline from current levels, increasing the net rate of return on European holdings. This would lead to an increase in U.S. portfolio allocations toward European assets and support an appreciation of the euro.

7. Remarks on European Financial Market Consolidation and Future Work

Financial market consolidation and maturation is a key goal of the EMU process. A substantial effort has been put forward in Europe to better understand the barriers to consolidation and the consequences of it. Many researchers feel that transactions costs matter for European investment. Our results suggest that that concern is correct.

In a recent study for the Center for European Policy Studies, Lannoo and Levin (2001) use operating profits of financial firms to show that domestic trades on a single national exchange within a country in Europe or on a U.S. exchange within the U.S. incur approximately the same clearing cost. But, since the individual exchanges in Europe are much smaller and offer fewer investment opportunities compared with the U.S. market, a European investor cannot find diversification in his own domestic market. A European investor would therefore want to trade across national exchanges, and in so doing, would bear higher settlement and, more importantly, higher intermediation costs. Euroclear (an international custodian securities depository that services the intra-European market as well as the international market) estimates that 60 percent of the costs of intermediating a cross-border equity trade arises from the maintenance of back-office operations and staff to service multiple markets. An additional 35 percent of the cost of intermediating a cross-border trade arises from the need to have local agents who know the peculiarities of the individual markets.

Lannoo and Levin conclude: "The cost issue is not only a question of domestic versus cross-border, but rather *intra* versus *inter* systems. Since no truly integrated European infrastructure exists for securities settlement, moving securities from one system, to another will necessarily be more expensive than staying within one system." (p. i). Thus, what matters for transactions costs intra-Europe is less the cost of the *exchange per se* and more the cost of the *intermediation process*. Intra-European trades across exchanges can cost up to eight times more than domestic trades or trades with the United States (Lanoo and Levin, tables 4, 5, and 10). Differences of this magnitude should affect portfolio allocations; we establish econometrically in the cross-section analysis that they do and make similar inferences using the portfolio poll data.

In future work, we hope to use bilateral equity holdings for European countries to investigate the role played by transactions costs. These results, together with our results for U.S. equity holdings, will allow us to estimate the effects of a change in transactions costs on holdings and derive an implication for the euro/dollar exchange rate.

*Catherine L. Mann is a senior fellow at the Institute for International Economics. Ellen E. Meade is a professor at the Center for Economic Performance of the London School of Economics. The authors appreciate comments from Frank Warnock. A more extensive version of this paper is Mann and Meade (2002) June.

Notes

1. "Market impact" measures the percentage movement of the buy or sell price from a daily benchmark average of open, close, high, and low prices.

2. Although PSW redefine AGW's bias measure to exclude closely held shares, the authors do not use the re-defined bias measure in regressions.

3. We include the HOME dummy rather than drop the U.S. from the sample, as in the AGW and PSW papers.

4. There are two caveats on the poll data worth noting. First, the *Economist* poll included 13 firms, but we excluded three firms from the sample owing to an insufficient number of observations on each firm. Second, there were two mergers over the period, and we have treated the merged firms as a single firm for the purposes of our analysis.

References

Ahearne, A., W. Griever, and F. Warnock, 2001, "Information Costs and Home Bias: An Analysis of U.S. Holdings of Foreign Equities," Federal Reserve Board, discussion paper, May.

Adjaouté, K., and J. Danthine, 2001a, "EMU and Portfolio Diversification Opportunities," Center for Economic Policy Research, working paper, October.

_____, 2001b, "Portfolio Diversification: Alive and Well in Euroland!," Center for Economic Policy Research, working paper, November.

Alquist, R., and M. Chinn, 2002, "Productivity and the Euro-Dollar Exchange Rate Puzzle," National Bureau of Economic Research, working paper, March.

Branson, W., and D. Henderson, 1985, "The Specification and Influence of Asset Markets," in *Handbook of International Economics Volume II*, R. Jones and P. Kenen, eds., Amsterdam: Elsevier Science Publishers.

Brooks, R., H. Edison, M. Kumar, and T. Sløk, 2001, "Exchange Rates and Capital Flows," International Monetary Fund, working paper, November.

Domowitz, I., J. Glen, and A. Madhavan, 2000, "Liquidity, Volatility, and Equity Trading Costs Across Countries and Over Time," Penn State University, working paper, January.

Domowitz, I. and B. Steil, 2001, "Innovation in Equity Trading Systems: The Impact on Transactions Costs and Cost of Capital," in *Technological Innovation and Economic Performance*, R. Nelson, D. Victor, and B. Steil, eds., Princeton, NJ: Princeton University Press.

Economist Ltd., The, 1992–2001, "Portfolio Poll," *The Economist*, selected issues.

Fender, I., and G. Galati, 2001, "The Impact of Transatlantic M&A Activity on the Dollar/Euro Exchange Rate," *BIS Quarterly Review*, December, pp. 58–68.

Fratzscher, M., 2001, "Financial Market Integration in Europe: On the Effects of the EMU on Stock Markets," European Central Bank, working paper, March.

Frenkel, J., and M. Mussa, 1985, "Exchange Rates and the Balance of Payments," in *Handbook of International Economics Volume II*, R. Jones and P. Kenen, eds., Amsterdam: Elsevier Science Publishers.

International Monetary Fund, 2001, *International Capital Markets: Developments, Prospects, and Key Policy Issues*, Washington, DC.

Lannoo, K., and M. Levin, 2001, "The Securities Settlement Industry in the EU: Structure, Costs and the Way Forward," Center for European Policy Studies: Brussels.

La Porta, R., F. Lopez-de-Silanes, A. Shleifer, and R. Vishny, 1998, "Law and Finance," *Journal of Political Economy*, Vol. 106, December, pp. 1113–1155.

Levich, R., 1985, "Empirical Studies of Exchange Rates," in *Handbook of International Economics Volume II*, R. Jones and P. Kenen, eds., Amsterdam: Elsevier Science Publishers.

Lewis, K., 1999, "Trying to Explain Home Bias in Equities and Consumption," *Journal of Economic Literature*, Vol. 37, June, pp. 571–608.

Mann, Catherine L., and Ellen E. Meade, 2002, "Home Bias, Transactions Costs, and Prospects for the Euro: A More Detailed Analysis," Center for Economic Performance, London School of Economics, discussion paper, and Institute for International Economics, working paper, June.

Meese, R., and K. Rogoff, 1983, "Empirical Exchange Rate Models of the Seventies: Do They Fit Out of Sample?," *Journal of International Economics*, Vol. 14, February, pp. 3–24.

Meredith, G., 2001, "Why Has the Euro Been So Weak?," International Monetary Fund, working paper, October.

Obstfeld, M., and K. Rogoff, 2000, "The Six Major Puzzles in International Macroeconomics: Is There a Common Cause?," National Bureau of Economic Research, working paper, July.

Pagano, M., O. Randl, A. Roell, and J. Zechner, 2000, "What Makes Stock Exchanges Succeed? Evidence from Cross-Listing Decisions," Center for Studies in Economics and Finance, working paper, December.

Pagano, M., A. Roell, and J. Zechner, 2002, "The Geography of Equity Listing: Why Do Companies List Abroad?," *Journal of Finance*, Vol. 57.

Pinkowitz, L., R. Stulz, and R. Williamson, 2001, "Corporate Governance and the Home Bias," National Bureau of Economic Research, working paper, December.

Portes, R., and H. Rey, 1999, "The Determinants of Cross-Border Equity Flows," National Bureau of Economic Research, working paper, September.

Schröder, M., 2002, "Benefits of Diversification and Integration for International Equity and Bond Portfolios," Center for European Economic Research/Zentrum für Europäische Wirtschaftsforschung, January.

Sinn, H., and F. Westermann, 2001, "Why Has the Euro been Falling? An Investigation into the Determinants of the Exchange Rates," National Bureau of Economic Research, working paper, July.

Tesar, L., and I. Werner, 1995, "Home Bias and High Turnover," *Journal of International Money and Finance*, Vol. 14, August, pp. 467–492.

Tille, C., N. Stoffels, and O. Gorbachev, 2001, "To What Extent Does Productivity Drive the Dollar?," *Current Issues in Economics and Finance*, Vol. 7, August, pp. 1–6.

U.S. Department of the Treasury, 2000, "Report on U.S. Holdings of Foreign Long-Term Securities," April.

Warnock, F., 2002, "Home Bias and High Turnover Reconsidered," *Journal of International Money and Finance*, Vol. 2.

Warnock, F., and C. Cleaver, 2002, "Financial Centers and the Geography of Capital Flows," Federal Reserve Board, discussion paper, April.

Appendix

Codes for Developed and Emerging Markets (Figure 1, p. 409)

Country	Codes	Country	Codes
United States	USA	France	FRA
New Zealand	NZL	Italy	ITA
Luxembourg	LUX	Philippines	PHL
Hungary	HUN	Chile	CHL
Argentina	ARG	Sweden	SWE
Peru	PER	Greece	GRC
Brazil	BRA	Korea	KOR
Venezuela	VEN	Spain	ESP
Netherlands	NLD	Switzerland	CHE
Turkey	TUR	Germany	DEU
Ireland	IRL	Australia	AUS
México	MEX	Denmark	DNK
Portugal	PRT	Great Britain	GBR
Indonesia	IDN	Hong Kong	HGK
Czech	CZE	Malaysia	MYS
Finland	FIN	Japan	JPN
Canada	CAN	South Africa	ZAF
Norway	NOR	Belgium	BEL
Austria	AUT	India	IND
Singapore	SGP	Taiwan	TWN
Thailand	THA		

Source: United Nations web site at www.un.org/depts/dhl/maplib/docs/geoname.pdf

Chapter 29
Comments on "Valuation and New Economy Firms"

Lawrence Slifman*
Board of Governors of the Federal Reserve System

For the most part, discussions about asset price bubbles and firm valuation are the domain of financial economists and the analytical tools of finance. However, as a macroeconomist, I prefer to use the notion of a production function as the basic organizing principle. What are the values and quantities of a firm's inputs and outputs, and how are a firm's inputs combined to create output and value?

Steve Kaplan's paper focuses on a key characteristic of the output of Internet firms—lower transaction costs. He then discusses the implications of this characteristic for the valuation of Internet firms. Using the notion of a production function, I would like to look not only at some important characteristics of the output of new economy firms, but also at some important characteristics of the inputs used by new economy firms.

In his paper, Kaplan talks only about Internet firms. But, as the title of this session—"Technology, the New Economy, and Asset Price Bubbles"—makes clear, this conference is about more than just Internet firms. So, the first questions I would like to raise are: What do we mean by "new economy firms," and what are some of their distinguishing characteristics?

The hallmark of new economy firms seems to be their heavy reliance on intangibles and, in many cases, rapidly evolving equipment as sources of firm value and productivity. That definition obviously includes more than just Internet and related firms; indeed, it includes more than information technology firms broadly defined. For example, the definition also includes many cutting-edge pharmaceutical and biotechnology companies—and, to my mind, rightly so. By this definition, then, new economy firms are distinguished by their inputs and not their outputs.

But the outputs of new economy firms also seem to have a common characteristic. As Kaplan's analysis makes clear, the output of new economy firms somehow involves quality change: lower transactions costs for Internet firms, thinner wafers for semiconductor manufacturers, or more effective life-saving medicines for pharmaceutical makers. Of course, quality change is not unique to new economy firms; old economy firms such as automakers are constantly improving the quality of their output, as well. In other words, improving output quality is a necessary characteristic of new economy firms but not a sufficient characteristic.

These common characteristics—heavy reliance on intangibles, use of equipment subject to rapid technological change, and changing output quality—play an important role in the valuation of new economy firms. They are also at the heart of some of the most difficult questions in production theory: What is capital? What are intangibles—assets to be capitalized or intermediate inputs? How should intangibles be valued? And, what is the appropriate way to measure changes in output quality?

Looking at the inputs in the production function of new economy firms, I would like to turn to some questions regarding the valuation of their tangible assets. The first issue I want to raise is obsolescence versus decay. As we all know, computers, unlike cars or machine tools, typically suffer very little physical decay or loss of productive services as they are used over time. But the value of those computers on the used-computer market falls very rapidly because of rapid technical improvements over time; that is, they become obsolete quickly. Thus, the balance sheet of a firm, which values tangible assets at historical cost, could well overstate the market value of those assets. Such overstatement probably isn't important for a start-up dot-com, whose tangible assets, it has been said, typically consist of a Sun server and a copy of Oracle software. But it could well be important, for example, for a long-haul fiber optic firm if the DWDM (dense wave division multiplexing) equipment used to light multiple channels on the fiber becomes obsolete quickly.

The case of long-haul fiber optic carriers raises another critical consideration regarding the value of a new economy firm's tangible assets—utilization. My colleague, Mark Doms, has estimated that for long-haul carriers, only about 30 percent of the fiber-miles installed are actually lit.[1] But with the right equipment, a strand of fiber can transmit data on multiple channels. More importantly, changes in the technology of the equipment used to transmit multiple channels of data over fiber have during the past five years exceeded the pace of Moore's law. Doms estimates that if the latest technology were employed on all of the installed fiber, then the utilization rate could be as low as 2 percent or 3 percent. Clearly, looking just at the book value of the tangible assets of a long-haul carrier would not give an accurate impression of the revenues that those assets are generating under current demand conditions.[2]

A final issue that I would like to raise about tangible assets is relevant for any firm (or household, for that matter). Tax laws, accountants, and our national economic accounts all assume fixed distributions of retirements for different classes of tangible assets based on some assumptions about decay. But, in fact, the decision to retire (scrap) an asset depends not just on its age and physical condition. Retirement decisions are also affected by the business cycle, among other things. Firms are much more likely to extend the productive service life of an asset by increasing outlays for maintenance and repair during a cyclical downturn than during an economic expansion. They are also more likely to stretch out replacement cycles for equipment subject to rapid technical change. This endogenous scrapping could be very important for translating gross investment into net investment and for predicting a firm's capital expenditures. Research by Cohen and Greenspan (1999) presented data that showed the cyclicality of automobile scrappage rates, and my colleague Jason Cummins is currently investigating the implications of endogenous scrapping for investment in business equipment.

Let me turn now to the critical input of new economy firms—their intangibles. Kaplan is far more expert on this subject than I am, but my reading of the literature and my conversations with business people suggest to me that organizational infrastructure and human capital are among the most crucial intangibles of new economy firms. Moreover, like such old economy giants as Coca Cola, many new economy firms spend heavily on developing brand equity. The issue, of course, is how to place a value on these intangibles. Some of the most insightful thinking on that question has been done by Baruch Lev; what I have to say on this subject is borrowed largely from his work.[3] Lev describes several features of intangibles that seem to apply with great force to valuing the inputs of new economy firms.

One feature of intangibles highlighted by Lev is that they can depreciate quickly. An idea that at one moment is an extremely valuable asset of a firm can be quickly displaced by a competitor's better idea, thus diminishing its value significantly and perhaps rendering it worthless. Another example is advertising ("brand equity"). Who remembers most of the extraordinarily expensive advertising that aired on the Super Bowl telecast just three months ago? The value of that spending has almost entirely dissipated. The implication for valuation is quite simple: Even though a firm may be spending huge amounts of venture capitalists' money on investing in intangibles, the *net* addition to the stock of a firm's intangibles might well be quite small.[4]

Lev also points out that, with one noteworthy exception, firms often find maintaining exclusive control over many of their intangible assets to be difficult. A firm *can* exclude a competitor from access to its installed base of physical capital. In contrast, a firm's competitors generally are free to try to lure away the cream of its human capital crop. So, a group of researchers that might appear to be a valuable asset for AstraZeneca one day could be gone the next day and be part of the Johnson & Johnson human capital stock. As a consequence of rapid depreciation and nonexcludability, the value of certain intangibles to a particular firm can be quite evanescent.

The one notable exception to the nonexcludability of intangibles is organizational infrastructure. As Lev puts it, "A company's organizational infrastructure is an amalgam of systems, processes, and business practices ... aimed at streamlining operations toward achieving the company's objections." By its very nature, then, organizational infrastructure is unique to a particular firm. You can't go out and buy organizational infrastructure the way you can buy a new computer, or advertising, or Ph.D. scientists. Just buying labor, tangible assets, and advertising doesn't mean you can create another Yahoo!. Because organizational infrastructure is idiosyncratic and cannot be bought and sold in an active market, it has no true market price.[5] Naturally, then, the lack of market prices makes the accurate valuation of firms that rely heavily on organizational infrastructure extremely difficult.

The implication of these characteristics of intangibles—that is, they are very difficult to value and their value at any time is evanescent—reinforces one of the points Kaplan makes in his paper. The overly ebullient profit forecasts of many investors, undoubtedly based in part on overly ebullient valuations of the intangible assets of dot-coms, boosted the equity prices of such firms far beyond levels that were consistent with the actual value of the firms' intangible assets.

Finally, I would like to return to a major theme raised in Kaplan's paper—the output of new economy firms somehow involves quality improvements. As someone who spends at least part of his time thinking about the measurement of output and productivity, I find quality improvements in the output of a firm to be critically important.[6] If buying a book from Amazon.com truly makes me better off than paying the same out-of-pocket cost and buying the book from my local bricks-and-mortar bookstore, then that improvement in my well-being (utility) should be reflected in the consumer price index for books. However, with the current measurement system, it isn't. More generally, to the extent that the quality improvements associated with the output of new economy firms are not adequately captured in price statistics, the nation's output and productivity will be understated. But that's a subject worthy of a conference of its own.

*Lawrence Slifman is an associate director in the Division of Research and Statistics at the Board of Governors of the Federal Reserve System. As a member of the staff of the Board of Governors, his work is not copyrighted.

Notes

1. Doms (2002) has a discussion of some economic issues related to the long-haul fiber optic industry. The utilization figures are from a conversation with Doms.

2. The perpetual inventory method for transforming investment into productive or wealth capital stocks will not fare well, either. Fundamentally, the perpetual inventory method relies on a fixed pattern of quality change for calculating depreciation. If the technology undergoes radical advances, then capital stocks can't be constructed with the usual set of tools.

3. See Lev (2001).

4. Corrado, Hulten, and Sichel (2002) also emphasize this point.

5. Jason Cummins (2002) discusses this in a recent paper.

6. See, for example, Corrado and Slifman (1999).

References

Corrado, Carol, Charles Hulten, and Daniel Sichel, 2002, "Measuring Capital and Technology: An Expanded Framework," paper prepared for the Conference on Research in Income and Wealth, Measuring Capital in the New Economy, National Bureau of Economic Research, April 26–27.

Corrado, Carol, and Lawrence Slifman, 1999, "Decomposition of Productivity and Unit Costs," *American Economic Review*, Vol. 89, May, pp. 328–332.

Cummins, Jason, 2002, "The Value of Intangible Capital: Estimates from Firm-Level Panel Data," paper prepared for the Conference on Research in Income and Wealth, Measuring Capital in the New Economy, National Bureau of Economic Research, April 26–27.

Doms, Mark, 2002, "Communications Equipment: What Has Happened to Prices?," paper prepared for the Conference on Research in Income and Wealth, Measuring Capital in the New Economy, National Bureau of Economic Research, April 26–27.

Greenspan, Alan, and Darrel Cohen, 1999, "Motor Vehicle Stocks, Scrappage, and Sales," *The Review of Economics and Statistics*, Vol. 81, August, pp. 369–383.

Lev, Baruch, 2001, *Intangibles: Management, Measurement, and Reporting*, Washington, DC: Brookings Institution Press.

PART VII

IMPLICATIONS OF BUBBLES FOR MONETARY POLICY

Chapter 30
Asset Prices in a Flexible Inflation Targeting Framework

Stephen G. Cecchetti*
Ohio State University and National Bureau of Economic Research

Hans Genberg
University of Geneva

and

Sushil Wadhwani
Bank of England

1. Introduction

Inflation targeting is being adopted by an increasing number of central banks. Almost every day another country is added to the list that contained only a handful a few years ago. It is surely no coincidence that inflation rates (actual as well as expected) have decreased substantially and, so far, durably in countries that have adopted this strategy for the conduct of monetary policy.

But what is the essence of inflation targeting, and how should it be implemented in practice? The straightforward answer to the first of these questions is that the central bank should strive to maintain inflation as close to a clearly specified target level as possible, while at the same time limiting fluctuations of real economic activity.[1] Interpreted in this way, inflation targeting is a statement of the objectives of monetary policy alone that allows for different methods of implementation.[2] It is sometimes suggested that a practical strategy for achieving the inflation-targeting objective is to follow a Taylor rule, whereby a short-term interest rate instrument responds to deviations of expected future inflation from the target rate and to deviations of output from its full-employment level.[3]

Several practical questions must be addressed before such a strategy can be implemented. The policymaker must choose the relative weights to attach to inflation and output, the precise horizon for expected inflation and output, the difficulties associated with measuring the full-employment output level, and whether there is any role in the policy rule for variables other than expected inflation and the output gap. This paper is about the last of these questions. Specifically, we ask whether there is any role of asset prices in the formulation of monetary policy in a flexible inflation-targeting framework.

The most common answer to this question is contained in Bernanke and Gertler's influential study. They conclude that:

"The inflation targeting approach dictates that central banks should adjust monetary policy actively and preemptively to offset incipient inflationary and deflationary pressures. Importantly, for present purposes, it also implies that policy should *not* respond to changes in asset prices, except insofar as they signal changes in expected inflation."

Bernanke and Gertler, 1999, p. 78

The primary exception to the view that asset prices do not belong in a Taylor-type interest-rate reaction function has arisen in an open-economy context. Ball (1999) finds that adding the exchange rate to the Taylor rule improves macroeconomic performance in a model where the exchange rate has a significant role in the transmission mechanism of structural shocks and monetary policy.[4]

Cecchetti, Genberg, Lipsky, and Wadhwani (CGLW) claim, however, that a more general case can be made for central banks to react to asset prices in the normal course of policymaking. There we argue that:

"[A] central bank concerned with both hitting an inflation target at a given time horizon, and achieving as smooth a path as possible for inflation, is likely to achieve superior performance by adjusting its policy instruments not only to inflation (or to its inflation forecast) and the output gap, but to asset prices as well. Typically, modifying the policy framework in this way could also reduce output volatility. We emphasize that this conclusion is based on our view that reacting to asset prices in the normal course of policymaking will reduce the likelihood of asset price bubbles forming, thus reducing the risk of boom-bust investment cycles."

CGLW, 2000, p. 2

Before we proceed, it is crucial to emphasize what we mean by this statement. It is our view that central banks can improve macroeconomic performance by *reacting* to asset price misalignments. We are not now saying, nor have we ever said, that policymakers should *target* asset prices.[5]

In the remainder of this paper, we first summarize the main arguments made in CGLW (section 2). In section 3, we discuss some of the recent work in this area. The implications of the recent research for our original view of the role of asset prices in the formulation of monetary policy are summarized in the final section of the paper. To anticipate, we believe that our original views remain valid. Criticisms have either adopted a too mechanical view of the conduct of monetary policy or assumed that central bankers are incapable of distinguishing (even approximately) between different types of macroeconomic disturbances. As we explained in detail in our previous study, and as we reiterate below, we take a different view on both issues.

2. Asset Prices and Central Bank Policy: Cecchetti, Genberg, Lipsky, and Wadhwani

In this section we restate the arguments presented in CGLW (2000) for how asset price misalignments should be used to guide central bank policy. We are primarily interested in examining whether and how asset price misalignments should influence monetary policy once other factors, such as the inflation outlook and the output gap, have been taken into account. In addition, we make a few brief comments both about the use of asset prices directly in the inflation measure targeted by the central bank and about the information content of asset prices for inflation forecasts.

To avoid confusion or misunderstanding, we want to emphasize that we are *not* advocating that asset prices should be *targets* for monetary policy, neither in the conventional sense that they belong in the objective function of the central bank, nor in the sense that they should be included in the inflation measure targeted by the monetary authorities. Instead, our principal claim is that central banks can improve macroeconomic performance by reacting systematically to asset price misalignments, over and above their reaction to inflation forecasts and output gaps. It is our view that central banks seeking to smooth output and inflation fluctuations can improve these macroeconomic outcomes by setting interest rates with an eye toward asset prices in general, and misalignments in particular. The main reason for this is that asset price bubbles create distortions in investment and consumption, leading to excessive increases and then falls in both real output and inflation. Raising interest rates modestly as asset prices rise above what are estimated to be warranted levels, and lowering interest rates modestly when asset prices fall below warranted levels, will tend to offset the impact on output and inflation of these bubbles, thereby enhancing overall macroeconomic stability. In addition, if it were known that monetary policy would act to "lean against the wind" in this way, it might reduce the probability of bubbles arising at all, which would also be a contribution to greater macroeconomic stability.

The rationale for our conclusions comes both from the intuition gained from simple theoretical models and from quantitative simulation results. In the remainder of this section we summarize these arguments.

2.1 The Intuitive Argument

The first illustration of the potential usefulness of reacting to asset prices is an application of the basic insight of Poole (1970), that leaning against the wind of interest rate changes is useful when disturbances originate in the money market. In CGLW we generalized this argument slightly to allow for movements in equity (or real estate) prices in an economy where the stock market (or the housing sector) is particularly important and to allow for changes in the exchange rate in an economy where the external sector is crucial.

A straightforward application of Poole's analysis shows that moderating changes in asset prices diminishes fluctuations in economic activity so long as the underlying reason for the asset price movement can be traced to a disturbance in the demand and/or the supply of the asset in question. To be sure, the same logic implies that when asset prices change as a result of disturbances in other markets—for example, if equity prices increase because of favorable productivity shocks—then the case for leaning against the wind of the asset price change disappears. It is important not to react automatically to any and all changes in asset prices, but to evaluate each situation separately and act accordingly.

The second illustration given in CGLW is based on a model due to Kent and Lowe (1997). Their model is dynamic and explicitly incorporates the notion of asset price misalignments. In their setup, when a bubble develops in equity markets, standard wealth effects drive current inflation up. Importantly, though, expected inflation may not change since there is a probability that the bubble will disappear by itself, reducing future inflationary pressures. A forward-looking central bank that sets the current interest rate in response to expected inflation (and does not take the equity price bubble into account) would not tighten monetary policy under such circumstances. As a result, the bubble in the equity market will bring about even higher inflation in the future if it continues and an even stronger economic slowdown if it collapses from an even higher level. Although expected inflation (i.e., the probability weighted average of these two future scenarios) may be on target, the country will suffer from highly variable economic activity as a result of the stance of monetary policy. By contrast, a policy of pre-emptively tightening in response to the emerging equity price bubble reduces this variability.

Similar mechanisms play a pivotal role in models in which monetary policy is transmitted via credit channels, and where the financial accelerator plays a significant role. In these cases, an emerging financial market bubble leads to higher investment as, given the higher value of their collateral, firms find it easier to borrow. More investment does stimulate aggregate demand and output in the short run, but in the end creates overcapacity and results in a sharp downturn. Even if average inflation is not affected significantly, the asset market bubble leads to higher output volatility. A central bank that reacts to the root cause of the instability—the asset price misalignment—will reduce the overall volatility in economic activity.

At an intuitive level, these arguments establish a prima facie case for taking asset price misalignments into account in the normal course of determining monetary policy, not only because they have an impact on expected inflation, but also because misalignments lead to unnecessarily large business cycle fluctuations. These conclusions are confirmed by the simulation results to which we now turn.

2.2 Reacting to Asset Prices in Three Macro Models

We summarize results from three simulation experiments. The first uses the small closed-economy model employed by Bernanke and Gertler (1999) to investigate the appropriate reaction of monetary policy to stock market bubbles. The second utilizes the small-scale open-economy model due to Batini and Nelson (2000) in which the exchange rate plays an important role. The third set of simulations explores the properties of a version of John Taylor's multi-country model originally developed to analyze international economic interdependence.

2.2.1 A Closed-economy Model Subject to a Stock Price Bubble

The Bernanke-Gertler model can be characterized as a standard dynamic new-Keynesian model, modified to allow for financial accelerator effects and exogenous asset price bubbles. Briefly, the economy comprises three sectors: households who consume and save; a government that manages fiscal and monetary policy; and a business sector composed of firms that hire labor, invest in new capacity, and produce goods and services.

Firms finance the acquisition of capital both through the use of internal funds and through external borrowing. The existence of credit market frictions means that there is a premium on external finance that affects the overall cost of capital and thus the real investment decisions of firms. This external finance premium depends inversely on the financial condition of potential borrowers. An improvement in a borrowing firm's position translates into a fall in the premium, which serves to magnify investment and output fluctuations. So, for example, an increase in a firm's share price, raising the net worth of the owners, will make the firm more creditworthy, reduce the external finance premium, thereby increasing borrowing and investment. This financial accelerator mechanism provides an additional channel through which monetary policy can affect spending. With a fall in real interest rates, for example, asset prices will rise, reducing the cost of external borrowing and providing an extra stimulus for investment.

For the purpose at hand, the crucial aspect of the Bernanke-Gertler model is the introduction of financial bubbles through the possibility that observed stock prices differ persistently from fundamental values, and that this difference grows exponentially. The consequence of this is that the bubble affects the quality of a firm's balance sheet, and so the cost of capital falls systematically when stock prices exceed fundamental values. The result is an increase in investment, resulting in both higher current aggregate demand and higher future potential output. When the bubble bursts, the financial accelerator operates in reverse leading to a reduction in both inflation and output.

To investigate the potential for monetary policy to moderate the influence of the financial bubble on the economy, CGLW study the consequence of the central bank setting the short-term interest rate according to the reaction function,

1) $R_t = \gamma_\Pi E_t \pi_{t+1} + \gamma_y(y_t - y_t^*) + \gamma_s s_{t-1} + \gamma_R R_{t-1}$,

where R is a policy-determined short-term interest rate, y is the log of real output, y^* is the log of potential or full-employment output, s is asset price misalignment, and E is the expectation operator. We assume that policymakers seek to minimize a loss function of the form,

2) $L = \alpha \text{var}(\pi) + (1 - \alpha)\text{var}(y)$,

where α is the relative weight on inflation variability in the objective function. CGLW examine whether the optimal value of $\gamma_s > 0$, i.e., can loss L be reduced by reacting to the stock price bubble?

The conclusion of the simulation experiments reported in CGLW was that "In the majority of the cases we study, it is strongly advisable for interest rates to respond [to stock price bubbles]. While the reaction may not be very large, it should clearly be there," (p. 25).

2.2.2 Monetary Policy and the Exchange Rate in a Small Model of an Open Economy

CGLW present a second set of simulations designed to investigate whether a central bank in an open economy should pay attention to exchange rate movements when it sets interest rates. We employ a variant of the Batini-Nelson (2000) model. This is a relatively conventional small open-economy model based on an aggregate demand and an aggregate supply relationship together with an equation determining the exchange rate. Aggregate demand depends on expected future income in addition to the expected real interest rate, aggregate supply is modeled according to a partially forward-looking Phillips curve, and the exchange rate is determined by the condition of uncovered interest parity.

In the simulations we consider two types of shocks: pure financial shocks, corresponding to deviations from strict uncovered interest parity, and pure aggregate demand shocks, unrelated to disturbances in income or the real interest rate. As before, CGLW were interested in finding out whether in addition to reacting to expected inflation, the central bank's interest-rate target should or should not respond to the exchange rate.

Not surprisingly, we found that the answer depends on the nature of the shock being considered. When financial disturbances hit the economy are the sole source of shocks, it is desirable to lean against the wind of exchange rate changes. Doing so prevents these shocks from destabilizing the real sector of the economy. When the objective of the central bank is to minimize some combination of variability of inflation and output from their respective target values, taking action to eliminate the effects of financial disturbances is a good thing. On the other hand, when aggregate demand shocks are important as well, changes in the exchange rate typically serve a useful function of absorbing some of the adjustment, thereby lessening the fluctuations in prices and output. Leaning against the wind of such exchange rate changes is then counterproductive. The simulation results presented in CGLW confirm this reasoning.

It is possible that these simulation results actually understate the benefits from a monetary policy rule that, in part, works to counteract exchange rate misalignments. To take a concrete example, suppose that a bubble creates an unwarranted appreciation of the exchange rate, and that *the bubble can be affected by monetary policy*. Then it might make sense to keep interest rates lower than would be necessary to, say, have expected inflation at a fixed time-horizon equal to target, because such a policy would mitigate the domestic deflationary impact of the bubble and reduce the deviation of inflation from the target today, with the added benefit of reducing the size of the "shock" from the bubble while it lasts. Moreover, since the bubble will be smaller on average under the proactive monetary policy, the destabilizing effects of the bursting of the bubble will also be also smaller. Hence, in this case, a monetary policy that takes the exchange rate misalignment into account could, under certain circumstances, reduce the average size of the (absolute) deviations of inflation from target measured over the entire future.[6]

2.2.3 Reacting to the Exchange Rate in a Large Multi-country Model

In a study designed to evaluate the consequences for macroeconomic stability, if Switzerland were to join the euro-area, Genberg and Kadareja (2000) provide evidence on the desirability of making Swiss monetary policy react to exchange rate movements. In contrast to the two previous sections, this is done in the context of a multi-country econometric model estimated with actual data. Specifically, Genberg and Kadareja adapt the model originally developed by John Taylor in the early 1990s. Taylor's framework is useful for studying monetary policy interactions and spillovers between the countries and the role of different types of exchange rate arrangements.

The Taylor model is a sophisticated Mundell-Fleming model with two important additions: a set of wage-price relationships on the one hand and rational expectations on the other. Genberg and Kadareja modified the original setup by substituting Switzerland for Canada and re-estimating the model with data from 1980 to 1996.[7,8]

In the stochastic simulations of the model the equations were shocked with random draws from a multivariate normal distribution with the covariance structure estimated from the data. In all cases the simulated outcomes were compared, variable-by-variable, with a baseline simulation of the model assuming no shocks. When comparisons between different monetary policy rules were made, the standard of reference was the root mean square percentage deviation from the baseline path.

Genberg and Kadareja proceeded to investigate the consequences of having the Swiss National Bank (SNB) react to the exchange rate (relative to the euro) *in addition to* inflation and the output gap. The results indicated clearly that some leaning against the wind of exchange rate changes is always better than free floating, regardless of the relative weight put on output and inflation in the overall loss function, α in equation 2. How much exchange rate smoothing is optimal, however, depends on this relative weight.

It is important to keep in mind that the Genberg-Karadeja results were obtained under the assumption that the SNB did not observe the underlying shock to the economy. Rather, the central bank simply reacted to the observed change in the inflation, output gap, and the exchange rate. Had the authorities been able to distinguish shocks to asset markets from shocks to goods markets, a more sophisticated strategy, whereby the SNB reacts differently to the exchange rate depending on the nature of the underlying shock, would have been preferred.

These results are clearly consistent with those obtained using the Batini-Nelson model. In both cases we conclude that the results depend critically on the source and relative importance of the shocks that are hitting the economy. It is important to emphasize, however, that the Genberg-Kadareja results indicate that a policy of leaning against the wind would have been desirable given the estimated distribution of shocks over the 1980–96 period. (More on this in section 3 below.)

3. Selected Opinions in the Recent Literature

Not surprisingly, our view that monetary policy should react to asset price misalignments has generated responses from other economists, e.g., Professors Bernanke and Gertler and Drs. Batini and Nelson have produced simulation results that, at first sight, do not seem to support our view.[9] In this section we review their studies in an effort to determine why there is an apparent disagreement. Our conclusions are straightforward. The relationship between movements in equity prices and exchange rates on the one hand, and inflation and output on the other, depend critically on the underlying sources of shocks to the economy. It is, therefore, important that monetary policy does not react mechanically and in the same way to all changes in asset prices. Judgment needs to be exercised in reacting to exchange rates changes and share price movements just as it has to be in the interpretation of and reaction to fluctuations in the estimated output gap. Some believe that there is little hope of being able to infer anything from asset price movements that is useful for monetary policy purposes, partly because asset prices are so volatile and partly because central banks do not possess more information about equilibrium valuations than the private sector.[10] For reasons that we explained in some detail in CGLW and that we will summarize below, we believe that central banks can improve macroeconomic performance if they judiciously incorporate information in asset prices in their decisions on monetary policy.

A similar conclusion emerges from a recent paper by Professors J. Stock and M. Watson on the information content in asset prices for inflation forecasts.[11] As we stressed in CGLW, it is difficult to find univariate relationships between asset price movements and future inflation that are stable across countries and over time. The reason presumably is that such relationships depend both on the institutional structure of an economy and on the shocks that were experienced during the historical episode in the recorded data. Again, the implication is that monetary policy cannot be based on a mechanically fixed reaction to all asset price movements, but instead must depend on whether current asset prices can be justified by underlying fundamental determinants or are the results of misalignments due to portfolio shifts.

In the last part of this section we take note of the analysis in the 2001 *Annual Report* of the Bank for International Settlements (BIS) which takes a sympathetic, if not openly supportive, view of the belief that monetary policy can have a role to play in reducing the imbalances caused by occasional misalignments in asset prices, especially in emerging markets.

3.1 Responding to Asset Price Bubbles in Simulation Models

The conclusions in CGLW are, in part, based on results from simulations of two theoretical macroeconomic models: Batini and Nelson's minimal open-economy model in which the exchange rate plays an important role in the transmission of monetary policy, and Bernanke and Gertler's somewhat larger closed-economy model in which credit markets play a crucial role in the monetary transmission process. Two recent papers by the authors of these models reconsider the issue of what role asset prices should play in the formulation of monetary policy. In this section we review the conclusions of these papers and relate them to our own.

3.1.1 Batini and Nelson (2000): Reacting to the Exchange Rate May Be Counterproductive

Recall from section 2.2.2 that the Batini-Nelson model we used for our simulations is a three-equation model of an open economy that determines the rate of inflation, the level of output, and the exchange rate. The three equations are an aggregate demand relationship in the form of a forward-looking IS curve, an expectations augmented (new) Phillips curve that serves as an aggregate supply relationship, and an uncovered interest parity condition linking domestic and foreign interest rates with the expected rate of change in the exchange rate. Shocks to aggregate demand, aggregate supply, and the interest parity condition lead to fluctuations in the endogenous variables. The role of the central bank is to set the domestic interest rate so as to minimize the induced fluctuations in inflation and output around their respective target levels.

Batini and Nelson (2000) introduce an exogenous bubble into the exchange rate process and study how the central bank should react to exchange rate movements in the course of setting the interest rate. Crucially, they presume that policymakers are unable to distinguish whether financial or real shocks are the source of the exchange rate movement. As a benchmark, Batini and Nelson use a policy reaction function in which authorities react only to expected inflation rate and the lagged interest rate itself.

Their conclusions can be summarized in three points:

1. When the economy is subject only to the three structural shocks (aggregate demand, aggregate supply, and interest parity), there is no benefit to be obtained from reacting explicitly to the exchange rate, so long as policy's reactions to the expected inflation rate and the lagged interest rate are optimal.

2. If the exchange rate is also subject to a bubble process in addition to the structural shocks, then a central bank that systematically leans against the wind of exchange rate changes will stabilize output somewhat, but it will destabilize inflation, the interest rate itself, and, surprisingly, the exchange rate. Again, when the responses to expected inflation and the lagged interest rate are re-optimized, there is no gain from reacting separately to the exchange rate.

3. If the uncovered interest parity condition is replaced by a more ad hoc, but arguably less empirically flawed relationship, and exchange rate changes have a strong direct influence on inflation, then a policy that responds to the exchange rate over and above the response to expected inflation and the lagged interest rate appears desirable.

How, if at all, should our previous conclusions be modified in light of these results? First, result one confirms our view that the appropriate reaction of monetary policy to movements in endogenous variables such as the exchange rate depends on the underlying source for these changes. We illustrated this by showing that leaning against the wind of financial shocks is useful, whereas doing the same in the presence of real shocks is not. Batini and Nelson subject their model to a particular combination of shocks in their simulations. Apparently, when real shocks are sufficiently important, leaning against the wind of exchange rate fluctuations becomes counterproductive.[12]

Conclusion two is surprising. If short-run exchange rate changes correspond to the prediction of the interest parity relationship and the private sector knows that a bubble is present and expects it to last indefinitely, then reacting to the exchange rate may be counterproductive. Batini and Nelson's simulations suggest that, under these circumstances, the interaction between the fully forward-looking behavior of the private sector and the central bank rule creates a type of instability.

We suspect that the result is model-specific and its interpretation should in any case be tempered by the following considerations. First, is it realistic to assume that the private sector expects the bubble to last indefinitely even if the central bank is actively attempting to prevent the exchange rate from following the bubble path? It might be plausible to assume that a monetary policy that reacts to exchange rate misalignments affects both the probability of the bubble emerging in the first place and the length of its duration. We suspect that this might reverse their results, though introducing it formally into the simulations is difficult because it would require a model of the formation of the bubble in the first place.[13]

Second, perhaps the authorities should not react in a similar way to exchange rate bubbles as they do to normal exchange rate fluctuations. After all, these two types of exchange rate movements are fundamentally different, and so one would think that they should generate different policy responses. We, therefore, stand by the general conclusion in CGLW that monetary policy reactions to asset price fluctuations should be conditioned by the underlying sources of these movements and that leaning against the wind can be helpful in certain circumstances.

Finally, there is the issue of the empirical failure of the uncovered interest parity condition. Batini and Nelson clearly recognize this as a problem and so examine the impact of potential substitutes. But what should the uncovered interest rate parity condition be replaced with? As conclusion three reveals, the answer is crucial for the implications we should draw for monetary policy.

3.1.2 Bernanke and Gertler (2001): Central Banks Should Not Respond to Movements in Asset Prices

In a brief article in the May 2001 issue of the *American Economic Review*, Bernanke and Gertler disagree with our view that it is desirable for a central bank to respond modestly to stock market bubbles over and above its reaction to inflation and the output gap. Using a modified version of their 1999 model (which they had kindly provided to us for the simulations described in CGLW), they maintain their judgment that reacting to share price misalignments is counterproductive. What accounts for such different conclusions?

We believe that the apparent disagreements are largely due to different assumptions about whether a central bank can distinguish between financial and technology shocks. Let us explain why. The most comparable set of simulation results is the one in which there are no shocks to the fundamentals. In this case Bernanke and Gertler show that reacting to stock prices *instead of* reacting to the output gap results in inferior economic performance.[14] What this implies is that the central bank should not ignore the output gap and treat share prices as a substitute for other information about the economy. We certainly subscribe to this view, and indeed all our results show that both the output gap and the stock price should be included in the information that the central bank uses. However, we also argued that taking account of share prices in the process of setting monetary policy leads to an improvement of economic performance once inflation *and* the output gap has been accounted for. We continue to believe that this is the case.

In the simulations underlying their 2001 article Bernanke and Gertler introduce a second source of shocks that influence stock prices.[15] Whereas their original work examined the consequences of nonfundamental bubbles alone, now they have added the possibility of fundamental technology shocks as a source of movements in equity values. We did not study the appropriate policy response to technology shocks in our simulations, but argued on theoretical grounds that the monetary policy response to such shocks should be different from the response to financial shocks. Their simulation results confirm this.

Of course, if we simulate an economy where several types of shocks are present simultaneously, and assume that the central bank has no possibility to differentiate between underlying sources of movements in endogenous variables, then it is quite possible that it is best to ignore certain variables when we formulate policy. This would be the case, for example, when stock prices have increased, but we do not know whether this is due to a positive productivity shock in the economy or to a financial bubble.[16] There is no controversy here. The bottom line therefore is whether central banks should try to infer from information in financial markets as to what kind of underlying disturbance is affecting the economy. We certainly believe that they should, and that some useful information can be obtained from asset price movements. We shall return to this issue in the final section of the paper.

3.2 Asset Prices, Inflation Forecasts, and Monetary Policy

Stock and Watson (2000) present an up-to-date review of the literature on the reliability of econometric forecasts of inflation and output growth for Group of Seven countries, together with some new evidence of their own.[17] What stands out in their study is the difficulty of finding any indicator variable(s) that reliably predict future rates of inflation or growth. The literature contains many papers that report significant in-sample Granger-causal relationships linking some current asset price variable with future inflation, but these relationships frequently prove to be unstable when the sample period is altered. More importantly, in-sample performance usually breaks down in more realistic out-of-sample forecasting tests.

In CGLW we describe a possible reason for the potential instability between asset price changes and subsequent computer price index inflation. It is as follows. Equity prices and exchange rates respond endogenously to disturbances that also affect inflation with a lag. Depending on the source of the underlying shocks to the economy, the relationship between an increase in an asset price and future inflation can vary in, both, size and direction. Econometric models measure the average relationship over a particular historical period, and to the extent that certain types of disturbances were dominant in some samples and other disturbances were more frequent in others, the relationship between asset prices and inflation will appear unstable in simple reduced-form models. Uncovering a stable relationship requires finding a way to control for the nature of the underlying disturbance.

In our earlier work we emphasize that monetary policy should react only to asset price misalignments, not indiscriminately to all asset price changes. It is crucial that policymakers differentiate between those asset price changes that are justified by underlying fundamentals and those that are not. It is only the latter that create the potential for significant future volatility.

A common attitude vis-à-vis the role of asset prices in the formulation of monetary policy is that they should be taken into account only insofar as they affect a fixed-horizon inflation forecast. The empirical evidence reviewed and presented by Stock and Watson (2000) implies that even this view does not allow us to be agnostic about the underlying source of asset price changes. The reason is that the signal carried by the asset price change about future inflation will be different depending on the source of the underlying disturbance that has created the changes in the first place.

According to this interpretation of the empirical evidence, we seem to be forced to take one of two positions about the role of asset prices in the formulation of monetary policy. On the one hand, we can argue that it is hopeless to identify underlying causes of asset price changes, and, therefore, we will never be able to extract reliable signals from them about future inflation. This is the view that there is no role, direct or indirect (via inflation forecasts), for asset prices in the conduct of monetary policy. Alternatively, we can adopt the position that it is possible to extract useful information from asset prices, which can be used both in inflation forecasts and in signaling future volatility. We clearly take the second of these views.

3.3 Financial Liberalization, Cycles, and Policy Response in Emerging Markets

Chapter VII of the 2001 Annual Report of the BIS argues that liberalization of financial markets "... has increased the scope for pronounced financial cycles ..." and that "The damage caused by financial instability has been particularly serious for emerging market countries," (BIS, 2001, p.123). The report contains an informative review of the mechanism by which developments in financial markets can lead to instability in the real sector of the economy. The particular role of property prices is discussed in detail, with an emphasis on its importance for inflation measurement and the problems it can create that require policy response.

The BIS report focuses primarily on the risks posed by financial instability and the regulatory and supervisory measures that can be instituted to make the financial system more resilient. The report is appropriately skeptical in our view of the possibility of using discretionary changes in the regulatory framework as a way of dealing with perceived misalignments as they occur. Although it points to difficulties in identifying asset price misalignments, the BIS report goes on to argue that "These difficulties need not rule out the very occasional use of monetary policy in this way," (p. 141). In this context it also makes the very useful point that "The case for a policy response need not depend on the ability of policymakers to make better judgments than the private sector. Rather, the fact that policymakers have different responsibilities and incentives may well mean that they respond quite differently to the same assessment of current trends," (p. 136). For example, market participants who feel that the stock market is "overvalued" may find it difficult to maintain an investment stance that is reflective of their views if the "bubble" is relatively prolonged. By contrast, policymakers may well be subject to less *short-termist* performance-related pressure.

4. Where Do We Stand Now?

In CGLW we set out to examine whether there is any role for asset price developments in the formulation of monetary policy. Our analysis was set in a flexible inflation-targeting framework in which the objective of monetary policy is to stabilize the inflation rate and the output level around some attainable target levels. In practice this is usually implemented by the central bank setting its interest rate instrument in response to deviations of an inflation forecast at a chosen horizon (usually somewhere between one and two years) from the target rate and, sometimes, a measure of the deviation of actual output from its potential level. We argued that if the central bank were to also react to estimates of misalignment of asset prices, macroeconomic performance could be improved.

Has subsequent research led us to modify our view in this respect? The short answer is no.

In a very general sense, the differences of opinion seem semantic. Virtually everyone agrees that information contained in asset prices should be taken into account insofar as they have a direct or indirect impact on inflation in the future. Hence, if we take a sufficiently wide view of "having an impact on future inflation," all the relevant information is already incorporated into the policy decision.[18]

In practice, however, inflation forecasts that enter policy decisions often refer to a fixed horizon, at least in public statements by the central bank. This means that consequences of asset price misalignments that may emerge at some other frequency might not be given sufficient weight in policy decisions. Furthermore, to the extent that asset price changes are included in forecasting equations in the manner suggested in the recent literature, the potential effects of such misalignments may not be captured at all.[19] Yet, as the BIS (2001) argues, financial cycles brought about in part by asset price movements can create real economic imbalances, and it is indeed possible to point to concrete examples where this has occurred. We, therefore, continue to believe that monetary policy decisions must be based on more than a fixed-horizon inflation forecast combined with an estimate of the current output gap.

A nontrivial and unresolved issue relates to the communication challenges presented by our proposal. Setting policy on the basis of conscious deviations of expected inflation from target at, say, the two-year horizon could hurt credibility. There is a significant risk that policy becomes less predictable and less transparent, thereby potentially jeopardizing accountability. In practice, attempts to set interest rates at a level that is different from what is necessary to achieve the target level at a two-year horizon must be accompanied by a justification that is explained simply and that commands broad agreement. Policymakers who consciously aim away from their target at a two-year ahead horizon (in order to reduce inflation volatility at other horizons) will attract suspicion if their explanation for doing so is complex and not well-understood, or, even worse, if a significant group of commentators does not agree that aiming away from the two-year ahead target will actually reduce inflation volatility. We recognize these to be critically important considerations when deciding on the implementation of our proposal.

What about the recent simulation results of Batini and Nelson and Bernanke and Gertler? These show clearly that it is important not to react mechanically to all asset price changes regardless of their source. We certainly do not want to quarrel with this view, which is why our original argumentation emphasized the need to identify asset price changes that can be justified by underlying fundamentals and those that cannot.[20] This, of course, requires a certain amount of judgment on the part of policymakers, but that is par for the course.

It has been suggested that central bank officials will never be able to determine whether asset prices are misaligned in the sense we use the term here. After all, the argument goes, markets have incorporated all available information into prices and what do policymakers know that market participants do not?

We find this argument to be specious because it assumes that "incorporating all available information" automatically eliminates misalignments. But unless strong-form market efficiency holds in practice, this is not the case. Furthermore, our proposal does not call for central banks to respond to small misalignments. We agree that these are difficult to detect and are unlikely to have very strong destabilizing effects in any case.

On the other hand, there are clearly times when egregious misalignments exist. Recent examples include Japanese stock and land prices in 1989 and the NASDAQ in late 1999 and early 2000. While some portion of these high price levels may have been justifiable based on fundamentals, few people would deny that a significant component was due to asset market disturbances. Ultimately, in terms of reducing inflation and output volatility, it is important that central bankers respond to these large relatively "obvious" misalignments.

As we have already discussed, central bankers might find it easier to respond to long-lived bubbles that generate these "obvious" misalignments as compared to the skeptical market participants who may have been steadily impoverished by the longevity of the bubble.

While we agree that it is difficult to estimate the degree to which an asset price is misaligned, it is not obvious that it is easier to estimate an output gap or the NAIRU (non-accelerating inflation rate of unemployment), measures that are commonly used in helping frame monetary policy. Indeed, one could argue that assumptions about asset price levels, and the extent of misalignments, are essential inputs into the process of estimating something like an output gap. The output gap estimate depends importantly on underlying productivity growth (which affects prospective potential output) and the equilibrium equity risk premium (which affects corporate investment, which in turn, affects trend growth)—the same uncertain inputs that are to be necessary to estimate the degree of stock price misalignment. Moreover, one's estimate of the prospective output gap also depends on what is likely to happen to the actual level of output, which, through the standard wealth effect, depends directly on the degree to which asset prices are misaligned. As we see it, if you cannot estimate asset price misalignments, you cannot forecast inflation either.

Putting our argument slightly differently, we are not persuaded that one should ignore asset price misalignments simply because they are difficult to measure. The standard response to noisy data is to use econometric methods to extract the signal. This is common practice in the use of statistics in a policymaking environment. If central bankers threw out all data that was poorly measured, there would be very little information left on which to base their decisions.

Two additional points have at times been suggested in arguing that asset prices should be ignored. The first is based on the view that there are times when different asset prices give conflicting signals. For example, housing prices may suggest potential inflationary pressures, whereas movements in the exchange rate point in a different direction. This clearly complicates the inference one might be able to draw from asset prices, but it does not imply that one should ignore them. Instead, it means that one should look at *all* relevant asset prices.

Another argument notes that asset price misalignments in small economies may be caused mainly by developments in financial markets elsewhere and that monetary policy in the small country will be unable to alter them significantly. Again, this does not invalidate our proposal. We are not arguing that monetary policy should target any particular level of share prices, and so the fact that these prices are determined mainly abroad does not prevent reacting to them. In addition, the potentially destabilizing effects of asset price misalignments can occur regardless of what causes these misalignments. Economic policy, therefore, must be ready to respond.

The conclusions we reached in "Asset Prices and Central Bank Policy," therefore, remain. Monetary policy that pursues an inflation-targeting strategy should attempt to identify and respond to asset price misalignments. Counter-arguments claiming that it is difficult to interpret asset price movements are correct, but they apply to other aspects of inflation targeting as well, so they do not eliminate the case for taking account of asset price misalignments in the conduct of monetary policy.

*Stephen G. Cecchetti is a professor of economics at Ohio State University and a research associate at the National Bureau of Economic Research. Hans Genberg is a professor of international economics at the Graduate Institute of International Studies at the University of Geneva. Sushil Wadhwani is a member of the Monetary Policy Committee of the Bank of England. The authors thank Kathy McCarthy, Ed Nelson, and Peter Rodgers for their comments on an earlier draft. The views in this paper are entirely those of the authors and should not be taken to represent those of their employers.

Notes

1. For more detailed discussions about the meaning of inflation targeting see, for example, Bernanke, Laubach, Mishkin, and Posen (1999) and Svensson (2001).

2. See also Genberg (2001).

3. While it can be useful to characterize monetary policy in this way in theoretical models, in practice monetary policy is never implemented according to a rigid rule. Furthermore, in their communication with the public, some inflation-targeting central banks speak only of reacting to an inflation forecast, making no explicit statements about responding to the output gap.

4. See also Svensson (2000).

5. As was the case in our previous work, this paper is *not* about what the central bank objective should be. Instead, we are concerned with how an inflation-targeting central bank can most effectively fulfill its objectives.

6. See Wadhwani (2000) for further discussion.

7. The countries retained were France, Germany, Italy, Japan, Switzerland, the United Kingdom, and the United States.

8. The most comprehensive reference to the specification and performance of Taylor's model is Taylor (1993). The re-estimation of the entire model and the specification/estimation of the Swiss module are described in detail in Kadareja (2000).

9. See Bernanke and Gertler (2001) and Batini and Nelson (2000).

10. In his comment on our argument, Mishkin (2001) brings up these same points. In addition, he erroneously claims that our arguments imply that central banks should *target* asset prices. As we emphasize at the outset, this is definitely not the case.

11. Stock and Watson (2000).

12. Recall the simulation results of Genberg and Kadareja, who, on the basis of the estimated distribution of shocks over the 1980–96 period, arrived at the opposite conclusion. Hence, this is clearly an empirical issue.

13. See Allen and Gale (2000) for a theoretical model that might be supplemented.

14. Here and in the following we are, of course, assuming that the central bank reacts forcefully to the expected rate of inflation. On this there is no controversy.

15. They also introduce some minor modifications of the model in the latest simulations. These relate to the response of investment to equity prices and the production function in the capital goods sector. But these changes are not responsible for our disagreement. Bernanke and Gertler also now allow the size of the stock price bubbles to be stochastic, while our simulations were, like their earlier simulations, based on fixed-size bubbles.

16. The same principle would also lead us to be very cautious if the latest statistics showed an increase in output, but we had no way of telling whether or not that corresponded to an increase in the natural rate of output.

17. See also, Goodhart and Hoffmann (2000) for some similar evidence.

18. This is certainly true if the objective of policy can be expressed in terms of inflation and output stability alone. If stability of asset prices has an independent role, then there might be an additional reason to react to asset price changes. Note in this context that stability of the interest rate is often included in the policy objective in order to rationalize the sluggishness of interest rate adjustments observed in practice. Whatever argument justifies this inclusion could perhaps be extended to other asset prices, such as the exchange rate.

19. For example, Cecchetti, Chu, and Steindel (2000) and Stock and Watson (2000).

20. This is not unique to asset prices. For example, an increase in inflation that is due to a fall in aggregate supply should in principle be treated differently from the same increase due to an increase in aggregate demand.

References

Allen F., and D. Gale, 2000, "Bubbles and Crises," *The Economic Journal*, Vol. 110, January, pp. 236–255.

Ball, Laurence, 1999, "Policy Rules for Open Economies," in *Monetary Policy Rules*, J. Taylor, ed., Chicago: University of Chicago Press.

Bank for International Settlements (BIS), 2001, *Annual Report*, Basel: BIS.

_____, 1998, "The Role of Asset Prices in the Formulation of Monetary Policy," BIS conference papers, Vol. 5, Basel: BIS.

Batini, N., and E. Nelson, 2000, "When the Bubble Bursts: Monetary Policy Rules and Foreign Exchange Market Behavior," mimeo.

Bernanke, Ben, Thomas Laubach, Frederic Mishkin, and Adam Posen, 1999, *Inflation Targeting: Lessons from the International Experience,* Princeton, NJ: Princeton University Press.

Bernanke, Ben, and Mark Gertler, 1999, "Monetary Policy and Asset Price Volatility," in *New Challenges for Monetary Policy: A Symposium Sponsored by the Federal Reserve Bank of Kansas City,* Federal Reserve Bank of Kansas City, pp. 77–128.

Bernanke, B., and M. Gertler, 2001, "Should Central Banks Respond to Movements in Asset Prices?," *American Economic Review*, May.

Cecchetti, S., R. Chu, and C. Steindel, 2000, "The Unreliability of Inflation Indicators," *Current Issues in Economics and Finance,* New York: Federal Reserve Bank of New York.

Cecchetti, Stephen, Hans Genberg, John Lipsky, and Sushil Wadhwani, 2000, *Asset Prices and Central Bank Policy,* Geneva Report on the World Economy 2, CEPR and ICMB.

Fama, E. F., 1981, "Term Structure Forecasts of Interest Rates, Inflation and Real Returns," *Journal of Monetary Economics*, Vol. 25, pp. 59–76.

Flemming, J., 1999, "Monetary Policy: Questions of Adequacy, Design and Presentation," *Economic Outlook,* Vol. 24, No. 1, October, pp. 9–13.

Genberg, H., and A. Kadareja, 1999, "The Swiss Franc and the Euro," Graduate Institute of International Studies, unpublished manuscript.

Gerlach, S., 1995, "The Information Content of the Term Structure: Evidence for Germany," Bank for International Settlements, working paper, No. 29.

Goodhart, C., and B. Hoffman, 2000, "Do Asset Prices Help to Predict Consumer Price Inflation?," unpublished manuscript.

Jorion, P., and F. Mishkin, 1991, "A Multicountry Comparison of Term Structure Forecasts at Long Horizons," *Journal of Financial Economics*, Vol. 29, pp. 59–80.

Kent, C., and P. Lowe, 1997, "Asset-Price Bubbles and Monetary Policy," Economic Research Department, Reserve Bank of Australia, Research Discussion Paper, No. 9709.

Mishkin, F., 2001, "The Transmission Mechanism and the Role of Asset Prices in Monetary Policy," NBER, working paper, No. 8617.

Poole, W., 1970, "Optimal Choice of Monetary Policy Instruments in a Simple Stochastic Macro Model," *Quarterly Journal of Economics*, Vol. 88, pp. 197–216.

Stock, J., and M. Watson, 2000, "Forecasting Output and Inflation: The Role of Asset Prices," paper presented at the Sveriges Riksbank and Stockholm School of Economics Conference on Asset Markets and Monetary Policy, Stockholm, June 16–17.

Svensson, Lars E. O., 2000, "Open-Economy Inflation Targeting," *Journal of International Economics,* Vol. 50, pp. 155–183.

Wadhwani, Sushil B., 2000, "The Exchange Rate and the MPC: What Can We Do?," Bank of England, *Quarterly Bulletin*, August.

Chapter 31
Interest Rate Policy Should Not React Directly to Asset Prices

Marvin Goodfriend*
Federal Reserve Bank of Richmond

1. Introduction

Central banks have made great strides in bringing inflation under control. Low and steady inflation is generally credited with improving macroeconomic stability around the world. The progress against inflation, however, did not put an end to financial instability. For instance, there was the run-up and sharp correction in U.S. equity prices in 1987 and in Japanese equity and land prices a few years later. More recently, the prices of U.S. technology stocks tripled between early 1999 and early 2000, and fell back again by 2001. These examples of extreme asset price volatility were associated with instability in the macroeconomy more generally.

Such developments have led economists and policymakers to wonder whether central banks should take greater account of asset price movements in making interest rate policy. The idea would be for interest rate policy to react directly to large asset price movements in order to pre-empt the cyclical instability often associated with extreme asset price fluctuations.[1]

This paper assesses the case for taking greater account of asset price movements in making monetary policy. The assessment is meant to apply primarily to monetary policy in large developed countries such as the United States and Japan and to the Euro area. The analysis reported in the paper along with a reading of the historical record suggest that monetary policy should not react directly to asset prices.[2] Under this recommendation, asset prices would continue to play an important indirect role in policy by helping to forecast aggregate demand and inflation. But asset prices would not in addition influence interest rate policy actions directly.[3]

Section 2 presents an overview of the relationship between asset prices and monetary policy. Among other things, it shows that there can be no presumption that interest rate policy actions ought to be correlated in any particular way with asset price movements. Section 3 provides three examples of how asset prices can mislead interest rate policy in practice. The analysis in sections 2 and 3 focuses on equity prices. Section 4 argues that it is counterproductive to take direct account of the foreign exchange rate in making monetary policy. Section 5 extends the argument by showing that there was little scope to improve monetary policy by reacting directly to asset prices in Japan in the late 1980s and in the United States in the late 1990s. A brief summary concludes the paper.

2. An Overview of the Relationship between Asset Prices and Monetary Policy

Monetary policy itself was an important source of macroeconomic instability during the period of go/stop policy prior to the stabilization of inflation in the early 1980s; it was a source of asset price volatility, as well. The go/stop era was characterized by periods of excessively easy and excessively tight monetary policy within a context of generally rising inflation and inflation expectations. Policy was excessively easy during the go phases because the central bank was inclined to wait until inflation and inflation expectations began to rise before tightening policy.

Asset prices would tend to fall for three reasons as policy was tightened in the stop phase of the policy cycle. First, rising inflation expectations would push long-term interest rates up. Second, higher real short-term interest rates brought about by tighter monetary policy would drive the real component of long rates higher. Third, monetary policy worked to bring inflation down by creating a deficiency of aggregate demand. The resulting output gap would cause a decline in current and future firm profits. Equity prices would tend to fall at the beginning of the stop phase of the policy cycle because lower expected future earnings were discounted at a higher rate of interest.

Once inflation was stabilized to its satisfaction, the central bank would initiate the go phase of the policy cycle with lower real short-term interest rates to stimulate spending. Asset prices would be inclined to rise at this point because both the real and the inflation expectations components of long-term interest rates would move lower. Moreover, the outlook for firm profits would improve as the recovery took hold.

However, the relationship between asset prices and monetary policy was relatively loose during the go/stop era for a number of reasons. Asset prices are forward looking. So, asset prices have the potential to lead the business cycle, to be out of phase, or to shift forward. Moreover, because asset prices are forward looking they can move prematurely and then reverse field in anticipation of cyclical fluctuations that are delayed or fail to materialize at all.

The relationship between monetary policy and asset prices seems likely to weaken even further with the attainment of price stability. Low and stable inflation expectations will anchor long-term interest rates more firmly. Employment and earnings should become more cyclically stable. And, real short-term interest rates should fluctuate in a narrower range than during the inflationary go/stop era.

The Federal Reserve's tightening of monetary policy in 1994 illustrates the point. In 1994, the Fed acted pre-emptively by raising short-term real interest rates after early warning signs of inflation appeared but before inflation itself began to rise. The

Dow fell by about 100 points when the Fed began to raise the federal funds rate in February. The long bond rate signaled an inflation scare, rising by about two percentage points during the year to peak at around 8.2 percent in November. But the Dow fell only slightly even as the Fed increased its federal funds rate target by 300 basis points from 3 percent to 6 percent. With inflation then running around 3 percent, the tightening amounted to a three-percentage point increase in the real short-term interest rate. When it became clear that monetary policy had successfully pre-empted rising inflation, the inflation scare subsided, bond rates came down, journalists began to talk of the death of inflation, and the Dow resumed its climb.

As the 1994 episode shows, there is little reason to think that interest rate policy actions should influence asset values one way or the other when monetary policy acts pre-emptively to maintain a low and stable rate of inflation. By adjusting its federal funds rate target to stabilize inflation, the central bank moves short-term real interest rates to make aggregate demand conform to movements in potential gross domestic product (GDP) in order to stabilize the output gap. Instead of being a predominant source of destabilizing go/stop shocks to the economy, monetary policy actually steers real short rates in a way that stabilizes the output gap and inflation against shocks to aggregate supply and demand.

In order to appreciate this point more fully, consider how interest rate policy should respond to aggregate demand and supply shocks, respectively, in order to stabilize inflation. Consider first an increase in aggregate demand unaccompanied by a conforming shock to potential output. The central bank ought to restrain the increase in aggregate demand by raising short-term interest rates. Since shocks are difficult to identify promptly in practice, that restraint is usually incomplete. Yet, firms are disinclined to raise their prices very much if they believe that the central bank will correct any excess of aggregate demand over supply before too long, that is, if the central bank has credibility for low inflation. In this case the price level will be sticky. Consequently, employment, firm profits, short-term interest rates, and equity values will all rise in response to an expansionary shock to aggregate demand. In general, short-term interest rates and equity prices would co-vary positively in response to a shock to aggregate demand when the central bank seeks to stabilize the output gap and inflation.

Now consider a shock to aggregate supply, for example, a temporary shortfall of productivity below its trend growth path. An adverse shock to productivity would temporarily reduce the level of noninflationary potential output. To stabilize inflation, the central bank should again raise short-term interest rates, this time to make aggregate demand conform to the negative shock to aggregate supply. The unexpected shortfall of productivity growth relative to its trend would tend to reduce profits and cause equity values to fall. In this case, short-term interest rates should rise even as equity prices fall. In general, short-term interest rates and equity prices would covary negatively in response to a shock to aggregate supply when the central bank seeks to stabilize the output gap and inflation.

The important point is that the unconditional correlation between asset prices and real short-term interest rates generated by monetary policy geared to maintaining price stability could be either negative or positive. The direction and size of the unconditional correlation would depend on the size, frequency, and duration of aggregate demand and supply shocks, the central bank's power to identify the shocks promptly, and the size and duration of the interest rate responses needed to maintain price stability.

To sum up, two things are clear. Even though short-term interest rates are managed by a central bank, when policy is undertaken to achieve an objective such as price stability, short rates and equity prices both should be regarded as endogenous variables that respond to underlying shocks in specific ways. There can be no presumption that interest rate policy actions should be correlated in any particular way with equity price movements.[4]

3. Three Situations in which Asset Prices can Mislead Interest Rate Policy in Practice

This section describes three practical situations in which asset prices can mislead interest rate policy. These situations are characterized, respectively, by an inflation scare, a profit squeeze, and rising trend productivity growth. To set the stage for the first two of these situations, imagine that initially the public is confident that the price level will remain stable for the foreseeable future. If expectations of inflation are firmly anchored, then labor markets can get surprisingly tight without triggering inflationary wage pressures. Firms would be inclined to hold the line on price increases even in the face of rising labor costs. Inflation expectations in long bond rates might be firmly anchored in spite of a buildup of inflationary pressures. And, other warning signs of inflation might not work well, either.

Seeing no threat of inflation, a central bank might be inclined to delay raising interest rates even as output moved above presumed non-inflationary potential output. A kind of wishful thinking could develop. The public might come to believe that the economy has become less prone to inflation, regardless of what the central bank does. Such optimism could support an unsustainable boom in spending by households and firms, especially if the central bank is reluctant to raise interest rates. The plausibly persistent increase in the economy's noninflationary productive potential could be reflected in a run-up in equity, real estate, and other asset prices.[5]

If, however, the economy continued to operate significantly above potential, then at some point the boom would self-destruct. The expansion would end either with an inflation scare and an outbreak of inflation or with a profit squeeze and a collapse of asset prices if the latter were to occur before an outbreak of inflation. Each of these possibilities provides an example of how sharply changing asset price movements can be a misleading guide for interest rate policy.

3.1 An Outbreak of Inflation

In this case tightness in labor and product markets eventually triggers an outbreak of wage and price inflation to which the central bank reacts by raising interest rates. The outbreak of inflation would reflect the collapse of an implicit reputational equilibrium in which wage and price setters kept their part of an implicit bargain by not inflating as long as the central bank was expected to use monetary policy to maintain conditions conducive to price stability.

The inflation scare would raise expected inflation and send long bond rates up.[6] The central bank would increase real short rates to restore low inflation and bring aggregate demand back in line with noninflationary potential output. Equity prices would fall because prior valuations would be seen to be excessive in light of the overestimation of the economy's productive potential. Higher interest rates would reduce the present discounted value of future earnings. Finally, the central bank would create slack in the labor market temporarily in order to bring inflation back down. Earnings would fall during the ensuing recession and pull equity prices down even more.

Thus, asset prices could fall considerably if a boom collapsed with an inflation scare and an outbreak of inflation. Nevertheless, the central bank would follow through with higher real short-term interest rates to bring inflation down and restore credibility for low inflation.

3.2 A Profit Squeeze

In this case the central bank's credibility for low inflation remains intact, and the expansion comes to an end with a profit squeeze and a realization that asset prices are unsustainably high. This could happen if wage growth accelerated due to excessively tight labor markets, and firms were not willing to raise prices because they believed that the central bank would restore conditions conducive to price stability before too long. If such a situation persisted, then unit labor costs would rise, and firm profits and asset prices would fall. Again, the fall in asset values would reflect a more realistic evaluation of the economy's productive potential and a more realistic valuation of equities. Reduced asset values would tend to precipitate a slowing of the growth of aggregate demand. Nevertheless, the central bank would refrain from lowering short-term interest rates until it saw evidence that aggregate demand growth had slowed persistently and sufficiently to restore a balance between aggregate demand and supply. The central bank might even raise interest rates somewhat if the growth of aggregate demand did not slow enough to eliminate the inflationary potential.

3.3 Rising Trend Productivity Growth

In this third scenario higher trend productivity growth induces firms and households to borrow against their improved future income prospects in order to spend some of the expected increase in future income currently. When actual and expected trend productivity growth both increase, an initial interest rates aggregate demand may rise even faster than current potential output. Employment increases as firms hire more labor to meet the growth of aggregate demand in excess of the current growth of productivity. Real wages rise as firms bid for more labor. Yet, if productivity growth continues to rise, then unit labor costs may remain stable, or even fall. Firms may be able to finance rising wages out of increasing productivity with room to spare. Inflation pressures may take time to build up, and disinflation is possible. The central bank may be inclined to put off raising short-term interest rates even as higher profit growth is reflected in rising equity prices. In fact, if inflation is already very low, the central bank may reduce short-term rates to avert deflation.

Eventually, trend productivity growth will stop rising. And competition for workers will cause real wages to catch up to the higher labor productivity. Real wages will grow faster than productivity and firm profits will grow more slowly during this transition period. The slowdown in profit growth may slow the rise in equity values or cause them to fall. By that time, however, inflation may be more of a threat than before. Labor markets will be tighter, and firms will find it harder to finance wage growth out of productivity. At that point, the central bank may have to raise short-term interest rates to hold the line on inflation, even if equity prices fall.

4. It is Counterproductive to Take Direct Account of the Foreign Exchange Rate

The role of a central bank in foreign exchange rate policy varies greatly depending on a nation's overarching goals for monetary policy. For instance, a central bank can use monetary policy to maintain a fixed exchange rate. Doing so, however, causes the central bank to lose the power to conduct independent monetary policy geared to domestic objectives. Today none of the world's major central banks, for example, the Bank of Japan, the Eurosystem, or the Federal Reserve, maintain a fixed exchange rate. These central banks manage monetary policy in a framework that emphasizes independent policy actions disciplined by an explicit or implicit mandate for low inflation. For the most part, their exchange rates float freely. The focus on domestic price stability at the expense of exchange rate stability seems appropriate for these large and largely closed economies.

Nevertheless, from time to time a central bank may become involved in operations aimed at directly influencing its exchange rate. Such an initiative could originate in the Treasury, or in the committee of Treasuries in the Eurosystem's case. The Treasury could invite the central bank to cooperate in achieving its exchange rate objective. That request might involve an adjustment of monetary policy. Or, the Treasury could request only that the central bank undertake sterilized operations in the foreign exchange market in support of the exchange rate objective.

It can happen that the objective for domestic monetary policy is fully compatible with an objective for the foreign exchange rate. For instance, if deflation of the domestic price level happens to be accompanied by an excessive appreciation of the foreign exchange rate, then easier monetary policy can act simultaneously against both the deflation and the high exchange rate.

More often, however, the domestic policy objective is apt to conflict with an exchange rate objective. For instance, the real exchange rate tends to appreciate when monetary policy tightens in an effort to restore or maintain domestic price stability. Exporters hurt by the temporarily high real exchange rate can pressure the government to intervene against the appreciating currency. Likewise, a country may need to ease monetary policy sharply to act against deflation. Yet, doing so could depreciate the real exchange rate and generate pressure from the nation's trading partners, hurt by the loss of competitiveness, to intervene against the depreciating currency.

As a mechanical matter, a central bank can undertake sterilized interventions in the foreign exchange market in support of an exchange rate objective without changing the stance of monetary policy, that is, without changing the short-term interest rate target. There is little evidence, however, that sterilized interventions alone can have a sustained effect on the exchange rate. Therefore, a central bank's participation in foreign exchange operations inevitably creates doubt about its commitment to maintain domestic price stability. Even the intermittent pursuit of exchange rate objectives by the central bank has the potential to create problems for monetary policy by destabilizing actual inflation and inflation expectations.[7]

5. Two Case Studies of Monetary Policy in the Presence of Extreme Asset Price Fluctuations

The purpose of this section is to review the course of monetary policy in two relatively recent periods marked by a large rise and a subsequent fall in asset prices. The first is the period of large asset price appreciation and decline in late 1980s and early 1990s Japan. The second is the recent run-up and collapse of technology share prices in the United States in the late 1990s and early 2000s. The question is whether interest rate policy plausibly could have been improved during these periods by reacting directly and pre-emptively to the asset price movements.

5.1 Japan in the Late 1980s

By the mid 1980s, the Bank of Japan was well on its way to acquiring a credibility for low inflation that was the foundation for the real boom in the second half of the decade.[8] The Bank of Japan handled the oil shock of the late 1970s and early 1980s well. Japanese inflation as measured by the GDP deflator moved only slightly above 5 percent in the aftermath of the oil shock. The Bank of Japan acquired more credibility for low inflation at mid-decade in the aftermath of the 1985–86 recession and the fall in oil prices.

Japanese real GDP growth averaged around 4 percent per year from 1987 until 1991. The strong growth during those years took the real GDP output gap as measured by the Organization of Economic Cooperation and Development from –4 percent to +4 percent.[9] The Bank of Japan steered real short-term interest rates from a range of 2.5 percent in mid 1986 to 1 percent in early 1989. Remarkably, there was a drop of nearly 1.5 percentage points in late 1988, even though by then the output gap had virtually disappeared and the economy was growing rapidly. The Bank of Japan began to bring real short rates up in the second half of 1989 only after the real GDP gap had become negative.

At first the Consumer Price Index (CPI) inflation rate remained very low, in keeping with the credibility for low inflation that the Bank of Japan had earned through its inflation-fighting actions earlier in the decade. This favorable inflation performance probably contributed to the Bank of Japan's willingness to keep real short rates so low for so long during the boom. In retrospect, it seems that both the Bank of Japan and the Japanese public may have been fooled to a degree by the recently acquired credibility for low inflation into thinking that the economy had become inherently more inflation-proof. That belief may have contributed to the spectacular rise in Japanese asset prices. The Nikkei Stock Average rose from just above 20,000 at the start of

1988 to peak at nearly 40,000 in early 1990. The Nikkei was to fall sharply to the 25,000 range by the end of 1990 and below 20,000 again by 1992. Japanese land prices also rose sharply during this period, following stock prices with a lag.[10]

Eventually, the overestimate of the economy's noninflationary potential and the delay in raising short-term interest rates created doubts about the sustainability of low inflation. Consumer Price Index inflation began to rise in mid 1989, moving up by three percentage points from below 1 percent in early 1989 to nearly 4 percent by mid 1990. The growth of unit labor costs rose by five percentage points from 2 percent in 1989 to more than 7 percent by 1992. Rising inflation expectations probably helped move long bond rates up by five percentage points from 4 percent in the first half of 1989 to 9 percent by mid 1990.

Having been insufficiently pre-emptive, the Bank of Japan moved to restore credibility for low inflation by raising real short-term interest rates sharply in the second half of 1989, raising real short rates by around three percentage points to 4 percent. The bank raised real short rates by another two percentage points to a peak of around 6 percent in 1990, and held them there until 1991 when the economy began to move into recession. In retrospect, the boom and bust cycle can be seen to reflect inflationary go/stop monetary policy of the kind discussed above.

The bank appears to have been reluctant to undertake preemptive tightening and, indeed, may have eased monetary policy in 1988 out of concern for the appreciation of the yen on the foreign exchange market.[11] The yen/dollar rate fell from around 155 in early 1987 to 125 in the spring of 1988. It held in that range and then rose again throughout 1989 to peak at around 160 in the spring of 1990. Japanese authorities may have delayed the tightening of monetary policy until after the yen depreciated significantly in 1989 and 1990 so as not to produce a further appreciation in 1988 and early 1989 at a time when the yen's value was already regarded as relatively high.

In retrospect, clearly the Bank of Japan should have raised real short rates sooner than it did and could have justified doing so on the basis of conventional indicators of the output gap and related data on resource utilization. Specifically, the bank should probably have raised real short rates in 1988, and raised them further in the first half of 1989, instead of cutting short rates in late 1988 and waiting until late 1989 to raise rates sharply.

Could the Bank of Japan reasonably have justified tighter monetary policy in reaction to rising equity prices in 1988 and 1989? The Nikkei did begin its spectacular rise in 1988. But the equity price rise was not so large by then to signal clearly what was to come. It was only later, in mid 1989, that the rise in the Nikkei came to appear highly unusual. As described above, however, by then other data were signaling clearly that monetary policy needed to be tightened sharply. So it is not plausible that interest rate policy could have been made much more pre-emptive by taking the course of equity price movements into account.

It is more plausible to think that tighter policy could have been justified in 1988 and early 1989 because both equity and land prices were already rising rapidly by then. The problem with this argument is that there would seem to be little reason to exclude foreign exchange from the class of assets whose prices should have influenced interest rate policy. However, we saw above that to the extent that interest rate policy was influenced strongly by the foreign exchange rate, that influence was in the wrong direction. Thus, it is far from clear that policy plausibly could have been more pre-emptive by reacting directly and aggressively to a broad index of asset prices.

5.2 The United States in the Late 1990s

To understand the long expansion and subsequent U.S. recession in the late 1990s and early 2000s, one must begin with the monetary policy tightening in 1994 and early 1995.[12] As discussed above, that pre-emptive policy action anchored inflation and inflation expectations more securely than ever before. Core CPI inflation stayed in the 2.5 percent to 3 percent range and has remained there ever since. The long-bond rate came down and ranged between 5 percent and 6 percent during the last two years of the decade, even as the unemployment rate fell to 4 percent during the period.

There was probably a tendency for the Federal Reserve and the U.S. public to overestimate the economy's noninflationary potential in the second half of the 1990s. And, there was probably some tendency for the central bank's credibility for low inflation to delay interest rate policy actions necessary to maintain overall macroeconomic stability. Moreover, with inflation and inflation expectations firmly anchored, there was greater risk that insufficiently pre-emptive interest rate policy actions would set off an unsustainable real boom. Excessively optimistic beliefs about the economy's noninflationary productive potential were probably also reflected to some degree in the run-up in asset prices. Such factors probably played a role in the long U.S. boom in the late 1990s, just as they probably played a part in the Japanese boom of the late 1980s.

The U.S. expansion differed from the Japanese, however, in one important respect: Trend productivity growth rose throughout the late 1990s. There was little evidence of that in late 1980s Japan. Rising productivity growth had two important implications for monetary policy. First, rising productivity growth reinforced the perception that the economy had become more inflation-proof. Even as labor markets became ever tighter and wage growth increased, rising productivity growth enabled firms to pay higher wages with little upward pressure on prices.

Second, although rising productivity growth would make the economy seem more inflation-proof in the short run, higher trend productivity growth would require higher real interest rates in the longer run. Higher real interest rates are needed in a faster growing economy to make households and firms accept a steeper spending profile that conforms to the faster productivity growth.

Adding to the forces acting on Federal Reserve interest rate policy were the East Asian financial crisis in 1997 and the Russian default in 1998. These two crises helped to keep short rates lower than they otherwise would have been.

It was particularly difficult to know how to manage interest rate policy in such circumstances. And, the Federal Reserve chose to wait before tightening interest rate policy very much until the need for restrictive policy became more obvious. This occurred in the second half of 1999 when the pool of available workers—unemployed plus discouraged workers—looked to be approaching an irreducible minimum. There was then no point in continuing to allow aggregate demand to outstrip the growth of aggregate supply, even if inflation had not yet begun to rise. With that logic, the Federal Reserve began its first concerted monetary tightening during the period. It raised the federal funds rate in three 25 basis point steps in June, August, and November of 1999. The Fed raised the federal funds rate by another one percentage point between November 1999 and May 2000 to a peak of 6.5 percent, where it was held until January 2001.

Could Federal Reserve interest rate policy have been improved by reacting more strongly to equity prices? Technology stock prices in the United States tripled between early 1999 and early 2000. Arguably, 1999 was the crucial year in which paying greater attention to equity prices plausibly should have made policy more pre-emptive. A closer look, however, indicates that the tech stock price rise only came to be seen as truly extraordinary sometime after the middle of the year, about the same time that the pool of available workers reached a bottom. By then, the Federal Reserve clearly recognized the need for significantly tighter policy.

One might argue that the extraordinary increase in tech stock prices in the second half of 1999 should have signaled the Federal Reserve to increase its federal funds rate target more aggressively than it did. After all, with core CPI inflation then running at around 2.5 percent, the real short rate was only about 4 percent at its peak in 2000. By comparison with other occasions of concerted monetary tightening in the past, the real short rate was not then particularly high.

In retrospect, one can see why this would not have been a good idea. First, the Federal Reserve had not yet lost credibility for low inflation, and so it did not need high real short rates to create slack in the labor market in order to bring the inflation rate down. The objective in 2000 was merely to bring the growth of aggregate demand down to the growth of noninflationary potential output. Second, a number of factors then clearly suggested that the economy was operating well beyond its sustainable growth rate: Labor markets were tightening excessively, investment in productive capacity looked excessive, and unit labor costs looked set to rise as wage growth overtook productivity growth. Thus, the previously projected path for profits looked unsustainable. In such an environment it seemed likely that equity values and tech stock values in particular were set to fall, perhaps considerably. The collapse of equity values would reflect a more realistic assessment of the economy's productive potential, and signal that fact to the broader public with negative consequences for aggregate demand.

In the event, even the Federal Reserve's relatively modest increase in real short-term rates was sufficient to slow the growth of aggregate demand because it was accompanied by a reduction of equity values. The combined effect of modestly higher real short-term interest rates and lower equity values slowed aggregate demand enough to avert an increase in inflation. An outbreak of inflation almost surely would have led to a deeper and more prolonged recession than the one that actually occurred. One reason that the U.S. recession was so mild is that inflation did not rise during the boom years. Having retained near full credibility for low inflation during the boom, the Fed could lower real short-term interest rates sharply to fight recession in 2001 without fear of an inflation scare.

6. Conclusion

The analysis presented above suggests that monetary policy should not react directly to asset prices. The key components of the argument are these: First, there can be no theoretical presumption that appropriate interest rate policy actions should be correlated positively with equity price movements. Second, it is relatively easy to imagine practical situations in which it might be appropriate for interest rate policy to move in the opposite direction from asset price movements or not to react at all. The point was illustrated in connection with the reaction of policy to an outbreak of inflation, a profit squeeze, and rising trend productivity growth. Third, it is counterproductive for the central bank of a large and largely closed economy that pursues an explicit or implicit mandate for low inflation to take direct account of the exchange rate in making interest rate policy.

Finally, a critical reading of monetary policy in Japan in the late 1980s and in the United States in the late 1990s suggests that interest rate policy could not have been improved by reacting directly to asset prices. Reacting directly to equity prices would have been helpful in both Japan and in the United States if doing so plausibly could have made interest rate policy more pre-emptive. However, in both the Japanese and the U.S. cases equity prices were not yet so high in the early part of the respective periods in which policy should arguably have been tighter to signal clearly what was to come. Moreover, by the time that equity price rises clearly came to appear unduly elevated, other data were already signaling that monetary policy should be tightened sharply. At that point it was not advisable to move short rates up more aggressively in reaction to the high equity prices because equity prices then seemed at risk of falling, perhaps considerably, with a potentially large adverse effect on economic activity.

In the case of Japan, where equity and land prices were both rising rapidly, it seems plausible that monetary policy could have been more pre-emptive by reacting to a broad index of asset prices. However, a broad index would naturally include foreign exchange rates as well as equity and land prices. We saw above that to the extent that monetary policy was influenced by the exchange rate during the period, that influence was in the wrong direction. Hence, it is not clear that Japanese interest rate policy in the late 1980s could have been made more pre-emptive by reacting directly and aggressively to a broad index of asset prices.

*Marvin Goodfriend is a senior vice president and policy advisor at the Federal Reserve Bank of Richmond. The views are those of the author and not necessarily of the Federal Reserve Bank of Richmond or the Federal Reserve System.

Notes

1. For example, the case for taking greater direct account of asset prices in making monetary policy is made in Cecchetti, Genberg, Lipsky, and Wadhwani (2000) and in Goodhart (1995).

2. See Bernanke and Gertler (1999), in particular, for an analysis suggesting that monetary policy should not react directly to equity prices. Batini and Nelson (2000) reach a similar conclusion with respect to the foreign exchange rate.

3. This recommendation does not preclude reacting to a collapse of equity prices that threatens to disrupt financial markets more generally. See Stock and Watson (2001) for an assessment of the power of asset prices to forecast output and inflation.

4. The analysis in the preceding paragraphs and in the following section is based on the "new neoclassical synthesis" approach to monetary policy developed in Goodfriend and King (1997 and 2001).

5. Borio and Lowe (2001), Goodfriend (2001), and Taylor (2001) explore this kind of instability.

6. Goodfriend (1993) describes how the Federal Reserve handled inflation scares from 1979 to 1992.

7. This argument is developed at length in Broaddus and Goodfriend (1995). See Schwartz (2000) for a more recent appraisal of foreign exchange intervention as a policy tool.

8. This section draws on Goodfriend (1997).

9. Organization of Economic Cooperation and Development (1994), p. 12.

10. See Okina, Shirakawa, and Shiratsuka (2001), page 399.

11. Okina, Shirakawa, and Shiratsuka (2001) discuss how concerns about yen appreciation influenced Bank of Japan interest rate policy during the late 1980s. See, especially, pages 419–421, 436–440, and 447. Note that the Bank of Japan was not made independent of the Ministry of Finance until the late 1990s.

12. See Goodfriend (2002) for a more extensive reading of U.S. monetary policy in the 1990s.

References

Batini, Nicoletta, and Edward Nelson, 2000, "When the Bubble Bursts: Monetary Policy Rules and Foreign Exchange Market Behavior," Bank of England, manuscript.

Bernanke, Ben, and Mark Gertler, 1999, "Monetary Policy and Asset Price Volatility," *Economic Review*, Federal Reserve Bank of Kansas City, 4th quarter, pp. 17–51; also presented at the Federal Reserve Bank of Kansas City's symposium, New Challenges for Monetary Policy, in Jackson Hole, WY, August 1999.

Borio, Claudio, and Phillip Lowe, 2001, "Asset Prices, Financial and Monetary Stability: Exploring the Nexus," Bank for International Settlements, manuscript.

Broaddus, J. Alfred, Jr., and Marvin Goodfriend, 1995, "Foreign Exchange Operations and the Federal Reserve," *Annual Report*, Federal Reserve Bank of Richmond, pp. 3–20.

Cecchetti, Stephen G., Hans Genberg, John Lipsky, and Sushil Wadhwani, 2000, "Asset Prices and Central Bank Policy," prepared for the conference Central Banks and Asset Prices, organized by the International Center for Monetary and Banking Studies, Geneva.

Goodfriend, Marvin, 2002, "The Phases of U.S. Monetary Policy: 1987 to 2001," prepared for the "Charles Goodhart Festschrift" conference, also in *Economic Quarterly,* Federal Reserve Bank of Richmond, Vol. 88.

_____, 2001, "Financial Stability, Deflation, and Monetary Policy," *Monetary and Economic Studies, Special Edition,* Bank of Japan, Vol. 19, February, pp.143–167.

_____, 1997, comment on K. Udea, "Japanese Monetary Policy, Rules or Discretion? A Reconsideration," in *Towards a More Effective Monetary Policy,* Iwao Kuroda, ed., London: MacMillan Press, pp. 289–295.

_____, 1993, "Interest Rate Policy and the Inflation Scare Problem: 1979–1992," *Economic Quarterly,* Federal Reserve Bank of Richmond, Winter, pp.1–24.

Goodfriend, Marvin, and Robert King, 2001, "The Case for Price Stability," in *First ECB Central Banking Conference, Why Price Stability?,* European Central Bank, pp. 53–94, and the National Bureau of Economic Research, working paper, No. 8423.

_____, 1997, "The New Neoclassical Synthesis and the Role of Monetary Policy," in *National Bureau of Economic Research Macroeconomics Annual 1997,* Ben Bernanke and Julio Rotemberg, eds., Cambridge, MA: MIT Press, pp. 231–282.

Goodhart, C. A. E., 1995, "Price Stability and Financial Fragility," in *Financial Stability in a Changing Environment,* Kuniho Sawamoto, Zenta Nakajima, and Hiroo Taguchi, eds., Japan: The Bank of Japan, pp. 439–497.

Okina, Kunio, Masaaki Shirakawa, and Shigenori Shiratsuka, 2001, "The Asset Price Bubble and Monetary Policy: Japan's Experience in the Late 1980s and the Lessons," *Monetary and Economic Studies, Special Edition,* Bank of Japan, Vol.19, February, pp. 395–450.

Organization of Economic Cooperation and Development, 1994, *OECD Economic Surveys: Japan,* Paris.

Schwartz, Anna J., 2000, "The Rise and Fall of Foreign Exchange Market Intervention as a Policy Tool," *Journal of Financial Services Research,* Vol. 18, No. 2/3, pp. 319–339.

Stock, James H., and Mark W. Watson, 2001, "Forecasting Output and Inflation: The Role of Asset Prices," Harvard University and Princeton University, manuscript.

Taylor, John, 2000, "Low Inflation, Pass Through, and the Pricing Power of Firms," *European Economic Review,* Vol. 44, pp. 1389–1408.

Chapter 32
Comments on Implications of Bubbles for Monetary Policy

Benjamin M. Friedman*
Harvard University

It is useful to begin by asking what lies behind the great interest today in the potential implications of asset prices for monetary policy. I suggest three separate motivations. First, despite the recent noteworthy success of monetary policy, both in the United States and elsewhere, there is always the laudable desire to seek improvement. Second, and more specifically, there is a more acute desire to draw what lessons we can from the Japanese debacle of the last 10 years. Many observers believe that this sorry experience might well have gone differently if the Bank of Japan (BOJ) had taken account of the sharp rise and fall in the country's equity and real estate markets in a different way than it did. Third—and this is the thrust of my reactions to the two papers under discussion today—I think there is also at issue here a form of disguised reaction against the increasingly narrow interpretation of what monetary policy is all about, especially in central banks outside the United States, including in particular the increasingly widespread adoption of "inflation targeting."

What, then, is the issue that these two papers address? A proposition with which I suspect nobody today disagrees is that the central bank should take account of asset prices to the extent that asset prices bear incremental information about the macroeconomic goals of monetary policy, whatever they may be. In the United States, under prevailing legislation, these goals explicitly include inflation as well as output and employment. In other settings the list could be longer. In some countries it is limited to just inflation.

I formulate the proposition in this manner, rather than in terms of asset price *misalignments*, because for purposes of this discussion whether asset prices are "correct" or not—that is, whether they do or don't incorporate all relevant information that the efficient markets hypothesis says they should reflect—is not important. It is easy to think of examples in which asset prices are correct from the standpoint of discounting future expected earnings but, nonetheless, bear an influence on aggregate demand that monetary policy might well seek to offset. The issue here is not whether asset prices are correct, therefore, but whether they contain incremental information that bears on the goals of monetary policy.

Given the universal agreement that monetary policy should respond to asset prices if they do contain such information, the operative question for debate is what to do if asset prices do *not* contain such information. The majority view today among monetary economists, which is the view expressed in Marvin Goodfriend's paper, is that if asset prices do *not* contain incremental information about the macroeconomic goals of monetary policy, the central bank should ignore them.

A second familiar view is that because the central bank cares about the consequences of asset prices for the financial markets, it should take asset price movements into account even if they do not directly contain incremental information about the macroeconomic goals of monetary policy. Federal Reserve Chairman Alan Greenspan, for example, has argued, " ... that there is a form of asymmetry in response to asset rises and asset declines ... [C]entral banks do not respond to gradually declining asset prices. We do not respond to gradually rising asset prices. We do respond to sharply reduced asset prices, which will create a seizing up of liquidity in the system," (Greenspan, 1999, p 143). By referring to potentially damaging implications for the liquidity of the financial markets, Chairman Greenspan gave a cogent explanation for why the central bank would plausibly react to asset prices even if they did not bear information that is directly useful for predicting future outcomes of the macroeconomic goals of monetary policy.

The paper by Stephen Cecchetti, Hans Genberg, and Sushil Wadhwani seeks to lay out yet a third position on this question. As in Chairman Greenspan's view, here too the answer is that the central bank should react to asset prices even if they do not contain incremental information about the macroeconomic goals of monetary policy. But the reasoning is entirely different. In brief, the Cecchetti-Genberg-Wadhwani argument is that the central bank should respond to asset prices because asset prices contain information about macroeconomic goals that a central bank has, and indeed ought to have, but either cannot or will not admit out loud in public discussion that it has.

In what ways does the Cecchetti-Genberg-Wadhwani view differ from what I have labeled the majority view? Their paper focuses on what the authors call "medium-run macroeconomic stability." (In other words, their focus here is on the second moment of real economic outcomes.) Medium-run macroeconomic stability, as they define it, is certainly a plausible enough goal for monetary policy to pursue, presumably alongside the goal of low and stable price inflation. If asset prices usefully inform the best available forecast of prospects for such medium-run macroeconomic stability, therefore, why is this not simply a specific case of the general proposition on which everybody already agrees? The answer lies in the fact that Cecchetti et al. take as given—indeed, they applaud—the monetary policymaking framework now often called "inflation targeting."

As the standard theory of economic policy articulated by Tinbergen nearly 50 years ago made clear, if a policymaker, in this case the central bank, has at its disposal only *one policy instrument*, then (in the absence of a degenerate model or some other analogous pathology) the intended trajectory for any *one policy target* is sufficient to describe the policy as a whole, no matter how many goals the policymaker has. Why, then, choose inflation as the single target variable for this summary purpose? Two distinct rationales have featured prominently in the "inflation targeting" literature. First, most economists accept the theory that money is neutral over long horizons—in other words, that while monetary policy can and does affect inflation over any horizon, over longer horizons there are reasons for doubting that monetary policy systematically affects real variables like output and employment. A second argument, however, following the literature of time inconsistency, is that it is also important to make "transparent" the central bank's "commitment" to low inflation. Interpreted in this second way, inflation targeting is, therefore, a way of shaping—if one were to take a negative view, one would say "manipulating"—the public's expectation of future inflation.

It is useful to pause at this point to ask whether inflation targeting, as actually practiced today by those central banks that have adopted this framework, really represents transparency in monetary policy or, perhaps, the opposite of transparency. The answer depends on whether the impression given to the public, by the articulation of central bank policy via the vocabulary and analytical framework of inflation targeting, is accurate or not. I believe that it is, in many cases, a misrepresentation.

As Lars Svensson (among others) has usefully shown, the "inflation targeting" framework is fully consistent with the central bank's having goals for both inflation and real outcomes. In this case the central bank's concern for real outcomes leads it to seek to return inflation to the targeted rate only gradually, rather than immediately, after any departure from that rate due to unanticipated shocks. Indeed, most central banks that have adopted inflation targeting do follow this kind of gradualist approach. But what is noteworthy is that the officials of these central banks are almost never willing to discuss in public the extent to which they have policy preferences with respect to any variables other than inflation. As Mervyn King, for example, has frequently argued, these officials maintain this silence about the real economic goals that also underlie their inflation targeting strategy for fear of being misinterpreted. The mere explicit mention of output or employment, the officials fear, will somehow lead the public to believe that the weight the central bank attaches to real outcomes, compared to that on inflation, is vastly greater than, in fact, it is.

It is in this context that we can best understand how their commitment to the rhetoric (as opposed to the required logic) of inflation targeting—in particular, the fear of ever mentioning out loud any real objectives that monetary policy might be pursuing—has shaped the approach that Cecchetti et al. take in their paper. Their position is schematically as follows. First, the central bank's objectives do include medium-run macroeconomic stability, as they define it. Second, the authors' reading of the empirical evidence is that asset prices do contain incremental information about this aspect of economic behavior. Third, therefore—just as the reasoning of the usual majority view would conclude—monetary policy should respond to asset prices. But, importantly, they cannot acknowledge this chain of reasoning as the standard view because to do so would be to acknowledge openly that the central bank includes real macroeconomic stability among the goals of monetary policy.

As a result, Cecchetti et al. are led to represent their view as a contradiction of the standard majority view, when in reality it is simply one specific statement of the majority view. Their characterization of the majority view is as follows: "A common attitude vis-à-vis the role of asset prices in the formulation of monetary policy is that they should be taken into account only insofar as they affect a fixed-horizon inflation forecast," (p. 15 of their manuscript). Yes, of course, *if* the fixed-horizon inflation forecast is the central bank's only goal variable, then this is merely a restatement of the standard majority view. But if the central bank also has other objectives—for example, real macroeconomic stability—then whether or not asset prices contain useful information about the fixed-horizon inflation forecast is *not* all that the standard majority view would want the central bank to know before deciding whether to respond to them.

The difference between the position on this question that they advance in their paper and the standard majority view that Cecchetti et al. are at such pains to emphasize, therefore, comes from the authors trying to force the conversation to stay within the narrow rhetorical confines of inflation targeting, when they fully recognize that in reality the central bank has more objectives than merely inflation. To repeat, in principle there is no contradiction between the central bank's having those other objectives and its pursuing an inflation targeting strategy in the formal sense articulated by, for example, Svensson. The problem is rather that the central banks that have adopted such inflation targeting strategies do not want to admit publicly that inflation is not their sole objective. Cecchetti et al. structure their argument about the potential role of asset prices within the confines of that denial. It is only for this reason that they are led to argue that their view is something other than the standard majority view.

Finally, what about the positive question at issue here? *Do* asset prices contain incremental information that bears on the macroeconomic objectives of monetary policy?

Cecchetti and coauthors say "Yes," arguing on the basis of model simulations. Importantly, however, in making this argument they are referring not just to asset prices in the sense that is most familiar in this discussion—namely, the stock market and perhaps also the real estate market—but also to the foreign exchange rate. But the bearing of exchange rates on macroeconomic behavior is hardly controversial. In an open-economy setting it is entirely familiar for exchange rate movements to have predictive power with respect to either inflation or real macroeconomic outcomes or, more likely, both. It is fairly uncontroversial, therefore, that the central bank should take exchange rates into account in setting monetary policy.

By contrast, Goodfriend addresses the positive question of whether asset prices are incrementally informative with respect to the macroeconomic goals of monetary policy squarely in reference to equity and real estate prices. He answers in the negative. His analysis focuses on the two concrete examples that are most at the forefront of the recent discussion of this issue: Japan during the "bubble" and "post-bubble" periods and the United States during the late 1990s stock market boom and the subsequent selloff.

Goodfriend analyzes each of these specific cases by asking a form of the "Richard Nixon question:" What did the central bank know and when did it know it? And, what did it do on the basis of what it knew? Further, what *could* it have done on the basis of what it knew? After all, what matters for purposes of monetary policy is not whether some clever econometrician can come along after the fact and discover, through sophisticated exploration, that such and such an asset price series did have predictive content if only one had known how to specify the exact price variable and run the right regression. The issue for monetary policy is whether, in real time—that is, in advance—one can draw inferences that are useful for policy decisions.

Goodfriend's answer, based on his analysis of these two cases, is "No." His reading of the Japanese example is that asset prices were simply redundant. In real time, they told the BOJ only what the bank could have known, and in fact did know, from other sources. His reading of the U.S. example is that asset prices were in part redundant and in part misleading.

Where do these two papers leave us, then, on the positive question of whether asset prices do or don't contain useful information with respect to the macroeconomic outcomes that matter for monetary policy? I offer three summary remarks.

First, everyone recognizes that, in open economies, exchange rates bear useful information for monetary policy. The question at issue is the stock market and in some countries the real estate market.

Second, Goodfriend's argument that stock and real estate prices did not contain such useful information in his two case studies is pertinent and, to a large degree, persuasive. His paper establishes a burden of proof: Those who argue for the information content of stock prices or real estate prices in this context should have to meet the standard of showing how, *in real time*, the asset prices that everybody knew were the right asset prices to watch were actually informative. (To be explicit on this point, Goodfriend's paper shows that in Japan stock prices were redundant, but useful information may have been contained in land prices. But how was the BOJ to know to base monetary policy on land prices rather than stock prices? In the Cecchetti et al. paper, the emphasis is on the NASDAQ index. But the movement of the NASDAQ differed from the movement of the Standard & Poor's 500, which, in turn, differed from the movement of the Dow Jones. How was the Federal Reserve to know that the NASDAQ was the right stock price index to watch?)

Third, it is important to remember that this issue is an empirical question, not an a priori matter. Most of the a priori reasoning on this subject, in both the Cecchetti et al. paper and the Goodfriend paper, amounts to establishing that mechanical univariate extrapolations from asset price movements are not likely to be helpful for making monetary policy. But this is not the issue. The question under debate is whether there is a role for asset prices in a more fully thought-out model, and in the end that is an empirical issue. What makes monetary policy challenging is that actions taken today affect the economy in the future. Information about the future is scarce, and, therefore, monetary policy should exploit relevant and useful information from wherever it comes—including asset prices. The positive empirical question is whether, in real time, asset prices contain such information.

*Benjamin M. Friedman is the William Joseph Maier Professor of Political Economy at Harvard University.

Reference

Greenspan, Alan, 1999. "Untitled Remarks," in *New Challenges to Monetary Policy*, Kansas City, MO: Federal Reserve Bank of Kansas City.

PART VIII

IMPLICATIONS OF BUBBLES FOR PRUDENTIAL REGULATORY POLICY

Chapter 33

The Historical Pattern of Economic Cycles and Their Interaction with Asset Prices and Financial Regulation

Charles A. E. Goodhart*
London School of Economics

1. Introduction: The Changing Nature of Business Cycles

1.1 1945–80

In the decades after World War II, business cycles were unusual in certain historical respects. So also was the underlying conjuncture; this was a period in most developed countries of unusually fast growth, rapid improvements in productivity, and low unemployment. However, these positive developments were achieved at the expense of steadily worsening inflation, which appeared to increase from cycle to cycle; this was the only peace-time period to exhibit such severe inflation, at least in the UK, as shown in figure 1.

During these decades, much of the impetus to growth arose from a high and frequently rising level of public sector expenditures. This interacted with large-scale private sector investment initially brought about by postwar restructuring and then maintained by rapid growth and the introduction of new technologies. Moreover, there was in many countries some attempt at Keynesian demand management (sometimes also influenced by reliance on the historical, downwards-sloping Phillips curve), which, along with other political and social factors, led to the authorities aiming to maintain unemployment at a rate that would lay somewhat below the natural rate.

In certain cases the upswing was led by private sector investment. In other cases the upswing was led by increased fiscal deficits; these could on occasion be due to additional social security expenditures (the Great Society) and in other cases due to an increased demand for defense (Cold War)—and in some cases both together (guns and butter). As a generality during this period, and certainly in the UK, fiscal policy was seen as the major tool of demand management and the instrument the authorities might best use to equilibrate the economy.

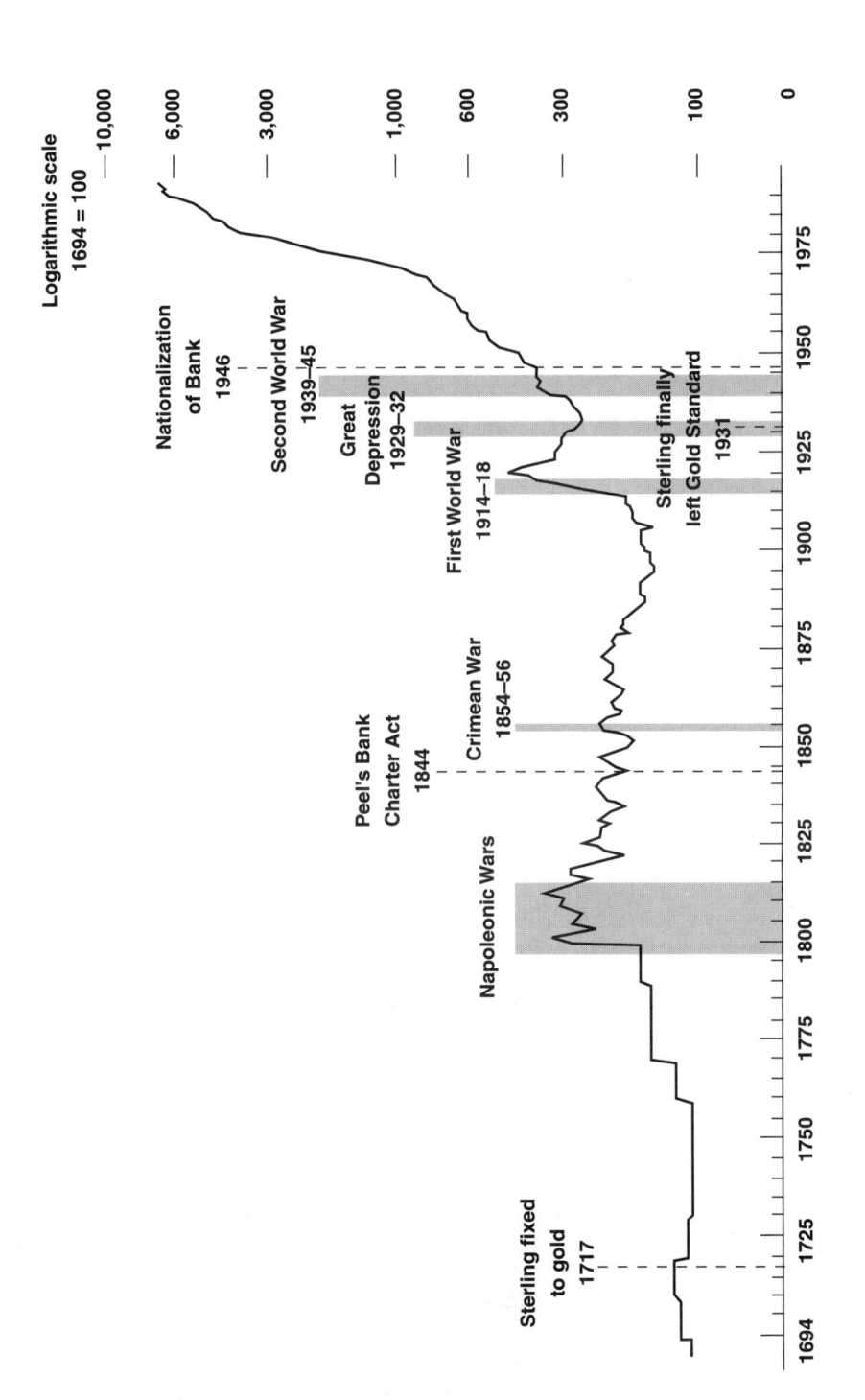

Figure 1: Economic Cycles in the UK

Interest rates were more frequently varied, at least in smaller open economies, in order to try to influence capital flows, so as to maintain the pegged exchange rate under the Bretton Woods system. In any case, variations in interest rates were not thought likely to be effective in controlling demand, and in those countries with large debt burdens, such as the UK, there was considerable reluctance to vary interest rates for internal demand management purposes, in part because of the side effect on the debt burden and the fiscal deficit. So, attempts to use monetary policy for demand management purposes were more frequently undertaken through direct controls on bank credit expansion, rather than by varying interest rates. With interest rates, thus, quite largely determined by external considerations, and/or held stable in order to ease the debt burden of the government and of industrial borrowers, monetary policy was relatively accommodating.

Not perhaps surprisingly under these conditions the crisis at the peak of the cycle and the subsequent downturn were generally caused by inflationary (excess demand) pressures. In the case of smaller open economies, such pressures were normally largely evidenced and exhibited by worsening current account deficits. Such worsening external deficits and rising inflation led to sharp increases in interest rates in those countries having difficulty in maintaining their pegged exchange rates. Where the inflation seemed most worrying, or the current account deficit was most intractable, the authorities would tend to augment the increase in interest rates with fiscal retrenchment.

In this context, as already noted, bank lending to the private sector was constrained, often by direct controls, in order to provide more room for lending to the public sector as well as certain favored (export) industries and also to restrain monetary growth, without having to raise interest rates to levels that were considered as unduly high. Such direct constraints on bank lending (actual physical controls on the volume of lending that banks could undertake) not only required the relevant lending institutions, in particular the banks, to be cartelized, but also led the authorities to reinforce and encourage the maintenance of cartelized, oligopolistic financial systems. Within such oligopolies, competition was limited, with the active support of the authorities, and the system was run in such a way that financial intermediaries were able to make regular stable profits. Such restrictions on competition reduced innovation and efficiency, but they did lead to banking systems and to financial markets that were safe, even if they were not very dynamic. These three or four decades were characterized by a remarkable absence of banking failures, as shown in figure 2, abstracted from Bordo et al. (2001, figure 1, p. 56).

1.2 Business Cycles before 1939 and after 1985

Whereas the cycles in the period from 1945 to 1979 were, therefore, somewhat special and unusual historically, the business cycles before 1939 and after 1985 could be described as more "normal," with such normal characteristics described further below. Note that the period between 1980 and (about) 1985 can be regarded as an intermission between the previous inflationary period, which culminated in the 1970s, and the return to peacetime normality after 1985. This intermission was, of course, largely brought about by the change introduced by former Federal Reserve Chairman Paul Volcker to the monetary policy regime in the United States in October 1979. This led

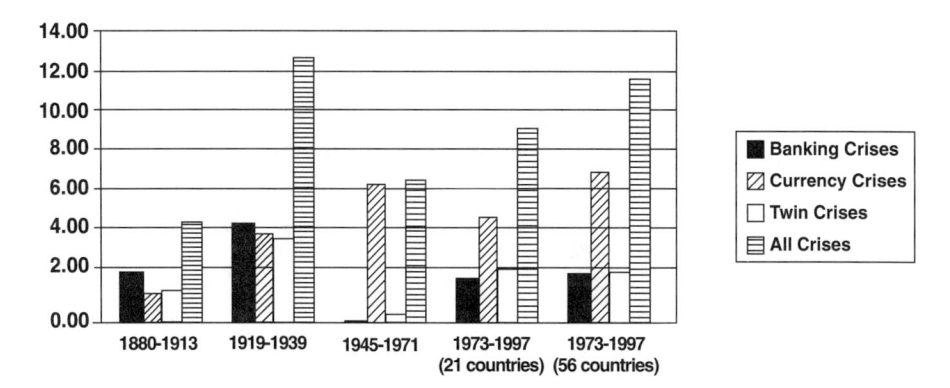

Figure 2: Crisis Frequency (Percent Probability Per Year)

to a dramatic period of very high and extremely volatile interest rates. The recession that this brought about in the early 1980s had a particularly severe effect on developing countries. Following the oil shock in the early 1970s, the international monetary system had devised a way of channeling large-scale capital flows from the oil-rich developing countries to the oil-importing developing countries. During the 1970s, with a combination of high inflation, low real interest rates, rapidly rising export prices denominated in dollars, and a reasonable growth in the volume of such trade, this pattern of international capital flows not only seemed sustainable, but also one of the great triumphs of the modern economy. All these features were effectively reversed by Volcker's policy regime change. This led to one of the world's great crises, the less-developed-country debt crisis in 1982; much of the period between 1982 and the mid 1980s was taken up with the need to resolve this difficult and long-lasting crisis. It was only really towards the middle of the 1980s that the world returned to a new, lower-inflation, (potentially sustainable) equilibrium.

Although sweeping generalizations, (such as this!) are always subject to necessary qualifications, business cycles in more normal periods, as occurred before 1939 and after 1985, have been mainly driven by fluctuations in private sector expenditures, notably in private sector investment and exports, and in associated fluctuations, frequently even more extreme, in asset prices, notably equity and property prices. I have attempted to document this commonality of experience in a paper, with Robert Delargy (1999), for which the subtitle is "Plus ça change, plus c'est la même chose."

During the recovery and boom periods of such cycles, the expansion phase is usually driven by rising private sector investment, owing often to technical progress or to the opening up of new trade, particularly export, prospects. During such a period, both business investment and profits are rising. Such increases in profits and the prospects of future higher profits cause asset prices to rise, and the expansion of profitable investment leads to sharp increases in borrowing and credit expansion by banks.

More often than not during such a boom the fiscal deficit remains low. The expansion leads to an increase in tax revenues, with constant tax rates, and with given public expenditure plans, the increase in output actually can lead to a slight fall in the ratio of public sector expenditures to total expenditures. Although exports are rising, these are frequently accompanied by sizable capital inflows so that imports rise even faster than exports. Nevertheless, despite a current account deficit, during the main part of the expansionary phase, the country often has a strong exchange rate, which appreciates if the exchange rate is floating. In the meantime, although wages are rising, the wage/price spiral will be held down by increasing productivity, so that unit labor costs do not rise at the same rate as nominal wages. Moreover, with a strong exchange rate tending to hold down the price of imports, there are further gains to the employee in terms of higher real wages. So, in these circumstances, a recovery can continue for a long time without leading either to an unsustainable fiscal deficit, or to significantly worsening inflationary pressures. Unlike the period between 1945 and 1980, the boom under these circumstances will not necessarily be brought to an end either by a necessity to tighten policy in order to restrain inflation, or to limit the extent of the external or the fiscal deficit.

Instead, the crisis, and subsequent bust, will frequently be caused by overinvestment, especially in property, leading to falling profitability and the reversal of the previous virtuous cycle. When this cycle goes into reverse, investment and profits fall, bringing with that falling asset prices, frequently showing dramatic declines, which in turn can lead to a weakening of the solvency of the banking system and to a contraction of credit expansion. That reduction in credit expansion feeds back onto falling investment and falling profits, leading to a further round of a vicious cycle of debt deflation.

In smaller open economies there is yet a further danger. The danger is that capital outflows, to avoid the weakness of asset prices and potentially insolvent banking systems, could lead to very rapidly falling exchange rates. Such falls in exchange rates could not only put further pressure on domestic borrowers who have borrowed in foreign currency, but could also lead to a revival of inflationary pressures just at the moment when the domestic economy is particularly weak. This can lead to a devastating combination of seriously worsening inflation and falling output just at the same moment.

Such a possibility of a debt/deflation cycle, interacting with fragile banking systems, was initially pointed out by Irving Fisher, whose message was subsequently taken up by Kindleburger and Hy Minsky. This process has subsequently been formalized by Kiyotaki and Moore.

There are, alas, all too many examples of such severe cycles in recent years. This general picture fits the examples of Japan from the mid 1980s onwards, of Scandinavia in the early 1990s, of Asia in the late 1990s, and, finally, of the United States between 1995 and now.

2. Which Asset Prices Are Most Important in this Context?

As already described at the end of the last section, in this normal cyclical pattern there is a crucial interrelationship between fluctuations in asset prices and in the economy more widely. That leads on to the general question of which set of asset prices has been most important in this respect.

In a number of empirical studies done on this subject with my colleague Boris Hofmann, the general answer that we have found is that it has been *property* prices, that is, the prices of housing and land, that have been most important in the interaction between fluctuations in output, bank lending, and asset prices. The United States has been somewhat atypical in this respect, since fluctuations in equity (share) prices—often an insignificant factor in cycles in other countries—have been relatively more important in the United States than elsewhere.

Some reasons for the greater importance of equity prices in the United States have been:

1) There is a wider shareholding, with a larger proportion of the population holding shares, and such holdings representing a larger share of personal wealth than in other countries (see table 1). In many other countries, most equity shareholdings, outside those owned within the company sector, are held indirectly to the benefit of individuals through financial intermediaries, notably pension funds, insurance companies, and even banks themselves.

2) For a variety of reasons, housing price fluctuations overall seem to be have been less extreme in the United States than in many other countries, for example, Scandinavia, Australia, the UK, and Japan. This is, perhaps, partly because the United States is such a large economy; there have been regions within the country where housing price fluctuations have been much greater than in other economies overall; for example, certain regions in New England and California have faced housing price fluctuations just about as large as those in smaller European countries.

Furthermore it is possible that the elasticity of housing supply in the United States is significantly greater than it is in smaller, older, and more densely populated countries. It is probably easier and quicker to get planning permission to build new houses in the United States than in these other countries. Moreover, the ability to use wooden construction, and the greater availability of wood as a building material, may make it quicker and easier to meet an increased demand with an increased supply of housing than is the case in many other countries.

3) Again, in the United States, there have probably been more links between bank lending and share prices, whether such lending is collateralized on shares or is for the finance of share purchases, than has been the case in other countries.

	Housing assets	Equity	Other financial assets	Other tangible assets
United States	21	20	50	8
Japan	10	3	44	43
Germany	32	3	35	30
France	40	3	47	9
Italy	31	17	39	13
UK	34	12	47	7
Canada	21	17	39	23

Note: Data refer to 1998 (1997 for France).
Source: OECD Economic Outlook, December 2000, Table VI.1

Table 1: Composition of Household Total Assets (in Percent)

Certainly in the early years of the 20th century, and in the interwar period, the interaction between the equity market and the banking system, for example, through the call loan market in New York, was considerably closer than the case in many other developed countries.

And, that leads to a question: Is the wealth effect on consumption of housing wealth considerably greater than the wealth effect on consumption of equivalent variations in equity prices (see, for example, Case, Quigley, and Shiller, 2001)? Did consumption in the United States, at least before the atrocity in September 2001, hold up reasonably strongly because housing values remained strong, despite the downturn in share prices?

Most attention has generally been paid to fluctuations in equity prices. Nevertheless, it is certainly arguable, and my work with Boris Hofmann (2000a; 2000b; 2001), strongly suggests that it is movements in property prices that have had far more effect in driving expenditures. By the same token it has been movements in real estate prices that have been most closely associated with the ability and willingness of the banking system to extend loans, and this has been a major driving force in the strong cyclical fluctuations in many countries in the past. There were many examples, especially before 1914, of crises related to property cycles. This, for example, occurred in Australia in 1893, in Italy in 1893 and 1907, in Argentina in 1890, and in Austria in 1873.

Let me present a few tables, which are mainly taken from the paper by Boris Hofmann and myself presented at the Swedish Riksbank on "Financial Variables and the Conduct of Monetary Policy." The first table shows the ratio of equity wealth to property wealth in percent (table 2); the data show that, as a generality, property wealth has been more important than equity wealth in our economies. The next table (table 3) shows the share of loans secured by real estate collateral.

Indeed, there is evidence that the single variable that has had the greatest effect on new business start-ups in the UK has been the price of housing, since most beginning entrepreneurs only have housing as an asset against which they can collateralize, at least in part, their loans from the banks (see Black, de Meza, and Jeffreys, 1996). Also note the major importance that de Soto, in his book *The Mystery of Capitalism*, attaches to the ability to collateralize housing value as the engine of capitalism.

In one of our recent papers (2001), Hofmann and I sought to construct a financial conditions index analogous to the monetary conditions index, once utilized by Canada and New Zealand. We did this in two ways, first looking at reduced form estimates of the effects of such asset price variations on output and second, from Value-at-Risk (VaR) impulse responses. The results, shown in table 4, generally show that housing

	Ratio		Ratio
Australia	27	Finland	18
Canada	43	Germany	18
Japan	45	Sweden	32
United States	45	UK	52

Source: Author's calculations based on Borio, Kennedy, and Prowse (1994), table A1.2, p. 80
Note: Data refer to 1988–92 (Sweden 1970–92, UK 1985–92).

Table 2: Ratio of Equity Wealth to Property Wealth (in Percent)

	Share		Share
Australia	34	Netherlands	36
Belgium	34	Spain	33
Canada	56	Sweden	>61
France	41	UK	59
Germany	36	United States	66
Italy	40		

Source: Borio (1996), table 12, p. 101
Note: Data refer to 1993 (Sweden 1992).

Table 3: Share of Loans Secured by Real Estate Collateral (in Percent)

price fluctuations are considerably more closely related to subsequent variations in real output than are either exchange rates or equity prices.

3. Financial Regulation and Asset Prices

How should macro monetary policy react to such asset price fluctuations? To the extent that such asset price fluctuations can be predicted to lead to general inflation in goods and service prices, that is, that they bring about subsequent changes in the Consumer Price Index (CPI) or retail price index, then there is a consensus that monetary policy needs to be countervailing in order to offset fluctuations in inflation around the target. However, there is much less agreement on the question of whether the authorities should be concerned with asset price fluctuations, even when they are not expected to lead directly to straightforward goods and service price inflation. This remains a contentious subject. There are arguments on both sides; Cecchetti et al. (2000) argue that for a variety of reasons, for example that output fluctuations may well become even more extreme as a result of asset price fluctuations, the authorities ought to have concern for asset prices directly. On the other hand, Bernanke and Gertler (1999) argue that it is only to the extent that asset price fluctuations are predicted to affect general inflation that the authorities should respond.

Whatever the difficulty of deciding how to adjust *macro monetary* policy in the face of large-scale asset price fluctuations may be, the problems for financial regulation are just as difficult, if not worse. The close connections, in both directions, between banking and asset price fluctuations means that strongly rising asset prices, for example in housing, tend to be accompanied by low bad debts, considerably improved collateralized margins, and strong bank profits. Bank share prices rise, and new equity is easy to raise. And this, of course, reverses in slumps.

So capital control regulations typically do not bite in booms at all, but tighten significantly during recessions. Financial regulation is inherently procyclical. Indeed, the more sensitive the capital requirements are to the current measurement of risk, the worse the procyclicality is likely to be. This has turned out to be the case with the proposals put forward at the beginning of 2001 by the Basel Regulatory Committee. Such procyclicality has been noted by a number of authors, for example, Borio et al. (2000) and Danielsson et al. (2001). Moreover, the use of VaRs, especially when based

	Interest rate	Exchange rate	House prices	Share prices
Canada	0.42	0.22	0.18	0.18
	0.59	0.28	0.10	0.04
France	0.54	0.19	0.18	0.09
	0.41	0.04	0.51	0.04
Germany	0.61	0.12	0.18	0.09
	0.43	0.08	0.46	0.03
Italy	0.52	0.19	0.16	0.13
	0.54	0.13	0.29	0.03
Japan	0.42	0.08	0.44	0.06
	0.43	0.04	0.48	0.05
UK	0.46	0.25	0.14	0.15
	0.45	0.17	0.35	0.03
United States	0.54	0	0.30	0.16
	0.37	0.02	0.58	0.03
Average	0.50	0.15	0.23	0.12
	0.46	0.10	0.40	0.04

Note: The table shows in each cell first the weight derived from the reduced form estimates and then the weight derived from the VaR impulse responses.

Table 4: FCI Weights

on a relatively short-run data period and using a model, such as generalized autoregressive conditional heteroscedasticity (GARCH), which puts a comparatively heavy weight on recent volatility, (and the more finely tuned risk sensitivity in the internal risk based models), are all likely to worsen such procyclicality. All this was set out in Danielsson et al. (2001), a Financial Markets Group Special Paper.

As Andrew Crockett and others at the Bank for International Settlements have emphasized, "Risk is assumed during (asset price) booms, but realized during the subsequent depression."

An obvious, but nevertheless, major problem is that asset price boom and bust cycles only become clearly apparent after the event. Asset price expansions are usually connected with certain extremely good innovations on the technological supply side, for example, the development of canals, railways, electricity, information technology, etc. So each expansionary phase invokes plausible stories about a "new economy." Even to the somewhat limited extent that asset price characteristics do exhibit historical stationarity, for example profit/earnings ratios and housing value/income ratios, there will be claims during any expansion that the future will not be like the past and that the business cycle has been eliminated. Moreover, there is little regularity to the business cycle, indeed, so little that it is hard to use the phrase "cycle," since this tends to denote regularity. Indeed, the onset of a subsequent recession following the start of an initial recovery seems to occur almost randomly, with an equal probability in each period (Love, 2002). So there is virtually no way that one can predict when a boom will end and a recession will occur. But it always has. For all such reasons, trying to estimate asset price "misalignments" will prove hardly possible. (Indeed, many doubt whether "misalignments" can occur in rational efficient markets, though recent movements in share prices, notably on the NASDAQ Exchange, and in the valuation of dot-com companies have cast considerable doubt on the hypothesis of rational efficient markets).

So what should we do under these circumstances? We can barely assess whether "misalignments" have occurred, nor their extent, nor when they will end. Even to the extent that we or the authorities do believe that we can observe such "misalignments," there are serious differences of opinion of what can and should be done about them. Nevertheless, the Basel II proposals appear to be yet further increasing the extent to which regulatory controls will cease to be effective in booms and have a stronger restrictive effect on bank expansions during slumps, which, from a systemic point of view, is exactly the time when one wants bank lending in aggregate to be increasing rather than reducing. So, what to do? This is a problem that the regulators at Basel are now having to address, because the point has been made forcefully both by regulators and by outside commentators.

What are the alternatives? There are perhaps three main alternative routes:

1) Do nothing. Insofar as there may be a problem of regulatory procyclicality, that should be left to a (more aggressive) countercyclical macro-policy. I find this difficult to accept on two grounds. The first is a point of principle. The major purpose of official regulation in the banking field ought to be to try to prevent and/or lessen the effect of systemic contagious problems, with potentially massive externalities for the economy as a whole. If regulation is going to be procyclical, and therefore enhance the likelihood of systemic problems, then there is a serious question of whether the whole exercise is doing any good at all.

The second issue is a more practical one; this is whether it would be possible to rely on monetary policy committees (MPCs) doing enough, and sufficiently aggressively, if the banking system should get stuck in a recession. The example of Japan is not encouraging. Central bankers are hardly typified as aggressive; their quality is more often one of caution. Under such circumstances, would it really be safe to rely on the ability of MPCs to vary interest rates and monetary growth sufficiently strongly if the regulatory system were actually acting as a drag-anchor, taking the banking system in the wrong direction from a systemic, aggregate point of view?

2) A second approach would be to abandon the pursuit of risk-sensitive regulatory requirements. Instead, one could just fix a, considerably higher, minimum capital ratio in relationship to overall liabilities. Such an approach has been advocated by some, for example in the U.S. Shadow Financial Regulatory Committee, for example, Statement No. 156, 1999. It can be argued that attempts by officials, however well meaning, to get involved in addressing risk-sensitivity requirements will lead to a system that is too complex, too intrusive, and too likely to distort in unforeseeable and unforeseen ways, as the banks react to the regulations.

Similarly, one may posit that, especially as the system changes and responds in ways that cannot be foreseen, regulation ought to be simple and broad-brush, or it would tend to get lost in the thickets of complexity and innovation.

3) The final alternative is to try to impose risk-related requirements on the basis of the understanding that risk is assumed during booms, whereas it only becomes concretely realized in slumps. This is not easy for many of the reasons already given, that is, that you cannot exactly assess where you are in the cycle, nor the degree of any asset price misalignment. Other reasons for the difficulty of this approach is that tax (Inland Revenue) officials, accountants and auditors, and a whole range of other commentators, will insist on linking taxes, profits, accounts, etc. ... to actual recorded details of what actually *has* happened in any one year, not to what *might* (stochastically) happen over some uncertain future. We live in a world with a requirement for annual records; such short-run annual periodicity exerts a tyranny over the way that we see and order events.

Nevertheless, there are a few tentative ideas, which may be worth considering. Some of these are:

a) Use the idea adopted in Spain of pre-provisioning for loan losses over the course of the cycle.

b) If it is necessary to endorse VaR models, then give incentives to use as long a historical period as possible and to use historical simulations rather than GARCH-type models.

c) Relate requirements on loans, such as loan to value ratios, which are related to specific assets, to the real percent change in such asset prices (that is, deflated by the CPI) over the last n years, with n perhaps equal to 3 or 4. The idea is that if real asset prices have been rising (falling) rapidly recently, the required (capital/collateral) cover would increase (decrease) sharply in line with the rise in asset prices. Whereas there is always dispute and uncertainty about the existence and size of misalignments, at least the rate of change, relative to recent trends, in asset prices is easily and unambiguously estimated, though the period of time over which one might try to relate regulatory, prudential requirements to the rate of change of asset prices would have to be analyzed and estimated more carefully.

d) Somewhat similarly to "c," condition capital adequacy requirements to the rate of growth (relative to trend) of bank lending to the private sector. Such (abnormal) growth has been one of the few reliable forward-looking indicators, at both the micro and macro levels, of trouble and failure several years ahead.

e) There may well be other possibilities and ideas. Indeed, I am waiting with bated breath and keenly for the ideas that my discussants will present when they come to comment on my own paper. I trust that it will be profitable for all of you to read their works.

---

*Charles A. E. Goodhart is the Norman Sosnow Professor of Banking and Finance at the London School of Economics.

References

Bernanke, B., and M. Gertler, 1999, "Monetary Policy and Asset Price Volatility," Federal Reserve Bank of Kansas City, *Economic Review*, 4th quarter 1999, pp. 17–51.

Black, J., D. de Meza, and D. Jeffreys, 1996, "House Prices, the Supply of Collateral and the Enterprise Economy," *Economic Journal*, Vol. 106, No. 343, January, pp. 60–75.

Bordo, M., B. Eichengreen, D. Klingebiel, and M. Martinez-Peria, 2001, "Is the Crisis Problem Growing More Severe?," *Economic Policy*, Vol. 32, April, pp. 53–82.

Borio, C., N. Kennedy, and S. Prowse, 1994, "Exploring Aggregate Asset Price Fluctuations Across Countries: Measurement, Determinants and Monetary Policy Implications," Bank for International Settlements, economic papers, No. 40, April.

Borio, C., 1996, "Credit Characteristics and the Monetary Policy Transmission Mechanism in Fourteen Industrial Countries: Facts, Conjectures and Some Econometric Evidence," in *Monetary Policy in a Converging Europe*, K. Alders, K. Koedijk, C. Kool, and C. Winder, eds., Boston: Kluwer Academic Publishers, pp. 77–115.

Borio, C., C. Furfine, and P. Lowe, 2001, "Procyclicality of the Financial System and Financial Stability: Issues and Policy Options," Bank for Internatioinal Settlements, papers, No. 1.

Case, K., J. Quigley, and R. Shiller, 2001, "Comparing Wealth Effects: The Stock Market Versus the Housing Market," Yale University, Cowles Foundation, discussion paper, No. 1335, October.

Cecchetti, S., H. Genberg, J. Lipsky, and S. Wadhwani, 2000, "Asset Prices and Central Bank Policy," *Geneva Reports on the World Economy*, No. 2.

Danielsson, J., P. Embrechts, C. Goodhart, C. Keating, F. Muennich, O. Renault, and H. Shin, 2001, "An Academic Response to Basel II," London School of Economics, Financial Markets Group, special paper, No. 130, May.

De Soto, H., 2000, *The Mystery of Capitalism*, London: Bantam Press.

Fisher, I., 1933, "The Debt-Deflation Theory of Great Depressions," *Econometrica*, Vol. 1, pp. 337–357.

Goodhart C., and P. Delargy, 1998, "Financial Crises. Plus ça change, plus c'est la même chose," *International Finance*, Vol. 1, No. 2, December, pp. 261–287.

Goodhart, C., and B. Hofmann, 2001, "Asset Prices, Financial Conditions and the Transmission of Monetary Policy," paper presented at the conference Asset Prices, Exchange Rates, and Monetary Policy, March 2–3.

_____, 2000a, "Do Asset Prices Help to Predict Consumer Price Inflation?," *The Manchester School*, Vol. 68, supplement, pp. 122–140.

_____, 2000b, "Financial Variables and the Conduct of Monetary Policy," Sveriges Riksbank, working paper, No. 112.

Kindleberger, C., 1989, *Manias, Panics, and Crashes*, second ed., London: Macmillan.

Kiyotaki, N., and J. Moore, 1997, "Credit Cycles," *Journal of Political Economy*, Vol. 105, pp. 211–248.

Love, R., 2002, "The Inter-Temporal Nature of Risk," appendix to C. Goodhart, Marjolin Lecture at Société Universitaire Européenne de Recherches Financières Conference in Brussels, October 27, 2001.

Minsky, H., 1986, *Stabilizing an Unstable Economy*, New Haven, CT: Yale University Press.

Shadow Financial Regulatory Committee, 1999, "Statement on 'The Basel Committee's New Capital Adequacy Framework,'" statement No. 156, administrative office c/o Prof. G. Kaufman, e-mail: gkaufma@luc.edu.

Chapter 34
Asset Price Bubbles and Prudential Regulation

Jeffrey Carmichael*
Australian Prudential Regulation Authority

and

Neil Esho
Australian Prudential Regulation Authority

1. Introduction

In the nine years to December 2000, real gross domestic product (GDP) grew at an annual average rate of 3.8 percent in the United States, 2.0 percent in the major European economies, 2.7 percent in the UK, 6.1 percent in Taiwan and at 4.3 percent in Australia. Against the trend of strong economic growth the Japanese economy has struggled throughout the past decade, with real GDP growth averaging only 1.2 percent.[1] The relatively low growth rate has occurred despite the Japanese government's large fiscal stimulus packages and the reduction of nominal interest rates to almost zero. The cause of Japan's decade of poor economic performance has been attributed, *inter alia*, to the collapse of property and stock price bubbles in 1990, which led to a massive increase in bad debts and a severely weakened financial system that continues to constrain the real economy.[2] Japan, of course, is not alone in having had its economic progress and financial stability severely disrupted by sharp reversals in asset prices. The dramatic currency reversals of several Southeast Asian countries and subsequent economic turmoil in 1997 are familiar to all.[3]

While a considerable amount of research has been devoted to the question of whether or not pre-emptive monetary policy should be used to influence asset prices, there has been comparatively much less discussion of the effectiveness, desirability and nature of pre-emptive regulatory policy in this context.[4] What literature there is generally supports the use of regulatory policy based on three main propositions: 1) Monetary policy is either inappropriate or relatively ineffective in bursting bubbles;

2) Procyclicality of the financial system can be reduced with appropriate regulatory policies; and 3) A strong banking system that correctly measures and prices risk can reduce the likelihood of asset price bubbles developing. Beyond this consensus they offer a wide range of possible approaches.[5]

Justifying a role for prudential regulation in controlling bubbles, however, requires more than just the ineffectiveness of monetary policy. It requires evidence:

- that bubbles actually cause damage to the real economy;
- of a reliable relationship between the formation and bursting of bubbles and the behavior of banks; and
- that regulation can influence this behavior without material side effects, either for the economy or for the other objectives of prudential regulation.

In what follows we take as given that asset price bubbles can cause damage to the real economy. That issue is the subject of other papers at this conference and is beyond the scope of this paper. We also avoid any debate over the definition of bubbles and whether or not they are rational or otherwise. For our purposes it is sufficient that asset prices can and do fall sharply from time to time and that these falls cause economic disruption; whether these falls are simply excessive price swings or genuine bubbles is not addressed. Our focus is primarily on the relationship between these price movements and the behavior of banks and on the way in which prudential regulation might affect that relationship.

We begin in section 2 with a brief review of the Australian experience with price cycles. While this evidence amounts to casual rather than rigorous empiricism, it does highlight some interesting aspects of the relationship. In particular it suggests that, on the Australian experience at least, banks have been neither the sole cause of bubbles, nor the main victims of them. There is, nonetheless, evidence of a positive relationship between rapid credit expansion and price bubbles and therefore a *prima facie* case for regulatory intervention.

Section 3 turns to the ways in which prudential regulation might seek to influence the banking system for the purpose of controlling price swings. We examine four possible sources of regulatory response: portfolio restrictions, adjustments in capital requirements, adjustments in provisioning requirements, and the use of stress testing. Of these we suggest that the first two are too blunt and potentially costly in terms of economic efficiency. We find that there is a case for using adjustments in provisioning requirements to control bubbles. The challenge is how best to calibrate the policy responses to avoid unnecessary side effects. In this respect, stress testing and internal risk models offer some prospects for refining this calibration as they become better integrated into regulatory methodology in coming years.

2. Asset Prices, Banking, and Economic Swings—the Australian Experience

In this section we provide a brief historical overview of the relationship between asset prices and economic and banking performance in Australia over the past 120 years. Given the unavoidable changes in data reporting and range of sources associated with collecting historical data, the aim is to present the data in a manner that maximizes comparability within each of four time periods 1880–20, 1920–44, 1960–80, and 1980– 2001. The discussion focuses on the state of the financial system and the development of asset price bubbles, with brief reference to the macroeconomic causes of the depressions and recessions during the past 120 years. The data are summarized in figures 1 to 4.

2.1 First Episode: 1880–1920

In April and May 1893, Australia experienced a widespread collapse of its banking system, with 12 out of 22 note-issuing banks (banks which issued notes that were used as a medium of exchange and subject to legislation) suspending payment.[6] The catalyst for the banking panic was the suspension of payment by the Commercial Bank of Australia on April 5, 1893.[7] By May 17, an additional 11 banks had suspended payment (due mainly to depositor runs) and remained closed for periods ranging from 31 days to 130 days.[8] At this time, the note-issuing banks controlled roughly 70 percent of total financial institution assets, while the banks that suspended payment accounted for roughly 50 percent of deposits with the note-issuing banks.[9] The suspending banks went through a process of reconstruction, which allowed them to recapitalize and increase liquidity before reopening. Depositors, however, faced substantial delays in gaining access to their funds. While most depositors were repaid by 1901, some were not repaid until 1918.[10] After reopening briefly, the City of Melbourne Bank failed a second time and was liquidated in 1895. Six banks merged between the period 1917–27, while the remaining five reconstructed banks were still operating in 1945.[11]

As shown in figure 1, real GDP grew at an average rate of roughly 5 percent per annum over the 10 years leading up to 1889, but with considerable yearly variation. Despite these annual fluctuations, there was little inter-state variation in real GDP growth between New South Wales (NSW) and Victoria, the two dominant Australian colonies leading up to 1889. In 1890, however, the Victorian economy moved into a much deeper and more sustained depression than NSW.[12] The financial boom and collapse was also more concentrated in Victoria, which in part explains the steeper and more prolonged fall in Victorian output.[13]

The period leading up to the price crash in 1889 shows signs of price bubbles in both property and mining stock prices, both of which rose by around 400 percent over the four years to 1889.[14]

Over the same period, the condition of the banking system was generally deteriorating, with both capital and liquidity ratios declining steadily. The rapid growth in bank credit, both in nominal terms and as a percentage of nominal GDP, highlights the role of credit growth in fuelling the investment boom. The weakening of the banking system left it highly vulnerable to the sharp downturn in prices in 1889. Moreover, the data understate the deteriorating condition of the financial system and true expansion of credit, as they exclude "other" banks (often referred to as "land" banks and "fringe" banks) and nonbank financial intermediaries such as building societies and finance companies. These institutions grew rapidly prior to the depression, were not regulated

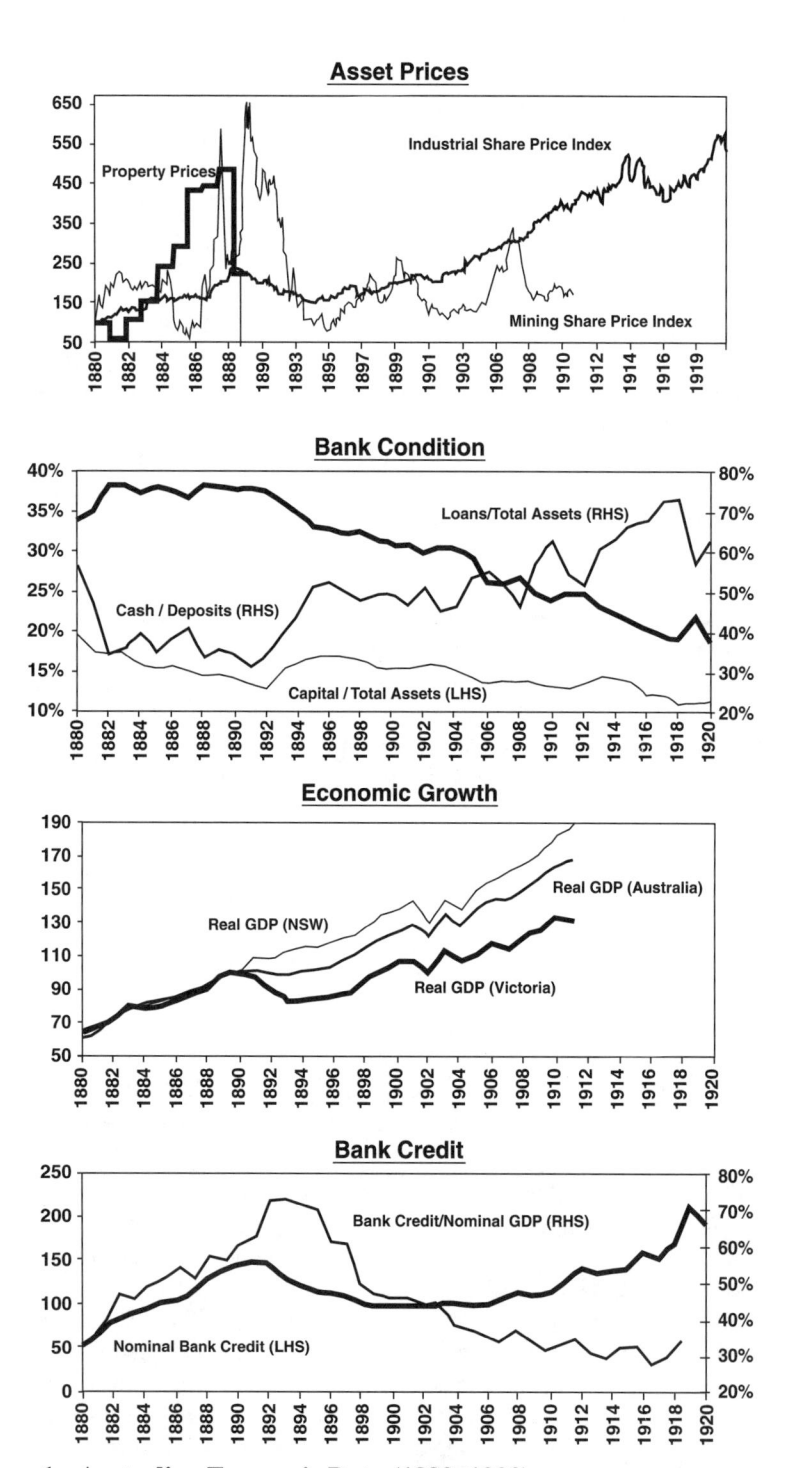

Figure 1: Australian Economic Data (1880–1920)

or supervised, and were highly exposed to the investment boom. As a result, a large number of these "other" banks and nonbanks failed when the property price boom collapsed and the economy contracted. During the period July 1891 to March 1892, 41 companies in Sydney and Melbourne that were involved in building and real estate finance and that accepted deposits from the public suspended payments.[15] The extent of the financial crisis among banks and nonbanks contributed to the depth and length of the economic downturn.

2.2 Second Episode: 1920–44

In contrast with the earlier period, a feature of the 1930s depression in Australia was the resilience of the banking system. Unlike the widespread banking collapses experienced in the United States and UK, only three banks failed in Australia. This included the failure of two small trading banks with combined deposits of less than 1 percent of total Australian trading bank deposits and the failure of the Government Savings Bank of New South Wales (GSB). The GSB was the largest savings bank in Australia and the second largest savings bank in the British Empire, with total deposits of £70.6m in June 1930 which, by the time of its closure in April 1931, had fallen to £54.2m.[16] The GSB was a strong and prudently managed bank, with over 70 percent of its credit exposure directly related to, or guaranteed by the NSW government. Ironically, the heavy exposure to the NSW government was the main reason for the bank's failure. In the midst of the 1930 state election campaign and deliberations about government responses to the depression, the operation of the GSB became a political battleground. Rumors prior to the election led to a steady deposit drain from the bank, while the incoming NSW government's policy of debt repudiation meant the bank was destined to fail. The failure of the GSB had more to do with political instability and insolvency of the NSW government than with the solvency of the bank.

The price rise in this period is less bubble-like than in the earlier period. The data in figure 2 show a steady increase in stock prices up to their quarterly peak in September 1929, before declining sharply. In the nine years to its peak, stock prices grew at an average quarterly rate of 2 percent. Property prices grew at a similar rate. Property prices, however, declined at a slower rate than stock prices and took substantially longer to recover to their pre-depression peaks.[17]

Although nominal bank credit, and to a lesser extent bank credit as a percentage of GDP, grew quickly in the 1920s, bank capital ratios increased steadily, while the ratios of loans to total assets increased marginally. Moreover, banks maintained a high proportion of government securities on their balance sheets; though, as noted above, this was not always a source of strength.

The 1930s depression in Australia was driven largely by external developments.[18] The combination of large overseas borrowing by governments, sharp falls in world commodity prices, and a drying up of external capital inflow were the main factors behind the severity of the depression. While it is true that domestic factors also weakened the economy, these domestic weaknesses had little to do with the health of the financial system or unrealistic asset price increases. There are no obvious signs of a domestic asset price bubble, and both bank and nonbank financial institutions acted prudently and survived the depression relatively unscathed.

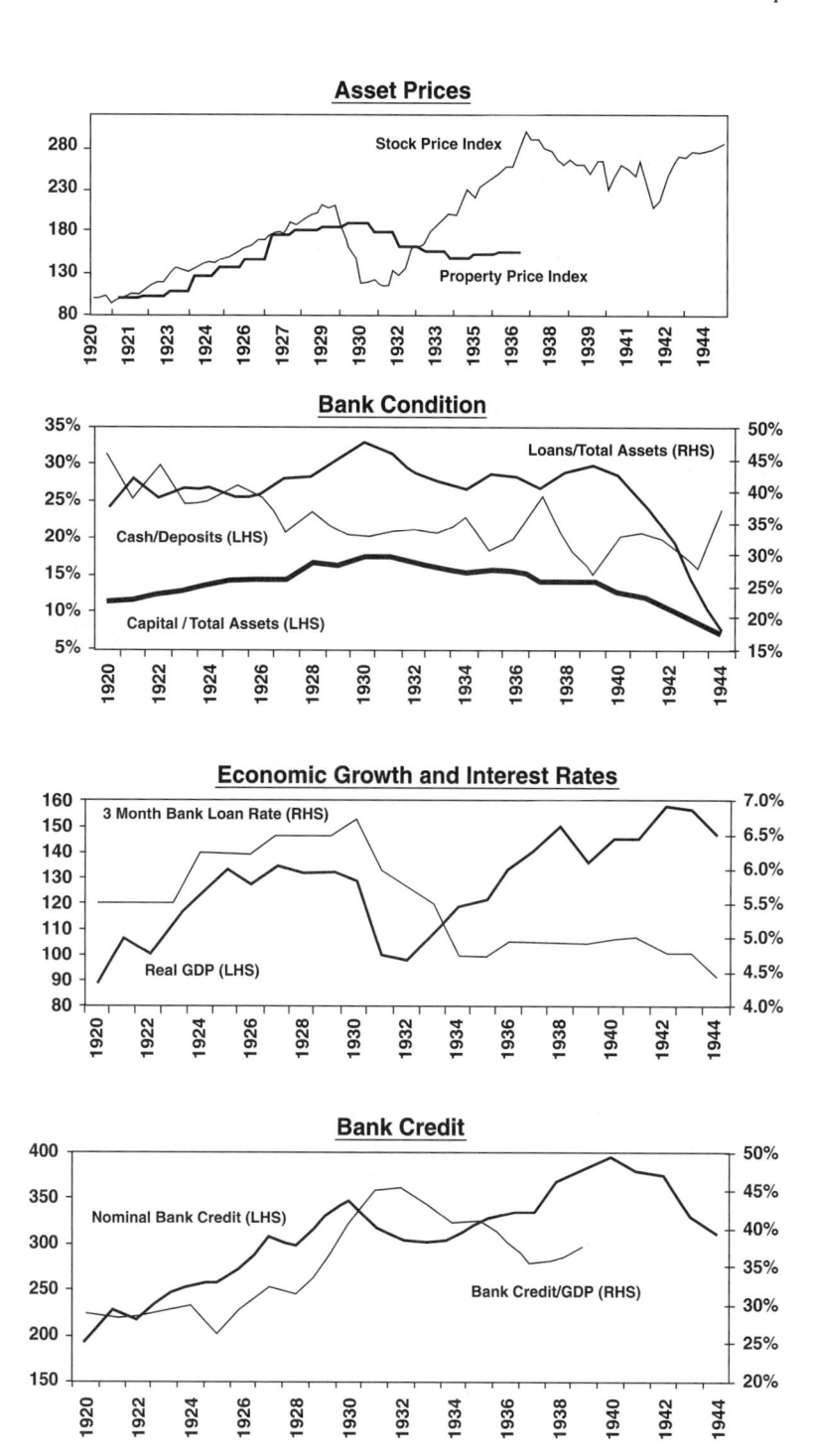

Figure 2: Australian Economic Data (1920–1944)

2.3 Third Episode: 1960–80

The Australian financial system in the 1970s again experienced difficulties (figure 3). These difficulties were, however, largely confined to the failure of finance companies that had become heavily exposed to the booming property market in the early 1970s and to several Queensland-based building societies. While the major banks were not directly involved in the property boom in a major way, some banks had substantial exposures to the property market via their direct equity holdings in finance companies.

The charts in figure 3 show the rapid increase in property prices from the late 1960s to their peak in 1974, followed by a crash and the beginning of a recovery in 1978. The stock market, which had risen sharply in the late 1960s on the back of a mining boom and rising property prices, also collapsed in 1974, falling to levels not experienced since mid 1959.

The government responded to rising inflation in mid 1973 with a rapid series of interest rates increases. The high interest rate policy, however, was also directly targeted at the property price bubble.[19] The tight interest rate policy was short lived, but did contribute to bursting the property price bubble which, in turn, created problems for property developers and financiers.

The failure in September 1974 of the Cambridge Credit Corporation, which was both a property developer and financier, reduced public confidence in the financial system. The following day, simultaneous depositor runs began on building societies in South Australia, Victoria and Queensland. It is unclear why the runs occurred in South Australia and Victoria, given that the societies were fundamentally strong and eventually survived. The building societies in Queensland were, however, less sound and found it difficult to operate in the high interest rate environment of 1974. While the societies survived the initial runs, between March 1976 and September 1977, eight Queensland building societies were either closed, forced to merge, or suspended payments.

Regulatory restrictions on bank lending largely insulated the banking sector from the problems in the real economy. Capital adequacy generally increased over the period, and the highly regulated bank environment severely limited opportunities for bank risk-taking.

2.4 Fourth Episode: 1980–2001

The 1990s saw the largest failures of the Australian financial system since the crash of the 1890s, and many authors have commented on the similarities of these two episodes of Australian economic history.[20] By the mid 1980s the Australian financial system had undergone major deregulation: Restrictions on interest rates and foreign exchange markets were removed; ceilings on bank interest rates and limits on bank lending volumes were removed; and 16 foreign banks were invited to enter the local market. The banks responded to the increased freedom and competition by competing vigorously for market share. However, after decades of rationing credit to high-quality borrowers, banks did not have the credit risk assessment expertise or sufficiently developed risk management systems in place to appropriately price and manage the large volume of new lending that followed. The accumulation of risky loans in

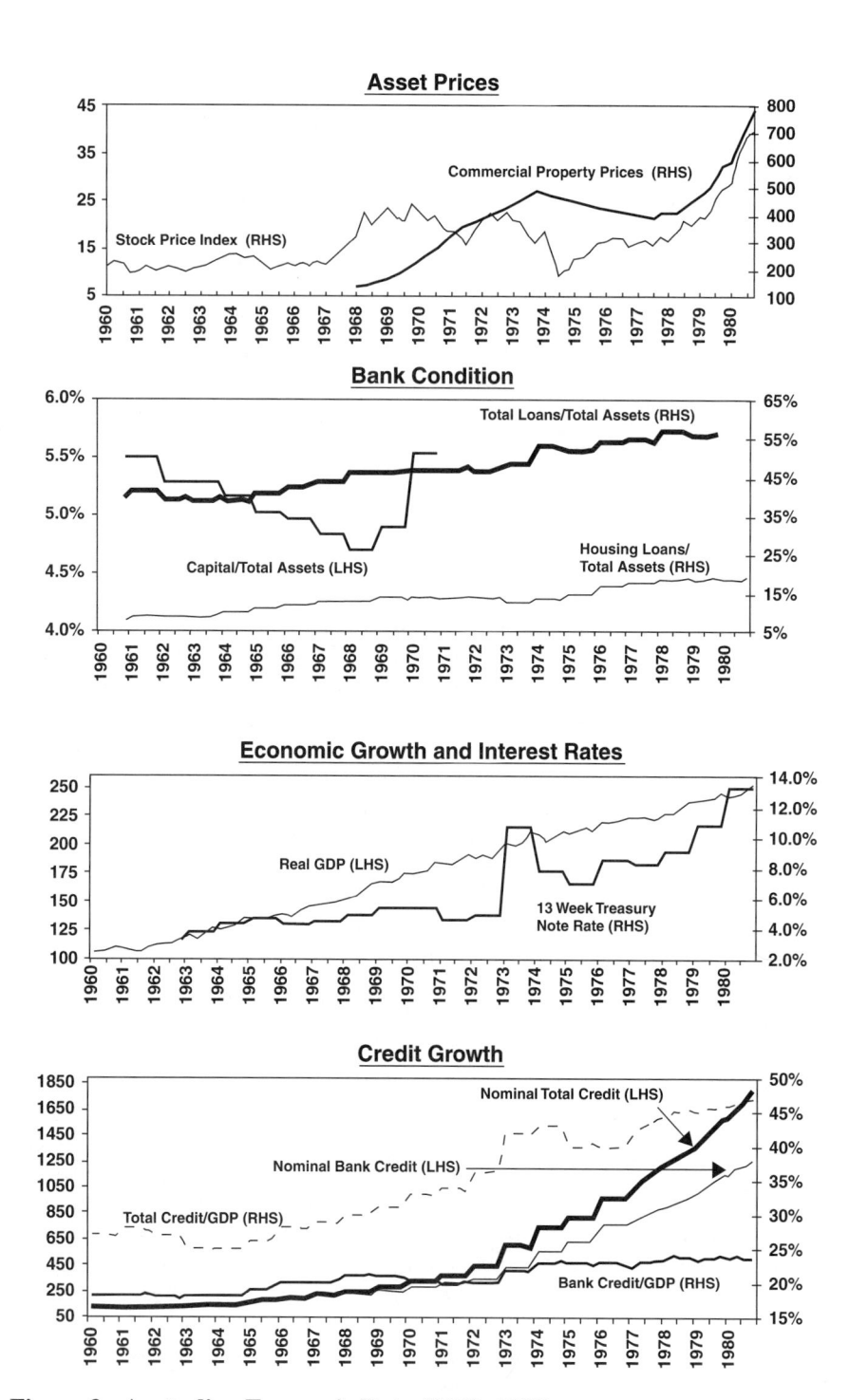

Figure 3: Australian Economic Data (1960–1980)

the mid to late 1980s resulted in a large increase in bad debts in the early 1990s. By March 1991, nonperforming loans totaled $25 billion or 5 percent of banking assets.[21]

The asset price cycle in this period was largely confined to commercial property (see figure 4). The boom in construction led to an oversupply of office space in the early 1990s, followed by a dramatic fall in property prices and a deep recession. The rapid rise and fall in stock prices preceded the collapse of property prices. However, as was the case elsewhere in the world, the collapse of stock prices in October 1987 had little immediate effect on either property prices or economic output.

Bank credit increased at an average quarterly rate of 4.9 percent in the seven years to March 1990, despite very high nominal and real interest rates. (In December 1985 nominal and real interest rates were 18 percent and 10 percent, respectively.) Credit demand was fuelled by rising share prices and later by rising property prices. Another factor affecting the demand for credit was the increased demand for highly leveraged, tax-driven asset acquisitions in an environment of high inflation expectations.[22] The easing of monetary policy that followed the collapse in stock prices was reversed in early 1988 and remained restrictive up until the beginning of the downturn in 1990.

As noted, the condition of the banking system leading up to the recession in 1991 was heavily influenced by deregulation. From June 1983 to June 1988 significant shifts occurred in the portfolio composition of Australian banks. The ratio of business loans to total assets increased from 56 percent to 68 percent, while the ratio of housing loans and personal loans to total assets declined from 38 percent to 30 percent. The economy-wide shift to business lending is even more apparent when nonbank lending is included. The ratio of total business credit to GDP doubled between 1980 and 1990, from 26 percent to 58 percent.[23] Thus, while overall credit growth appears to have been important in fuelling the property price boom in the late 1980s, changes in the portfolio composition of banks were possibly even more so.

While banks sustained substantial losses following the price crash in 1990 they generally entered the period with sufficient capital to survive. The exceptions were the state banks. The State Bank of Victoria (SBV) and State Bank of South Australia (SBSA) required large capital injections from their respective state governments to avoid outright failure. As with the experience of the 1970s, most of the losses in the SBSA and the SBV were due to property exposures in finance company and merchant bank subsidiaries, rather than direct bank exposures. The new foreign banks also incurred large losses. Losses at four of the new bank entrants exceeded initial start-up capital and retained earnings, requiring capital injections from their foreign parent institutions.[24]

Nonbank financial institutions fared equally badly. In 1990, the Farrow group of building societies, which controlled more than 50 percent of building society assets in Victoria, failed.[25] At the time of its failure, the balance sheets of the Farrow group of building societies bore little resemblance to those of traditional building societies; they were dominated by high-risk commercial loans and had a heavy reliance on large wholesale deposits for funding.

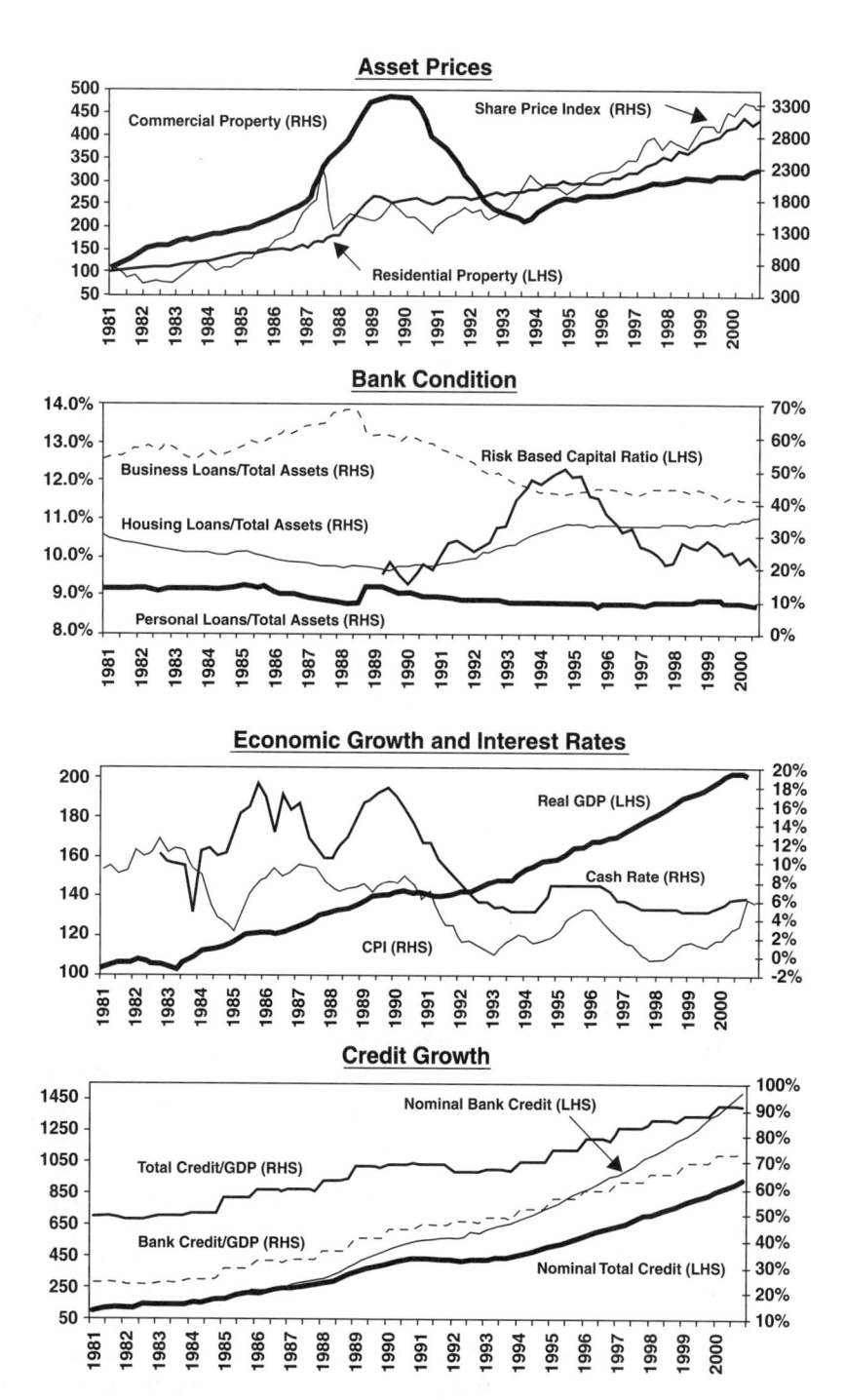

Figure 4: Australian Economic Data (1980–2000)

2.5 Asset Price Bubbles, Financial Activity and Regulation: Lessons from the Australian Experience

This brief summary of Australia's experience with asset price bubbles and banking crises is far from definitive. It nonetheless suggests a few features that are relevant in considering the role that might be played by financial regulation in addressing asset price bubbles:

- First, the bursting of asset price bubbles can have a significant negative impact on the real economy and that impact is amplified where the price crash leads to a financial crisis in the banking system. Put another way, there is much to be said for having a prudentially sound banking system.
- Second, while banks are often the major source of finance to speculative booms, they are not the only source. Heavy-handed regulation encourages unregulated institutions to fill the credit void.
- Third, even when the expansion in total credit is not excessive, asset price bubbles in a particular sector may be fuelled—or at least accommodated—by changes in portfolio composition, such as occurred in the Australian banking system in the late 1980s.

3. Using Regulation to Control Bubbles—Consideration of the Options

The first issue to be resolved is whether or not dealing with bubbles lays within the normal responsibility range of prudential regulators. While there is no universally agreed upon definition of what should motivate prudential regulation, there is growing acceptance of the idea that all forms of financial regulatory intervention should by justified in terms of counteracting market failure. Thus competition regulators intervene to correct market failure arising from market dominance and to ensure that competitive forces prevail in financial markets. Market conduct regulators intervene to correct market failure arising from market misconduct and to ensure that markets are fair and efficient. The market failure associated with prudential regulation is usually described as asymmetric information failure.

This form of market failure arises where products or services are so sufficiently complex that disclosure, by itself, is insufficient to enable consumers to make informed choices. This arises where buyers and sellers of particular financial products or services will never be equally well informed, regardless of how much information is disclosed. The issue is one of complexity of the product and of the institution offering it. The regulatory response in these cases is to interpose a regulatory body between the supplier of the service and the consumer to establish a set of behavioral rules for the supplier, to ensure that the promises being made by the supplier have an acceptably high probability of being met.

But systemic instability also involves a type of market failure. It is a fundamental characteristic of parts of the financial system that they operate efficiently only to the extent that market participants have confidence in their ability to perform the roles for which they were designed. The more sophisticated the economy, the greater its dependence on financial promises and the greater its vulnerability to failure of the financial system to deliver against its promises. The importance of finance and the potential for financial failure to lead to systemic instability introduces an "overarching externality" that warrants regulatory attention. The most familiar case of such an externality is that associated with bank runs, where failure of one institution to honor its promises leads to a general panic as individuals fear that similar promises made by other institutions may also be dishonored.

While bank runs are the most common form of this type of market failure, they are by no means the only one. Asset price bubbles also have some of the characteristics of this type of market failure. For example, it may be optimal for individual banks to contract credit to a sector that has just experienced a sharp downturn in prices but, if all banks follow the same policy, the economic downturn will be amplified by the contraction of credit.[26]

It has become increasingly common in recent years among countries that have separated banking supervision from their central banks to assign the correction of asymmetric information failure to the prudential regulator and the correction of systemic instability to the central bank. To the extent that asset price bubbles fall into the systemic instability category and to the extent that they contain genuine market failure, they would appear on this allocation of responsibilities to be more in the bailiwick of monetary policy than of prudential regulation. This separation, however, has been more a matter of practicality than of principle. There can be little argument that sound prudential regulation adds to systemic stability. Thus, regulation to correct asymmetric information failure and to correct systemic instability are complementary rather than mutually exclusive.

How prudential tools might be used to deal with bubbles remains to be assessed. Supervisors assess and influence risk-taking in financial institutions through a range of qualitative and quantitative methods. These techniques include restrictions on portfolio composition, risk-based capital requirements, loan loss provisioning, and stress testing of market risk exposures. In this section we examine the appropriateness of these regulatory policy options for dealing with asset price bubbles.

3.1 Restrictions on Portfolio Composition

Portfolio restrictions have historically been used as a tool of both bank supervision and monetary policy. To limit the risk of asset price bubbles, Schwartz (2001) suggests that regulation should be particularly concerned with bank portfolio composition and that regulators should give financial institutions an incentive for self regulation by linking deposit insurance premiums to a benchmark asset portfolio, where the weights for loans secured by each class are set by the regulator.

Her argument for influencing portfolio composition in this way is based on the U.S. experience of the 1920s and more recently the Japanese experience of the 1980s. Schwartz notes that it is not necessarily an increase in the total supply of bank credit that facilitates rising prices, but rather portfolio shifts, an observation that is consistent with the Australian experience in the late 1980s.

By linking bank portfolio composition to capital requirements or deposit insurance premiums, regulators would impose increased costs on banks that deviate from the benchmark portfolio. There are, however, several practical difficulties in applying portfolio constraints as suggested by Schwartz.

First, the construction of a suitable set of weights for the benchmark portfolio is problematic. It requires regulators to form judgments about the optimal structure of the real sector—an area in which their expertise would have to be questioned. Second, it involves substituting the judgement of regulators for the judgement of bank management—something that runs counter to the risk-based philosophy that has been emerging in banking regulation over recent decades. Third, high growth industries, by definition, tend to make greater demands on new credit than do stable or declining industries. A decision to effectively limit the amount of new credit supplied to a particular sector may inhibit growth in areas of the economy in which the country has a genuine comparative advantage. Final, institutions that wish to deviate from the benchmark portfolio because of their expertise in a particular market segment, such as small business lending, would be penalized for doing so.

While we accept that shifts in portfolio composition can play an important role in facilitating the development of asset price bubbles, introducing a system of benchmark portfolio weights and penalizing deviations from these benchmarks would be an extremely costly and inefficient way of dealing with the problem. It would also be a retrograde step in the evolution of regulatory philosophy away from directives that substitute the commercial judgements of regulators for those of bank management.

3.2 Capital Adequacy

Minimum capital ratios have been the mainstay of banking regulation for many years. Several options for varying these minima have been suggested as ways of dealing with asset price bubbles.

Kaufman (1998) points to the high leverage of banks as the source of most bank failures and suggests that increasing the required minimum capital ratio is a relatively costless but effective way of insulating banks and the real economy from the bursting of bubbles. His assertion that additional capital is effectively costless is based on the proposition that regulated banks are able to exploit lower capital ratios than unregulated institutions because of their implicit government guarantee through deposit insurance. He also recommends a wider application of structured early intervention, with higher trigger capital ratios as a fundamental element of this strategy. We have several reservations about the general applicability of this approach.

First, while there is nothing magical about the 8 percent minimum capital required by the Basel Accord, and it is a truism that higher capital is safer than lower capital, increasing required capital is not costless in practice. While Kaufman may be correct that alterations to the capital ratios of banks is largely a pricing issue from the perspective of the markets, the availability of credit, and therefore the cost of credit, is not independent of the debt/equity ratios of banks; in the extreme, a system of pure equity banks is likely to charge considerably more for credit than a very highly-leveraged banking system. Second, this framework offers no guidance as to how much capital is sufficient. Third, while higher capital requirements (and tougher structured early intervention) may reduce the likelihood of a financial crisis following the bursting of a bubble, they do not address the role that banks play in supporting the formation of bubbles. Fourth, raising the capital requirement would require international agreement—at a time when the world's regulators are considering revisions that will make capital requirements more flexible and, in the case of lower-risk banks, less costly. Finally, increasing capital requirements on banks could encourage the growth of unregulated nonbank alternative providers of credit.

Another aspect of capital adequacy that has been discussed in this respect is the way in which the regulatory minimum ratio is treated over the business cycle. It has long been recognized that there is an element of contradiction in the idea of a minimum capital requirement that is invariant across the cycle. The minimum capital adequacy ratio is supposed to provide a buffer of lower priority claimants to protect depositors in times of distress and to provide a buffer of time for regulators to merge troubled banks with stronger banks before they become insolvent. This buffer, however, is not independent of the stage of the cycle. In the upswing, retained earnings are likely to add to capital, while in the downswing, losses are likely to reduce capital. The very idea of capital as a buffer suggests that it should absorb such movements over time. However, if the capital requirement is a strict minimum, banks will need to hold higher than the minimum on average, in order to remain above the minimum during downswings.

This has led some to argue that the Accord's 8 percent minimum capital should be reinterpreted as an average over the cycle, rather than as a strict minimum. Alternatively, if the 8 percent represents a fixed lower bound banks need to establish their own buffers above that level, with the knowledge that choosing too low a buffer may result in the loss of their franchise. This debate is largely about the level of capital and, as such, is a variant of Kaufman's argument.

Of more relevance is the suggestion that the minimum capital ratio might be adjusted cyclically. In practice this line of argument has not had much support, as much as anything because of the difficulty of identifying a business cycle *ex ante*. The idea of cyclical capital requirements has, however, been highlighted by the recent Basel proposals to allow banks to use their internal models as the basis for determining capital adequacy.

The essence of the Basel proposal is that capital should be sufficient to meet both expected and unexpected losses. In a default mode credit model both of these are determined largely by assumptions about default probabilities and recovery rates. The concern among many bankers is that default probabilities and recovery rates are highly correlated, with defaults rising and recoveries falling during an economic downturn. Thus, unless these models are sufficiently forward looking, they will increase required capital in recessions and decrease it during booms. This potential procyclical response in capital requirements runs exactly counter to the principle of allowing capital to absorb losses in difficult times and could lead to an increase in forced exits.

One approach to this problem would be for regulators to require banks to use cycle neutral estimates of default probabilities and recovery rates—or more conservatively, to use historically worst case estimates. In both these cases, required capital would exceed banks' estimates of economic capital during booms. With worst case estimates required capital and economic capital would coincide in recessions. While this adjustment would not necessarily reduce the contribution of banks to the formation of pricing bubbles (relative to the exiting cyclically fixed 8 percent rule) it would remove the potential procyclical impact of the Basel proposals.

3.3 Loan Loss Provisioning

During an economic expansion, bank credit increases, while loan losses and provisions for loan losses typically fall; the opposite occurs during recession. This procyclical tendency for provisions arises because traditional provisioning methodology, based on general and specific provisions, tends to be backward looking, rather than based on future expected losses. The traditional approach to provisioning for loan losses is based on the view that provisions should reduce the value of loan assets to the lower of cost and net realizable value. Under this approach provisions are not generally established until a loan is recognized as impaired. The behavior of reserves under the traditional approach accentuates the boom and bust cycle and can, therefore, contribute both to creating price bubbles and to financial crises once the bubble has burst.

The procyclical nature of the traditional provisioning methodology has raised concerns for regulators. In response, the Basel Committee first issued a consultative paper on the topic in October 1998 and a revised paper for further comment in July 1999. The committee's key guidance in this area was for banks to recognize impaired loans once it became probable that the bank would not collect all amounts due under the loan contract. Banks were encouraged to estimate the extent of probable losses and to set provisions to cover the expected losses. Despite the introduction of the concept of expected loss, provisioning tended to remain generally reactive rather than anticipative, for reasons largely related to tax and accounting rules (both of which deny recognition of expected losses as a basis for provisioning).

In recent years, however, banks have begun adopting variations of what is known as dynamic provisioning. The philosophy underlying dynamic provisioning is that provisions should cover expected losses, while capital should be available to cover unexpected losses. Expected loss, EL, for a particular borrower is defined as:

$$EL = PCE \times EDF \times LIED,$$

where PCE is the potential credit exposure, EDF is the expected default frequency (probability of default) and $LIED$ is loss in the event of default (as a percentage of the exposure). Dynamic provisions are more responsive to the true state of the credit portfolio, and recognize expected losses as a cost of doing business. In principle, a good dynamic provisioning model should recognize the business cycle and possible asset price bubbles in all three of the components of the expected loss calculation.[27]

The problem at this stage of development of the credit modeling technology is that models and modeling assumptions are still institution specific. One of the reasons that the Basel Committee has not progressed further than it has in the use of internal models for regulating risk is the lack of common standards and approaches among the models used by international banks. To add to the difficulty, many smaller and regional banks do not use models and would find it difficult to justify the expense and level of sophistication required, given the risks to which they are exposed.

The question is whether there is a relatively simple way for banking regulators to impose a provisioning rule that captures the essence of the modeling approach and does so in a way that has the opposite effect to that of the traditional approach to provisioning. One such approach has been pioneered by Spanish banking regulators.

De Lis, Pagés, and Saurina (2000) outline the statistical provisioning requirements introduced by the Spanish central bank. The essence of the Spanish approach is to require three levels of provisioning. The first two, specific and general provisions, are as conventionally defined. To these core provisions they add a statistical provision that is anticyclical—increasing in periods of expansion and being run off in downswings. While cyclicality is not necessarily eliminated, provisions are considerably smoothed over the cycle. The statistical provision is built up during the economic expansion phase, while specific provisions remain low. As the economy enters a downturn, and specific provisions start to increase, the statistical provision is run down. This not only ensures that banks are in a better position to manage an economic downturn, but also leads to lower volatility in bank profits.[28]

To test the impact of this approach, we simulated its application to Australian banks as a group over the period 1990 to 2001.[29] In the absence of details about individual loan books we used actual provisions as a proxy for the general and specific provisions required by the Spanish model. The divergence between actual total provisions and the simulated total provisions is, therefore, due entirely to the simulated statistical provisions.

As illustrated in figure 5, the actual provisions of Australian banks display a strong countercyclical pattern over the 1990s. The simulated total provisions including the statistical provisions, however, are considerably more stable over the cycle; the procyclical pattern of general and specific provisions is offset by the countercyclical pattern of statistical provisions. Simulated total provisions including the statistical provision are relatively stable and are generally just below 2 percent while the balance in the statistical fund remains positive.[30]

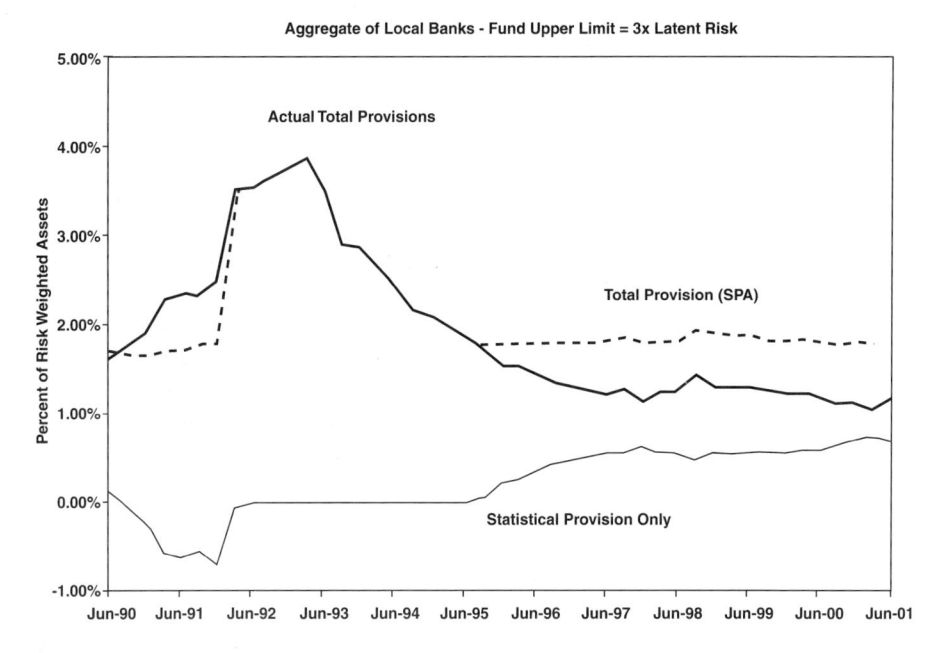

Figure 5: Actual and Statistical Provisioning: Australian Banks

Interestingly, for the most recent period, the simulation suggests that actual provisions in the Australian banking system, as at 2001, are almost half the levels that the Spanish approach would require for the current stage of the business cycle.

Given that the four major Australian banks all use a form of dynamic provisioning, we would have expected their total provisions to be more stable than the total for all banks. In practice, however, our simulations showed a broadly similar pattern for each of the major banks individually to that shown in figure 5 for Australian banks as a group. The one exception was the National Australia Bank (NAB), for which the simulated total provisions remained relatively stable, reflecting the smaller increase in specific provisions for the NAB during the early 1990s.[31]

While there are definite attractions in the Spanish approach, implementing such an approach in many countries would require resolution with the accounting profession, which would be no easy task. An alternative, worthy of further consideration and analysis, might be to apply the principles underlying the Spanish provisioning approach to capital adequacy.

3.4 Stress Testing

In its report on stress testing by large internationally active financial institutions, the Bank for International Settlements (BIS, 2000), defines stress testing as "various techniques used by financial firms to gauge their potential vulnerability to exceptional but plausible events." In essence, stress testing involves subjecting a bank's model of its business to particular scenarios in order to gauge the responsiveness of its profitability and capital to those scenarios. Whereas statistically-based risk measures such as Value-at-Risk (VaR) identify the maximum loss that is likely to be incurred at any given confidence level, stress testing identifies the precise loss that is likely to be incurred under a given scenario. It has the advantage of being able to test the bank's resilience to extreme shocks. Common stress tests conducted at banks surveyed by the BIS are given titles such as "1987 stock market crash" and "1994 bond market crash." The aggregation of firm level exposures to such risks provides potentially valuable information for supervisors to use in assessing the systemic risks faced by the banking sector in the event of an asset price bubble.

In Australia for example, banks adopting the internal models approach to market risk are required to undertake a range of standard stress tests. For the equity portfolio, standard stress tests require banks to report changes in the market value of their portfolios to assumed shocks to prices and volatility. While these tests are limited to the traded market portfolios of banks, and therefore ignore the effects of the shocks transmitted through the banks' lending portfolios, the data give at least some indication of the banking industry's direct exposure to particular asset prices.

The use of stress testing as a regulatory tool is, however, still in the developmental stages and is subject to several limitations. First, its use is primarily in identifying risk rather than in controlling it. The response of the regulator to an assessed exposure of financial stability to the bursting of an asset price bubble is still a matter of judgment. Second, the results of stress tests are only as good as the risk models developed by the banks for their own internal use. As noted earlier, the cost of developing sophisticated risk measurement models may not be a justifiable expenditure for many banks.

Third, even where the models exist, the complexity, cost and time needed to run reliable stress tests makes frequent testing infeasible and limits the scenarios that may be analyzed.

Notwithstanding these current limitations, as internal models become more reliable and more widely used, stress testing may prove to be the most effective means of identifying the extent of financial sector exposure to price reversals.

4. Concluding Thoughts

This paper is not a definitive coverage of the role of prudential regulation in either controlling the emergence of asset price bubbles or in limiting the financial damage from their aftermath. From the Australian experience and our review of the four main regulatory approaches to bubbles we, nevertheless, draw several conclusions.

First, until the methodology for identifying price bubbles becomes more advanced, there is little to be gained—and possibly significant potential costs—in trying to use regulation as a means of dampening the emergence of asset price bubbles. To the extent that there is a role for regulation in dealing with bubbles it is in preventing banking crises in the wake of an asset price collapse. Since this requires a prudentially sound banking system, in which capital increases commensurate with the risks being undertaken, introducing a systemic stability objective in this way does not create any conflicts with the existing objectives of regulators.

Second, since credit can be provided in many countries by unregulated financial institutions, and since unregulated financial institutions can also precipitate a financial crisis, sound bank regulation is at best a partial solution to the problems created by asset price bubbles.

Third, in addition to overseeing the general prudential strength of banks, regulation can contribute to financial stability by:
- amending and improving prudential standards so as to remove the inherent tendencies that some of these have to exacerbate asset price cycles and the real cycles that accompany them;
- adjusting, where feasible, provisioning and/or capital requirements so as to introduce a counter-cyclical element; and
- monitoring, through stress testing, sectoral exposures and the vulnerability of the banking sector to asset price reversals and, where circumstances warrant, taking steps to limit or reduce that vulnerability.

*Jeffrey Carmichael is chairman of the Australian Prudential Regulation Authority. Neil Esho is a staff member in the Department of Policy, Research, and Consulting of the Australian Prudential Regulation Authority. The views and opinions expressed in this paper are those of the authors and do not necessarily reflect those of the APRA. The authors thank Wayne Byres, Phillip Lowe, Claudio Borio, Anthony Coleman, Alvin Liaw, Marianne Gizycki, and Terry Pittorino for helpful comments, and Patrick

D'Arcy for providing data. We also wish to thank our two discussants at the conference, Ramon Moreno and Joaquim Levy, for helpful comments.

Notes

1. RBA Bulletin, April 2001.

2. See Heffernan (2001) and Schwartz (2001).

3. See, for example, Miller (1998).

4. The questions of how to recognize asset price bubbles and whether or not monetary policy should respond to bubbles has been addressed in both the academic literature and the popular press by, among others, Bernanke and Gertler (1999), Cecchetti et al. (2000), Goodhart (2001), Kent and Lowe (1997), Frank and Browning (2001), Kaufman (1998), Bordo and Jeanne (2002) and Schwartz (2001).

5. For a more comprehensive review of the literature on this subject see Carmichael and Esho (2001).

6. The Federal Bank of Australia had previously been liquidated on January 18, 1893 (Boehm, 1971). Another two banks were liquidated and one acquired in 1892, and one bank failed in 1891 (see Butlin, 1971).

7. It is interesting to note that the Commercial Bank's 300,000 shares of £10 each were only partly paid to £4. While depositors viewed this as a sign of strength, no call on shareholders was made prior to suspension. A feature of the reconstruction of the bank was a fully paid £6 per share.

8. Boehm (1971).

9. Fisher and Kent (1999, pp. 9–12).

10. Fisher and Kent (1999, p. 13).

11. Butlin (1971, p. 104).

12. Estimates of real GDP during this period vary to some degree by source. According to Butlin (1962) Australian real GDP at factor cost fell by 24 percent from 1891 to 1893 and did not return to 1891 levels until 1904. According to Boehm (1971), real per capita GDP did not pass pre-depression peaks until 1907–09.

13. Haig (2001, p. 22).

14. The property price series is only available for Melbourne. Fisher and Kent (1999) provide an Australia-wide measure of property prices, which shows a similar spike in property prices. Their capital value indicator includes changes in volume and quality of properties and tends to lag the series presented. The capital value indicator, reflecting valuations by city councils for tax purposes, are likely to have lagged changes in market prices.

15. Boehm (1971, p. 262). Due to a combination of fraudulent and unsound practices, changes in legislation and easing of the money market in 1889–90, the institutions were able to conceal and delay their failure until July 1891, almost two years after the peak of the speculative boom.

16. Sykes (1988, table 12.2).

17. It should be noted that the property price measure used in this period is the capital value indicator developed by Fisher and Kent (1999). In the earlier period, these data suggested a slower rate of price increases and lagged the data obtained from Silberberg (1975).

18. See Valentine (1987) for a brief discussion and references on the role of domestic and external factors in causing and prolonging the 1930s depression.

19. On September 9, 1973, the Australian Prime Minister, Gough Whitlam said "If as a consequence, the higher interest rates have the effect of curbing the speculative rush into land and property, that will be all too good," (Sykes, 1988, p. 437).

20. Pope (1991).

21. Thompson (1991, p. 1,260).

22. MacFarlane (1991).

23. Macfarlane (1991, p. 178).

24. Ferguson (1991, p. 159).

25. Fitz-Gibbon and Gizycki (2001).

26. Borio et al (2000).

27. For an example of how this could be applied in the case of an amortizing mortgage, see Carmichael and Esho (2001).

28. The methodology is outlined further in the appendix.

29. In simulating the effects of the Spanish provisioning requirement we used the capital adequacy risk weight divided by 100 for each loan category as a proxy for s_j.

30. An underlying assumption of the Statistical Provisioning Approach (SPA) is that the statistical fund should not be depleted. In the Australian simulation the fund is depleted by early 1992, leading to an immediate sharp rise in total provisions to the level of actual provisions. Actual provisions and provisions using the SPA are identical from this point until mid 1995, at which point the specific provisions again begin to accumulate.

31. We also simulated the 1990 to 1995 cycle forward based on current provisioning levels, with very similar results. This suggests that a repeat of the cyclical increase in bad loans experienced in the first half of the last decade would produce a similar cyclical increase in provisions.

References

Bernanke, Ben, and Mark Gertler, 1999, "Monetary Policy and Asset Price Volatility," Federal Reserve Bank of Kansas City, *Economic Review*, 4th quarter.

Boehm, Ernst A., 1971, *Prosperity and Depression in Australia 1887–1897*, Oxford: Clarendon Press.

Bordo, Michael D., and Olivier Jeanne, 2002, "Boom-Busts in Asset Prices, Economic Instability, and Monetary Policy," mimeo.

Borio, Claudio, Craig Furfine, and Philip Lowe, 2000, "Procyclicality of the Financial System and Financial Stability: Issues and Policy Options," *BIS Papers Marrying the Macro- and Micro-Prudential Dimensions of Financial Stability*, No. 1.

Butlin, Noel G., 1962, *Australian Domestic Product, Investment and Foreign Borrowing 1861–1938/39*, Cambridge: Cambridge University Press.

Butlin, S. G., A. R. Hall, and R. C. White, 1971, "Australian Banking and Monetary Statistics 1817-1945," Reserve Bank of Australia, occasional paper, No. 4A.

Carmichael, Jeffrey, and Neil Esho, 2001, "Asset Price Bubbles and Prudential Regulation," Australian Prudential Regulation Authority, working paper, September.

Cecchetti, Stephen, Hans Genberg, John Lipsky, and Sushil Wadhwani, 2000, "Asset Prices and Central Bank Policy," Geneva Report on the World Economy 2, Center for Economic Policy Research and International Center for Monetary Banking Studies.

Committee on the Global Financial System, 2000, "Stress Testing by Large Financial Institutions: Current Practice and Aggregation Issues," Bank for International Settlements.

Ferguson, Rob, 1991, "Banking Deregulation—A Virtue or a Necessity?," in *The Deregulation of Financial Intermediaries*, Ian McFarlane, ed., Reserve Bank of Australia, pp. 143–168.

Fernández de Lis, Santiago, Jorge M. Pagés, and Jesús M. Saurina, 2000, "Credit Growth, Problem Loans and Credit Risk Provisioning in Spain," paper presented at the Bank for International Settlements Autumn Central Bank Economists' Meeting.

Fisher, Chay, and Christopher Kent, 1999, "Two Depressions, One Banking Collapse," Reserve Bank of Australia, research discussion paper, No. 1999-6.

Fitz-Gibbon, Bryan, and Marianne Gizycki, 2001, "A History of Last Resort Lending and Other Support for Troubled Financial Institutions in Australia," Reserve Bank of Australia, research discussion paper, No. 7.

Frank, Stephen E., and E. S. Browning, 2001, "Busting of the Tech Bubble Has a Familiar 'Pop' to It," *The Wall Street Journal*.

Goodhart, Charles, 2001, "What Weight Should Be Given to Asset Prices in the Measurement of Inflation?," Dutch National Bank, staff reports, No. 65.

Haig, Bryan, 2001, "New Estimates of Australian GDP: 1861–1948/49," *Australian Economic History Review*, Vol. 41, No. 1, pp. 1–34.

Heffernan, Shelagh A., 2001, "Japanese Finance: Reform or Ruin?," *The Financial Regulator*, Vol. 6, No. 1, pp. 48–59.

Kaufman, George G., 1998, "Central Banks, Asset Bubbles, and Financial Stability," Federal Reserve Bank of Chicago, working paper, No. 98-12.

Kent, Christopher, and Philip Lowe, 1997, "Asset Price Bubbles and Monetary Policy, Reserve Bank of Australia, research discussion paper, No. 97-09.

Miller, Merton H, 1998, "The Current Southeast Asia Financial Crisis," *Pacific-Basin Finance Journal*, Vol. 6, pp. 225–233.

McFarlane, Ian, 1991, "The Lessons for Monetary Policy," in *The Deregulation of Financial Intermediaries*, Ian McFarlane, ed., Reserve Bank of Australia pp. 175–199.

Pope, David, 1991, "Bank Deregulation Yesterday and Today: Lessons of History," Australian National University, Economic History, Research School of Social Sciences, working paper, No. 156.

Reserve Bank of Australia (RBA), 2001, *Bulletin*, April.

Schwartz, Anna J., 2001, "Asset Price Inflation and Monetary Policy," paper presented at the Annual Meeting of the American Financial Association Meeting, New Orleans, January 7.

Silberberg, R., 1975, "Rates of Return on Melbourne Land Investment, 1880-92," *The Economic Record*, Vol. 51, pp. 203–217.

Sykes, Trevor, 1988, *Two Centuries of Panic, A History of Corporate Collapses in Australia*, North Sydney: Allen & Unwin Australia.

Thompson, Graeme, 1991, "Prudential Supervision," in *The Deregulation of Financial Intermediaries*, I. McFarlane, ed., Reserve Bank of Australia, pp. 115–142.

Valentine, Tom J., 1987, "The Causes of the Depression in Australia," *Explorations in Economic History*, Vol. 24, No. 1, pp. 43–62.

Appendix

The Spanish Model for Bank Provisioning

In addition to general and specific provisions, the Spanish Central bank has introduced a system of statistical provisioning. Application of the methodology is relatively simple and is illustrated below.

1) $TP_{it} = SP_{it} + GP_{it} + StP_{it}$

where TP_{it} is total provisions for bank i in period t; SP_{it} is specific provisions for bank i in period GP_{it}; t is general provisions for bank i in period t; and StP_{it} is statistical provisions for bank i in period t.

2) $SP_{it} = \sum_j e_j \Delta M_{jt}$

3) $GP_{it} = \sum_j g_j \Delta L_{jt}$

4) $StP_{it} = \sum_j s_j L_{jt} - SP_{jt}$,

where e_j, g_j, and s_j are provisioning weights for loan category j, which are multiplied respectively by the change in problem loans for each loan category (ΔM_{jt}), the change in the volume of each loan category (ΔL_{jt}), and the outstanding balance of each loan category L_{jt}. The provisioning weights may be determined by a standard or internal based model.

The annual statistical provision accumulates over time, so that

5) $StF_{it} = StP_{it} + StF_{it-1}$, subject to $0 \leq StF_{it} \leq 3 \sum_j s_j L_{jt}$,

where StF_{it} is the balance of the statistical provision fund for bank i in period t, and $s_j L_{jt}$ is also referred to as latent risk.

In strong economic periods specific provisions will be below latent risk, with the result that the statistical provisions will be positive and the statistical fund will be built up, subject to the imposed limit. In periods of economic downturn, specific provisions increase above latent risks, implying a negative contribution to the statistical provision. That is, the statistical fund will be run down. In aggregate, this results in much less cyclical provisioning. It is important to note that the statistical provision is not a tax deductible expense.

Chapter 35
The Morning After: Restructuring in the Aftermath of an Asset Bubble

Michael Pomerleano*
World Bank

In the 1980s, asset bubbles occurred in Norway, Finland, and Sweden. In the 1990s in Japan, real estate and stock prices collapsed, following their meteoric rise in the late 1980s. And in mid 1997, a real estate bubble occurred in Thailand, and real estate and equity market bubbles occurred in Malaysia. This paper presents the hypothesis that the buildup, duration, and severity of bubbles in equity and real estate markets, as well as the restructuring that occurs in their aftermath, are related to the availability of skills in financial sector services. Countries with capable professionals such as appraisers, analysts, and insolvency experts recognize and respond more swiftly to asset bubbles than countries with a limited set of skills in the financial sector. In addition, countries benefit from the development of market instruments that spread risks (such as secondary markets in distressed debt), mitigate the magnitude of bubbles, and expedite the mop-up process. In short, the paper examines the micro-institutional dimension of bubbles and offers policy recommendations.

1. The Context: Theoretical and Empirical Evidence

In the end, conventional macroeconomic responses are not sufficient in the absence of complementary micro-level restructuring. Theoretical and empirical evidence in the academic literature points to the influential role that limited financial sector skills play in precipitating price bubbles and in delaying restructuring in the aftermath of a bubble.

Allen and Gale (2000) develop a model of asset price bubbles based on an "agency problem" and the amount of credit provided for speculative investment. Their model suggests that the lack of transparency and the exacerbation of the agency problem in an opaque financial system are determining factors in the buildup of asset price bubbles. The analysis recognizes that investors in real estate and stock markets borrow from banks. Risk is shifted if the ultimate providers of funds—banks—are unable to analyze their investments due to the lack of financial sector expertise and resulting opacity. The shifting of risk increases the return to investment in the assets and causes investors to bid up asset prices above their fundamental value.

Allen and Gale's hypothesis is supported by evidence from Sweden, Indonesia, Thailand, and other countries that liberalized their financial systems rapidly without building adequate regulatory and supervisory infrastructure and without developing a sufficient base of skills. For example, the crisis in Sweden was preceded by rapid expansion of credit following the deregulation of financial markets; in the span of five years, private borrowing grew from 85 percent to 135 percent of gross domestic product. Prior to liberalization, Sweden's financial system did not have a base of skills or experience in assessing and evaluating risks. As a result, credit was misdirected, and a significant proportion was used for speculation in real estate and other financial assets. At the peak of the crisis, bank loans to real estate, or collateralized by real estate, accounted for more than 60 percent of all loan losses. The real estate speculation culminated in a bubble that burst in 1990–91. Indonesian, Malaysian, and Thai banks also misdirected credit and built up a large exposure to real estate, precipitating the Asian crisis.

Limitations on the availability of skills in the financial sector affect stock valuations, as well. In a paper with Zhang (1999), I examine the relationship between corporate fundamentals and stock market performance in Asia. Using corporate and stock market data, we demonstrate not only that Southeast Asian corporate equities earned poor risk-adjusted returns, but also that these returns did not, on average, cover the cost of capital. In this respect, capital markets in Asia did not allocate capital effectively. This may reflect both the lack of disciplined corporate budgeting processes and the lack of market analysis in emerging markets.

Similar evidence comes from recent research at ING Barings (Rosgen 2001). Rosgen explores which stock valuation ratios worked in the past 11 years across nine Asian markets lacking qualified investment analysts in the financial sector. He finds that share prices were almost irrelevant in making profitable investment decisions in Asia. Rather, the winning strategy was to buy shares in those companies that achieved the highest returns on equity in the previous accounting period, irrespective of their current market value. Discounting cash flows—a traditional tool of financial analysis—appears to be an unreliable method in Asia; cash flow projections are wild guesses, as is the discount rate applied to them.

Fischer (2001) suggests that corporate restructuring should be closely coordinated with bank restructuring but that they often are not because capacity and data are lacking. Further, corporate restructuring requires a broad set of instruments and institutional arrangements. For instance, a legal-administrative framework must exist to deal with insolvency (creditor rights, collateral recourse), and the tax structure must avoid perverse incentives that encourage excess leverage and discourage debt restructuring (see, for instance, Sundararajan and Seelig, 2001).

William Mako (2001) offers several prerequisites for effectively restructuring distressed companies in a systemic crisis:

- strong legal protection in the bankruptcy law for creditors and an ability to impose losses on debtors;

- an efficient framework to support out-of-court corporate restructuring efforts;
- government imposition of losses on shareholders of local financial institutions and government pressure to revalue assets;
- flexibility and readiness to lay off workers and accept foreign control over companies;
- removal of tax, legal, and regulatory impediments to corporate restructuring;
- creation of a central body responsible for driving financial sector restructuring and making adequate corporate restructuring a condition for bank recapitalization;
- sufficient professional capacity to conduct due diligence, structure and negotiate workouts, conclude asset sales, and manage converted equity; and
- crisis efforts to resolve immediate corporate distress, supplemented by measures to promote long-term corporate health.

I complement this prescription by focusing on financial sector services and instruments.

2. Critical Skills and Professions

Two diametrically opposed experiences illustrate the need for expert financial professionals. First, Sweden's successful restructuring can be attributed to the rapid response and the use of strict valuation rules from the onset of restructuring (Heikenstein, 1998). All banks had to mark-to-market their real estate assets. The Bank Support Authority hired expert professionals on valuation of various types of assets to ensure that banks did not overestimate or underestimate their value. As a result of the regulatory discipline applied, the mop-up was rapid.

In contrast, other crisis countries have been slow to dispose of bad property loans, and a huge oversupply exists due to excessive investment in the property sector. In Japan and Thailand, the lack of expert appraisers hindered rapid valuations and transparent market transactions in the aftermath of their respective asset bubbles. In the absence of credible valuations and market mechanisms for disposing of property and the presence of legal and tax distortions, the number of transactions is minimal. Due to lack of credible valuations that reflect market values, rents and real estate prices have dropped slowly despite high vacancies and further increases in supply (Eschweiler, 1999a). Therefore, adjustments in the property sector in Japan and Thailand are lagging, and this is slowing their recovery. In short, the absence of skills and of market-based financial instruments that price risk and value assets leads to distorted price signaling.

When a country's financial system relies heavily on its banks, systemic vulnerabilities increase. The Asian financial crisis provides ample evidence. According to Federal Reserve Chairman Alan Greenspan (1999), "This leads one to wonder how severe East Asia's problems would have been during the past eighteen months had those economies not relied so heavily on banks as their means of financial intermediation ... Had a functioning capital market existed, the outcome might well have been far more benign ... The lack of a spare tire is of no concern if you do not get a flat ... East

Asia had no spare tires." Nonbank financial institutions, consisting of capital markets, insurance companies, pension funds, and other nonbank financial institutions, provide an alternative mechanism for mobilizing and allocating savings, for managing risk and liquidity, and for facilitating government debt management. The nonbank financial sector reduces the financial vulnerability of enterprises through improved access to equity markets and less dependence on short-term bank debt, through the refinancing risks of governments in a domestic public debt market, and through the banking system's term transformation risks. Financial markets with depth and breath manage crisis better than markets without them.

Development of nonbank financial institutions, such as insurance schemes and collective investment instruments, requires a high level of professional expertise. The strong correlation among the base of skills, the growth of nonbank financial intermediation, and the stability of the financial system, lead to the conclusion that poor contingency planning and weak responses to financial crisis are attributable to inadequate skills in the financial services sector. This, in turn, exacerbates the magnitude and costs of crises.

Financial sector services seem to play a small role in many emerging market countries (United Nations, 1997). Employment in finance, insurance, real estate, and business services as a percentage of total employment is lower in countries such as Brazil (1.9 percent), Indonesia (0.8 percent), the Philippines (2.4 percent), Poland (2.6 percent), and Russia (0.7 percent) than in the United States (11.4 percent). For instance, in the tiger economies, the past growth model emphasized production and exports. The crisis highlighted the weakness of a growth model that does not promote services (Eschweiler, 1999b).

Economic theory instructs that complete markets lead to better resource allocation. One essential condition for a functioning, complete financial market is an adequate base of professional financial skills. In the United States, many of the needed professions and reforms grew out of crisis. The U.S. debacle with the savings and loans in the 1980s, which cost taxpayers $200 billion, led to the certification process for appraisers, which was established only 10 years ago. The regulation was in direct response to evidence of appraisal problems and misconduct inside U.S. financial institutions. The evidence, brought to light in the U.S. Congress, concluded that fraud and self-dealing by officers, directors, and insiders caused or contributed to half of all financial institution failures. Faulty or fraudulent real estate appraisals were used systematically to overvalue collateral and to make unsafe real estate loans. In the United States, the Appraisal Subcommittee of the Federal Financial Institutions Examination Council was created to oversee appraisers and ensure that real estate appraisers are sufficiently trained and tested so that they are competent, independent, and ethical and use uniform, high professional standards. The United States is not perfect; it just experienced and responded to its crisis earlier than other countries.

The following discussion examines professions critical to the process of restructuring: insolvency experts, lawyers, accountants, appraisers, financial analysts, and actuaries. See table 1 for the number of insolvency experts, appraisers, and actuaries by country.

	Appraisers		Insolvency experts		Actuaries	
Economy	Number per million population	Number	Number per million population	Number	Number per million population	Number
Argentina	—	—	0.92	34	4.54	168
Australia	—	—	31.57	606	—	—
Austria	—	—	2.84	23	—	—
Belgium	—	—	0.68	7	—	—
Brazil	29.39	5,000	—	—	2.40	408
Canada	—	—	34.89	1,071	—	—
Czech Rep.	535.37	5,500	1.56	16	—	—
China	10.64	13,420	0.01	8	0.01	8
Finland	28.96	150	—	—	18.73	97
France	29.74	1,750	2.53	149	21.78	1,282
Germany	97.38	8,000	0.99	81	20.22	1,661
Hong Kong (China)	159.46	1,084	—	—	29.27	199
Hungary	—	—	2.20	22	12.87	129
India	0.34	350	0.03	33	0.11	111
Indonesia	6,665	1,400	0.02	4	0.03	7
Israel	—	—	0.16	1	—	—
Italy	—	—	0.80	46	—	—
Japan	44.96	5,700	0.04	5	6.73	853
Korea, Rep. of	36.47	1,724	0.02	1	0.23	11
Lithuania	126.01	466	—	—	—	—
Malaysia	21.50	500	1.12	26	—	—
México	30.62	3,000	0.02	2	1.95	191
New Zealand	—	—	49.86	191	—	—
Nigeria	—	—	0.03	4	—	—
Norway	—	—	2.00	9	—	—
Pakistan	—	—	—	—	0.10	14
Philippines	—	—	0.01	1	0.90	68
Poland	77.62	3,000	0.28	11	0.10	4
Romania	—	—	0.62	14	—	—
Russia	27.48	4,000	—	—	—	—
Singapore	129.17	519	2.74	11	20.41	82
South Africa	—	—	7.13	305	—	—
Spain	—	—	0.30	12	—	—
Sweden	56.38	500	1.58	14	27.74	246
Switzerland	—	—	0.84	6	48.05	345
Thailand	—	—	0.13	8	0.21	13
United Kingdom	334.79	20,000	27.02	1,614	79.75	4,764
United States	284.14	80,000	6.54	1,841	53.16	14,968

— Not available.
Sources: For insolvency, the International Federation of Insolvency Professionals membership database; for appraisers, the International Valuation Standards Committee; for actuaries, the International Actuarial Association

Table 1: Appraisal, Actuarial, and Insolvency Professionals by Country

2.1 Insolvency Experts

Insolvency practitioners analyze the business and financial viability of a real estate project or a company and choose between restructuring and liquidation. They require expertise to negotiate approval of, implement, and monitor the restructuring plan and to manage operations of the company. If liquidation is needed, insolvency practitioners arrange for the orderly disposition of the company's assets and the creditor's claims. Their expertise and integrity must be above reproach.

The International Federation of Insolvency Professionals (INSOL) is a worldwide federation of national associations for accountants and lawyers who specialize in insolvency. The members are engaged in formal insolvency proceedings, advise creditors, and advise and restructure businesses in financial difficulty. The INSOL has 29 member associations worldwide with more than 8,000 professionals. The INSOL's membership reveals a wide disparity of skilled professionals across countries: Japan has five members of the INSOL, while Canada has 1,071 and the United States has 1,841.

The qualifications to be an insolvency expert vary among local organizations and from country to country. For instance, in the United Kingdom, any of seven recognized bodies can authorize an insolvency practitioner to act. Memberships in local associations typically are made up of qualified accountants or lawyers. Accountants tend to take insolvency appointments in the common law system, and lawyers tend to lead in the civil law system and in the United States. However, there are considerable differences in the training and licensing of insolvency professionals. In a very few nations (United Kingdom, Canada, Australia, and some others), insolvency practitioners are examined, licensed, and regulated either by their professional bodies or by the state. In other countries (France), the court list of liquidators and administrators is highly restricted. In the vast majority of nations, however, insolvency work is carried out by accountants or lawyers who also undertake other professional services. Some may specialize in insolvency work, but they might have no formal qualifications or accreditation that distinguish them from other practitioners.

In many countries, any remotely qualified person—whether an accountant or a notary—can be appointed by the court as a liquidator, as long as the person is disinterested. Often the appointed "expert" lacks ability, independence, or both. For instance, there is no registration of insolvency practitioners in New Zealand. Disqualifications for accepting an appointment are set out in the Companies Act 1993, section 280, and include persons of less than 18 years of age, creditors, shareholders, directors, auditors, or receivers of the company. Similarly, in the People's Republic of China the draft of a new insolvency law only requires the administrator to have not been struck off as a lawyer or accountant within the last five years. There is not even a requirement that the administrator be an accountant or a lawyer.

2.2 Appraisers

Appraisers are needed to value property, including commercial, industrial, residential, machinery, and personal. Appraisers reduce risk by assigning credible values to property based on a standard method: All participants recognize the methodology, and the valuation is consistent. However, standards of certification are lacking in many emerging markets, and minimum uniform standards of appraisal and minimum qualifications are needed. Professionally recognized training and certification programs are needed to ensure the professional expertise, integrity, and responsibility of appraisers.

The International Valuation Standards Committee is an association of professional valuation associations from some 50 countries. There are wide differences in the availability of appraisal services in select markets. The frequency ranges from 335 appraisers per million population in the United Kingdom to 0.3 appraisers per million population in India.

The standard methodology for appraisals relies on the market, income, and cost approaches. On the qualitative side, perhaps the most striking point is that not all countries abide by appraisal based on market value—for example, the use of comparable transactions in order to establish market value. In Japan valuations rely on the cost approach. Appraisals of property often are based on the value of land (land price index) and, rarely, the sales comparison and income approach. The reliance on cost basis is due to the lack of data: Market data are scarce due to lack of information disclosure and the failure to collect transaction data. Further, architects and engineers are most common in the property valuation profession, and their bias is to use cost basis for appraisals. Therefore, the real estate market is not transparent.

Across countries, there is no consistent treatment of the appraisal and valuation profession with respect to training and regulation. Similarly, in many countries—for example, Argentina—there are no uniform standards of valuation. In others—for example, France and México—there is no state-appointed or self-regulatory body for the supervision of real estate valuation. In many countries, the regulation and development of the profession usually have followed a crisis of some sort—the savings and loan crisis in the United States, the property crash in the 1980s in Europe, the reform of the centrally planned economies in Eastern Europe, and the recent financial crisis in Asia.

Similarly, the United Kingdom's experience with instilling training and licensing requirements for surveyors is instructional of best practices. The Royal Institution of Chartered Surveyors (RICS) is the premier global professional body that represents, regulates, and promotes chartered surveyors and technical surveyors. To become either a technical or professional member of the RICS, candidates have to complete an approved academic qualification followed by two years of structured training in the workplace. Following the minimum training period, candidates are then assessed via submissions and an interview. Successful assessment allows members to be upgraded to technical or professional membership. After they have been full members for at least five years, they can apply to become fellows. The members are bound by the rules of conduct and bylaws outlined in the RICS charter.

All countries are in the process of establishing a mortgage lending market and introducing mortgage-based instruments in their capital markets; therefore, there is a need to improve the standards of valuation. Clearly, there is a need for added effort in many countries to ensure that appraisal standards are correctly applied and regulated. This can be accomplished by establishing professional standards of valuation, educational requirements, methodology, ethics, and oversight in developing real estate markets.

2.3 Financial Analysts

Disciplined financial decisionmaking demands expertise. Such financial analysis is employed in a variety of functions—securities analysis, portfolio management, and the budgeting process. Financial analysts practice in various industries, including investment management, banking, and insurance. Expert financial analysis requires education, standards of professional conduct, and standards of practice. The Association for Investment Management and Research (AIMR) was created to educate and certify investment managers and analysts and to sustain high standards of professional conduct. Although the AIMR is an international organization, 82 percent of its members practice in North America.

2.4 Actuaries

Actuaries traditionally work in the insurance and employee benefits industries and the health and retirement benefits sectors. They make it possible to share and disperse risks and, in a market economy, help to stabilize the financial system. Nevertheless, actuaries are scarce in developing countries. The International Actuarial Association (IAA) is the global body that brings together the actuaries in their member countries; its members are actuarial associations worldwide. The IAA is dedicated to the research, education, and development of the profession and of actuarial associations. Among its functions are to review and implement the rules for the accreditation of individual members and to recommend educational guidelines and a syllabus for an internationally recognized actuarial qualification.

Some economies have professions that are properly trained and regulated and have commonly accepted standards of business that produce an institutional structure better able to withstand bubbles. Why do Hong Kong and Singapore have more financial sector professionals per capita than Japan and Korea? Does that make their economies more immune to crisis and more flexible in their response? There are several possible answers. One explanation is rooted in the differences in legal traditions—common law versus civil law. To a remarkable degree, legal traditions seem to affect the development of professions. The evidence suggests that professions develop more rapidly in the common law tradition to adapt to new circumstances. Common law countries, including Australia, Canada, Hong Kong, Singapore, and the United States, are former British colonies and rely on independent judges and juries and legal principles supplemented by precedent-setting case law to respond to evolving circumstances. Civil law is not adept at responding to the changing needs of the economy—doing so requires new rules regarding property valuation and regulation of new financial products such as insurance. Civil law countries, including Indonesia, Japan, Korea, and Latin American countries, rely on legal codes that contain very specific rules.

There are two other possible explanations. First, Japan and Korea, as well as other Asian countries and Latin American countries, rely on banking financial intermediation. In some of these countries, the savings are channeled largely by directed credit from banks to businesses. In many instances, the credit decisions are made without reference to risk, and an implicit safety net is in place. In such instances, there is less need for professionals to manage risks. Therefore, the lack of professions is a direct result of the savings intermediation process. Second, in Asia and Latin America groups of affiliated companies—*keirtsu* in Japan, *chaebol* in Korea, *grupos* in Latin America—are integrated both vertically and horizontally, are organized around their own trading companies and banks, and are involved in a variety of industrial, resource, and service sectors. Due to a developed internal market for financial resources, these companies rely less on external markets, so there is less need for the financial skills of external experts.

3. Critical Financial Products

Countries with a rich set of financial sector skills can develop a wider range of investment and risk management mechanisms that can help to transfer liquidity, market, and credit risks and thereby dampen the volatility of the financial system. However, in order to develop sophisticated financial market instruments, countries first need to acquire a base of human capital. A secondary market for debt, securitization of performing and impaired assets, corporate financial restructuring funds, corporate restructuring vehicles, and real estate investment trusts are some of the instruments designed to mitigate the severity of bubbles as well as support remedial measures to deal with their after-effects. Two of the products—corporate financial restructuring funds and corporate restructuring vehicles—are from Korea, which sought to develop market solutions to facilitate the restructuring process in the aftermath of the crisis. The Korean initiative might serve as a model for other countries.

3.1 Secondary Market for Distressed Debt

Development of a secondary market in distressed corporate debt would: 1) help troubled banks to dispose of poorly performing loans and, therefore, enable more efficient management of loan portfolios; 2) create a process for signaling the market valuation of troubled loans; and 3) allow prospective acquirers to accumulate a strategic equity interest in corporations or real estate projects and to exert influence over the restructuring. After the Loan Syndication and Trading Association in New York established codes of practice for the industry, the volume of trading in secondary loans exploded in the United States. Between 1991 and 1999, volume grew more than 1,200 percent. In 1991, $8 billion (face amount) of loans were traded in the secondary market, according to the Loan Pricing Corporation. In 1999, $110 billion (face amount) in loans were traded.

Secondary markets for distressed debt are relatively underdeveloped in emerging markets. Lengthy due diligence and lack of standard documentation, which lead to protracted settlement periods, high potential for failed transactions, and substantial legal costs, discourage transactions in the secondary market. Several measures can foster the development of a secondary market for debt in developing countries: standardization and simplification of the sale agreement for loans, establishment of standard settlement procedures, establishment of codes of practice for market activity (such as a protocol related to due diligence), and establishment of mechanisms for transparent valuation of loans. Such measures would bring greater transparency and efficiency, improve market liquidity, and encourage companies to trade their debt in the secondary market.

3.2 Securitization of Performing and Impaired Assets

Securitization is the issuance of marketable securities backed by the expected cash flow from specific assets (Thompson, 1995). Securitization generates gains for originators, consumers, and investors, including more efficient financing, better balance sheet structure, and better risk management. Securitization enables financial institutions to eliminate interest rate mismatches and investors to make investment decisions independent of the credit standing of the originator and focus on the degree of protection provided by the repayment capacity of the assets securitized.

Residential mortgages are the most commonly securitized asset. In the United States, mortgage-backed securities account for 55 to 60 percent of all outstanding residential mortgages. The U.S. experience demonstrates that the government can nurture and guide the development of markets. Much of the growth in the mortgage-backed securities market is due to standardization following the savings and loan crisis of the 1980s and guided by the Resolution Trust Corporation.

Securitization can be used to sell performing and impaired assets and holds great promise for banks seeking to dispose of assets in developing countries. The lack of securitization products in many countries hinders the mop-up in the aftermath of a bubble, largely because of the prerequisites required for securitization: a supportive legal environment, a transparent accounting environment, an effective regulatory environment, a supportive tax environment, and back-office systems. Many developing countries lack the robust financial infrastructure that can facilitate securitization transactions. Therefore, securitized assets impose significant compliance or administrative costs on the originator and do not provide adequate protection to investors.

In Asia, the legal and regulatory framework obstructs securitization, and legislative initiatives are needed. For instance, China faces three legal impediments to securitization transactions. First, as a civil law country, China lacks the legal concept of trusts. Therefore, the structure of trusts required for securitization—limited-purpose entities that issue securities backed by the assets acquired—is not recognized. Special legislation establishing trusts is needed to develop the securitizations market. Second, the transfer of assets to the trust and the income of the trust are deemed taxable events. Tax legislation is needed to establish tax neutrality for transferring the underlying assets to a trust, as well as to establish the trust as a pass-through vehicle. Finally, in the event of the bankruptcy of the trust originator, the trust can be a party to the bankruptcy process. This process undermines the objective of securitization, which is designed to "ring fence" the credit risk of the trust from the underlying credit risk of the originator. Therefore, insolvency legislation needs to clarify that the trust is not a party to a bankruptcy process.

A separate set of impediments is due to shallow financial systems. In most developing countries, bond markets are not developed and do not accommodate issuance of asset-backed bonds. It is instructional that Korea introduced the legislative changes designed to enable securitization only after the 1997 crisis. However, securitization transactions seem to defy the intended objectives by offering *full recourse* to the buyers of securities and by circumventing regulatory objectives. The notable exception is Malaysia, where the national mortgage corporation (Cagamas) introduced mortgage-backed securities and promotes the secondary mortgage market. However, a secondary market is lacking in all other developing countries.

Over the past three years, changes in Latin America's legal systems coupled with a deeper understanding of securitization by regulators and key participants have led to a sizable increase in securitization transactions: nine transactions in 1998 valued at $2.1 billion and 27 transactions in 1999 valued at $5.4 billion (see Standard & Poor's, 2000). Argentina is at the forefront of asset securitizations, with the largest number of transactions. The market developed after Argentina established the required legal and regulatory environments (the trust law was enacted in January 1995) and began to focus on the development of mortgage transactions. In other Latin American countries—Brazil, México—securitizations remain cross-border and secured by future receivables. The situation highlights the immature development of local capital markets and the lack of suitable assets for securitization. Virtually the same legal impediments inhibit the development of real estate investment trusts.

3.3 Corporate Financial Restructuring Funds

Corporate financial restructuring funds, which were developed in Korea, offer an interesting mechanism for developing and embedding market discipline in the restructuring process. The Korean government created these funds in an effort to facilitate the restructuring of small and medium businesses. The government asked 23 Korean financial institutions to contribute to a corporate restructuring fund, raised $1.3 billion, and appointed Korea Development Bank as manager. Several major U.S.-based investment managers received $250 million in balanced mandates of debt, equity, and private equity. These funds were a hybrid of a private equity fund and a mutual fund investing in listed equity and debt; private equity funds are the closest analogy in the United States. They confined their investments in new issues of equity and debt of troubled companies and emphasized operational restructuring. In the process, they also reduced leverage, improved cash flow, and improved the profitable use of capital. The western managers also engineered improvements in corporate governance standards, accounting standards, and transparency and promoted the development of the domestic mutual fund industry.

3.4 Corporate Restructuring Vehicles

Corporate restructuring vehicles, which also originated in Korea, focus on the operational restructuring of medium and large workout (distressed) companies. Although bank workouts can provide financial stability, banks in Korea and elsewhere are not equipped to inject fresh equity or to engage in operational restructuring (for example, the sale of noncore assets and affiliates, cost reductions, a focus on core competencies). These elements of restructuring are needed to preserve viable businesses and maximize recoveries to financial institutions. In corporate restructuring vehicles, the financial institutions' loans in workout companies are aggregated and consolidated in a special-purpose vehicle and converted to debt and equity. Control of the restructuring process is transferred to an experienced strategic investor, which provides financing and makes operational and financing decisions. Complex legal, tax, and valuation issues need to be overcome, but the payoff—the preservation of ongoing concerns—is high. Again, this market-based approach to restructuring offers several benefits. First, outside investors provide expertise that is lacking in the public sector (that is, operating and turnaround skills and industry knowledge). Second, corporate restructuring vehicles offer a private sector–funded solution to a market problem. Finally, they provide a degree of flexibility and expertise for banks, investors, and regulators that the traditional approach of centralized, government-owned asset management companies does not.

3.5 Real Estate Investment Trusts

Real estate investment trusts (REITs) are companies that own and, in most cases, operate pools of income-producing real estate, such as apartments, shopping centers, offices, and warehouses. Some also finance real estate. They mobilize debt and equity in the capital markets, creating a direct link between real estate valuations and the cost of capital. These trusts link the real estate industry closely to prices in financial markets and provide a venue to diversify real estate risks. About 300 REITs with total assets of more than $300 billion are operating in the United States. About two-thirds of these trade on the national stock exchanges. The advent of the REIT industry and of the commercial mortgage-backed securities and secondary loan market has diversified methods of real estate lending and allowed lenders to spread underwriting risk and mitigate credit risks. Other benefits include increased liquidity, the ability to hedge against cyclical credit crunches, and increased diversification of borrowers and collateral. Overall, the REIT industry has reduced volatility in the real estate industry.

4. Conclusions and Policy Recommendations: A Market-Based Approach to Restructuring

Restructuring is a tedious and demanding process composed of incremental and complementary institutional measures, including the development of financial sector skills and market instruments. The absence of skills to manage restructuring and market-based instruments weighs heavily on countries, and they are not likely to restructure rapidly and efficiently.

International standards are needed to strengthen public financial institutions, particularly in securities and bank regulation. There is an equal need to strengthen the capacity of the private financial sector through international standards in the essential professions and improvements in the institutional setting. Specifically, effort is required along three dimensions: *regulations* to facilitate the growth of the financial services professions, *incentives* to induce individuals to enter these professions, and *opening* of the financial sector to foreign competition.

Regulation is needed to ensure that practitioners have appropriately high levels of competence and skills, that practitioners have integrity and independence, and that a procedure is available for dealing effectively with enforcement. An effective regulatory regime instills credibility in these professions. Leadership is needed to foster professional associations for appraisers, actuaries, and insolvency experts, among other professions. Incentives are needed to encourage the development of skills and instruments by outsourcing contracts for securitization to the private sector and to promote expertise by hiring and outsourcing service contracts in auditing and appraisals only to licensed professionals. Incentives also are needed to encourage the presence of foreign banking, insurance, and securities by dropping the restrictions on foreign entry. Policy measures—directed at developing market-based instruments in distressed debt, corporate restructuring funds, and real estate investment trusts—are needed to bring greater transparency, efficiency, and liquidity to these markets. Policies also are needed to remove legal impediments to the development of a market for securitization through legislation enabling a legal structure for trusts, tax neutrality, and amendments to the insolvency legislation. Similarly, standard documentation for trading distressed corporate loans is needed to improve consistency, transparency, and, therefore, liquidity in the distressed debt market.

*Michael Pomerleano is the program manager for the Financial Sector Learning Program of the World Bank. The author is indebted to Bozena Krupa for research assistance. Jeff Carmichael, Mansoor Dailami, Ben Friedman, George Kaufman, Bob Litan, Bill Mako, Paul Masson, and Bill Shaw provided very helpful comments. The findings, interpretation, and conclusions expressed in this paper are entirely those of the author. They do not necessarily represent the views of the World Bank.

References

Allen, Franklin, and Douglas Gale, 2000, "Bubbles and Crises," *Economic Journal,* Vol. 110, January, pp. 236–255.

Eschweiler, Bernhard, 1999a, "Asia's Property Morass is Still Deep," in *Asian Financial Markets,* New York: Morgan Guaranty Trust Company, Economic Research, October 29.

_____, 1999b, "Asia's Top Economies Must Focus on Services," in *Asian Financial Markets,* New York: Morgan Guaranty Trust Company, Economic Research, April 30.

Fischer, Stanley, 2001, "Financial Sector Crisis Management," remarks before the seminar on "Policy Challenges to the Financial Sector in the Context of Globalization," The World Bank Group, International Monetary Fund, and Board of Governors of the U.S. Federal Reserve System, Washington, DC, June 14.

Greenspan, Alan, 1999, "Lessons from the Global Crises," remarks before the World Bank Group and the International Monetary Fund, Program of Seminars, Washington, DC, September 27.

Heikenstein, Lars, 1998, speech by the deputy governor of the Bank of Sweden at a seminar arranged by the Swedish embassy, Seoul, Korea, July 15.

Mako, William P., 2001, "Corporate Restructuring Strategies: Recent Lessons," paper presented at the Asian Regional Seminar on Financial Reform and Stability, International Monetary Fund, Hyderbad, India, March 29.

Pomerleano, Michael, and Xin Zhang, 1999, "Asian Corporates and Capital Markets," in *Financial Markets and Development: The Crisis in Emerging Markets,* Alison Harwood, Robert Litan, and Michael Pomerleano, eds., Washington, DC: Brookings Institution.

Rosgen, Markus, 2001, "Share Valuation in Asia: Throw out the Rule-Book," *Economist,* May 24.

Standard & Poor's, 2000, *Structured Finance: Securitization in Latin America,* New York: Standard & Poor's.

Sundararajan, Vasudevan, and Steven A. Seelig, 2001, "Corporate Financial Restructuring," paper presented at the Asian Regional Seminar on Financial Reform and Stability: Systemic Issues, International Monetary Fund, Hyderabad, India, March 29.

Thompson, J. K., 1995, *Securitization: An International Perspective,* Paris: Organization for Economic Cooperation and Development.

United Nations, 1997, *Statistical Yearbook 1997,* New York: United Nations.

Chapter 36

Comments on "The Historical Pattern of Economic Cycles and Their Interaction with Asset Prices and Financial Regulation"

Joaquim Vieira Levy*
Ministry of Planning, Brazil

It is a pleasure to discuss these papers, which undoubtedly complement each other. I was asked to focus my remarks on Professor Charles Goodhart's paper, and I will do so, albeit also touching upon the other two papers.

Goodhart's argument can be divided into three parts. First, he proposes that the nature of business cycles has changed and that this justifies reviewing the policy actions taken in response to economic downturns. He next notes that in recent business cycles, large swings in asset prices are a prominent feature of the economic landscape, begging the question of whether this feature is also important. Finally, he inquires about what instruments could be used to minimize the impact of such cycles and how the information in asset prices could help in this effort.

With respect to the changing nature of business cycles, Goodhart points out that economic upswings in the 1945–80 period were often propped up by fiscal policy and accompanied by increasing inflationary pressures. This was in contrast with cycles before and after this period, which have been mainly driven by private investment, often in the wake of some technological change. In these supply-driven cycles, the upswing would not be accompanied by inflationary pressures, but asset prices would increase quite rapidly above the Consumer Price Index.

The increase in asset prices would fuel an increase in lending backed by such assets that would result in over-investment, which eventually would reduce profitability. This drop would be translated into falling asset prices, a weakening of the solvency of the banking system and a contraction of credit expansion. In this typical business cycle, the financial sector played a key role in, allow me to borrow a word from the psychological disciplines, enabling private investors in the upswing and in hindering them, perhaps too much, at the downturn.

A similar contrast between the dynamics of demand- and supply-driven cycles was made in the case of small open economies.

A conclusion of this analysis seems to be that if business cycles are not caused by excess demand induced by the government (e.g., reflected in inflation), tightening fiscal and monetary policy—including credit conditions—after the internally generated downward phase of the cycle starts may not be the right policy response. This conclusion is relatively uncontroversial, except perhaps for aspects of the short-term management of the exchange rate in small open economies, for which high interest rates may be required during a short period of time after the bursting of a bubble to avoid an uncontrolled devaluation and the onset of an inflationary process.

Turning to the prominence of changes in asset prices, Goodhart proposes that some of these changes are important. He highlights the quality of the information associated with property prices, noting that Value-at-Risk estimations suggest that fluctuations in prices of housing are more closely related to subsequent variations in real output than are fluctuations in either exchange rates or equity prices.

The final part of his paper suggests ways to use the information on asset prices and the volume of loans backed by such assets in designing prudential rules to reduce the feedback of asset prices on economic cycles and the vulnerability of the financial sector to these cycles. The rationale for emphasizing such suggestions appears to come from the more prominent role of financial institutions in the new-old type of cycle, in contrast with their lesser role in the typical 1945–80 cycle.

Unfortunately, current prudential regulations are mostly procyclical. The quest, thus, is to find anticyclical prudential regulations. Goodhart argues that increases in required capital or provisions based on changes in asset prices and the volume of lending backed by these assets would be well suited to respond to this need. By contrast, capital requirements based on the volatility of asset prices at the moment of the crisis can exacerbate financial instability. I believe this is also largely supported by recent literature, especially in the aftermath of the Asian crisis. Nonetheless, the contour of a strategy along these lines still needs to be detailed, and Goodhart's paper stimulates this discussion.

The paper, indeed, puts forward creative approaches. On the other hand, it leaves an uncomfortable impression, even if unintentionally. This impression arises from the apparent contrast between monetary policy and prudential rules resulting from the emphasis on the role of prudential regulation in helping avoid crises. This apparent shift of responsibilities looks awkward, and Carmichael and Esho actually appear to defend their institutions from being assigned to carry out this role.

Goodhart's paper sometimes also gives the impression that the choice is in part between rules and discretion, to the extent to which monetary policy can be seen as imparting more discretion than prudential regulations, when forbearance is left out. One of the problems with contrasting the two approaches is that the instruments considered within the realm of prudential regulation rather than belonging to the arsenal of monetary policy vary with time. For instance, Goodhart highlights that credit limits and restrictions on portfolio composition were viewed as instruments of monetary policy back in the 1960s and 1970s, while Carmichael and Esho include them squarely among possible prudential rules.

The sharing of the responsibility for avoiding bubbles between monetary policy and prudential authorities also needs to take into account the scope of regulated financial institutions. The example of housing loans brought forward by Goodhart illustrates this point. A large part of housing loans in the United States is repackaged in such a way that the risk can be transferred away from banks. If this is the case, penalizing the stock of bank mortgages may not do much to avoid bubbles, since original loans may not be in bank balance sheets anymore.

Moreover, it is not completely clear why prudential regulations should include concerns about housing prices if it is argued that monetary policy should respond to changes in these prices. Of course, there are cases—especially when considering the more current understanding of monetary policy as the use of interest rates—where monetary policy is not fully effective to address the problems in one particular sector or region, in which cases supervision may acquire a greater role (this point was made in Belaisch, Kodres, Levy, and Ubide, 2001, with respect to the European Union). However, this is not entirely clear from Goodhart's presentation.

Also, the presentation of the role of real estate prices—and in particular, housing prices—admits several readings. I believe the paper could distinguish more the effects of real estate prices in general from the effects of housing prices, both for monetary policy purpose and financial regulation. To the extent to which both prices move together, perhaps one may act as a proxy for the other. But, since the 1980s, the gravest problems of real estate loans have often been associated with loans to developers of commercial property, rather than housing. Also, the distinction is important because the mechanisms through which each sector influences the cycle can be quite different. For instance, Goodhart emphasizes the importance of housing as collateral (e.g., to small loans in England and Latin America), i.e., housing prices as a fuel to investments in other sectors. By contrast, rises in commercial real estate prices typically reflect speculation using profits taken from other sectors. Thus, the implications for monetary policy or prudential regulations of information from each market can be different. Interestingly, data presented by Carmichael and Esho show that housing loans in Australia fell on the eve of the last banking crisis, while business loans (commercial real estate included? backed by equity on houses?) increased sharply.

Turning back to the issue that "prudential" instruments and monetary policy indeed share a common ground, one can point out to the case of capital flows to small open economies. As observed by Goodhart, it is often the case that economic indicators of small open economies look fine during economic booms, although the economy is fragile. Hence, a surge in capital inflows, for instance, can be easily rationalized, even if trouble is brewing underneath, as these flows finance investments that ultimately will prove not profitable.

In light of this, indicators related to banks' foreign liabilities could be added to the tentative ideas presented by Goodhart as risk-related requirements. A difference between this risk-related requirement and those proposed by Goodhart is, of course, that it will largely price the liability composition rather than the asset composition of banks. The paper of Carmichael and Esho, however, suggests that this is reasonable. The paper shows a synchrony between crises in Australia and other noncentral markets—including South America. This suggests that risks in Australia were not related only to idiosyncratic errors in the evaluation of the prospects of land or sheep prices, but also to the ability of banks to raise cheap money from international markets. In this case, domestic interest rates, i.e., standard monetary policy instruments, may be ineffective to slow down credit creation.

Of course, this proposed "novel" prudential instrument is close to some measures taken in emerging markets in the last two decades, especially those increasing the cost of internalizing short-term capital. Examples of such instruments are the unremunerated reserve requirements imposed by Chile to target short-term capital inflows, as well as similar taxes imposed by Brazil on short-term flows and constraints on the ability of importers to use foreign loans to invest in domestic financial assets. These were not quantitative controls, like those of the 1960. Instead, they left the final decision to the investor, satisfying a criterion stated by Carmichael and Esho.

These examples also highlight the importance of not putting too much trust in single automatic mechanisms. The effectiveness of those instruments, when taken in isolation, has often been under doubt. The International Monetary Fund (IMF) has, for instance, noted that Bank for International Settlements statistics using data from lending countries tended to indicate that the share of short-term capital flows to Chile was larger than what was suggested by Chilean statistics (IMF, 1998). Cardoso and Goldfajn (1997) show that capital control mechanisms adopted by the Brazilian authorities in the 1990s often lost their "power" in a relatively short period of time. On balance, the effectiveness of such instruments appears to depend on several factors. The performance of Chilean financial institutions in the 1990s reflected also the conduct of fiscal policy and other macro fundamentals. Similarly, the ability of the Brazilian financial system to weather the 1999 devaluation was in large part due to a steady improvement in prudential regulations and the financial sector reform started in 1995 when price stabilization acted as the bursting of an asset bubble and accelerated changes in that sector.

As a practical matter, trust in more stringent prudential regulations should also be tempered by the observation that a natural consequence of tightening regulations in one sector is to deviate business to other sectors. Most recently, the reaction of the corporate sector in some Latin American and Asian countries where more rigorous prudential rules for banks have been enforced is a good example of this behavior. A rapid shift of credit activities from regulated banks—whose corporate business has dwindled—to inter-firm lending has been observed in some of these countries, where large corporations that have access to capital markets have started acting as lenders to suppliers and a host of related businesses. In some, the apparent calm in the financial sector, sometimes dominated by large, solid foreign banks, may be hiding shaky practices in unregulated sectors.

Before closing my observations on Goodhart's paper, I would like to mention another factor that can help strengthening the role of prudential regulations. Then, I will leave the discussion of these rules—in particular, the Spanish provision rules—to the other discussants. One can certainly establish equivalence between provisions and capital requirements, and both prudential mechanisms contribute to increasing the cost of the banking business. Therefore, the coordination of prudential regulation and taxes remains quite important. On this issue, I think the example of Portugal—where the central bank has, or at least used to have, a voice on the determination of which provisions are tax-deductible—is worth considering. The example of Switzerland is also noteworthy, not the least because perhaps it's less open to discretion. Indeed, since the mid 1990s, all provisions can be tax-deductible, with reversions being immediately taxable (Confoederatio Helvetica, 2001). Swiss banks have used this opportunity with reportedly good results.

In sum, prudential regulation certainly has a role in reducing risks before the bursting of a crisis and in minimizing the effects of this bursting. It is, however, unlikely to be possible to shift much of the burden from monetary policy, and it is difficult to envisage rules so effective that they could replace a minimum degree of discretion.

Finally, if allowed, I would like to add a couple of observations regarding the Pormeleano paper—which deals with the aftermath of bubbles, rather than their avoidance. First, I think that the paper offers a new, interesting angle to the discussion. Also, the Brazilian experience supports some of the views expressed there, even if the data presented on the cost of banking crises and other indicators could be questioned. Undoubtedly, the existence in Brazil of a developed financial sector with a range of tradable instruments proved to help resolve problems in the banking sector and cushion the economy from domestic and foreign shocks. Second, I would venture that in some countries—especially the more developed ones—the difficulties in solving banking issues go beyond the lack of trained people.

*Joaquim Vieira Levy is chief economist at the Ministry of Planning in Brazil.

References

Belaisch, A., L. Kodres, J. Levy, and A. Ubide, 2001, "Euro-Area Banking at the Crossroads," International Monetary Fund, working paper, No. 01/28.

Cardoso E., and I. Goldfajn, 1997, "Capital Flows to Brazil—The Endogeneity of Capital Controls," International Monetary Fund, working paper, No. 97/115.

Confoederatio Helvetica —The Federal Authorities of the Swiss Confederation, 2002, Federal Income Tax Act (LHID, RS 642.11 and RS 642.14), available on the Internet at http://www.admin.ch/ch/f/rs/rs.html.

International Monetary Fund, 1998, "Chile's Experience with Capital Controls" in *International Capital Markets,* annual report.

Chapter 37
Comments on "Asset Price Bubbles and Prudential Regulation"

Ramon Moreno*
Federal Reserve Bank of San Francisco

Jeffrey Carmichael and Neil Esho provide a very interesting overview of Australia's historical experience with asset price booms and busts or other shocks that led to financial fragility and bank failures. They then discuss alternative prudential policies that might be applied to deal with bubbles. The discussion is of particular value because it provides insights about a case that is most likely not very familiar to readers outside Australia.

In my comments, I would like to focus on three topics that come up in reading the paper: 1) the policy assignment: Should monetary authorities or prudential authorities be responsible for responding to asset price bubbles? 2) the lessons from Australia's experience and possible prudential implications; and 3) the possible use of alternative prudential policy tools to deal with asset price bubbles.

1. Asset Prices and the Policy Assignment

What is the most appropriate policy tool to deal with asset price fluctuations and their effects? Should monetary authorities assume primary responsibility for managing the risks posed by asset prices? Should prudential authorities? Or, should each play a complementary role? Carmichael and Esho interpret (without necessarily endorsing) the recent literature as being "generally against the use of monetary policy to control or burst bubbles" while being "generally positive about using prudential regulation to burst bubbles."

The argument that monetary authorities should adopt inflation targeting and not respond directly to asset prices rests in part on the idea that inflation targeting can prevent financial imbalances that might be caused by asset price fluctuations. For example, if a sharp increase in asset prices is inflationary, an inflation targeting regime will lead, appropriately, to tighter monetary policy. However, there are a number of episodes in East Asia, such as Japan in the second half of the 1980s, in which we observe asset prices rising without very marked increases in inflation. Under these conditions, a monetary policy that relies only on inflation targeting may not curb increasing exposure to a booming property market. It remains an open question whether prudential authorities may then play a role in dealing with the financial imbalances that may result.

Proponents of inflation targeting also assume that monetary authorities cannot distinguish between fundamentals and a bubble. As shown by Bernanke and Gertler (1999), under these conditions, responding directly to an increase in asset prices that is partly due to a technological innovation and partly due to a bubble may choke off the output effects of the innovation, as well as of the bubble. An inflation targeting policy would, it is argued, take care of the effects of the bubble only.[1] This is worth highlighting because if it is assumed that monetary authorities cannot distinguish between bubbles and fundamentals, it cannot be assumed that prudential authorities can do so either, at least *ex ante*. In such a case, the response to asset price volatility, if any, must be assigned to prudential authorities only if the costs of any mistakes they might make is lower than the costs of any mistakes monetary authorities might make. Further research and discussion of this question is needed (see, for example, Borio and Lowe, 2002).

2. Australia's Experience with Boom and Bust Cycles

The authors discuss four episodes of boom and bust cycles in Australian economic history from the 1880s to the 1990s. The description suggests that the conditions under which Australian financial institutions were vulnerable to boom and bust cycles were broadly in line with international experience. In particular, rapid growth in asset prices and exposure to property markets appear to be associated with banking distress (Hutchison and McDill, 1999; Gonzalez-Hermosillo, 1999).

Australia's experience highlights at least three conditions that may make the financial sector vulnerable and may warrant special attention from prudential authorities:

i. *Exposure to property markets*—In all crisis episodes, the vulnerability of Australian financial institutions was related to their exposure to the property market. There was the early collapse of 41 property-market oriented "other" banks and nonbanks in 1891–92; the failure of finance companies and building societies in the 1970s; and the bank losses related to property exposures in finance companies and merchant banks, as well as the failure of the Farrow group of building societies in the 1990s. In contrast, the financial sector was relatively stable in the 1930s depression, when property-market oriented institutions were less important. A recent study by Marianne Gizycki (2001) highlights the continuing relevance of property market exposure in Australia by providing estimates of the impact on banks of such exposure in Australia in 1990–99. She finds that a one percentage point slowdown in commercial property price inflation increases the impaired assets ratio by 0.06 percentage points, and that each percentage point increase in the share of construction in aggregate activity increases the impaired assets ratio by almost 0.4 percentage points. This is broadly in line with cross-country evidence suggesting that exposure to property markets has implications for banking distress (Gonzalez-Hermosillo, 1999).

ii. *The coexistence of banks and other less regulated financial institutions, or near banks*—Carmichael and Esho suggest that near banks emerged to avoid the regulations imposed on banks. One could argue that if these near banks pose no systemic risk or make no claim on government deposit insurance, they are of no special concern to regulators. However, there are examples in many countries in which the failure of near banks leads to government intervention, whether due to concerns about systemic stability or for political reasons. In any case, near banks appear to have had implications for systemic stability in Australia. The collapse of near banks in the 1890s was followed by growing uncertainty and the subsequent collapse of a number of banks. In the 1990s, the financial condition of major banks was impaired due to their ownership of near banks (finance company and merchant bank subsidiaries). We know that this problem is not unique to Australia. The 1997 crises in Thailand and Korea were, respectively, led by finance companies and merchant banks, which apparently also emerged to exploit less stringent regulation. Thai finance companies were exposed to a domestic asset price boom. Korean merchant banks were exposed to booms in a number of emerging markets outside Korea as well as to troubled Korean corporate borrowers.

iii. *Financial liberalization and rapid credit growth*—Repeating a familiar cycle, the most recent Australian crisis followed an episode of financial liberalization and rapid credit growth. Rapid credit growth also played a role in the boom phase of a number of earlier crisis episodes.[2] Financial liberalization poses special challenges for prudential authorities because banks with little experience in risk management may rapidly increase lending. It is also worth asking whether the connection between rapid credit growth and crises should be a consideration in deciding whether to adopt monetary or inflation targeting. This may be particularly relevant in emerging markets where the banking sector still plays a dominant role, so that money may still "matter" (Moreno and Glick, 2002).

3. Alternative Prudential Tools

The authors highlight the disadvantages of alternative prudential tools that might be used to deal with asset price bubbles. Restrictions on portfolio composition appear impractical, as regulators do not know better than banks what the best portfolio is. Increasing capital requirements would be too costly. Stress testing as a regulatory tool in Australia is at an early stage, and is too costly for many banks. The authors do espouse a loan loss provisioning technique that is based on anticipated losses, offsetting the tendency for loan loss provisions to be backward-looking.

The discussion brings up a number of issues pertinent not only to Australia, but also to the general analysis of capital requirements and loan loss provisioning. For example, the relationship between capital requirements and loan loss provisioning is worth exploring further. In discussing capital requirements, the authors cite the need for a buffer that adjusts over the business cycle. However, a mechanism for providing such a buffer is also available via dynamic provisioning for loan losses. There may be an optimal assignment of different types of risk between capital and loan loss provisions that warrants further investigation.[3]

It would also be useful to examine further the implications of uncertainty about whether there is a bubble in applying the proposed Spanish model of loan loss provisioning. On the one hand, if there is a bubble, underprovisioning may encourage further lending by banks in a way that misallocates resources, fuelling the inefficiencies highlighted by Dupor (2001) and contributing to fragility that may disrupt economic activity when the bubble bursts. On the other hand, if there is no bubble but a possible technology shock, overprovisoning will supply less credit than is desirable during the expansion phase. The authors' illustration of how an assumed bubble affects potential credit exposure suggests that the effects can be very large. The next step would be to determine, for Australia and perhaps more generally for other countries, how much weight should be assigned to a "bubble" scenario. This would help clarify whether regulators should focus more on the costs of potential underprovisioning or the costs of potential overprovisioning.

It would also be desirable to investigate further why banks appear to underprovision. In their recent study of 1,200 banks in 37 countries over the period 1988–99, Laeven and Majnoni (2002) find that banks tend to underprovision during good times, so that they end up eating into their capital during bad times. Gonzalez-Hermosillo (1999) finds that low capital equity and reserve coverage of problem loans signal a high likelihood of near-term failure, so underprovisioning has significant effects on the financial sector. One explanation for underprovisioning, noted by Carmichael and Esho, is that traditional provisioning tends to be backward looking and is not based on expected losses. However, Carmichael and Esho also find that the major Australian banks, which all use a form of (forward-looking) dynamic provisioning, are provisioning at roughly half the level suggested by a regulatory (Spanish) model of statistical provisioning. Possible explanations are not immediately obvious. Is it tax disincentives? Is there an implicit expectation of bailouts? Some of these possibilities warrant further research, as the answer may determine the appropriate regulatory strategy.

*Ramon Moreno is a research advisor in the International Studies Section and associate director, Center for Pacific Basin Monetary and Economic Studies, Economic Research Department, Federal Reserve Bank of San Francisco. The opinions expressed in this paper are those of the author and do not necessarily reflect the views of the Board of Governors of the Federal Reserve System or the Federal Reserve Bank of San Francisco.

Notes

1. Bernanke and Gertler also argue that responding to a bubble directly can induce more output volatility than an inflation targeting policy can. However, there are scenarios in which this is not the case, as long as it is assumed that authorities can identify bubbles or the source of a shock. See Dupor (2001) or Cecchetti, Genberg, and Wadhwani (2002).

2. Gizycki (2001) finds that the relationship between the share of bank impaired assets and real credit growth was positive and statistically significant in the 1990s.

3. Laeven and Majnoni (2002) offer one interpretation. They propose that loan loss reserves be seen as a buffer for expected losses that may vary over the business cycle, while capital provides the fixed buffer for "unexpected" losses that are the at the far end of the tail of the distribution.

References

Bernanke, Ben, and Mark Gertler, 1999, "Monetary Policy and Asset Price Volatility," Federal Reserve Bank of Kansas City, *Economic Review,* 4th quarter.

Borio, Claudio, and Philip Lowe, 2002, "Asset Prices, Financial and Monetary Stability: Exploring the Nexus," paper prepared for the conference: *Asset Price Bubbles: The Implications for Monetary, Regulatory, and International Policies,* Federal Reserve Bank of Chicago and The World Bank Group, Chicago, April 22–24.

Cecchetti, Stephen, Hans Genberg, and Sushil Wadhwani, 2002, "Asset Prices in a Flexible Inflation Targeting Framework," paper prepared for the conference: *Asset Price Bubbles: The Implications for Monetary, Regulatory, and International Policies,* Federal Reserve Bank of Chicago and The World Bank Group, Chicago, April 22–24.

Dupor, Bill, 2001, "Nominal Price versus Asset Price Stabilization," University of Pennsylvania, Internet manuscript, accessed April 19, 2002, at http://finance.wharton.upenn.edu/~dupor/spid_nov01.pdf.

Gizycki, Marianne, 2001, "The Effect of Macroeconomic Conditions on Banks' Risks and Profitability," Reserve Bank of Australia, research discussion paper, No. 2001-06.

Gonzalez-Hermosillo, Brenda, 1999, "Determinants of Ex-Ante Banking System Distress: A Macro-Micro Empirical Exploration of Some Recent Episodes," International Monetary Fund, working paper, No. 99/33.

Hutchison, Michael, and Kathleen McDill, 1999, "Are All Banking Crises Alike? The Japanese Experience in International Comparison," *Journal of the Japanese and International Economies,* Vol. 13, No. 3, pp. 155–180, previously issued as working paper PB99-02, Center for Pacific Basin Monetary and Economic Studies, Federal Reserve Bank of San Francisco.

Laeven, Luc, and Giovanni Majnoni, 2002, "Loan Loss Provisionings and Economic Slowdowns: Too Much, Too Late?," the World Bank Group, working paper, No. 2749.

Moreno, Ramon, and Reuven Glick, 2002, "Is Money Still Useful for Policy in East Asia?," in *Inflation Targeting: Theories, Empirical Models and Implementation in Pacific Basin Economies,* The Bank of Korea, ed., proceedings of the 14th Pacific Basin Central Bank Conference, November 15–18, 2001, Seoul; also, Federal Reserve Bank of San Francisco, Center for Pacific Basin Monetary and Economic Studies, working paper, No. PB11-02.

Chapter 38
Comments on "The Morning after ... "

Eric Rosengren*
Federal Reserve Bank of Boston

A substantial literature has developed to address what causes bubbles and what policies would be appropriate to prevent or mitigate bubbles. However, relatively little research has focused on what policies would be appropriate to mitigate the impact of a bubble bursting. This is an important question because the aftermath of burst asset bubbles has varied widely across countries. Some countries have experienced only short-lived effects from burst bubbles, such as the Scandinavian and American experiences with real estate bubbles bursting in the early 1990s. In contrast, the bursting of the stock and real estate bubbles in Japan in the early 1990s resulted in more than a decade of subpar growth.

These divergent results are critical to understand given the uncertainty surrounding how policymakers should react to potential bubbles. Given the difficulty in identifying asset bubbles and determining appropriate policy responses, few countries have aggressively attacked what they perceive as emerging bubbles. Given these difficulties, this passive response may be appropriate if the economic costs generated by a burst asset bubble can be contained. If reactive responses can quickly restore the economy to its potential economic growth path, than proactive policies against bubbles, particularly given the uncertainty surrounding those proactive policies, probably cannot be justified.

Michael Pomerleano's paper, "The Morning After: Restructuring in the Aftermath of an Asset Bubble," provides a first step in understanding what factors contribute to mitigating the impact of a burst asset bubble. He provides a cross-country analysis of the aftermath of bursting asset bubbles to determine what factors reduce the economic impact. While he finds an important role for fiscal policy, monetary policy, and financial infrastructure, he emphasizes the importance of developing the supply of human capital and market-based financial instruments. The emphasis on developing the supply of human capital is an area that is often overlooked and needs further investigation. Despite the importance of a supply of skilled financial professionals, the political willingness to make tough financial choices that may result in significant

short-run economic pain may be more critical in explaining what has happened in those countries where the aftermath of a bubble bursting has lingered for many years.
The next section will briefly contrast the collapse of bubbles in several countries. The second section will examine the role of the supply of human capital and possible other factors in those countries where the recovery from an asset collapse has been particularly extended. The final section will provide some conclusions.

1. The Problem: Significant Differences in the Aftermath of Asset Bubbles

One of the interesting observations in the Pomerleano paper is how different recoveries from asset collapses have been across countries. Perhaps the most interesting example is Japan. Japan has been afflicted by two asset price collapses—stock prices and real estate prices. The Nikkei reached a peak of 40,000 in the fourth quarter of 1989 and dropped to 15,000 by the third quarter of 1990. It is particularly striking that stock prices have remained depressed for more than 12 years, with the Nikkei only slightly above 10,000 as of the second quarter of 2002. Similarly, commercial real estate prices began to decline in 1990 and continued to decline over the following 12 years, with several real estate indices falling by as much as 60 percent. The aftermath of these asset price collapses has been severe. Over the 12-year period since the collapse, the Japanese economy has experienced subpar growth, rising unemployment rates, and a banking system that remains impaired.

The experience with asset bubble collapses in the United States has been quite different. Commercial real estate prices experienced sharp declines from 1989 to 1992, with the declines particularly acute in New England, where commercial real estate prices were 50 percent of their peak level by 1991. Unemployment rates in New England tripled, and 15 percent of New England banks failed. Despite these problems, the recovery was quick. By 1995 the unemployment rate, which had peaked at over 9 percent, had declined to below 5 percent. Commercial real estate prices reached their earlier peak by 1998 and then continued to climb. Banks experienced significant consolidation, but by the end of the decade almost all the remaining banks were on strong financial footings.

A second more recent example is the collapse of the NASDAQ, which declined from a peak of over 5,000 in the first quarter of 2000 to a level of 1,500 by the third quarter of 2001. While it is still too early to fully evaluate the response to the collapse, initial effects seem quite modest. Most economic forecasters expect growth in 2002 to exceed 3 percent, while commercial prices have experienced only modest declines, and very few banks have become impaired.

These brief descriptions of asset bubble collapses indicate that the effect can differ greatly across countries. While the United States has had large declines in real estate and stock prices, the impact on the real economy has been far less dramatic than in Japan. It is these differences that the Pomerleano paper seeks to explain.

2. Cross-sectional Differences in the Effect of Asset Bubble Collapses

The Pomerleano paper examines the differences in asset price collapses across countries. Such regressions can be difficult to estimate because of the vast differences in the economic setting across countries. However, several patterns do emerge. First, many of the factors that are important in causing asset bubbles also have an impact on the effect of the bubble bursting. Thus, differences in fiscal policy, monetary policy, and financial infrastructure (e.g., bankruptcy code) can all explain some of the cross-country differences. However, Pomerleano's thesis is that human capital and market-based financial instruments have not received sufficient attention.

Human capital is an essential complement to an effective financial infrastructure. A bankruptcy code requires professional financial experts able to restructure firms. Given the importance of real estate in many asset bubbles, professional real estate skills such as those of appraisers and liquidators are required to transfer real estate assets. Ideally, developing thick secondary markets for assets enables asset transfers to be done more efficiently. With sufficient liquidity, secondary market instruments can aid in providing a broader spectrum of investors able to participate in the market.

The human capital skills do not develop in a vacuum. Pomerleano suggests three ways that the supply of professional skills can be developed. First, regulating professional qualifications provides a baseline of expectations needed to be considered a professional. Exams and course requirements are an essential part of developing appraisers, actuaries, and insolvency experts. Second, the government frequently ends up owning troubled assets, and the government should respond by encouraging securitization and the movement of these assets to the private sector. Third, foreign direct investment can infuse highly skilled financial professionals into the domestic economy.

Development of secondary market instruments can also be encouraged by the government. The government needs to provide appropriate tax and legal structures to encourage markets in distressed debts. Providing economic incentives for the development of real estate investment trusts and vulture funds provides a broader base of investors who can participate in the market for distressed assets.

The suggestions by Pomerleano have not received sufficient attention in most countries. Human capital is essential to restructuring after an asset bubble collapse. Governments can definitely provide greater encouragement to develop financial professionals and provide an infrastructure that encourages the development of secondary markets. Nonetheless, these developments are necessary but not sufficient for minimizing the impact of an asset bubble collapse.

The lack of a supply of skilled labor is not sufficient to explain the extended problems in Japan. While the scarcity of these skills in the labor market was a problem in 1990, it does not fit Japan today. In March 2002 alone, Japanese companies issued ¥578 billion in asset backed securities. These securities included commercial mortgage backed securities as well as the more traditional credit card and residential mortgage backed securities. In addition, Japanese commercial and investment banks are global and have participated in these markets in Europe and the United States. Thus, internal development of human capital and importation of skills through exposure to foreign markets have provided the ability to securitize distressed assets.

Many of the current problems reflect a demand, not a supply, problem. Distressed assets have remained on the books of the government and financial institutions for more than a decade in Japan. The government has not been willing to risk depressing asset prices by quickly disposing of troubled assets and requiring financial institutions to do the same. Because the government is not a particularly effective custodian of these assets, the value of these assets has diminished over time. In addition, the large overhang created by the supply of distressed assets has discouraged private investors fearful that the government may at some point change course and rapidly dispose of their inventory of distressed assets.

To the extent that the supply of human capital is creating a problem, it is in the public rather than the private sector. Bank supervision in Japan has been far less proactive than in the United States, in part, because the staff is small and does not include a sufficient number of skilled professionals. Staff must be able to evaluate models of credit, market, and operational risk. These skills are highly technical, often requiring advanced degrees in finance or economics, but are essential for effective supervision of large banks. In addition to the modeling, the evaluation of collateral, residual values, and securitized assets requires the same professional skills utilized by private sector firms. To attract and retain such skilled individuals requires the ability to provide significant salaries and opportunities for advancement. The supervisory demand for highly skilled staff will only increase, but the governmental response in Japan has been inadequate to date.

A second area that needs increased attention is the role played by financial institutions more generally. The collapse of the NASDAQ has had relatively little impact because it did not impair the financial infrastructure in the United States. Banks in the United States hold significantly less stock than their Japanese counterparts. As a result, stock declines have macroeconomic effects through the reduction in wealth, but financial institutions are still able to provide financing for worthwhile projects. In Japan, the large cross-shareholding of stock is a critical institutional difference. Declines in stock prices reduced hidden reserves and caused many Japanese banks to become capital constrained. Thus, credit flows are impaired by stock price declines in Japan, and will continue to be a potential problem as long as Japanese banks hold substantial portfolios of stocks.

When asset prices impair the financial infrastructure, the recovery process is impacted. Not only does the economy suffer a loss of wealth, but it is also affected by the disruption of financial intermediation. Because banks are critical to the transmission of monetary policy, a major policy tool becomes less effective because of the financial impairment. Under such circumstances, macroeconomic responses are unlikely to be sufficient; microeconomic changes are also required. These microeconomic changes often have fiscal implications, as governments usually have significant financial liability that results from implicit or explicit guarantees on bank deposits.

3. Conclusion

While the supply of financial professionals can clearly impede the economic response to an asset bubble collapse, it is a necessary but not a sufficient factor. Asset bubble collapses can have a very different impact depending on whether the collapse primarily affects wealth or whether it also has a significant impact on financial intermediaries. When financial intermediaries are affected, the supply of skilled professionals to do workouts in the public as well as the private sector is important. In addition, two factors are critical—the willingness of the government to quickly dispose of troubled assets that it holds directly or encouraging disposal of troubled assets through supervisory intervention at financial institutions.

Many analysts have been skeptical of the ability of financial regulators to be proactive in preventing asset bubbles. Bubbles are difficult to distinguish from fundamental changes in the economy. Furthermore, even if a bubble is identified, it is problematic determining the appropriate time to react and which tools to use so that an excessive response is avoided. An important factor in whether financial regulators should be proactive is whether they can mitigate the effect of an asset bubble, and thus reactive responses are sufficient.

Our knowledge of factors that mitigate the impact of an asset bubble collapse is too rudimentary to assume that reactive policies will be sufficient to avoid severe outcomes. While improving the supply of skilled financial professionals is part of the answer, the willingness of governments to forcefully react to an asset bubble collapse has not been present in many of the countries with the worst outcomes. This is particularly true when financial intermediaries have been severely impaired by declining asset prices.

Nonetheless, the impairment of financial intermediaries may be mitigated in the future as financial intermediaries become more sophisticated in risk management. Improvements in risk modeling that are being suggested in the Basel proposals will require banks to allocate more capital for loans with higher probabilities of default and greater losses given default. In addition, the Basel proposals are encouraging greater use of stress-testing exercises that should make banks more cautious when faced with the possibility of irrational exuberance in asset markets.

*Eric Rosengren is the senior vice president and director of the Supervision and Regulation Department at the Federal Reserve Bank of Boston. The view expressed is that of the author and does not necessarily reflect official positions of the Federal Reserve Bank of Boston or of the Federal Reserve System.

PART IX

LOOKING FORWARD: PLANS FOR ACTION TO PROTECT AGAINST BUBBLES

Chapter 39
Banking Provisions and Asset Price Bubbles

Jaime Caruana*
Bank of Spain

One of the central topics of debate among economists has traditionally been the reasons for economic cycles, including the factors that may amplify or smooth them, whether the authorities should aim to iron them out and, if so, how this can be done. More recently, the role of the financial sector in the dynamics of economic cycles has emerged as a key question in this debate.

I would like to focus today on some problems posed to regulators and policymakers by asset price bubbles and the credit cycle, and to share with you some thoughts on a regulatory device we have recently introduced in Spain to deal with some of these problems—the so-called forward-looking provisioning, also referred to as the dynamic or statistical provision.

The procyclical behavior of the banking sector, which is now generally accepted in the literature, is receiving greater attention by academics, policymakers, and market participants. There is a growing feeling that the financial sector contributes to the swings in real activity and may even intensify and accelerate them. Feedback effects between credit growth and rises in asset prices are increasingly evident, although not yet well understood. Transmission channels from the financial sector to the real sector are becoming more and more flexible, rapid, and complex. This is particularly clear for industrial countries, whose financial markets are more sophisticated, but it is also affecting emerging markets, as a logical consequence of their rapid integration into global financial markets.

In the first part of my speech, I will focus on these issues, and in particular on whether the recent behavior of financial markets is exacerbating the volatility and cyclicality of the real economy. Insofar as this is the case, the next question we regulators should ask ourselves is whether this occurrence might be a result of the increasing weight of the financial sector in the economy or of spontaneous financial market developments, such as new risk management techniques by market participants, and/or a byproduct of prudential regulations that might unintentionally amplify financial cycles.

This debate has gained momentum recently in the context of the discussions for a new Basel Capital Accord. One of the issues identified in the discussions was to precisely what extent there are factors in the old or new regulations favoring excessive procyclicality. But we should not overemphasise this point. It is true that a certain degree of cyclicality in risk management techniques and regulations is not only unavoidable but also sensible. We regulators ask banks to be more risk-sensitive, and risk-sensitive usually means procyclical behavior.

The second part of my address will deal with the forward-looking provisioning system recently adopted in Spain. The merit of this regulation is that it introduces incentives for better risk management by banks, while at the same time attenuating the cyclicality of the financial sector and, thereby, swings in the real economy.

In my concluding remarks I will try to summarize the main lessons we have learned in discussing, designing, and implementing the new system, with an emphasis on the broader economic view rather than on the purely supervisory one. Let me bring forward my main conclusion: There are regulatory mechanisms, like dynamic provisioning, that provide incentives for sound risk management and are anticyclical by nature and can, therefore, moderate cyclical swings.

Recent experiences in a number of countries show that *credit expansion and asset price increases—and bubbles—are mutually reinforcing processes* (see figure 1). Asset prices may start to rise in an economy because new investment opportunities appear or simply because of overly lax financial conditions. When asset prices rise so does the value of collateral, which makes financing easier, increasing the demand for assets. That, in turn, pushes asset prices upward. In the downturn, as the value of

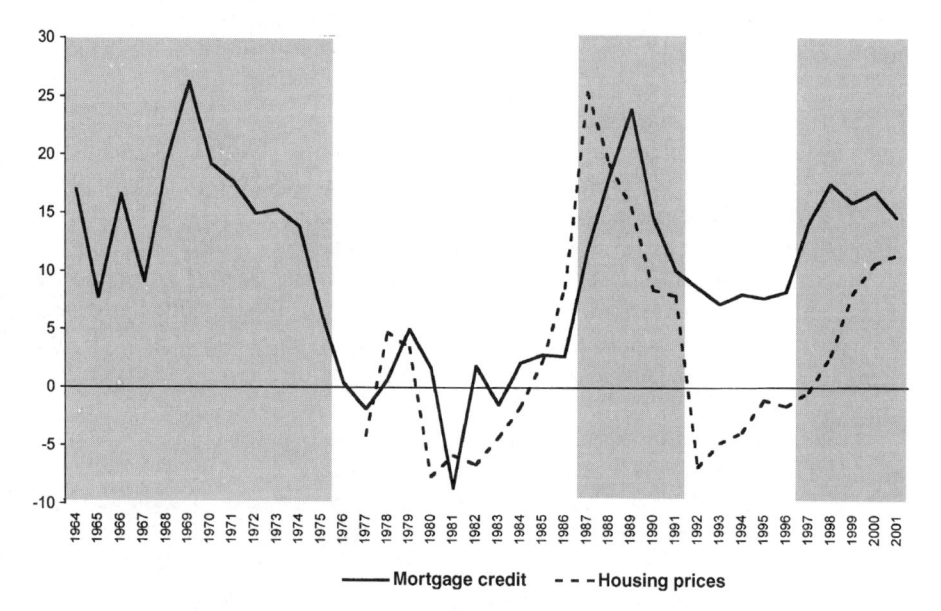

**Figure 1: Mortgage Credit and Housing Prices in Spain
Annual Real Growth Rates (Percent)**

collateral drops, financing possibilities decline, as does credit growth, a process often reinforced by financial institutions pursuing much more cautious credit policies as they are incurring losses or making smaller profits in this phase of the cycle. Tighter credit policies reinforce recessionary forces and provoke additional reductions in asset prices.

This sequence affects different categories of assets (commercial property, residential property, and equity), whose impact on the real economy and transmission channels differ. Commercial property seems particularly linked to the business cycle, while residential property has a larger impact on consumption. Equity prices are intertwined with business profits and investment but are also related to spending through wealth effects, depending on the role equity plays in the determination of financial wealth.

This interaction between credit cycles and asset price bubbles poses a number of challenges, both in the monetary policy and financial stability domains, for the authorities and regulators. In the upswing, inflationary pressures related to excessive credit growth are compounded by financial imbalances resulting from unwarranted optimism on the part of corporations and households and excessive risk-taking on the part of financial institutions. In the downturn, recessionary and deflationary forces are aggravated by credit contraction as a result of excessive risk aversion by lenders.

The possible explanatory factors of this potential amplification of the cycle in the financial sector are many-faceted and complex. First, heightened competition in the banking sector and in financial markets leads in an upturn to riskier strategies that are only corrected when the rise in bad debts becomes evident in the downturn. Second, there seems to be a tendency for economic agents to overreact to changes in their environment, leading to over-optimism in good times and over-pessimism in bad times. Third, herding usually reinforces existing trends and causes overshooting. Fourth, the use of common assessment and risk management tools by market participants and, finally, an excessive and shortsighted focus on "shareholder value" may also amplify swings. Prudential regulations may have also occasionally proved conducive to an excessive emphasis on the short term when assessing risks.

What can the authorities do to counter these tendencies? Debate among academics, policymakers, and market participants has been intense in recent years and is far from settled. This is an area particularly open to discussion, where new ideas and new evidence are forthcoming. Indeed, the way monetary stability and financial stability interact with each other seems a particularly complex topic, and the impact of specific measures on both fields is uncertain.

As far as *monetary policy* is concerned, the debate on whether it should react to asset prices has been one of the most interesting of recent years. Insofar as asset prices contain useful information that helps predict future price—and output—developments, they should clearly be included in the set of indicators the central bank uses for decisionmaking. This is not, however, as easy as it may sound. First, because empirical evidence on the usefulness of asset prices in predicting future price and output developments is not conclusive. And second, because the integration of asset prices in macroeconomic models poses a series of practical difficulties.

Going one step further, a related question is whether monetary policy should react directly to asset prices, over and above the impact of the latter on inflationary prospects. The argument would be that deflating an asset price bubble at an early stage contributes *per se* to long-term financial and monetary stability. Against this view, I tend to share the position of those arguing that asset price bubbles are very difficult to identify in practice and, even assuming that they were correctly recognized, there is a lot of uncertainty as to how asset markets would react to policy changes. Furthermore, this strategy may prove difficult to communicate to the public.

Concerning *financial policy*, the regulators' task of ensuring the long-term soundness of the financial system entails creating the right incentives for market participants—not reacting in excess in a given cyclical position and avoiding excessive misalignments. To this end, first it is essential to encourage better knowledge of the risks assumed, a long-term orientation to analyses, and, consequently, more prudent management within financial institutions. Second, a greater heterogeneity among financial market players to avoid mimetic behavior seems desirable, although this is something the markets would normally develop by themselves. Third, greater transparency and disclosure by the authorities and private institutions would help market participants to focus on fundamentals. Fourth, a better understanding and evaluation of liquidity patterns in financial markets is needed on the part of both market participants and supervisors. Finally, the regulatory authorities should obviously not introduce rules promoting short-term strategies.

Let me focus now on the *relationship between bank credit, loan losses, and provisions for loan losses*. There is ample international evidence on the cyclical pattern of credit, which is very strongly correlated to gross domestic product (GDP) growth, as shown in figure 2 for the case of Spain (with an elasticity higher than one, meaning that when real product grows, credit tends to grow more, and when

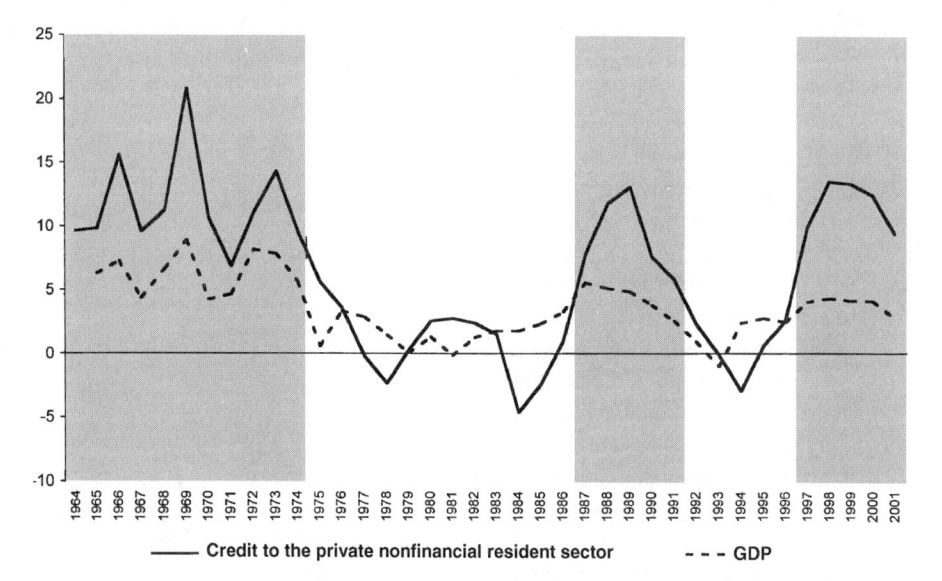

**Figure 2: Long-Term Behavior of Credit in Spain
Credit and GDP Annual Real Growth Rates (Percent)**

real product falls, credit likewise tends to fall even more). Demand and supply effects are difficult to disentangle in credit cyclical dynamics. On the one hand, more economic activity tends to cause more credit demand. At the same time, credit rationing tends to diminish when the economy is booming and tightens when the economy is in recession. Both demand and supply seem to account, therefore, for credit cyclical swings.

Competition is a key factor in explaining credit supply dynamics. Strong competitive pressures may exacerbate the trend towards looser credit conditions in the upturn because the fight for a market share coincides with the observation of low nonperforming loans, leading towards an over-optimistic perception of low risk.

The probability of losses exists from the moment the loan is granted, but it will only become apparent ex post, with the emergence of default problems. Most credit risk mistakes are actually made during the expansionary phase, when optimism is prevailing, although, only in the downturn will they become evident.

Empirical estimates show that there is a strong correlation between credit growth and bad loans, with an average lag of around three years (see figure 3). This means that a credit expansion process is likely to lead to some credit quality problems in roughly that time horizon. The average duration of the economic cycle (from boom to bust) is similar. This implies that if banks only look at contemporary bad loans to determine their credit risk policies, they will restrain credit and increase risk premia in the downturn. The higher cost of funding for bank-dependent borrowers will feed back to activity, reinforcing recessionary forces.

I turn now to provisions. In Spain, until 2000, loan loss provisions were strongly procyclical (as in many other countries), because they were largely linked to the volume of contemporaneous problem assets. These static provisions are backward-looking; they are based on past events. They are only accounted for loan by loan when borrowers fail to repay or in some cases when the situation of the borrower deteriorates significantly.

As a consequence, the ratio of provisions to total loans fell, therefore, during periods of economic growth and tended to rise considerably during downturns (see figure 4). As a result, the latent risk of loan portfolios was not properly recognized in

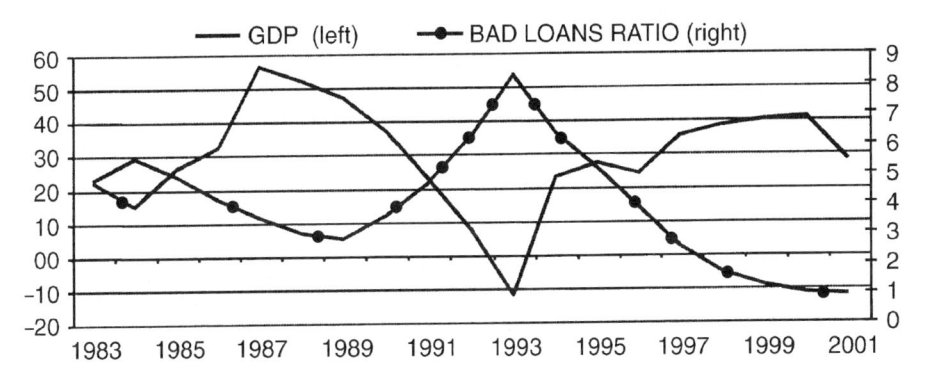

Figure 3: GDP and Bad Loans Ratio in Spain

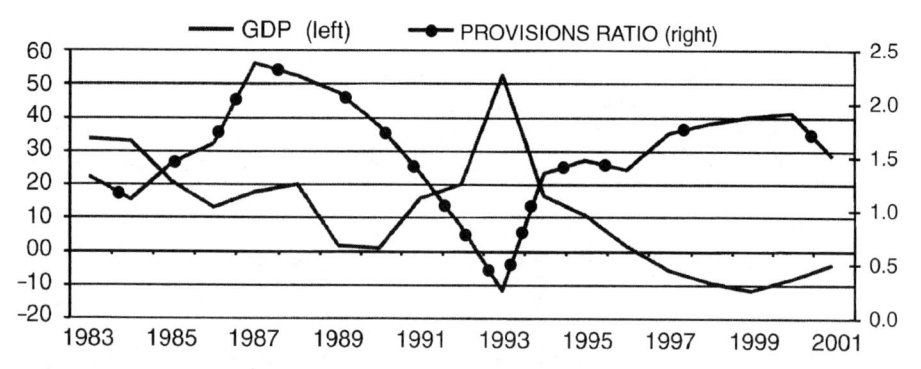

Figure 4: GDP and Provisions Ratio in Spain

the profit and loss account under the old system. In periods of economic expansion the decrease in doubtful loans went hand in hand with the decrease in provisions, which, in turn, allowed bank managers to improve bottom-line profits.

However, one can argue that there is something wrong in the level of profits shown if the latent credit risk in the loan portfolio is not properly taken into account. Intrinsically, every loan has an expected (or potential) loss that should be recognized as a cost by means of an early provision. Otherwise, the picture of the true profitability and solvency of the bank over time could be distorted. More dangerously, the overvaluation of profits might lead to an increase in dividends that could undermine the solvency of the bank. Therefore, the acknowledgement of latent losses is a prudent valuation principle (similar to the mathematical reserves set aside by insurance companies) that contributes to correcting the cyclical bias that currently exists in the profit and loss account. The management of credit risk in the banking sector has perhaps something to learn from insurance practices.

Theoretical papers on bank *credit risk management* also go in the same direction, stressing the importance of proper pricing (i.e., the interest rate charged should cover expected losses as well as the cost of holding capital for unexpected losses). Estimating expected losses when the bank assesses the borrower is the first step for sound risk management.

Proper risk management is obviously a primary task of bank managers and shareholders. But we, as bank supervisors, should evaluate the effectiveness of a bank's policies and practices for assessment of loan quality and provisioning practices. The ability of a bank's loan review system to identify, classify, monitor, and address loans with credit quality problems in a timely manner should be assessed by the supervisor on a regular basis as part of a risk-based approach. A misclassification of assets (and the corresponding underprovisioning) is always present in banks heading for profitability and solvency difficulties.

Sound credit risk management practices at the banks' level, including acknowledgement of expected losses in due time, collide to a certain extent with the current accounting framework. The problem stems from the fact that this framework does not support the notion of provisions on the basis of expected losses, with the result that the recognition of losses is frequently delayed. Some of the answers (i.e., full fair value accounting) to this problem given by those whose set accounting rules may have other important drawbacks. I will touch upon this later.

Let me briefly *summarize the content of our dynamic provision*. In December 1999, the Bank of Spain introduced a new solvency provision, the so-called statistical or dynamic provision, focusing on the statistical risk embedded in the unimpaired portfolio. The provision started to apply in July 2000.

The main idea behind this provision, together with the other provisions of the Spanish system, is to try to capture expected losses. From the very moment that a loan is granted, and before any impairment on this specific loan appears, there is a positive default probability (no matter how low it might be) following a statistical distribution with an expected loss. The expected loss is known in a statistical sense but not yet identified in a specific loan operation or borrower. As the risk appears at the beginning of the operation, so does the statistical provision requirement. With this system, provisions run in parallel to revenues and are, therefore, distributed through the cycle, allowing for a better mapping between income and costs in the profit and loss account.

The statistical provision that we have established works in practice as an addition to the "old" existing provisions: When "old" provisions are well below expected losses, the "new" dynamic provision is added. In good years the net "specific" provisions are very low (or even negative, if there are substantial recoveries), so the new provision accumulates. But in bad years the "specific" provisions increase sharply, eventually exceeding the gross burden of the statistical provision. The net result is that with this system provisions are distributed over the cycle, providing a better recognition of expected losses.

More specifically, the amount of the statistical provision is the difference between the measure of latent risk (i.e., expected losses) and the specific provision (that covering impaired assets). In good times, the specific provision is low and the statistical provision is positive. However, in a slowdown, as the impaired assets rise, the specific provision requirements increase and the statistical provision becomes negative. This means that the statistical fund (accumulated in previous years) starts being used, with its proceeds (the difference between the latent risk and the specific provision) being credited to the profit and loss account. Therefore, thanks to the mechanism of the statistical provision, the burden of credit risk on the profits of banking institutions is better spread over the cycle and more in accordance with the evolution of expected losses.

The new scheme offers banks two options: First, to use their own internal measurements of the statistical credit risk and, second, to use a standard method. The Bank of Spain expects that in the future an increasing number of institutions will be able to show robust computations, in the framework of an integrated credit risk management system. However, probably in the next year or two, most banks will use the standard method.

In the standard system the supervisor sets the parameters. The portfolio is distributed in six blocks, according to the relative riskiness of the different assets, or off-balance-sheet items with credit risk. A vector of coefficients (ranging from 0 percent to 1.5 percent) is applied to the exposures contained in the six blocks. The resulting figure is the estimated expected loss for the bank portfolio.

The computation produces an aggregate annual gross burden (i.e., the expected loss) that, in relative terms, should equal the average annual net insolvency burden borne by the Spanish banking system in the last 14 years. This time span covers more than a full economic cycle.

You might note that the internal approach to calculate the expected losses or the latent risk squares perfectly with Basel II developments.

The new provision has started with a vector of coefficients that will result in a burden lower than this average. This takes into account the improvements in risk management since the last cyclical peak (1993/94), and facilitates acceptability of the scheme among institutions. The scheme will probably be adjusted in coming years, on the basis of the experience gained with its application.

A limit of three times the annual gross burden has been put on the accumulated statistical provision, to avoid an unnecessary or excessive accumulation of funds in the event of a prolonged cyclical bonanza.

At present, the impairment of assets and other credit risk is at an historical low in Spain, and it will remain so in the foreseeable future, due to good economic conditions. Thus, the new provision should accumulate a significant amount of funds, with a reasonable, acceptable impact on the bottom line of the profit and loss account. Those funds should allow extra solvency losses to be covered when the tide turns.

Technically, the new provision is considered a value adjustment. In the published accounts the provision will be deducted from the book value of the credit items that produce it. The provision is not considered a reserve to be integrated in the bank's own regulatory funds. The annual accounts shall report the various solvency provisions (or value adjustments) and their method of computation.

The statistical provision is not a tax-deductible expense, although banks can use an asset account of anticipated taxes (i.e., the impact on the profit and loss is neutral but still negative in terms of cash flows).

Finally, given the considerable internationalization of our banking system in recent years, it is important to keep in mind that the statistical provision is required on an individual level of all the members of a consolidated banking group. It is not possible to counter a positive statistical provision requirement in one bank with a negative one in another bank of the same group. This individual bank approach reinforces the statistical provision requirement and squares well with the fact that expected losses arise at an individual bank portfolio level.

By now, you are probably wondering about the real impact of the statistical provision in the Spanish banking system. As far as the profit and loss account is concerned, the statistical provision for depository institutions represented around 12 percent of 2001 total operating margin. At the end of 2000, the statistical fund reached 15 percent of its maximum amount (remember there is a cap of three times the latent risk), and at the end of 2001 it stood at 27 percent. At current rates, the statistical fund will reach its peak at the end of 2004.

As for the cyclical behavior of banks, it is too soon to say, but we tend to think that the anticyclical nature of the statistical provision is influencing bank behavior.

I must confess that gaining acceptance among banking institutions for our new provisioning scheme was not easy. Banks were reluctant to see their bottom line profits effected, arguing that the Spanish provisioning system was already demanding (including tight asset classification rules plus on-site monitoring and enforcement by Bank of Spain inspectors, not to mention high solvency ratios by international standards).

Apart from banks' initial—and understandable—criticism, some other voices have been raised, although not very loudly, against dynamic provisioning. Some of them can be readily refuted. Others merit careful discussion because the alternatives they propose may affect financial stability.

The most obvious criticism is that a system of dynamic provisioning smoothes bank profits. It is true that the statistical provision tends to smooth profits over the course of the cycle. But it is no less true that the current ex post provisioning system (i.e., setting aside a specific provision when the impaired asset appears) artificially increases the volatility of banks' profits. More importantly, this increased volatility in the latter case has less to do with economic fundamentals (i.e., expected losses) than with accounting rules. If expected losses appear from the beginning of the operation, banks should start to provision them at the very outset. This means an increase in provisions and a decline in bank profits during expansionary periods, just when credit risk expands the most. When the downturn arrives and expected losses turn into real losses, the impact of provisions on profits will be lower since a significant amount of the expected loss had been previously acknowledged.

To the extent that the extra volatility of bank profits is the result of an insufficient recognition of expected losses, dynamic provisioning only restores part of the distortion created.

From a prudential point of view, it is clear that dynamic provisioning limits dangerous capital erosions in times of plenty, requiring banks to provision expected losses and avoid paying out dividends (remember the insurance case). Some observers mention that there is no need for ex ante provisioning since future margin income is enough to cover expected losses. For supervisors, however, to rely on future margin income might be an overly adventurous stance.

Let me expand on this. First of all, experience has painfully shown us that the pricing of a loan is not always properly adjusted to the risk involved in the operation (even taking into account fees and future customer relationships). I have already talked about strong competition for market share or over-optimism. Second, even if the risk is properly priced, the proceeds from a high margin could have been paid out to shareholders by the time the impairment appears. Moreover, dynamic provisioning allows for a timely recognition of both the income and costs stemming from bank loan portfolios.

An alternative to the current accounting framework is being promoted at some international forums. I am talking about full fair value accounting (FFVA). I underline "full." It is quite clear to me that FFVA has, for the time being, insurmountable drawbacks, both of a theoretical and practical nature, for commercial banks. I would place a big question mark over FFVA feasibility.

Dynamic provisioning is a reasonable approach to the fair value of a loan without the numerous drawbacks of FFVA. The statistical provision facilitates prudent risk management and does not increase volatility of profits.

To conclude, let me emphasize that this provisioning regulation in Spain was introduced for prudential reasons. The regulation has three main advantages. First, it provides banks with incentives for better risk management (i.e., risk appraisal, pricing, internal models, etc. ...). Second, the provisioning regulation reconciles good risk management with sound and prudent accounting practices. And finally, the regulation is anticyclical in nature (therefore mitigating the tendency to reinforce cycles). Overall, these three advantages can be summarized as one: Dynamic provisioning reinforces the soundness of each single banking institution and of the whole system.

My answer to the first question posed at the beginning of this speech is that, although risk management techniques may induce risk-sensitive behavior, and risk-sensitive usually means procyclical, that is not necessarily the case when some good regulatory practices, such as dynamic provisioning, are adopted. Such measures contribute to taming economic and financial cycles.

Let me finish by adding a word of caution. Regulatory devices *per se* alone will not attain a safe and sound banking system. A proper risk management culture deeply ingrained in banks' practices is also a necessary condition to reach that goal. Consequently, banks and regulators should work hand in hand to improve financial stability.

*Jamie Caruana is governor of the Bank of Spain.

Chapter 40
Looking Forward on Monetary and Supervision Policies to Protect against Bubbles

Takatoshi Ito*
*University of Tokyo
Hitotsubashi University
and National Bureau of Economic Research*

1. Introduction

This paper, prepared for the concluding panel of the conference, "Asset Price Bubbles," contains a summary of conference papers and discussions at the conference with respect to the question of what the central bank should do when asset prices are increasing (but the general prices are not). My own contributions to this question are added at the end of the summary.

The damage from a bubble is obvious. When asset price prices rise by a magnitude of 300 percent to 500 percent, and then collapse, many distortions and dislocations may occur. Those who have borrowed to invest in real estate and equities suffer from price declines, and in extreme cases, go bankrupt. Banks that lend to (near-) bankrupt borrowers suffer from nonperforming loans and resulting losses. With weakened banks and corporations, the economy likely goes into a prolonged recession. The examples are abundant: a bubble in the 1920s followed by the Great Depression in the early 1930s in the United States; a bubble in the 1980s followed by a "lost decade" of the 1990s in Japan; and the NASDAQ (tech) bubble and its burst in the 1990s in the United States, to name a few. In the first two cases, the crash was accompanied by the severe strain on the economy and financial institutions; in the third case the tech bubble has produced only a brief decline in the economic activities, at least to date.

The rest of this paper is organized as follows. In the next section, the key question will be raised, and the answers will be examined in the sections that follow.

2. Key Question

What should a central bank do when asset prices are rapidly rising, but the Consumer Price Index (CPI) is not?

There are several points that may qualify this question. First, I hasten to add that "CPI is not rising" means not only that the current CPI inflation rate is low, but a regular inflation forecasting model does not show any sign of CPI inflation to come. Second, asset prices include stock prices and real estate (land and structures) prices. An answer to this question may depend on what kind of asset prices are rising. Even in the real estate prices, housing and commercial properties may have different consequences (there are fewer defaults on owner-occupied housing)—as emphasized by the Herring and Wachter paper of this conference.

One possible answer to the question is "do nothing." Price stability is the foremost important objective of the central bank. An increase and decrease in the asset prices may produce some gains and losses to investors. However, that kind of income transfer is not a concern of the central bank. Asset prices will be relevant if, and only if, they signal future CPI price inflation, or they may be relevant from the financial stability reason. The CPI inflation rate is a policy objective, and actions on the part of the central bank are not required until there is a sign of asset price increases signaling the CPI inflation to come. Asset prices will prompt a cautious vigilance, but not an action. The interest rate hike can be delayed until the moment that a regular inflation forecast model flashes the rising CPI inflation rate in the near future. If the interest rate hike is too early, it might kill an economic boom.

However, "do nothing" may prove to be a failure in some cases. Many regard the interest hike by the Bank of Japan in the last phase of the bubble of the 1980s to have been too late. There are three possible answers to the key question that contradict the "do nothing" policy. When asset prices are rising and there is no (forecast of) CPI inflation:
1. Raise the interest rate for the stability of the CPI prices.
2. Raise the interest rate for the stability of the financial system.
3. Take no action. Financial system stability should be protected by supervision.
Let me explain these positions in turn.

3. Price Stability

Suppose that asset prices are increasing, while the CPI inflation rate is stable and forecast to be stable in the future in the regular policy reaction function. This was the case in Japan from 1985 to 1988, and also in the United States from 1995 to 1998. A question in each episode is at which point the interest rate could have been raised due to inflation concern. Asset prices are supposed to influence the gross domestic product (GDP) gap and CPI inflation in the future, but asset prices are not included in the (usual) policy reaction function directly. A crucial question is whether the asset prices should influence the policy decision over and above the regular CPI price forecasts.

One possible answer to the key question is that even in the absence of signs of the CPI inflation, the interest rate should be raised in response to asset price inflation. Asset price increases do eventually result in the CPI inflation rate. The most likely channel is through wealth effects. Asset price increases stimulate consumption and investment and, without supply responses, result in inflation. But, this may take a long time. As a precaution, the interest rate should be raised in advance of the (regular) inflation forecast model.

The Cecchetti et al. paper and the Bryan et al. paper of this conference, as well as Cecchetti, Genberg, Lipsky, and Wadhwani (2000), argue for pre-emptive tightening. In its implementation, there could be two ways to have similar effects. The reaction function can be modified to include asset prices, or the CPI index can be modified to include asset prices.

Criticism of this position and possible rebuttals are as follows. First, it is difficult to identify whether asset price increases are a permanent boom (productivity increase) or a bubble, in the middle of the asset price inflation. It could be too late (the Bank of Japan would have found it difficult to raise the interest rate before 1988, when the interest rate was already high); or, it could be too early (when Federal Reserve Chairman Alan Greenspan warned of irrational exuberance, the Dow was at 6,500 in 1996, long before the peak). They insist that it is easy to identify overpriced assets. Second, there is an uncertain lag. It can be long before the CPI starts to rise. There is no theoretical, reliable reason that the rise in the interest rate would stop asset price increases, as argued by Goodfriend (of this conference). Third, since asset prices are volatile, monetary policy would become too volatile if it reacts to asset prices, as argued by Mishkin (of this conference). Fourth, even when monetary policy responds to asset prices, how much difference it could make is difficult to assess. The magnitude of difference an early action of monetary policy can make is unclear.

Rebuttals can be possible. First, Cecchetti et al. argue that it is not impossible to identify the overvaluation of asset prices. Second, all variables (including M3 at the European Central Bank) as well as the CPI and asset prices, not to mention the usual GDP gap and inflation, are examined anyway.[1] Third, Bryan et al. (of this conference) argue that monetary policy should be aimed at the CPI of *permanent* consumption, and this justifies a position that monetary policy is to be adjusted to asset prices.

4. Financial Stability

Even if it may be difficult to justify the increase in the interest rate due to a lack of (signs of) CPI inflation, there is another reason that could justify the interest rate hike. A bubble and its burst most likely damage financial stability, as asset price volatility tends to produce nonperforming loans. The protracted instability of the banking system in Japan in the 1990s is rooted in the bubble of the 1980s. This view has been put forward by Okina and Shiratsuka (of this conference).[2]

According to this view, the bubble should be contained in order to maintain financial stability, even if there is no sign of CPI inflation. Whether financial stability is threatened in the future when asset prices are rising may be judged by various indicators, including credit growth, among others. Credit growth has been identified as a common denominator in many bubble episodes.

There was a consensus among participants of this conference that if the damage to financial stability is feared, the central bank can mitigate the damage by aggressive easing and providing ample liquidity.

Although the view seems sensible, some criticisms may apply. First, identification of a boom and a bubble may be difficult. (This criticism is the same as the one in the preceding section.) Second, not all bubbles and their bursts result in the damage of the financial system (e.g., the U.S. tech bubble in the 1990s). Mishkin and White (of this conference) emphasize this point.

Which asset prices are increasing may be relevant for possible financial instability in the future. It seems that real estate prices, commercial properties in particular, are more damaging than stock prices, when prices crash. In many countries, with Japan being an important exception, banks do not hold equities, so the financial system is unlikely to be affected by stock price volatility.

5. Financial Supervision

The third possible answer to the key question is that the interest rate can be left alone when CPI inflation is (predicted to be) not rising, and even when there is some concern about the financial stability due to a possible bubble. This answer depends on the premise that a bubble problem should be dealt with by (tightening of) supervision and regulation. Strong supervision and regulation would ensure financial stability even with asset price volatility—the bubble and its burst. Therefore, what the supervision authorities—that is, the central bank in some countries, the treasury in others, and independent financial supervision agency in Japan and the United Kingdom—should do when asset price increases are observed is to make sure that banks and other financial institutions do not accumulate risky loans. This view pays little attention to monetary policy as a possible problem of a bubble and seems to be supported by Mishkin and White, Cochrane, Goodfriend, Goodhart, and Carmichael and Esho, all at this conference.

This view is attractive because bubbles are everywhere all the time, as Bordo et al. (of this conference) have shown. It is better to learn to live with it, rather than trying to kill it.

According to this view, a principal problem of the 1980s in Japan was not whether the interest rate could be raised in the summer of 1988 instead of May 1989, but that the supervising agency (then the Ministry of Finance) did not pay much attention to the potential risk building up by financial institutions. An increasing share of real estate lending should have sounded an alarm. The rising loan/value ratio in the bank lending should have prompted a yellow card. Indeed, in March 1990 the Ministry of Finance did issue a directive (administrative guidance) to set a ceiling on real estate lending. This was too late.

Even though this position seems to be sensible, its implementation may be difficult. It is easy to say that bank balance sheets should be soundly maintained. However, balance sheets of the Japanese banks appeared strong at the end of the 1980s.[3] Credit rating was high, and almost all borrowers were performing well. Their holdings of equities had low book values, but high market values. The latent capital gains seemed to provide enough buffers for any unexpected losses. In fact, it is difficult to say whether financial institutions are sound or not by just looking at the current balance sheets.

6. Further Thoughts on Supervision and Regulation

With the above discussions in mind, some concrete measures of supervision and regulation can be devised. My thoughts are based on experiences of the Japanese bubble.[4] These supervision and regulatory measures are either independent of or complement monetary policy.

First, more transparency can be enhanced. In the phase of asset price rising, short-selling of individual stock options should be introduced. This will encourage investors taking a position against a bubble. Mishkin and White, Trichet, and Cochrane mentioned this position at the conference.

Second, the loan/value ratio of bank lending to real estate prices should be carefully watched. In Japan, the loan/value ratio increased toward the end of the bubble period, while it was guided lower when the real estate prices went up in Hong Kong. This kind of direct regulation may sound like too much intervention by the supervision authority. However, if a risk model of a bank is properly designed, risk of price declines should be taken into account as asset prices increase. Therefore, the loan/value ratio should be lowered as a result of risk model simulation (or a stress test). Similar results can be obtained either by a direct regulation or by a stress model.

Third, similarly, banks may be regulated (or be induced by a risk model) so as not to concentrate lending to real estate related sectors. Indeed, in March 1990 the Japanese Ministry of Finance regulated that each bank would not increase the total size of real estate lending. Looking back, this was too late.[5] (The peak of the stock price bubble was the end of December 1989.) If this regulation had been implemented earlier, could it have made a difference? Although this kind of direct regulation is harmful during normal times, it may be justified to limit systemic instability under the bubble circumstance.

Fourth, taxes can be adjusted to prevent self-fulfilling speculation (not just during a bubble period, but during normal times). In Japan, the inheritance tax system has been identified as such a mechanism. The inheritance tax is assessed on reduced value of real estate, while the full mortgage can be deducted. Therefore, investing in real estate with a high leverage ratio has tended to reduce the total assessed values for inheritance taxes. When real estate prices went up sharply, many elderly people started to worry about the inheritance tax, so they invested into real estate more. Other tax measures that don't cause distortions that encourage procyclical asset price movements can be examined.

Fifth, public lands should be released if at all possible when asset prices increase. Hong Kong and Singapore did this, while Japan restricted the sale of public lands in the (mistaken) belief that supply would increase speculative activities.

7. Concluding Remarks

Although strict regulation and sound supervision are hard to argue against, many think that most regulations are procyclical. The Value-at-Risk (VaR) model is known to have procyclical effects: A cyclical downturn would cause downgrading of borrowers and banks, and that, in turn, would restrict lending from banks. Similarly, a strict application of capital adequacy regulation (just like Japanese banks did toward the end of the 1980s) would not bite into the boom, but bites can make situations worse when the situation becomes difficult (like Japanese nonperforming loan problems in the 1990s). How to deal with this is a difficult question that begs answers. Goodhart (of this conference) provides some hints.

In order to discuss problems arising from asset price increases and decreases, not only monetary policy but also supervision and regulatory policies have to be considered. The conference papers cover a wide range of issues surrounding monetary and supervision policies. More discussions and research is needed.

*Takatoshi Ito is a professor at the Research Center for Advanced Science and Technology at the University of Tokyo and at the Institute of Economic Research at Hitotsubashi University and a research associate at the National Bureau of Economic Research.

Notes

1. Governor Trichet in his keynote address at this conference argued that M3 possibly gives additional information toward distinguishing a boom from a bubble.

2. A similar view is expressed also in Okina, Shirakawa, and Shiratsuka (01).

3. This was pointed out by Aliber's comments during the conference.

4. See Ito (1992, chapter 14).

5. In addition, there were some loopholes to this regulation. Lending to nonbank financial institutions was used to get around the regulation.

References

Cecchetti, Stephen G. Hans Genberg, John Lipsky, and Sushil Wadhwani, 2000, *Asset Prices and Central Bank Policy*, Geneva Reports on the World Economy, Vol. 2, Geneva: International Center for Monetary and Banking Studies.

Ito, Takatoshi, 1992, *Japanese Economy*, Cambridge, MA: MIT Press.

Okina, Kunio, Masaaki Shirakawa, and Shigenori Shiratsuka, 2001, "The Asset Price Bubble and Monetary Policy: Japan's Experience in the Late 1980s and the Lessons," Bank of Japan, *Monetary and Economic Studies* (Special Edition), February, pp. 395–450.

Chapter 41
Planning to Protect against Asset Bubbles

Vincent R. Reinhart*
Board of Governors of the Federal Reserve System

Making plans to protect against asset bubbles involves issues at the intersection of the economic profession's understanding of how assets are priced, how monetary policy works, and how the public responds to regulatory policies. That so many different topics and viewpoints were brought up over the course of the discussion at this conference indicates that the cards are stacked against me drawing useful generalizations. But against these odds, I will assert that four properties of asset prices in general and their aberrant behavior dubbed "bubbles" in particular imply five lessons for policymakers.

1. Four Properties

First, I will start with what should be a self-evident proposition. The Federal Reserve Bank of Chicago and the World Bank could not have sustained a two-and-a-half-day conference were it not for the fact that asset prices—in particular, the values of equity claims on capital and real estate—matter for spending decisions and help to forecast economic activity. High and rising share values make households more willing to spend and to take on debt and businesses more eager to acquire capital. In addition, because equity prices importantly depend on investors' expectations of future economic conditions, their behavior might be read directly as a leading indicator of economic activity. While the relative importance of equity prices in economic forecasting varies across industrial countries, the fact that they are an element in constructing a near-term projection does not.[1] But, in that regard, the role of equity prices is one among many important determinants of spending, including long-term interest rates, the exchange value of the currency, private spending propensities, the government's fiscal position, and economic activity abroad.

Bubbles in asset prices may put particular strains on activity, and they may produce a significant misallocation of resources. In an environment of ready capital gains, households might be consuming and building up debt on the basis of ephemeral additions to wealth and firms might be adding to capacity simply because the inflated market values of their existing capital stocks were high relative to replacement costs. These purchases of durable goods, to the extent that they were viewed with regret once equity prices fell back into their proper alignment, would have the potential to amplify cyclical swings in economic activity.

Second, the profession does not understand how assets are priced particularly well in general or what inflates an asset price bubble in particular. That is not to say that economists do not appreciate the critical roles long-lived assets serve in helping households to smooth their consumption over time and to insure against shocks to income prospects. Rather, those explanations appear to account for only a small fraction of the observed variation in the prices of long-lived assets, consistent with those values depending importantly on attitudes toward risk and expectations of earnings that stretch well into the future.[2] And, the anomalies known as asset price bubbles are even more puzzling both in real time and ex post. There is no clearer example of that than the fact that Peter Garber (1989) has suggested that the canonical example of a bubble—the tulip mania that history books tell us gripped Holland in the second half of the 1630s—may, in fact, have represented the rational adjustment to changed circumstances. Indeed, Garber's reading is that tulip mania and the Mississippi and South Sea Bubbles "... probably looked a lot like a normal day in a pit of the Board of Trade," (Garber, 1990, p. 36).

Third, while our understanding of equity prices may be imprecise, marked changes in economic prospects are likely to have large consequences for them. This follows because an equity share represents a claim on a stream of future earnings. Even a small change in the anticipated growth of those earnings—or the rate at which they are discounted—could have a large effect on its price. For instance, the Gordon equation links the ratio of dividends (D) to the price (P) of a share to the discount rate (r), the equity risk premium (ρ), and the expected growth rate of dividends (g), as in:

$$D / P = r + \rho - g.$$

In this construction, for a given level of dividends, a change in the expected growth rate of dividends will prompt a proportional change in share prices equal to the initial price/dividend ratio,

$$\frac{\Delta P}{P} = \frac{P}{D} \Delta g.$$

This is a large number—currently around 70 for the Standard & Poor's 500 index–and suggests both that an analyst's view of the appropriate level of equity prices depends importantly on his or her expectation of the growth of the economy and that a revision to growth prospects can trigger a substantial revaluation. Of course, all else is seldom equal. An uptick in the growth of the economy's overall potential to produce, which presumably would pull up the path of prospective dividends, would probably also raise the appropriate discount rate because it implies higher returns to all forms of capital. Thus, a higher path for dividends evermore would be discounted at a higher rate, with ambiguous effects on share values.[3]

It is easy to imagine situations, at least for an industry, in which the sudden introduction of a key innovation would raise growth prospects for some firms relative to the discount rate, setting off a large capital appreciation. Whether that appreciation would be contained to the increase dictated by changed fundamentals is an open question. Chancellor (1999) provides a long list of episodes where inventions inflated asset bubbles, or manias, that were induced in Schumpeter's words "... by a preceding period of innovation which transformed the economic struggle and upset the pre-existing state of things."[4] Indeed, when the innovation introduces important economies of scale, there can be a stretch of time when many firms race to become large enough in the field to exploit those economies, setting the stage for the excess accumulation of physical capital witnessed by the crazy quilt of rail lines outside London and the miles of unlit fiber beneath our streets.[5]

Fourth, participation in financial markets is likely to become increasingly democratic over time. It is not unreasonable to think that the willingness of households to take on risk has a greater-than-unitary income elasticity, in line with their likely higher education and increased resources to absorb shocks. For any year, participation in the equity market reported in our triennial Survey of Consumer Finances (SCF) rises as the income bracket rises (shown moving down any of the columns of table 1).[6] But also over time, advances in computer technology, communications, and financial engineering, as well as the force of deregulation, have lowered the cost of transacting in financial markets, making it easier for households to participate in less intermediated forms of finance. This probably explains why direct and indirect ownership by households of corporate equities reported in the SCF has risen over the years (shown moving across the rows of the table).

The increased presence of the household sector in equity markets matters for two reasons. For one, financial wealth has the potential to influence an increasing share of spending.[7] For another, episodes of inflating asset prices resonate in history when they were marked by broad retail participation. Large run-ups in share values followed by a crash matter to more than financial historians when they leave their

Family characteristics	Families having stocks holdings, direct or indirect			
	1989	1992	1995	1998
All families	31.6	36.7	40.4	48.8
By income (1998 dollars)				
Less than 10,000	**	6.8	5.4	7.7
10,000–24,999	12.7	17.8	22.2	24.7
25,000–49,999	31.5	40.2	45.4	52.7
50,000–99,999	51.5	62.5	65.4	74.3
100,000 or more	81.8	78.3	81.6	91.0

Note: Indirect holdings are those in mutual funds, retirement accounts, and other managed assets.
**Ten or fewer observations.

Table 1: Direct and Indirect Holdings of Stock

imprints on household spending and attitudes toward risk-taking. Writing about the tulip mania, Mike Dash noted that:

> *It was the province not of financiers experienced in the way of business, but of country people and poor city dwellers who had, when they started dealing in bulbs, almost certainly never owned a single share in their whole lives.*

Dash (1999, p. 132)

Almost 300 years after those events, F. Scott Fitzgerald would describe in *Babylon Revisited* how the chief barman of the American Bar in Paris had become rich dabbling in equities and would, while it lasted, be chauffeured to work each day—but dropped off a discreet distance away.

2. Five Lessons

My task now is to take lessons from this experience for monetary policymakers in particular.

First and foremost, attention must be paid to asset prices. The effects of monetary policy on spending and inflation are neither immediate nor certain. As a result, to further the ultimate goal of price stability with the least disruption to economic activity, central banks typically try to act in advance to offset potential slack or pressure on resources. But acting in that pre-emptive manner requires making forecasts of future economic outcomes. Asset prices enter into that process to the extent that they are important determinants of current and future spending, and so of pressures on inflation. Of course, the attention paid to equity prices might be increased should they change by a large amount. Simply, a large realignment may be a reason to treat the near-term outlook as more uncertain for two reasons. For one, large changes in asset prices may try the robustness of relationships embedded in conventional economic models. For another, a large swing in equity values may reflect a considerable change in the market's assessment of fundamentals. That market participants could change their outlook in a way that triggers a sudden, sizable revaluation in a key financial market price may be enough of a reason for monetary policymakers to revisit their own assessment of fundamentals. But, of course, the same could be said of any other instrument that was influential in shaping the economic outlook or that appeared broadly on financial market balance sheets, including foreign exchange, long-term debt instruments, and real estate.[8]

Second, there are many means to deal with systemic strains that might result from sharp declines in asset prices. Several central bank policies can strengthen the financial system's ability to absorb stresses emanating from the equity market. Working with supervisors to ensure that depositories and other intermediaries maintain adequate standards (including collateral and margin requirements), keeping mandatory capital ratios high enough that intermediaries can remain viable even under extremely adverse conditions, and requiring exchanges and clearing entities to conduct stress tests of critical systems are all mechanisms that are routinely relied upon to ensure that financial markets can weather equity market storms. And, should a storm break, a central bank can inject reserves in abundant volume through open market operations, lend freely at the discount window, encourage participants to continue to take on credit exposure, and provide technical expertise to help clearing processes.

Third, and as a consequence of the first two lessons, macro policy should be focused on macro outcomes. Tightening monetary policy beyond that required to achieve desired macroeconomic outcomes in response to high and rising equity prices or other asset values would involve trading off among goals. The central bank would be tolerating some straying from the fundamental goal of the stability of the prices of goods and services, at least in the near term, in order to lessen the risks of future systemic problems or severe macroeconomic dislocations down the road. It is by no means obvious that the mandates of most central banks in industrial countries permit such a trade-off. Moreover, a systematic policy response that reduces the fluctuations of one asset price may only shift those pressures to other market prices. In some cases, the systematic response of monetary policy to an asset price need not even make that asset price more stable. Simply, when the central bank acts as a feedback trader, it adds to, not lessens, volatility.[9]

A central bank may be inclined to act because of concerns about dynamic inefficiencies and systemic risks. In doing so, however, policymakers must believe themselves to have a firmer view of fundamentals than the market and a lack of confidence that market forces would correct the imbalance in a timely fashion, a belief that is particularly problematic if asset bubbles tend to occur when the economy's longer-term growth prospects are being re-evaluated. Policymakers' confidence that they understand market dynamics would have to extend to the belief that they could calibrate their action to have the desired effect on equity values.

My last two lessons relate to the structure of financial markets, first at a point in time and then over time.

As a fourth lesson, we should appreciate that diversified financial systems tend to be more resilient. The wonder of the events of the fall of 1987 (when tumbling share values broke all records), of the fall of 1998 (when changing attitudes toward risk dried up market liquidity), or of 2000 and 2001 (when a reappraisal of the fortunes of the technology sector trimmed 60 percent from the NASDAQ) was not the initial movement in asset prices but the subsequent resilience of the U.S. economy. To an important extent, this resilience owed to the existence of multiple channels of intermediation. At times of market stress, when investors' risk aversion intensified, a healthy depository sector filled the gap to satisfy those firms reliant on external funding. This also simplified the Federal Reserve's task, in that the increased emergency provision of liquidity was quickly channeled by market forces to those in need.[10]

My last lesson for the last session in a conference on asset bubbles is simple: Get used to them because financial prices have become more volatile. It is true that equity prices show no trend in volatility over the past century. However, eight of the 10 largest daily percent changes in the Dow Jones Industrial Average (in absolute value) since 1946—or over the period when monetary authorities have been held more responsible for macroeconomic stability—have been recorded in the past 15 years (table 2).

Date	Percentage point change
October 19, 1987	−22.6
October 21, 1987	10.2
October 26, 1987	−8.0
October 27, 1997	−7.2
October 13, 1989	−6.9
January 8, 1988	−6.9
September 26, 1955	−6.5
August 31, 1998	−6.4
October 20, 1998	5.9
May 28, 1962	−5.7

Table 2: Ten Largest One-Day Percentage Point Changes in the Dow Jones Industrial Average Since 1946

3. Conclusion

Financial markets price a changeable future, and price movements are likely to leave an increasingly more distinct imprint on spending behavior. The more resilient the financial structure is, the more able the economy will be to absorb that variability. To the extent that the effects of those price changes on spending and inflation pressures are forecastable, a pre-emptive monetary policymaker will take them into account. When they come by surprise, a central bank has other means to respond to the resultant strains.

Accepting those uncertainties allows the economy to enjoy the efficiencies associated with a free and open capital market. But that argument was put quite clearly during the English parliamentary debate in 1825 on the repeal of the South Sea Bubble Act. One speaker noted:

> *The evil (of speculation) was certainly one which deserved to be checked; though he hardly knew how the check could be applied. The remedy would be worse than the disease, if, in putting a stop to this evil, they put a stop to the spirit of enterprise.*
>
> Chancellor (1999, p. 109)

The inherent tension for policymakers posed by open capital markets—that they improve mean outcomes but may make those outcomes more uncertain—can be seen in the simple observation that the speaker 177 years ago was Alexander Baring, a man whose family name would recur in the litany of financial crises to come.

---

*Vincent R. Reinhart is director of the Division of Monetary Affairs at the Board of Governors of the Federal Reserve System and an economist for the Federal Open Market Committee. He thanks Jim Clouse, Bill English, Don Kohn, Dave Lindsey,

Brian Madigan, Steve Oliner, and Carmen Reinhart for their helpful comments and Jeff Slone for his research assistance. The views expressed are those of the author and do not necessarily reflect those of the Federal Reserve Board of Governors or any other members of its staff.

Notes

1. For example, Gerlach (1998) found that incorporating recent movements in equity prices helped to sharpen predictions of industrial production in Canada, the United Kingdom, and the United States. However, in other countries in his sample (France, Germany, Italy, and Japan), the effect either differed insignificantly from zero or was significant but of the sign opposite to intuition.

2. John Cochrane gives a concise review of the difficulties consumption-based asset pricing models have in explaining share values in Chapter 21 of *Asset Pricing* (Cochrane, 2001). While there are many ways of stating the puzzle of equity prices, perhaps the easiest is the observation that, given the smoothness of consumption, it takes a risk aversion coefficient with an implausibly high value of around 250 to explain the equity premium observed in U.S. history.

3. That is, both g and r in the Gordon equation would rise. In a deterministic setting, the standard consumption-smoothing relationship predicts that consumption (C) grows according to:

$$\frac{\Delta C}{C} = \frac{r - \theta}{\gamma},$$

where θ is the rate of time preference and γ is the constant relative risk aversion. Along a balanced growth path, consumption expands at the same pace as the economy overall, σ, implying that

$r = \gamma\sigma + \theta.$

Thus, a unit increase in the economy's growth potential increases the real rate by a factor of γ, the risk aversion term.

4. Quoted in Chancellor (1999, p. 92).

5. Chancellor (1999) details the excesses of the English railroad boom of the 1840s in Chapter 5.

6. Kennickell, Starr-McCluer, and Surette (2000) describe the results of the 1998 SCF.

7. It is worth noting that economies with market- as opposed to bank-dominated intermediation seem to exhibit higher marginal propensities to consume out of wealth, at least as reported in the most recent *World Economic Outlook* of the International Monetary Fund (2002, Chapter 2).

8. This is also a message stressed by Bernanke and Gertler (1999), among others.

9. In Reinhart (1998), I examine the consequences of such feedback rules to equity prices in a simple model. In a related context in Reinhart (2000), I show that capital controls to limit variations in one market raised volatility in another market.

10. See Federal Reserve Chairman Alan Greenspan's speech at the World Bank in April 1999 emphasizing the importance of a "spare tire" in the intermediation system.

References

Bernanke, Ben, and Mark Gertler, 1999, "Monetary Policy and Asset Price Volatility," Federal Reserve Bank of Kansas City, *Economic Review*, pp. 17–51.

Chancellor, Edward, 1999, *Devil Take the Hindmost: A History of Financial Speculation*, New York: Farrar, Straus, Giroux.

Cochrane, John H., 2001, *Asset Pricing*, Princeton, NJ: Princeton University Press.

Dash, Mike, 1999, *Tulipomania*, New York: Crown Publishers.

Gerlach, Stefan, 1998, "The Information Content of Equity Prices: Some Results for the G-7 Countries," Bank for International Settlements, working paper.

Garber, Peter M., 1990, "Famous First Bubbles," *Journal of Economic Perspectives*, pp. 35–54.

_____, 1989, "Tulipmania," *Journal of Political Economy*, pp. 535–560.

Greenspan, Alan, 1999, "Currency Reserves and Debt," Board of Governors of the Federal Reserve System speech, available at http://www.federalreserve.gov/boarddocs/speeches/1999/19990429.htm.

International Monetary Fund (IMF), 2002, *World Economic Outlook*, Washington, DC: IMF.

Kennickell, Arthur B., Martha Starr-McCluer, and Brian J. Surette, 2000, "Recent Changes in U.S. Family Finances: Results from the 1998 Survey of Consumer Finances," Federal Reserve Board *Bulletin*, pp. 1–29.

Reinhart, Vincent, 2000, "How the Machinery of International Finance Runs with Sand in its Wheels," *Review of International Economics*, pp. 74–85.

_____, 1998, "Equity Prices and Monetary Policy in the United States," in *The Role of Asset Prices in the Formulation of Monetary Policy*, Basel, CH: Bank for International Settlements.

Conference Program

Asset Price Bubbles: The Implications for Monetary, Regulatory, and International Policies

Cosponsored by
Federal Reserve Bank of Chicago and World Bank Group

April 22–24, 2002
Federal Reserve Bank of Chicago
Chicago, Illinois, USA

Monday, April 22, 2002

6:00 pm – 7:00 pm	Registration and Reception
7:00 pm	Dinner

Welcoming and Opening Remarks
Michael H. Moskow, President,
Federal Reserve Bank of Chicago

Cesare Calari, Vice President,
World Bank Group

Moderator:
Michael H. Moskow, President,
Federal Reserve Bank of Chicago

Keynote Speaker:
Randall S. Kroszner, Member,
Council of Economic Advisers

Tuesday, April 23, 2002

7:30 am – 8:40 am Breakfast

Moderator:
Manuel Conthe, World Bank Group

Asset Price Bubbles and Their Implications for Monetary Policy and Financial Stability

Keynote Speaker:
The Honorable Jean-Claude Trichet, Governor, Bank of France

8:45 am – 10:40 am **Session 1: Recent Experience with Asset Price Bubbles**

Moderator:
Uri Dadush, World Bank Group

Papers:
UNITED STATES
U.S. Stock Market Crashes and Their Aftermath: Implications for Monetary Policy
Frederic S. Mishkin, Columbia University
Eugene N. White, Rutgers University

JAPAN
Asset Price Bubbles, Price Stability, and Monetary Policy: Japan's Experience
Kunio Okina, Bank of Japan
Shigenori Shiratsuka, Bank of Japan

EAST ASIA
Lending Booms, Real Estate Bubbles, and the Asian Crisis
Charles Collyns, International Monetary Fund
Abdelhak Senhadji, International Monetary Fund

LATIN AMERICA
Tropical Bubbles: Asset Prices in Latin America, 1980–2001
Santiago Herrera, World Bank Group
Guillermo Perry, World Bank Group

Discussants:
Takeo Hoshi, University of California, San Diego
Ignazio Visco, Organization for Economic Cooperation and Development

10:40 am – 10:55 am Break

10:55 am – 12:30 pm **Session 2: Theory and History of Asset Price Bubbles**

Moderator:
Manuel Conthe, World Bank Group

Papers:
Stocks as Money: Convenience Yield and the Tech-Stock Rollercoaster
John H. Cochrane, University of Chicago

Bubble Psychology
Werner De Bondt, University of Wisconsin, Madison

Bubbles in Real Estate Markets
Richard Herring, The Wharton School,
 University of Pennsylvania
Susan Wachter, The Wharton School,
 University of Pennsylvania

Discussants:
Robert S. Chirinko, Emory University
Bertrand Renaud, Formerly World Bank Group

12:30 pm – 2:00 pm   Lunch

Moderator:
W. James Farrell, CEO,
Illinois Tool Works, Inc.

Rational and Irrational Bubbles

Keynote Speaker:
Allan Meltzer, Carnegie Mellon University

2:10 pm – 3:50 pm   **Session 3: Empirical Dimensions of Asset Price Bubbles**

Moderator:
Ravi Jagannathan, Northwestern University

Papers:
Asset Prices, Financial and Monetary Stability: Exploring the Nexus
Claudio Borio, Bank for International Settlements
Philip Lowe, Bank for International Settlements

The Stock Market Crash of 1929: Irving Fisher was Right
Ellen R. McGrattan, Federal Reserve Bank of Minneapolis
Edward C. Prescott, University of Minnesota and
 Federal Reserve Bank of Minneapolis

A Stochastic Index of the Cost of Life:
An Application to Recent and Historical Asset Price Fluctuations
Michael F. Bryan, Federal Reserve Bank of Cleveland
Stephen G. Cecchetti, Ohio State University
Róisín O'Sullivan, Ohio State University

Discussants:
Andrew J. Filardo, Council of Economic Advisers and
    Federal Reserve Bank of Kansas City
Bruce Lehmann, University of California, San Diego

3:50 pm – 4:10 pm   Break

4:10 pm – 6:00 pm   **Session 4: International Transmission of Financial Shocks**

Moderator:
Cesare Calari, World Bank Group

Papers:
Globalization and Changing Patterns in the Transmission of Shocks in Financial Markets
Michael D. Bordo, Rutgers University and
    National Bureau of Economic Research
Antu Panini Murshid, University of Wisconsin,
    Milwaukee

Asset Price Bubbles and Stock Market Interlinkages
Franklin Allen, The Wharton School,
    University of Pennsylvania
Douglas Gale, New York University

Banking Policy and Macroeconomic Stability:
An Exploration
Gerard Caprio, Jr., World Bank Group
Patrick Honohan, World Bank Group

A Global Perspective on Extreme Currency Linkages
Philipp Hartmann, European Central Bank and
    Center for Economic Policy Research
Stefan Straetmans, University Maastricht
Casper de Vries, Erasmus University Rotterdam

Discussants:
Ashoka Mody, International Monetary Fund
Anna J. Schwartz, National Bureau of Economic Research

6:00 pm – 7:00 pm   Reception

7:00 pm Dinner

Moderator:
Jack B. Evans, CEO,
The Hall-Perrine Foundation

Keynote Speaker:
Robert J. Shiller, Yale University

Wednesday, April 24, 2002

7:30 am – 8:15 am Continental Breakfast

8:15 am – 9:45 am **Session 5: Technology, the New Economy, and Asset Price Bubbles**

Moderator:
Robert J. Darnall, Chairman,
Board of Directors of Federal Reserve Bank of Chicago

Papers:
Valuation and New Economy Firms
Steven N. Kaplan, University of Chicago

Transactions Costs and Home Bias: Can They Explain Euro Depreciation?
Catherine L. Mann, Institute for International Economics
Ellen E. Meade, London School of Economics

Discussant:
Lawrence Slifman, Board of Governors of the
  Federal Reserve System

9:45 am – 10:05 am Break

10:05 am – 12:05 pm **Session 6: Implications of Bubbles for Monetary Policy**

Moderator:
Robert Flood, International Monetary Fund

Papers:
Asset Prices in a Flexible Inflation Targeting Framework
Stephen Cecchetti, Ohio State University
Hans Genberg, Graduate Institute of International
  Studies, Geneva
Sushil Wadhwani, Bank of England

Interest Rate Policy Should Not React Directly to Asset Prices
Marvin Goodfriend, Federal Reserve Bank of Richmond

Discussant:
Benjamin M. Friedman, Harvard University

12:15 pm – 1:45 pm Lunch

Moderator:
Michael H. Moskow, President,
Federal Reserve Bank of Chicago

Keynote Speaker:
Michael Mussa, Institute for International Economics

1:45 pm – 3:40 pm **Session 7: Implications of Bubbles for Prudential Regulatory Policy**

Moderator:
James Nelson, Federal Reserve Bank of Chicago

Papers:
The Historical Pattern of Economic Cycles and Their Interaction with Asset Prices and Financial Regulation
Charles Goodhart, London School of Economics

Asset Price Bubbles and Prudential Regulation
Jeffrey Carmichael, Australian Prudential Regulation Authority
Neil Esho, Australian Prudential Regulation Authority

The Morning after: Restructuring in the Aftermath of an Asset Bubble
Michael Pomerleano, World Bank Group

Discussants:
Joaquim Vieira Levy, Ministry of Finance, Brazil
Ramon Moreno, Federal Reserve Bank of San Francisco
Eric Rosengren, Federal Reserve Bank of Boston

3:40 pm – 4:00 pm Break

4:00 pm – 6:00 pm **Session 8: Looking Forward: Plans for Action to Protect against Bubbles**

Moderator:
Robert Z. Aliber, University of Chicago

Panel:
Banking Provisions and Asset Price Bubbles
The Honorable Jaime Caruana, Governor, Bank of Spain

Looking Forward: Plans for Action to Protect against Bubbles
Anthony Neoh, China Securities Regulatory Commission

Looking Forward: Plans for Action to Protect Against Bubbles
Takatoshi Ito, Hitotsubashi University

Planning to Protect against Asset Bubbles
Vincent R. Reinhart, Board of Governors of the Federal Reserve System

6:00 pm Reception
Buffet Dinner and Adjournment

Organizing Committee: W. Curt Hunter, Federal Reserve Bank of Chicago
George G. Kaufman, Loyola University Chicago and Federal Reserve of Chicago
Michael Pomerleano, World Bank Group

Index

accountability, 10–12, 439–440
accounting, 11–12, 222
  full fair value, 545
actuaries, 510–511
agency problems, 324–330, 384–384, 387, 503–504
amplification mechanisms, 38
analysts, 210, 234, 510
appraisers, 508–509
arbitrage
  and banks, 92–93
  cost of, 234
  dependence on, 211
  and dollars/T-bills, 182
  in market efficiency, 232, 234
  rational, 211
  and 3Com/Palm, 177–178
Argentina, 4, 153–154, 380n7
Asia
  asset price cycles, 104–109
  bank regulation, 520
  banks, 112, 115, 123
  and capital, 112, 504, 505–506
  credit in, 109, 115, 121–122
  crises transmission, 313
  currency linkages, 375
  equity prices, 104, 129
  financial imbalances, 257
  financial professionals, 510
  monetary policy, 124
  1997 crisis, 368, 505
  property price decline, 115–120
  public policy, 112, 123–124
  real estate, 120–122, 241
  regulation in, 112, 123
  and risk-taking, 112, 123
  and securitization, 512
  See also specific countries
asset price gap, 251–255
asset returns, 142
audit systems, 11
Australia
  banks, 258, 482–491, 496–497, 525
  international credit, 519–520
  loan loss provisioning, 496–497
  real estate, 519, 524–525
autoregressive distributed lag (ARDL), 133–134
availability heuristics, 222, 223

balance sheet effects, 153–154
balance sheets
  of banks, 342–346, 550
  and equity market, 54–55, 168–169, 431
  tangible asset value, 420
banks
  absorptive capacity, 346–353
  Asian, 112, 115, 123
  Australian, 258, 482–491, 496–497, 525
  balance sheets, 342–346, 550
  capital, 227, 351, 493–494, 505
  competition between, 223, 224, 329–330
  and deposit insurance, 492
  deposit shocks, 346–353

banks (*continued*)
  and disasters, 221–223, 241
  equity holdings, 532
  and exchange rates, 471
  expected payoff, 329
  foreign liabilities, 519
  foreign-owned
    benefits, 338, 341–342, 349, 356
    risks, 520
  international trades, 351–353
  Latin American, 241, 520
  and liquidity, 224
  versus market-based finance, 240–241
  merchant, 525
  and public policy, 224–226
  and real estate, 220–226, 240–241, 551
  risk management, 21, 123, 223–227
  role of, 339, 342–346
  safety net effect, 224–226
  stock-holding, 532
  stock prices of, 341
  See also central banks; credit
banking regulation
  and asymmetric information, 492
  and deposit fluctuations, 349
  and financial crises, 338
  and government corruption, 341
  and nonbank credit, 491, 520
  short- and long-term effects, 353–356
  and short-term lending, 339–340
bank runs, 224–225, 492
bankruptcy, 504–505, 512
behavioral finance, 207–209, 212–213, 234–236
benchmarks, 19, 189
beta, 198, 200–201, 206
  See also volatility
bond markets, 189, 449, 512
book value, 193, 305
brand equity, 421
Brazil, 155–156, 380n7, 520, 521
bubbles
  amplification mechanisms, 38
  burst period, 81–82, 89–91
  and crashes, 139–141, 294
  definitions, 23, 35, 165
  determinants, 141
  empirical dimensions, 291–296
  identifying, 4–7, 12, 42–43, 165–168, 261–262
  long-term impact, 147–149
  minimizing factors, 164
  nonrational, 26–28
  precipitating factors, 38–39
  prevention, 164
  puncturing, 155–156, 164, 169

  rational, 24–26, 165, 198–199, 293
  testing for, 131–137
Buffet, Warren, 213n7
building costs, 285–286
Bulgaria, 155
Bundesbank, 76
Bush, George W., 9–10
business cycles
  and capital adequacy, 494
  and credit, 538–540
  and equity prices, 471–474
  and exchange rates, 470–471
  and fiscal policy, 467–468
  and housing, 472–474, 518
  and inflation, 469, 517
  post World War II, 467–469
  and real estate, 472–474
  and regulation, 474–478, 518–521
  and risk, 475, 476–478
  supply-driven, 469–471, 517
  and VaR, 471, 518, 551–552
buyout investors, 397

capital
  and Asia, 112, 504, 505–506
  of banks, 227, 351, 493–494, 505
  cost of, 146–147
  and emerging markets, 520
  equity market capitalization, 27
  ex ante real rates, 305
  external acquisition, 431
  global allocation, 340
  information technology, 235
  intangible, 272, 301–305
  versus loan loss provisioning, 525–526, 527n3
  market value, 302–303
  net rental rates, 305
  and 1929 crash, 27
  and public policies, 112
  requirements for, 493–494
  short-term, 520
  tangible, 272
  Tobin's q, 16, 146–147
capital accounts, 124
capital adequacy, 493–494
capital flows, 141–142, 154, 471, 519–520
capital gains, 302
capital markets, 506, 509
cash flow, discounting, 504
central banks
  and asset prices, 49, 459–460
  and booms, 17
  and cost of life, 279
  and credit availability, 329–332, 385–386

credit tightening, 49–50, 255–256, 430
crises prevention, 255–256
and employment, 461
and equity market, 54, 556–557
and financial imbalances, 261–263
and financial (in)stability, 74–75, 492, 549–550
and inflation, 89, 439, 446, 448–449 (*see also* inflation-targeting)
Japanese, 84, 89, 164, 451–453
and loan provisioning, 543–546
and misalignments, 439
and monetary policy, 16–17, 49–50
and output gap, 433, 436–437, 446–447
and price stability, 547–548
real objectives, 461
and risk-taking, 17
and segmented markets, 93
sterilized interventions, 450–451
and stock market, 74–76
supervisory role, 550–551
Swiss, 433
and tax-deductibility, 520–521
See also Federal Reserve; interest rates; monetary policy
Chile, 153–154, 520
China, 189, 512
civil law countries, 510
closed-economy model, 431–432, 436–437
collateral
loan-to-value ratios, 477
real estate as, 155, 219, 221, 325, 506, 519
housing, 473
stocks as, 155, 325, 472–473
Colombia, 153–154
commodities, 188
common law countries, 510
communications costs, 399
competition
and credit cycles, 541
and exchange rates, 450
and intangible assets, 421
interbank, 223, 224, 329–330, 539
and Internet firms, 394, 397, 399
conflicting signals, 441
conflict of interest, 11–12
construction costs, 285–286
Consumer Price Index (CPI)
and housing prices, 109
and inflation, 278, 284
and interest rates, 284
in Japan, 86, 451
stability of, 548–552
consumption
and equity prices, 15, 146–151, 553, 558

future, 278, 279
growth of, 559n3
and housing, 473, 539
and inflation, 277–279, 299–301
in Latin America, 146–151
consumption tax, 86
contracts, enforcement of, 96n1
contrarians, 214n8
convenience yield
defined, 175
description, 187–191, 233–234
limitations, 239–240
and price distortions, 233–234
and tech stocks, 175–178, 187–191, 193–197
corporations
audit systems, 11
officer accountability, 10–12
restructuring, 504–505, 513–514
value assessment, 272
corruption, 341
cost of life
and asset prices, 278–280
change estimates, 280–281
versus cost of living, 279, 281–284, 286–287, 288n3, 291–292
dynamic factor index, 281–287
and inflation, 299–301
and interest rates, 286–288, 288n3
cost of living index
versus cost of life, 279, 281–284, 286–287, 288n3, 291–292
crash identification, 55–56
crash minimization, 168–169
Crash of 1929
as benchmark, 55
and bubbles, 46–47, 294
and capitalization rate, 27
causes, 273–274
Federal Reserve role, 61–63, 273–274, 294
and volume, 192
credibility, 260, 266n20, 439–440, 453–454
credit
aggregate, 329–332, 346, 385–386
in Asia, 109, 115, 121–122
and asset prices, 19, 249–256
availability of, 228n11, 329–332, 385–386
bank-based, 91–93, 96
and bubbles, 141
and business cycles, 538–540
constraints on, 469
cyclicality, 538–541
domestic growth, 141–144
and equity prices, 147, 228n11
and euro, 407

credit (*continued*)
   expansion, 249–256, 266n12, 525, 538–540
   against future income growth, 449–450
   and housing, 151–154
   inter-firm, 520
   international markets, 519–520
   in Japan, 91–93, 96
   and land prices, 219
   in Latin America, 141–142, 151–156
   loan-to-value ratio, 223–224, 477, 550
   loss provisioning, 471, 495–497, 502, 520–521, 526, 540–546
   and mimetic behavior, 20
   and monetary policy, 16, 18
   versus own money, 326, 384
   public *versus* private sectors, 469
   and real estate, 101–104, 121–122, 155, 220–221, 551 (*see also* agency problems)
   regulation of, 155, 491–498, 520
   REIT-based, 123
   secondary markets, 519, 531, 5511–513
   short-term, 339–340
   and stock market crashes, 54–55, 64, 66, 69, 72
   stress testing, 497–498
credit gaps, 250–255
currency
   Argentine peso, 4
   emerging markets, 368–370, 373–379
   euro, 406–407, 414–415
   extreme movements, 366–370
   of industrialized countries, 370–373, 376–378
   in Latin America, 141, 155–156, 375
   linkage measurement, 364–366
   speculation, 363
current account deficits, 149, 469

debt/deflation cycle, 471
debt flows, 124
decision-making, 206–209, 212, 222
deflation, 284–287, 471
demand
   and asset value decline, 449
   and business cycles, 468–469
   for commercial real estate, 219–220
   and equities, 177, 200
   and Federal Reserve, 453–454
   and herding behavior, 212
   and interest rates, 447, 469
   in Japan, 531–532
   and short selling, 200
deposit insurance, 492
depreciation, 301–304, 421
developing countries
   bond markets, 512

crisis transmission, 310–313, 316–319
   debt crisis, 470
   financial sector, 506
   housing in, 155
   recovery in, 506
   See also emerging markets
direct pressure, 283–274
disaster myopia, 221–224, 241
diversity, 557, 4008–409
dividend discount models, 206
dividends
   and earnings, 303–304
   and equity prices, 132–135, 231–232, 554
   expected growth, 554
   and fundamental value, 272–272
   timing issues, 157n18
dollar volume, 191–192
downsizing, 505
dynamic factor index, 281–287

earnings, 210, 235
eBay, 394
economic indicators
   equity prices as, 553
   and European monetary policy, 18
   exchange rates, 462, 519
   of financial crises, 250–256, 295, 550
   for future inflation, 437
   investor behavior as, 553
   See also forecasting
economy of scale, 555
efficient markets model, 232
emerging markets
   currency, 368–370, 373–379
   real estate, 220
   risk management, 379, 511
   short-term capital, 520
   volatility, 340
   See also developing countries
Employee Retirement Income Security Act (ERISA), 9–10
employment, 399, 453–454, 461, 467
   downsizing, 505
Enron, 72
equipment, 419–420, 419–421
equity markets
   Asian, 104
   versus bank financing, 240–241
   capitalization, 27
   in China, 189
   European, 410–415
   float, 182
   and forecasting, 205
   fundamental values, 271–273

Index

home bias, 404–414
individual investors, 555–556
and inflation, 266n19, 430
and information, 8, 190
institutional factors, 211
and interest rates, 72–73
international linkages, 324–325, 332–334, 386–387
interwar, 284
in Japan, 451–452
in Latin America, 141, 142–144
and monetary policy, 72–76
in 1990s, 4–7, 15, 27–28, 44–45
portfolio allocation, 404–407
psychological factors, 17, 210–212
and sentiment, 398, 400
share supply, 195–197
trading frequency, 190, 192
valuation, 274, 293–294, 504
  overvaluation, 190, 236n3, 271–274
  undervaluation, 274
winning strategies, 504
See also stock market crashes
equity prices
of banks, 341
and business cycles, 471–474
and consumption, 15, 146–151, 553, 558
and credit supply, 147, 228n11
and demand, 177, 200
and dividends, 132–135, 231–232, 554
as economic indicators, 553
and firm growth, 306
fundamental value, 134–135, 431
Gordon model, 231–232
and growth rates, 232
index inclusion, 200
and inflation, 266n19, 449
information in, 462–463
and interest rates, 30
in Japan, 451–453, 532
in Latin America, 128–129, 146–151
and monetary policy, 454, 455
price-to-max value ratio, 139–140
and productivity, 559n1
psychological factors, 210–212
and required return, 189
versus return on equity, 504
risk aversion coefficient, 559n2
and share supply, 195–197, 200
in United States, 4–7, 15, 27, 472–474
variability perception, 209
volatility, 557–558
and volume, 191–194
euro, 406–407, 414–415

Europe
and crisis transmission, 318, 319
equity markets, 410–415
investor behavior, 404–405
market consolidation, 415
monetary policy, 18
See also specific countries
European Central Bank, 18
European Union, 319
exchange market pressure, 310–315
exchange rates
in Asia, 115, 120, 375
and banks, 471
and business cycles, 470–471
currency movements, 366–370
and domestic policy, 450
emerging markets, 368–370, 373–379
euro/dollar, 406–407, 414–415
fixed, 317–319
free floating, 433
and globalization, 310–315
and industrialized countries, 370–373, 376–378
and inflation, 435
and interest rates, 512, 518
linkage measurement, 364–366
and monetary policy, 42, 432–433, 435–436, 450–451, 452–453
and portfolio allocation, 406–407
as predictors, 462
and rational bubbles, 25
and risk-shifting, 325
and shock transmission, 361–362
in small open economies, 471, 518
stability, 258, 442n18
yen/dollar, 452
expectations
of credit, 228n11
and financial imbalances, 259–260
of future inflation, 461
and interest rates, 16
of Internet stocks, 393–395
in Japan, 95–96, 240
modeling, 28–29
and NASDAQ bubble, 231–233
of profit, 16
and psychology, 205 (*see also* psychology)
rational, 23, 24, 197–198
explanations, 49–50, 197–200
external finance premium, 96n1
extreme value analysis, 363

Fama-MacBeth statistics, 193–194
Federal Reserve
and equity markets, 274

Federal Reserve (*continued*)
   and financial instability, 168
   and inflation, 65, 69
   in late 1990s, 453–454
   and Latin America, 141
   and liquidity, 74–75, 164
   and LTCM crisis, 170
   and NASDAQ bubble, 170
   1994 action, 446–447
   pre-emptive action, 446–447
   and September 11, 74–75
   and stock market crashes, 63–72
      crash of 1929, 61–63, 273–274, 294
   See also monetary policy
fiber optics, 420
finance companies, 525
financial analysts, 210, 234, 510
financial crises
   Asian, 368, 505
   and asset prices, 253
   and emerging countries, 310–313
   enhancement factors, 18–20
   indicators, 250–256, 295, 550
   international transmission, 312–321, 338, 441
   regional, 316–320, 363
   source, 432–433
   stages, 211–212
   timing, 251
financial diversity, 408–409, 557
financial imbalances, 257–263
financial (in)stability
   and asset prices, 294–296
   and central banks, 549–550
   determining factors, 249–256
   and globalization, 309–321
   and inflation, 256–257
   international, 309–320
   in Japan, 89, 91–93, 549
   and monetary policy, 256–263
   and policy intervention, 168
   and stock market crashes, 72–74
   systemic, 491–492
   systemic nature, 491–492
   See also business cycles; medium-run macroeconomic stability
financial sector
   critical products, 511–514, 515, 531
   in developing countries, 506
   expertise, 505–511, 514–515, 521, 531–533
   foreign presence, 515
fiscal policy, 467–468
float, 182
forecasting
   and behavioral finance, 209–210

   and equity markets, 205
   and equity prices, 553, 559n1
   of inflation, 437
   and pre-emptive action, 556
   productivity, 29, 559n1
   See also economic indicators
foreign entry, 515
foreign liabilities, 519
foreign ownership, 338, 341–342, 349, 356
France, 15
fraud, 506
frequency
   and profitability, 222–223
   and real estate, 240
   of shocks, 221–223
   of stock trades, 239
   See also timing
frictionless rational pricing, 197–198
full fair value accounting (FFVA), 545
fundamental value
   assessment of, 261–262, 272–273
   deviation from, 16
   and equity prices, 134–135, 431
   and investment money source, 326, 384
   permanent change, 166
   and productivity, 170
   of spin-offs, 176–178

General Electric (GE), 399
General Motors (GM), 177
Germany, 319
globalization
   and banks, 351–353
   crisis incidence, 315–321
   and equity markets, 324–325, 332–334, 386–387
   exchange markets, 310–315
   international credit, 519–520
   pre- and post-World War I, 309–321
   and small economies, 441
   and VaR, 317–319
gold standard, 310, 317, 319
Gordon model, 189, 197, 232, 554
Granger causality, 157n18, 437
Great Depression, 61–64
Greenspan, Alan
   on Asian crisis, 505–506
   on asset prices, 46
   impact of, 213n4
   irrational exuberance, 30
gross domestic product (GDP), 89, 97n6

hedge funds, 19, 120
herding
   by analysts, 210

Index 575

and asset prices, 19–20, 212
and banks, 226, 340
and contrarians, 214n8
and liquidity, 212
and VaR, 21
heuristics, 209
home bias, 404–414
Hong Kong, 102, 120, 240, 551
housing
　and business cycles, 241, 472–474, 518
　and consumer price index, 109
　and consumption, 539
　in cost of life, 282, 285
　and credit, 151–154
　　mortgages, 512–513, 519
　in developing countries, 155
　and inflation, 109
　as investment, 241
　in Latin America, 151–154
　and real output, 473–474
　secondary markets, 155
　in United States, 472
H.R. 2269, 10
H.R. 3763, 10
human capital, 505–511, 514–515, 521, 531–533
hyperinflation, 188

income taxes, 301–302
indexes
　cost of living, 279, 281–284, 286–287, 288n3, 291–292
　and Japan, 455
　and mutual funds, 19–20
　Standard and Poor's, 200
indicators. *See* economic indicators
Indonesia, 120
industrialized countries, 370–373, 376–378
inflation
　in Asia, 121
　and asset price information, 30–31, 97n6
　and bond markets, 449
　and business cycles, 469, 517
　and cash, 188
　and central banks, 89, 439, 448–449
　and commercial real estate, 524–525
　and Consumer Price Index, 278, 284, 292
　and consumption, 277–279, 299–301
　and cost of life, 299–301
　and credit, 121, 257–260
　and crises, 257–260
　and equities, 266n19, 430
　and exchange rates, 435
　expectations of, 461

　financial imbalances, 257–260
　and financial stability, 256–257
　forecasting, 437
　future, 437
　and housing prices, 109
　hyperinflation, 188
　and interest rates, 121, 286–288, 446
　and long bond rates, 449
　low levels, 257–263, 523–524
　and monetary policy, 260
　and output gap, 89
　and productivity, 259
　views of, 49–50
inflation-targeting
　and consumption, 279
　and financial imbalances, 260–261
　and macroeconomic stability, 95, 461–462
　rationale for, 460–461
　short- *versus* long-term, 263
　and Taylor rule, 427–429
information
　about monetary tightening, 49–50
　and agency problems, 9
　in asset prices, 30–31, 97n6, 459–463
　and asset pricing, 8
　asymetric, 224, 491–492
　complexity of, 491
　and credit gaps, 251, 266n14
　disclosure of, 10–12
　on earnings, 235
　and equities, 8, 190, 462–463
　and external finance premium, 96n1
　and herding, 20–21
　and Internet, 392
　and NASDAQ prices, 235
　and pension reform, 9–10
　and public policy, 7–9
　in real estate prices, 462–463
　regulation of, 491–492
　and stock market crashes, 54
　transparency, 20–21, 212, 511, 515
　uncertain, 29
information technology, 235–236
infrastructure
　financial, 532
　organizational, 421
initial public offerings (IPOs)
　lock-ups, 195, 395
　3Com/Palm, 176–188
　underperformance of, 200
　and venture capitalists, 396–397
innovation, 305, 555
insolvency experts, 508
institutional investors, 8–9, 211, 326, 384

institutional rationality, 214n10
insurance, 492, 506, 510–511
intangible assets, 301–305, 419–422
intellectual capital, 421
interest rates
  after-tax real, 273
  in Asia, 115, 120, 121
  and asset prices, 431, 446–455
  and CPI, 284, 548–549
  and credit availability, 329–330
  and crisis transmission, 317–319
  and demand, 447, 469
  and equities, 30, 72–73
  and exchange rates, 512, 518
  and expectations, 16
  and inflation, 121, 286–288, 288n3, 446
  in Japan, 93–95, 455, 549
  lowering, during bubble, 170
  and money supply, 182
  1994 tightening, 446–447
  parity, 435–436
  and price stability, 548–549
  and productivity, 267n25, 453
  short term, 317–319, 431–432, 446–447, 450–451, 453–454
  spread, 56
  stable *versus* sluggish, 442n18
  and supply, 447
  and timing, 549
  See also monetary policy
intermediation, 349, 510–511, 559n7
Internet, 391–392, 394–395, 398–399
Internet stocks
  and monetary policy, 43–44, 50
  and profitability, 27, 391–392, 398, 399
  and short sales, 194, 395
  valuations, 392–395, 419–422
  and venture capitalists, 395–398
  See also tech stocks
intrinsic bubble model, 137–139
inventions, 555
investment
  and equity prices, 146–151, 431
  and financial crises, 251–255
  in Latin America, 146–151
  and overcapacity, 430
  overinvestment, 149
  with own money, 326, 384
investment decisions, 206–207
investment gaps, 251–255
investment horizons, 19, 21
investors
  buyout, 397
  European, 404–405, 410–414

individual, 555
institutional, 8–9, 211, 326, 384
U.S., 395–398, 404–410
venture capital, 395–398
irrationality, 30, 197, 199

Japan
  asset price booms, 32n2, 82–84, 89–91, 325, 523–524
  rational, 26–27
  banks, 91–93, 96, 532, 549
  bond trading, 189
  central bank, 89
  Consumer Price Index, 86, 451
  credit, 91–93, 96
  danger signals, 550
  demand, 531–532
  equities, 451–453, 532
  expectations, 95–96, 240
  financial imbalances, 257
  financial stability, 89, 91–93, 549
  interest rates, 93–95, 455, 549
  liquidity, 93, 97n12, 164
  loan-to-value ratio, 550, 551
  monetary policy, 47–49, 84, 89–93, 170, 451–453
  output gap, 86–88
  recovery, 505, 530
  risk-shifting, 385
  stock-holding banks, 532
  taxes, 86, 551
  and United States, 318
  valuation expertise, 505
jobs. *See* employment; labor

Kalman filter, 281
  See also dynamic factor index
Keynes, John Maynard, 206
Korea, 120, 512–514, 525

labor, 259, 449, 453–454
land, 218–220, 227n2, 455, 551
Latin America
  and Australia, 519–520
  banking crises, 241
  bank regulation, 520
  bubbles, 134–141
    determinants of, 141–144
    testing for, 131–134
  consumption, 146–151
  crashes, 139–141
  and crises transmission, 313
  currency, 4, 141, 155–156, 375
  equities, 128–129, 141, 142–144, 146–151

financial professionals, 510–511
housing, 151–154
investment, 146–151
public policy, 154–156
real estate, 129, 139, 142–144, 154–156
stabilization programs, 258
U.S. impact, 141, 142–144
See also specific countries
leveraging, 223, 226, 242
liquidators, 508
liquidity
  and banks, 224
  and European monetary policy, 18
  and Federal Reserve, 74–75, 164
  and herding, 212
  and herding behavior, 212
  in Japan, 93, 97n12, 164
  and secondary market, 511
  and stock market crashes, 64, 74
loan-loss provisioning
  description, 495–497
  in Portugal, 520–521
  in Spain, 502, 526, 540–546
loan-to-value ratios, 223–224, 477, 550, 551
log dividend-yield, 134
Long-Term Capital Management (LTCM) crisis, 45, 170, 368

M3, 18
macroeconomic stability, 50, 95, 460–462
macro markets, 155
Malaysia, 120, 512–513
market efficiency
  definition, 232
  and modern finance, 206–207
  and NASDAQ bubble, 232–233
  and public policy, 8, 9–12
  semi-strong, 8
  strong form, 8
  and tech stocks, 206
market value, 305
mass media, 212
medium-run macroeconomic stability, 460–461
mental frames, 208
merchant banks, 525
México, 153–154, 325
millenium, 45
mimetic behavior. *See* herding
misalignments, 439–441, 459–460, 476
  and central banks, 429
monetary policy
  and Asia, 124 (*see also under* Japan)
  and asset prices, 16–22, 41–49, 428–441, 462
  and business cycles, 518–521

closed-economy model, 431–432, 436–437
credibility, 260, 266n20, 439–440, 453–454
and credit, 519–520, 539–540
and equities, 72–76, 454, 455
in Europe, 18
and exchange rates, 42, 432–433, 435–436, 450–453, 462
and financial stability, 256–263
and fluctuations *versus* bubbles, 295
Greenspan role, 213n4
international, 433, 441, 519–520
intervention rationale, 438–439
in Japan, 47–49, 84, 89–93, 170, 451–453
and macroeconomic stability, 50
and 1929 crash, 294
open economy model, 432–433, 435–436
pre-emptive, 446–447, 452, 455
and price stability, 17–18
versus prudence, 481–492, 518–526
public explanations, 49–50
recession prevention, 31
and shock type, 432–433, 436–437
in small open economies, 432–433, 435–436
and stock market crashes, 73–76
and tech stocks, 454
tightening, 49–50, 255–256, 430, 446–447, 557
time horizon, 439–440
timing, 263, 295–296, 462–463
transmission channels, 16
See also central banks; inflation-targeting; interest rates
moral hazard. *See* risk-taking
mortgage-backed securities, 242, 512–513, 519
mutual funds, 8–9, 19–20

NASDAQ bubble, 191–200
  aftermath, 530
  and expectations, 231–233
  and Federal Reserve, 170
  and information, 235
Nelson, E., 432–433
new economy
  and business cycles, 475
  characteristics, 419–421
  and equity pricees, 15
  impact, 391–392, 398–399
  intangible assets, 421–422
New England, 506
1929. *See* Crash of 1929
noise-to-signal ratio, 252–253, 265n11, 266n12
nonrational bubbles, 26–28

obsolescence, 419–421
Olympic model, 206–207

OPEC, 69
open economies. *See* small open economies
ordinary least squares (OLS), 193
Organization for Economic Cooperation and Development (OECD), 166
output gap
　and central banks, 433, 436–437, 446–447
　estimation of, 440
　euphoria effect, 96n3
　and inflation, 89
　in Japan, 86–88
overcapacity, 430
overconfidence, 190
overinvestment, 149
overvaluation, 144, 166–168
　of equities, 166–168, 190, 236n3, 271–274
　Palm, 180
　identification of, 549
　of real estate, 144

Pakistan, 368
Palm, 175–188
　convenience yield, 175–178, 187–191, 233–234
　options trading, 186, 194
　price and volume, 180–181
　share supply, 182–184
　and short selling, 182–183
　as spin-off, 176–178
　3Com linkage, 184–186
　volatility, 179–180, 185
pension funds, 275n3, 506
pension reform, 9–10
P/E ratios, 166, 169
perpetual inventory method, 422n3
personnel, 508–511
petroleum, 69
Philippines, 120, 368
portfolio composition, 406–407, 492–493, 518, 543–544
Portugal, 520–521
precipitating factors, 38
pre-emptive action
　and financial imbalances, 263
　and forecasting, 556
　and Japan, 455
　monetary policy, 446–447, 452, 455
　regulatory, 481–482, 533
prevention, 31, 164
price-earnings (P/E) ratios, 166, 169
price manipulation, 11
price stability, 17–19, 21, 548–549
pricing
　rational, 197–198, 233–234

versus value, 206
process innovation, 305
productivity
　change, permanence of, 25–26
　economy of scale, 555
　and equity prices, 559n1
　forecasting, 29, 559n1
　and fundamental value, 170
　growth, impact of, 449–450, 453
　and inflation, 259
　and interest rates, 267n25, 453
　and output gap, 440
　and technology, 27, 391–392, 399–400
　in U.S., 25–26, 170, 259, 407, 453
profitability
　of Internet firms, 27, 391–392, 398, 399
　and low-frequency events, 222–223
　steady-state pre-tax, 272–273
　and technology, 27, 391–392, 399
profit expectations, 16
profit squeeze, 449
protection, 556–559
provisioning. *See* loan loss provisioning
psychology
　behavioral finance, 207–209, 212–213, 234–236
　belief perseverance, 210–211, 214n10
　decision-making, 206–209, 212, 222
　disaster myopia, 221–224, 241
　euphoria, 96n3
　of financial behavior, 209–210
　herding, 19–20, 210, 212, 214n8
　impact of, 210–212
　intuitive judgment, 212
　Keynes view, 206
　perverse incentives, 223–226
　rational assumptions, 206–207, 213n4
　rational *versus* behavioral, 234–236
　See also behavioral finance; herding
public policy
　in Asia, 112, 123–124
　and banks, 224–226
　and behavioral finance, 235–236
　bubble identification, 4–7, 12
　bubble pricking, 169
　under George W. Bush, 9–12
　and exchange rates, 450
　and financial instability, 168–169
　implementation of, 168–169
　information availability, 7–9
　and investor psychology, 212
　in Latin America, 154–156
　and market efficiency, 8, 9–12
　and real estate, 124, 154–156, 225–226, 228n5

recession prevention, 31
and risk, 123
quality, 419–420
flight to, 380n10
rate of return, 178, 329–330, 407
rating agencies, 340
rational adjustments, 554
rational arbitrage, 211
rational bubbles, 24–26, 165, 198–199, 293
rational expectations, 23, 24, 197–198
rationality
  assumptions of, 206–207, 213n4, 234–235
  of society, 214n10
rational paradigm, 206–207
rational pricing, 197–198, 233–234
real estate
  appraisals, 506, 508–509
  and Asian banks, 112
  in Asian countries, 120–122, 241
  and banks, 220–226, 240–241, 551
  and business cycles, 242, 472–474
  as collateral, 155, 219, 221, 325, 506, 519
  and credit, 101–104, 121–122, 155, 220–221
    (see also agency problems)
  cyclicality, 103–104, 120–122, 241–242
  in emerging markets, 220
  as equity hedge, 159n35
  income-producing, 241–242 (see also real estate, commercial)
  information in, 462–463
  and inheritance tax, 551
  land, 218–220, 227n2, 455, 551
  in Latin America, 129, 139, 142–144, 154–156
  leveraging, 223, 226, 242
  price determinants, 218–221, 228n11
  and public policy, 124, 154–156, 225–226, 228n5
  and regulation, 155, 220
  rent, 228n12
  and risk, 103–104, 221–226, 242, 324
  and short selling, 218–219, 228n5, 241
  traditional views, 241
  See also housing; real estate, commercial
real estate, commercial
  in Australia, 519, 524–525
  and credit expansion, 539
  demand factor, 219–220
  and inflation, 524–525
  leveraging, 223–226, 242
  in New England, 530
  short sales of, 241
real estate investment trusts (REITs), 123, 155, 242, 514

recessions, 17, 31
recommendations, 210
recovery
  critical products, 511–514, 515
  in developing countries, 506
  foreign presence, 515
  human capital role, 505–511, 514–515, 521, 531–533
  in Japan, 505, 530
  variations, 530–533
regional crises, 316–320, 363
regulation
  in Asia, 112, 123
  and behavioral finance, 235–236
  and business cycles, 474–478, 518–521
  of capital adequacy, 493–494
  and financial professions, 514
  implementation, 168–169
  of information, 491–492
  in Latin America, 155
  of portfolio composition, 492–493, 518, 543–544
  pre-emptive, 481–482, 533
  and real estate, 220
  of real estate, 155
  recommendations, 474–478
  See also banking regulation
Regulation Q, 74
rent, 228n12
residual income, 304
residuals-augmented least squares (RALS), 133–134
restructuring, corporate, 504–505, 513–514
return on equity, 504
risk
  and business cycles, 475, 477
  and equity prices, 559n2
  and growth potential, 559n3
  and high frequency trading, 239
  nondiversifiable, 206
  and process innovation, 305
  and real estate, 242
  and return, 206
  versus uncertainty, 28–29, 30
risk management
  and business cycles, 476–478
  corporate restructuring, 513–514
  and credit cycles, 540
  distressed debt market, 511
  and emerging market, 379, 511
  for financial institutions, 21, 123
  impact of, 20
  provisioning, 471, 495–497, 502, 520–521, 526, 540–546

risk management (*continued*)
  real estate (REITs), 123, 155, 242, 514
  versus savings intermediation, 510–511
  secondary markets, 155, 511–513, 519, 531
  securitization, 512–513
  stress testing, 497–498
risk premium, 166–168, 171n2, 198, 440
risk-shifting, 324–330, 384–384, 387, 503–504
risk-taking
  in Asia, 112, 123
  by banks, 223–227
  and central banks, 17
  factors, 207, 214n10
  and individual investor, 555–556
  and mutual funds, 8–9
  public policy, 123
  and real estate, 103–104, 221–226
  and stock market crashes, 54–55, 64
  versus uncertainty, 28–29
Russia, 45, 368

saving, 149
savings and loan crisis, 506
savings intermediation, 510–511
scrappage, 420–421
secondary markets, 155, 511–513, 519, 531
securitization, 512–513
segmented markets, 93
Self-Exciting Threshold Autoregression (SETAR), 140, 141
September 11, 2001, 74–75
shareholders, 225, 505
shocks, high- and low-frequency, 221–223
short selling
  and convenience yield, 190
  and demand, 200
  of Internet stocks, 194, 395
  of land, 218–219, 228n5, 241
  and pessimists, 200
  of stock options, 551
  and tech stocks, 182–183, 194
short-termism, 19, 21
short-term lending, 339–340
Singapore, 102, 120, 124, 240
small open economies
  capital flows, 471, 519
  exchange rates, 471, 518
  monetary policy, 432–433, 435–436
  See also developing countries
South Africa, 375
Spain, 477, 502, 526, 537–546
speculation, 363, 558
spinoffs. *See* Palm
stability. *See* financial (in)stability

stabilization programs, 258
Standard Augmented Dickey-Fuller tests (ADF), 133–134
stock market crashes
  1903, 56–59
  1907, 58–59
  1917, 59–60
  1920, 60–61
  1937, 63–64
  1940, 64–65
  1946, 65–66
  1962, 66
  1970, 66–68
  1974, 68–69
  1987, 45, 55, 69–71
  1990, 71
  2000, 71–72
  and bubbles, 46–47, 139–141, 294
  and financial stability, 72–74, 76
  identification, 55–56
  and information, 54
  and liquidity, 64, 74
  minimization, 168–169
  and risk, 54–55, 64
  See also Crash of 1929
stress testing, 21, 497–498
supervision, 550–551
supply, 259, 430, 443n20, 447, 532
  and business cycles, 469–471, 517
Sweden, 505
Switzerland, 433

tax deductibility, 520–521
taxes
  on consumption, 86
  on income, 301–302
  in Japan, 551
tax neutrality, 512
tax rates, 293, 470, 551
tax revenues, 470
Taylor rule
  and asset prices, 428
  augmented, 169
  data for, 87, 97n8
  description, 88, 427
  and exchange rate, 428
  and Japan, 85, 86, 91, 95
Tchebysheff inequality, 220
technology, 27, 391–392, 399
  See also information technology
technology shocks, 437, 475
tech stocks
  asset valuation, 419–420
  and monetary policy, 454

Index

myths, 205–206
and risk-shifting, 329
theoretical explanations, 197–200
valuation, 166–168
See also Internet stocks; NASDAQ bubble; Palm
terms of trade, 141–144, 154
testing, 131–137
Thailand, 120, 123, 505, 525
3Com. *See* Palm
threshold heuristics, 222
timing
and bank capital, 351
and crisis indicators, 251
horizons, 439–440
and interest rates, 549
and monetary policy, 263, 295–296, 462–463
See also frequency
Tobin's q, 16, 146–147
trading frequency, 239
transaction costs
within Europe, 415
and foreign exchange, 406–407
Internet impact on, 391–392, 394–395, 399
and portfolio allocation, 404–410
transparency, 20–21, 212, 511, 515
See also information
Treasury bills, 178–179, 180, 182, 190
trusts, 512
t statistics, 193
tulip mania, 232, 554, 556

uncertainty, 28–29, 30
underwriting standards, 223–224
United Kingdom, 318, 473, 509
United States
equity premiums, 559n2
and equity prices, 4–7, 15, 27, 472–474
financial expertise, 506
intrinsic bubble model, 137
investor behavior, 395–398, 404–410
and Japan, 318

and Latin America, 141, 142–144
New England, 530
productivity, 25–26, 170, 259, 407, 453
savings and loan crisis, 506
See also Federal Reserve; monetary policy; NASDAQ bubble; stock market crashes

valuation, 199, 363
of tech stocks, 166–168, 392–395, 419–422
See also under equity markets; overvaluation
value
and asset prices, 24
of company, 191
of equities, 271–273
of intangible assets, 421
of land, 227n2
perception of, 209–211, 212
versus price, 206
and turnover, 193
See also fundamental value
Value-at-Risk (VaR)
and Asian real estate, 121–122
and business cycles, 471, 518, 551–552
effects of, 20, 21
and international crises, 317–319
versus stress-testing, 497
venture capitalists, 395–398
volatility, 340, 557–558, 559n9
See also beta
Volcker, Paul, 469–470
volume, 191–194, 198, 240
vulnerability factors, 250–256

wages, 449–450, 453
weak-form market efficiency, 8
wealth effect, 15, 539
workout loans, 225
World War I, 59–61
World War II, 64–65

Y2K, 45